Vermont
AN EXPLORER'S GUIDE

A quiet country road leads into Roxbury

VTD

Vermont
AN EXPLORER'S GUIDE

Fifth Edition

Christina Tree & Peter Jennison

The Countryman Press
Woodstock, Vermont

Library of Congress Cataloging-in-Publication Data
Tree, Christina.
    Vermont, an explorer's guide / Christina Tree and Peter Jennison—5th ed.
        p. cm.
    Includes index.
    ISBN 0-88150-227-8
    1. Vermont—Description and travel—1981—Guide books.
I. Jennison, Peter S.   II. Title.
F47.3.T73   1992
917.4304'43—dc20   91-28232
                                                                  CIP

Maps by Richard Widhu

Cover design by Frank Lieberman

Cover photograph by Richard W. Brown

Printed in the United States of America.

10 9 8 7 6 5 4 3 2

Dedications

Timothy Alfred Davis
— C.T.

Keith Warren Jennison
— P.S.J.

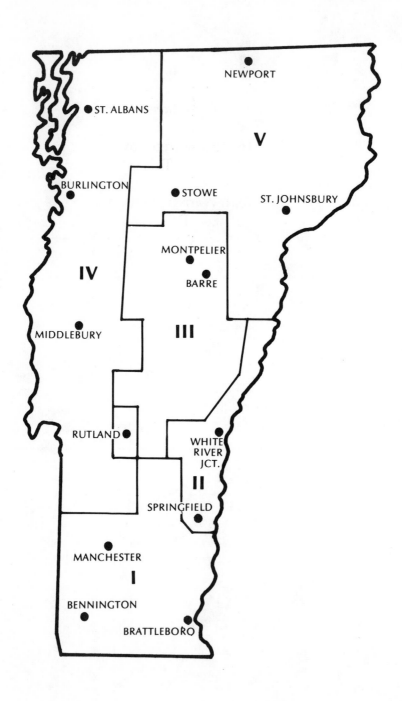

Contents

A Note to the Reader

No entries for any of the establishments appearing in the Explorer's Guide Series have been solicited or paid for.

Please note two things: The prices cited in the book are those available at press time in early 1992 and do not include the 8 percent state rooms and meals tax. We have tried to note the addition of a 15 percent gratuity where applicable.

Smoking: Most bed & breakfasts are now smoke-free, and several inns have nonsmoking rooms, as do larger restaurants. If this is important to you, ask when you call for reservations.

The Special Value symbol (☞) appears next to selected lodgings and restaurants that combine exceptional qualities with moderate prices.

In this fifth edition of *Vermont: An Explorer's Guide,* we have included specific prices for entries in the "Dining Out" section of each chapter.

Restaurants featuring a prix fixe menu have been noted accordingly.

Price categories do not appear in the "Eating Out'" sections, in that these establishments are inexpensive by definition. All prices listed were those available at press time. Increases are possible.

Introduction: "Contrary Country"

Welcome to Vermont, the Switzerland of North America (as Lord Bryce, the British ambassador and historian called it in 1909), and to this fifth edition of the most comprehensive guide to its assets and charms, hidden and obvious. It is intended for Vermont residents, as well as visitors. No other portrait of the state gathers so much practical information between two covers.

The book divides Vermont into areas, whose boundaries usually coincide with those of the local chambers of commerce. Each section begins with a verbal snapshot of the surroundings and historical vignettes, followed by words of guidance, getting around, things to see and do, and descriptions of just about every legal form of recreation—skiing, horseback riding, sailing, hiking, swimming, canoeing, golf, or whatever else is handy. Then come capsule descriptions, with prices, of places to stay, representing roughly two-thirds of the local lodging. Obviously, we can't go on about each place the way inn and B&B guides do, but we are frank (even about a sacred cow or two). We visit regularly (many innkeepers tell us they see us far more frequently than authors of the specialized guides), and we describe many reasonably priced options, some of them real gems, which are found in no other book. We should also say that we charge nothing to be included, while a large percentage of lodging guides charge lodging places a "processing fee," anywhere from $250 to $2,500.

After lodging descriptions each chapter includes painstaking critiques of the local upscale restaurants (*Dining Out*) and the everyday options (*Eating Out*), listings of local theaters and other entertainment, of shops worth walking into, and of special events.

Vermont's popularity as a summer resort for the city-weary means that you might want to look outside the prime attractions of Manchester, Woodstock, and Stowe (unless you haven't ever visited them) and seek out the less-traveled areas like the verdant lower Champlain Valley, the pristine hill villages, the Islands, and, of course, the Northeast Kingdom.

Every Green Mountain village offers something of interest: an unusual small inn, antique or craft shop, cheese maker, gourmet restaurant, or simply vistas of such breathtaking beauty that they demand mention. And Vermont is full of surprises. No matter how many trips a visitor makes, the unexpected is always around the corner: a spectacular view, a splendid house or barn, even a cluster of tarpaper shacks in a hollow of appalling poverty within two miles of a posh summer or winter playground for the affluent.

Today's visitor is more likely than not to be welcomed by ex-visitors. Innkeepers, shopkeepers, and craftspeople tend to be here by choice rather than birth: 40 percent of the state's population of 560,000 came "from away." This post–World War II stage of Vermont's colorful history is as worthy of note as its 14 years as an independent republic.

The years of sovereignty, between 1777 and 1791, stamped Vermont with the indelible "contrary country" brand, to borrow a phrase of the late Ralph Nading Hill. Some contemporary Vermonters, surveying the murky horizons of the 1990s, mutter conspiratorially about secession. But when basically conservative Vermonters voted in nearly 200 town meetings in 1982 for a bilateral nuclear arms freeze, they were not just being ornery. They acted traditionally, in the spirit that animated Ethan Allen's Rabelaisian Green Mountain Boys, who wrested independence from the grip of Hampshiremen and 'Yorkers as well as from "The Cruel Minestereal Tools of George ye 3d"; and in the abolitionist fervor that impelled Vermonters to flock to the colors in record numbers when President Lincoln called for troops to preserve the Union. They voted their consciences with much the same zeal when, in both world wars, the legislature declared war on Germany, in effect, before the United States did; and with the prescience that prompted Vermont to lead the nation in the enactment of protective land-use laws.

The portrait of the legendary Vermont Yankee—frugal, wary, taciturn, sardonically humorous—has faded somewhat in today's homogenized, shopping-center culture. The Vermonter has made some concessions to the microchip age, but as Ralph Nading Hill, the Vermont historian, wrote in *Yankee Kingdom*, "his individuality has not yet been eroded away. And the character of the countryside that Bernard DeVoto said is every American's second home remains largely the same. The valley towns, white and serene, seem to have become a universal symbol of nostalgia—of belonging somewhere, even to those who have seen only pictures of them reproduced on calendars. The reason is, perhaps, that the people of a rootless age find something admirable about a slice of hill country that has resisted being made over into the latest fashionable image."

A principal reason for this sense of permanence is that, prudently, Vermonters have not torn down the past; rather, abandoned farmhouses have been restored, and in a score of towns, adaptive preservation techniques have been thoughtfully used to convert obsolete

Harness racing at the Tunbridge Fair

woolen mills into enclosed markets. The former State Penitentiary in Windsor, once the oldest in the country still in use, has been transformed into low-income housing units. The post-war infusion of light industry, moreover, has been carefully sited in ways that leave the surrounding landscape mostly undisturbed.

As the flatland author, born in Hawaii, raised in New York City, and living near Boston, Chris Tree defends her expertise about Vermont. Her infatuation with the state began in college. "The college was in Massachusetts, but one of my classmates was a native Vermonter whose father ran a general store and whose mother knows the name of every flower, bird, and mushroom. I jumped at her invitation to come 'home' or to 'camp' and have since spent far more time in Vermont than my friend. As a travel writer for *The Boston Globe*, I have spent more than twenty years writing newspaper stories about Vermont towns, inns, ski areas, and people. I interviewed John Kenneth Galbraith about Newfane, Pearl Buck on Danby. I rode the Vermont Bicentennial Train, froze a toe on one of the first inn-to-inn ski treks, camped on the Long Trail and in state parks, paddled a canoe down the Connecticut, slid over Lake Champlain on an ice boat, soared over the Mad River Valley in a glider, and hovered above the Upper Valley in a hot air balloon. I have also tramped through the woods collecting sap, ridden many miles with Vermont Transit, led a foliage tour, collided with a tractor, and broken down in a variety of spots ranging from Stowe's Main Street to the village of Marshfield—'Can't fix it here. No way for you to get out of here. No place to stay either.'

"Of all my experiences, the most prized has been getting to know Vermonters, something which I find increasingly difficult in resort areas, and one reason why I frequently head for the rolling farm country on the high plateaus east of the Green Mountains in central Vermont and in the Northeast Kingdom. The other reason is that rental cottages or 'camps' are far cheaper off the beaten path, a consideration when you travel as a family of five. Which isn't to say that we don't enjoy Stowe, Woodstock, the Mad River Valley, and Southern Vermont. My excuse for remaining a flatlander is an embarrassment of riches in both senses: aside from lacking the funds to move, we simply cannot decide which part of Vermont to move to."

Peter Jennison, the "born again" Vermonter, returned to his native heath in 1971, because, like many latter-day immigrants, he was tired of working in New York City and being held hostage by the New Haven Railroad. When he is asked "How long have you lived in Vermont?" he is apt to reply, "Since 1769," thinking of the miller, John Saxe, who settled in Highgate. Indeed, he is the fifth generation to have been born in the same room in the family's former Swanton dairy farm. Since returning to Vermont, he has founded a publishing company ("necessity being the mother of ingenuity"), written several books about Vermont, notably *The Roadside History of Vermont*, and served as a trustee of the Vermont Historical Society. "I haven't done half the things Chris has," he admits, "but in over fifty years I have almost qualified to join the 251 Club—whose numbers aspire to visit every town and gore—and I've seen how the state has been transformed from an almost wholly agrarian society to a far more sophisticated place to live, a land of infinite variety where people still mind their own business. We have freedom and unity—the state motto."

Peter added a quotation from Charles T. Morrissey's *Vermont: A History*: " . . . the entire state is a reminder of the American past, a remnant from the agrarian culture which once we were. It is understandable why Americans come here from other states in search of the mystic chords of memories, and why some want to build a fence around Vermont in order to preserve it as a specimen of Americana, a national park of the Yankee spirit which infused our national psyche."

The authors wish to thank the staffs of the Vermont Travel Division and of local chambers of commerce for their assistance in providing information for the book and express their boundless gratitude, individually and collectively, to all of their Countryman Press colleagues, particularly Robin Dutcher-Bayer and Clare Innes; and to Jean Forden, Tony Egan, Barbara Thomke, and Richard Courcelle, for their encouragement, support, and patience.

Christina Tree
Peter S. Jennison

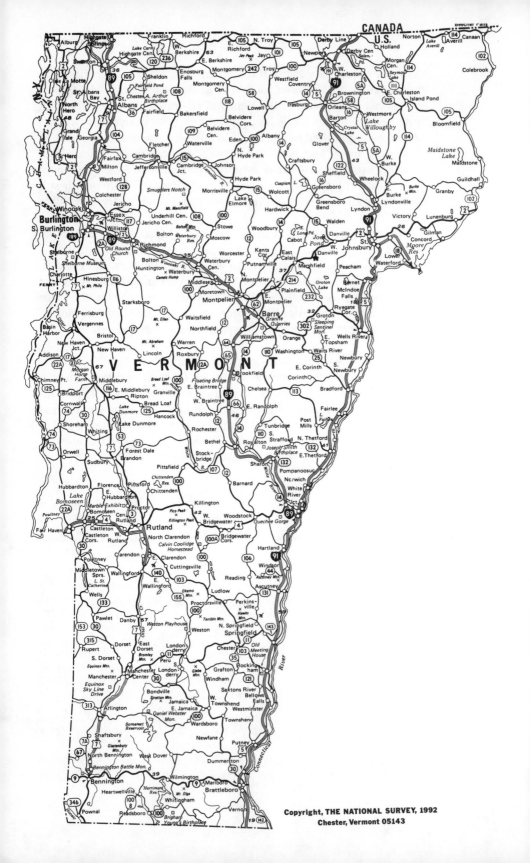

What's Where in Vermont

AGRICULTURAL FAIRS "Vermont Agricultural Fairs and Field Days," a pamphlet available from the Vermont Department of Agriculture (828-2500), Montpelier 05602, lists the major events, beginning with the **Vermont Maple Festival** in St. Albans in April and filling every weekend in July, August, and September. The most famous are the **Champlain Valley Exposition**, Essex, around Labor Day; **Orleans County Fair** in Barton (five days) and the **Bondville Fair** (two days), both in late August; the **Vermont State Fair** in Rutland (nine days, the biggest); and the **World's Fair** in Tunbridge (four days, the most colorful of all).

AIR SERVICE Burlington International Airport (863-3489) currently offers most of the scheduled service in Vermont. Carriers include: **Business Express** (Delta Connection), Burlington to Boston: 800-221-1212. Also serves Lebanon (NH) Regional Airport: 800-345-3400. **Continental Airlines** connects Burlington with most major US cities: 800-221-1212. **Northwest Airlines** offers flights to Lebanon (NH) Regional Airport: 800-225-2525. **United Airlines** connects with most US points via Chicago: 800-241-6522. **US Air** flies in from New York and Boston: 800-428-4322. **Northwest Airlines** offers an air link from Boston: 800-225-2525. **Adirondack Airlines** has daily service from Rutland to Newark and Islip: 800-441-2304.

AIRPORTS Vermont offers 65 private and 10 state-owned airports, only one (above) with scheduled flights but all accessible to private and some to charter planes. Request a copy of the Vermont Airport Directory from the Vermont Agency of Transportation, RAPT: 828-1711.

AMTRAK AMTRAK offers service between Washington and Montreal with stops as listed below. Phone: 800-USA-RAIL.

Northbound		Southbound
3:15 AM	Brattleboro	12:15 PM
3:50 AM	Bellows Falls	11:40 PM
5:00 AM	White River Jct.	10:40 PM
6:15 AM	Montpelier	9:15 PM
6:30 AM	Waterbury	9:00 PM
7:05 AM	Essex Junction	8:30 PM
7:40 AM	St. Albans	8:00 PM

ANTIQUARIAN BOOKSELLERS "Old Books in the Green Mountain State," a listing of the 40 or more current members of the Vermont Antiquarian Booksellers Association, is available from its member stores. See "Brattleboro," "Middlebury," and "Rutland" chapters under *Selective Shopping*.

The VABA has an annual fair at the Woodstock Inn the first or second Sunday of August.

ANTIQUING A pamphlet guide, "Antiquing in Vermont," listing more than 120 members of the Vermont Antiques Dealers' Association, is available by sending a self-addressed #10 envelope to Muriel McKirryher, 55 Allen Street, Rutland 05701. Major concentrations of dealers can be found in **Bennington, Brandon, Burlington, Middlebury, Manchester**, and **Woodstock**.

APPLES During fall harvest season, there is a demand not only for bushel baskets already filled with apples but also for an empty basket and the chance to climb a ladder and fill it with MacIntosh, Red Delicious, or others among the many varieties of apples grown in Vermont—primarily in the **Champlain Valley** and in the **Lower Connecticut River Valley** between Springfield and Putney. Detailed listings can be found under descriptions of these areas and by requesting the "Vermont Apples" pamphlet from the Vermont Department of Agriculture, 116 State Street, State Office Building, Montpelier, VT 05602.

AREA CODE The area code for all of Vermont is 802, the reason we have omitted listing it at all within the text.

ARTS COUNCILS Vermont has local arts councils that organize films, festivals, and concerts throughout the year. The ones listed are the largest and are good sources for what's happening in their area: Arts Council of Windham County, Brattleboro (257-1881); Catamount Film and Arts Center, St. Johnsbury (748-2600); Crossroads Arts Council, Rutland (775-5413); Onion River Arts Council, Montpelier (229-9408); Pentangle Arts Council, Woodstock (457-3981). The overall information source is the Vermont Council on the Arts (828-3291) in Montpelier.

ART GALLERIES Vermont's principal collections of art (painting, sculpture, and decorative arts) are found in the **Bennington Museum** (works by Grandma Moses), the **Robert Hull Fleming Museum** at the University of Vermont, Burlington; the new **Arts Center** at Middlebury College; the **Athenaeum** in St. Johnsbury; the **Shelburne Museum** in Shelburne; the **Chaffee Art Gallery**, Rutland; the **Southern Vermont Art Center**, Manchester; the **Thomas Waterman Wood Art Gallery**, Montpelier; the **Dana House,** Woodstock (John Taylor Arms); the **Helen Day Art Center** in Stowe; the **Chandler Gallery** in Randolph; and in such private galleries as the **Peel Gallery of Fine Art** in Danby, **Gallery Two** and **The Woodstock Gallery and Design Center** in Woodstock, and the **Tontine Gallery** in East Barnard. The **Vermont Studio Center** in Johnson includes a gallery showcasing the work of the (constantly changing) professional artists who gather to work here (see "North of the Notch").

AUCTIONS Most major upcoming auctions are announced in the Thursday edition of the Vermont newspapers, with a listing of items that will be up for bid. Auctions may be scheduled at any time, however, during summer months, advertised primarily on local bulletin boards and in shop windows. Among well-known auctioneers and auction houses: William Dupras of Randolph Center; Butch Sutherland, Woodstock; C. W. Gray of East Thetford, every Monday night, year-round (livestock); Arthur Hicks, Hick's Commission Sales, Morrisville.

BALLOONING Year-round champagne flights are offered by Brian Boland and Ruth Ludwig at Post Mills Airport (333-4883). Also inquire at the Stoweflake Resort, in Stowe (253-7355). The state's major ballooning events are the **Lake Champlain Balloon Festival,** held in early June, and the **Annual Balloon Festival** in Quechee, in late June.

BARNS Many barns along the highways and byways have distinctive touches, such as ornate Victorian cupolas, and still more are connected to farmhouses in the "extended" architectural style that served as shelter for the farmer's trips before dawn in deep snow.

Just a dozen round barns survive in Vermont, all built between 1899 and World War I. The concept of the round barn is thought to have originated with the Shakers in Hancock, Massachusetts, where the original stone barn, built in 1824, is now the centerpiece of a museum. The Vermont survivors include: the **Moore barn** in East Barnet; the **Hastings barn** in Waterford; the **Metcalf barn** (Robillard Flats) in Irasburg; the **Parker barn** in Grand Isle, converted into a housing center for the elderly; two barns in Coventry; the **Powers barn** in Lowell; the **Parker barn** in North Troy; one in Enosburg Falls; **Southwick's** in East Calais; and the **Joslin round barn** (now a cultural center attached to a B&B), Waitsfield. Note that the name ascribed to each barn belongs to the builder rather than to present owners. Round barn addicts should check at local general stores for location and secure permission to photo-

VTD

Country auctions offer free family fun

graph the structures. Among other Vermont barns open to the public are the vast five-story, 416-foot-long, Norman-style **Farm Barn** and the impressive stable and carriage house at **Shelburne Farms** in Shelburne. The round barn once in Passumpsic has been moved to the Shelburne Museum.

BED & BREAKFAST Bed & breakfasts are listed under their respective locations in this book, and new ones appear each month, replacing the old guest house (which serves no meals at all) in towns and the "farmhouse vacation" (which traditionally serves all three meals) in the country. The bed & breakfasts that we have inspected range from working farms to historic mansions, from $50–150 per room.

BICYCLING An estimated 15,000 pedal pushers, representing a wide span in ages (but not counting camp groups) and biking abilities, annually join organized tours through Vermont. **Vermont Bicycle Tour-**ing (better known as VBT) introduced the whole notion of guided bike tours for adults back in 1971. Its founder, John Freidin, is the author of *25 Bicycle Tours in Vermont* (Backcountry Publications), the bible of independent bicyclists. Now owned by Bill Perry, VBT (Box 711, Bristol 05443) offers a choice of more than 50 different tours (varying lengths) on more than 350 days, spring through fall. At latest count, there were nine cycle touring groups based in Vermont, most furnishing equipment, guides, a support van (the "sag wag"), and lodging at country inns. **Vermont Country Cyclers** (Box 145, Loomis Hill Road, Waterbury Center 05677) is the other big operator and features elegant lodging. **Bike Vermont** (PO Box 75, Grafton 05146, and Box 207, Woodstock 05091), headed by Bob McElwain, features smaller groups than the other two. **Bicycle Holidays** (RD 3, Box 2394, Middlebury 05753), **Clearwater Sports** (Route 100, Waitsfield 05673), and **Viking Biking** (RR 1, Box 70, Little Pond Road, Londonderry

05148) also offer inn-to-inn tours. In the past few years, touring options have been increased by companies like **Vermont Mountain Bike Tours** (Tom Yennerell, PO Box 685, Pittsfield 05762) and **New England Bicycle Tours** (John McKeon, PO Box 26, Randolph 05060), featuring wide-tire, sturdy-framed mountain bikes, ideal for exploring dirt roads. There are now three outstanding places to come, stay, and improve mountain biking skills on an extensive network of cross-country ski trails (**Craftsbury Mountain Bike Center**, Box 31, Craftsbury Common 05827) and on a combination of back roads and alpine ski trails at **The Mountain Bike School and Touring Center** at Mount Snow, West Dover, and Killington, where lifts service 25 miles of trails spread over three of the ski resort's six peaks. Neophytes as well as experienced bikers are welcome at all mountain bike centers. There are also two outfits—**Country Inns Along the Trail** (c/o Churchill House Inn, RD 3, Brandon 05733) and **Cycle Inn Vermont** (c/o Okemo Inn, RFD 1, Box 133, Ludlow 05149)—composed of innkeepers whose establishments are a comfortable bike ride from each other. Participants are largely on their own, but rental equipment is available and baggage is transferred from inn to inn. In addition, a growing number of bicycle shops are not only renting bikes but offering guided tours. We've noted **Lake Willoughby Bike Rental** and **Guided Tours in Westmore**, but there are more, many more who offer self-guided tours with rentals (these are noted in each chapter).

Stowe's bike path and rental mountain bikes make it an ideal place to sample the sport. And there are other bike paths. The Burlington Bike Path follows the shore of Lake Champlain for seven miles (rentals available), the Bennington Historic Bike Route leads bikers around local sights, and the 34-mile D&H Recreation trail follows an abandoned railroad bed almost 20 miles from Castleton to West Rupert, with the remainder in New York State. A "Bicycle Touring in Vermont" information sheet is available from the Vermont Travel Division (828-3236), 134 State Street, Montpelier 05602. Within each chapter, we have described sources for local bike rentals.

BIRDING   A handy booklet, "Check List for Birds of Vermont," is available from either the Green Mountain Audubon Society, Box 33, Burlington 05401, or Vermont Fish and Game, Montpelier 05602. Outstanding birding areas include the **Missisquoi National Wildlife Refuge** in Swanton and the 4,970-acre **Victory Basin** east of St. Johnsbury. The 230-acre **Green Mountain Audubon Nature Center** in Huntington (434-3068) is open year-round, Tuesday–Friday 9–5, and weekends 1–4. The Vermont state bird is the hermit thrush.

The **Vermont Institute of Natural Science** (457-2779), Woodstock 05091, sponsors bird walks in all parts of the state, frequently led by Walter G. Ellison, author of "A Guide to Bird Finding in Vermont," available from VINS for $5.95 plus $1.50 mailing charge per copy. The Institute's **Vermont Raptor Center** introduces visitors to the owls, hawks, and eagles of northern New England (26 species are in residence).

BOATING   The pamphlet "Vermont Boating, Rentals & Marinas," available from the Vermont Travel Division (see *Information*) includes an annually updated list of boat (motor, sail, and canoe) rentals. Also see *Canoeing, Cruises,* and *White Water.* The official state map (also see *Information*) notes public boat launch areas. A booklet, "Laws and Regulations Governing the Use and Registration of Motorboats," is available from the Vermont Department of Public Safety, Marine Division, Montpelier 05602.

BOOKS   For a complete bibliography, write for the "Books about Vermont" catalogue from the Vermont Historical Society, 109 State Street, Montpelier 05602. In addition to the books we mention in specific fields or on particular subjects, here are some of the most useful current titles: *The Vermont Atlas and Gazetteer,* compiled and published by David DeLorme and Company, Freeport, Maine; *Vermont: A History,* by Charles Morrissey (W. W. Norton); *Vermont Place Names: Footprints in History,* by Esther Swift (Stephen Greene Press); *Lake Champlain: Key to Liberty,* by Ralph Nading Hill (Countryman Press); *Contrary Country,* by Ralph Nading Hill (Shelburne Museum); the three gorgeously illustrated albums put out by *Vermont Life—Vermont, a Special World, Vermont For Every Season,* and *The Vermont Experience—*and *Fast Lane on a Dirt Road,* by Joe Sherman (Countryman Press). *The Roadside History of Vermont,* by Peter Jennison (Mountain Press, Missoula, MT), is an informal narrative of what happened where and when along main travel routes. For children, *Vermont, The State with the Storybook Past* by Cora Cheney (New England Press) is the best. Keith Jennison's classic collections of Vermont humor, like *Yup . . . Nope & Other Vermont Dialogues* (Countryman Press) are in most bookstores and many gift shops. A basic reference directory is *The Vermont Year Book,* published annually by the National Survey, Chester.

BOOKSTORES   There are good general bookstores in Barre, Bennington, Brattleboro, Bridgewater, Burlington, Chester, Essex Junction, Hardwick, Londonderry, Lyndonville, Manchester, Middlebury, Montpelier, Morrisville, Newport, Randolph, Rutland, St. Albans, St. Johnsbury, Shelburne, South Burlington, Springfield, Stowe, Waitsfield, Wilmington, Winooski, and Woodstock. Several of them with special significance, like **Johnny Appleseed, Bear Pond, North-shire, Chassman & Bem,** and the **Vermont Bookshop,** are mentioned in the text under *Selective Shopping* in their respective towns. The most complete stock of Ver-montiana is on sale in the **Vermont Historical Society Shop** in Montpelier.

BREWERIES   Microbreweries are multiplying. **The Catamount Brewery** in White River Junction is the oldest and largest of this breed. Founded in 1987, it now produces 6,000 barrels per year (figure 31 gallons per barrel). It brews porter (a dark, rich ale), also fold and amber lagers and a seasonal Christmas ale. **The Vermont Pub and Brewery** in Burlington produces the most varieties, more than a dozen. The most popular in its pub (opened in 1988) is Burley Irish Ale. **Mountain Brewers** in Bridgewater produce Long Trail Ale, a ruddy English ale, also Northern Light (fewer calories). **Otter Creek Brewers** in

Middlebury produces a malty ale and a wheat beer.

BUS SERVICE   Vermont Transit. For a current timetable, contact Vermont Transit Co., Inc. (864-6811 or 800-451-3292), 135 St. Paul Street, Burlington 05401. The major routes are: (1) up the western side of the state from New York City and Albany via Bennington, Rutland, and Burlington to Montreal; (2) from Boston via White River Junction and Burlington to Montreal; (3) Boston to Burlington via Rutland; (4) Quebec to New York City with connections to Boston via Newport and St. Johnsbury. Read the timetable carefully, and you will find that most corners of the state of Vermont—and a number elsewhere in northern New England—are served. Children under 12 years travel half price; one child under five can travel free. Vermont Transit Tours, geared to Vermont residents who want to get out for a day (to Boston's Quincy Market) or for a weekend (to New York City or Montreal) or for more than two weeks (to Florida and other points south), are described in newsletters available from the Burlington office.

CAMPS, for children.   There are 55 summer camps for boys and girls in the state; for a listing, contact the Vermont Camping Association, RD 1, Box 162, Salisbury 05769.

CAMPGROUNDS   Private. A listing of the 90 private campgrounds that belong to the Vermont Association of Private Campground Owners and Operators (VAPCOO) can be found on the state map; a brochure detailing the locations, facilities, services, and numbers of sites at each is available from the Vermont Travel Division (828-3236).
    State Campgrounds. Thirty-five fine campgrounds are maintained by the Department of Forests, Parks and Recreation (244-8711), described in the State Parks brochure available from their office at 108 South Main Street, Waterbury 05676. They offer more than 2,000 campsites, many with lean-to shelters, none with hook-ups. There are two classes of state park campgrounds: Class A, which have beaches and swim-

ming, and Class B, which do not. Anytime after January 3, a campsite can be reserved for six days to two weeks. Reservations for less than six days cannot be accepted before June 1. Reservations for three or more nights are accepted at most parks after May 15. In 1992, camping fees range from $9 per night for a tent or trailer site in a Class B area to $14 plus 8 percent state rooms and meals tax (would you believe?) in a Class A area.

The State Parks brochure describes each park and gives details on group camping sites. Vermont state park campsites are all screened by trees from neighboring sites and are well maintained; many parks have organized programs: hikes, campfire sings, films, and lectures. Most parks are relatively uncrowded, especially midweek when the only sites likely to be filled are in Branbury, Stillwater, Groton Forest, and Lake St. Catherine. We have provided details, including phone numbers, for each park as it appears within the text. A listing can also be found on the state map. A separate pamphlet, "Guide to Primitive Camping on State Lands," is available from the Department of Forests, Parks and Recreation.

Green Mountain National Forest Campgrounds. Within the 300,000-acre preserve, 94 fine, well-developed campsites are offered. They are available on a first-come, first-serve basis for a maximum 14-day period at a modest charge, posted at the entrance to each area. Camping is also permitted, without fee or prior permission, virtually anywhere on National Forest land. Before pitching your tent, however, we recommend that you visit one of the three district ranger offices, in Manchester Center, Middlebury, or Rochester, and inquire about proper places to camp. A free mini-map is available from the Green Mountain National Forest (773-0300), 151 West Street, Rutland 05701.

U.S. Army Corps of Engineers. The Department of the Army, New England Division, Corps of Engineers, has constructed two camping areas in Vermont. The Winhall Brook Camping Area at Ball Mountain Lake in Jamaica offers 108 campsites near flush toilets, showers, and swimming, free on a first-come, first-serve basis; for details contact the Basin Manager,

Upper Connecticut River Basin Office, North Springfield Lake, 98 Reservoir Road, Springfield 05156. The Corps of Engineers also built the 30-site camping area of Quechee Gorge near the North Hartland Dam, now maintained by the state.

CANOEING Organized canoe trips have increased dramatically in recent years. For details, contact: **Battenkill Canoe,** Box 65, Route 313, West Arlington 05250 (day-trips, inn-to-inn tours throughout the state); **Clearwater** (Route 100, Waitsfield 05673) offers guided tours, instruction, and special expeditions. **The Stone House Inn** (North Thetford 05054) is a stop on multiday, inn-to-inn expeditions on the Connecticut River. **Canoe USA** (728-3261), based in Randolph, also offers inn-to-inn tours, and **Vermont Voyageur** (Montgomery Center 05471) offers a wide variety of guided tours and will tailor them to the needs of families. **Connecticut River Safari** (Route 5, Brattleboro 05301) in the southeastern corner of the state and **Pine Ridge Adventure Center** (1075 Williston Road, Williston 05495) also offer guided tours. **Mannsview Inn** (800-937-MANN) in Jeffersonville offers rental canoes and shuttle service on the Lamoille River, as does **Silver Maple Lodge** (800-666-1946) in Fairlee for the upper Connecticut.

Helpful publications include: *AMC River Guide—New Hampshire/Vermont*, good for detailed information on canoeable rivers, available from the Appalachian Mountain Club, 5 Joy Street, Boston, MA 02108. "Vermont Guide to Fishing Map," free from Vermont Fish and Wildlife Department, Waterbury 05676, notes falls, rapids, boulder fields, dams, and other potential dangers. *Canoe Camping Vermont & New Hampshire Rivers* (Backcountry Publications) is a handy guide. "Winooski River Canoe Guide" is $2 from the Winooski Valley Park District, Ethan Allen Homestead, Burlington 05401. (Also see *White Water.*)

CANOE RENTALS Rentals are available from the canoe outfitters listed above and from the boat rental sources listed in the free "Vermont Boating Rentals and Marinas" pamphlet, available from the Travel Division (see *Information*).

CHEESE A century ago, almost every Vermont town had its cheese factory to which farmers brought their daily surplus milk. Today the two most widely distributed Vermont cheeses are Cabot's and Seward's. **Cabot Farmer's Co-op**, the state's most famous cheese factory, is a modern plant producing 12 million pounds of cheese a year, maintaining a slick visitor's center with a video orientation, plant tour, and gift shop. **The Seward Family** produces a Genuine Vermont Cheddar in their East Wallingford plant; they showcase and sell it in the Seward Family Restaurant on Route 7 in Rutland. The family has been in the business since the Civil War and prides itself on a sharp cheddar, aged over nine months. **Grafton Village Cheese Company** in Grafton had its beginnings around 1890 and was resurrected by the Windham Foundation in 1966; visitors view the cheese-making from outside, through a picture window. **The Plymouth Cheese Corp.**, founded in 1890 by Col. John Coolidge, father of President Coolidge, is now operated by John Coolidge, son of the president. The factory shop is open (see Plymouth) year-round, producing an old-fashioned Vermont Granular Curd Cheese. At **Shelburne Farms** (open daily, year-round), near Burlington, Alec Webb makes cheddar from a single herd of Brown Swiss cows. In New Haven, **Orb Weaver Farm** produces a creamy, aged, Colby-type cheese made in small batches, entirely by hand (available in two-pound wheels and one-pound waxed wedges). In Hinesburg, **International Cheese Company** produces a line of traditional cheeses; in Enosburg Falls, **Hahn's** produces bakers' cheese and fresh cheesecake; and in Middlesex, **1782 Settlement Cheese** produces a farmstead cheese. **Vermont Butter & Cheese Co.** in Websterville makes goat cheese.

CHILDREN (especially for) **Alpine Slides** delight children of all ages at Bromley (where there is also a **Mountain Rafting Ride**) as well as at Pico and Stowe.

Alpine Lifts, which operate in summer, are also a way of hoisting small legs and feet to the top of some of Vermont's most spectacular summits. **Mt. Mansfield**, Vermont's highest peak, is accessible via the gondola. **Killington Peak**, second highest

in the state, can be reached via chair lift on weekdays and by a 3½-mile gondola ride on weekends. **Jay Peak**, commanding as dramatic a view as the others, is accessible on a smooth-riding tram. In southern Vermont, **Stratton's** gondola runs daily all summer and fall, and **Mount Snow's** chair lift runs on weekends in summer, daily during foliage season.

Santa's Land in Putney is the only commercial attraction geared specifically to children.

The Discovery Museum in Essex Junction is a rewarding, hands-on experience; exhibits range from small animals and snakes through computers.

The Shelburne Museum has many exhibits that please youngsters, as does the **Fairbanks Planetarium and Museum**, St. Johnsbury, which is filled with stuffed animals, birds, and exhibits from near and far. **The Montshire Museum of Science** in Norwich and the **Billings Farm Museum** and **Vermont Institute of Natural Science,** both in Woodstock, are child pleasers.

Skiing. Over the past few years, as ski areas have come to compete for family business, most ski resorts have developed special programs for children: See *For Children* under each ski area described in the text. In summer, a growing number of ski areas—Bolton Valley, Smugglers' Notch, Sugarbush, Stratton, Killington, and Mount Snow—offer full day-camp programs for children. Also see *Farms* and *Railroad Excursions.*

CHRISTMAS TREES A listing of Christmas tree growers, most of them cut-your-own places, is available from the Vermont Department of Agriculture, 116 State Street, Montpelier 05602.

COLLEGES A brochure listing all the state's colleges, giving details on what is offered, is published by the Consortium of Vermont Colleges, available from the Vermont Travel Division (see *Information*).

COVERED BRIDGES The state's 110 surviving covered bridges are marked on the official state map.

CRAFTS More than 1,000 Vermonters make their living from craft work. There are also more than 100 retail craft outlets in the state, ranging from back kitchens to the two nonprofit **Vermont State Craft Centers**, one in Windsor (674-6729) and the other showcasing over 250 professionals at Frog Hollow (388-4871) in Middlebury, with a small offshoot in Burlington. Within this book, we have described outstanding local craftspeople and crafts shops as they appear geographically. We have also included major crafts festivals. Among the most outstanding: in July, the **Woodstock Craftsmen's Fair**; **Burklyn Summer Fair of Vermont Arts & Crafts**; **The Killington Art Show**; **Art on the Mountain** at Haystack Ski Area in Wilmington; and the **Southern Vermont Craft Fair** in Manchester. In September: the **Stratton Arts Festival** (four weeks, until mid-October). In October: the **Mt. Snow Craft Fair** and the **Fall Festival of Vermont Crafts** in Montpelier; and in November: the **Burlington Craft Fair.**

CRUISES   If you don't own a yacht, there are still plenty of ways to get onto Vermont rivers and lakes. Possible excursions include the *Belle of Brattleboro* that plies the Connecticut from Brattleboro; the *Spirit of Ethan Allen*, a paddle-wheeler-style excursion vessel based in Burlington; *The M/V Carillon*, a sleek replica of an old lake boat, offers narrated cruises from Larrabees's Point in Shoreham up and down Lake Champlain near Fort Ticonderoga; and the *Heather Sue* sails on Lake Whitingham from Wilmington. For details, check under respective locations in this book. Three-hour sails are available from **McKibben Sailing Vacations** in Burlington, and excursions on small passenger boats, specializing in scuba charters, are offered by **Inland Sea Charters** in Milton and **Marine Explorers** in Shelburne.

DINERS   Vermont will not disappoint diner buffs. Hearty meals at reasonable prices can be found at the **Miss Newport** (good coffee), East Main Street, Newport; at **Henry's Diner** (known for its Yankee pot roast, lobster roll, and generally good three squares) and **The Oasis**, both on Bank Street, Burlington. The **Parkway Diner** at 1696 Williston Road, South Burlington, is

known for its Greek salad, lobster roll, and Parkway Special: roast beef on pumpernickel roll. The **Miss Lyndonville Diner** on Bond Street, Lyndonville, is admired for its pies (a breakfast special) and has been augmented by the nearby **Miss Vermont** (Route 5, St. Johnsbury Center), though lines are still long on Sunday morning. **Blue Benn Diner,** 102 Hunt Street in Bennington, serves imaginative vegetarian as well as standard diner fare. Add to these the **Green Mountain Diner**, Main Street in Barre, **Cindy's Diner** in St. Albans, **Don's Diner** in Bennington, **Jad's Family Diner** (try the turkey) in Brattleboro, **Anthony's** in St. Johnsbury, and **Delaney's Country Girl Diner** in Chester. **Miss Bellows Falls Diner** is on the National Register.

EMERGENCIES   Emergency numbers are given on the inside cover of Vermont phone books and on the official state map. Within this book, we have furnished the number of the medical facilities serving each area at the end of each chapter.

EVENTS   Almost every day of the year some special event is happening somewhere in Vermont. Usually it's something relatively small and friendly like a church supper, contra dance, community theatrical production, concert, or crafts fair. We have worked up our own "Calendar of Events" but would like to mention here that up-to-date, detailed listings of current events are available from the Vermont Travel Division, 134 State Street, Montpelier 05602. Check also in local weekly newspapers and area shopping guides.

FACTORY OUTLETS   Within the book, we have mentioned some, but not all, of the factory outlets in the state of which we are aware. Our bias has been to favor distinctly made-in-Vermont products. Among our favorites: **Johnson Woolen Mills** (outstanding wool clothing for all ages) in Johnson; **Bennington Potters** (dinnerware, planters, etc.) in Bennington and Burlington; **Vermont Marble** in Proctor; **Weston Bowl Mill** in Weston; **Townshend Furniture** in Townshend; **Kennedy Bros.** (woodenware) in Vergennes; **American Maple Products** in Newport. Manchester is known for its dozens of "factory direct" stores specializing in quality clothing.

"Vermont Factory Outlets," a pamphlet compiled by the Vermont Chamber of Commerce is available from the Vermont Travel Division, 134 State Street, Montpelier 05602.

FARMERS' MARKETS   From mid-June to early October you can count on finding fresh vegetables, fruit, honey, and much more at farm prices in commercial centers throughout the state. Check the times and places in Burlington, Enosburg, Morrisville, Newport, St. Johnsbury, Norwich, Fair Haven, Middlebury, Montpelier, Rutland, Brattleboro, Manchester, Waterbury, and Windsor. Current details about the farmers' markets are found in "The Farmers' Market" and "Vermont Fruits & Vegetables" pamphlets; both are available from the Vermont Travel Division (see *Information*).

FARMS   In 1991, Vermont had less than 2,500 full-time dairy farms (compared to 26,490 in 1945), and less than 850,000 acres—out of the state's total 6 million acres—were being cultivated. Still, the farmhouse and barn are a symbol of Vermont to out-of-staters, and the highlight of a Vermont vacation for most children is a visit to the barn. "Farm Vacation Opportunities in Vermont" lists the farms that take in guests and is available from the Vermont Travel Division (see *Information*). We have also described each of these places as they appear within their areas. They include **Berkson Farms** in Enosburg Falls, **Knoll Farm Country Inn** in Fayston, **Liberty Hill** and **Harvey's Mountain View**, both in Rochester.

FARM STANDS   The handy "Vermont Fruits & Vegetables" pamphlet contains descriptive listings of roadside stands as well as pick-your-own places and farmers' markets. It's produced by the Vermont Department of Agriculture, 116 State Street, Montpelier 05602.

FERRIES   On Lake Champlain, a number of car-carrying ferries ply back and forth between the Vermont and New York

shores, offering splendid views of both the Green Mountains and the Adirondacks. The northernmost, the **Plattsburgh Ferry**, crosses from Grand Isle, Vermont, on Route 314 (year-round: 12 minutes). From Burlington, the **Lake Champlain Ferries** cross to Port Kent, New York (1 hour). The **Essex Ferry** crosses from Route F-5 near Charlotte, Vermont, to Essex, New York (20 minutes). Check schedules (864-9804) for hours of operation and rates. All three of these are operated by the Lake Champlain Transportation Company, descendant of the line founded in 1828 claiming to be "the oldest steamboat company on earth." Near the southern end of the lake, the **Fort Ticonderoga Ferry** (897-7999) provides a scenic shortcut between Larrabees Point, Vermont, and Ticonderoga, New York. This small, car-carrying ferry makes the six-minute crossing continuously between 8 AM and 9 PM during the summer season and on a shorter schedule in spring and fall. Service runs from late April through the last Sunday in October. Officially, the "Fort Ti Ferry" has held the franchise from the New York and Vermont legislatures since 1799.

FIDDLING   Vermont is the fiddling capital of the East. Fiddlers tend to include concert violinists, rural carpenters, farmers, and heavy equipment operators who come from throughout the East to gather in beautiful natural settings. The season begins over the July 4 weekend with the **Annual Fiddler's Concert**, Kents Corner, Calais. They follow, in sequence: **Ryegate Fiddle Festival**, South Ryegate; **Crackerbarrel Fiddle Festival**, Newbury; **Burklyn Old-Time Fiddler's Contest**, Burke Mountain Base Lodge, East Burke; **Annual Old-Time Fiddling Contest**, Chelsea; the **Certified State Championships**, Bellows Falls; and in late September, the **National Championship Fiddle Contest**, Barre. Fiddle festivals tend to start around noon and end around dusk. The **Northeast Fiddling Association**, which publishes newsletters of all events, can be contacted at RFD 1, Stowe 05672.

FISHING   Almost every Vermont river and pond, certainly any body of water serious enough to call itself a lake, is stocked with fish. Brook trout are the most widely distributed game fish. Visitors age 15 and over must have a five-day ($20), fourteen-day ($20), or a nonresident ($30) license good for a year, available at any town clerk's office, from the local fish and game warden, or from assorted commercial outlets. Since these sources may be closed or time consuming to track down on weekends, it's wise to obtain the license in advance from the **Vermont Fish & Wildlife Department** (244-7331), Montpelier 05602; request an application form and ask for a copy of "Vermont Guide to Fishing," which details every species of fish and where to find it on a map of the state's rivers and streams, ponds, and lakes. Boat access, fish hatcheries, and canoe routes are also noted. A list of contoured depth charts for more than 80 Vermont lakes and ponds is available from the **Vermont Department of Water Resources (Depth Charts)**, Montpelier 05602; prices vary; minimum order is $1.

The state's most famous trout stream is the **Batten Kill** in the southwest, focus of a fly-fishing school offered by the **Orvis Company** in Manchester Center, which has been in the business of making fishing rods and selling them to city people for more than a century (it also maintains an outstanding museum devoted to fly fishing). In Stowe, **REC Corp.** (253-7346) now rivals Orvis as a producer of fly-fishing equipment and has its own fly-fishing school. Many inns, notably along Lake Champlain and in the Northeast Kingdom, offer tackle, boats, and advice on where to catch what. Land-locked salmon can be found in some northern lakes, and the Atlantic salmon has begun to return to the Connecticut River; other common species include bass, walleyes, northern pike, and perch.

Federal fish hatcheries can be found in **Bethel** (234-5241) and **Pittsfield** (483-6618), and state hatcheries are in **West Burke** (467-3660), **Bennington** (442-4556), **Grand Isle** (372-3171), **Roxbury** (485-7568), and **Salisbury** (352-4471).

Northland Trout Tours (496-6572) in North Fayston offers half, full, and two-day fly-fishing clinics. They also shepherd fishermen to high, hidden streams and offer a variety of guided canoe trips. **Strictly Trout** (869-3116) in Westminster West offers a full guide service, furnishing gear and advice, with or without guide and instruction.

Virtually every Vermont body of water has one or more fishing access areas, and they are used year-round. Ice anglers can legally take every species of fish (trout only in a limited number of designated waters) and can actually hook smelt and some varieties of whitefish that are hard to come by during warmer months; the **Great Benson Fishing Derby** held annually in mid-February on Lake Champlain draws thousands of contestants from throughout New England. The **Lake Champlain International Derby**, based in Burlington (phone 862-7777 for details), is a big summer draw.

Books to buy include *The Vermont Atlas and Gazetteer* (David DeLorme and Company, Freeport, Maine), which offers town-by-town maps and gives details about fishing species and access; *The Atlas of Vermont Trout Ponds*, $11.95, and *Vermont Trout Streams*, $19.95, both from Northern Cartographic Inc. (Box 133, Burlington 05402); and *Fishing Vermont's Streams and Lakes* by Peter Camman, published by Backcountry Publications, Woodstock, Vermont.

FOLIAGE   For very good reason, Vermont takes its foliage seriously. The Travel Division (see *Information*) maintains a foliage number and sends out weekly bulletins on color progress, which is always earlier than assumed by those of us who live south of Montpelier. Those in the know usually head for northern Vermont in late September and the very first week in October, a period that coincides with peak color in the area as well as with the **Northeast Kingdom Fall Foliage Festival** (see "St. Johnsbury Area"). By the following weekend, central Vermont is usually ablaze, but visitors should be sure to have a bed reserved before coming, because organized bus tours converge on the state from throughout the United States, with a growing contingent each year from Canada and the rest of the world. By the Columbus Day weekend, when what seems like millions of

Even the smallest towns have parades like this in Brookfield

Robert Eddy

Bostonians and New Yorkers make their annual leaf-peeking expedition, your odds of finding a bed are dim, unless you take advantage of those chambers of commerce (notably Middlebury, Woodstock, Brattleboro, Manchester, and St. Johnsbury) that pride themselves on finding refuge in private homes for all comers. During peak color, we recommend that you avoid Vermont's most heavily trafficked tourist routes, especially Route 9 between Bennington and Brattleboro; there is plenty of room on the back roads, especially those unsuited to buses. We strongly suggest exploring the high roads through Vermont's "gaps" (see *Gaps, Gulfs, and Gorges*) during this time of year or, if possible, avoiding roads entirely; this is ideal hiking season.

FORESTS AND PARKS   More than 300,000 Vermont acres are managed by the US Forest Service. They are traversed by 512 miles of trails, including the Appalachian/Long Trail that follows the ridge line of the main range of the Green Mountains (see *Hiking*). The forest harbors six wilderness areas. Use of off-road recreational vehicles is regulated. Information—printed as well as verbal—about hiking, camping, skiing, berry picking, and birdwatching is available from the ranger stations in Manchester Center, Middlebury, and Rochester. For details (request a free "mini-map" and "Winter Recreation Map"), contact the Green Mountain National Forest (773-0300), PO Box 519, Rutland 05701. Also see *Campgrounds*.

The **Department of Forest, Parks and Recreation** (244-8711), Waterbury 05676, manages a total of 157,000 acres of land, offering opportunities for hunting, fishing, cross-country skiing, snowmobiling, and primitive and supervised camping. The 40 exceptionally well groomed state parks, including 35 camping and 35 day-use areas, are described in the invaluable "Vermont State Parks" brochure available from the department. The state forests are largely undeveloped for hiking: Trails can be found in the Mt. Mansfield State Forest and in Willoughby State Forest (overlooking Willoughby Lake). Many of the trails detailed in current guidebooks (see *Hiking*) traverse state forests; for current cross-country ski trail information contact the Vermont Travel Division, Montpelier (see *Information*).

GAPS, GULFS, AND GORGES   Vermont's mountains were once much higher before they were pummeled some 100,000 years ago by a mile-high sheet of ice. Glacial forces contoured the landscape we recognize today, notching the mountains with a number of handy "gaps" through which men eventually built roads to get from one side of the mountain to the other. Gaps frequently offer superb views and access to ridge trails. This is true of the **Appalachian**, **Lincoln**, **Middlebury**, and **Brandon** gaps, all on the Long Trail; and of the **Roxbury Gap** east of the Mad River Valley. Gaps at lower elevations are "gulfs," scenic passes that make ideal picnic sites: Note **Granville Gulf** on Route 100, **Brookfield Gulf** on Route 12, and **Williamstown Gulf** on Route 14. The state's outstanding gorges include: 140-foot-deep **Quechee Gorge**, which can be viewed from Route 4 east of Woodstock; **Brockway Mills Gorge** in Rockingham (off Route 103); **Cavendish Gorge**, Springfield; **Clarendon Gorge**, Shrewsbury (traversed by the Long Trail via footbridge); **Brewster River Gorge**, south of Jeffersonville off Route 108; **Jay Branch Gorge** off Route 105; and (probably the most photographed of all) the **Brown River** churning through the gorge below the Old Red Mill in Jericho.

GENERAL STORES   Still the hub of most small Vermont communities, general stores retain some shreds of their one-time status as the source of all staples and communication with the outside world. The most famous survivor is the **Vermont Country Store** in Weston, a genuine family business that has expanded into a Vermont version of L. L. Bean. Still, its 119-page catalog is a source of long underwear and garter belts, Healthy Feet Cream, shoe trees, and gadgets like a kit that turns a plastic soda bottle into a bird feeder. By contrast, the state's least commercial, most evocative emporium is the **W. E. Pierce Country Store** in North Shrewsbury (17 miles northwest of Weston). "Pierce's store" has been in the family for 150 years, and Glendon and Marjorie Pierce devote their days to sharing a sense of the way it worked in their childhood. Most current Vermont country stores fall somewhere in between these two extremes. Within each chapter, we have described some of our personal favorites in Pawlet, East Poultney, Jericho Center, East Burke, Montgomery

Center, Craftsbury, and West Danville. "The General Store in Vermont," an oral history by Jane Beck, is available from the Vermont Folklife Center in Middlebury.

GOLF   Golfers find Vermont's 52 courses generally less crowded, less expensive, and more scenic than other links. Roughly half are 18 holes, and a half dozen are justly famed throughout the country. A full program of lodging, meals, and lessons is available at **Mount Snow**, **Killington**, **Stratton Mountain**, **Sugarbush**, and **Stowe**. The **Woodstock Inn** and others also offer golf packages. The Manchester area boasts the greatest concentration of courses. A complete list of courses can be found on Vermont's official state map, and a descriptive list of golf courses is available from the Vermont Travel Division, 134 State Street, Montpelier 05602.

Vermont Golf Courses: A Player's Guide, by Bob Labbance and David Cornwell, is a useful new book that describes all 50 of the courses open to the public, including detailed course maps, yardages, fees, opening/closing dates, starting times, and more. The 144-page, trade paperback may be ordered from the New England Press, Box 575, Shelburne 05482, for $14.95 plus $1.50 postage.

HERBS   Herb farms are a growing phenomenon in rural Vermont—sources of live perennials and herbs; herbs dried into fanciful wreaths; sachets, potpourri, or seasonings, distilled as scents. In our wanderings we have happened on: **Meadowsweet Herb Farm**, attached to a handsome farmhouse on a back road in Shrewsbury; **Cambridge Herbary**, the source of 88 different kinds of herbs raised and processed by Vermonter Sally Bevins west of Jeffersonville; **Talbot's Herb and Perennial Farm** in Hartland, east of Woodstock off Route 4; **Rathdowney**, 3 River Street, Bethel 05032. A pamphlet guide to 28 "Vermont Perennial & Herb Display Gardens" is available from the Vermont Department of Agriculture (828-2416), 116 State Street, Montpelier 05602.

HIKING AND WALKING   There are over 700 miles of hiking trails in Vermont—which is 162-miles long as the crow flies but 255-miles long as the hiker trudges, following the Long Trail up and down the spine of the Green Mountains. But few hikers are out to set distance records on the **Long Trail**. The path from the Massachusetts to the Canadian border, which was completed in 1931, has a way of slowing people down. It opens up eyes and lungs and drains compulsiveness. Even diehard backpackers tend to linger on rocky outcrops, looking down on farms and steeples. A total of 98 side trails (175 miles) meander off to wilderness ponds or abandoned villages, mostly maintained, along with the Long Trail, by the **Green Mountain Club** (223-3463), founded in 1910, which also maintains 70 shelters, many of them staffed by caretakers during summer months. The club's *Guide Book of the Long Trail* ($7.95 for members, $9.95 for nonmembers, plus $1.25 for postage and handling) gives details on trails and shelters throughout the Long Trail system. The club also publishes a *Day Hiker's Guide to Vermont* ($7.95 to members, $9.95 to nonmembers, plus $2.00 to mail) as well as smaller guides: "Day Hiking in Vermont," a pamphlet guide to 19 day hikes and "The Long Trail" brochure are free with SASE. Contact the Green Mountain Club, PO Box 889, 43 State Street, Montpelier 05602. The Appalachian Trail Conference (PO Box 807, Harpers Ferry, West VA 25425) includes detailed descriptions of most Vermont trails in its *A Guide to New Hampshire and Vermont* ($18.95), and a wide assortment of trails are nicely detailed in *Fifty Hikes in Vermont* (Backcountry, $11.95); *Walks & Rambles in the Upper Connecticut River Valley* (Backcountry, $9.95) is also helpful and nicely written. (Also see *Forests and Parks* and *Campgrounds*.) Note: On public land, you may camp and build fires only at designated areas. On private land, you must have the permission of the landowner to build a fire between April and November and, of course, you must seek permission to camp.

Backpackers who are hesitant to set out on their own can team up with **Vermont Voyageur Expeditions** (Montgomery Center 05471; 326-4789). Hikers who prefer solid beds and gourmet meals to sleeping bags and trail food can take advantage of treks available through **North Wind Inn**

Touring (244-5726), based in Waitsfield, **Pathways Through Vermont**, offered by Betsy Allen (824-3830) in Londonderry, **Four Seasons Touring**, offered by Charles Marchant (365-7937) in Townshend, and **Vermont Hiking Holidays** (453-4816) in Bristol, an off-shoot of Vermont Bicycle Tours.

There is also **Vermont Walking Tours**, a program offered by the Inn on the Common in Craftsbury (586-6919). Two groups of inns have also offered support services (route planning, baggage transfers) as well as meals and lodging. **Country Inns Along the Trail** is based at the Churchill House (RFD 3, Brandon 05733; 247-3300) and **Walking Inn Vermont** involves inns between Ludlow and Chester (PO Box 243, Ludlow 05149-0243; 228-8799).

"Walking" Vermont's dirt roads and less strenuous paths has, in fact, become the "inn" thing to do in the past couple years. Contact **Walking Tours of Southern Vermont** in Arlington (375-1141) and **Country Walkers** (244-5766) in Waterbury.

HISTORIC HOUSES AND SITES Vermont itself is close to being "living history." A "Guide to Historic Sites" is available from the Vermont Division for Historic Preservation (828-3226), 58 E. State Street, Montpelier 05602. Our personal pick of historic sites are the **Calvin Coolidge Birthplace** at Plymouth Village; **Brownington Village** in the Northeast Kingdom; and **Shelburne Farms** on Lake Champlain. Historic places are listed on the official state map.

HORSEBACK RIDING A list of riding stables, specifying trail and sleigh rides, is included in the free booklet, "Vermont Traveler's Guidebook," available from the Vermont Travel Division (see *Information*). **West River Lodge** in Brookline and **Mountain Top Inn** in Chittenden both offer inn-based trail rides, and it's worth noting that inn-to-inn treks are offered by **Kedron Valley Stables** in South Woodstock, by **Shanagary Farm** in Westminster Station, and by **Icelandic Horse Farm** in Waitsfield. Within the book, we have also noted trail riding in the regions it's offered; check under **Jeffersonville, Bristol, Castleton, Craftsbury Common, Island Pond, More-**

town, **Morgan**, **Manchester Center**, **Stratton**, **Waitsfield**, and **Warren**.

HOSTELS The hostels in Vermont are affiliated with **American Youth Hostels** (AYH), 1332 I Street NW, Suite 800, Washington, D.C. 20005, from which you can secure a handbook describing all US facilities. Hostels are open to all travelers who are AYH members (membership costs adults $25, children $10, and families $35). Nonmembers may use hostels for an additional $8 per night. They supply simple lodging and cooking facilities and are geared to bicyclists and skiers. The Vermont hostels are in **Colchester**, **East Jamaica**, **Rochester**, **Stowe** (open to students only in winter), **Warren**, **Waterbury Center**, **Woodford**, and **Craftsbury Common**. The AYH booklet comes free with membership. Hostelers are expected to carry their own sleeping sack and personal eating utensils, to reserve bunkspace ahead, and to arrive between 5 and 8 PM. Hostels customarily close between 10 AM and 5 PM; checkout is by 9:30 AM; alcohol is not permitted on the premises.

HUNTING "Vermont Guide to Hunting," a free pamphlet, lists and locates major wildlife management areas in the state and is available, along with a current **"Digest of Fish & Wildlife Laws,"** from the Vermont Fish and Wildlife Department, Montpelier 05602. A nonresident small game hunting license costs $35, a regular hunting license is $75, a combined hunting and fishing license is $95. A limited bow and arrow license is $50; a regular bow and arrow license is $15 on top of the regular hunting license. A nonresident trapping license is $300; an alien, nonresident trapping license is $500; both of these can be obtained only through the Fish and Wildlife Department. Of special interest may be the nonresident small game license, five-day for $20. A resident hunting license is $12, and trapping is $20. **Deer season** begins 12 days before Thanksgiving and lasts for 16 days. **Bow and arrow season** also lasts 16 days beginning the first Saturday in October; **hare and rabbit** season extends from the last Saturday in September to the second Sunday in March; **gray squirrel** from the last Saturday in September to the

last Thursday before regular deer season. **Partridge and ruffed grouse** may be shot between the last Saturday in September and December 31, with a limit of four daily, eight in possession. **Black bear** season is determined annually. Licenses may be secured from local town clerks or wardens, or ahead of time by mail from the Fish and Wildlife Department. In order to purchase a Vermont hunting or combination license, a person must show or submit either a certificate proving he has satisfactorily completed a hunter safety course or a previous hunting or combination license issued to him.

ICE CREAM Vermont's quality milk is used to produce some outstanding ice cream as well as cheese. The big name is, of course, **Ben and Jerry's,** proud producers of what *Time* has billed "the best ice cream in the world." Their plant on Route 100 in Waterbury (featuring factory tours, free samples, real cows, and a gift shop full of reproductions in every conceivable shape) has quickly become one of the state's most popular tourist attractions. Other good Vermont ice creams include **Seward's** in Rutland, **Page's Ice Cream** in West Brattleboro, **Wilcox Brothers** in Manchester, and **Mountain Creamery** in Woodstock.

INFORMATION The Vermont Travel Division (828-3236), 134 State Street, Montpelier 05602, is the source for four excellent, free aids to exploring the state: (1) **Vermont's Official State Map** includes symbols locating covered bridges, golf courses and picnic spots, ski areas, recreation sites, and boat launch ramps. On the reverse side are descriptive listings of museums, galleries and historic places, fishing and hunting rules and license fees, state and private campgrounds, state liquor stores, and hospital emergency rooms. (2) "Vermont Vacation Guide," a 24-page booklet, is filled with details about where to find what. (3) A "Vermont Events" tabloid lists the myriad small happenings that spice any visit to the Green Mountain State, as well as year-round attractions, seasonal attractions, and information sources throughout the state. (4) The "Four Season Vacation Rentals" booklet (see *Rental Cottages*) gives up-to-date accommodation information. The state maintains three pamphlet-filled **Welcome Centers**: at Fair Haven (265-4763), on Route 4A at the New York border; in Guilford (254-4593), on I-91 at the Massachusetts border; in Highgate Springs (868-3244), on I-89 at the Canadian border.

A handy piece of basic exploration equipment is available from the Vermont State Chamber of Commerce (223-3443), Box 37, Montpelier 05602: "Vermont Traveler's Guidebook" contains paid listings of lodging, restaurants, camping, shops, and attractions. Within this book, we have noted local chambers of commerce, town by town. In towns not served by a chamber, inquiries are welcomed by the town clerk.

First-time visitors may be puzzled by Vermont's Travel Information System of directional signs that replace billboards (banned since 1967, another Vermont "first"). Stylized symbols for lodging, food, recreation, antiques and crafts, and other services are sited at intersections off major highways, at interstate rest areas, at incoming border Welcome Centers, and at other key points of travel interest. Travel Information Plazas should be consulted to get oriented to the system. They are indicated on the state map.

INNS We have described many inns in their respective towns, quoting 1991–1992 rates. These prices are, of course, subject to change and should not be regarded as gospel. Summer rates are generally lower than winter rates (except, of course, in lake resorts); weekly or ski-week rates run 10–20 percent less than the per diem price quoted. Many inns insist on MAP (Modified American Plan—breakfast and dinner) in winter but not in summer. Most resorts have AP (American Plan—three meals); and we have shown EP (European Plan—no meals) where applicable. We have attempted to note when 15 percent service is added, but always ask if it's been included in a quoted rate. There's always the 8 percent state tax on rooms and meals. It's prudent to check which, if any, credit cards are accepted. We have noted places in which children are unwelcome and have attempted to mention the few places that accept pets. It's safe to say that our authors have visited more Vermont inns, more fre-

quently, than anyone living today. We do not charge for inclusion in this book, and we attempt to give as accurate and detailed a picture as space permits. In this edition, for the first time, we noted inns that offer exceptional value.

"**Vermont Country Inns,**" a descriptive listing of more than 200 lodging places, is available from the Vermont Travel Division, 134 State Street, Montpelier 05602 (828-3236).

For quick reference, note our Lodging Index.

LAKES The state famed for green mountains and white villages also harbors more than 400 relatively blue lakes: big lakes like **Champlain** (150 miles long) and **Memphremagog** (boasting 88 miles of coastline but most of it in Canada), smaller lakes like **Morey**, **Dunmore**, **Willoughby**, **Bomoseen**, and **Seymour**. Lakes are particularly plentiful and people sparse in Vermont's **Northeast Kingdom**. A century ago, there were many more lakeside hotels; today just a half dozen of these classic summer resorts survive: **Quimby Country** in Averill, **Highland Lodge** in Greensboro, the **Tyler Place** in Highgate Springs, the **Basin Harbor Club** near Vergennes, **Eagle's Nest Resort**, and the **Lake Morey Club**. There are a half dozen smaller, informal inns on scattered lakes, but that's about it. Still, you can bed down very reasonably within sound and sight of Vermont waters either by renting a cottage (more than half of those listed in "**Four Season Vacation Rentals,**" available from the Vermont Travel Division, are on lakes) or by taking advantage of state park campsites on Groton Lake, Island Pond, Maidstone Lake, Bomoseen, Lake Carmi, Elmore, Lake St. Catherine, and Silver Lake (in Barnard). On Lake Champlain, there are a number of state campgrounds, including those on **Grand Isle** (accessible by car) and on **Burton Island** (accessible by public launch from St. Albans Bay). See *Campgrounds* for details about these and the free campsites on **Ball Mountain Lake** maintained by the Army Corps of Engineers. There is public boat access to virtually every Vermont pond and lake of any size. Boat launches are listed on the state map.

LIBRARIES   The small village of **Brookfield** boasts the state's oldest, continuously operating public library, established in 1791. Most libraries that we mention here date, however, from that late nineteenth-century philanthropic era when Andrew Carnegie's largesse filtered down to places like **Swanton** or when wealthy native sons were moved to donate splendidly ornate libraries to their home towns. Notable examples are to be found in **Barre, Chester, Ludlow, Wilmington, Rutland, Newport, Woodstock, St. Johnsbury**, and **Brattleboro**.

Two of our favorite libraries lie within a short drive of each other; one on the Common in **Craftsbury Common**, and the second—a converted general store—in **East Craftsbury**, where there is a special back room for youngsters, with a ping-pong table amid the books. Unfortunately, visitors may not check out books unless they happen to be staying within the community that the library serves. However, visitors are free to use Regional Libraries, open 8:30–5 Monday–Friday, and 9–5 on Saturdays, closed on Saturdays in July and August. Regional libraries are located in St. Johnsbury; Berlin, near Barre; in Georgia, near St. Albans; Dummerston, near Brattleboro; and in Rutland.

For research, the **Vermont Historical Society Library** in Montpelier is a treasure trove of Vermontiana and genealogical resources, as is the Wilbur collection of the **Bailey-Howe Library** at the University of Vermont and the Russell Collection in Arlington. Three of the Vermont State Colleges—Castleton, Johnson, and Lyndon—have collections of Vermontiana in the Vermont Rooms of their libraries.

LLAMA TREKKING   Northeast Kingdom Llama Expeditions (584-3198), Windy Hill Farm in Groton, offer half-day ($45), all-day ($70), and overnight treks into adjacent 26,000-acre Groton State Forest. Gale and John Birutta have six llamas (four "packers") and include a catered snack or lunch in every expedition.

MAGAZINES   *Vermont Life*, the popular and colorful quarterly published by the Agency of Development and Community Affairs and now edited by Tom Slayton, is an outstanding contemporary chronicle of Vermont's people and places, featuring distinguished photographers. Single issues cost $2.50; $9 a year, $23 for three years; 61 Elm Street, Montpelier 05602.

Vermont Magazine, the upbeat, statewide bimonthly launched in 1989, covers major issues, townscapes, new products, and personalities, and reviews inns and restaurants. $18 a year from Box 288, Bristol 05443.

Vermont History, a quarterly scholarly journal, is published for members of the Vermont Historical Society, Montpelier.

Upper Valley is a glossy bimonthly published at $6 a year at 89 Main Street, West Lebanon, New Hampshire 03784.

The Prosper Publishing Company, Barnard 05031, publishes the quarterly *Woodstock Common*.

Vermont Business Magazine is a well-written, tabloid-sized monthly that provides investigative reportage, analysis, and overview of the state's economic doings from politically conservative and entrepreneurially aggressive points of view. Subscriptions are $15 per year; free to Vermont businesses and government agencies. Manning Publications, Inc., PO Box 6120, Brattleboro 05301.

MAPLE SUGARING   Vermont produces an average of 500,000 gallons of maple syrup each year, more than any other state. No less than 2,400 maple growers tap an average of 1,000 trees each. One-fifth to one-quarter gallon of syrup is made per tap, boiling down 30–40 gallons of sap for each gallon of syrup. The process of tapping trees and boiling is stubbornly known as "sugaring" rather than syruping, because the end product for early settlers was sugar. Syrup was first made in the early nineteenth century but flagged when imported cane sugar was easy to come by. The Civil War revived the maple sugar industry: Union supporters were urged to consume sugar made by free men and to plant more and more maples. The annual pamphlet listing **"Maple Sugarhouses Open to Visitors"** indicates which producers sell sugar and maple cream along with syrup; many do, but the big product now is the "liquid sunshine" for which people have learned to pay a high price in recent years.

For our money, the only place to buy syrup is at a sugarhouse during the season. The trick is finding one in full steam. Traditionally, sugaring season begins with Town Meeting (first Tuesday in March). The fact is, however, that sap runs only on those days when temperatures rise to 40 and 50 degrees during the day and drop into the 20s at night. And when the sap runs, it must be boiled down quickly. What you want to see is the boiling process: sap churning madly through the large, flat evaporating pan, darkening as you watch. You are enveloped in fragrant steam, listening to the rush of the sap, sampling the end result on snow or in tiny paper cups. Sugaring is Vermont's rite of spring. Don't miss a sugar on snow party: plates of snow dribbled with hot syrup, accompanied by donuts and dill pickles. The "Maple Sugarhouses Open to Visitors" pamphlet (available from the Vermont Travel Division, 134 State Street, Montpelier 05602) lists more than 100 maple producers, giving their phone numbers (be sure to phone before going to check if there is sugaring that day) and the method used for collecting sap. Many farmers now use plastic pipeline that runs directly from tree to collecting tank, but there are still some oxen and horses out there, pulling the collecting tank around from tree to tree. There is one big **Maple Festival** each spring in **St. Albans,** a three-day happening that includes tours through the local sugarbush (usually the second weekend in April). At **Maple Grove,** "the world's largest maple candy factory" in St. Johnsbury, factory tours are offered Monday through Friday year-round, and the Maple Museum and gift shop is open May through late October. At **American Maple Products** (year-round) in Newport, you can see a movie about maple production; the story of sugaring is also dramatized in the **New England Maple Museum** in Pittsford and in the maple museum at **Sugarmill Farm** in Barton. We have listed maple producers in the areas in which they are most heavily concentrated.

MAPS   The Official State Map (see *Information*) is free and extremely helpful for general motoring in Vermont but will not suffice for finding your way around on the webs of dirt roads that connect some of the most beautiful corners of the state. Among our favorite places in which you can be guaranteed to get lost using the state map: the high farming country between Albany, Craftsbury, and West Glover; similar country between Chelsea and Williamstown; south from Plainfield to Orange; and between Plymouth and Healdville. There are many more. We strongly suggest securing a copy of *The Vermont Atlas and Gazetteer* (David DeLorme and Company, Freeport, Maine) if you want to do any serious back road exploring, or *The Vermont Road Atlas and Guide* from Northern Cartographics, PO Box 133, Burlington 05402.

MONEY   Don't leave home without MasterCard or Visa, the two credit cards that are far more readily accepted in Vermont than American Express or personal checks. Each inn has its own policy about credit cards and checks; some accept cash only.

MOTORING   The Official State Map, updated annually (see *Maps*), comes free from local chambers of commerce information booths as well as state information centers (see *Information*). Motorists should bear in mind that gas stations can be infrequent in rural areas and often close early in the evening. **State highway rest areas** with pay phones and bathroom facilities, indicated on the state map, are found on I-91 at Guilford (a Welcome Center), northbound; at Bradford, north- and southbound; at Barnet, northbound; at Derby, southbound; and Coventry, northbound. On I-89 there are rest areas at Sharon, north- and southbound; and at Randolph, north- and southbound. Note the work of Vermont sculptors commissioned for these rest areas by the Vermont Council on the Arts in cooperation with the Vermont Marble Company. In 1982, the Vermont stretch of I-89 was dedicated to honor veterans and casualties of the war in Vietnam.

Picnic sites with tables and benches are scattered along most major routes throughout the state; picnic tables are clearly marked on the state map. **AAA Emergency Road Service:** 800-222-4357.

MOUNTAIN TOPS While Vermont can boast only seven peaks above 4,000 feet, there are 80 mountains that rise more than 3,000 feet and any number of spectacular views, six of them accessible in summer and foliage seasons to those who prefer riding to walking up mountains. **Mount Mansfield**, at 4,343 feet the state's highest summit, can be reached via Mountain Auto Road. This midnineteenth-century road brings you to the small Summit Station at 4,062 feet, from which a half-mile Tundra Trail brings you to the actual summit. The Mt. Mansfield Gondola, a four-passenger, enclosed lift, hoists you from the ski area's main ski lodge up to the Cliff House (serving light meals all day), from which a trail also heads up to the Chin. **Killington Peak**, Vermont's second highest peak at 4,241 feet, can be reached via another $3\frac{1}{2}$-mile gondola ride (operating weekends only) and by a $1\frac{1}{4}$-mile ride on a chair lift. Both lifts take you to a summit restaurant and a nature trail that even the small children can negotiate. **Jay Peak**, a 3,861-foot summit towering like a lone sentinel near the Canadian border, is accessible via a 60-passenger tram (daily except Tuesdays), and a "four-state view" from the top of **Stratton Mountain** is accessible via the ski resort's six-passenger gondola, "Starship XII" (daily in summer and fall). Toll roads include the Auto Road to the 3,267-foot **Burke Mountain** in East Burke, the Toll Road to the 3,144-foot summit of **Mt. Ascutney** in Ascutney State Park, and the road to the top of **Mt. Equinox** in Sunder-land. There are also chair lift rides to the top of Bromley (you don't have to take the Alpine Slide down) and Mount Snow (weekends in summer, daily in foliage season).

MUSEUMS Vermont museums vary from the immense **Shelburne Museum** with its 36 buildings, many housing priceless collections of Americana, plus assorted exhibits like a completely restored lake steamer and lighthouse, to the **American Precision Museum**, an 1846 brick mill that once produced rifles. They include a number of outstanding historical museums (our favorites are the **Sheldon Museum** in Middlebury, the **Old Stone House Museum** in Brownington, and the **Dana House** in Woodstock) and some collections that go beyond the purely historical: **Bennington Museum** (famed for its collection of Grandma Moses paintings as well as early American glass and relics from the Revolution) and the **Fairbanks Museum and Planetarium** in St. Johnsbury. The **Billings Farm and Museum** in Woodstock shows off its Blue Ribbon dairy and has a fascinating, beautifully mounted display of nineteenth-century farm life and tools. A detailed, 150-page catalogue, "Vermont's Museums, Galleries & Historic Buildings," is available from The Museum & Gallery Alliance, c/o Shelburne Museum, Dept. VTM, Shelburne 05482 ($5.95, plus $1.50 postage and handling). Within this book, we have included all museums in their respective areas.

MUSIC The Green Mountains are filled with the sounds of music each summer. The internationally famous **Marlboro Music Festival** (254-8163), at Marlboro College, presents chamber music under the direction of Rudolf Serkin on weekends from early July through mid-August. The **Vermont Mozart Festival** (862-7352) is a series of 20 concerts performed at a variety of sites ranging from beautiful barns at the University of Vermont and Shelburne Farms to a Lake Champlain ferry boat, and including some striking classic and modern churches and a ski area base lodge. Other concerts are presented at the **Summer Music School** in Adamant (229-9297), at the Town House in Hardwick by the **Craftsbury Chamber Players** (888-3158), and in Stowe, for a week in late July, the **Performing Arts Festival** (253-7321). In Putney, a series of three-evening chamber music concerts each week are presented in the **Yellow Barn** (387-6637). Other concert series are performed at the **Southern Vermont Arts Center** (Thursday and Sunday, 362-1405); at the **Fine Arts Center**, Castleton State College (468-4611, ext. 285); at the **Dibden Auditorium**, Johnson State College (635-2356); and at **Johnson Hall,** at Middlebury College (388-2763). The **North Country Concert Association** (43 Main Street, Derby Line) performs at sites throughout the Northeast Kingdom lake area. The **Vermont Symphony Orchestra**, oldest of the state symphonies, figures in a number of the series noted above and also performs at a variety of locations, ranging from Brattleboro's Living Memorial Park and the State House Lawn to Wilson Castle, throughout the summer. In Weston, the **Kinhaven Music School** offers free concerts on summer weekends.

OPERA HOUSES   Northern New England opera houses are a turn-of-the-century phenomenon: Theaters built as cultural centers for the surrounding area, stages on which lecturers, musicians, and vaudeville acts, as well as opera singers, performed. Many of these buildings have long since disappeared, but those that survive are worth noting. The **Hyde Park Opera House**, in Hyde Park, built in 1910 has been restored by the Lamoille County Players, who stage four annual shows—one play, two musicals, and an annual foliage season run of "The Sound of Music." The **Barre Opera House**, built in 1899, is an elegant, acoustically outstanding, second-floor theater, which is the home of the Barre Players; productions are staged here year-round. In **Derby Line**, in the second-floor **Opera House** (a neo-classic structure that also houses the Haskell Free Library), the audience sits in Vermont watching a stage that is in Canada. The **Chandler Music Hall** in Randolph has been restored for varied uses.

PICK YOUR OWN   A list of orchards and berry farms open to the public, also a "Vermont Apple" brochure detailing all major orchards, can be secured from the Vermont Department of Agriculture, 116 State Street, Montpelier 05602. **Strawberry** season is mid- to late-June. **Cherries**, **plums**, **raspberries**, and **blueberries** can be picked in July and August. **Apples** ripen by mid-September and can be picked through foliage season.

QUILTS   A revival of interest in this craft is especially strong in Vermont, where quilting supply and made-to-order stores salt the state. For information, contact the **Green Mountain Quilters Guide**, c/o L. Leister, RD 2, Bethel 05032, which sponsors several shows a year. The **Vermont Quilt Festival** is held for three days in mid-July

in Northfield, including exhibits of outstanding antique quilts, classes and lectures, vendors, and appraisals. Shelburne Museum has a good quilt collection.

RAILROAD EXCURSIONS   Vermont's rail excursions are not in heavily touristed places. The **Green Mountain Flyer** runs between Bellows Falls on the Connecticut River and Chester (13 miles), with special foliage runs for another 14 miles to Ludlow. Named for the fastest train on the old Rutland Railroad, the excursion is run by the employee-owned Green Mountain Railroad, which also hauls talc, lumber, and limestone slurry between Bellows Falls and Rutland (see "Bellows Falls" for details). Based in Morrisville, 10 miles north of Stowe, there is also **Vermont Land Cruises**, offering 35-mile runs to Joe's Pond in summer and during foliage season, operated by the Lamoille Valley Railroad, another small freight line (see "Stowe" for details). The **St. J. and LC Railroad** is under new management and hopes to continue the foliage runs.

RENTAL COTTAGES AND CONDOMINIUMS   "Four Season Vacation Rentals," an annual booklet available from the Travel Division (828-3236), Montpelier 05602, lists upwards of 200 properties, most of them either lakeside cottages or condominiums near ski areas but also including a variety of housing, ranging from wooded summer camps by a stream to aristocratic brick mansions with priceless views. We have found this publication indispensable for exploring the state—as a family of five—at all seasons. Rentals average $350 per week, usually more in winter, less in summer; incredible bargains by any standard.

RESTAURANTS   Culinary standards are rising every day: One can lunch simply and inexpensively nearly everywhere and dine superbly in a score of places where the quality would rate three stars in Boston or New York but is at least a third less expensive. Fixed price menus (prix fixe) have been so noted.

We were tempted to try to list here our "favorites," but the roster would be too long. Restaurants that appeal to us appear in the text in their respective areas. The range and variety are truly extraordinary. Note: A pamphlet, "Vermont Guide to Smoke-Free Dining," listing restaurants with smoke-free sections, is available from the Vermont Lung Association (800-642-3288). Note that we divide restaurants in each chapter into *Dining Out* (serious dining experiences) and *Eating Out* (everyday places).

ROCKHOUNDING "Rockhounding in Vermont," a good writeup of Vermont's rockhounding sites, special events, and the state's geological history, is available free from the Vermont Travel Division, Montpelier 05602 (828-3236). The most obvious sites are: **Rock of Ages Quarry and Exhibit** in Barre and the **Vermont Marble Company Exhibit** in Proctor (a film, free samples). Major exhibits of Vermont fossils, minerals, and rocks may be viewed at **Perkins Geology Hall**, University of Vermont, Burlington; the **Fairbanks Museum** in St. Johnsbury; and the **Melendy Mineral Museum**, South Londonderry (phone for an appointment). An annual **Rock Swap and Mineral Show** is held in early August, sponsored by the Burlington Gem and Mineral Club. Gold, incidentally, can be panned in a number of rivers, notably Broad Brook in Plymouth; Rock River in Newfane and Dover; Williams River in Ludlow; Ottauquechee River in Bridgewater; White River in Stockbridge and Rochester; Mad River in Warren, Waitsfield, and Moretown; Little River in Stowe and Waterbury; and the Missisquoi in Lowell and Troy.

SHEEP Sheep are multiplying quickly in Vermont and may someday again outnumber cows, as they did in the midnineteenth century. Their modern appeal is primarily for their meat, but a number of farmers specialize in processing wool, notably the **Boutchers** in Whiting and **Gisela Gminder** of Morrisville (who offers weaving lessons at her Stowe Wool and Feathers Shop). "**Vermont Sheep Plus,**" a descriptive listing of the members of the Vermont Sheep Breeders Association, is available from the Vermont Department of Agriculture (828-2500), 116 State Street, Montpelier 05602. A number of colorful festivals are presently staged by and for sheep breeders.

SHIPWRECKS Well-preserved nineteenth-century shipwrecks are open to the public (licensed divers) at three Underwater Historical Preserves in Lake Champlain near Burlington. *The Phoenix,* the second steamboat to ply Lake Champlain, burned to the waterline in 1819. *The General Butler,* an 88-foot schooner, fell victim to a winter gale in 1876. A coal barge, believed to be the *A.R. Nowes,* broke loose from a tug and sank in 1884. Contact the Division of Historic Preservation: 828-3226.

SKIING, CROSS-COUNTRY Cross-country centers and tours are listed in the free "Vermont Winter Guide" co-published by the Vermont Chamber of Commerce and the Vermont Travel Division (see *Information*). We have included each commercial touring center as it appears geographically. Given the dearth of natural snow in recent years, the importance of checking current conditions is more important than ever. In the winter of 1991–1992, the information number is 229-0531.

Vermont's most dependable snow can be found on high elevation trails in **Stowe**, at **Craftsbury Center** in Craftsbury Common, at **Hazen's Notch** in Montgomery Center, at **Bolton Valley** resort (between Burlington and Stowe), and at **Blueberry Hill** in Goshen. **Mountain Top Inn** in Chittenden (handy to Killington and Rutland) offers snow-making on a loop trail.

A number of centers are part of the Catamount Trail, on which skilled cross-country skiers have made their way from the Massachusetts to the Canadian border. For details, contact the Catamount Trail Association, Box 897, Burlington 05402.

Packaged inn-to-inn tours, with baggage transported for you, can be found in all parts of Vermont. For details, contact the **Churchill House Inn**, Brandon; **North Wind Tours**, Waitsfield; **Craftsbury Center** in Craftsbury Common; **Mountain Top Inn** in Chittenden (483-6089); and **Viking Ski Touring Center** in Londonderry.

Konari Outfitters in Vergennes (featuring ski or snowshoe tours with sleds), RD 1, Box 441B, Vergennes (759-2100), and **Vermont Voyageur** offer mountaineering and winter camping as well as inn-to-inn. **Four Season Touring** (365-7937) in Townshend and Hazen's Notch also offer guided tours. For details about marked cross-country trails in state preserves, contact the Department of Forests, Parks and Recreation (244-8711), Waterbury 05676, and for those within the Green Mountain National Forest, request the "Winter Recreation Map" (see *Forests and Parks*). Other possibilities are described in *25 Ski Tours in Vermont* by Stan Wass (Backcountry Publications).

SKIING, DOWNHILL Since the 1930s, when America's commercial skiing began with a Model-T Ford engine pulling skiers up a hill in Woodstock, skiing has been a Vermont specialty. There are 22 ski areas in Vermont. The Vermont Chamber of Commerce publishes a glossy "Vermont Winter Guide" in conjunction with the Vermont Travel Division (from whom it's available free; see *Information*). Unfortunately, this guide includes no rates. Watch for the November ski section in major newspapers that compile these crucial data. In 1991–1992, lift tickets range from $26 per adult at Mad River Glen, a famously challenging old ski area with the state's lowest percentage of snow-making (15 percent) but frequently excellent conditions (especially in late winter), to $41 per adult at Okemo and at Killington, the largest ski resort (107 trails) in the East. Mount Snow, Vermont's second largest area (under the same ownership as Killington), also charges $40. Increasingly, over the past decade, a number of long-established Vermont ski areas have become self-contained resorts. Both Bolton Valley and Smugglers' Notch cater to families; Okemo, Stratton, and Sugarbush offer varied skiing and facilities, appealing to a full range of patrons. Though no longer Vermont's biggest, Stowe remains Ski Capital of the East when it comes to the quantity and quality of inns, restaurants, and shops. Bear in mind that lodging, lifts, and lessons all cost far less by the week than for a weekend, especially during nonholiday stretches. We have described each ski area as it appears geographically. A 24-hour snow condition report for the state is available by phoning: 229-0531 (November–June).

SLEIGH RIDES A list of sleigh rides is available from the Vermont Travel Division (see *Information*). It's also contained in the "Vermont Winter Guide" (see *Skiing*).

SNOWMOBILING Some 2,200 miles of well-marked, groomed trails are laced together in a system maintained by the **Vermont Association of Snow Travelers.** VAST's corridor trails are up to eight feet wide and are maintained by 200 local snowmobile clubs; for detailed maps and suggestions for routes, activities, and guided tours, contact the **Vermont Association of Snow Travelers** (229-0005), Box 839, Montpelier 05602. Vermont has a reciprocal registration agreement with New York, Maine, New Hampshire, and Quebec; otherwise registration is required to take advantage of trails within the state. Snowmobile rentals and tours are listed in the "Vermont Winter Guide" (see *Skiing*).

SOARING **Sugarbush Soaring** (496-3730), Sugarbush Airport, Warren. The Mad River Valley is known as one of the prime spots in the East for riding thermal and ridge waves, and the **Sugarbush Airport** is a well-established place to take glider lessons or rides or simply to watch the planes come and go. The **Fall Wave Soaring Encampment** held in early October draws glider pilots from throughout the country. Gliders and airplane rides are also available at the **Morrisville/Stowe State Airport** (888-5150) and at **Post Mills Aviation** in Post Mills (333-9254), where soaring lessons are also a specialty along with simply seeing the Connecticut Valley from the air.

SPAS Vermont is the setting for a select few of the country's finest spas. The oldest of these is **New Life Spa,** directed by Jimmy LeSage at Killington. **Topnotch** in Stowe and the **Equinox Hotel** in Manchester both offer full spa programs.

SUMMER SELF-IMPROVEMENT PRO-GRAMS Whether it's improving your game of tennis or golf, learning to take pictures, to weave, cook, identify mushrooms, fish, bike, or simply to lose weight, there is a summer program for you somewhere in Vermont. See *Tennis, Golf, Canoeing,* and *Fishing* for lodging and lesson packages. Prestigious academic programs include the **Russian School** at Norwich University (Russian only is spoken in all social as well as class activities; both undergraduate and graduate courses are offered) and **intensive language programs** at Middlebury College and a **writers' program** at the college's Breadloaf summer campus. Senior citizens can take advantage of some outstanding courses offered at bargain prices that include lodging as part of the **Elderhostel program**. For details, write to Elderhostel, 80 Boylston Street, Boston, Massachusetts 02116. The state's oldest, most respected **crafts program** is offered by Fletcher Farm Craft School, Ludlow 05149: off-loom weaving, creative needlework, quilting, pottery, raku, and stained glass, plus meals and lodging (minimum age 18).

The **Vermont Studio Center** in Johnson is relatively new but already has a national reputation. Working artists come to renew their creative wellsprings or to explore completely new directions during intensive sessions that feature guidance and criticism by some of the country's premier artists. For details, phone: 635-7000.

Craftsbury Center in Craftsbury has summer programs for all ages in running and sculling, and Lyndon State has a running camp.

SWIMMING On the official state map, you can pick out the 36 day-use areas that offer swimming, most with changing facilities, maintained by the State Department of Forests, Parks and Recreation ($1 per adult, $.50 per child). A similar facility is provided by the Green Mountain National Forest in Peru, and the US Army Corps of Engineers has tidied corners of its dam projects for public use in Townshend and North Springfield. There are also public beaches on roughly one-third of Vermont's 400 lakes and ponds (but note that swim-ming is prohibited at designated "Fishing Access Areas") and plenty on Lake Champlain (see Burlington, Charlotte, Colchester, Georgia, and Swanton). Add to these all the town recreation areas and myriad pools available to visitors, and you still haven't gone swimming Vermont-style—until you have sampled a Vermont swimming hole. These range from deep spots in the state's ubiquitous streams to 100-foot-deep quarries (Dorset Quarry near Manchester and Chapman Quarry in West Rutland are famous) and freezing pools between waterfalls (see the Mad River Valley). We have included some of our favorite swimming holes under *Swimming* in each section but could not bring ourselves to share them all. Look for cars along the road on a hot day and ask in local general stores. You won't be disappointed.

TENNIS Vermont claims as many tennis courts per capita as any state in the union. These include town recreation facilities and sports centers as well as private facilities. Summer tennis programs, combining lessons, lodging, and meals, are offered at **Bolton Valley**, **Killington**, the **Village at Smuggler's Notch**, **Stratton**, **Topnotch Resort** in Stowe, and two **Sugarbush** resorts (Sugarbush Inn and the Bridges). Check *Tennis* under entries for each area.

A listing of Vermont tennis courts is included in the "Vermont Traveler's Guidebook" available from the Vermont Travel Division, 134 State Street, Montpelier 05602.

THEATER Vermont's two long-established summer theaters are both in the Manchester area: the **Dorset Playhouse** and the **Weston Playhouse**. The **Green Mountain Guild** presents a series of summer musicals at the **Killington Playhouse**. Other summer theater can be found in Castleton, in Waitsfield (the **Valley Players**), in Warren (**Phantom Theater**), and in Stowe (the **Stowe Playhouse** and the **Lamoille County Players** in Hyde Park), and year-round in White River Junction (**River City Arts**). For a complete and current listing, consult the "Vermont Traveler's Guidebook" available free from the Vermont Travel Division (see *Information*).

TRAINS   See *AMTRAK*

WATERFALLS   Those most accessible include: the falls at **Brewster River Gorge** in Jeffersonville; in **Bristol Memorial Forest Park**, Bristol; **Buttermilk Falls** (a popular swimming hole) in Ludlow; **Carver Falls** in West Haven (126 feet high); the falls in **Clarendon Gorge; Cow Meadows Ledges** in Newbury; **Duck Brook Cascades** in Bolton; the **East Putney Falls** and **Pot Holes; Glen Falls** in Fairlee; **Great Falls** of the Clyde River in Charleston; **Hamilton Falls** in Jamaica; **Little Otter Creek Falls** in Ferrisburg; **Middlebury Gorge** in East Middlebury; **Moss Glen Falls** in Granville Notch; the seven falls on the **Huntington River** in Hanksville; **Shelburne Falls** in Shelburne; **Texas Falls** in Hancock; **Cadys Falls** in Morrisville; **Bingham Falls** in Stowe; and **Northfield Falls**, Northfield. We have spent some time looking without success for Big Falls in Troy (we gave up after learning that a few people had died there in recent years) and could not penetrate the swampy ground around Moss Glen Falls in Stowe. Most of these sites can be located on *The Vermont Atlas and Gazetteer* maps (see *Books*).

WEATHER REPORTS   For current weather information in Vermont, dial the following numbers: for **Northern Vermont:** 862-2475; **North Central**: 476-4101; **South**: 464-2111; and **South Central**: 773-8056. Listen to "An Eye on the Sky" on Vermont Public Radio. Produced by the Fairbanks Museum and Planetarium, Mark Breen and Steve Maleski make their reports on life's most constant variable both entertaining and informative.

WHITE WATER   During white-water season beginning in mid-April, experienced canoeists and kayakers take advantage of stretches on the **White**, the **Lamoille**, and the **West** rivers, among others. Thousands gather in Jamaica for races on the West River between the flood control dams.

For guided white-water weekend and midweek trips in northern Vermont (for the novice and intermediate canoeists), contact **Vermont Voyageur Expeditions,** Montgomery Center 05471.

WILDFLOWERS   Vermont boasts five times the natural flora growing in other northeastern states, some 1,927 varieties, and in a few places this wealth has been gathered into compact spaces for viewing. In Charlotte, on Route 7, the **Vermont Wildflower Farm** invites you to stroll its six acres of pathways, fields, and woodlands in which species are labeled for the layman; open daily from mid-May through Christmas; $2 admission per adult. We must also mention the **Putney Nursery** in Putney, founded and nurtured by the late George Aiken, dean of Vermont politicians and author of the classic *Pioneering with Wildflowers*; and the **Vermont Institute of Natural Science** in Woodstock, which offers fern walks on its own land and field trips for "bog-trotters." The **Montshire Museum of Science** in Norwich has a 1.5-mile trail that loops beside the Connecticut River and up a ridge, providing a look at several habitats in a short distance. It's possible to find an occasional southern plant species that has migrated up the river valley. In the fall of 1990, the museum will open a wildflower trail.

Old Bennington's First Congregational Church

I. Southern Vermont

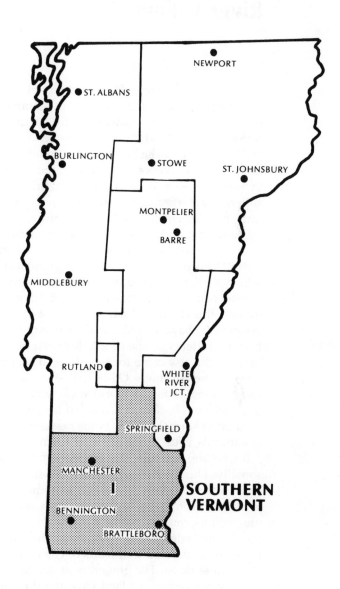

NEWPORT

ST. ALBANS

BURLINGTON

STOWE

ST. JOHNSBURY

MONTPELIER

BARRE

MIDDLEBURY

RUTLAND

WHITE RIVER JCT.

SPRINGFIELD

MANCHESTER

I

SOUTHERN VERMONT

BENNINGTON

BRATTLEBORO

The Lower Connecticut and West River Valleys

The southeast corner of Windham County falls within the bailiwick of the Brattleboro Area Chamber of Commerce. This area includes the Connecticut River towns of Putney and Westminster, the West River towns of Newfane and Townshend, the Whetstone River town of Marlboro, and the beautiful backroaded hills between these valleys. All three rivers and, of course, the roads that follow them meet in Brattleboro—as do the residents of this area whenever they go to a supermarket, discount store, or movie. But "Brat," as it is locally known, is so entirely different from the villages—and each of the villages from each other—that it is impossible to talk about them all at once. Permit us, therefore, to introduce them one by one.

Brattleboro is "a college town without a college"—or so we were told by a fellow customer at the Common Ground, an unusual worker-owned restaurant on newly fancied Elliot Street. For more than a decade, this restaurant has served as a rallying point for the young people who have moved into the surrounding hills. Many came here first as students at one of a half dozen nearby educational institutions, and a few came for the music at Marlboro or one of the burgeoning music centers. Others come to study with the Experiment in International Living, a world-wide educational exchange organization that dates back to 1932 and has trained thousands of Peace Corps volunteers since the 1960s. Some newcomers have opened shops and restaurants, causing the old river town to take on a new look.

It's not the first time that Brattleboro has taken on a different personality. During its long history the state's largest town has shed many skins. The very site of Fort Dummer, built in 1724 just south of town, has been obliterated by the Vernon Dam. Gone too is the early nineteenth-century trading and resort town; no trace remains of the handsome Federal-style commercial buildings or the two elaborate hotels that attracted trainloads of customers who had come to take their water cures. The gingerbread station itself is gone, along with the wooden casino in Island Park and the fine brick town hall, complete with gilded opera house. And the great slate-sided sheds up on

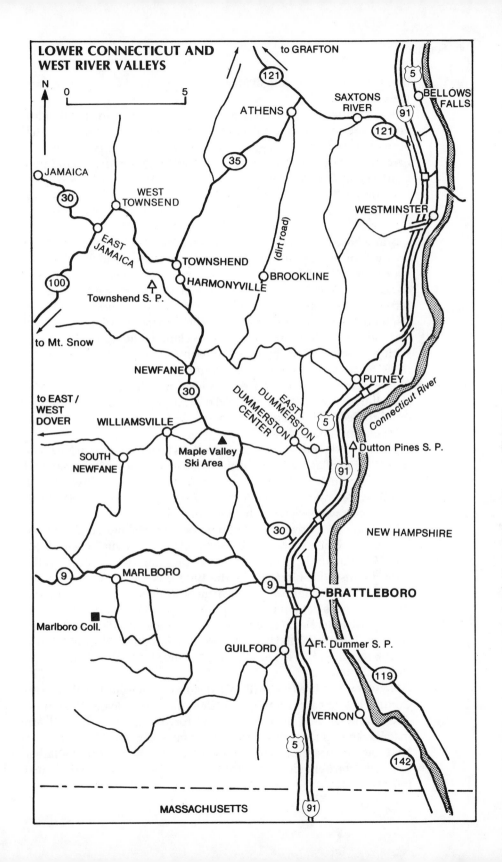

LOWER CONNECTICUT AND WEST RIVER VALLEYS

N

0   5

to GRAFTON

121

ATHENS

SAXTONS RIVER

BELLOWS FALLS

5

91

121

JAMAICA

30

WEST TOWNSEND

35

WESTMINSTER

EAST JAMAICA

100

TOWNSHEND

HARMONYVILLE

BROOKLINE

(dirt road)

Townshend S. P.

to Mt. Snow

NEWFANE

30

PUTNEY

Connecticut River

to EAST / WEST DOVER

WILLIAMSVILLE

EAST DUMMERSTON

DUMMERSTON CENTER

5

Dutton Pines S. P.

SOUTH NEWFANE

Maple Valley Ski Area

91

30

NEW HAMPSHIRE

9

MARLBORO

9

BRATTLEBORO

Marlboro Coll.

GUILFORD

Ft. Dummer S. P.

119

5

VERNON

142

MASSACHUSETTS

91

Birge Street are the sole evidence that thousands of Estey organs were once made here.

Still, a motorist bogged down in the eternal Main Street bottleneck notices Brooks House, built splendidly in 1869 as an 80-room hotel, now converted to housing, offices, and shops. If you park, you will find that Elliot Street has been fitted out with new lights and specialty shops, and that the Latchis Hotel, a couple of blocks down, has been restored to its 1930s high art deco glory (inside as well as out). The surviving rail station is now the Brattleboro Museum and Art Center, filled with historical and changing exhibits.

Brattleboro is actually full of pleasant surprises. For example, there are the beautiful grounds of the Brattleboro Retreat and the extensive sports facilities at Living Memorial Park. Live theater, music, and dance are presented without hoopla. The fanfare seems to be reserved for the annual winter carnival, begun eons ago by Fred Harris, who is also famed for founding the Dartmouth Winter Carnival and the U.S. Eastern Amateur Ski Association. The carnival climaxes with a cross-country ski race, the granddaddy of all such "citizen races" currently held around the country.

VILLAGES   Newfane. A columned courthouse, matching Congregational church, and town hall—all grouped on a handsome green—are framed by dignified white clapboard houses, including two of Vermont's most elegant inns.

When Windham County's court sessions began meeting in Newfane in 1787, the village was about the same size as now: 20 houses and two hotels. But in 1787 the village was two miles up on Newfane Hill. Beams were unpegged and homes moved to the more protected valley by ox-drawn sleighs in the winter of 1824.

Newfane inns have been famous for more than a century; first, because the whitewashed jail accommodated 25 paying guests, feeding them (an 1848 poem says) "good pies and oyster soup" in the same rooms with inmates. By the time this facility closed (in the 1950s), the Newfane Inn—which incorporates much of its hilltop structure—was beginning to acquire a reputation for gourmet fare. Economist John Kenneth Galbraith, a summer resident in the area since 1947, helped publicize the charms of both the village and inn—whose one-time chef eventually opened the Four Columns Inn at the rear of the Green.

Newfane has bred as well as fed famous men. In the Windham County Historical Society (open Memorial Day–October, Wednesdays, Sundays, and holidays 2–5 and for special events), you learn that Eugene Field of nursery rhyme fame (Wynken, Blynken, and Nod, etc.) came from a line of local Fields; a portrait of his father Roswell, who defended Dred Scott in *U.S. v. Scott*, hangs in the courtroom.

Newfane Village is more than just a fine place to dine, sleep, and stroll. It is the site of one of the state's oldest and biggest Sunday flea markets. There are two general stores: One is owned by former flatlanders specializing in exquisite quilts; the other has been run by the same family for decades. Beyond the stores and the remnants of the railway station (which served the narrow-gauge Brattleboro-Londonderry line from 1880 to 1936), there is an unusually fine cemetery in which a local, Sir Isaac Newton (his given name), lies buried beneath a marble obelisk.

Townshend. The next full village center above Newfane is Townshend, a much-photographed community. Its Green is a full two acres bordered on one side by a classic white, 1790 Congregational church, complete with green blinds, amidst clapboard homes. On the other side of the Green is a columned and towered stucco town hall and the fine buildings of the new Leland and Gray Union High School (originally founded as a Baptist Seminary in 1834). At the junction of Routes 30 and 35, a short white clapboard block contains an apothecary, a hardware store, and a grocery, even a reasonably priced soda fountain. The big annual event is Hospital Fair Day when the Common is filled with booths and games, all to benefit 21-bed Grace Cottage Hospital. The hospital grew, unbelievably, out the backside of a rambling old village home. (Known for the quality of its service, this is Vermont's first hospital to have installed a birthing bed.)

This small town also contains a furniture factory (see *Outlets*), a state forest, a public swimming area, Vermont's largest single-span covered bridge, 15 cemeteries, and, atop one of its wonderfully abrupt hills, a welcoming inn (check *Windham Hill* under *Lodging*). An old tannery in West Townshend is now a moderately priced restaurant and tavern.

Westminster. Sited in a mile-wide plain above the Connecticut, this village is one of Vermont's earliest settlements. The unusually wide main street was designed as a militia training ground, and it was here in 1775 that locals barred New York court officials from their courthouse. The uprising, known as the "Westminster Massacre," was quelled and is considered one of the opening shots of the Revolution. Here also at a convention held in 1777, Vermont declared itself a free and independent state. Today, Westminster is a quiet valley town, noted for its farm stands and burying ground. In the Westminster Historical Society (open Sundays 2–4), you can see copies of the state's first newspaper (the famous press itself is now in the Vermont Historical Society Museum; see "Montpelier").

Marlboro. Turn off busy Route 9 and you enter another, more tranquil world. In summer, flowers brim from window boxes, and the air is filled with the sounds of the Marlboro Music Festival. In other seasons, students purposefully stride from building to building on the small, attractive Marlboro College campus, which, incidentally, maintains a fine network of cross-country ski trails. Check under *Shopping* for the three fine crafts studios here. The Marlboro Historical Society with its collection of pictures, old farm tools, and antique furniture, is open Saturdays 2–5, July–Labor Day.

Putney. This village's riverside fields have been heavily farmed since the mideighteenth century, and its hillsides produce more than one-tenth of all the state's apples. Putney is an unusually fertile place for progressive thinking, too. Back in the 1840s, it spawned a group who practiced "Bible Communism," the sharing of all property, work, and wives. John Humphrey Noyes, the group's leader, was charged with adultery in 1847 and fled with his flock to Oneida, New York, where they founded the famous silverplate company. Today, the town is best known for Putney School, a very unusual co-ed, college preparatory school founded in 1935. It stresses the individual aptitudes of its students and has a regime that entails rising at 6:30 each morning and helping with chores, which include raising animals on the school farm. Landmark College is the country's first college specifically for dyslexic students and occupies the former multi-million dollar Windham College campus designed by Edward Durrell Stone.

The River Valley Playhouse, also on the campus, now stages year-round performances, films, concerts, lectures, and art shows.

Many young people who come to Putney for schooling never move away. The changing population is evidenced by the range of gourmet items available in the Putney Food Co-op (one in a lineup of three general stores at the village center) and in the fact that more than 40 established craftspeople now live in town (see *Shopping*). Putney's native sons are no slouches either. They include the late George Aiken, who founded and developed the Putney Nursery and served as governor before going on to Washington as a senator in 1941, a post he held until retirement in 1975. He was also the author of the classic *Pioneering with Wildflowers*. Frank Wilson, a genuine Yankee trader who was one of the first merchants to enter Red China, built the first of his six Basketvilles, "The World's Largest Basket Stores," in the village. The Putney Historical Museum, open Wednesdays and Saturdays 2–5, is housed in the town hall. There is a seasonal information booth just off Route 5 at the I-91 access ramp in front of the Putney Inn.

GUIDANCE   **Brattleboro Area Chamber of Commerce** (254-4565), 180 Main Street, Brattleboro 05301. Open year-round, Monday–Friday 8–5. Besides the Main Street office, there are two seasonal information booths run by knowledgeable senior citizens in warm weather months—on Route 9 in West Brattleboro and on Route 5 at the Common, just north of the junction with Route 30. There is also a seasonal information booth, maintained by Putney merchants, in front of the Putney Inn, just off Route 5.

GETTING THERE   By bus: Greyhound/Vermont Transit offers service from New York and Connecticut. Peter Pan Bus Co. serves Boston via Springfield. The bus stop is on Route 5 at the junction with Route 9 west.

By train: See *AMTRAK* in "What's Where."

TO SEE AND DO   **Brattleboro Museum and Art Center** (257-0124), Canal and Bridge streets, Brattleboro. Open Tuesday–Sunday 12–6, May 11–November 3; closed holidays. The town's 1915 rail station makes a handsome home for historical exhibits such as an Estey organ, a photo of Naulahka (the now-private house in which Rudyard Kipling wrote his *Jungle Books*), and photos of the Brattleboro Kipling knew during his 1892–1896 stay. There are also changing exhibits, frequent concerts, and other live presentations.

Brooks Memorial Library (254-5290), 224 Main Street, Brattleboro. This modern facility includes changing exhibits of art and sculpture and a permanent collection of works by Larkin G. Mead, the Brattleboro boy who first achieved national fame by sculpting an eight-foot-high angel from snow one night and placing it at the junction of Routes 30 and 5. The replica of this snow angel is here.

Santa's Land (387-5550), Route 5, Putney. Open May–December 24 daily; Igloo Pancake House open all year. A Christmas theme park with some unusual animals. Sleigh rides are available January–March by appointment, minimum 10 people.

MG Car Museum (722-3708), Westminster. (See "Bellows Falls.")

Molly Stark Trail, Route 9 between Brattleboro and Bennington, is dedicated to the wife of General John Stark, hero of the battle of Bennington. It is a winding, heavily trafficked route, lined for much of the way with tourist-oriented shops and restaurants. We advise avoiding it in foliage season.

Vermont Yankee Energy Information Center (257-1416), Vernon. The exhibit and information center at this (Vermont's only) nuclear power plant on Governor Hunt Road is open weekdays 10–2, Saturdays in summer. Phone to check because hours may change.

Connecticut River Fish Ladder, Vernon. The 984-foot fish ladder helps American shad and salmon return to spawning grounds; 51 pools in a 35-foot vertical rise. Best viewing is from May 25–July 16, 8–5 daily.

FARMS TO VISIT   One of the state's concentrations of farms and orchards is here in the lower Connecticut River Valley, some offering "pick-your-own," others welcoming visitors to their farm stands, sugaring houses, or barns.

Harlow's Sugar House (387-5852), Route 5 in Putney, is one of the most visitor-oriented operations, permitting you to pick your own apples, blueberries, and strawberries and offering sleigh rides during sugaring season. Syrup prices tend to be high.

Hickins Mountain Mowings (254-2146), Black Road, Dummerston. Located off the high, wooded back route that my children call the "Gnome Road" (between Route 5 in Putney and Route 30 in West Dummerston), this is an outstanding family farm, noted for the quality and variety of its vegetables, flowers, maple syrup, pickles, jams, jellies, and fruitcakes. Open year-round until sunset.

Green Mountain Orchards (387-5851), West Hill Road, Putney. Open daily in season. Pick-your-own apples and blueberries; cider available in season.

Dwight Miller & Son (254-9158), Putney. Open daily year-round, offering pick-your-own apples, strawberries, and peaches. Also selling pears, plums, and turnips; follow signs from Route 5 across from KOA campground.

H & M Orchard (254-2711), Dummerston Center. Selling apples and strawberries; offering pick-your-own strawberries. One of the most accessible sugar shacks to observe "boiling" during sugaring season.

Dutton Berry Farm and Stand (365-4168), Newfane. You can pick your own vegetables and berries at the farm on the Brookline Road or buy from the ample stand on Route 30.

Whetstone Valley Farm (254-9638), Route 9, West Brattleboro, opens its sugarhouse to visitors and sells syrup year-round.

COVERED BRIDGES   In Brattleboro, the reconstructed Creamery Bridge forms the entrance to Living Memorial Park on Route 9. North on Route 30 in West Dummerston, a town lattice bridge across the West River is the longest, still-used covered bridge in the state (for the best view, jump into the cool waters on either side; this is a popular swimming hole on a hot summer day). Vermont's longest single-span bridge stands by Route 30 in West Townshend just below the Townshend Dam but is closed to traffic. There is also a covered bridge across the Green River in Guilford and another in the delightful back road town of Williamsville.

PARKS AND FORESTS   **Sandy Pond State Park** (257-7406), Guilford. This former 125-acre estate with a large pond is good for swimming and boating, circled by a nature path that leads to a five-acre perennial garden.

Fort Dummer State Park (254-2610), RFD 3, Brattleboro 05301. Located two miles south of Brattleboro on South Main Street. There are 61 campsites, including nine lean-tos, a dump station, playfield, and a hiking trail through hardwoods with views of the river valley.

Dutton Pines State Park (254-2277), Brattleboro. On Route 5, five miles north of town, this is a picnic area with a shelter. $.75 per adult, $.25 per person under 14.

Townshend State Forest (365-7500), Townshend. There are 30 campsites here (camping fees same as Fort Dummer). There is swimming nearby at Townshend Dam and a short (2.7 miles) but very steep climb to the summit of Bald Mountain; trail maps are available at the park office. Adults pay $.75, children $.25.

Living Memorial Park, just west of Brattleboro on Route 9. This is an unusual facility for any community. It includes a swimming pool (mid-June–Labor Day, $.50), ice-skating rink (early December–mid-March, $1.75 adults, $1.00 students), tennis courts and playground, camping sites ($4.00 per site per night), lawn games, a nine-hole golf course, and a ski hill serviced by a T-bar.

BICYCLING   **Putney Bicycle Club**, the oldest in Vermont, sponsors an extensive program of tours through the nearby back roads. Check the **West Hill Shop** (387-5718), just off Exit 4 of I-91, across from the Putney Inn, for local information, advice, and rentals, including fat-tired bikes. **The Country Inn** in Williamsville (348-7148) rents mountain bikes.

RIVER TOURS AND CANOEING   The 32 miles from Bellows Falls to the Vernon Dam is slow-moving water, as is the 6-mile stretch from below the dam to the Massachusetts border.

The Belle of Brattleboro (254-7120), Putney Road. The new, 49-passenger, mahogany-trimmed riverboat offers several kinds of cruises Tuesday–Sunday and holidays, Memorial Day–Columbus Day.

West River Canoe (896-6209), Route 100, Townshend, rents canoes by the hour, day, week, or month in season; sailboats, sailboards, and paddleboats are also available at Townshend Dam.

Connecticut River Safari (254-3908), located at the cove at West River Bridge, Putney Road, has rental canoes, guided camping adventures for singles, families, and groups.

FISHING   In the **Connecticut River**, you can catch bass, trout, pike, pickerel, and yellow perch. There is an access on Old Ferry Road, two miles north of Brattleboro on Route 5, another from River Road on the New Hampshire shore in Westmoreland (Route 9 east, then north on Route 63).

The **West River** is a source of trout and smallmouth bass; access is from any number of places along Route 30.

Strictly Trout (869-3116), RFD 3, Box 930, Westminster West, offers a guide service, also lodging and camping packages for fly fishermen.   In Vernon, there is a boat access on **Lily Pond** and in Guilford, on **Weatherhead Hollow Pond** (see *The Vermont Atlas and Gazetteer*, DeLorme).

GOLF   **Brattleboro Country Club** (257-7380), Upper Dummerston Road, nine holes.

HIKING   In Brattleboro, there are two pleasant walks. One is along the West

River, following the abandoned West River Railroad bed. Access is off Route 5 north of town; take the second left turn after crossing the iron bridge; look for the trail by the Maple Farms milk plant. There is also a pleasant path up to the Retreat Tower, a nineteenth-century overlook. The trail begins beside Linden Lodge on Route 30. **Wantastiquet Mountain**, overlooking Brattleboro from across the Connecticut River in New Hampshire, is a good 1.5-hour hike from downtown and is great for picnics and views of southeastern Vermont. Also see **Fort Dummer State Park** for a wooded trail south of town, overlooking the Connecticut, and a steep trek up **Bald Mountain** (see *Townshend State Forest*). There is a trail to the top of **Putney Mountain** between Putney and Brookline, off the Putney Mountain Road.

Four Season Tours (365-7937), Townshend. Charles Marchant offers walking tours of old cemeteries, wilderness treks, moonlight trips, featuring local history and lore; $20 per person per day, $14 per half day; group rates.

HORSEBACK RIDING   West River Lodge and Stable (365-7745), Hill Road, Brookline. The small inn, stable, and riding school were all established in 1930 and have a loyal, year-round following. Guests are encouraged to bring their own mounts, but neophytes are also welcome. Trail rides offered, also sleighing in winter. There are also "centered riding" clinics, teaching improved riding posture using the Alexander technique. All-day trail rides in spring and fall are a tradition. Just two miles from Newfane, a short ways off Route 30, this is a frequently by-passed place, a real find for anyone who loves horses.

South Mowing Stables (254-2831), Hinesburg Road. Lucile Bump offers instruction.

Taffy Morgan (365-4228 or 874-4384), Townshend, offers buggy rides to elegant picnics (see *Dining Out*).

Shanagary Farm (722-3548), Route 5, Westminster Station, offers inn-to-inn rides.

HORSE RACING   Hinsdale Racetrack (336-5382), Route 119, Hinsdale, NH. Pari-mutuel betting. Tuesday–Saturday 8 PM. Saturday and Sunday matinee at 1:30. Runs year-round. Greyhounds mid-August–mid-June. Harness racing mid-June–mid-August. Full dining room. Closed Monday.

SAILBOARDING   New England Sailboard Co. (874-4178), Route 30, Jamaica, and **West River Canoe** (896-6209), Route 100 (off Route 30), Townshend; both offer sailboard instruction and rentals.

SWIMMING   In Brattleboro, there is a pool in **Living Memorial Park (mid-June–Labor Day, $.50). The nearest beach for this area is Wares Grove in Chesterfield, NH (nine miles east on Route 9, the next left after the junction with Route 63). This pleasant beach on **Spofford Lake** is good for children; there is a snack bar and makeshift changing facilities. In Guilford, there is swimming at **Weatherhead Hollow Pond.** The biggest swimming hole by far is at the **Townshend Dam**, off Route 30 in West Townshend. You drive across the top of this massive structure, completed in 1961 as a major flood prevention measure for the southern Connecticut River Valley. Swimming is in the reservoir behind the dam, ideal for children. Changing facilities provided, small fee.

The West River offers a few swimming holes, notably under the covered bridge on Route 30 in West Dummerston, and just off Route 30, a mile or so up (on the South Newfane Road), the Rock River swirls through a series of swimming holes, some favored by skinny-dippers. There's parking and a small beach at the covered bridge, and cars line the road above the Rock River (there's a steep path down).

CROSS-COUNTRY SKIING   Brattleboro Outing Club Ski Hut (254-4081), Upper Dummerston Road. Trails through woods and golf course, 15 km machine tracked, rentals, instruction.

Four Season Tours. Charles Marchant (365-7937), Box 132, Townshend 05353, offers guided moonlight and other cross-country tours in the Townshend area.

In **Living Memorial Park**, (254-4081) Brattleboro, a six-km trail through the woods is not only set but lighted for night skiing.

DOWNHILL SKIING   The big ski areas are a short drive west into the Green Mountains, either to Mount Snow (Route 9 from Brattleboro and then up Route 100 to East Dover—see the "Mount Snow Area") or up Route 30 to Stratton and beyond to Bromley and Magic mountains (see "Manchester and the Mountains").

Maple Valley (254-6083), Route 30, West Dummerston.
Lifts: 2 double chair lifts, 1 T-bar.
Trails: 13 trails and slopes.
Vertical drop: 1,000 feet.
Facilities: cafeteria, ski shop, lounge, rentals, repairs, snow-making
Ski school: American technique, PSIA certified.
Open: Daily, Wednesday–Saturday for night skiing.
Rates: $25 adult, $19 junior on weekends but $12 for everyone midweek; $12 adult, $10 junior for night skiing. There's also a $45 ski club membership that entitles you to half price on any ski tickets and lessons.

In Brattleboro itself, a T-bar serves the ski hill in **Living Memorial Park**, and there is a ski jump near the Brattleboro Retreat.

SKATING   Living Memorial Park, Brattleboro; rink is open daily, evenings until 9.

Rollerdome, Route 5 north of Brattleboro, roller skating Friday and Saturday, 7:30–10:30; Saturday and Sunday, 2–5.

LODGING   Old Newfane Inn (365-4427), Newfane 05345. The long, low-beamed dining room was a part of the original inn built up on Newfane Hill (see *Newfane Village*), and there is a seemly sense of age to this landmark, with its formal atmosphere. The 10 guest rooms, nine with baths, furnished with antiques are spotless, as are the public rooms. Famous for outstanding French–Swiss cuisine. Closed in November and April. Rates: $95–135 double with bath, $125 for a suite (living room, bath, and bedroom); two-night deposit required to confirm reservation. Continental breakfast.

Four Columns Inn (365-7713), Newfane 05345. Built in 1830 by General Pardon Kimball to remind his southern wife of her girlhood home, this is a classic Greek Revival mansion, now converted to 15 rooms, each with private bath and antique beds, surrounded by 155 acres for strolling along the pond, stream, and through the gardens. Your hosts are Pamela and Jacques Allembert. The highly rated restaurant is one of the best in Vermont. $100–170 double occupancy, including breakfast. MAP only during foliage season.

Windham Hill Inn (874-4080), West Townshend 05359. Poised high above the West River Valley, this 1825 brick farmhouse offers an unusual retreat. Each of the 15 guest rooms (all with private bath) is carefully furnished with antiques and interesting art; five are in the White Barn Annex, two with a large deck looking down the valley. Common rooms in the inn itself include an airy sun porch with woodstove and TV, wicker chairs, and sofa. Other sitting rooms are "country elegant," with oriental carpets, wing chairs, and silver candelabra on the formal, Queen Anne central dining table; smaller tables for two in the Frog Pond Room. There are also informal spaces for relaxing. Guests congregate for cocktails before dinner—a six-course, candlelit affair. In winter, there is a small pond for skating and a cross-country ski center on the 160-acre property. $175 per couple MAP in summer and fall, $125 single; packages available.

The Inn at South Newfane (348-7191), South Newfane 05351. This elegant inn is sited just off the beaten track in a picture-perfect village, complete with covered bridge. There are 6 large guest rooms, all with high ceilings and private bath. The public rooms are nicely appointed, and the porch, a great place for evening cocktails, overlooks a sweeping lawn shaded by weeping willows (a hammock is strung between two), with a swimming pond at its center. The innkeepers are Connie and Herb Borst and their daughter, Lisa, a graduate of the Culinary Institute of America and the chef who has put this place on the Vermont dining map. $90–100 per person per day MAP, double occupancy, $15 less B&B. Closed November and April.

☞**Latchis Hotel** (254-6300), 50 Main Street, Brattleboro 05301. A downtown art deco–style hotel first opened in 1939 and then reincarnated after a thorough and loving restoration in the summer of 1989. It has remained in the Latchis family throughout. Push open the door into the small but spiffy lobby, and you smell fresh popcorn from the adjacent (also beautifully restored) movie theater—to which guests receive free passes. Other surprises include highly polished terrazzo marble floors, fresh flowers, a sprinkling of 1930s furniture, air-conditioning, sound-proof windows (a real blessing), and cheerful, brightly decorated rooms. There are 38, including suites, all accessible by elevator. Rates: $40–62 for double rooms, $54–68 for mini-suites, and $76–98 for suites, includes continental breakfast. You might want to request a corner room looking up Main Street or an upper floor with views of the river and New Hampshire woods.

Hickory Ridge House (387-5709), RFD 3, Box 1410, Putney 05346. This is a find: an 1808 brick mansion, complete with Palladian window, set on 12 acres on a country road near the Connecticut River. There are seven airy guest rooms, painted in soft, authentic colors like rose and peach, decorated with antiques and interesting art, but not enough to clutter. The original Federal-era bedrooms are large, with Rumford fireplaces; those in the back wing are smaller, off a cozy upstairs sitting room. Hosts Jacquie Walker and Steve Anderson come to innkeeping from backgrounds that include college teaching, cooking, and chimney-sweeping. Steve can greet you in German, Russian, and French. Breakfast features their own jams and jellies, baked goods, eggs from their chickens, honey from their bees, and local maple syrup. In summer, a swimming hole lies within walking distance and in winter, there are miles of cross-country touring trails nearby. $45–80 per room, B&B; $18 for an extra person in the room.

☞**West River Lodge** (365-7745), RR 1, Box 693, Newfane 05345, off Route 30, Hill Road, Brookline. Since the 1930s, this inn has catered to horse lovers, doing so exclusively through the 1970s and up until Gill (pronounced Jill, short for Gillian) and Jack Winner, both former college professors, bought it a few years ago. Riding is still a big draw: English-style riding instruction is offered in the ring next to the big barn, and there are trail rides. This is also a place you can bring your own horse or carriage. Some of the finest back road bridle paths are right out the door. In winter, there are sleigh rides. Nonriders too can enjoy the isolated feel of this white farmhouse, just a mile or two off busy Route 30. There's a swimming hole across the meadow, and guests have access to nearby tennis courts. Watercolor workshops are also offered. Rooms are cheerful, unpretentious, and country comfortable. Meals are what Gill describes as country cooking but with a Welsh accent to match her own. Guests dine around a common table in the low-beamed dining room and gather around the fire in the friendly, old-style parlor. $65–75 per double room B&B, $100–115 double room MAP; weekly and single rates also available.

Longwood Inn (257-1545), Marlboro 05344. Formerly a dairy farm set back above Route 9, this attractive inn has nine, nicely furnished guest rooms, and there are four efficiency studios (accommodating three to six) in the Carriage House. The more expensive rooms have fireplaces, and one has a whirlpool. Two comfortable rooms are reserved for guests to relax downstairs in the inn, and there is a large public dining room with an ambitious menu and strong local following. The fish pond out front is well stocked. In winter, a cross-country trail leads to Hidden Lake. Rates are $120–160 per room, $175 in an extra-large room with fireplace and whirlpool bath, MAP; $85–135 B&B. Add 15 percent to all rates.

The Putney Inn (387-5517), Putney 05346. One of the oldest farmhouses in the area, this red clapboard landmark was built by the first settlers. In the early 1960s, when the land was divided for construction of I-91, it was sold to local residents who renovated the farmhouse without disturbing the post and beams or the central open hearth. Plants and antiques add to the pleasant setting of the entry and large dining rooms. Twenty-five guest rooms occupy a motel-like wing, each with Queen Anne reproduction furnishings, baths, color TV and phone. Rates: $68 double, $54 single, includes full breakfast.

BED & BREAKFASTS   "40 Putney Road" (254-6268), at that address, Brattleboro, recently opened by Jim Fairbanks and Alain Beret, takes full advantage of a formal French-style town house. Three comfortably furnished guest rooms with private baths plus a small sitting room upstairs; big sitting room, garden room, elegant dining room; classically landscaped grounds make a pleasant setting for breakfast on the patio. $68 per room double, $45 single, with full breakfast. Nonsmoking.

Boardman House (365-4086), Village Green, Townshend 05353. An 1840s Greek Revival house tucked into a quiet (away from Route 30 traffic) corner of one of Vermont's standout Commons. Sarah and Paul Messenger offer five comfortable guest rooms, each with private bath. There's also a two-bedroom suite, a parlor with fireplace, and airy, old-fashioned kitchen. Breakfast usually includes fresh fruit compote and oven warm muffins, and a creative main dish. $60–85 per room.

Mugwump Farm (348-7761), Williamsville 05362. An eighteenth-century farmhouse, 2.5 miles from Maple Valley ski area, a shade off the beaten path. Marian Fickett offers three simple, clean, and inviting rooms, $45–50, shared bath; continental breakfast included.

Rainey Brook Farm (874-4889), Route 30, West Townshend 05359. Leete Ekstrom offers four guest rooms which vary in beauty; request the back room. $45 double, $35 single, breakfast included.

General Fletcher Homestead (874-4853), West Townshend 05359. A 220-year-old home set off in its own grounds just off Route 30.

Common rooms are dark, but the three guest rooms are attractive. President Eisenhower slept here in 1948 while fishing in the West River across the road. $55–60 includes a full breakfast.

Mapleton Farm (257-5252), Route 5, East Dummerston 05346. The former Dutton Farm, built in 1803, is set on 25 acres; rates are $55–75 double, including continental breakfast.

Dalem's Chalet (254-4323), West Brattleboro 05301. Set back from Route 9, this chalet-style motel is a family find, offering tidy rooms with two double beds and TV, indoor and outdoor swimming pools, game room and sauna, a pond with swans, and best of all, a fine little restaurant specializing in Swiss dishes; $38–68 per room.

Anthony Jones House (365-7029), 5 Church Street, Newfane. This eighteenth-century house on the Common offers rooms with fireplaces and a two-bedroom unit with kitchenette (ask for rate), ranging from $40–105, including continental breakfast.

DINING OUT   **Inn at South Newfane** (348-7191), Dover Road, South Newfane. A nicely decorated dining room in a former mansion (see *Lodging*) is the setting for gourmet meals prepared by Lisa Borst, a graduate of the Culinary Institute of America who has been collecting more than her share of culinary medals in the past few years. The menu is unusually varied. You might begin with char-grilled quail in Yucatan-style marinade or with fresh-shucked mussels, sweet sausage and tomato in white wine, followed by boneless breast of duck with a green peppercorn-mustard sauce, milk-fed veal with apple-wine sauce, or a wild game special. Entrées $16–20. No credit cards.

The Four Columns Inn (365-7713), Newfane. The dining room is housed in a converted barn with a large brick fireplace as its centerpiece. Proprietor Jacques Allembert formerly owned Le Bistro in New York City. The menu is French with emphasis on herbs (homegrown) and locally raised lamb, and trout from the adjacent pond. Appetizers feature cold, smoked salmon mousse and smoked trout with chive cream cheese, black bread and horseradish sauce, and the wide choice of entrées might include sautée of lobster and shrimp, assorted vegetables, with green and red pepper corn bread or marinated quail, grilled with pesto couscous and greens. Entrées $16-22.

Longwood Inn (257-1545), Route 9, Marlboro. The attractive dining room in this old inn is well known for the quality of its fare. You might dine on poached salmon in Scotch cream sauce, roasted Cornish game hen with herbed rice stuffing, or pan-blackened rib-eye steak or grilled breast of duckling. Appetizers might include smoked duck sausage or skewered shrimp. Leave room for the chocolate bourbon pecan pie with maple whipped crème. Entrées $15–20.

Townshend Country Inn (365-4141), Route 30, Townshend. This pleasant country restaurant may just offer the best dining value in southern Vermont. Since acquiring this old house—the oldest part dates back to 1776 and was a summer home for Grandma Moses—a few years ago, Joe Peters (fresh from seven years of managing the Yankee Pedlar in Holyoke, MA) has created a mix of ambience and quality dining at prices well below the norm. You had better come early for the Sunday Vermont Buffet Brunch. Specialties vary with the night. Thursday it's "New England Clambake"; Friday it's prime rib. Pasta primavera, roast Long Island duckling, and pork medallions Milanese are perennial favorites. Entrées $12.95–20.

The Putney Inn (387-5517), just off I-91, Exit 4 in Putney. An eighteenth-century house is now a popular restaurant, good for "just a plain ole burger" or unlimited salad bar at lunch, or for dependable fare, ranging from baked lasagna to broiled lamb chops for dinner. Try the maple mousse for dessert. All three meals are served. Dinner entrées $10.95–18.

Old Newfane Inn (365-4427), Route 30, Newfane Village. The low-beamed old dining room is very formal, open for both lunch and dinner. Chef-owner Eric Weindl offers a Swiss-accented continental menu with choices like white asparagus in "sauce verte," sautéed bay scallops, veal Roulade, and rack of lamb for two. For 20 years, this has been a dining landmark. Closed Mondays. Dinner entrées $15–22.

Taffy Morgan's Elegant Picnics (874-4384), Townshend. Taffy transports guests in an open buggy or enclosed rockaway to a grassy field or mountain top where she lays out a gourmet picnic lunch, served on linen, with crystal and china. The feast might begin with lobster quiche, include braised Cornish game hens or butterflied leg of lamb. $50 per person.

Peter Haven's (257-3333), 32 Elliot Street, Brattleboro. Just 10 tables in this nifty new place; continental cuisine with the accent on seafood, such as grilled swordfish Geneva. Open 6–10, Tuesday–Saturday. Entrées: $11–16.

EATING OUT   The Common Ground (257-0855), 25 Elliot Street, Brattleboro. By no means the most elegant or expensive restaurant in town, this is a unique and rewarding place. The dining rooms occupy the high-ceilinged second floor of an old industrial building, and there is a pleasant glass-walled solar terrace. At the beginning of each month, a leaflet is printed up showing the specialties available each day; these run the gamut from Russian vegetable pie through lasagna to spanakopita. Other specialties include fresh fish, organic chicken, and sandwiches, depending on the day. Beverages range from banana yogurt shakes through beer and wine. Customers help themselves to tea, coffee, and side dishes. Strangers are encouraged to sit down at the same table and talk to each other; there is a rare friendly feel to this place. There are monthly art shows, occasional lectures, and live entertainment. Monday–Saturday for lunch and dinner;

closed Tuesdays; Sundays for brunch 10:30–1:30, and dinner 5:30–9.

Panda North (257-4578/4486), Route 5 north of Brattleboro (Exit 3 off I-91), near the Quality Inn. Chinese-restaurant buffs will delight in this excellent source of Hunan and Szechuan dishes. Lunch specials like shredded pork with black beans, shrimp with garlic sauce.

West Townshend Village Café (874-4162), Route 30, West Townshend. Hidden down below the road by the West River, this former tannery makes a delightful lunch or dinner stop. There is a children's menu with burgers and hot dogs, also a variety of salads and sandwiches served all day, but you can also dine on shrimp parmesan, baked stuffed rainbow trout, or prime rib au jus. In summer there is dining on the deck.

Jad's Family Restaurant (257-4559), Canal Street, Brattleboro. A good bet for families; homemade soup, diner fare, fried foods, children's menu.

Shin La Restaurant (257-5226), 57 Main Street (across from the Latchis Hotel), Brattleboro. Open 11–9, a small, new Korean restaurant specializing in homemade soups, dumplings, and Korean dishes. There are sushi specials on Tuesdays.

Walker's Restaurant (254-6046), 132 Main Street, Brattleboro, closed Sundays except during foliage and Christmas. This is a great downtown way stop: spacious dining rooms with bare brick walls, oak tables and bar, soft lighting. For lunch there is a wide choice of burgers, soups, quiche, and sandwiches (note that only fresh potatoes, cut on the premises, are used for french fries). The dinner menu includes steak, seafood, fish, and chicken, basics like fried clams and sirloin steak, not-so-basics like mustard-herbed baked chicken.

T.J. Buckley's (257-4922), 132 Elliot Street, Brattleboro, open Tuesday–Sunday at 6 PM.

West River Marina (257-7563), Route 5 just north of Brattleboro. Spring–fall 11:30–midnight, Sundays 10–9. Live music, Thursday and Friday. Sandwiches, soups, fresh fish entrées served on a riverside deck. Reasonably priced.

Jade Wah (254-2392), 40 Main Street, Brattleboro. This unpretentious family place offers Szechuan–Mandarin cuisine, some Cantonese dishes, Chinese hors d'oeuvres, seafood dishes, and some American food. It has a full liquor license. Open Monday–Thursday 11:30 AM–11 PM; Fridays and Saturdays 11:30–midnight; Sundays noon–11 PM.

Latchis Grille and Windham Brewery (254-4747), in the Latchis Hotel, serves lunch and dinner daily. One can tour the brewery that produces ales, porters, and lagers.

Curtis' Barbeque. On fair summer days, follow your nose to the blue school bus parked on Route 5 in Putney, just off I-91 Exit 4. Curtis cooks up pork ribs and chicken, seasoned with his secret bar-

becue sauce, also foil-wrapped potatoes, grilled corn, and beans fla-
vored with Vermont maple syrup. By far the best barbeque in the
Northeast! He's there Thursday–Sunday 9–9.

The Putney Summit (387-5806), Route 5, one mile north of
Basketville, open daily for breakfast, lunch, and dinner.

ICE CREAM AND SNACKS   Page's Ice Cream, Route 9, West Brattleboro.
Outstanding ice cream with frequent special flavors, made on the
spot. There's a coffee shop, too, that's open from 6 AM to 8 PM.

The Upper Crust (257-1991), Brooks House Mall, Brattleboro. Located just off the Harmony Parking Lot, this irresistible store is a
source of a variety of good breads, cakes, croissants, cookies, linzers,
tarts, eclairs, and such. There is a small sit-down area; juices, sodas,
coffee, and a variety of teas are served. Monday–Thursday 7–5:30,
Friday 7–6, Saturday 7–5. Closed Sundays.

Hamelman's Bakery, Elliot Street, Brattleboro. European pastries,
breads, rolls, cakes. Many locals prefer it to The Upper Crust.

MUSIC   Marlboro Music Festival at Persons Auditorium, Marlboro College (254-8163 or 254-2394). Concerts, primarily chamber music, are
offered on Fridays, Saturdays, and Sundays, early July–mid-August.
Tickets are usually sold out by May, but seats can often be found on
the screened-in porch attached to the concert hall. Pablo Casals preceded Rudolf Serkin as artistic director here. Festival members are
limited to 70 and their public performances are incidental to their
work together. For advance tickets write: Marlboro Music Festival,
135 South 18th Street, Philadelphia, PA 19103 (215-569-4690); after
June 6: Marlboro Music Festival, Marlboro 05344.

Yellow Barn Music Festival (387-6637), Putney. Begun in 1969,
this is a series of three-evening chamber music concerts each week in
July and August. Performances are in a 150-seat barn located behind
the Public Library in Putney Village. Artists include both well-known
professionals and students from leading conservatories.

Brattleboro Music Center (257-4523), 15 Walnut Street, Brattleboro.
Housed in a former convent, this burgeoning music school sponsors
a wide variety of local music events and festivals, some of them
staged at the River Valley Playhouse and Art Center (see below).
Each fall it features the outstanding New England Bach Festival's
chamber orchestra and chorus.

Friends of Music at Guilford (257-1969/1028), Guilford; a series of
concerts throughout the year at various locations.

PLAYS, CONCERTS, LECTURES   River Valley Performing Arts Center
(387-5454), on the Landmark College campus, Route 5, Putney. Built
as the art center for former Windham College, this facility now serves
the community with its 400- and 100-seat theaters.

Opera at the Latchis Theater, Main Street, Brattleboro. Several
productions are staged in the ornate 1,200-seat theater in the course

of the year. Phone the Brattleboro Music Center (above) or the Latchis Hotel (254-6300) for details.

NIGHTCLUBS   **Mole's Eye Café** (257-0771), Brattleboro. A live music club. **River Bend Inn's Echo Room** (365-7352), Newfane. Lively band Saturday nights until 1 AM.

FILMS   **The Latchis Theater**, Main Street, Brattleboro, and **First Cinema** (at Fairfield Plaza, Route 5 north of Brattleboro), show first-run films.

SELECTIVE SHOPPING   *Brattleboro*   **Vermont Artisan Design** (257-7044), 115 Main Street. This attractive shop displays the work of more than 80 Vermont craftspeople.

Sam's Army & Navy Dept. Store (254-2933), 74 Main Street. This family business now fills two floors of two buildings with a full stock of hunting, camping, and sports equipment. Prices are reasonable, but people don't shop here for bargains. The big thing is the service—skilled help in selecting the right fishing rod, tennis racket, or gun. There are also name-brand sports clothes and standard army and navy gear. Sam's is usually open 8–6, until 9 on Fridays, closed Sundays. On the first day of hunting season (early November), the store opens at dawn and serves a hunter's breakfast (it also sells licenses).

Borter's Jewelry Studio-Gallery, 1 Harmony Place. Bob Borter is a gem cutter who designs gold and silver jewelry. Worth a stop.

Delectable Mountain (257-4456), 6 Elliot Street, Brattleboro. Fine fabrics, Harris tweeds, silks, all natural imported laces, museum-quality quilts (owner Jan Norris makes them all).

Wildwater Outfitters (254-4133), 20 Elliot Street, an unusual building full of outdoor gear, canoes, kayaks, sailboards, skis, books, and magazines.

Tom and Sally's Handmade Chocolates, Harmony parking lot (home of the Vermont Cow Pie); and **Wilson's Chocolate Shop,** 111 Main Street, both in Brattleboro, fuel sweet-toothers (also see *Bookstores* and *Factory Outlets*).

Putney   **The Putney Woodshed and Putney Artisans** (387-4481), Route 5, Putney Village 05346. Open daily 9–5, Sunday 12–5; closed February. In the barn behind her house, Margot Torrey has created a showcase for work by more than 140 craftspeople, many who live in and around Putney. Woodcuts, cards, things woven, sculpted, forged, and printed are among the unusual wares for sale here. Note that the Putney Artisans stage occasional open-studio tours.

Blossom Handweaving (387-4189/5205), Main Street. Judy Zemmel weaves and sells an exceptional array of clothing, also rag rugs; children's books are also stocked.

Oak Grove, an adjacent shop, carries a wide range of yarns handspun or spun at local mills and hand-dyed by local artists.

Putney Clayschool (387-4395), Kimball Hill, open 10–5 daily, except Thursday. A great variety of pitchers, teapots, batter bowls, other functional stoneware and earthenware made, displayed, and sold.

Silver Forest of Vermont (387-4149), center of the village, a clothing store worth checking.

Green Mountain Spinnery (387-4528). Just off I-91 Exit 4. Founded as a co-op ten years ago, now employing 13 people, this is a real spinning mill in which you can watch undyed, unbleached wool from local flocks being sorted, scoured, picked, carded, spun, skeined, and labeled. You can also buy the resulting wool in various plys—all in natural colors. Knit-kits and patterns are sold too. Open Monday–Saturday, 10–5:30.

Basketville (387-5509). The first of the "world's largest basket stores" now scattered between Venice, Florida, and Milo, Maine. Founded by Frank Wilson, an enterprising yankee trader in the real sense, this is a family-run business. The vast store features woodenware, wicker furniture (filling the entire upstairs), wooden toys, and exquisite artificial flowers as well as baskets and myriad other things, large and small. Prices are generally 40 percent below retail. Open daily from 8–9 in busy seasons and 8–5 in slack seasons.

Putney Nursery (387-5577), Route 5. This roadside nursery, begun and fostered by former Senator George Aiken, offers an unusually wide selection of wildflowers, also ferns, perennials, and herbs. Open Monday–Saturday 8–5.

Marlboro   **Turnpike Road Pottery** (245-2168). Open Saturdays 1–4. Malcolm Wright makes wood-fired pottery.

Applewoods (254-2908). Daily 10–6. There are furnishings made from burls and other wood forms.

Vermont Wood Artisans (464-5425), Butterfield Road. Sat Singh Khalsa makes widely respected tables, dressers, armoires—whatever you need. The lines are simple and the craftsmanship is so exceptional that the pieces are striking. His wife, Sat Kaur, crafts equally striking pottery lamps in a range of soft hues, marketed under the name of Hawk Wing Potters.

Lucy S. Gratwick (257-0181) welcomes visitors to her studio, which displays a colorful range of apparel in cotton, silk, and wool.

Along Route 30   **Newfane Country Store** (365-7916). Mary and Peter Loring have filled their store with quilts, Vermont cheese and maple syrup, plus toys and Christmas ornaments. The quilts and things quilted are truly outstanding.

Carriage House Comforters (257-0407, 800-828-DOWN), Williamsville (four miles north of Brattleboro on Route 30, south of Newfane). Goose-down comforters, pillows; silk and flannel nightshirts at factory store prices.

Lawrence's Smoke House (365-7751), Route 30, Newfane 05345.

Corncob-smoked hams, bacon, poultry, fish, specialty meats, and cheese are the specialty of the house. Catalog and mail order.

Alia (365-7932), Route 30, Harmonyville. A small roadside shop in which shell and inlaid mosaic jewelry is made and sold.

Black Mountain Antiques Center (254-4384), two miles north of Brattleboro on Route 30. A mall with 60 dealers, open year-round 10–5.

BOOKSTORES   **The Book Cellar** (254-6026), 120 Main Street, Brattleboro. An outstanding, long-established, full-service bookstore, particularly strong on Vermont and New England titles.

Green Mountain Bookstore (257-7777), 29 High Street, Brattleboro. Another fine bookstore in which browsing is encouraged, and there are occasional poetry readings and other special events.

Basket's Paperback Exchange (257-4221), 12 Elm Street, Brattleboro. A great selection of new and used paperbacks.

Everyone's Books (254-8160), 71 Elliot Street, Brattleboro. This is an earnest and interesting alternative bookstore, specializing in women's books, also a great selection of children's titles.

Brattleboro Books (257-0177), 34 Elliot Street, 9:30–6 daily, except Sunday. An extensive selection of used and out-of-print books bought.

OUTLETS   **The Outlet Center** (254-4594), Canal Street, Brattleboro. Open daily 9–9; Exit 1 off I-91. This former factory building produced handbags up until a few years ago. The Factory Handbag Store still carries the brand that was made here (it's now manufactured in Massachusetts) and a variety of other bags of all sizes. Fifteen stores now fill the building; ample parking.

Spring Tree Chocolate Factory Outlet, Route 5, Exit 3 (I-91), Putney Road, Brattleboro. Over 150 fine sweets and snacks from bins. Open Monday–Saturday 10–5:30; noon–5 on Sundays.

Londontown Factory Outlet Store (257-7056), Fairfield Plaza north of Brattleboro on Route 5. Open Monday–Saturday 10–6; Friday until 9. A large selection of discounted rainwear, outerwear, jackets, leathers, and slacks for men, women, and children.

Townshend Furniture Company (365-7720), Route 30, Townshend. Attached to the factory itself is a genuine outlet for traditional furniture in a variety of woods. Forty percent off many pieces. Open daily 10–5.

Pine Tree Table Store, Route 142 in Vernon, next to the Fire Department, open daily. Firsts and seconds of all the pine furniture manufactured in the plant next door.

SPECIAL EVENTS   February: **Brattleboro Winter Carnival**. Many events in Living Memorial Park, a full week of celebrations climaxed with the Washington's Birthday Race.

Late June: **Dummerston Center Annual Strawberry Supper**, Grange Hall, Dummerston.

July and August: **Marlboro Music Festival** in Marlboro, **Yellow Barn Music Festival** in Putney.

July 4: A big parade winds through Brattleboro at 10 AM; games, exhibits, refreshments in Living Memorial Park; fireworks at 9 PM.

Late July (last Saturday): Annual sale and supper sponsored by the Ladies Benevolent Society of Brookline; old-fashioned affairs with quality crafts.

Early August: **Grace Cottage Hospital Fair Day**, exhibits, booths, games, rides on the Green in Townshend.

Early September: **Heritage Festival Benefit** in Newfane, sponsored by Newfane Congregational Church. **Putney Artisans Festival**, Putney Town Hall.

Labor Day Weekend: **Annual two-day music festival** in Guilford's Organ Barn (257-1961). Concerts are free.

October: **Bach Festival**, sponsored by the Brattleboro Music Center (257-4523).

Early December: **Christmas Bazaar** on the Common, Newfane. Frequent auctions, bazaars, and church suppers are listed with the Chamber of Commerce and in the *Brattleboro Reformer*, the area's daily newspaper. **Farmer's Markets** are held weekly with time and place heavily promoted in the *Brattleboro Reformer*.

MEDICAL EMERGENCY   Brattleboro, Dummerston, Marlboro, Putney (254-2010); Brookline, Newfane (603-352-1100); Townshend (365-7676); Westminster (463-4223). **Brattleboro Memorial Hospital** (257-0341), 9 Belmont Avenue, Brattleboro. **Grace Cottage Hospital** (365-7357), Townshend.

Mount Snow/Wilmington Area

Mount Snow made its splashy debut as a ski destination in 1954. Reuben Snow's farm was transformed by ski lifts and trails, lodges, a skating rink, and an immense, floodlit geyser. Ski lodges mushroomed for miles around, varying in style from Tyrolian to fifties futuristic. The impact of all of this hasty development on the small village of West Dover helped to trigger Vermont's environmental protection law, Act 250.

By the early 1970s, bust had followed boom, and the ski area was absorbed by one company after another, finally acquired in 1977 by S.K.I. Ltd., owner of Killington (Vermont's largest ski resort by far). Mount Snow now incorporates Haystack, a few miles down the valley. A cross-country ski ridge trail connects the two downhill areas. There are also three commercial cross-country ski centers maintaining an extensive system of touring trails. The town of Dover, which includes Mount Snow, was Vermont's fastest growing community with hundreds of new condominium units—all neatly clustered behind screens of greenery—built in the 1980s.

The village of Dover is a small knot of white clapboard buildings on the crest of a hill. It isn't even marked from Dover Hill Road. West Dover, down on Route 100, is the actual center of town. It remains picturesque enough, a lineup of church, inn, and town offices. But much of Route 100 between Wilmington and Mount Snow is a visual history of the ups and downs of the ski industry since the late fifties.

Beyond this narrow, nine-mile-long strip of motels and shops, however, mountains rise steeply. On the west, the upper Deerfield Valley is edged with the backbone of the Green Mountains, and on the east, the hills rise tier upon tier. Drive north a mile beyond Mount Snow, and you enter some of the least touristed countryside in Vermont. The same is true a mile south of Wilmington.

Although the surrounding hills were once lumbered extensively, they are now hauntingly empty. At one time, there were more local lumbering villages than there are ski areas today. Many are ghost towns, two of them—Mountain Mills and Somerset—at the bottom of reservoirs. Wilmington, the village at the junction of Routes 9 and 100, looks much the way it did when sheep were being herded down its streets.

GUIDANCE   **Mount Snow/Haystack Region Chamber of Commerce** (464-8092), PO Box 3, Wilmington 05363. Good for inquiries by phone or in writing. A seasonal information booth is maintained at the junction of Route 100 south and Route 9. *Deerfield Valley News*, the local weekly, is good for current events information.

GETTING THERE   By train: You can take AMTRAK to Brattleboro, or Vermont Transit to Brattleboro or Bennington, but there's no dependable way of getting from there to Wilmington.

By car: The obvious route to Mount Snow from points south and east is I-91 to Brattleboro, then Route 9 to Wilmington. There are two scenic shortcuts that are useful to know about during foliage season and winter weekends especially: (1) Route 30 north from Brattleboro, 11.1 miles to the marked turnoff for Dover; follow the road through the covered bridge in south Newfane past Dover to West Dover; (2) Turn off I-91 onto Route 2 in Greenfield, MA; follow Route 2, 3.6 miles to the Colrain Road (turn at Duck Pond Tavern) and proceed 17.3 miles to Jacksonville, where you pick up Route 100 into Wilmington.

GETTING AROUND   Limousine/Taxi Service: Mount Snow Vermont Tours, Inc.—also known as Buzzy's Taxi and Shuttle Service (464-2076)—offers charter service to Boston, NYC, Hartford, Albany, and Keene, also meets buses, planes, and trains. There's also Valley Taxi (464-3280).

TO SEE   **Whitingham Village**. Brigham Young, the Mormon prophet who led his people into Utah and is hailed as the founder of Salt Lake City, was born on a hill farm here, the son of a poor basketmaker. Two sites in town commemorate Young: One is a monument that sits high on Town Hill (the view is spectacular), near picnic benches, grills, a playground, and parking area. The second is on Stimpson Hill (turn south at Brown's General Store); on the right a few hundred yards up, there is a small marker that proclaims this to be the homestead site of "Brigham Young, born on this spot 1801 . . . a man of much courage and superb equipment." Before leaving the village, note the "floating island" in the middle of Sadawga Pond. The village was once a busy resort thanks to a mineral spring and its accessibility via the Hoosuc Tunnel and Wilmington Railroad. It still retains an inn (see *Lodging*) and an auction barn (see *Shopping*).

Green Mt. Flagship Co. (464-2975), Route 9 west from Wilmington. Richard Joyce offers seasonal excursions on Lake Harriman aboard the *M.V. Mt. Mills*, a twin-stacked pontoon vessel accommodating 50 people. Joyce caters to bus groups, but there are usually at least a half dozen seats left over. His narration of the lumbering history of the area is often accompanied by live music.

North River Winery (368-7557), Route 112, six miles south of Wilmington. Open daily 10–5, except for January–May when it is open 11–5 Friday–Sunday. An 1850s farmhouse and barn in this small village contain an interesting, small winery dedicated to producing fruit wines. We can speak for the full-bodied apple blueberry, neither too dry nor too sweet. Green Mountain apple, cranberry apple, and a number of other blends are offered. Free samples come with the tour.

Luman Nelson Wildlife Museum (464-5494), Route 9, across from the Skyline Restaurant, Marlboro, east of Wilmington. Open year-round 9–5. This is a great little museum, featuring stuffed birds and animals. Nominal admission; gift shop.

LIVING HISTORY   The New England Plantation (464-7213), Route 100, Wilmington, at the corner of Cold Brook Road, sponsors special events during the summer: authentic reenactments of French and Indian War clashes, a Seventeenth Century Muster, Civil War Days, and a show of World War II military vehicles, for example.

STATE PARK   Molly Stark State Park (464-5460), Route 9 east of Wilmington Village. This 158-acre preserve offers 34 campsites, including eight lean-tos. A hiking trail leads through the forest to 2,415-foot Mt. Olga, from which there is a panoramic view. See *State Parks* in "What's Where" for fees, reservations, and information.

SCENIC DRIVES   Dover Hill Road, accessible from Route 100 either via Dorr Fitch Road in the village of West Dover or via the East Dover Road farther south (just below Sitzmark). The road climbs steeply up past the tiny village center of Dover. Here you could detour onto gravel-surfaced Cooper Hill Road for a few miles to take in the panoramic view of mountains that spread away to the northwest. On an ordinary day, you can pick out Mount Monadnock in New Hampshire beyond Keene. You can either loop back down to Route 100 via Valley View Road or continue down the other side of the hill, through East Dover to the general store, covered bridge, and picturesque village center in South Newfane, returning the way you came. If you are out for a real ride, follow this road all the way to Route 30, then continue south to Brattleboro and return via Wilmington on Route 9, the Molly Stark Trail.

Handle Road runs south from Mount Snow, paralleling Route 100, turning into Cold Brook Road when it crosses the Wilmington line. The old farmhouses along this high, wooded road were bought up by city people to form a summer colony in the late 1880s. It's still a beautiful road, retaining some of the old houses and views.

Kelley Stand Road is a 20-mile road heading west from Wardsboro through the village of Stratton (very different from the ski area by that name on the other side of the mountain), past the Daniel Webster Monument (Webster spoke here to 1,600 people at an 1840 Whig rally), through National Forest all the way to Arlington. The hiking trail into Stratton Pond that begins near the monument is the most heavily hiked section of the Long Trail.

AIR RIDES **North Air** (464-2196), Mount Snow Airport off Country Club Road, West Dover, offers scenic air rides.

BOATING Sailboats, canoes, and rowboats can be rented by the hour or day at **Lake Front Restaurant** (464-5363), located west of Wilmington on Route 9, across from Harriman Reservoir.

BOWLING **North Star Bowl and Mini Golf** (464-5148), Route 100, Wilmington, opens daily at noon for candlepin bowling, videos, pool tables.

CHAIR-LIFT RIDES **Mount Snow** (464-3333), chair operates on weekends in summer and daily throughout foliage season, and the view is truly spectacular: $9 adult, $5 juniors.

FISHING **Harriman Reservoir** is stocked with trout, bass, perch, and salmon; a boat launch is off Fairview Avenue.

Somerset Reservoir, five miles west of Wilmington, then 10 miles on the Somerset Road; offers bass, trout, and pike. There is a boat launch at the foot of the nine-mile-long lake. Smaller Sadawga Pond in Whitingham and Lake Raponda in Wilmington are also good for bass and trout; there is a boat launch on the former. Fishing licenses are available at Parmelee & Howe and at Coomb's Sugarhouse.

GOLF **Mt. Snow Country Club** (464-3333). Weekend and five-day midweek Golf School packages are offered May–October; 18-hole Cornish-designed championship golf course also open on daily basis. Note that the Pumkin Patch Nursery at Mount Snow offers a full program of hiking, swimming, and games for children ages six weeks to eight years while parents are doing their thing.

Sitzmark Golf & Tennis Club (464-3384), Wilmington; 18 holes, club and cart rentals.

Haystack (464-8301), Mann Road, off Cold Brook Road, Wilmington; clubhouse, 18 holes designed by Desmond Muirhead; full pro shop.

HIKING Aside from the trails already mentioned in the two state parks and a short, self-guiding trail atop Mount Snow, there are a number of overgrown roads leading to ghost towns. The Long Trail passes through the former logging town of Glastenbury (261 residents in 1880), and a former, colonial highway within Woodford State Park leads to a burying ground and eighteenth-century homesites. Somerset is another ghost town.

HORSEBACK RIDING **Flame Stables** (464-8329), Route 100, Wilmington. Western saddle trail rides, half-hour wagon rides.

HUNTING **The Hermitage Sporting Clays and Hunting Preserve** (464-3511), Wilmington 05313, consists of 500 acres and provides guided shoots with dogs, or you can try your hand at a round of 100 sporting clays. It is possible to use your own dog for a shoot, but there are no kennels available for overnight lodging. Reservations required.

MOUNTAIN BIKING **The Mountain Bike School and Touring Center at Mount Snow** (464-7788, 800-451-4211) bills itself as "America's first and foremost mountain-bike school." Two- and four-day sessions geared to everyone from beginners to racers are offered on local terrain ranging from back roads to ski trails. Note that the same day care is available as that described under *Golf*.

Cross-Country Bike Shop (464-0432), Route 100, Wilmington. Rentals, accessories, repairs; NORBA race series. Open Wednesday–Sunday from 10–5.

The Cupola (464-8010), Route 100, West Dover. Sales/rentals of Reflex mountain bikes. Open daily 8–6.

FITNESS CENTERS **Snow Lake Lodge** (464-3333); **Sugarhouse Health and Racquet Club** at Timber Creek (464-3508), off Route 100, West Dover.

SWIMMING There are two beaches on 11-mile-long Harriman Reservoir, also known as Whitingham Lake. **Mt. Mills Beach** is one mile from Wilmington Village, posted from Castle Hill Road. **Ward's Cave Beach** is on Route 100 south from Wilmington—right at Flame Stables and follow signs. (Ask about skinny-dipping at the Ledges.)

Sitzmark Lodge (464-3384), north of Wilmington on Route 100, has a pool that is open to the public free of charge. Snacks and bar available poolside.

TENNIS The municipal courts at Baker Field in Wilmington are available, also eight courts at Sitzmark (see above), four courts at the Andirons Motel (464-2114), and six at Tara (464-3050), Route 100 in West Dover.

CROSS-COUNTRY SKIING **Hermitage Ski Touring Center** (464-3511), Wilmington. Outstanding 35-km, machine-tracked network (50 km total) includes a ridgetop trail with superb views, elevations of 1,867–3,556 feet. Instruction, rental, repair, telemark guided tours (also see *Lodging*, *Restaurants*). Guided tours are offered along the ridge trail connecting Haystack and Mount Snow; inquire at the Hermitage.

Sitzmark Ski Touring & Learning Center (464-5498), Wilmington. Open fields, golf course with orchards and woodlands above, 25 km total tracked. Rentals, instruction, café, change rooms, headlamp tours, telemark lessons, guided tours.

The White House Ski Touring Center (464-2135), Wilmington. A total of 22 groomed trails meander through the woods at elevations of 1,573–2,036 feet. Instruction, rentals, lodging, ski weeks.

Timber Creek Cross Country Touring Center (464-0999), West Dover. Just across Route 100 from the entrance to Mount Snow; a high elevation, wooded system of trails that holds its snow cover; rentals, instruction available.

DOWNHILL SKIING **Mount Snow** (main number: 464-3333; information: 464-2151; and reservations, including the Country InnVitation Package: 800-245-SNOW), West Dover 05356. In the 15 years that S.K.I. has owned Mount Snow, it has boosted snow-making from 7 percent to 84 percent of the trails, which have also multiplied with the ab-

Mt. Snow/Fred McKinney

Mount Snow's Sunbrook slopes

sorption of the former Carinthia ski area, and has leased the Haystack Ski Area. Downplaying its old image as a singles' and snowbunnies' haven, it now stresses family and couples packages, has a strong children's program, and offers extensive expert skiing. With the addition of Haystack, there are 127 trails (47 miles) on nearly 600 acres. You can ski Mount Snow in the morning and Haystack in the afternoon, or vice versa.

Lifts: 24, including two quad chairs, 9 triple chair lifts, 10 double chair lifts, 1 T-bar, and 2 rope tows.

Trails: 127—22 "easier," 59 "more difficult," and 19 "advanced." There are five distinct areas here: the Main Mountain, the expert North Face, the Sunbrook Area, Carinthia Slopes, and Haystack.

Vertical drop: 1,700 feet.

Snow-making: 80 percent of the mountain.

Facilities: Five base lodges, an upper lodge near the summit, and a Vacation Center (ski week registration and Pumkin Patch Nursery), also the Snow Barn (nightclub with entertainment, dancing).

Ski School: 85 instructors, ATM method.

For children: SKIwee for children ages 6–12, Pumkin Patch for children aged 6 weeks to age 2, Peewee SKIwee for ages 3–5 (a combination of day care and light lessons).

Special programs: Free skiing for children age 12 and under during special "Teddy Bear" ski weeks; "Romancing the Snow" couples' ski weeks.

Rates: $36 daily, $40 Saturday–Sunday; $70 for 2 days, adult; $155 for 5 days, adult; $36 for two days, junior.

Haystack at Mount Snow (464-3333)

Lifts: 3 triple, 2 double chair lifts, 1 T-bar.

Trails: 43 trails—12 expert, 15 intermediate, 16 novice.

Vertical drop: 1,400 feet.

Snow-making: 90 percent.

Facilities: Attractive base lodge set above the beginner slopes; ski shop, rentals, ski school nursery; outstanding new base lodge at the bottom of the main mountain.

Rates: $24 Monday–Friday; $32 Saturday and Sunday.

OTHER WINTER RECREATION   **Ice fishing** is available on Harriman and Somerset reservoirs. **Sleigh rides** are available at the William Adams Farm (464-3762), at Flame's Stables (464-8329), and at Matterhorn Lodge (464-8011), where dinner is also served. Guided **snowmobile rides** using rental machines are available from Henry Wheeler (464-5225), Route 100, Wilmington.

LODGING   There are some 90 lodging facilities in the area, ranging from intimate country inns to impersonal, motel-like facilities, designed to accommodate groups. **The Mount Snow Lodging Bureau and Vacation Service** (800-245-SNOW) operates year-round: November–March 8–9; otherwise, 8–5. The Mount Snow brochure, available by writing to the Bureau (200 Mountain Road, Mount Snow 05356), includes descriptive listings of inns and lodges, plus chalet and condo rentals.

INNS   *Wilmington 05363*   **The White House of Wilmington** (464-2135, 800-541-2135). Built in 1915 on a knoll on Route 9 as a summer mansion for Martin Brown, founder of Brown Paper Co., its public rooms are huge, airy, and light but also manage to be warm in winter—with the help of yawning hearths. There are 12 luxurious guest rooms, all with private bath, four with fireplaces, and one suite. Guests gather around the sunken bar. There is tennis and a fine old pool, 45 km of cross-country trails in winter, also a health spa complete with indoor pool. Full breakfast and highly rated dinner served daily. Skiers' lunch in winter. Cash or checks preferred for accommodations. Rates: $95–110 per person, MAP in winter.

☞**Misty Mountain Lodge** (464-3961). Just 20 people can be accommodated in this informal old farmhouse set high up on a hillside, surrounded by its 150 acres. Rooms are plain, but there is an agreeable feel to the inn, which features home-cooked meals and singing around the hearth while innkeeper Buzz Cole plays the guitar after dinner; children feel welcome. This is, in fact, one of the very few inns in Vermont run by Vermonters, one of the few that looks like a Vermont home. And some guests who have never stayed in a Vermont house are a bit put off at first. "A couple pulled up one night," Buzz Cole told us, "and they stayed out there in the car for the longest time, deciding whether to come in. When they did they said they would eat somewhere else. But then they smelled the roast beef and agreed to have dinner. They got talking to other guests—lawyers, engineers, people who have been coming here for years—and they joined in the singing after dinner. The next evening they came back with champagne for everyone in the house." The farmhouse has been in the family since 1916, and Buzz and Elizabeth have been taking in guests since 1954. Elizabeth makes the quilts on all the beds. $72 per person MAP for a two-day winter weekend, $140 per person for a five-day ski week, $30 per person B&B, $42 MAP.

Nutmeg Inn (464-3351). A delightful, eighteenth-century, roadside farmhouse on the edge of the village offering 13 rooms, each nicely decorated with new wallpaper, quilts, and braided rugs; spacious two- and three-bedroom suites with fireplace and color TV. There is a cozy living room, library, and BYOB bar, plus three intimate dining rooms for full, complimentary breakfasts. Centrally air-conditioned. Mini-driving range and pitching area on the extensive grounds. Rates: $65–130 summer weekdays; $85–155 foliage season; $95–180 winter. Cash or checks preferred.

Trail's End, A Country Inn (464-2727), Smith Road, off East Dover Road. So fancifully designed and decorated that a gnome would feel at home. There's a wonderfully in-the-woods feel to the unusual spaces, which include a library and game room, a large living room with a two-story, fieldstone fireplace, another balcony-level sitting room, and a great dining space divided between an area with large round copper and intricately tiled tables for a number of guests to gather around and "the bar" lined with wooden booths. There are 18 rooms, each decorated differently, all with private baths; two fireplace suites with canopy beds, refrigerators, and Jacuzzis. In summer, there is a clay tennis court, nicely landscaped pool, and inviting paths leading out into the gardens and up the hill. Mary and Bill Kilburn pride themselves on the four-course dinners served Saturdays, when the number of guests warrants, and on full breakfasts. Guests have access to their own fridge, too, a luxury especially in summer when no one wants to stray too far from the pool for lunch. $70–110 per room with breakfast in winter, $120–160 for the suites, plus 10 percent gratuity; less in summer.

The Hermitage (464-3511). Innkeeper Jim McGovern breeds dogs and game birds and collects wines and art for this unusual and popular hostelry, which combines fine dining with cross-country skiing. There are some lovely rooms in the farmhouse annex; 15 of the 29 guest rooms are in the former Brook Bound, a mile down the road. Rates vary widely: from $65–125 per person MAP. Credit cards not accepted for final payment.

The Red Shutter Inn (464-3768). A gracious, big, 1890s house on the edge of the village with nicely furnished guest rooms and fireplace suites, one with a whirlpool built for two. The dining room, furnished with an assortment of old oak tables, has a good reputation and is open to the public. From $80–155 per room B&B.

In Dover and West Dover 05356 **The Inn at Sawmill Farm** (464-8131), off Route 100. Rod Williams is an architect, his wife Ione, an interior decorator, and their son Brill, an accomplished chef. Together the team have created one of Vermont's most elegant inns, a world-class hideaway in the Relais & Chateau category, filled with antiques. In summer, flowers are everywhere, inside and out; there is a swimming pool, tennis court, and trout pond. There are 22 beautifully appointed guest rooms, each different, some with working fireplaces; $280–320 double MAP.

Shield Inn (464-3984/6585). John and Marijke Sims have expanded this attractive place which now has 12 rooms, seven with fireplaces and six with Jacuzzis; five of these semi-suites have both. In the winter, a five-course, family-style dinner is served to guests. Winter weekend rates range from $119–189 per person MAP for two nights. In the summer, $55–95 per person B&B.

The Austin Hill Inn (464-5281; 800-332-RELAX), Route 100. Several of the recently renovated 12 guest rooms have balconies, and all come with private baths.There's a big common room with a fireplace and an outdoor swimming pool. Robbie Sweeney is the lively innkeeper, who serves full country breakfasts, afternoon tea, and a five-course candlelight dinner for two on Saturday nights and occasionally arranges "Murder Mystery Weekends." Rates vary by the season: $275–305 two-night fall and winter weekends for two MAP; $110–125 for two B&B; $220–250 spring, $80–95 summer. Children over seven are welcome, but no pets or smoking in the inn.

Doveberry Inn (464-5652), Route 100. A spacious, well-built inn just a minute's drive from the Mount Snow access. There's a comfortable, large living room with fireplace, and upstairs each of the eight rooms is immaculate and bright, each with private bath and full vanities (some of them copper), also with cable TV and video players (there's a video library). Request a back room, overlooking the woods. Innkeeper Pat Rossi and her sister Kathy are both culinary school graduates; Pat cooks breakfast, and Kathy, dinner (see *Dining Out*); $100–120 per person B&B for a winter weekend, plus 15 percent; $75–85 per room midweek in summer.

West Dover Inn (464-5207; 800-732-0745), Route 100. Built as the village inn in 1846, there are eight rooms with private baths and color TV, and two fireplace suites with whirlpool tubs. Guests share a living room with a hearth and a public dining room. $75–195 per couple B&B, three-night minimum required during holiday periods.

Deerhill Inn (464-3100), PO Box 397. A quiet, elegant retreat set on the shoulder of a hill with lovely views. Joan and Robert Ritchie have added an English accent to this upscale lodge and turned it into a gracious English country house, the kind with oriental carpets, plush couches, flowery wallpapers, and afternoon tea. The 17 rooms vary immensely so ask for a description of options. The dining room is popular (see *Dining Out*), but an upstairs sitting room offers privacy for guests. $170 per person per weekend in winter MAP, less in summer.

Cooper Hill Inn (348-6333), Cooper Hill Road, East Dover 05341. High on a hilltop on a quiet country road, Pat and Marilyn Hunt's sprawling colonial home has 13 guest rooms, most with private baths, including two-room family suites, living room, dining room, game room, and roomy covered porch. Meals served family-style; BYOB. $98 per person MAP for a two-day winter weekend.

BED & BREAKFASTS   **Snow Den Inn & Gallery** (464-9355),   West Dover 05356. A small country inn on the National Register of Historic Places in the middle of the village, neat and cozy. Five of the eight rooms have fireplaces, and all have private baths. Works by local, national, and international artists featured. Summer, $75 per room; $95 per person for a two-day weekend, breakfast included.

☞**Weathervane Lodge** (464-5426), Dorr Fitch Road, West Dover. Well away from Route 100 with a fine view, this chalet-style lodge run by Liz and Ernie Chabot can accommodate as many as 35 guests in nine rooms and a nice, big suite. All but one room and the suite share baths. Two large, casual lounges with fireplaces have a rather cluttered but warmly homey quality; the one on the lower level has a set-up BYOB bar, soda and ice machines, and a refrigerator for guests' use. Rates range from $25 per person B&B during the week to $44 per person for the suite on holidays and weekends; plus 15 percent gratuity.

Engel House (368-2974), Jacksonville. Charles and Charlene Rinaldi offer bed and breakfast in their gracious 1840s house right in the village of Jacksonville. There are three rooms with shared bath, $35–75, breakfast included. The Carriage Stop is just up the street for lunch and dinner, and North River Winery is across the way.

LODGES   These are distinctly different from inns. They are larger, usually with motel-style rooms, and designed with skiers in mind—with such amenities as pools, saunas, game rooms, and lounges.

Snow Lake Lodge at Mount Snow (800-451-4211, 464-7788), 100 Mountain Road, Mount Snow 05356. This 94-room lodge is known for its indoor hot and cold "leisure pools" surrounded by a bit of tropical jungle. The newly renovated building also offers an attractive dining room, game room, lounge, complete fitness center, outdoor pool, and tennis. Rates: on request.

Nordic Hills Lodge (464-7788, 800-326-5130), Wilmington 05363. A fairly large (27-room) lodge near Haystack with a warm, family-run feel, plenty of common space, Jacuzzi, sauna, outdoor heated pool in summer when rooms are $52, including breakfast; $44 midweek; $68 during foliage; $109 per person for a two-day weekend in winter.

Grey Ghost Inn (464-2472), Box 938, West Dover 05356. On Route 100, 27 rooms with bath, lounges, dining areas, game room, sauna, color cable TV, group rates. $90 per person B&B for a two-day weekend, $150 per five-day ski week.

MOTELS   The Vintage Motel (464-8824), Wilmington 05363. The Vintage offers 18 pleasant rooms with baths; comfortable common room with woodburning stove. Heated pool and some air-conditioned rooms available. The village shops are just down the road. Rates $49–64 per person for a two-day weekend, lower off season; midweek and weekend specials.

CONDOMINIUM UNITS   Condominium development has been recent and intense in this area. The Mount Snow brochure describes a half dozen major complexes. Haystack has its own mushrooming units.

Mount Snow Resort Center Condominiums (464-7788; 800-451-4211). There are four distinct condominium developments at the base of Mount Snow, each with its own pool, sauna, whirlpool, and other amenities; $540 is the average rate for a two-day weekend for a unit sleeping four to six people. These are nicely designed; a real bargain in the summer.

Associated Rental Management (464-2323, 800-882-5467), Box 191, West Dover 05356, represents Timber Creek, Snow Mountain Village, Bears Crossing, Snowtree, and Handlewoods. Moderately priced condominiums to luxury town houses, whose amenities can include indoor pools, spas, sauna, fitness center, and, at Timber Creek, cross-country ski center and trails.

Crafts Inn (464-2344), West Main Street, Wilmington 05363. The old hotel in the middle of the village (designed by Stanford White in 1896) has been renovated as a time-share resort. The 29 rental units each have a bedroom, sleep sofa in the living room, and kitchen. There is an indoor heated pool, four hot tubs, two saunas, a racquetball court, and a weight room. Summer rates: $100–140 weekdays, $120–160 weekends.

Haystack Mountain Real Estate (464-5321/7458). Two- and three-bedroom condo town houses are spread out along the Golf Club fairways and slope-side at Haystack at Mount Snow.

Snow Resorts Hospitality Group (464-2177, 800-451-MTSNOW), PO Box 757, West Dover 05356. Condos at the base of Mount Snow and nearby.

DINING OUT   Sawmill Farm & Restaurant (464-8131), West Dover. Dinner only, 6–9. The main dining room is fabricated from the innards of an old barn but hung with fine old portraits, the linen-covered tables set with sterling and garnished with fresh flowers; there is also a smaller, sun-and-plant-filled dining room. Eighteen main dishes are offered regularly; specialties include roast duck in green peppercorn sauce, rack of lamb, and soft shell crab; generally there is also a choice of 16 appetizers and irresistible desserts. One of the best in the state. Entrées $18–25.

The Hermitage (464-3759), Wilmington. A widely acclaimed restaurant that has recently been expanded: French doors, fine art on the walls, long tablecloths, and a mixture of arm and wing chairs all make for the elegance due the dishes. You might begin dinner with Norwegian smoked salmon or game bird pâté, proceed to chicken almandine, frogs legs Provencal, or the game bird selection, with a wine chosen from 2,000 labels. Main courses $14–25.

Le Petit Chef (464-8437), Route 100 north, Wilmington. Open daily except for Tuesdays, 6–9. Elegant French dining in an old roadside house. This is a local favorite. Chef/owner Betty Hillman's menu might include shrimp Dijonnaise (baked in mustard, garlic, and herb sauce), noisettes of venison (sautéed with Shitaki mushrooms), or a fresh vegetable sautée. Main courses in the $13–22 range (rack of lamb for two is $46).

Brush Hill (896-6100), Route 100, West Wardsboro. Off by itself and up a hill, a small restaurant with a huge hearth and wide view, accommodating just 25 people for a leisurely dinner. Michael and Lee Sylva specialize in what they call "contemporary cuisine." You might begin with "New Wave Antipasto" or lobster corn fritters with avocado and dine on quail with sautéed fresh herbs; about $60 per couple. Open Wednesday–Sunday 6–10.

Doveberry Inn (464-5652), Route 100, West Dover. Sisters Kathleen Snyder and Patricia Snyder Rossi are both graduates of the New England Culinary Institute in Montpelier. Kathy is the dinner chef, serving a choice of dishes, from citrus pork chops (lean chops in a light orange sauce) and chicken stir fry to rack of lamb and scallops poached in court-bouillon; there are always two fresh fish selections. Entrées $15–23; closed in the summer.

The Capstone (464-7264), Route 100, West Dover. The dining room at the West Dover Inn has a new chef, Anthony Tomanelli, who specializes in colorfully presented tangy dishes like seafood ravioli, chicken with peppers, steak, and duck; creative desserts. Main courses are $13–20. Closed Wednesday.

Two Tannery Road (464-2707), Route 100, West Dover. A popular spot for dining on the likes of Hotsteinschnitzel (veal cutlet, breaded and pan-fried with capers) or a mixed skillet of chicken and shrimp with Marsala, cream, and veal stock. Open Tuesday–Sunday. Entrées $16.50–23.00.

The Red Shutter Inn (464-3768), Route 9, Wilmington. The pleasant, oak-filled dining room provides a "night out" atmosphere, and the menu ranges from Coquilles Saint-Jacques through a variety of seafood to prime ribs; entrées include a "personalized salad" (patrons fill out a checklist when they order to concoct a salad from any or all of the 15 ingredients). Open Wednesday–Saturday in the winter; daily except Tuesday in summer. Entrées $13–22.

Deerhill Inn (464-3100), West Dover. Closed Mondays and during mud season, otherwise open for dinner. Applauded as one of the best places to dine in the valley. There are two dining rooms in this hillside inn, one with a cozy fireplace and a larger room with windows and French doors overlooking Mount Snow. Tables are elegantly set with candles, linen, and crystal. Chef Jay Christensen's menu is classic: roast rack of lamb (roasted with garlic and rosemary) and filet mignon in pastry (with Roquefort butter and pancetta), but there's also a stir fry vegetable dish with shrimp and scallops. Entrées $12.95–23.95.

The White House of Wilmington (464-2135). The wood-paneled dining room is warmed by a glowing hearth. The menu is ambitious, including Wiener Schnitzel, Coquilles Saint-Jacques, boneless duck stuffed with apple, grape, and walnut stuffing, and veal with Marsala plus 13 other entrées from $13.50–18.95.

EATING OUT   **Poncho's Wreck** (464-9321), Wilmington. Newly rebuilt, open daily for dinner; lunch Friday–Sunday. A delightful, casual atmosphere; specialties are Mexican dishes, fish and smoked meats. Located in the village, moderately priced, tends to fill up so it's advisable to come very early or late.

☞**Elsa's Epicurean Deli and Cafe** (464-8425), Route 100, Wilmington. Popular for lunch; gourmet shop and takeout. Also open for dinner; closed Tuesdays. There's a long Sandwich Basket list, ranging from bagel, cream cheese, and lox to Havarti and cucumber; also burgers, salads, and "main events," like cheese fondue for two in winter and charcoal-grilled, smoked pork chops with a green salad. Beer and wine.

Dot's Restaurant (464-7284), Wilmington, is open from 5:30 AM until 3 PM and to 8 PM Friday and Saturday. This is a cheerful, pine-sided place in the middle of the village. There's a long formica counter as well as tables, fireplace in back, and wine by the glass. Stop by for a bowl of the hottest chili in New England. The soup and muffins are homemade, and the Reubens are first-rate.

Cup'N'Saucer (464-5813), Wilmington. Open 6–6, a small, reasonably priced place on Route 100 north; pies a speciality.

Skyline Restaurant (464-5535), Route 9, Hogback Mountain, Marlboro. For more than 40 years, Joyce and Dick Hamilton have operated this restaurant with "the 100-mile view." The knotty pine dining room has worn, shiny tables, fresh flowers, and a traditional

New England menu. In winter, there's a fire. Specialties include home-made soups, homebaked brownies, pies and turnovers, and a Ver-monter sandwich. Moderately priced.

Deerfields (464-5634), Route 100, just a half-mile north of the lights in Wilmington. Boasting the best BBQ ribs in town, deep-dish pizzas, fabulous fajitas, fresh seafood. Open for breakfast, lunch, dinner.

Truffles Restaurant (464-5608) at the Viking Motel, Route 100, Wilmington. A large roadside dining room with a large menu, in-cluding Wiener Schnitzel and roast duckling. You can also get by for dinner with a steak sandwich or quiche and the salad bar. Moderate.

B.A.'s Red Anchor (464-5616), South Main Street, Wilmington. Ad-jacent and related to Poncho's Wreck, an informal fish place with a raw bar, fried clams, and daily specials like fried salmon slices in bacon or a sautéed mixed grill with lemon pepper sauce, plus ribs. Sunday brunch for $8.95.

Fannie's Main Street Restaurant and Tavern (464-1143), West Main Street, Wilmington, has good family fare at reasonable prices; deli and carry-out too.

Alonzo's Pasta and Grille (464-2355), at the Crafts Inn, West Main Street, Wilmington. Open daily for lunch and dinner, breakfast on weekends. "Create your own grille" specials (teriyaki steak, Andouille sausage, etc.); full children's menu at $1.99.

Panda North (464-5861/5864), Mountain Park Shopping Plaza, Route 100, West Dover. This latest outpost in the spiffy chain of superior Chinese restaurants serves lunch and dinner daily, with many Hunan and Szechuan house specials, plus takeout.

ENTERTAINMENT   **Mountain Park Cinema** (464-6477), Route 100, West Do-ver, has two theaters for first-run films.

Peaches Place (464-7705), Route 100 at Michael's, Wilmington, stages live theatricals and concerts.

APRÈS SKI   During ski season, the following establishments feature live en-tertainment or DJs on most nights. In summer, they come to life on weekends. On Route 100, between Wilmington and Mount Snow, look for **The North Country Fair** (464-5697), **Sitzmark Lodge** (464-3384), **Andirons** (464-2114), **Deacon's Den** (464-9361), and **Snow Barn Entertainment Center** (the old Rubin's Barn at Mount Snow). In town, check out **Poncho's Wreck** (464-9320).

SELECTIVE SHOPPING   **Quaigh Design Centre** (464-2780), Main Street, Wilmington. This is a long-established showcase for top Vermont crafts; imported Scottish woolens are also a specialty.

John McLeod, Ltd. (464-8175), Route 9, Wilmington. Unusual wooden shapes to decorate your homes (clocks, mirrors, cutting boards, etc.) are sold in the showroom of this woodworking shop on the western verge of the village; open daily.

Coomb's Sugarhouse (368-2345), Jacksonville. Free tours and samples at Coombs Candy Kitchen; pure maple syrup and candies.

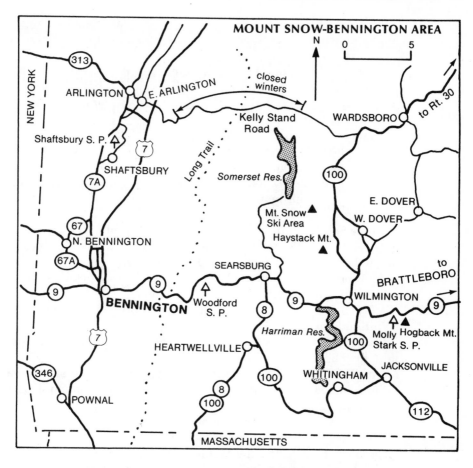

Bartleby's Books and Music (464-5425), North Main Street, Wilmington, is a cheerful shop for new books (mostly paperbacks), greeting cards, cassettes, and compact disks.

Wilmington Antique and Flea Market (464-3345), junction of Routes 9 and 100, Wilmington. Open Saturday and Sunday, Memorial Day–Labor Day.

1836 Country Store Village (464-5102), West Main Street, Wilmington, has an eclectic stock of decorative brasses, pierced tin lanterns, cotton calicoes, quilting supplies, cheese, and the usual souvenirs, plus Lyman House Restaurant, which serves breakfast all day.

Parmelee & Howe (464-5435), Wilmington. Under the same ownership for the past four generations, this is a serious pharmacy, a first-rate hardware store, and a good bet for most summer vacation needs, from toys to fishing licenses.

Craft-haus (464-2164), Wilmington. Set high on a hillside, this is a gallery in Ursula and Ed Tancrel's home. The big attractions are

Ursula's cloisonné and enamel-plated jewelry that sells for far higher prices in urban stores. Open weekends 10–5 and at other times by appointment.

Swe Den Nor Ltd. (464-2788), Route 100, West Dover. A long-established (recently moved) store with a wide selection of Scandinavian, contemporary, and country furniture; also lamps, paintings, and gifts.

Klara Simpla (464-5257), Wilmington. A "Holistic Country Store" with a following stretching the length of Route 9: vitamins, homeopathic remedies, natural foods, a wide selection of books, and, of course, Birkenstock sandals. Upstairs are weekly sessions in massage therapy, yoga, chiropractic, acupuncture; also special workshops in nutrition, dowsing, etc.

Stone Soldier Pottery (368-7077), Route 100 south, Jacksonville. A nice selection of Vermont-made crafts in wood and ceramics, including Robert Burnell's work, made on the premises.

Hobson's Choice, Route 100, West Dover. Fresh vegetables, fruits, outstanding dried flower wreaths, much more.

SPECIAL EVENTS   Late January: **Harriman Ice Fishing Derby on Lake Whittingham** (464-8003).

March (St. Patrick's Day weekend): Valley-wide snow sculpture contest, torchlight ski parade.

April (Easter weekend): Nondenominational sunrise service on Mount Snow summit with continental breakfast, eggs hidden all over mountain, good for prizes.

Late May–early October: Mount Snow Golf School.

July–August: **Summer Fest at Mount Snow** (464-3333). The weatherproofed stage behind the Mount Snow base lodge is the scene of frequent performances: ballet, children's entertainment, and concerts, ranging from big name folk and jazz artists to symphony orchestras.

July–mid-August: **Marlboro Music Festival** (254-8163).

Late July–early August: **Art on the Mountain, Haystack** (464-5321): a nine-day exhibit, one of the largest and best gatherings of craftspeople and their wares, displayed in Haystack's unusual glass and wood base lodge, daily 10–5.

Mid-August: **Deerfield Valley Farmers Day,** Wilmington (464-8092). Old-fashioned agricultural fair with midway, livestock exhibits.

Mid-August: **NORBA National Mountain Bike Championships** (464-3333).

October (Columbus Day weekend): **Mount Snow Craft Fair.**

MEDICAL EMERGENCY   Jacksonville (368-2323); East Dover (348-7979).
Deerfield Valley Health Center (464-5311), Wilmington. Staffed by four doctors, four nurses, lab technician.

Ambulance/Rescue Squads: Wilmington and West Dover (464-5335); East Dover (365-7979); Jacksonville (368-2323).

Bennington/Arlington Area

Vermont's southwest corner is dominated by Bennington, the state's third largest city (15,815), which is undergoing something of an industrial renaissance, while retaining its historic luster. This has, in turn, spawned several new places to stay and eat. The first town settled west of the Connecticut River in the New Hampshire Grants, in 1749, and named for the avaricious Governor Benning Wentworth, Bennington became a hotbed of sedition when the "Bennington Mob," or Green Mountain Boys, formed in 1770 at Fay's Catamount Tavern under the leadership of Seth Warner and Ethan Allen to expel both the 'Yorkers (who claimed the territory) and, later, the British.

The Battle of Bennington (more precisely, the Battle for Bennington) on August 16, 1777, deflected General Burgoyne's occupation of the colonies when New Hampshire General John Stark's hastily mobilized militiamen beat the tar out of Colonel Baum's overdressed Hessians on high ground near the Wallomsac River, across the New York border.

Today, Bennington is nationally known as the home of distinguished Bennington College, established in the early 1930s (now the most expensive private college in the country), and remembered by collectors of Bennington pottery.

Although never formally the capital of Vermont, Arlington, on Route 7A, was the de facto seat of government during most of the revolutionary period. Fearing British attacks in the north, Vermont's first governor, Thomas Chittenden, moved south from Williston, liberated a Tory property in Arlington (the area known as "Tory Hollow"), and conducted affairs of state from there.

Many older visitors to Arlington fondly remember Dorothy Canfield Fisher, the author of 50 immensely popular, warm-hearted novels and a judge of the Book-of-the-Month Club for 25 years. Five years before her death in 1958, Mrs. Fisher published *Vermont Tradition, The Biography of an Outlook on Life*, in which she captured the essence of the state's character: ". . . Travel through Vermont—north, south, east, west, from Pownal to Canaan, Guilford to Highgate—nowhere will you find a township where overwhelming majority opinion does not support this unwritten law: that, except where the safety of others is in danger, everyone must be allowed to do, think, believe whatever seems best to him; that equality before the law is only the first step. Equality must extend to the protection of everybody's personal dignity, within the community; for the backroad farmer and his wife bringing butter and eggs to the kitchen door, no less and no more for the owner of the plywood factory."

Another famous resident was illustrator Norman Rockwell, who lived in West Arlington from 1939 to 1953. Many of his illustrations of small-town Americans were done in and around Arlington.

GUIDANCE   A good visitor's guide to Bennington County is provided by the **Bennington Area Chamber of Commerce** (447-3311), Veterans Memorial Drive, 05201, which also has a well-supplied information center.

GETTING THERE   By car: Bennington lies at the convergence of Routes 7, 7A, 9, 67, and 67A. Going north can be confusing; watch the signs carefully to choose between the limited-access Route 7 to Manchester or the more interesting but slower historic Route 7A, to Shrewsbury and Arlington.

By bus: Vermont Transit from Albany or hubs in Connecticut and Massachusetts.

TO SEE AND DO   **Historic Bennington Walking Tours**, self-guided with a keyed map-brochure from the Chamber of Commerce that describes Old Bennington, including the 306-foot, blue limestone shaft of the Bennington Battle Monument, dedicated in 1891; all the fine early houses along Monument Avenue; the Old Academy; Old First Church; the Burying Ground, where five Vermont governors and Robert Frost repose; and the venerable Walloomsac Inn, now a private home.

A second walking tour of the downtown area includes the 1898 railroad depot (now a restaurant), constructed of blue marble cut to resemble granite, old mills, and Victorian homes.

Bennington Museum (447-1571), West Main Street, Route 9, Bennington. Features memorabilia from the Battle of Bennington, especially the oldest American Revolutionary flag in existence, early American glass, furniture, dolls and toys, plus historic Bennington pottery, notably an extraordinary ten-foot ceramic piece created for the 1853 Crystal Palace Exhibition. Particularly popular is a gallery of paintings by "Grandma Moses" (Anna Mary Robertson, 1860–1961), who lived in the vicinity. Open daily 9–5 except for the months of December, January, and February. Admission: adults $4; seniors and college students $3; family $10; under 12, free.

The Park-McCullough House (442-5441), Route 67A in North Bennington. A splendid, 35-room Victorian mansion built in 1865 by Trenor W. Park, a Forty-niner who struck it rich as a lawyer in California and later as a railroader. He built the house on part of the farm owned by his father-in-law, Hiland Hall, a representative to Congress and governor of Vermont. Park's son-in-law, John G. McCullough, became governor of Vermont in 1902 and raised his family in this capacious house. It has been open to the public since 1965 and is on the National Register of Historic Places, functioning as a community arts center. There's an appealing children's playhouse replica of the mansion and a stable full of carriages; gift shop; lunch counter; afternoon tea on the veranda. Open for tours late May–October, Monday–Friday 10–4, Saturday 10–2; admission.

The Shaftsbury Historical Society, Route 7A, is gradually developing a cluster of five historic buildings, including two schools. Open summer weekends 2–4 and serendipitously when the curator happens to be handy.

Norman Rockwell Exhibition (375-6423), Route 7A, Arlington. Housed in a "Hudson River Gothic" church are some 500 of the artist's *Saturday Evening Post* cover illustrations and prints, plus a 20-minute film showing and a gift shop. Open daily 9–7, admission.

The Dr. George A. Russell Collection of Vermontiana, believed to be the third largest such collection, is housed in quarters behind the Martha Canfield Public Library, Arlington. Dr. Russell, the country doctor immortalized in the Rockwell print that hangs in thousands of doctors' offices, collected Vermontiana for most of his long life and left his collection to the town. The collection includes Dorothy Canfield Fisher materials, a large selection of Norman Rockwell's work, many photographs from the period 1860–1890, an extensive selection of town and country histories for Vermont and neighboring states, and a wealth of genealogical materials (deeds, letters, wills, account books, diaries, etc.) for the Arlington area and the state as a whole. Although not a museum (there are no displays), the collection is open to the public on Tuesdays or by appointment with the curators, David and Mary Lou Thomas (375-6307).

The Martha Canfield Library, Arlington (named for Dorothy Canfield Fisher's grandmother), holds a book sale under a tent on its lawn 10–5 on Fridays and Saturdays and 1–5 on Sundays from June 15 through foliage season. Books are sold at prices ranging from $.15 to $.50 per copy, and records and jigsaw puzzles are also available at moderate prices. During peak holiday seasons, the sale is sometimes held on weekdays as well.

Oldcastle Theatre Company (447-0564), Bennington. Based at Southern Vermont College (lodged in the Norman-style Everett mansion on the slopes of Mount Anthony), the company offers a full summer season of plays, sometimes performing also at Bennington College.

COVERED BRIDGES   Three just off Route 67A in North Bennington: Silk Road, Paper Mill Village, and the Burt Henry.

STATE PARKS   **Shaftsbury State Park** (375-9979), 10.5 miles north on Route 7A, has facilities for swimming, picnicking, boating, nature trail, on 26-acre Lake Shaftsbury.

Woodford State Park (447-4169), Route 9 east of Bennington. This

VTD

Covered bridge and swimming hole, Arlington

400-acre area includes 104 camping sites, 16 of them with lean-tos, swimming in Adams reservoir, a children's playground, picnic spots, canoe and rowboat rentals.

CANOEING   Battenkill Canoe Ltd. (375-9559), River Road, off 7A, Arlington, is the center for day-trips—with van service—canoe camping, instruction, rentals, and equipment. Customized inn-to-inn tours arranged.

SKIING   Prospect Mountain (442-2575/5283), Route 9 east of Bennington. An intimate, friendly family ski area, with cross-country (25 km), downhill, and telemark facilities, ski school, rentals and repairs, learn-to-ski packages, group rates, cafeteria, and bar. Moderate prices for all.

OTHER RECREATION   Mt. Anthony Club (442-2617), Bank Street (just below the Battle Monument): 18-hole golf course, tennis and paddle courts, pool, lunch, and dinner.

Green Mountain Racetrack (823-7311), Route 7 south in Pownal, just this side of the Massachusetts border, was built for horse racing, but now has a pari-mutuel season of greyhound races from the end of February to early October, Wednesday–Saturday 7:45 PM; Sundays, holidays 1:30 PM doubleheaders. Admission $1.

Back Road Country Tours (442-3876), by jeep from Bennington.

LODGING   *Bennington 05201*   Greenwood Lodge (summer 442-2547; winter 914-472-2575), eight miles east of Bennington on Route 9. Open July–Labor Day, this rustic lodge/hostel and its tent sites occupy 120 acres in Woodford, adjacent to the Prospect Mountain ski area. There are dorms for American Youth Hostel members and private family rooms; bring your own linen or sleeping bags. Three small ponds for swimming and fishing. Inquire about inexpensive rates and exclusive group use.

INNS   *Arlington 05250*   The Arlington Inn (375-6532), on Route 7A in the center of Arlington, occupies the 1848 Greek Revival mansion built by Martin Chester Deming, a Vermont railroad magnate, and has been used as an inn off and on since 1889. Thirteen attractively restored rooms are spacious and furnished with Victorian antiques. The inn serves award-winning American dinners and luxurious Sunday brunch. Room rates range from $95 double occupancy to $125, including continental breakfast. Open all year.

West Mountain Inn (375-6516), on Route 313 west of Arlington. A former summer home with splendid views of the mountains and valley converted and expanded into an inn. The attractive rooms are named after famous people associated with Arlington, and a copy of Dorothy Canfield Fisher's *Vermont Tradition* is in every room. Breakfast, dinner, and Sunday brunch served (no dinner on Sunday). The inn's property includes over five miles of walking and cross-country skiing trails. A number of special events are featured, such as a fly-tying weekend two weeks before trout season and a wild leek and fiddlehead fern weekend later in the spring. Innkeepers Mary Ann and Wes Carlson give complimentary African violet plants to guests who promise to take care of them. Rates $142–165 MAP. A two-bedroom housekeeping apartment is available on short-term or seasonal lease. Open all year.

Hill Farm Inn (375-2269), RR 2, Box 2015, Arlington. Located off Route 7A north of the village, this historic farmstead, now owned by the Hardy family, is set on 50 acres of land bordering the Batten Kill. There are six bedrooms on the second floor of the main building and five in the adjacent 1790 guest house; five of the 11 rooms have private baths. Several cabins and two two-room suites are available in the summer and fall. Guests can have a four-course dinner at 6:30 and full country breakfast. Licensed for beer and wine; smoking only in the common rooms. Double room rates range from $65 (hall bath or cabin) to $90 (private bath), B&B. Children welcome at special rates; guests receive complimentary homemade jam.

BED & BREAKFASTS *Bennington 05201*   **South Shire Inn** (447-3839), 124 Elm Street. This turn-of-the-century Victorian mansion is a most attractive guest house, featuring 10-foot ceilings with plaster moldings, a library with a massive mahogany fireplace, an Italianate formal dining room, and comfortable bedrooms furnished with antiques. The five guest rooms have private baths, some with fireplaces; two can be joined as a suite. $75–125 with breakfast; no smoking; older children preferred.

   Safford Manor (442-5934), 722 Main Street, Route 9 east, has six rooms in a 1774 house that displays some fine examples of colonial workmanship, plus a Victorian main parlor and library, $42–88.

   Molly Stark Inn (442-9631), 1067 East Main Street. Five rooms, one with private bath, $78–88.

   Baker's at Bennington (442-2263), Route 7A north, is a pleasant, five-bedroom place, $45 per room.

   The Four Chimneys Inn (447-3500), 21 West Road, Route 9, Old Bennington. This stately home offers three redecorated, luxurious rooms ($100–125) as adjuncts to Alex Koks' latest upscale restaurant (see *Dining Out*).

   Country Cousin (375-6985), Old Depot Road, off Route 7A, Shaftsbury 05262. This 1824 Greek Revival house has three bedrooms and baths, plus living and dining area, library, and music room; $46–55.

Arlington 05250   **The Inn on Covered Bridge Green** (375-9489), off Route 313, West Arlington. Fans of Norman Rockwell can now actually stay in his former home, a pretty white colonial next to a red covered bridge on the village Green where Ethan Allen mustered his Green Mountain Boys. Ron and Anne Weber opened the place in 1987 and offer five bedrooms (semiprivate baths), furnished with antiques. There's a tennis court, and full country breakfasts are events, served on bone china with Waterford glass and silver. Rates range from $45 single to $125 for a family room for four. No smoking.

   Ira Allen House (362-2284), Route 7A, Arlington. A smartly renovated old roadside home with nine guest rooms, some set up for families. The inn's property across Route 7A fronts on the Batten Kill, good for trout fishing and, for the warm-blooded, a dip in a 10-foot-deep swimming hole. Guest dining; $46–60 per room.

Shenandoah Farm (375-6372), five miles west of Arlington on Route 313, has three rooms with private baths and two rooms with a shared bath in an 1820 Colonial house. $40–65 per room with full breakfast.

The Willow Inn (375-9773), Route 7A, is a small, freshly decorated "English style" B&B with three rooms; $50 with shared bath, $60 with private.

Others: Whimsy Farm (375-6654), off Route 7A on Old Depot Road, north of Bennington; Shaftsbury Guest House (447-0907), five miles north of Bennington on Route 7A and Church Street.

MOTELS   Vermonter Motor Lodge (442-2529), Route 9, two miles west of Old Bennington, is an attractive mini-resort with newly redecorated rooms and cabins, cable TV, room phones, swimming, boating, bass pond, Sugar Maple Inne Restaurant; $45–75 per room.

Among others: Harwood Hill (442-6278), Route 7A north, has economy and deluxe units, $36–44; Ramada Inn (442-8145), intersection of Routes 7 and 7A, Kocher Drive, $74.

DINING OUT   The Four Chimneys Inn (447-3500), 21 West Road, Route 9, Old Bennington. Alex Koks, one of Vermont's preeminent chefs, has transferred his talents from the Village Auberge in Dorset to this redecorated, stately home. The elegantly sophisticated setting—three dining areas with pale rose walls and table linens, and a screened porch with red-and-white-striped canvas ceilings—reflects the equally superior cuisine. For lunch, one might savor a salad of grilled duck with spiced pecans, home-cured Gravad lox with sourdough toast and lemon-lime mustard, or sautéed shrimp with garlic pasta and chive butter. Dinner might include an appetizer such as galantine of goose liver mousse and an entrée of roast chicken, steak, rack of lamb, or a rib-eye steak flambéed with cognac and green peppercorns. Open daily, but check ahead, especially in late fall or early spring. Dinner entrées $10.50–19.00.

Bennington Station (447-1080), Depot Street, Bennington. Train buffs love this place, a splendidly converted Romanesque railroad station built in 1897 of rough-hewn blue marble for the Bennington & Rutland Railroad. The exceptionally attractive restaurant features a collection of historic photos and is open for lunch and dinner daily. For lunch, one could have Iron Horse Chili to start, Railroad Spikes (marinated and grilled beef strips), or a variety of salads and sandwiches. The dinner menu includes grilled duck salad, prime rib, New England chicken pot pie, fish, and various teriyakis and BBQ ribs. Main courses $6.95–16.95.

The Arlington Inn (375-6532), Arlington. Truly outstanding, innovative American cuisine in this mauve-walled formal dining room or attached solarium. Peppery Maine crabcakes with a light cream sauce is a delectable appetizer, as is smoked salmon wrapped around crab meat, topped with caviar. For entrées, salmon lasagna, rainbow trout, grilled turkey breast with mustard thyme butter, pear and mango chutney, or, in summer, scalopinne of veal with fresh strawberries. For Sunday brunch, chocolate chip and macadamia nut pancakes with smoked bacon, or grilled salmon with eggs Benedict. Luncheon served on summer weekends. Dinner entrées $13.95–22.95.

EATING OUT   **The Brasserie** (447-7922), 324 County Street, Bennington (in Pottery Yard), is open daily except Tuesday 11:30–8, serving inexpensive, exceptional, lighter fare—imaginative combinations of hearty soups (black-eyed pea with ham hocks and vegetables), quiche, pâté, salads, and such specialties as Mozzarella Loaf (cheese baked through a small loaf of French bread with anchovy-herb butter), or Rotelle with spinach, onions, and prosciutto in cream with parmesan.

The Publyk House (442-9861), Route 7A north, Bennington, is a remodeled barn with an indoor greenhouse and a fine view of Mt. Anthony. Open for dinner daily.

Blue Benn Diner (442-8977), Route 7, near Deer Park, Bennington, open from 5 AM; breakfast all day, or lunch, which combines "road fare" with more esoteric items like eggs Benedict, tabouli, falafel, and herb teas.

Occasionally Yogurt Natural Food Restaurant, 452 Main Street, Bennington.

Alldays & Onions (447-0043), 519 Main Street, Bennington. In this fish market deli café, you can build your own sandwiches at lunch daily, except Sunday, or splurge on rack of lamb with honey-thyme sauce for dinner (Thursday–Saturday).

The Villager Restaurant (447-0998), Route 67, North Bennington, is an intimate, popular, chef-owned bistro serving dinner 6–9:30 (bar menu, 5–12).

Phyllis' Food and Et Cetera, East Arlington, open May–October, combines a profusion of collectibles with church-supper goodies: chicken and biscuits, French silk pie, cheddar and ham sandwiches.

The Edgewood Restaurant (375-6604), Route 7A, Arlington, serves lunch and dinner, featuring a shrimp and salad bar, closed Tuesdays.

SELECTIVE SHOPPING   **Hawkins House** (447-0488), 262 North Street, Route 7, Bennington, is a crafts market complex for the work of some 250 artisans in silver and gold, unusual textiles, hand-blown glass, pottery, quilts, cards, books, music, prints and woodcuts, stained glass, candles, and more. Open daily except for Christmas and New Year's.

The Antique Center of Old Bennington & The Camelot Gift Gallery, Route 9 west, Bennington, which has several high-quality shops under one roof.

Bennington Potters Yard, downtown on County Street, Bennington, is the hi-tech place to get contemporary Bennington Pottery, Catamount Glass, well-designed ovenproof cookware manufactured in North Bennington, and to eat at the Brasserie.

Jonathan Logan Outlet, West Main Street, Bennington, at the Paradise Motel, has name-brand ladies apparel at discount.

Images from the Past (442-3204), West Main Street, Bennington. Fascinating ephemera: postcards, prints, holograms, historic house boxes. Open daily April–December, winter weekends.

Williams Smoke House Country Store, Route 9 east, Bennington, offers a free pound of bacon with its bone-in-hams; gift packs.

The Chocolate Barn, Route 7A north of Shaftsbury, is an unusual combination: two floors of antiques, 56 varieties of hand-dipped chocolates, fudge, and special orders from antique candy molds. (There's another store at Routes 30 and 100 in Jamaica.)

Candle Mill Village in East Arlington is a charming hamlet of specialty shops next to two waterfalls. It is located in the Candle Mill, operated locally, stocking 50,000 candles from all over the world, including one that weighs 248 pounds. There's also The Happy Cook, The Music Box Shop, Where Did You Get That Hat?, the Rosebud Toy Company, Aunt Dudy's, and the Bearatorium. Nearby are an Antiques Center, The Village Pedaler, and Scandinavian Dolls. One of the ubiquitous Green Mountain Boys, Remember Baker—the builder and first owner of the mill—is remembered by a monument.

The Beside Myself Gallery, Lathrop Lane, four miles north of Arlington off Route 7A. Open May 15–October 15, this gallery displays the work of contemporary regional artists: paintings, handmade paper, sculpture, and collages. Open 2–5 daily or by appointment.

The Cheese House and the Arlington Wood & Pottery Center, Route 7A, Arlington. From souvenir T-shirts to custom stained glass and other local crafts.

SPECIAL EVENTS   Late May: **Bennington Mayfest:** street festival, crafts, entertainment.

July: **Annual Bennington Museum Antique Show**.

August 16–18: **Bennington Battle Day Weekend**.

Mid-September: **Antique and Classic Car Show**.

October 3–5: **Annual Antique Show**.

MEDICAL EMERGENCY   Bennington (911); Arlington (447-7911) **Southwestern Vermont Medical Center** (442-6361), Bennington.

Manchester and the Mountains

Manchester is an up-and-down town consisting of several villages that seem to vary in status with their altitude. The highest, Manchester Village, is an elegant gathering of mansions, spread along marble sidewalks, around the venerable Equinox Hotel, the gold-domed county courthouse, and historic Hildene, a lavish summer retreat built by Robert Todd Lincoln, son of the president. Fine summer homes are sequestered away from view on River Road and up country lanes that radiate from Manchester Center and Manchester Depot. With art, music, nearby summer theater, and three golf clubs (only one of which is open to the public), Manchester remains a top summer address.

Manchester's old Dowager Queen Mary atmosphere has been replaced by a Princess Di quality, as moneyed young professionals flock to the snowy slopes of Bromley and Stratton and to the burgeoning number of "factory direct" stores. But beneath the town's bustling resort glamour still lies—as reliable as Harris tweed—the fabric of a thriving small town, woven by farmers, merchants, lawyers, carpenters, teachers, clergymen, doctors, housewives, and innkeepers.

It was the sharp contrast between old money and local poverty that prompted Manchester's socialist poet Sarah Cleghorn to write her famous quatrain:

The golf links lie so near the mill
That almost every day
The laboring children can look out
And see the men at play.

The stark contrast between the nineteenth-century resort village and mill town have disappeared with the mills, and the lines between the Center and Depot have been blurred by the lineup of shops, inns, and restaurants.

Manchester's "Mountains" are Mount Equinox, a stray member of the Taconic Range, looming grandly above Manchester Village on the west, and the Green Mountains, which include Bromley and Stratton ski areas on the east.

The spine of the Green Mountains, little more than a dozen miles west of Manchester, is traced on the map by Route 100. The road hugs the base, rather than the ridge of the mountains, and twists with the rivers that, in some places, have carved valleys just wide enough to hold small villages like **Weston,** one of Vermont's most beautiful resort communities. See *Villages* for more on Weston and three more of the area's unusual villages: **Dorset, Pawlet,** and **Danby.**

GUIDANCE   Manchester and the Mountains (362-2100), at Manchester Center, this clapboard Chamber of Commerce information booth is walled with pamphlets, good for general walk-in information. The chamber does not make reservations but does keep a running tally on space in member lodging places, short-term condo and cottage rentals.

    Area Lodging Service (824-6915), PO Box 519, Londonderry 05148, offers year-round help with local lodging. This is a commercial reservation service that transfers you directly to its member inns, B&Bs, and motels (most local lodging places) after determining what you want when. A detailed leaflet guide to local lodging, prices included, is available from them.

    Stratton Mountain maintains a reservation and information service—800-843-6867 (THE-MTNS) serves some 20 lodges, condo clusters, and inns on and around Stratton.

    In winter, the **Bromley-Magic Lodging Service** (824-5458) also makes reservations for condominiums and houses, as well as a number of its surrounding inns.

    Londonderry Area Chamber of Commerce (824-8178), maintains an information booth and an office in the Mountain Marketplace (the Londonderry shopping center) at the junction of Routes 11 and 100.

GETTING THERE   By car: From Bennington north, Route 7 to Manchester is a limited-access highway that's speedy but dull, except for viewing Mt. Equinox. One gets a more interesting taste of the area, especially around Arlington, by clinging to historic Route 7A. From the southeast, the obvious access is I-91 to Brattleboro, then Route 30 north.

    By bus: Vermont Transit offers good service from New York and Montreal to Manchester; connections with Boston are via Williamstown, MA, or Rutland.

MUSEUMS AND GALLERIES   Historic Hildene (362-1788), Route 7A, Manchester Village. Mid-May–October 10–4; fee. A house among historic houses, this 24-room Georgian Revival manor is set on 412 acres, including formal gardens and paths that lead down into the Batten Kill Valley. Bring a picnic lunch and plan to stay half the day. The tour begins with a wagon ride to the Carriage Barn, now a sophisticated Visitors Center with a slide show about Robert Todd Lincoln. You learn that he first came to the village as a boy with his mother for a stay at the Equinox House; his father was assassinated before the family could return, as they had intended, the following summer. It was Todd's law partner who later persuaded him to build this summer home adjacent to his own mansion. Todd died here in 1926, and members of the family lived here until 1975. Guides are familiar with at least one Lincoln and with the true character of the authentically furnished house. Tours include the restored formal gardens and a brief demonstration of the 1,000-pipe organ, which can be played both manually and with one of 240 player rolls on hand. Picnic tables outside command a view of the valley below, and there are numerous trails to stroll or—in winter when the Carriage Barn becomes a warming hut—to explore on skis. (see *Cross-Country Skiing*). In the summer, Sunday afternoon polo matches are a popular spectator sport. Inquire about organ concerts and other special events.

Southern Vermont Art Center (362-1405), West Road, Manchester Center. Memorial Day–mid-October, daily except Monday 10–5; Sunday noon–5; admission charged. This gracious old mansion, set on 375 acres of grounds, offers changing exhibits: paintings, sculpture, prints, and photography, also a summer-long session of classes in various art forms for both adults and children and a series of both concerts (held in the adjacent, 430-seat Pavilion hall) and films. Light lunches are also served in the Garden Café, and there are extensive trails through the woods, among them a botany trail featuring rock formations, 67 varieties of wildflowers, and birches.

The American Museum of Fly Fishing, Seminary Avenue and Route 7A, Manchester Village. Open May–October 10–4 daily, the museum displays more than a thousand rods and reels made by famous rodbuilders and owned by such luminaries as Daniel Webster, Bing Crosby, Ernest Hemingway, and presidents Hoover and Eisenhower. Don't miss it.

Farrar Mansur House (824-5894), Village Green, Weston. Built in 1797 as a tavern and inn, this is a rewarding museum of local history. Open weekends Memorial Day–Columbus Day, and in July and August, Wednesday–Saturday 1:30–4:30; $2 adult, $1 ages 7–12.

Weston Mill Museum, Weston, open in summer months 10–5. This is a working restoration of a vintage mill.

VILLAGES   In addition to Manchester (see chapter introduction), there are four more unusually picturesque villages in this area: **Weston**, 15 miles to the northeast; **Dorset**, eight miles to the northwest; **Pawlet**, another seven miles north on Route 30; and **Danby**, eight miles north of Dorset and 10 miles east of Pawlet.

Weston. Sited at the north end of the West River Valley, Weston is known for its summer theater and for the Vermont Country Store, New England's number one nostalgia outlet. The oval common is shaded with majestic maples. A band plays in the bandstand, and theatricals are performed in the Weston Playhouse, one of the oldest summer theaters in the country. It is also known for summer concerts presented by the Kinhaven Music School and for the music, Sunday liturgies, and retreats at Weston Priory, a small community of Benedictine monks.

Dorset. This pristine village is visible evidence that it takes money "to prevent the future." A fashionable summer refuge for years, few signs of commerce mar its state of carefully manicured nature. Today's tranquility, making it a haven for artists and writers as well as for the affluent, contrasts sharply with its hotheaded youth. In 1776, the Green Mountain Boys gathered in Cephas Kent's Tavern and issued their first declaration of independence from the New Hampshire Grants, signed by Thomas Chittenden, Ira Allen, Matthew Lyon, Seth Warner, and other Founding Fathers of Vermont. Today the Dorset Inn, said to be the state's oldest continuously operating hostelry, is the village focal point, along with the Dorset Playhouse (see *Entertainment*), one of New England's most venerable summer theaters. The first marble to be quarried in North America came from Dorset, and the local quarry is one of the most popular swimming holes around. There is also an 18-hole golf course (billed as the state's oldest) and a choice of places to stay (see *Lodging*).

Pawlet. Not far north of Dorset, this hamlet on Route 30 is an unexpected delight, with an intriguing mix of architectural styles in the buildings that cling to the rather steep slopes leading up from Flower Brook, over which Johnny Mach's General Store extends. Gib Mach has harnessed the rushing brook to a turbine that generates his electricity and has built a glass-topped counter at the end of a store aisle (between the sewing and the pet supplies) through which you can peer down at the water, surging through the narrow gorge below. Next door, a former railroad station is now The Old Station Restaurant and Ice Cream Parlor, and a clutch of nearby shops are worth investigating (see *Selective Shopping*).

Danby. A by-passed hamlet on Route 7 between Dorset and Wallingford, Danby is being re-born—again. This vintage village is known for its fine marble quarries and as home base for Silas Griffith, an 1850s lumber baron who is billed as Vermont's first millionaire. In the 1960s, novelist Pearl Buck bought seven buildings in the village and began to renovate them, and since her death, inns (see *Lodging*), restaurants (see *Dining Out*), and some intriguing shops (see *Selective Shopping*) have opened here.

MOUNTAIN TOPS   Mount Equinox (362-1113). The 3,825-foot-high summit of Mount Equinox, most of the mountain in fact, is owned by the Carthusian monks who occupy the monastery, which can be seen from the top. A toll road (open May–October 8–10; $5 per car) climbs more than five miles from Route 7 to the **Sky Line Inn** (362-1113) on top. This can be a spectacular ride on a clear day, even more dramatic if the mountain is in the clouds and the road keeps disappearing in front of you. Be sure to drive back down in low gear. There are also trails to the top; see *Hiking and Camping*.

Bromley Mountain (824-5522). This 3,284-foot-high mountain offers excellent views of Stratton and Equinox mountains. It is traversed by the Long Trail (see *Hiking and Camping*) and is also accessible by hiking up the ski trails from the midpoint get-off on the chair lift. This lift serves the **Alpine Slide** Memorial Day–mid-October, weather permitting, 9:30–6 (just until 5 after Labor Day); fee. This alpine slide was the first in this country. Lunch, snacks, and drinks are available at the base lodge, six miles east of Manchester on Route 11 in Peru.

Stratton Mountain (297-2200) offers a four-state view from its summit, accessible by "Starship XII" gondolas from the ski resorts (Route 30, Bondville). The gondola runs daily in summer and fall 11–5; $7 per adult, $4 per child, 6 and under free.

PARKS AND FORESTS   **Green Mountain National Forest** (362-2307), District Ranger Office, Manchester. A public information office serving the southern third of the 275,000-acre Green Mountain National Forest is located on Routes 30 and 11 east of Manchester, open Monday–Friday 8–4:30. Maps and details are available about where to fish, hike, cross-country ski, and camp. All National Forest campsites are available on a first-come, first-serve basis.

Emerald State Park (362-1655), North Dorset. On Route 7, this area offers 105 campsites, including 36 lean-tos, also hiking and nature trails, among them a 3.4-mile, round-trip trek to a natural bridge.

Merck Forest and Farmland Center (394-7836), Route 315, Rupert 05768. Some 2,800 acres of near wilderness, including Mt. Antone, were set aside in the 1950s as a foundation by George Merck of the Merck Drug Company, now maintained through donations. The forest area offers year-round facilities: foot and horse trails, picnic areas, a spring-fed swimming pond, 12 shelters, a farm museum, and a sugarhouse that produces 400 gallons of syrup. The Merck Forest Summer Camp has six one-week sessions for children. Reservations are required for overnight use of the shelters. An extensive network of trails is marked for cross-country skiing.

Jamaica State Park (874-4600), Jamaica 05343. This 758-acre wooded area offers riverside camping, swimming in a great swimming hole, a picnic area, and an organized program of guided hikes. An old railroad bed along the river serves as a trail to the Ball Mountain Dam. One weekend in spring and fall is set aside for white-water canoe races. There are 40 tent sites, including 15 lean-tos.

BICYCLING   In Manchester, bike rentals and touring information are available from **Battenkill Sports Cycle Shop** (362-2734), open daily 9:30–5:30, in the Stone House, junction of Routes 7 and 11/30.

Stratton Sports (297-2200), at Stratton Mountain, rents mountain bikes and offers terrain ranging from paved roads to cross-country ski trails and (for expert bikers) a combination of service and ski trails down from the summit (the gondola hoists bikes as well as riders to the top); a variety of guided tours are offered.

Viking Biking (824-3933), Little Pond Road, Londonderry, offers 16- to 18-gear rentals and self-guided bike tours along dirt roads either as day-trips or with baggage transferred from inn to inn; weekends are $200 per person, lodging and meals included.

CANOEING The **Batten Kill** makes for satisfying canoeing in the spring; the Manchester to Arlington section is relatively flat water but gets difficult a mile above Arlington. (See "Bennington/Arlington Area" for rentals from **Battenkill Canoe** and "Grafton, Chester, and Bellows Falls" for **Outdoors in Vermont**).

FISHING Fly fishing has been serious business in the Batten Kill since the midnineteenth century. Orvis Company began manufacturing bamboo rods in Manchester Village near the spot where they are still produced.

The **Batten Kill** is generally recognized as Vermont's best wild trout stream; access is available at a number of places off Route 8. Brown trout can also be found in **Gale Meadows Pond**, accessible via gravel road from Route 30 at Bondville. **Emerald Lake** in North Dorset is stocked with pike, bass, and perch; rental boats available at the state park facility.

The **Orvis Fly Fishing School** (362-3622 and 800-548-9548). The name in fly-fishing instruction as well as equipment; 2½-day courses, offered twice weekly April–mid-July, then weekends through August.

Rainbows End Guide Service (824-5241), Box 1214, Manchester Center 05255, invites you to fish for brook trout in the Mettowee Valley and nearby mountain streams as well as in the Batten Kill.

GOLF The 18-hole golf course at the **Equinox Country Club** (362-3223), which was established in the 1920s for guests of the Equinox House, has just undergone a $3 million renovation; the club also offers pleasant noontime dining.

The **Stratton Golf School** (800-843-6867), offers weekend and midweek sessions including professional instruction, use of the 27-hole course at Stratton Mountain, and a special 22-acre "training site."

Tater Hill (875-2517), Windham. A nine-hole course, built on the site of one of New England's largest and oldest potato farms. Facilities include a pro shop, carts, dressing rooms, and showers. (Note: There is also a swimming pool for non-golfing members of the family.)

East Dorset Driving Range (362-0040), Route 7, East Dorset. Open in season 10–7:30, lessons available.

HIKING AND CAMPING   (See also *Parks and Forests*) **Hapgood Pond Recreation Area**, Peru. Acquired in 1931, this was the beginning of the Green Mountain National Forest. There is swimming, fishing, and limited boating on the seven-acre pond. Removed from the picnic ground and beach, there are 28 campsites (first-come, first-serve basis). A pleasant, eight-mile forest trail threads the woods.

Golf at the foot of Mt. Equinox, Manchester

Greendale Campground, two miles north of Weston on Route 100. There are 14 sites.

From the District Ranger Office, request hiking maps to the following:

Lye Brook Wilderness, a 14,600-acre preserve south of Manchester with a 2⅓-mile trail to the Lye Brook Waterfalls.

Grout Pond, west of the village of Stratton, marked from the Kelley Stand Road. Deep in the Green Mountain National Forest, this is a great spot for a picnic, complete with grills and a small beach.

The Long Trail. This Massachusetts to Quebec path doubles as the Appalachian Trail throughout this area; portions of the trail make good day hikes, either north over Bromley Mountain or south over Spruce Peak from Routes 11 and 30. The most heavily hiked stretch of the entire trail is the relatively level trek in from the Kelley Stand Road to Stratton Pond; there are three shelters in the immediate area, and swimming is permitted. **Griffith Lake**, accessible from Peru and Danby, is a less crowded swimming and camping site on the trail. For details, consult the Green Mountain Club *Guide Book of the Long Trail*.

Ball Mountain Lake (886-8111), Jamaica 05343. This 85-acre lake, a dramatic sight among the wooded, steep mountains, can be viewed from the access road off Route 30. One hundred seven campsites are available on Winhall Brook at the other end of the reservoir, open mid-May–mid-September; accessible off Route 100 in South Londonderry, free. It is controlled release from this flood dam that provides the outstanding canoeing available on the West River below Jamaica each spring. This area is maintained by the U.S. Army Corps of Engineers.

Mount Equinox. Details about the rewarding, six-mile Burr and Burton Trail from Manchester Village to the summit are available in *Day Hiker's Guide to Vermont* (Green Mountain Club) and *Fifty Hikes in Vermont* (Backcountry Publications). At 3,825 feet, this is the highest mountain in the state that is not traversed by the Long Trail.

Walking Tours of Southern Vermont (375-1141), Route 2, Box 622, Arlington 05250. Guided tours throughout this area are offered with lodging at local inns.

HORSEBACK RIDING AND HORSE-DRAWN RIDES **Windhill Horses and Tack Shop** (362-2604), Manchester, North Road. Trail rides and lessons offered, open daily in riding season. Sleigh rides.

Deb's Magical Horserides (824-3750), South Road, Peru. Trail rides, riding lessons, overnight camping trips, even in winter, weather permitting; $25 per person for 1½ hours, $100 per half day, $200 per full day, $250 overnight.

Stratton Stables (297-2200), Stratton Resort; trail and pony rides, private lessons, sleigh rides, and carriage rides.

Chipman Stables (293-5402), Danby Four Corners. Trail rides.

SHOOTING **Orvis Company** (362-3622 or 800-548-9548) of Manchester (see *Fishing*) offers two-day shooting courses ($775) in July and August, three-day programs ($950) September–mid-October. Hunters move in groups of five through 10 stations in a simulated hunting course. Tuition includes guns and ammo, but no lodging is included.

SHUNPIKING For those of us who like to get off the main drag, this area offers some exceptional back roads, many of them shortcuts but most are worth exploring, especially during foliage season. Avoid in mud season.

Green Mountain National Forest Road Number 10, Danby to Landgrove. Closed in winter. The longest (14 miles) and most isolated of these byways, the road (beginning in Danby) climbs through the White Rocks Recreation Area, crossing a number of tempting hiking paths as well as the Long Trail. There are some fine views as you continue along, and you might want to picnic somewhere in the middle of the forest, as I did by a beaver pond. The road follows Tabor Brook, down into Landgrove, itself a tiny, picturesque village.

Peru to Weston. From the village of Peru, an enticing, wooded road is paved as far as Hapgood Pond, then continues smoothly

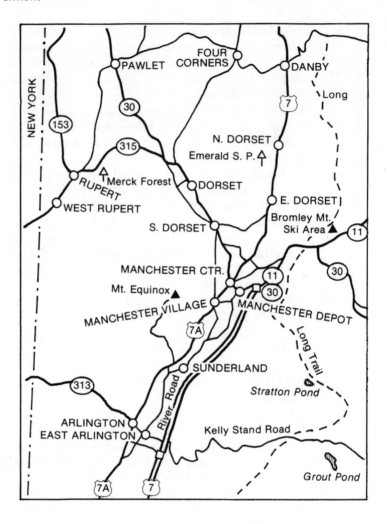

through Landgrove, a miniscule village with an outstanding inn (open to the public for dinner), set in rolling fields. The way to Weston is clearly marked.

East Rupert to Danby. This Danby Mountain Road is the logical shortcut from Dorset to Danby, and it's quite beautiful, winding up and over a saddle between Woodlawn Mountain and Dorset Peak; well-surfaced dirt, with long views in places. If you are coming from East Rupert, be sure to turn right at Danby Four Corners and follow Mill Brook into Danby.

SWIMMING   Dana L. Thompson Recreation Area (362-1439), Route 30 north, Manchester, is open daily in summer, but hours for general swimming are limited; nominal fee.

Dorset Quarry, off Route 30 on Kelley Stand Road between

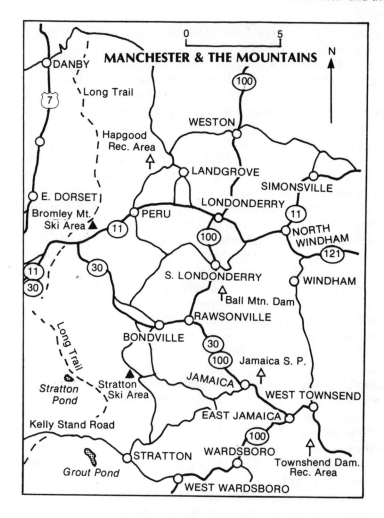

MANCHESTER & THE MOUNTAINS

Manchester and Dorset, is a deep, satisfying pool but not recommended for children. The upper quarry is the local skinny-dipping spot.

Hapgood Pond in Peru, with its sand and calm, shallow drop-off, is favored by families with young children.

Emerald Lake State Park (362-1655), Route 7, North Dorset, offers clear lake swimming.

Also see **Grout Pond** and the **Merck Forest** under *Hiking and Camping*.

TENNIS   **Stratton Mountain** (297-2200), offers weekend and midweek clinics. There are 15 outdoor and four indoor courts. Note: Stratton Mountain offers full day-care and day camp in the summer for children (aged six weeks to 10 years old) of parents enrolled in the golf and tennis programs. A Junior Tennis Day Camp is also offered week-days for children aged 7–15.

Dana L. Thompson Recreation Area, Manchester. Public courts are available with weekly memberships or on a per hour basis.

WINDSURFING   Lessons and rentals are available at **Stratton Lake** (874-4178).

CROSS-COUNTRY SKIING   **Viking Ski Touring Centre** (824-3933), Little Pond Road, Londonderry. The Viking trail system now includes 40 km of trails, 35 km groomed, 3 km lighted. There is a rental and retail shop and a café serving drinks, light breakfasts, and lunches. There are lessons, lunch tours to Weston, bed & breakfast and inn-to-inn tours using a total of four local hostelries. Owner Irving Gross also offers four bedrooms at the Touring Center, $55–60 per person, including breakfast, snacks, and trail pass. Trail fee: $11.

Wild Wings Ski Touring Center (824-6793), Peru. Tracy and Chuck Black run a family-oriented touring center located within the boundaries of the Green Mountain National Forest, 2½ miles north of Peru. Trails are narrow, geared to the intermediate skier, and adjoin an extensive public system that connects the center with Landgrove. This area tends to get a heavier snowfall than other local touring centers; the 20 km of trails are at elevations between 1,650 and 2,040 feet. Instruction, rentals, and free hot bouillon are found in the warming hut.

Stratton Ski Touring Center (297-1880), Stratton Mountain. Based at the Sun Bowl, a 20-km series of groomed loops plus adjoining backcountry trails. Guided backcountry tours as well as a variety of other tours are offered.

Nordic Inn Ski Touring Center (824-6444), Route 11, Londonderry. The center has 20 km of trails through neighboring woods. Lunch and dinner are served.

Hildene Ski Touring Center (362-1788), Manchester. The Lincoln Carriage Barn serves as a warming hut for this system of 21 km of groomed and mapped trails on the estate built by Robert Todd Lincoln. Trails meander through woods and fields on a promontory overlooking the Batten Kill Valley between Mt. Equinox and Lye Brook Wilderness. Lessons and equipment are available. Trail fees.

DOWNHILL SKIING   **Bromley** (824-5522). Located on Route 11 in Peru, eight miles east of Manchester. Founded in 1937 by the late Fred Pabst of the Milwaukee brewing family, this is among the oldest ski areas in the country. It was also one of the first to have snow-making, snow farming, a slope-side nursery, and condominiums. It retains its own following of those who like its friendly atmosphere and sunny trails.
Lifts: 1 quad and 6 double chair lifts, 1 surface lift, and 1 T-bar.
Trails: 35 trails—35 percent intermediate, 34 percent beginner, 31 percent expert.
Vertical drop: 1,334 feet.

Snow-making: 83 percent of terrain from base to summit.

Facilities: The base lodge offers two cafeterias, two more formal areas. Skiers unloaded right at the base lodge; the driver then parks in an area across Route 11 and rides back on a shuttle bus.

Ski school: ATM method.

For children: Nursery for ages one month to six years. Mighty Moose for ages 3 to 5, Discover Ski School for 6 to 14 year olds.

Rates: $36 adult, $24 junior, weekends; $24 adult, $12 junior, weekdays; also half-day and five-day rates; free under age six.

   Stratton (297-2200). Located atop a five-mile access road from Route 30 in Bondville; snow phone: 297-2211. Stratton is an unusually well groomed mountain. This goes for its trails, its facilities, lodges, and clientele. It ranks highly among Vermont's major ski resorts, a big mountain with two separate areas: the original North Face and the distinctly sunnier Sun Bowl, focus of a current expansion program, including a new base lodge, new quad chair, expanded trail system, and snow-making. Thanks to the quantity of lifts, skiers are generally dispersed over the trail network. Stratton Village, a complex that includes 25 shops, 3 restaurants, a 91-room condo-hotel, a 750-car garage, and 170 condominiums, dwarfs the base facility. A sports center includes a 25-yard-long pool, whirlpool, indoor tennis courts, racquetball courts, exercise equipment, and a lounge (also see *Lodging*).

Lifts: 1 gondola, 4 quads, 1 triple, 6 double chair lifts.

Trails and slopes: 92.

Vertical drop: 2,003 feet.

Snow-making: 252 acres.

Facilities: A restaurant and cafeteria in the base lodge, also cafeterias mid-mountain and in the Sun Bowl lodges. Chapel of the Snows at the parking lot, a little Bavarian-style church, has frequent nondenominational and Roman Catholic services. A shuttle bus brings skiers from inns on the mountain to the base lodge. Stratton Spots offers rentals and repairs.

Ski school: ATM and GLM methods, SkiWee.

For children: Day-care for six months to three years old. A separate base lodge for "Cubs"; combined ski and play programs are offered— Little Cubs (aged 4–6) and Big Cubs (aged 6–12).

Special program: Stratton Mountain School, a co-ed prep school for Alpine and cross-country racers, academic year and summer programs.

Rates: $39 per adult weekends and Saturdays, $32 weekdays, $22 junior, free under six, special packages.

SLEIGH RIDES   **Pfisters** (824-6320) in Landgrove offers the most remote, romantic sleigh ride around. Also inquire at **Windhill Farm Stable** (362-2604), North Road in Manchester, and at **Stratton Mountain** (297-2200).

SNOWMOBILING   A "Winter Recreation Map," available free from the Green Mountain National Forest District Ranger Office (362-2307), Manchester, shows trails presently maintained in this area by the Vermont Association of Snow Travelers.

RESORT INNS   **The Equinox** (362-4700; 362-1595; 800-362-4747). Route 7A, Manchester Village 05254. The white columned inn is composed of 17 distinct parts that have evolved over the past 220 years. It's still evolving. In the mid-eighties, it was revamped from its foundations up, an unavoidable process that left it sound but, many said, soulless. Thanks to a 1991 infusion of British funds and taste (Guiness Enterprises), the 174 guest rooms and suites, most of which are unusually spacious and furnished in pine reproductions, are acquiring modern plumbing and a brighter, more country feel. The B&B rates now include a sumptuous breakfast featuring Scottish salmon and oatmeal as well as Vermont maple syrup. It's served in a formal, oval dining room with an elegant vaulted ceiling. Service is friendly and impeccable, and meals are memorable (see *Dining Out*). Facilities for which guests pay extra include the newly revamped, 18-hole golf course, a fitness center with indoor pool, touring bikes, and tennis courts. In summer, complimentary children's program for ages 5–10 is also offered. Rooms: $174–194 per couple; suites, $249; town houses, $455 per night for up to six people. Weekend, midweek packages, children free, less off season.

   Wilburton Inn (362-2500/800-648-4944), River Road, Manchester 05254. This is a brick, baronial, turn-of-the-century mansion set on expansive grounds with long views of the Batten Kill Valley. The most splendid guest rooms are among the nine in the mansion itself, but many of the 25 recently renovated rooms in outlying cottages are very appealing, thanks to innkeeper Georgette Levis' touch with colors and chintz. The cottage rooms are better suited to families since they offer more privacy and direct access to the seemingly limitless lawn—which harbors a pool and tennis courts; guests also enjoy golf privileges at a nearby country club. Common rooms in the mansion are richly paneled, and the living room is immense, complete with piano, comfortable window seats and couches, oriental rugs, and an enormous hearth. An unusual quantity of original art is scattered through all the resort's rooms, guest as well as public rooms. Guests breakfast at wrought iron, glass-topped tables in the sunny Terrace Room, and dinner is served in the Billiard Room, reminiscent of an exclusive men's club. Open year-round, $85–140 per couple including a full breakfast and afternoon tea. (Dining room open to the public, except Tuesdays.)

   The Inn at Willow Pond (362-4733; 800-533-3533 outside of Vermont), Box 1429, Manchester Center 05255, 2.3 miles north on Route 7A, offers 40 spacious guest rooms and suites in three separate, contemporary, Colonial-style buildings on a hillside overlooking the Manchester Country Club's golf course. The Meeting House reception building contains the lofty main lounge, conference facilities for up to 200, and a fitness center with exercise equipment, two saunas, and a library. There's also an outdoor lap pool and a restaurant in a renovated 1780 house. The larger guest rooms feature fireplaces and sitting areas. Winter rates are $88 (for a small suite) to $138 for multi-room suites with fireplace and shared parlor; off season rates begin at $78 per room, and all include continental breakfast; full breakfast also served in the restaurant (see *Dining Out*). Midweek rates also available.

INNS AND BED & BREAKFASTS   *Manchester 05254* (unless otherwise indicated)   **1811 House** (362-1811), Manchester Village. "A place to feel pampered" is the way the owners of this magnificent building describe what they offer. Parts of this mansion date back to the 1770s. It has been an inn since 1811, except for a few years during which it was owned by President Lincoln's granddaughter, Mary Lincoln Isham. Public rooms are as elegant as any to be found in New England, and the 14 guest rooms are in keeping, each with private bath, many with hearths; TV and phones are available on request. Innkeepers Bruce and Marnie Duff dispel any stuffiness in this rarified world. There is an authentic-looking pub room with exposed rafters and an expansive lawn overlooking the Equinox Golf Course. There are also English-style flower gardens. A full breakfast is included in the room rate, from $100 for a cozy double to $170 for a suite with a queen four-poster canopy bed, fireplace, and sitting area. Children over 16 are welcome. Off season rates available.

   Birch Hill Inn (362-2761), West Road. A gracious, bright, and airy old home set away by itself up on West Road, amid lovely mountain scenery. Innkeepers Pat and Jim Lee welcome guests as they would into their own home, presiding over the dinner table, which seats 14. There are just five guest rooms plus a summer cottage. The house has been in Pat's family since 1917, which may be the reason the rooms look so homey and right. There is a piano and an endless jigsaw puzzle and supply of games in the attractive living room (children over 6 are welcome), and a pleasant sun room in which to read with a sense of the lawn beyond. A kidney-shaped pool and trout pond await in warm weather, and there are miles of touring trails for the winter. Hors d'oeuvres and set-ups are provided at the cocktail hour. $50–55 per person B&B plus 15 percent service charge. Dinner is offered several nights a week. Closed April and November.

   Reluctant Panther Inn (362-2568), Box 673, Manchester Village. Renowned for its gourmet fare (see *Dining Out*) this purple-painted village home also has 12 rooms and four suites, each decorated with bright wallpapers and antiques. Seven rooms and all the suites have fireplaces, and the Mark Skinner Suite features two woodburning fireplaces—one in an enormous bathroom with a double Jacuzzi center stage. All have room phones and cable TV. Breakfast is served to guests only, and, with the exception of dining hours, the living room and unique pubs make a peaceful and pleasant retreat. Innkeepers are Maye and Robert Bachofen. Closed after foliage until early December, again in mud season. $150–270 per couple, includes breakfast and dinner. No children under age 14.

The Inn at Manchester (362-1793), Box 452. A gracious old Main Street home, set back from Route 7A, with an expansive porch, big windows, gables, and a carriage house in back. There are 21 rooms, named for flowers and herbs, all but five with private bath. There are several two-bedroom suites with connecting bath, and four are in the Carriage House. The dining room and parlors are imaginatively and comfortably furnished, and there is a game room, warmed by an antique woodstove. In summer, there is a pool in back. Breakfast and—on holidays and winter weekends—dinner is prepared with flare and care by Harriet and Stan Rosenberg, currently celebrating their fourteenth year as innkeepers. $75–125 per room B&B plus 10 percent service charge. Ask about Wellness Weekends and midweek specials. Wine and beer served.

Manchester Highlands Inn (362-4565), PO Box 1754, Highland Avenue, Manchester Center 05255. Patricia and Robert Eichorn call their spacious Victorian inn "Manchester's best kept secret." It's on a quiet side street, a short walk from all the shops and restaurants but with an away-from-it-all feel, especially on the back porch and lawn (with its pool), all of which command an expansive view of Mt. Equinox. The 15 guest rooms are nicely decorated with family antiques and personal touches. Common rooms include a comfortable living room, a wicker-filled sunroom, and a TV room (with a library of movies to feed the VCR). In winter, the loss of the pool and porch is assuaged by the basement "Remedy Room" with its bar and games—connected by "the tunnel" (decorated with guest graffiti) to the rooms in the carriage house. A very full breakfast is served, and a four-course dinner ($18) is available. $60–85 single and $80–110 per person includes breakfast and an afternoon snack; 10 percent gratuity is added.

The Village Country Inn (362-1792), Manchester Village. This century-old inn (formerly The Worthy Inn) has been resurrected in lace and roses. There are 30 rooms and suites, all with private bath. The rooms are small but fun, furnished in antiques, dressed in lace curtains. Downstairs there are roses on the curtains and couches, and the predominant color is rose. The dining room is attractive, and there's an inviting pub and a pool out back. $135–185 per couple MAP, plus 15 percent gratuity year-round.

☞**River Meadow Farm** (362-1602/3700), Sugarhouse Lane, PO Box 822. Off by itself down near the Batten Kill south of Manchester Village, this is a beautiful old farm, built early in the nineteenth century to house the town's paupers. There are five bedrooms sharing two baths, and guests have the run of the downstairs with its welcoming kitchen, pleasant living room, and dining room. Outside there is ample space to hike and cross-country ski—with a splendid view of Mt. Equinox. Pat Dupree is a long-time Manchester resident who enjoys orienting her guests. Rates are $25 per person, full breakfast included.

Brook-n-Hearth (362-3604), Box 508, Manchester Center 05255. A gracious home, built in the 1940s to accommodate guests in four nicely furnished, second-floor rooms sharing a bath with shower. Guests have full use of the living room with its inviting hearthside sofas, games, books, and TV, also the pool table in the basement. The house sits high on the crest of Routes 11 and 30, overlooking the town. Trails run back to the brook. Larry and Terry Greene are helpful hosts; rates: $36–70 per room, $60–80 for a two-room family suite plus $12–24 per extra person.

Seth Warner Inn (362-2830), Manchester Center 05255. This imposing vintage 1800 house is set back from Route 7A, south of Manchester Village, and it's a beauty, carefully restored with open beams and stenciling, furnished in antiques, and curtained in lace, offering five bright guest rooms with country quilts and private baths. Common space includes a gracious living room, a hall library, and the dining room in which guests gather for a full breakfast. $70–85 per room including breakfast.

The Inn at Sunderland (362-4213), Route 7A. This 1840s Victorian farmhouse sits at the foot of the Mt. Equinox Skyline Drive and backs onto meadows that stretch down to the Batten Kill. The 10 guest rooms all have private baths and are furnished with antiques, and the common rooms include two sitting rooms and two small dining rooms—plenty of room to relax. Hosts Tom and Peggy Wall are knowledgeable about local dining and shopping. $70–115 per couple includes a full breakfast and complimentary canapés.

Danby 05739 ☞**Silas Griffith Inn** (293-5567) is the renovated 1891 mansion that once housed Vermont's first millionaire. Lois and Paul Dansereau have restored the hardwood floors, carved bird's-eye, curly maple and cherry woodwork, scrubbed the leaded windows, painted the tin ceiling in the dining room, and created an unusually comfortable, welcoming inn. The 17 guest rooms, 11 with private bath, are divided among the main house and converted carriage house, all furnished with antiques. You might want to request room #14 with its round porch (but no closet) or #16 with a huge bed made for the room, one of several rooms that can be a family suite sharing one bath. Common rooms include a large living room, well stocked with books, and a front parlor with a TV, accessed by a wonderful "moon gate" door. Lois is an acclaimed chef, and the restaurant (in the carriage house) is a locally popular dining place (see *Dining Out*). Danby's intriguing shops are just down the street, there's some outstanding hiking trails just a few minutes' drive into the Green Mountain National Forest, and Emerald Lake State Park is just three miles down Route 7. The inn's own 11 hilltop acres include a pool. Rates are $84 for a room with private bath, $69 shared, including full breakfast; discounts for weekdays or for a stay of several days. Rates are higher in foliage season.

The Quail's Nest (293-5099), Box 21, Main Street, Danby 05739, is a simple, pleasant B&B in an 1835 house. Each of its five guest rooms is furnished with antiques and handmade country quilts ($50–65 per room). The Edsons serve a tempting full breakfast.

Dorset 05251   **The Barrows House** (867-4455). This exceptional mini-resort features attractive, flexibly arranged accommodations (19 rooms, 9 suites) in the main house and seven adjacent cottages. The early nineteenth-century house is a short walk from the center of this historic village, but there is an out-in-the-country feel to the 12-acre grounds, which include a gazebo, a swimming pool, and a tennis court. In summer, bike rentals are offered, along with access to the nearby Dorset Golf Club. In winter, cross-country ski equipment is available. There are comfortable sitting rooms in the main house and the larger cottages, where large families or several friendly couples can be lodged. A convivial bar and game room is wallpapered to resemble a private library. Rates range from $160 to $210 per couple including breakfast and dinner, plus 10 percent service; less off season. The dining room is outstanding (see *Dining Out*).

The Dorset Inn (867-5500), Dorset Village, a National Historic Site and the state's most venerable hostelry (in continuous operation since 1796) faces Dorset's historic Green. It has been stylishly renovated by its owners, Sissy Hicks, former chef at the Barrows House, and Gretchen Schmidt. Known for its excellent cuisine and relaxing atmosphere, the inn has 34 guest rooms. It's within walking distance of the golf course and theater and offers a lineup of front porch rockers from which you might not want to stir. Rates: $70–120 double, including gratuity and a full breakfast.

Inn at West View Farm (867-5715), just south of Dorset Village, is a small, well-groomed lodge with an appealing personality, known especially for its exceptional cuisine. Known under previous ownership as "The Village Auberge," it has now reclaimed the name of the farm it was in the nineteenth and early twentieth centuries—when it included 20 outbuildings and 200 acres. The dining room remains the focal point of the inn (see *Dining Out*), but Helmut and Dorothy

Stein have added a very pleasant living room with a fireplace to the smaller, old front parlor. There's also an inviting wicker-filled sun porch. One downstairs room has been fitted for handicapped access, and the nine upstairs rooms, four of them new additions, are all furnished comfortably, fitted with bright paper and bright, crisp fabrics. Rates: $75–106 B&B or $140–171 MAP plus 15 percent service charge.

Cornucopia of Dorset (867-5751). This newly renovated, nineteenth-century Colonial home run by Bill and Linda Ley has four meticulously decorated bedrooms, each with canopy or four-poster bed and private bath; the corner room also has a fireplace. One common room is walled in glass, overlooking a manicured back lawn, and guests can also relax in the library, in a small living room with a fireplace, and on a back terrace. The cottage suite in the rear is a beauty, with a loft bedroom, living room with fireplace, kitchen, and sundeck. Rates are $80–165 double plus 10 percent service charge; includes a multi-course breakfast, which might include puff pancakes, gingerbread waffles, or quiche Lorraine. A wake-up coffee or tea tray and use of bikes and cross-country skis are also included. No smoking.

The Little Lodge at Dorset (867-4040). Allen and Nancy Norris have opened their attractive home to guests. It's a gem, set atop a rolling lawn, overlooking a small trout pond—with a fountain spouting from its center. There's a living room with a woodstove and a formal dining room in which guests breakfast around one long table, but the center of the house is the wood-paneled, open-beamed den with a fireplace and comfortable couches and armchairs and a corner BYOB bar, complete with fridge. The five guest rooms, all with private bath, are big enough to squeeze in an extra child, tastefully papered, and fitted with quilts, armchairs, and books. Golf, theater, and hiking are handy in summer, and in winter, there is cross-country skiing and skating on the pond. Guests are invited to store picnic fixings in the icebox, share the cocktail hour (set-ups and cheese provided), and socialize by the hearth. Rates: $80–90 per couple B&B, more in foliage season, less for longer stays.

Dovetail Inn (867-5747), PO Box 976. Federal-style inn on the Dorset Green with 11 bedrooms (all with private bath). Breakfast served in rooms or in the dining room; wine and beer served in the "keeping room"; outdoor pool. Rates: $65–125 (for "Hearthside" efficiency) double, breakfast included. Inquire about special packages.

Marble West Inn (867-4155), West Road. The day we stopped by, this attractive place was filled with a bicycle group, so we couldn't peek into any of the rooms, but we noted an inviting living room with a window seat and fireplace and gardens overlooking trout ponds. It's set on a back road, facing open fields, a mile and a half from the village of Dorset. $85–135 per couple including breakfast, plus 15 percent service charge.

Landgrove 05148   ☞**The Village Inn** (824-6673), RD Box 215. This red clapboard building rambles back and around, beginning with the 1820
house, ending an acre or two away with a 1976 addition housing a
whirlpool. The "Vermont continuous architecture" draws guests from
a handsome lobby, past 18 crisp, bright rooms (16 with private bath)
that meander off in all directions, through the inviting Rafter Room
Lounge (huge, filled with games and books), to the attractive dining
room in the original house. Many rooms are well suited to families,
and there is plenty here to busy children as well as adults: During
warm weather, there is a heated pool, tennis, a trout pond, and lawn
games. In winter, you can take a sleigh ride or step out onto the 15-
mile cross-country trail system that leads through the picturesque
village of Landgrove (just a church, former school, and salting of
homes cupped in a hollow), on into surrounding National Forest.
Bromley Ski area is just six miles away, and Stratton is a 20-minute
drive. Dining is by candlelight, and the menu is imaginative. The
Snyder family has been running this very special place for many
years; the Snyders currently at the helm are Else and Don. $68–85 per
person MAP in fall and winter (cheaper midweek, and $5–35 per
child in the same room); $65–85 per couple B&B in summer ($5–20
per child in the same room); dinner is still served in summer except
Wednesdays.

Londonderry 05148   **The Highland House** (824-3019), Route 100 between
Londonderry and Weston. A handsome house set above a sloping
lawn with nine rooms in the main house, eight in the adjacent Carriage House—which has its own sitting room, a good set-up for
groups. Amenities include a pool and tennis court, and the small
dining room is open to the public (see *Dining Out*). $100 per couple is
the average weekend rate, including tax, gratuity, and a full breakfast. Special midweek and off season rates.

Peru 05152   **The Wiley Inn** (824-6600), Route 11. This homey old inn is just one
mile from Bromley. Its core is an 1835 house containing a delightful
living room with fireplace, library, and dining room and a 1940s
motel-style wing, obviously tacked on to serve early skiers. There are
17 units (two of them two-bedroom suites), and the remaining 13 are
double rooms—all have private bath. Request a room in the old inn;
these are just a few dollars more and much nicer than those in the
new wing. Summer facilities include a backyard pool and play area.
Helga and Fred Sobek have prided themselves on their dining room
(see *Dining Out*). $65–70 per person MAP in winter, B&B rates avail-
able in summer when dinner is not served.

South Londonderry 05155   ☞**The Londonderry Inn** (824-5226), PO Box 301. A
large clapboard homestead that became a summer inn in the 1940s
and went year-round when it found itself handy to Stratton as well
as Bromley. There are 25 guest rooms, 20 with baths, some with two
rooms to a bath; good for families. Public rooms are large, bright, and

warm. Jim and Jean Cavanagh delight in helping plan guests' daily itineraries. Children are welcome. Rooms come big and small, and all are cheerful. There is an attractive dining room, a tavern, a game room with table tennis and billiard tables, and a swimming pool. Rates are $45–75 per couple including breakfast; $15–20 extra per person in a family room.

The Three Clock Inn (824-6327). This gourmet getaway is tucked up on a hilly village back street. Better known as a restaurant (see *Dining Out*), it also offers four lovely upstairs rooms, one with a canopy bed and fireplace, and an upstairs sitting room with woodstove to provide complete privacy from the dining crowd. In summer, the garden is a profusion of flowers, and in winter, Bromley is just a few minutes' drive, as are the cross-country trails at Viking. $70 per person plus 10 percent gratuity, MAP.

Weston 05161   ☞**Colonial House Inn & Motel** (824-6286), Box 138. A rare and delightful combination of nine motel units and six traditional inn rooms (shared baths), connected by a very pleasant dining room, a comfortable, sunken sitting room with dried flowers hanging from the rafters, and solarium overlooking the lawn; there's also a fully equipped game room. Innkeepers John and Betty Nunnikhoven make all ages feel welcome, and 75 percent of guests are repeats. Rates include memorable, multi-course breakfasts. Dinners are served family style: $9.95 for light fare and $16.95 for a full meal (children under 12 pay $7.95); BYOB. The inn is a few miles south of the village, with lawn chairs facing a classic farmscape across the road and most guest rooms overlooking a meadow. Rooms are $31.50–70.00, B&B, $8 per child 4–12 (free for infants), less for longer stays.

1830 Inn on the Green (824-6789), Route 100, PO Box 104. It's tough to beat the look or location of this elegant bed & breakfast, right across from Weston's handsome Common. A graceful, curved staircase (moved here from the Bellows Falls mansion of Hetty Green, "witch of Wall Street") leads to four guest rooms, the best overlooking the back garden. The large living room has lovely, long windows and an 1830s hearth, and hosts Sandy and Dave Granger make you feel welcome. $60–80 includes a full breakfast, featuring local syrup, jams, and herbs.

Wilder Homestead Inn (824-8172). A classic, Federal-style brick house, beautifully transformed for B&B guests by Peggy and Roy Varner. There are seven guest rooms, all with private bath, five with fireplaces, several with early nineteenth-century stenciling, each with a different decor. Guests gather for full, candlelight breakfasts around the long table in front of a huge hearth in the dining room; there's also an attractive library and living room. All the sights of Weston are within an easy walk, and there's a waterfall across the street. $60–85 per couple B&B. No smoking. No children under age six.

The Darling Family Inn (824-3223), Route 100. An 1830s house, exquisitely furnished with family antiques by Joan and Chapin Darling. The five guest rooms have private baths, canopied beds, fine quilts, and artistic touches. There are wide-planked floors throughout, and Joan has expertly hand painted the walls. Full country breakfasts are included in the rates, and candlelit dinners can be reserved. In summer, the pool adds a nice touch. $75–95 per room B&B, $85 per couple in one of the two attractive cottages out back (breakfast not included).

The Inn at Weston (824-5804), Box 56. This clapboard inn on the edge of the village is known for its dining room but also offers 20 rooms, which are pleasant but offer less value than other options in town. From $64 for a room with shared bath to $140 for a deluxe room in the Coleman House across the street. A 10 percent service charge is added, breakfast included.

SKI LODGES (open year-round)   *Near Bromley*   **Johnny Seesaw's** (824-5533), Peru 05152. Built as a dance hall in 1926 and converted into one of Vermont's first ski lodges in the 1930s, this is a wonderfully weathered, comfortable place, even more attractive in summer than in winter. Within walking distance of the slopes in winter, it offers tennis and a pool in summer. There are 28 rooms, ranging from dorms to doubles, and master bedrooms with fireplaces in the main house, including an unusual number of family suites; also four cottages with fireplaces, good for large families and small groups. The living room boasts Vermont's first circular fireplace, a long row of upholstered pads known as the "seducerie," and red leather chairs from the 1936 Republican Committee Headquarters in New York City. $40–50 per adult MAP in winter, $35 per adult B&B in summer.

At Stratton Mountain   **Stratton Mountain Inn** (800-777-1700), with 125 rooms, is the largest lodging facility on the mountain. Rooms have private baths, phones, and TVs, and facilities include a large dining room, saunas, and whirlpools. $89–119; per room without meals.

Stratton Village Lodge (800-843-6867), adjacent to the Stratton base lodge, has 91 studio-style units with kitchenettes. $89–300 rates run $135–200 without meals, less when combined with golf, tennis, or ski packages. All resort guests have access to the sports center with its indoor pool, exercise machines, racquetball, and tennis courts.

Birkenhaus (297-2000). A modern but intimate lodge owned by Ina and Jan Dlouhy; the smallest and coziest of the lodging options on Stratton Mountain. The 18 rooms are simply, comfortably decorated, and a sitting room with fireplace overlooks the ski slopes. An appealing bar, a beauty shop, and outstanding dining room (see *Dining Out*) are also a part of this picture. $84–158 per room MAP spring–fall, more in winter; EP rates also available.

MOTELS   The Barnstead Instead (362-1619), Box 88, Manchester 05255. Just up Bonnet Street, two blocks from the amenities of the Center, this is a genuine former hay barn, converted into motel units. It's all been done with consummate grace and charm, many small touches like braided rugs and exposed old beams. There is also a "gathering room" and outdoor pool. Rooms: $60–80.

The Weathervane (362-2444), Route 7, Manchester 05254. Set back from the road with two picture windows in each of its 20 large units, each room has TV, free coffee, and hot chocolate. There is also a "courtesy room," with books, games, and magazines, and a pool. $74–84 per couple, $7 per extra person, $10 more during foliage.

Best Western Palmer House (362-3600), Manchester 05255. A luxury motel with 31 rooms with color TV, free coffee. There are also meeting rooms, a pool, whirlpool, and sauna. $75–100 per couple.

Four Winds (362-1105), Box 1234, Manchester Center 05255, two miles north on Route 7, combines an 1854 house with pleasant motel units. A full-service breakfast is served in the inn; golf, tennis, and luncheon privileges at the Manchester Country Club. Double occupancy rates $65–90.

Manchester View Motel (362-2739), Manchester Center 05255. On Route 7 north of town with a variety of rooms, including some with fireplaces and fridges, some suites with living rooms and fireplaces, Jacuzzis. A former barn now holds a breakfast room and exercise space. Facilities also include an outdoor pool. $69–160.

Swiss Inn (824-3442; 800-847-9477), Route 11, Londonderry 05148. From its exterior, this looks like a standard motel, but once inside the differences are appealing. New owners Joe and Pat Donohue continue to feature Swiss dishes in their dining room (see *Dining Out*); they also offer a full breakfast. Rooms are large enough to accommodate families, and public space includes a library and a game room (with pool table) as well as a sitting room and bar. There's an outdoor pool. $59–129 (for two connecting rooms) in winter, less off season.

Emerald Lake Motel & Chalets (362-1636), Route 7, eight miles north of Manchester, North Dorset 05253 (next to Emerald Lake State Park). Motel units are available; chalets accommodate from 2 to 12 people, with living rooms, color TV, and fully equipped kitchens with linens, dishes, and cookware (but no maid service). Reasonable daily and weekly rates.

CONDOMINIUMS   **Bromley Village** (824-5458), PO Box 1130, Manchester Center 05255, is a complex of attractive one- and two-bedroom units adjacent to the ski area. Summer facilities include a pool and tennis courts. In winter, you can walk to the lifts; there is also a shuttle bus. From $35 per person midweek in winter.

Stratton Mountain Villas (800-843-6867), Stratton Mountain 05155. Roughly 100 of the resort's condominium units are in the rental pool at any given time, and they encompass a range of sizes and shapes, run $160 per night for a one-bedroom to $310 for a four-bedroom unit. All resort guests have access to the sports center with its indoor pool, exercise machines, racquetball and tennis courts (a fee is charged).

DINING OUT   **Chantecleer** (362-1616), Route 7A, East Dorset, 6–9:30, closed Mondays and Tuesdays. Long respected as one of Vermont's outstanding restaurants, this chef-owned establishment prepares such specialties as veal sweetbreads and sautéed quail Vinerone, chicken breast framboise, and Dover sole. Leave room for profiterole maison or coup Matterhorn. The setting is an elegantly remodeled old dairy barn with a massive fieldstone fireplace. There is an extensive wine list. Entrées: $16.75–22 (the Chateaubriand Bouquestiere for two is $48). Reservations essential.

☞**Three Clock Inn** (824-6327), South Londonderry. Dinner except Mondays. Chef Heinrich Tschernitz has a well-earned reputation for the quality of a varied menu that includes escargots maison and unusual veal dishes. You might begin with scampi maison, proceed to cutlet of veal zingara, or duckling a l'orange, and finish with chocolate mousse. The intimate dining rooms are low-beamed and cheery, tables garnished with fresh flowers and candles, and in summer there are tables on the flowery porch. Entrées run $14.75–21.50, well worth it. Reserve.

Mistral's at Old Toll Gate (362-1779), off Route 11/30 east of Manchester. Open for dinner daily, except Wednesday. A long-time dining landmark under new ownership located in the old toll house once serving the Boston to Saratoga road. During warm weather months, there is the sound of the brook rushing by just under the windows. Specialties such as salmon stuffed with lobster and vegetables and sautéed veal pesto with fusilli are accompanied by a very long wine list. Entrées run $15.95–44.00. Reserve.

The Barrows House (876-4455), Dorset Village. Open for dinner nightly, but weekends only in November. In a spacious, rather formal country dining room and its attached conservatory, both conscientiously appointed, diners can select à la carte or a prix fixe menu that changes seasonally; nightly specials are also offered. Smoked fish crêpes ($6.95) might be followed by sherry-marinated breast of chicken ($15.95) or apricot-glazed rack of lamb ($20.50). A "tavern menu," featuring entrées like Maine crabcakes ($8.95), is available every night but Saturdays. Reserve.

Auberge at the Inn at West View Farm (867-5715), Route 30, Dorset. Open for dinner except Monday. Check ahead for winter day closings. Known simply as "L'Auberge" under previous ownership, the current dining room has managed to maintain its old following and is gaining fame in its own right. The à la carte menu lists "Beginnings" such as "New England Shellfish Stew Au Sherry" and such entrées as duckling roasted with rosemary and thyme, stuffed with apple and sausage in a cider sauce. A tavern menu (available mid-day as well as in the evening) features a variety of sandwiches as well as a $6.50 pasta and $8.25 scrod.

The Black Swan (362-3807), Route 7A, Manchester Village (next to the Jelly Mill). Open for dinner daily except Wednesday; lunch daily Friday–Sunday July–October. The food in this crisply decorated and managed old brick Colonial house is a treat for the senses. A representative dinner might begin with chilled strawberry soup or escargots aux amandes and proceed to veal quennelles ($17) or vegetable bouillabaisse ($14.75). Lighter fare is served in the Mucky Ruck Bistro, open Sunday–Friday from 5:30 (except during foliage season).

Silas Griffith Inn (293-5567), Danby. This attractive, informal dining room, with a hearth and walls decorated with antique kitchen gadgets, is in the carriage house behind the converted carriage house. Dinner, served at 7 PM by reservation, might begin with brie baked with apple chutney or sausage-stuffed mushrooms, and the entrée (there's a choice of five) might be filet mignon cordon bleu or spicy shrimp in a tomato-mushroom sauce served on fresh linguini. The menu changes daily, $20 prix fixe.

Reluctant Panther (362-2568), Route 7A, Manchester Village. Open for dinner except Tuesday and Wednesday. The greenhouse dining room is particularly pleasant and can be the setting for a memorable evening, beginning with hors d'oeuvres in the sitting room. The menu changes nightly but might include escargots en croute and tenderloin of beef. Entrées $12.95–19.95. The wine list is extensive.

Birkenhaus (297-2000), Stratton Mountain. Open for breakfast, lunch (except Friday), and dinner daily. This small, modern lodge has a fine reputation for dining. The five-course, nightly changing menu includes French and Austrian specialties. Dinner might begin with seared andouille sausage with onions and peppers ($6.50), followed by spinach soup with parmesan ($4), a garden salad ($4), and Wiener Schnitzel ($17.50), or lamb noisettes with Provencal sauce ($18.50), topped off with apfelstrudel ($4.50) or linzer torte ($4.50).

The Dorset Inn (867-5500). Open daily for breakfast, lunch, and dinner. Chef Sissy Hicks can be relied on for outstanding New England fare, seven days a week. Begin dinner with smoked mussels, followed by a small Caesar salad and then roast rack of lamb, topped off with chocolate mousse cake or pumpkin pecan pie. Both a tavern menu and full dinner menu (entrées $16.50–19.50) are offered.

Wiley Inn (824-6600), Route 11 between Manchester and Londonderry (one mile east of Bromley). Open for lunch and dinner, Sunday brunch. The setting is an old country inn, the chef is Culinary Institute of America graduate Manfred Sobek, and the menu is a mixture of traditional (breast of chicken sautéed with white wine and tarragon) and venturesome (shrimp Pernod or roast venison with the lightest glaze of red wine, rosemary, thyme, and juniper berries). Entrées $14.50–19.75.

The Equinox (362-4700), Manchester Village. Dinner is served both in the formal, vaulted, blue-and-yellow dining room and in the more intimate Marsh Tavern. British specialties like steak and kidney pie are the specialty of the tavern, and the weekly "Victory Garden" buffets in the main dining room, featuring Vermont vegetables, cheeses, and desserts like maple mousse, get top billing in this valley. Entrées $12.50–21.50.

Dina's (362-4982), at the Inn at Willow Pond, Route 7 north of Manchester Center. Open for dinner except Mondays. This meticulously renovated 1780 farmhouse, with exposed beams, traditional, three-sided fireplaces, and raised Colonial paneling, resembles a Williamsburg tavern. Open for breakfast and dinner daily; chef-owned by Henri and Dina Bronson, specializing in "Modern American" cuisine that Dina describes as "stressing fresh ingredients and creative but not so creative that you don't know what you're eating." Dinner might begin with wild mushrooms and goat cheese in filo, followed by Dina's chowder and maybe a grilled game hen with rosemary and garlic, or veal scaloppine with pesto cream.

Wilburton Inn (362-2500), River Road, Manchester Village. Open Thursday–Sunday for dinner in summer season (see *Resort Inns*). This is a dress-up, grand country estate atmosphere. The richly paneled dining room is the setting for dining from a menu that might include pâté from the chef's terrine ($6), followed by chicken Florentine roulde ($15), poached salmon with dill wine sauce ($18), or rack of lamb seasoned with rosemary ($26).

The Londonderry Inn (824-5226), Route 100, South Londonderry. Closed Tuesdays. The large, attractive dining room is a pleasant place to dine on baked brie followed by veal Picatta ($14) or marinated swordfish en brochette ($12.75). There is a broad choice with daily specials; the constants are fresh ingredients and home baking. The huge tavern hearth is also a nice place to linger.

The Highland House (824-3019), Route 100, Londonderry. There are just six tables in the dining room of this old inn. The menu usually includes an antipasto and a choice of a dozen entrées ranging from stuffed breast of chicken ($14.95) to filet mignon with shrimp ($21.95).

The Inn at Weston (824-5804), Weston Village. Open for dinner year-round except Monday. Within walking distance of the Weston Playhouse, the inn's attractive dining rooms (no smoking) are known for fine dining. The menu usually includes a choice of eight entrées like salmon rouelles (medallions of salmon poached in saffron accented sauce) and veal Weston (Vermont veal prepared differently each day). Entrées $14.95–22.50. The wine list is extensive.

Swiss Inn (824-3442), Londonderry. Open for dinner, except Wednesday, to the public with a strong local following. While ownership has changed, specialties remain Swiss: Geschnetzeltes (veal à la Swiss), beef fondue, and chicken "Lugano" (chicken breast dipped in Gruyère cheese batter), also continental dishes like shrimp à la Marseille and veal tarragon. Entrées $13.95–17.00.

Johnny Seesaw's (824-5533), Route 11, Peru. A prohibition-era dance hall, then one of New England's first ski lodges, this atmospheric inn is well worth a dinnertime visit even if you don't happen to be staying there. The extensive menu usually includes a choice of veal and seafood dishes, pork chops Vermont style, and Johnny's sesame chicken (children can always get hamburgers or pasta as well as half-sized portions). Entrées from $11.95 for lemon walnut chicken.

Village Inn at Landgrove (824-6673), Landgrove-Weston Road, Landgrove. Dinner served by reservation except Wednesdays in summer; check ahead on weeknights off season and in winter. This fine old inn is off by itself up dirt roads at the edge of a tiny village. Dining is by candlelight from a reasonably priced menu. Complete dinners—beginning with steak Diane run $12.95–$18.00.

The Barn Restaurant Tavern (325-3088), Route 30, Pawlet. Open year-round for dinner. This is a genuine old barn with a huge fireplace and a view of the Mettawee River. The large menu offers something for everybody—homemade ravioli ($9.95), chicken Pawlet (marinated in buttermilk, baked and breaded with lemon shallot butter), or a 20-ounce charbroiled steak ($23.95). There's also a children's menu.

White Dog Tavern (293-5477), Route 7 north of Danby Village. Open for dinner Tuesday–Sunday. This is an 1812 farmhouse with a central chimney and four fireplaces, each serving as a centerpiece for a dining room. There's a cheery bar, an outdoor deck in summer, and a choice of smoking and nonsmoking dining rooms. The blackboard menu includes clams, shrimp, sandwiches, and the house special—chicken breasts à la Tom, served up with herbs, garlic, and melted cheese over spaghetti ($10.75); options might include blackened catfish ($10.75) and clams zuppa ($12.75).

The Mill Tavern Restaurant (824-3247), Londonderry. Open for dinner only, 5–9:30 nightly but check before coming. A genuine old mill building, its interior festooned with 10,000 handmade tools dating from the early 1700s through the late nineteenth century. In winter, there is a blazing hearth and après-ski atmosphere.

Nordic Inn (824-6444), Londonderry. Lunch, dinner, Sunday brunch. The glass-sided, greens-filled dining rooms at the rear of this inn welcome cross-country skiers for lunch, but at dinner, this is the scene of serious dining. The menu might include shrimp scampi ($15.50) or steak au poivre ($16).

EATING OUT   *Manchester*   **Garden Café** at the Southern Vermont Arts Center (262-1405), West Road, Manchester Center, open for lunch, June–mid-October, Tuesday–Saturday 11:30–2:30, brunch on Sunday at the same time. The food is fine and the setting is superb: a pleasant indoor room with views over the sculpture garden and the terrace outside; reasonably priced.

Quality Restaurant (362-9839), Main Street, Manchester Center. This used to be the local little place you stopped by for breakfast, lunch, and dinner, but with the gentrification of Manchester, the atmosphere and prices have risen. It's still a good bet for lunch and dinner. Sandwiches are served 11 AM to closing, along with blackboard dinner specials, wine, beer, and "kidsuppers."

Manchester Pancake House and Sandwich Shoppe (362-3496), Route 7A, Manchester Center. Open daily 7 AM–3 PM. This small brown house has no connection with the Pancake House chain; it's a family-run, family find for breakfast and lunch, a favorite with locals. You can breakfast all day on pancakes or omelets or settle for a sub or sandwich (my tuna salad was $2.99).

Grabber's (362-3394), Manchester. Lunch and dinner. Formerly the "Palace," this high Victorian brick building makes a colorful dining space; you can choose to dine in the pub, library, parlor, or garden room; specialties are barbecued spare ribs, prime ribs, and seafood, or you can dine from the salad bar.

Laney's Restaurant (362-4456), Routes 11/30. Open for lunch and dinner. The hot new spot in town, specializing in exotic pizza from a wood-fired brick oven, hickory-smoked ribs, grilled steaks, and salads; draft beer in frosted mugs.

Gurry's (362-9878), Route 11/30, east of Manchester Depot. Open daily 5–12. This is a locally favored, recently renovated but still friendly place for pizza, burgers, fried seafood, and such.

Sirloin Saloon (362-2600), Route 11/30, Manchester Center. This is a large, many-cornered, Tiffany lamplit, polished brass place that's always packed; there's a children's menu.

The Gourmet Café (362-1254), Factory Point Square, Manchester Center. Lunch year-round, daily, extended hours in summer. Tucked away in a corner of one of many shopping clusters, this attractive, small dining room has deli food; an outdoor café, weather permitting. Soups, salads, sandwiches, beers, and wine spritzers. Picnics-to-go.

Park Bench Café (362-2557), open from 5 PM daily, the town's singles' bar, featuring munchies like fried zucchini, veggies, and nachos; deli sandwiches and more substantial New York sirloin, ribs.

Marbleledge Lodge (362-1518), five miles north of Manchester Center on Route 7. A great find for reasonably priced home cooking; German specialties.

Golden Royal Dragon (362-4569/4560), Route 11/30, Manchester Center, open daily for lunch and dinner. This is a relatively small, attractive Chinese restaurant with a standard selection (also some really spicy Szechuan dishes) and reasonable prices; luncheon specials.

In Londonderry   **Jake's Marketplace Café** (824-6614), Mountain Marketplace at the junction of Routes 100 and 11. Open for breakfast from 5:30AM–10 PM. A local institution with a lively sports lounge, a lunch counter, and a pleasant pink dining room. Overstuffed sandwiches, salads, and burgers are the order of most days, along with pizzas, hoagies, and calzones counter.

The Garden Market, Route 11, Londonderry, 10–6 daily. A health food store with great sandwiches and deli takeouts, the perfect source for picnic pickings before you head for the woods (see *Hiking and Camping*, and *Shunpiking*).

Gran'ma Frisby's, Route 11 east of the village. When Magic Ski Area was open, you were lucky to get in the door of this wonderfully pubby place on a winter weekend. Open for lunch and dinner and known for its fries and fresh dough pizza, this is a friendly, reasonably priced find any time of year.

In Pawlet   **The Old Station Restaurant and Ice Cream Parlor**, open from 6 AM until 3 in winter, later in summer. If you think about it, railroad depots make perfect diners—with the counter and a row of stools down the length of the building and tables along the sides. This classic 1905 depot was moved here from another town and positioned above a babbling brook. It's a particularly pleasant place. Coffee cups bearing regulars' names hang by the door.

At Stratton Mountain   **Mulligans** (297-9293) also has a Manchester Village locale (362-3663), but there it's not as crucial to know about this spacious, pleasant, family-priced restaurant that's open for lunch and dinner, good for burgers, sandwiches, salads, and dinner options like Thai basil chicken and lobster and seafood manicotti (both $10.95). Children's specials include a Ninja Turtle Burger and Gorilla Cheese (both $1.50).

In Weston   **The Bryant House** (824-6287), Weston. Owned by the neighboring Vermont Country Store, this fine old house has belonged to one family—the Bryants—from the time it was built in 1827 until the family line petered out. Upstairs, a special room is set aside to look as it did in the 1890s. There are plenty of salads, sandwiches, and Vermont-style chicken pie. Lunch served 11:30–3.

ICE CREAM AND FUDGE   **Wilcox Brothers Dairy** (362-1223), Route 7A south, Manchester. Some of the creamiest, most delectable flavors in Vermont are made in this family-owned-and-run dairy, available at the farm and a variety of local restaurants.

Mother Myrick's Ice Cream Parlor & Fudge Factory (362-1223),

Route 7A, Manchester Center. Open daily 11–midnight in summer; fountain treats, cappuccino, baked goods, handmade chocolates, and fudge concocted daily.

ENTERTAINMENT   *Theater*   **Dorset Playhouse** (867-5777). The Dorset Players, a community theater group formed in 1927, actually owns the beautiful playhouse in Dorset. Winter performances by the Dorset Players. Mid-June–October 8:30 nightly, 5 PM and 9 PM Saturday. In summer, the "Dorset Theatre Festival": new plays as well as classics by a resident professional group.

Weston Playhouse (824-5288). This popular summer theater on the Common has been active for over 50 years and gives nightly performances from mid-July–September. The cabaret downstairs is open after performances.

Music   **Kinhaven Music School** (824-9592), Lawrence Hill Road, Weston, presents free concerts Fridays at 4:30, Saturdays at 2:30, July–mid-August; inquire about details.

Strattonfest (297-0100), Stratton Mountain, July and August. This series usually includes folk, jazz, classic, and country western music on successive weeks.

Manchester Music Festival (362-1956), summer, at the Southern Vermont Arts Center. Haig's in Bondville is the place for live music and dancing in the winter.

Film   **Derry Twin Cinema** (824-2221), Routes 11 and 100, includes a bar and tables in rear rows; shows two first-run movies nightly.

Manchester Cinema (362-1229), Manchester Center.

Equinox Twin Cinema (262-2633), Manchester Center.

SELECTIVE SHOPPING   **Orvis Retail Store**, Route 7A, Manchester Center. Supplying the needs of fishermen and Manchester's other visiting sportsmen since 1856. Known widely for its mail-order catalog, the second oldest in the country, Orvis specializes in the fishing rods made in the factory out back; also other fishing tackle and gear, country clothes, and other small luxury items—from silk underwear to welcome mats—which make the difference in country, or would-be country, living. Don't miss the "bargain-basement."

The Vermont Country Store, Weston Village, open year-round, Monday–Saturday 9–5. Back in 1944, the late Vrest Orton revived the business established by his grandfather and father in northern Vermont before the turn of the century. Gradually, that business—selling sensible clothing, gadgets, old-fashioned yard goods, and kitchen utensils—has expanded into a national tourist attraction, complete with a hefty mail-order catalog. Orton prided himself on reviving, among other things, the Vermont Common Cracker, first made in 1820, now produced in his Rockingham store. Son, Lyman, is now in charge.

ANTIQUE SHOPS   **The Danby Antiques Center** (293-9984), Main Street,

Danby, displays American country and formal furniture and accessories from 24 dealers in 11 rooms and the barn. Open 10–5 daily, April–December; Thursday–Monday, January–March.

East-West Antiques (325-3466), Route 30, offers antiques and artifacts from Indonesia and Ireland, also fabrics and women's clothing.

The 1812 House Antiques Center (362-1189), Route 7, north of Manchester Center. Open daily, displaying quality antiques representing 30 dealers.

ART GALLERIES   **The Peel Gallery** (293-5230), Route 7, two miles north of Danby Village, represents 50 American artists whose works are dramatically displayed in a restored eighteenth-century barn. Margaret and Harris Peel launched this showcase 17 years ago. Shows and receptions are scheduled between Memorial and Columbus Day. Among the artists represented are Patrick Farrow, Sidney and Barbara Willis, Larry Webster, and several other nationally known artists. The gallery is open 10–5 year-round, closed Tuesdays except in July and August.

Tilting at Windmills Gallery (362-3022), Routes 11/30, Manchester Center. Open daily. An unusually large gallery with a wide selection of market-geared art.

Todd Pottery, Fine Art and Craft Gallery, south edge of the village of Weston. Housed in an 1840s barn, an attractive gallery displaying an interesting mix of paintings and pottery.

BOOKSTORES   **The Northshire Bookstore**, Main Street, center of Manchester Center, is highly regarded as one of the most complete in New England. The Morrows have filled the venerable Colburn House with a wide range of unusually well displayed volumes, and in summer, books overflow onto the porch. An amazingly wide range of adult titles, children's books, and records are featured, along with an extraordinarily comprehensive stock of current and classic paperbacks.

Johnny Appleseed, Manchester. Housed in the square brick building built to house the Battenkill Bank in the early nineteenth century. In 1930, Ruth Hard opened the bookstore, relinquishing it in 1935 to her famous parents—newspaper columnist, state legislator, and poet Walter Hard and novelist and general Vermont raconteur Margaret Hard. Since 1965, the store has been owned by Fred Taylor, who likes to talk books—both old and new.

CRAFT SHOPS   **The Pawlet Potter** (325-3100). Marion Waldo McChesney works in her studio on the ground level of her restored, brick landmark house, where customers can watch her turn out one-of-a-kind pieces: vases, platters, and "seastones," amazing floating ceramic discs. Ceramic jewelry and a variety of unusual designs make this small studio—with a rocker in which you may want to just immerse yourself in the creative atmosphere—well worth a visit.

Danby Marble Company (293-5425), Route 7 north of Danby Village, open daily May–October and from November 20–December 30. At first glance, this is just another array of marble bookends, lamps, chessboards, candle holders, trivets, and vases. Look more closely and you will find that this is a showcase for marble from throughout the East. (Danby itself is the site of what's billed as "the largest underground marble quarry in the world.") Tom Martin, owner of this store, cuts marble to whatever sizes and shapes you may desire.

Weston House Quilt Collection (824-3636), Weston Village. Joanne and Richard Eggert have assembled one of the state's standout selections of both hand- and machine-made quilts.

The Stratton Arts Festival, Stratton Mountain, mid-September–mid-October daily. Serious crafts shoppers should not miss this splendid event, the oldest and largest showcase of art and a wide variety of pieces crafted by Vermonters.

GENERAL STORES **J. J. Hapgood Store**, Peru. Daily 8:30–6. A genuine general store with a potbelly stove, old-fashioned counters filled with food, and some clothing staples; geared to locals rather than tourists.

Peltier's General Merchandise (867-4400), Dorset Village. A village landmark since 1816: staples and then some, including almost any kind of fish on request, baking to order, Vermont products, wines, and gourmet items like hearts of palm and Tip tree jams. Since there are no lunch or snack shops in Dorset, this also serves the purpose; good for picnic fare.

Johnny Mach's General Store, Pawlet Village. The focal point of this genuine old emporium is described under Pawlet (see *Villages*), but the charm of this family-run place goes beyond its water view. Built as a hotel, it's filled with a wide variety of locally useful merchandise.

The Weston Village Store, Weston. Open daily. A standard country emporium catering to visitors.

Note: General store buffs should make the pilgrimage to North Shrewsbury, 17 miles northeast of Weston (see "Okemo Mountain/ Ludlow Area").

MANCHESTER'S FACTORY DIRECT SHOPS Manchester merchants refuse to call these stores "outlets." Prices are slightly higher than factory stores, lower than retail. The list is lengthening quickly. At present, the dozen plus factory outlets include Polo/RalphLauren, Ann Klein, Calvin Klein, Beneton, Van Heusen, Timberland, Dexter Shoe, Hathaway, Brooks Brothers, Cole Hann Company Store, and John Roberts. Shops that carry a number of brands include: **Manchester Commons, Campus Factory Outlet**, and **Battenkill Place.**

OTHER OUTLETS **J. K. Adams Co., Factory and Factory Store**, Route 30, has a complete line of its fine wood products: sugar maple butcher blocks, knife racks, spice racks, cheese and carving boards, with complementary accessories. Discounted "seconds" on the second floor.

Chris Tree

Everyone shops at Mach's, Pawlet

Weston Bowl Mill, Weston. Open year-round, 8–6 in summer, 9–5 in winter; 10–5 on Sundays. This classic old wood mill has long produced quality woodenware, available throughout the state and here at factory prices. There are an amazing variety of boxes, furnishings, toys, and furniture, as well as bowls; request a catalog.

OTHER STORES   **Herdsmen Leather**, Manchester Center. Open daily, year-round, billing itself as "New England's finest leather shop"; coats, boots, shoes, and accessories; watch for sales.

    Landau, Factory Point Square and Route 7A, across from Jelly Mill, Manchester Center. Billing itself as "the world's largest collection of Icelandic woolens," an unusual choice of Icelandic jackets, blankets, sweaters, coats, and accessories.

    The Enchanted Doll House, Route 7, north of Manchester Center. Daily 9–5, Sundays 10–5. Twelve rooms full of dolls, dollhouses, toys, miniatures, games, and books. For children as well as collectors.

    The Gallery of Danby Green (293-5550), Main Street, occupies the restored Greek Revival Hawden House. From parlor to kitchen, dining room to nursery, each room is appropriately decorated and stocked with upscale gifts and gadgets, mostly from Vermont, including wood and marble carvings. We came away with a great little pepper grinder.

    The Jelly Mill, Route 7A, Manchester Center. Daily 10–6. A three-story barn filled with folk art, crystal, cards, crafts, and other assorted gifts. You can watch the resident woodcarver and silversmith. Snacks and light meals available in the Buttery Restaurant on the second floor.

Equinox Valley Nursery, Route 7A, south, Manchester. An outstanding farmstand and spread managed by three generations of a family; good for picking vegetables, berries in season. Especially famous in the fall for the 100,000 pounds of pumpkins it produces, also for its display of scarecrows and pumpkin faces; sells pumpkin bread, pie, ice cream, and marmalade along with other farmstand staples. During January and February, the family usually makes 1,000 jars of jams and jellies.

Authentic Designs (394-7713), The Mill Road, Route 315, West Rupert 05776, creates fine reproduction Colonial and early American lighting fixtures, electrified or left unwired for candles, made of brass or maple. Open Monday–Friday 9–4, or by appointment on weekends.

Basketville, Route 7A, Manchester. South of the village, open daily, a very large branch of the Putney store: thousands of baskets, wicker furniture, dried flowers.

SPECIAL EVENTS   March: Spring skiing, sugaring.

April: Trout season opens; Easter parades and egg hunts at ski areas. White-water canoeing on the West River.

May: **Vermont Symphony Orchestra** performs; Hildene opens.

June: **Strawberry festivals in Dorset;** the annual vintage car climb to Equinox Summit; **Southern Vermont Art** series opens.

July: Fireworks and old-fashioned Fourth celebrations.

July–Labor Day: **Weston Playhouse** season.

July–mid-August: **Kinhaven Music School** concert series; Dorset Theater and Weston Playhouse open; a major antiques show held at Hildene in even years, at Dorset in odd ones.

August: **Southern Vermont Crafts Fair** (first weekend)–juried exhibitors, entertainment, food, and music; Manchester Dance (mid-August; **Manchester Horse Show** (late August).

August (first week): Polo matches and an antique show at Stratton Mountain.

September: **Annual Maple Leaf Half-Marathon, Stratton Wurstfest** on Labor Day Weekend; **Stratton Arts Festival** (beginning second weekend, running through mid-October), a major display of Vermont crafts and art, and a performing arts series in the base lodge at Stratton Mountain. The **Manchester Autumnfest** is a concurrent presentation of dance, theater, and music.

Peru Fair: just one day, usually the last Saturday in September, considered one of Vermont's most colorful, it includes a pig roast, also crafts, food, entertainment.

October: **Weston Antiques Show,** first weekend, one of the state's oldest and most respected, staged in the Weston Playhouse.

December: **Candlelight Tours of Hildene**, including sleigh rides, refreshments in the barn, music on the organ.

MEDICAL EMERGENCY   Manchester/Dorset Rescue Squad (362-2121).

Northshire Medical Associates (362-4440), Manchester Center.

Manchester Family Medical Care (362-1263).

Mountain Valley Medical Clinic (824-6901), Route 11, opposite the Flood Brook School, two miles west of Londonderry, three miles east of Peru.

Carlos Otis Clinic (297-2300) at Stratton Mountain.

Tri Mountain Rescue Squad: 824-3166.

Grafton, Chester, and Bellows Falls

These three, strikingly different towns form a collage of Vermont's past, present, even future—from the once-thriving industrial center of Bellows Falls to the oases for travelers in the villages of Grafton and Chester.

Grafton is Vermont's Cinderella. Unquestionably queenly today, it was—and not too long ago—a forgotten, decaying village.

Prior to the Civil War, Grafton boasted more than 1,480 souls and 10,000 sheep. Wool was turned to 75,000 yards of Grafton cloth annually; soapstone from 13 local quarries left town in the shape of sinks, stoves, ink wells, and footwarmers.

But then one in three of Grafton's men marched off to the Civil War, and few returned. An 1869 flood destroyed the town's six dams and its road. The new highway by-passed Grafton. The town's Tavern, however, built in 1801, entered a golden era. Innkeeper Marlan Phelps invested his entire California Gold Rush fortune in adding a third floor and double porches, and his brother Francis organized a still extant coronet band. Guests included Emerson, Thoreau, and Kipling; later both Woodrow Wilson and Teddy Roosevelt visited.

But by 1940, the Tavern was sagging, and nearly all the 80-some houses were selling—with plenty of acreage—for $3,000–$5,000.

Enter Matthew Hall, a New York financier and descendant of the town's first pastor, who had been summering here since 1936. Hall's "Aunt Pauline" Fiske, who often joined him, financed restoration of some fine, three-dimensional murals in the Congregational church. On her death, Miss Fiske left a fortune in trust to her two nephews, Hall and Dean Mathey of Princeton, New Jersey. A note requested its use be for an unusual worthy cause, something she would have liked. For five years, the men couldn't hit on a suitable scheme. Then one Vermont morning, Mathey woke Hall with the news that he had "found the answer to Aunt Pauline's money . . . Grafton."

Incorporated in 1963 under the name "Windham," the Foundation immediately focused on the town's rotting core. A restored version of the last store was opened, complete with lunch counter. After roofing a blacksmith shop, the Foundation went on to tackle the unwinterized Tavern. The architects of Old Deerfield left the rocking chairs on the Tavern's front porch and its handsome face unchanged. New heating, wiring, an elevator, 20 guest rooms, and 14 private baths were added.

The Windham Foundation has expanded the inn by adding 16 double rooms in restored homes across the way, also four complete houses and a luxurious stable for guests who want to bring a horse. It owns 21 buildings in town and, among other things, has built a cheese factory, opened a nursery and gift shop, and buried the village's electric, phone, and cable TV wires. There is a museum, with old vehicles, tools, and the innards of an old-time country store, that also contains displays on the wildlife management of its 1,300 acres. The Windham Foundation maintains a demonstration flock of 20 sheep and marked footpaths on which visitors can wander down past the sheep and pond, into the woods and home again.

Over the past few years, some fine guest houses have opened around town—along with art galleries and assorted shops. It all adds up to the biggest tourist destination within a radius of 10 miles—a sweep that happens to include the fine old Rockingham Meeting House and the Vermont Country Store in the village of Rockingham, the delightfully unrestored village of Windham, the village of Saxtons River (known for its own picturesque inn), and the lively town of Chester with its fine Historical Society and Art Guild, its outstanding shops and inns. The roads connecting these places are particularly scenic.

GUIDANCE   The **Bellows Falls Chamber of Commerce** (463-4280), Box 554, 55 Village Square, Bellows Falls 05101, maintains a downtown office generally open year-round; offers information about the town of Rockingham—which includes Bellows Falls, Rockingham Village, and Saxtons River.

The chamber has a most informative "Guided Walking Tour" brochure for the town's historic district, where adaptive preservation is under way.

The **Chester Chamber of Commerce** (875-3827), Chester 05143, maintains a booth in the center of town.

GETTING THERE   By bus: Vermont Transit from points in Connecticut and Massachusetts stops at Bellows Falls (at Fletcher's drug store in the square) and in Chester (at the Rexall next to the Chester Inn).

By train: See *AMTRAK*. Northbound, the "Montrealer" stops at 3:50 AM, but southbound it now arrives at an almost civilized 11:10 PM.

Taxi service for Bellows Falls: **Rick's Taxi Service** (463-9414).

TO SEE AND DO   **Green Mountain Flyer** (463-3069), PO Box 498, Bellows Falls 05101, created in 1984 by the local freight line—the Green Mountain Railroad—to fill the void left by Steamtown USA. Twice daily rides are offered July through Labor Day, and there is a weekend schedule before and after that; special foliage rides all the way to Ludlow are scheduled for foliage season. The regular, 13-mile (one-way) ride to Chester Depot is exceptionally beautiful. Rolling stock includes some turn-of-the-century cars, and the route is along the Connecticut River, past covered bridges, beside small villages and farms, and through wooded rock cuts, which include the spectacular Brockway Mills gorge.

MG Car Museum (722-3708), Route 5, Westminster, between Bellows Falls and Brattleboro. Assembled by Gerard Goguen, a former trumpet player with the Boston Symphony and sports car race driver, the museum is "the world's largest private exhibit of a single marque." Twenty-seven of the sleek models are on display, with ten more being restored. There's a 1927 14/28 Tourer Flatnose, the oldest MG in the United States and one of six known to exist; the J-4 that nearly took Goguen's head off at Watkins Glen; the 1955 EX-182 race car and the prototype of the MGA. The most elegant is a 1932 custom convertible created for Bernice Marshall of Montreal, Canada. Open daily except Monday 10–5, July and August; weekends during June and September and up to Columbus Day.

Chester encompasses three distinct villages within a few miles, each of them worth noting. There is the old core with the double-porched Chester Inn at its center, flanked by an attractive lineup of shops and restaurants and set back from the old highway (Route 11) by a stringbean Green. Across the road stands a fine old brick schoolhouse, now the **Historical Society and Art Guild**, in which you can see changing art exhibits and learn about the town's colorful history, including the story of Clarence Adams, one of Chester's most prominent citizens who broke into more than 50 businesses and homes between 1886 and 1902 when he was finally apprehended.

Don't miss Chester's **Stone Village** up on North Street (Route 103); a double line of 30 buildings faced in "gneiss," a rough-hewn gleaming mica schist quarried from nearby Flamstead Mountain. Cool in summer, warm in winter, stone houses are a rarity in New England. All of these are said to have been built by two brothers in the pre–Civil War decade, with hiding spaces enough to make them a significant stop on the Underground Railroad.

Midway between Main and North streets is **Chester Depot**, a pleasant old traffic center that resembles neither of these places. The well-kept Victorian depot serves as northern terminus for the Green Mountain Flyer (see above), spilling more than a hundred passengers at a time into the village center to browse in Cummings Hardware and Jameson's Food Market and to stroll by the steepled town hall. It's an appropriate terminus for a country railroad.

The peaceful village of **Rockingham** just off Route 103 between Chester and Bellows Falls is well worth a stop to visit the **Old Rockingham Meeting House**, Vermont's oldest, unchanged public building. Built in 1787, this Federal-style structure contains "pigpen"-style pews, each accommodating 10–15 people, some with their backs to the minister. The old burying ground is filled with thin old markers bearing readable epitaphs.

Sited by one of the biggest natural falls in the entire course of the Connecticut River, **Bellows Falls** itself cascades down a hill so steep that a stairway connects the commercial Westminster Street with the residential neighborhood above. Old paper mills and railroad-era buildings are crowded on yet another level down by the river— where you can still see carvings made centuries ago by members of the Pennacook tribe who gathered by the falls to fish. You can also see the remains of one of America's first canals, built in 1802 to ease river traffic around the great falls.

The **Fish Ladder and Visitors Center** (463-3226), New England Power Company, Bridge Street, is one of a series of ladders constructed on the Connecticut River to return Atlantic salmon and American shad to their native spawning grounds.

Here, too, is the **Adams Old Stone Gristmill Museum**. The mill ground grain from 1831 until 1961; the old machinery is all in place, and the adjacent museum exhibits relics of the town's long and varied industrial history (open usually Saturday and Sunday 2–4 and by appointment: 463-4280). There are more relics of local history to be found in the **Rockingham Free Library and Museum** (65 Westminster Street; open year-round, Monday–Friday 2–4).

Most shops and businesses are contained in nineteenth-century brick buildings lining the widened stretch of Westminster Street (Route 5) known as "The Village Square." There is a Florentine tower atop the town hall (which includes the Falls Cinema and Fletchers Drug). The bus stops here.

Bellows Falls was the home of Hetty Green (1835–1916), who parlayed a substantial inheritance into a $100 million fortune; she was called the "witch of Wall Street," to which she traveled by day coach, looking like a bag lady in threadbare bombazine.

Even if you do not stay in **Grafton**, you must come to see this restored village center, to visit the village shops, to walk the well-marked paths through the woods and fields, and to look into the **Grafton Historical Society Museum** (open Memorial Day–Columbus Day, 2:30–4:30 on Saturdays; also on Sundays in July and August plus holiday weekends and holiday Mondays; 843-2388). There are also wildlife exhibits, a replica of a country store, horse-drawn vehicles, and before and after pictures of the town—all housed next to the Windham Foundation on Townshend Road (open June–November daily 8:30–5).

The unusually shaped inn (see *Lodging*) and Vermont Academy (now a private, coed prep school) are the two most striking buildings in **Saxtons River**. **The Historical Museum**, housing a nineteenth-century parlor and kitchen as well as other local memorabilia, is open Saturday and Sunday, 2:30–5 in summer.

FARMS TO VISIT   **Saxtons River Orchards** (722-3396). Pick your own apples during September and October and enjoy the foliage from these hilltop orchards; choice of MacIntosh, Cortland, Delicious, and Spys. Off Route 121 west of the village.

Allen Brothers Farms & Orchards (722-3395), Bellows Falls. Open year-round, daily; located on Route 5, two miles south of Bellows Falls, offering pick-your-own apples and potatoes, also selling vegetables, plants and seeds, honey, syrup, and Vermont gifts.

Grafton Village Apple Company (843-2406), Route 121, Grafton. Open daily, 9–5. Selling apples, maple syrup, fresh-pressed cider in season, pumpkins, berries, also wines, gourmet items, and Vermont gifts.

COVERED BRIDGES   There are five covered bridges in the area: two in Bartonsville (one and a half miles north of Route 103, the other east off Route 103), two in Grafton, and one in Saxtons River off Route 121, noteworthy for its "flying buttresses" (replaced in 1982).

SUGARHOUSES   **Butternut Acres** (843-2429), Route 121, Grafton; **Valley Brook Farm** (843-2452), three miles south of Grafton on the Townshend Road; **Grouse Hill Farm**, Grafton, one mile north on Middletown Road; **Grafton Village Apple Company** (843-2406), Route 121, Grafton.

BICYCLING   **Neal's Wheels** (875-3627), Route 11 in Chester rents touring bikes, also available from **The Old Tavern** (843-2231) in Grafton and from **Fuller's General Store** in Grafton.

CANOE AND BOAT RENTALS   **Green Mountain Marine** (463-4973), Route 5, Missing Link Road, Rockingham 05101, on the Connecticut River; open April—October.

GOLF   **Tater Hill Club** (875-2517), Popple Dungeon Road, Windham (off Route 11, two miles south from junction of Windham Road and Route 121), offers 18 holes, a pro shop, instruction, and a restaurant.

The Bellows Falls Country Club (463-9809), Rockingham. Scenic nine-hole course, clubhouse with bar and lunchroom.

HORSEBACK RIDING   **Shanagary Farm** (722-3548), Westminster Station, offers guided "Equestrian Weekends," riding all day through backwoods and roads, dining and sleeping at the Saxtons River Inn (see *Lodging*).

Wagon rides (875-2760) from Chester Green are offered out into the countryside.

CROSS-COUNTRY SKIING   **Tater Hill Cross-Country Ski Center** (875-2517), Popple Dungeon Road, Windham. A total of 40 km of trails, 20 tracked: a mix of meadows and forests at elevations of 1,786–2,000 feet. Instruction, rentals, showers, change rooms, and restaurant, guided and headlamp tours.

VTD

Grafton has timeless charms for strollers

Grafton Ponds (843-2231), Grafton. The program is based at the Tavern and the trails are just down the road, meandering off from a log cabin warming hut, over meadows, and up into the woods on Bear Hill. Rentals and instruction offered.

LODGING   *Grafton*   All places listed below are in the 05146 zip code area.

The Old Tavern (843-2231). The brick core of this splendid building dates back to 1788, but the double-porched facade is midnineteenth century. The stylish interior (vintage 1965) tastefully recreates a formal early American setting worthy of Williamsburg or Old Deerfield. The 20 beautifully decorated bedrooms in the main building are supplemented by more in a less formal Annex and in six fine old village houses, which can be rented whole, ranging from Hillside Cottage ($110–125) with just a living room and bedroom to Tuttle House, sleeping nine, offering a full kitchen ($220 per day). It's frequently difficult to find space here during the summer and fall, easier in winter. Open year-round; in the summer, there are tennis courts and a sand-bottomed swimming pond; in winter, cross-country skiing. Doubles cost $80–140 per night B&B. There's a 20 percent discount for midweek stays of two or more nights in the winter. Youngsters are welcome—in the Annex and cottages.

The Inn at Woodchuck Farm (843-2398). Open May–October. This 1780s farmhouse sits high on a hill, up a back road above Grafton. The porch, well stocked with comfortable wicker, has a peaceful, top-of-the-world feel, and there are views from the elegant living room and dining room, too. Ann and Frank Gabriel have gradually expanded guest space since they opened in 1968, and even the two rooms with shared bath ($69) are more attractive than most you'll find, and some are real standouts. The inn can now accommodate 20 guests, and options include a "studio," with its own kitchen and deck, and the barn, fancifully transformed into retreat space for either a couple or family of four. The pond, good for swimming, fishing, and canoeing, is just below, and in all there are 200 rolling acres, laced with walking trails. A four-course dinner is served on request. Country antiques, stoneware jugs, and other old kitchenware are sold in the barn shop. Rooms and suites with private bath $89–98, $115 per couple and $195 for four, breakfast included.

Eaglebrook of Grafton (843-2564), a stately home diagonally across from the Tavern, has opened three guest rooms in addition to its gift and textile shop; $70 or $75 (private bath).

The Wayfarer at Grafton (843-2363) has spool beds and country antiques. This 1834 brick house is up-street from the Tavern and has four guest rooms, two with private bath, two shared, each with fireplace. $65–80 including continental breakfast. This, too, has a barn full of antiques. Open year-round, except during the Parks' vacations. By reservation only.

Hayes Guest House (843-2461), Kidder Hill Road, is located on a pleasant back street by a covered bridge. This is a comfortable old house with four guest rooms, the gem being on the first floor with a private bath, fireplace, and four-poster so high you need a stool to climb aboard. Reasonable rates ($65–75) include continental breakfast. Children and (a rarity) dogs are welcome.

Chester   All places listed below are in the 05143 zip code unless otherwise noted.

The Inn at Long Last (875-2444) (formerly the Chester Inn) is the revitalized centerpiece of this lively village. Innkeeper Jack Coleman, the former president of Haverford College, received a lot of national publicity when he worked incognito as a garbage man in Maryland and a ditch-digger (while returning to chair meetings of the Federal Reserve Bank of Philadelphia). He recorded these sabbaticals in a book, *Blue Collar Journal*, and then headed the Clark Foundation in New York, again impersonating a homeless vagabond and prison inmate. Each of the 30 individualized guest rooms in the renovated inn have been named for people or places he admires, Currier & Ives, Frederick Law Olmstead, George Orwell, Lord Peter Wimsey, the Brooklyn Bridge, and Boston. Each room is not only decorated but also equipped (with suitable books) to theme, and arriving guests are encouraged to stroll the halls, peeking into each available room before selecting. Books that Coleman happens to be reading himself are also strewn around the vast common room, and guests are encouraged to browse and borrow. This is a big hotel, and past owners have failed to "fill its britches," so to speak. Jack Coleman has managed to bring it to life. On the morning we woke up here, the lobby (common room) was filled with the music of the Weston monks, and hot coffee had been set out for early strollers. Meals are also outstanding, from hearty breakfasts to fine dining (see *Dining Out*). Amenities include a tennis court. All rooms are $160 for two, $90 for one, MAP, plus 15 percent gratuity.

Hugging Bear Inn & Shoppe (875-2412), Main Street, is a handsome Victorian home in the middle of an unusually handsome Vermont town, with a giant teddy bear sitting on its front porch. Inside there are teddy bears on the beds of six spacious guest rooms (each with private bath), and, in the "Shoppe" out back, are more than 4,000 stuffed bears. Innkeepers Georgette Thomas, her son and daughter-in-law Paul and Diane Thomas, believe that people don't hug enough. Everyone is invited to hug any bear in the house, and the atmosphere here is contagiously friendly. Rates are $55–60 single, $75–85 double (plus $5 during foliage season), $10 for children under age 14, breakfast included.

The Chester House (875-2205), on the Green across from the Inn at Long Last, was opened in 1987 by Irene and Norm Wright. A distinctive 1790s house on the National Register of Historic Places, the inn has a downstairs parlor, Keeping Room, and dining room decorated in early American style and the four guest rooms are quite luxurious and have private baths: The King Room includes a sitting area; the Queen Room has a canopied, queen-size bed and large Jacuzzi; and there's a canopied double in the Princess and twins in the Twin. $50–75 per room B&B, less for four nights or more.

The Stone Hearth Inn (875-2525), is an 1810 farmhouse. Its many additions (formerly the Cranberry Inn) ramble along behind a stockadelike row of fir trees that shield it from Route 11. The 10 guest rooms are nicely decorated with the same quality antiques that you see in the living room—which has a fieldstone fireplace. The dining room serves breakfast, lunch (Tuesday–Saturday, summer only), and dinner (Friday–Saturday). There is also an inviting Pub Room with a full liquor license and player piano. A large game room has ping pong, pool tables, and exercise equipment. There's also a Nutcracker gift shop. $50–70 per person including breakfast. Open year-round.

Greenleaf Inn (875-3171), PO Box 188, just off Main Street. Dan and Liz Duffield offer five rooms, all furnished with antiques, most of them found at local auctions. Liz is a member of the Chester Art Guild and exhibits works by other members in a small gallery here. Rooms with private baths are $70–80, including a full breakfast.

Night with a Native (875-2616), PO Box 327 (Route 103) in the village. Bill and Doris Hastings are sixth-generation Vermonters, and their house conveys a lively interest in many things. They obviously enjoy accommodating guests. There are two small bedrooms, sharing one bath. Breakfast features freshly baked (no cholesterol) muffins. $45–50, depending on the season.

Other Bed & Breakfasts: **Stone Village** (875-3914), Route 103; **The Henry Farm** (875-2674), off Route 11; **Inn Victoria** (875-4288), on the Green; and **Second Wind** (875-3488), on Grafton Road, $65–75 double.

Saxtons River   All places listed below are in the 05154 zip code area.

Saxtons River Inn (869-2110). The 21 rooms (11 with private baths) are divided between the high Victorian main inn and the Greek Revival mansion across the street. New proprietors Sandy and Ilene Freiman are upgrading this landmark. The sunny front room with big windows on the street is a cafélike bar, and there are inviting upstairs sitting rooms (away from the bar and restaurant traffic). The upstairs porch has been transformed into a comfortable roost. $60 per room with shared bath, $68 with private, including breakfast. Note that this is a stop on horseback riding, inn-to-inn treks; also popular with bicyclists and cross-country skiers (special packages available).

Moore's Guest House (869-2020), 57 Main Street. David Moore's restored Victorian town house with spacious veranda and six guest rooms is a good place for family reunions, since all meals can be catered by advance reservation. A rom with a private bath is $65, $55 shared. Cash or checks, please.

Bellows Falls   All places listed below are in the 05101 zip code area.

Rockingham Motor Inn (463-4536, 800-255-4756 outside Vermont), Route 5, north of town. The Ticino family, who took over the place in 1987, have made this a popular spot for family gatherings and community benefits. Its friendly atmosphere outweighs its rather utilitarian appearance. Doubles are $45 (foliage season surcharge); a two-day ski package, including lift tickets, breakfasts, and dinner, is available.

Horsefeathers (463-9776), 16 Webb Terrace (Route 5 north of town). An 1890s house with its own garden acreage and views over town to the river. Guests can claim two sunny rooms with a library, also a tempting porch rocker. The guest rooms, most with private baths, are $55–85, including breakfast.

☞**Blue Haven Guest House** (463-9008), RFD 1, Box 328, Route 5 south of Bellows Falls, has a distinctly French atmosphere. Not only does Helene Champagne speak it, but the big country kitchen where guests have breakfast has the touch of a contemporary *auberge*. There are five comfortable rooms, some with canopied beds, and four baths; *"Ange"* is especially appealing. The crude stone fireplace in the common room (once a schoolhouse) has stones from every state. $45 single, $85 double, with full breakfast. Credit cards; AARP discount. Smoke-free.

River Mist Bed & Breakfast (463-9023), 7 Burt Street. A Victorian town house with a big porch and modest rates starting at $25 per person with big breakfast.

Andover   All places listed below are in the 05143 zip code area.

The Inn at High View (875-2724), East Hill (formerly the Quilted Cat B&B), is now a full-service inn run by Gregory Bohan. Fine paneling ornaments the living and dining rooms; there's a rock garden pool, sauna, and cross-country trails. The eight rooms are $80–125 including breakfast; dinner with an Italian flair is served to guests on Friday and Saturday for $25.

Rowell's Inn (875-3658), Route 11, Simonsville. Truly exceptional, this place was built as a brick, double-porched stage stop in 1820 by Major Edward Simons. It has been serving the public off and on since then. After decades of neglect, it was meticulously restored by Lee and Beth Davis. Inside are Victorian touches like tin ceilings and some stained glass; tavern, parlor, dining room, and six comfortable guest rooms with private baths, one with a working fireplace. $140 double occupancy, MAP includes a five-course dinner and afternoon tea, as well as breakfast. The Antiques Shop is in the attached barn. Located midway between Londonderry, Weston, and Chester, it's off by itself with some fine walks and cross-country skiing out the back door.

DINING OUT   **The Old Tavern** (843-2231), Grafton, serves lunch, dinner, and Sunday brunch in the formal dining rooms or in the more casual sun room. The menu includes a baked cheddar turnover as an appetizer, and such entrées as chicken breast stuffed with pecans and Vermont goat cheese, grilled quail with currant BBQ sauce, venison stew, and buffalo rib-eye steak. Lunches are under $10, and there's a winter series of Renaissance Sunday Brunches featuring recitals. The dinner menu is traditional New England with a Continental touch: Green Mountain lamb chops and New England lobster pie, but there is also Colonial quail (three quail grilled and served with sour sherry sauce). Entrées $15–22.

The Inn at Long Last (875-2444), Chester, is open to the public for dinner Tuesday–Saturday. Chef Michael Williams recommends, from the extensive menu, pumpkin bisque with fried leeks and maple crème fraiche, panfried swordfish medallions with lemon-pepper crust and tomato-olive relish, or roasted venison leg with blackberry-sage sauce and beachplum compote; $14–20.

Leslie's (463-4929), Rockingham. Conveniently placed a short distance off the interstate, this one-time tavern with seven fireplaces and a Dutch oven serves lunch and dinner daily. There's a selection of beef entrées, including Leslie's Combo (sautéed shrimp and a seven-ounce sirloin), plus seafood (Cajun seafood stuffed shrimp) and such specialties as veal Zurichoise and Leslie's Alfredo (strips of chicken breast sautéed with garlic, tomatoes, mushrooms, parmesan, and cream served over fettucini). Entrées $12.95–20.00.

Joy Wah (463-9761), Rockingham Road (Route 5), Bellows Falls. Full-service Chinese fare in a Victorian farmhouse perched on a knoll overlooking the Connecticut River; includes all the familiar dishes on its lengthy menu. Open daily for lunch and dinner. Well under $20.

Saxtons River Inn (869-2110), Saxtons River. Dinner is à la carte, with a wide choice of entrées, ranging from seafood fettucini and vegetable lasagna to stuffed lobster tails and filet steak with roasted hazelnuts. Note: This is a favored dining spot before productions at the Saxtons River Playhouse. Entrées $14–20.

EATING OUT   **Raspberries and Tyme** (875-4486), on the Green, Chester (where the Deli used to be), serves delectable breakfasts 8–11, lunch 11:30–3. and tea 3–4. Closed Monday and Tuesday.

Beverly Restaurant & White Parrot Lounge (875-2400), on the Green, Chester. Open for dinner daily except Tuesdays; entrées $8.95–13.95, including a fine salad bar featuring shrimp.

Diamond Jim's (875-4040), Route 103 south, Chester, steak and seafood nightly from 4:30, Sunday 12 noon–8, in a cheerful new spot.

Delaney's Country Girl Diner, junction of Routes 11 and 103, Chester, is a homey, popular spot open Monday–Saturday 5:30 AM–8 PM, Sunday 7 AM–8 PM.

Miss Bellows Falls Diner, 90 Rockingham Street, Route 5, downtown Bellows Falls, is one of the few remaining Worcester Lunch Cars, and as such is on the National Register of Historic Places. Open Monday–Saturday 5 AM–9 PM, Sunday 6 AM–9 PM, it serves customary roadside fare and a few specials, like American chop suey.

SELECTIVE SHOPPING   **Grafton Village Cheese Co.** (843-2221), Grafton Village. You cannot tour this exceedingly tidy operation, but you can look through the large viewing window and watch the cheese being made. The shop, open Monday–Friday 9–4, and Saturdays from June 1 to October 21, sells its Covered Bridge Cheddar (the covered bridge has been positioned out back). It is milder than Cabot or Crowley cheese and comes both plain and sage.

Grafton Village Store (843-2348), Grafton, combines staples and convenience with Vermont crafts, syrup, cheese, and an upscale room

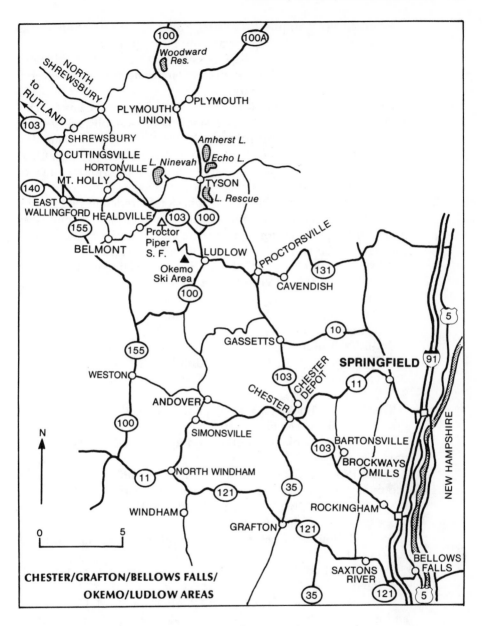

CHESTER/GRAFTON/BELLOWS FALLS/
OKEMO/LUDLOW AREAS

full of "Goodjam" products—vinegars, herbs, old and new kitchenware.

Tickle Your Fancy Gifts (843-2384), Main Street, Grafton. Open daily in summer and fall; otherwise by appointment. This is a great trove of lamps, shades, placemats, stationery, and unusual gifts; worth a stop.

Pickle Street Antiques (843-2203), Route 121 east, Grafton, stocks country furniture, folk art, tinware, quilts, and collectibles.

Wildacre Enterprises (843-2324), Grafton, offers custom cabinetry with one-of-a-kind and limited production furniture, using rosewood, black walnut, ebony, and bubinga.

Carpenter's Emporium (875-3267), on the Green in Chester. This 1870s store no longer houses Flamstead (a long-established clothing company), although in the summer of 1989, there were still a number of the distinctive Flamstead silk-screened skirts and dresses at bargain prices (upstairs); now the large store is filled with a variety of basic clothing, also notions, games, soaps, toys.

The National Survey (875-2121), Chester. Founded in 1912 by two sons of Chester's Baptist minister, the National Survey publishes maps for many states, foreign governments, industries, and groups throughout the world. In their Charthouse store—which occupies the ground floor of a lacy Victorian house on Main Street—you can find maps, books about Vermont, arts and crafts supplies. Open Monday–Friday 9–5, Saturday 10–4.

Brick Cottage Collectibles (875-3431), Route 11 east, Chester, stocks antiques and used books.

Bonnie's Bundles (875-2114), Stone Village, Route 103, Chester; and Townshend Road, Grafton. A doll-lover's find. More than 100 original, handcrafted stuffed dolls. Open daily February–December 9–5; Sundays 1–5.

Misty Valley Books (875-3400), on the Green, Chester, is a bright, growing, well-stocked bookshop where browsing is encouraged and which sponsors book-and-author readings. Open daily except Monday.

Weird Wood (875-3535), Route 11, Chester, connected to the Green Mountain Log Homes center, has racks of cherry, butternut, pine, maple, walnut, redwood, teak, rosewood, and even cherry burls for wood carvers and do-it-yourself projects.

Forlie-Ballou (875-2090), Chester. Upscale women's clothes, accessories, and gifts.

Oak Unlimited, Route 103, Chester, offers furniture and marvelous, handcarved animals.

Silver and Leather Tack (875-4527), off Main Street, Chester, has an impressive array of fine saddles, bridles, polo mallets, and other gear for the horsey set, plus silver jewelry.

Country Treasures (875-4377), on the Chester Green, open Wednesday–Sunday, is a snappy shop for quilts, wall hangings, folk art, dried flowers, with a Christmas corner.

Stonehouse Village (875-4477), Route 103 south, Chester, is a recently opened antiques mall with 125 dealers and a touristy collection of country crafts.

Vermont Country Store, Rockingham Village. An offshoot of the famous Vermont Country Store in Weston, this is also owned by Lyman Orton and actually houses his common cracker machine, which visitors can watch stamping out the hard round biscuits. The store also sells whole-grain breads and cookies baked here, along with a line of calico material, soapstone griddles, woodenware gadgets, natural-fiber clothing, and much more; there is an upstairs bargain room.

Big Red Barn, Route 5, south of Bellows Falls. Four floors of a 150-year-old barn are filled with baskets, candles, Vermont products, souvenirs, antiques. Open year-round.

Jelly Bean Tree (869-2326), Saxtons River. A craft cooperative run by several local artisans and carrying the work of many more on consignment: pottery, macramé, leather, weaving, batik, hand-sewn, knit, and crocheted items. Open daily 12–5.

ART GALLERIES   **Gallery North Star** (843-2465), Grafton. There are six rooms in this Grafton Village house, all hung with landscapes and graphic prints of birds, horses, and other animals, most of them by Mel Hunter whose atelier in the back is also open to visitors. Hunter specializes in minutely detailed graphic prints. Hunter's signed, limited graphics, which he prints on the premises, are priced from $125 up.

Thistledown Gallery (843-2340), Grafton (next to the Old Tavern). Open Memorial Day through October for New England crafts and fine art.

Crow Hill Gallery (875-3763), Flamstead Road, Chester, shows the work of Jeanne Carbonetti and other local artists.

Chester Art Guild, located across the road from the Chester Inn, is open June–October daily, except Mondays, 2–5.

ANTIQUES   Antique stores are particularly thick in this area. In Grafton, they include **Gabriel's Barn Antiques** at Woodchuck Hill Farm (843-2398), **Woodshed Antiques** (843-2365), **Frank E. Jones** (843-2424). In Saxtons River: **Studio Antiques** (869-2326), **Agape Antiques** (869-2273), **Sign of the Raven** (869-2500), and **Schoolhouse Antiques** (869-2332). In Chester: **Chester House Antiques** (875-2871), **Bill Lindsey** (875-2671), and **Lamplighter Antiques** (875-2612).

ENTERTAINMENT   **Saxtons River Playhouse** (869-2960), stages summer-long musicals and popular plays, Monday–Saturday at 8:30 PM; Sunday at 2.

The Green Mountain Festival Series (875-4473), based in Chester, presents concerts, magicians, and touring companies like the National Theater of the Deaf, staged in the Green Mountain Union High School auditorium.

SPECIAL EVENTS   February: **Chester Winter Carnival**.

July: In Chester, **St. Josephs Carnival, Horse Show and Community Picnic, Congregational Country Fair**. In Bellows Falls, **The Ver-**

mont State Certified Championship Old Time Fiddlers Contest.

August: In Chester, **Outdoor Art Show**. In Rockingham (first weekend in August), **Old Rockingham Days**, a full weekend of events–dancing, live entertainment, sidewalk dining, contests, fireworks.

MEDICAL EMERGENCY   Chester (875-3200); Bellows Falls, Grafton, Rockingham (463-4223); Gassetts (875-3200).

Health Center at Bellows Falls (463-3903), Bellows Falls.

Okemo Mountain/Ludlow Area

In contrast to all other Vermont ski towns, Ludlow is neither a tiny picturesque village nor a long-established resort. It boomed with the production of "shoddy" (fabric made from reworked wool) after the Civil War, a period frozen in the red brick of its commercial block, Victorian mansions, magnificent library, and academy (now the Black River Museum). In the wake of the wool, the General Electric Company moved into the steepled mill at the heart of town and kept people employed making small aircraft engine parts until 1977. Cashmere is still produced in the town's old Jewel Brook Mill, and an assortment of small industries has opened in the new Dean Brown Industrial Park. Ludlow is, furthermore, a crossroads market town, with stores supplying most of the needs for the small surrounding towns.

Ludlow also has 3,300-foot-high Okemo Mountain rising right from its heart. The ski area here dates from 1956, but until recently, it was a sleeper—a big mountain with antiquated lifts on the edge of a former mill town. Ski clubs nested in the Victorian homes, and a few inns catered to serious skiers.

Since 1982, however, when Tim and Diane Mueller bought Okemo, the old T-bars and Poma lifts have all been replaced with fast-moving, high-capacity chair lifts. Snow-making equipment and more than two dozen trails have been added, along with hundreds of condominiums. A total of 2,400 people can presently bed down on the mountain—which has doubled its number of patrons in as many years.

The effect on Ludlow has been dramatic. The old General Electric plant has been turned into condominiums, inns have multiplied, and the fire chief has tacked a tidy motel onto the back of his house. Local dining options now include a choice of six-course gourmet meals, as well as well-sauced dishes, and stained-glass atmosphere at Nikki's, and pasta at Valente's (where Mama pinches a child's cheek and tells him to "eata the meatballs").

Summer visitors tend to own or rent cottages on Lake Pauline, Reservoir Pond, or Lake Rescue. Lake Ninevah and Echo and Amherst lakes are just north of the town line. There are also those who come for programs at Fletcher Farm Crafts School or come simply because Ludlow's location makes an ideal base from which to explore much of southern and central Vermont.

"The resort business is the number-one employer now," observes Bob Gilmore, owner of Nikki's. "But this is still a real town."

West from Ludlow, Route 103 climbs steeply in beautiful hill country, through Mount Holly to Belmont or Hortonville and Shrewsbury. A turnoff through Mount Holly and Hortonville will be rewarded with spectacular views of the surrounding hills.

North from Ludlow, Route 100 links together the chain of lakes. South from town, it climbs Terrible Mountain for nine full miles before its descent into Weston. To the east, Route 131 follows the Black River through the picturesque mill villages of Proctorsville and Cavendish. Route 103 follows the Williams River to Chester. Handy to Weston, Grafton, Killington, and numerous activities, Ludlow is just far enough from everywhere to retain its own unmistakable identity.

GUIDANCE **Ludlow Area Chamber of Commerce** (228-5830), Ludlow 05149. A walk-in information office in the Jewell Brook Plaza, Route 100/ 103, in the middle of the village, is filled with menus, events listings, and lodging brochures, staffed daily in summer, also on weekends in winter. During foliage and winter seasons, however, the job of lodging visitors shifts to the **Okemo Mt. Lodging Service** (228-5571 or 800-78-OKEMO) at Okemo Mountain.

GETTING THERE By bus: Vermont Transit offers direct service from Boston, via Bellows Falls for New York and Connecticut, from Rutland for points north and west.

TO SEE AND DO **Black River Academy Historical Museum** (228-5050), Ludlow. Open Memorial Day–Columbus Day, Wednesday–Sunday 12–4. A steepled, brick school building, built in 1889. The academy's reputation drew students from throughout New England. One large room is dedicated to President Calvin Coolidge, class of 1890. Other rooms in the four-floor building are filled with exhibits about mining, lumbering, railroading, farming, and other segments in the history of the Black River Valley. Children and donations are welcome.

Joseph Cerniglia Winery, Inc. (226-7575; 800-654-6382), Winery Road, Proctorsville 05153. The winery is open daily 10–5 year-round; gift shop. There are tours every 15 minutes, and wine tastings constantly. The wines are premium apple varietal and won prizes at the Indiana State Fair and at the International Eastern Wine Competition.

Fletcher Library, Ludlow (Monday–Friday 10–5:30; Saturday 10–1, 6:30–8:30). One of Vermont's most beautiful town libraries: reading rooms contain marble inlays; fireplaces; old-style, green-shaded lights; and century-old paintings of local landscapes.

Cavendish Historical Society Museum, Cavendish. Open June–October, Sunday 2–5, housed in the former Baptist Church; this is a collection of weaving implements, old photographs, farm tools, articles used or made in Cavendish, changing exhibits, and a lecture program.

Mt. Holly Community Historical Museum, Belmont, open in July and August, Sundays 2–4. Even if it isn't open, the exercise of finding this appealing little museum is worthwhile. It sits just downhill from the center of the village of Belmont, as picturesque a village as any to be found in Vermont. The general store is a classic, and Star Lake is a great place for a swim.

SUGARHOUSE   Green Mountain Sugar House (228-7151), Route 100, four miles north of Ludlow. You can watch syrup being produced at this roadside sugarhouse in March and April; maple candy is made throughout the year on a weekly basis. Gift and produce shop open 9–6 "most of the time."

FISHING   Public access has been provided to Lake Rescue, Echo Lake, Lake Ninevah, Woodward Reservoir, and Amherst Lake. Fishing licenses are required (even for canoeing on these lakes), and this is strictly enforced. The catch includes rainbow trout, bass, pickerel. There is also fly fishing in the Black River.

BACK ROAD TOURS   Vermont Backroad Tours (226-7910), Box 64, Carlton Road, Cavendish. The Phillips family offer tours, June–mid-October, 9–4 Monday, Tuesday, Saturday, and Sunday. Tours frequently include the Crown Point Military Road, Cavendish Gorge, visits to local craftspeople, and a soapstone factory. $35 per person per day.

BICYCLING AND WALKING   Cycle Inn Vermont (228-8799), Box 243, Ludlow 05149-0243. Five inns in and around Ludlow combine to offer a flexible, self-guided service for bikers. It includes route planning, luggage transport from inn to inn, bike rentals, and emergency assistance. You can tour for two days or two weeks, cycle or walk a few or 50 miles.

Bicycles can be rented from **Dunnett Ski Rentals** (228-7547).

BOATING   Echo Lake Inn (228-8602) rents canoes and other boats. Rentals are also available at Camp Plymouth State Park (see *Swimming*) and at Hawk at Salt Ash (see "Killington").

HORSEBACK RIDING   Holly Hills Trails (259-2650), Mount Holly. The same trails are used for riding and cross-country skiing. $15 per person per hour.

Trail rides are also offered at **Salt Ash Stables** (see "Killington").

GOLF   Fox Run Resort (228-8871), Ludlow. A nine-hole course with a restaurant, lounge.

SWIMMING   The **Town Recreation Area** on West Hill includes a man-made beach (with lifeguard) on a small, spring-fed reservoir; also a snack bar and playground/picnic area.

Buttermilk Falls, near the junction of Routes 100 and 103. There is a swimming hole off Route 103. Turn at the VFW post just west of the intersection.

Camp Plymouth State Park, off Route 100 at Tyson. Beach on Echo Lake, picnic area, food concession.

TENNIS   **Town Recreation Park** on West Hill (end of Pond Street). Two courts available to the public.

CROSS-COUNTRY SKIING   **Fox Run Ski Touring Center** (228-8871), junction Routes 100 and 103, Ludlow. A café and rental shop are surrounded by the open roll of the golf course; there are also wooded and mountain trails adding up to 20 km, most of it tracked; guided tours.

Holly Hill Trails (259-2650), Mount Holly.

DOWNHILL SKIING   **Okemo** (228-4041/snow reports 228-5222), Ludlow. "Rip Van Mountain" is the image Okemo is presently projecting: a BIG mountain (boasting Vermont's fourth highest vertical drop) that's been sleeping since the fifties but is making up for lost time. Okemo is now a big destination mountain with a small resort feel. The trails are easily accessible. Just beyond the middle of town, you turn up a short access road to a relatively small parking lot. You walk through a hotel complex, find a smallish base lodge, and are off on a fast-moving chair lift (no wait). Surprises begin at the top of these lifts, where you meet a wall of three-story condominiums and find your way down to the spacious Sugar House base lodge from which the true size of the mountain becomes apparent. This is a mountain of many parts. Beginners and lower intermediate skiers can enjoy not only the lower southwest but also the upper northeast sides of the mountain—entirely different places in view and feel. From the summit, beginners can actually run a full 4½ miles to the base. Expert skiers, on the other hand, have the entire northwestern face of the mountain, served by its own chair. There are also a number of wide, central fall line runs down the face of Okemo. Basically, however, this is upper intermediate heaven, with literally dozens of trails with varying terrain. We became addicted to Upper and Lower World Cup, a long and steep but forgiving run with sweeping views across the Black River Valley to the Connecticut River. Solitude Peak, with eight totally snow-covered trails served by a quad chair, is another haven.

Lifts: Five quad chairs, three triple chairs, and two surface lifts.

Trails and slopes: 71—30 percent novice, 50 percent intermediate, 20 percent expert.

Vertical drop: 2,150 feet.

Snow-making: Covers 90 percent of trails, some with top-to-bottom snow.

Facilities: Base lodge with cafeteria; mid-mountain Sugar House base lodge with cafeteria; Beach House snack bar just below summit; two restaurants, hotel, rental shops, nursery, condo lodging.

Ski school: 150 instructors, ATM (American Teaching Method), Nastar races, outstanding childrens' programs—SKIwee for ages 4–8 and Young Mountain Explorers for ages 8–12.

Rates: $72 for two-day weekend adult ticket, $42 per weekend day; many packages.

LODGING   Okemo Mt. Lodging Service (228-5571 or 800-78-OKEMO) refers less than half its inquiries to slope-side condominiums. A wide variety of inns can be found within a 10-mile radius. (Note: This seems to be the one resort area in New England in which most lodging places add a 15 percent service charge to rates.) Also see *Guidance.*

COUNTRY INNS   *In Ludlow 05149* ☞**The Okemo Inn** (228-8834), Route 100, open except for two weeks in April and November. Ron Perry has been here longer than any other local innkeeper, and this 1810 home is well kept, effortlessly welcoming. There are 11 nicely furnished guest rooms, most with two double beds and private bath. There is a living room with a table made from old bellows in front of the hearth and a dining room with low, notched beams; also a TV room with color cable. Travel- or ski-weary muscles can be soothed in the sauna or summertime pool; 10-speed bike rentals and guide maps available. $65–85 per person MAP in winter, $45–55 B&B in the summer. Add 15 percent for service.

The Andrie Rose Inn (228-4846), 13 Pleasant Street, is on a quiet back street with surprisingly good views of Okemo. This is a turn-of-the-century house in which the old detailing has been carefully preserved, but the feel—thanks to bold flowery prints, pastel colors, and skylights—is light-filled and cheering. The 10 guest rooms have private baths (5 with whirlpool baths and some with good old clawfoot tubs) and antique iron or wood beds. Small details like a basket "of things you may need," fresh flowers, bathroom amenities, and complimentary hors d'oeuvres all add to the sense of someplace special; five-course continental dinners ($30–50) are available on weekends. $70–110 per couple includes a full breakfast buffet. Add 15 percent service charge.

Echo Lake Inn (228-8602 or 800-356-6844), Route 100 in Tyson, but the mailing address is Ludlow. One of the few survivors of the many Victorian-style summer hotels (although parts of the building are older) that once graced Vermont lakes, the inn is four-stories tall with a long, white porch, lined in summer with pink geraniums and red rockers. Now winterized, it offers 26 rooms, 12 with bath. There are six condo units in the adjacent building. The cheapest rooms are under the eaves on the fourth floor, a find for families. The top price is for spacious suites with antiques. The living room is homey and informal, with hooked rugs and wooden chairs grouped around the fireplace and TV. There's also an inviting Stoned Tavern and a low-beamed dining room, both open to the public. Summer facilities include tennis and swimming in the pool or at the private beach on Echo Lake across the road, where rental boats and canoes are available to guests. No smoking in guest rooms. $55–75 per person MAP. Add 15 percent for service.

The Governor's Inn (228-8830), 86 Main Street, open except in April. William Wallace Stickney, governor of Vermont from 1900–1902, built this fine Victorian house with its ornate slate, hand-painted fireplaces. The eight guest rooms, all with private baths, are smallish but antique-filled, coated with flowery paper, windows fitted with country curtains. Guests find cordials and other nice touches next to their quilt-covered beds. There is a small pub and game room as well as the elegant living room and dining room, open to the public, featuring a table d'hote menu of six courses (see *Dining Out*); five-course breakfasts and tea are served in a cheery back room, "warmed by the sun and a woodstove." $170–180 double occupancy, MAP; add 15 percent for service, B&B rates also available. No smoking.

Black River Inn (228-5585), 100 Main Street. A fine, 1835 Federal-style home with hand-carved, oak staircases and marble fireplaces is now a very gracious inn. Boasting Ludlow's first indoor tub and a carved bed in which Lincoln slept, it offers 10 antique-furnished guest chambers, eight with private bath. Facilities also include a Jacuzzi and game room. Rates are $70–95 per couple B&B; singles from $55. Children welcome; dinners available by reservation.

Ginger Place (228-3000), 1000 South Main Street. Gerard and Virginia Snyder's nineteenth-century farmhouse sits right on the road but offers some standout rooms, notably the family space with four beds adjoining the family's own playroom (where guest children are welcome). There's also an East Wing Suite with two bedrooms, a living room and kitchen. Lace, quilts, and antiques throughout. Our only reservations are about the two downstairs, roadside rooms.

In Proctorsville 05153   **The Golden Stage Inn** (226-7744), PO Box 218, open except April and November. Under Kristen Murphy and Marcel Perret, this inn is a find, offering exceptional food and elegantly comfortable rooms. Built as a stage stop in 1796, this spacious, white clapboard house also served as a stop on the Underground Railroad and as home for actress and writer Cornelia Otis Skinner. There are six guest rooms with private baths, four that share two baths. There are antique quilts on the beds, rockers where you want them. The large, plant-filled living room is lined with books round a cheery fireplace. For summer, there is an outdoor pool set in four acres of rolling lawns; note the borders of varicolored shrub roses and many perennial beds, as well as a large herb garden from which Marcel culls seasonings. Both are former professionals in the food business.

Dinner is a five-course gourmet event, along with evening hors d'oeuvres and a full breakfast in the $135–145 per room rate. Add 15 percent for service.

Castle Inn (226-7222), Box 157, open except for November and mud season. Built in 1904 by Allen Fletcher, another Vermont governor, this is a truly palatial stone mansion with an abundance of mahogany and oak paneling, ten hearths, elaborately carved ceilings and mantels. An inn since 1964, it offers ten guest rooms, eight with private baths. Breakfast is served to guests, dinner is open to the public (see *Dining Out*); $75–90 per person MAP. The hot tub and sauna operate year-round, and the new pool and tennis court are open in the summer. Add 15 percent service charge.

Okemo Lantern Lodge (226-7770), Box 247, a former mill owner's mansion, rich in ornately carved butternut and stained glass. The dining room takes center stage downstairs, and it's usually filled with aromas from the adjacent kitchen. The ten guest rooms are on the small side, but all have private baths; our favorites are on the third floor. $65 per person MAP; $45 B&B. Add 15 percent service charge. Pool. Public dining by reservation.

BED & BREAKFASTS   *In the hills to the west of Ludlow.*

☞**Maple Crest Farm** (492-3367), Box 120, Cuttingsville 05738. This handsome, white brick farmhouse sits high on a ridge in the old hilltop center of Shrewsbury. It was built in 1808 as Gleason's Tavern and is still in the same family. In the 1860s, they began taking in guests and have done so off and on ever since. The Smiths offer bed and breakfast in four antique-filled rooms at $50 per couple ($25 single) and in two charming apartments ($65), which can accommodate small families. "Every piece of furniture has a story," Donna Smith says—and she knows the story. Ask about a rocking chair or spool bed, and you will begin to sense who has lived in this unusual house down through the years. Books and magazines are everywhere, and if you look closely, you'll see they're carefully selected, focusing on local and Vermont tales and history. The Smiths are noted for the quality of their maple syrup, produced in the sugarhouse at the peak of the hill; the same sweeping view can be enjoyed in winter on cross-country skis. You can walk off in any number of directions.

The Buckmaster Inn (492-3485), Lincoln Hill Road, Shrewsbury Center 05738, was built as the Buckmaster Tavern on a hilltop in 1801. Actually, it's right across from the Maple Crest Inn, and the two handsome B&Bs continue to compete in a friendly way. This gracious house is owned by Sam and Grace Husselman, and it accommodates six guests in spacious, comfortable rooms. There are two living rooms, one with an organ, another with a TV and fireplace, and you will have no trouble finding something to read. The Husselmans are warm hosts who can tell you where to hike. Rates are $50 double for a room with a shared bath, $60 for the room with private bath, and $40 single; breakfast specialties include Grace's cranberry or banana bread and blueberry muffins.

The Parmenter House (259-2009), PO Box 106, Belmont 05730. This is a very Victorian house in a small, unusually picturesque village just off the beaten track. The house retains its Victorian detailing, including a handsome mantel made from local marble, but it has been opened to take advantage of its rear view out over Star Lake. The four guest rooms are furnished with appropriate antiques. Children welcome, bikes and canoes available. $65–95.

Hortonville Inn (259-2587), off Route 103 in Hortonville, RFD 1, Mount Holly 05758. This large white house sits high on a hill and, along with the classic church across the road, forms the center (in fact, about all there is) of Hortonville. Two rooms have private baths; the other three share another. Each room has a VCR; 250 tapes on hand. There's a swimming pool, and you can rent a horse or bikes. The views are magnificent, and there are 13 acres out back with trails cut for hiking and cross-country skiing. The summer rates of $50–60 per couple (foliage and winter, $65–75) include a three-course breakfast, nightly wine and hors d'oeuvres, herbal teas, and coffee with cookies on tap all day.

The Leslie Place (259-2903), Box 62, Belmont 05730. We came to Belmont looking for the Leslie Place and couldn't find it. No one in this tiny village knew where it was. The old farmhouse that Mary Gorman has restored (there were no baths, no plumbing or electricity when Mary bought it 16 years ago) features a three-bedroom apartment with its own delightful living room, fully equipped kitchen, and private entrance. There's also a spacious room (it can sleep four) on the other side of the house above Mary's living space, which she cheerfully shares along with advice on where to walk on the 100 rolling acres and beyond. $45–50 single, $44–65 double B&B; the apartment begins at $35 per person. No smoking or guests.

Austria Haus (259-2441), Box 2, Mount Holly 05758 (off Route 103). A century-old farmhouse surrounded by 100 acres, it offers four guest rooms, two with private bath, grand views, and cross-country skiing outside the door. $32 single, $45–50 double with full breakfast.

MOTEL   **Best Western Ludlow Colonial Motel** (228-8188), 93 Main Street, Ludlow 05149. A few years ago, Fire Chief Rick Harrison built a 14-unit motel unit onto the back of his 1825 home, and he built it well. His wife Betty Ann tastefully decorated the standard rooms (two double beds, air conditioning, cable TV with HBO, phone) and family suites; with pool and garden. They added a two-bedroom unit with a full bath and living room in their home, then built another building full of condominiums next door and remodeled two old houses at the other end of the village (near the Okemo access road) into more condominiums. Everything is nicely done and reasonably priced. Prices are $43–53 midweek, $73–83 weekend. (The condos are not part of the Best Western chain.) Less in summer.

CONDOMINIUMS   **Okemo Mountain Lodge** (228-5571), RFD 1, Ludlow 05149. This three-story condo hotel at the entrance to the area is really a cluster of 76 one-bedroom condos, each with a sleeping couch in the living room. There's a compact kitchen with eating counter and a fireplace, enough space for a couple and two children. $170–270 per night per couple in winter, many packages; less in summer.

Kettle Brook Condominiums at Okemo, same phone and address as the lodge. Salted along trails, units range from efficiencies to three-bedroom units, nicely built. $135–230 per couple in winter, many packages, less in summer.

Winterplace, same phone and address as the lodge. These are Okemo's luxury condominiums, set high on a mountain shelf with access to an indoor pool and, in summer, tennis courts. From $260–395 for four people in winter, less in summer.

Okemo Trailside Condominiums (228-8255), PO Box 165, Ludlow 05149. Scattered along the Lower Sachem Trail, many of these condos date back more than 15 years; the 100-acre development is under different management from Okemo Mountain. There are some 200 one- to four-bedroom units, half of them in the rental pool.

The Mill (228-5566), 145 Main Street, Ludlow 05149. The town's beautiful, centerpiece mill (see the introduction) has been converted into one- to three-room condo units. These are attractive but rather dark rooms with back balconies overlooking the Black River. Offers the advantage of being able to walk to all amenities in town. $62–247 depending on time; five days from $250–740.

Strictly Rentals (228-3000), 1000 South Street, Ludlow. This service, based at Ginger Place, represents 40 seasonal and 150 short-term rentals ranging from lakeside summer cottages to winter condominiums. $70–375 per day in winter.

Country Home Management (259-2682), in Belmont, represents a range of rentals priced from $125 per night and $450 per week in winter.

Tiki & Associates (228-3500), Ludlow, manages rental properties ranging from condos to farmhouses, good for all seasons.

SELF-IMPROVING VACATIONS   **Fletcher Farm** (228-8770), Ludlow 05149. Operated since 1948 by the Society of Vermont Craftsmen, this old farm on the eastern edge of town offers dorm-style lodging, pleasant studio and relaxing space, and June–October programs (basically two-week sessions) in weaving, spinning, potting, other crafts, art, and folk dancing. Meals are family-style. The store sells handcrafted items, art and craft supplies.

Green Mountain at Fox Run (228-8885 or 800-448-8106), Box 164,

Ludlow 05149. A former resort and, for the past 19 years, "an educational community for weight and health management." This was one of the first anti-diet programs in the country and continues to attract clients from 50 states and many foreign countries. With the exception of the months of January and February, Fox Run offers one to four week-long programs that offer a daily regimen of exercise and lectures with a remarkably high success rate. From $1,075 for one week.

DINING OUT   **Nikki's** (228-7797), Sunshine Market Place, Ludlow. Open for dinner and Sunday brunch. Positioned at the foot of Okemo's access road, this is one of Vermont's most pleasant restaurants. Bob Gilmore has been in business for more than a dozen years now, and the dining areas and menu have continued to evolve. The dining rooms are up-and-down spaces with plenty of stained and beveled glass, exposed wood and brick, booths, with-it prints and naperies. You can choose a casual corner and order off the bistro menu or go for the linen-dressed tables and a special, like shrimp mousse with seafood cream. The chocolate-mandarine entremet with hazelnut-praline sauce, incidentally, came in first one year in the Taste of Vermont. Children's menu available. Entrées $9.95–19.95.

Golden Stage Inn (226-7744), Proctorsville (between Route 103 and 131). The dining rooms are attractive, and the food is receiving rave reviews. Innkeepers Marcel Perret and Kristen Murphy were both formerly "flavor experts" employed by a national company. They grow most of their vegetables, fruit, berries, and herbs. Marcel is the entrée chef, and Kristen supervises the baking and desserts. A much abridged sample menu features potato chervil soup with Pernod to begin and includes salmon steaks with chive sauce, tortellini with pesto, lime sorbet with gin, chicken prosciutto in cream sauce with fresh sage, and a walnut tart. Prix fixe, moderate to expensive. Reservations must be made by 11 AM for the 7 PM serving.

The Governor's Inn (228-8830), 86 Main Street, Ludlow. Owned by Chef Deedy Marble and her husband Charlie, this is Ludlow's most famous restaurant. Dinner, by reservation only, is served every day except Tuesday and begins at 6 PM with hot hors d'oeuvres and cocktails served in the parlor. Guests then move on to the Victorian dining rooms where they are served by waitresses in period dress. Each evening's menu and its price is fixed. You might begin with sherried apricot soup and feast on the Governor's braised quail. Prix fixe $35.

Echo Lake Inn (228-8602), Route 100 north in Tyson. Open to the public for breakfast, lunch, and dinner. The dining room with its print wallpaper and mauves is attractive, and Phil and Kathy Cocco have developed quite a following. Dining options usually include roast country duckling, sautéed veal medallions, artichoke hearts, tomato, garlic and pinenuts finished with a demiglace; also boneless chicken filled with goat cheese and prosciutto topped with a lingonberry sauce. There are also nightly fish, pasta, and house specials. A friend recommends Kathy's chocolate decadence with raspberry sauce. Entrées $12.95–16.95.

Harry's Cafe (259-2996), Route 103, Mount Holly, open 5–10 Tuesday–Sunday. At this writing, Harry's is the hottest dining and eating out spot between Weston and Killington. Trip Pierce took the funky old Backside Restaurant and turned it into a light, airy space with good art and a woodstove. "It's open season on whatever you want to eat," is the way Pierce describes the wildly ecclectic menu: Thai-style teriyaki and red curry, shrimp and tortellini, fish and chips, and New York sirloin. Specialties include "Flauta": grilled steak or chicken thinly sliced, wrapped with lots of jack cheese and onion in a flour tortilla, topped with more cheese and baked until golden; served with salsa and sour cream. Another favorite is Fritto Misto: a platter of deep-fried shrimp, scallops, and fish in a crispy batter served with fresh angel hair pasta with basil marinara. Dinner entrées are $9.95–13.95, but you can also dine on tapas like chicken and ginger wantons or Thai clear noodle salad. Cheeseburgers, pizza, and big burritos are also available all day.

Priority's (228-2800), Okemo Mountain Resort. Housed right under the clock tower at the entrance to Okemo, a bright, spacious area with delightfully deep booths for lunch and a variety of spaces for dinner; also a sports bar and live music and dancing (no cover) on weekends. House specialties include chicken and steak teriyaki and seafood fettucini Alfredo. It's a large menu ranging from fish and chips to prime rib. Great burgers, burritos, and pizza at lunch. Entrées $5.95–14.95.

Castle Inn (226-7222), Ludlow. The interior of this stone mansion is a rich blend of American oak, Mexican mahogany, and French marble. Before dinner, guests are invited to meet in the library for cocktails, then to move to the paneled dining room for a five-course meal that can commence with pâté or escargots and include roast duckling or veal scalloppine. Moderate to expensive.

Michael's Seafood and Steak House (228-5622), Main Street, Ludlow. A large old dining landmark with a large, upscale pub. Open for dinner nightly with midweek specials, a Sunday buffet lunch. Groups are a specialty here. You might order pasta and sausage, stuffed flounder, coq au vin, or seafood Newburg for six ($29.95–48.95).

DJ's Restaurant (228-5374), 146 Main Street, Ludlow. Open from 4:30 for dinner. A former downtown eatery that's been upscaled, this place is best known for its broiled scallops and shrimp, extensive salad bar, and nightly specials. Moderately priced.

EATING OUT   **The Hatchery** (228-8654), Main Street at the stoplight, Ludlow, open 5 AM–3. A storefront coffee shop with a café atmosphere; great for breakfast omelets or pancakes, for luncheon quiche or soups.

Pot Belly Pub (228-8989), 130 Main Street, Ludlow. Open for dinner nightly and lunch most days. First opened in a storefront in 1974, this zany place has expanded into a great space, good for live entertainment (swing and blues bands, jug band music, and rock'n'roll on weekends) and victuals ranging from popcorn shrimp or pot belly chicken or ribs to chocolate peanut butter pie. Belly burgers or the Cajun chicken sandwich are good bets at lunch, and you can always get a belly burger at dinner too or go for the pot belly ribs ($12.95) or Mexican chicken ($11.95).

Valente's Italian Restaurant (228-2671), Main Street, Ludlow. An old-fashioned, downtown restaurant, this is locally respected Italian food the way Mama makes it.

See Dining Out *for Harry's Cafe and Priority's*

SNACKS   **Sweet Surrender**, Sunshine Marketplace, Ludlow. Open from 5 AM to bake fresh doughnuts and breads; there are a few tables; coffee, cream soda, and papers are also sold.

Baba-à Louis Bakery (226-7178), corner of Depot Street and Route 131 in Proctorsville (across from the post office). Open 7–6, Tuesday–Saturday, it developed a wide following in Chester before moving to this location in 1984. Everything is made on the spot from fresh ingredients. The breads are outstanding, so are the croissants, the cheese twists, and a wide assortment of munchies.

SELECTIVE SHOPPING   In **Sunshine Marketplace** at the Okemo access road, check out **Mountain High** (228-5216), closed Tuesdays. Peter Manship's jewelry workshop has evolved into a two-story crafts gallery selling work by 55 craftspeople and artists, still featuring handmade jewelry.

The Quilt Patch and Cook's Cupboard, 140/160 Main Street, Ludlow. Two adjoining stores, the first specializes in customized creations, fabrics, and notions, and the second in cookware and gadgets with some reasonably priced antique furniture thrown in.

Singleton's Store, downtown Proctorsville. A long-established family business in the middle (it's not hard to find) of Proctorsville has kept abreast of the demands of the area's condo owners while continuing to cover the basics. Fine wines, choice meats, a standout deli, and a gun shop are all part of the scene; the specialty of the house is smoked meat (an average of 350 pounds of meat sold per day).

Wild Bill's Bargain Outlet, Proctorsville, open 10–6 daily and until 8 Fridays. Housed in the town's defunct old mill, a mishmash of genuine bargains. We always come away with something we didn't realize we needed.

Green Mountain Sugar House (228-7151), Route 100, four miles north of Ludlow. You can watch syrup being produced in March and April; maple candy is made throughout the year on a weekly basis. This is also a place to pick strawberries in June and July, to find freshly pressed cider in September; the gift and produce shop is open daily 9–6 "most of the time."

Vermont Industries Factory Store (800-826-4766, 492-3451), Route 103, Box 301, Cuttingsville, occupies a big barn full of hand-forged, wrought iron products—free-standing sundials, sconces, candle holders, corn driers, hanging planters, chandeliers, and a wide range of fireplace accessories. We could kick ourselves for not buying one of the distinctive floor or wall lamps that we have since seen selling for substantially more in other stores.

In Shrewsbury **W. E. Pierce General Store**, North Shrewsbury. Closed Sundays, otherwise open 7:30–6, located at a four corners at which signs point variously to Rutland 10, Cuttingsville 4, Shrewsbury Center 2, Bridgewater 9, Plymouth 9. Glendon and Marjorie Pierce carry on the business that their father Willie began in 1918. And Willie bought it from a cousin, so they can well claim that it's been in the family for 150 years. It remains one of the most genuine, old-fashioned, and beloved general stores in all Vermont. Stock has dwindled in recent years, but what the Pierces share with visitors is precious, priceless. "The counters used to be piled high with horse blankets, and the shelves were filled with syrup cans, everything farmers needed to keep their tractors running, canning jars," Glendon muses. "We used to sell a car-load of grain a week, and people would bring their own containers to take home the sugar, flour, and beans we kept in bulk. Years ago we used to keep open evenings, and the men would come in after working in the fields all day and play cards or checkers and talk until 8 or 9." It's easy to imagine the scene around the pot belly stove—which continues to heat the store. "Salada Tea" is still lettered in porcelain on the window, and the stereograph still clicks through a half-dozen pictures if you put in a penny.

Carrara's Mountain Country Store (492-3617), Shrewsbury. This new variety store is about a mile below Pierce's General Store, on the road back down to Shrewsbury Center. Larry Carrara keeps the hours and a full stock of staples that Marjorie and Glendon Pierce no longer fuss with. He also sells copies of his book, *A Moose for Jessica*, which photographs and narrates the famous love affair between a moose and one of Larry's cows. The moose hung around for many months between 1986 and 1987, and the story ran in papers across the country. The store also carries other Vermont books, products, and souvenirs.

Meadowsweet Herb Farm (492-3565), North Shrewsbury. The Herbshed attached to Polly Hayne's handsome old farmhouse on a back road (follow the signs) is a studio and retail shop in which herb wreaths, potpourri, and culinary blends are made from more than 175 herbs and scented geraniums. A number of perennial herbs and geraniums are grown year-round in the solar greenhouse and sold as seedlings and seeds. The farm and Renaissance Gardens are open daily, May–October, Monday–Saturday during November and December.

SPECIAL EVENTS   January: **Okemo Winter Carnival** is celebrated for nine days, including two weekends in the middle of the month; tug-of-war, tobogganing, snow sculpture contest, fireworks, ski races, torchlight parade, etc.

July 1: **Fletcher Farm Arts and Crafts Fair.**

July 4–Labor Day: Band concerts on the Green.

Labor Day weekend: **Game Fair and Outdoor Exposition.**

MEDICAL EMERGENCY   Ludlow (911); Cavendish (226-7283); Mount Holly (775-3133).

Black River Health Center (226-7262), Cavendish.

II. Upper Connecticut Valley

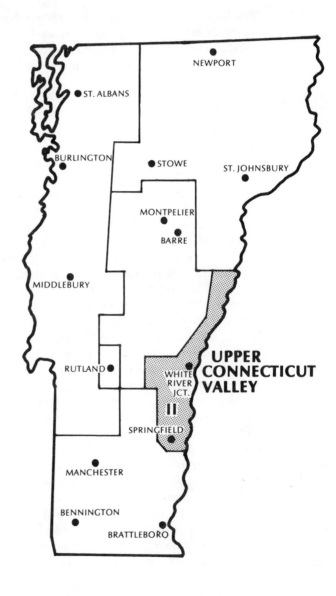

Upper Valley River Towns

The Upper Valley ignores state lines to form one of New England's most beautiful and distinctive regions. Its two dozen towns are scattered along both the Vermont and New Hampshire banks of the Connecticut River for some 20 miles north and south of Dartmouth College.

"Upper Valley" is a name coined in the 1950s by a local daily, *The Valley News*, to define its two-state circulation area. The label has stuck, interestingly enough, to the same group of towns that, back in the 1770s, tried to form the state of "New Connecticut." But the Dartmouth-based, pro–New Connecticut party was thwarted by larger powers, namely New York and New Hampshire, along with the strident Vermont independence faction, the Green Mountain Boys. On July 2, 1777, delegates met at Elijah West's tavern in Windsor to declare Vermont a "free and independent state," bounded on the east by the Connecticut River.

The Valley itself prospered, a fact that's obvious from the exquisite Federal-era meetinghouses and mansions still salted through this area. And while it has had its ups and downs, it is growing now far more quickly than either Vermont or New Hampshire.

Admittedly, there are far fewer bridges than there once were (from Springfield on the south to Newbury on the north, just ten out of dozens survive), but they include the longest covered bridge in the United States (connecting Windsor with Cornish), and the Upper Valley is still an undeniable entity.

The Upper Valley area phone book includes towns on both sides of the river (it's a local call back and forth, no area code needed), and Hanover's Dresden school district reaches well into Vermont. Several Independence Day parades start in one state and finish across the bridge in the other. And the Montshire Museum (which recently moved, lock, stock, and barrel, across the bridge from Hanover to Norwich) combines both states in its very name.

The cultural center of the Upper Valley remains Dartmouth Green (now graced with a major theater and museum) in Hanover. With the nearby medical complex and the West Lebanon shopping center strip (a popular escape route from Vermont sales tax), it forms a genuine hub, handy to the highways radiating, the way rail lines once did, from White River Junction.

Since the 1820s, the Valley's industrial center has been in Springfield and Windsor, both of which have produced far more than their share of inventors. And for a century, summer inns and camps have lined the shores of Lakes Morey and Fairlee.

Beyond these red brick towns and old resort enclaves, farms still spread comfortably along the river, all the way from Weathersfield Bow to Newbury. They are backed by steep hills, one of them (Mt. Ascutney) skiable. The stretch of both road (Route 5) and river north from Wilder Dam to the oxbow in Newbury offers unexpected vistas of the Presidentials in New Hampshire (New England's highest mountains). Inns cater to bicyclists and canoeists.

GETTING THERE   By car: Interstates 91 and 89 converge in the White River Junction, VT/Lebanon, NH, area, where they also meet Route 5 north and south on the Vermont side; Route 4, the main east-west highway through central Vermont; and Route 10, the river road on the New Hampshire side.

By bus: White River Junction is a hub for Greyhound/Vermont Transit (293-3011) service with express service to Boston. This is the hub of the area's bus transportation, also noteworthy in that it is one of New England's few pleasant bus stations with clean, friendly dining and snack rooms.

By air: The Lebanon (NH) Regional Airport has service to and from Boston and New York via **Business Express (Delta)** (603-298-5178, 800-345-3400) and **Northwest Airlines** (603-298-5651, 800-225-2525).

GUIDANCE   The *Connecticut River Valley Tourism Council* (800-544-NHVT) puts out a useful brochure listing members' services and attractions. A free "Dining Guide" to the area is published by Mammoth Enterprises, Box 61, Thetford 05074, and the glossy *Upper Valley Magazine* ($1.95 per copy) is available from 89 Main Street, West Lebanon, NH (603-298-5515).

The specific area information sources are: **Springfield Chamber of Commerce** (885-2779), 55 Clinton Street, Springfield 05156; open Monday–Friday 8–5.

Windsor Area Chamber of Commerce (674-5910), PO Box 5, Windsor 05089. The friendly walk-in information office in Windsor House is open Monday–Friday, 7–3 year-round.

Greater White River Chamber of Commerce (295-6200), PO Box 697, White River Junction 05001; office open weekdays 8–4:30.

TO SEE *Springfield* **Springfield Art & Historical Society** (885-2415), 9 Elm Street. Lodged in a Victorian mansion are collections of pewter, Bennington pottery, toys and dolls, primitive paintings, costumes, and periodic shows by area artists. Open May–mid-October, Tuesday–Saturday, varying times.

The Eureka Schoolhouse, Route 11, near I-91. The oldest (1790) schoolhouse left in the state. Open 9–4, mid-May–mid-October. Nearby is a century-old covered bridge.

Windsor **The American Precision Museum** (674-5781), South Main Street. An important, expanding collection of hand and machine tools, assembled in the 1846 Robbins, Kendall & Lawrence Armory, itself a National Historic Landmark. The firm became world famous in 1851 because of its displays of "the American system" of manufacturing interchangeable parts, especially for what became the renowned Enfield rifle. Open May 30–November 1, 9–5; $2 adults, $.75 children.

Old Constitution House, North Main Street. This is Elijah West's tavern (but not in its original location), where delegates gathered July 2, 1777, to adopt Vermont's constitution. It now holds an intriguing collection of antiques, prints, documents, tools and cooking utensils, tableware, toys, and early fabrics. Theoretically open daily, late May–mid-October, but staffed by volunteers, so you can never be sure. Small fee.

Vermont State Craft Center at Windsor House (674-6729). An attractive retail showcase-gallery of Vermont craftspeople: glass, ceramics, furniture, jewelry, prints, toys, plus a series of instructional programs. (Most of the craftspeople displayed are within an easy drive and welcome visitors who call ahead.) Windsor House itself opened in 1840 as the best public house between Boston and Montreal. The columned, brick building was saved from the wrecker's ball by a band of determined local preservationists who organized Historic Windsor, Inc., in the early 1970s and continue to offer advice and specific courses on preservation. Open 9–5 Monday–Saturday, year-round; also 12–5 Sundays, June–January.

On your stroll around town, note the **Old South Congregational Church**, designed by the famed Asher Benjamin and built in 1798; it was renovated in 1844, 1879, and again in 1922 but fortunately retains its classic beauty.

St. Francis of Assisi Roman Catholic Church. The most significant example of contemporary religious art since the Rothko Chapel in Houston may be seen here in the series of the "Seven Sacraments" panels contributed to the newly built church by George Tooker, the noted American painter who lives in nearby Hartland.

St. Paul's Episcopal Church, on the common, built in 1832, is the oldest Episcopal church in Vermont still in regular use.

The Townsend Cottage, across the square, dating from 1847, is a striking example of "Hudson River Bracketed" or "Carpenter Gothic" style.

And across the longest and sole surviving covered bridge on the Connecticut River, in Cornish, NH, **The Saint-Gaudens National Historic Site** (603-675-2175), Cornish, New Hampshire. Includes the

Hugh Sadlier

Windsor-Cornish bridge before recent restoration

sculptor's summer home, barn/studio, sculpture court, and formal gardens, which he developed and occupied between 1885 and his death in 1907. The property was accepted by the National Park Service in 1964. Augustus Saint-Gaudens loved the Ravine Trail, a quarter-mile cart path to Blow-Me-Up Brook, now marked for visitors, and other walks laid out through the woodlands and wetlands of the Blow-Me-Down Natural Area. Saint-Gaudens was one of several artists who formed a summer colony in Cornish, a group that included poets Percy MacKaye, Witter Bynner, and William Vaughan Moody; Winston Churchill, the American novelist whose summer estate was used as the vacation White House by President Woodrow Wilson in 1914 and 1915; Ethel Barrymore, Charles Dana Gibson, Finley Peter Dunne, and Maxfield Parrish. Summer visitors can enjoy examples of the artist's work and bring a picnic lunch for Sunday outdoor concerts. Open daily late May–October.

White River Junction   Located at the confluence of the Connecticut and White rivers and the intersection of Interstates 91 and 89, and once a bustling, often raucous railroad hub, White River Junction is expanding its peripheral reach to accommodate the concentration of brand-name motels, a new post office, professional offices, and fast-food stops. The downtown seems to resist renewal, except for the venerable

Hotel Coolidge, and you can almost feel the aura of steam and cinders that cling to the locomotive and railroad cars parked across from the hotel. (And how many residents or visitors know that Horace Wells of White River Junction was the first person to use laughing gas as an anesthetic for pulling teeth in 1844?)

The Catamount Brewery (296-2248), 28 South Main Street, White River Junction. Grateful quaffers applauded the recent introduction of this zesty, English-type ale; tours and tastings by appointment.

Hanover, New Hampshire   **Dartmouth College**. Chartered in 1769, Dartmouth is the ninth oldest and one of the most prestigious colleges in the country with 4,000 undergraduate men and women and 1,000 graduate students. Dartmouth's handsome buildings frame three sides of its elm-shaded Green, and the fourth side is lined with visitor-friendly buildings: the large, college-owned **Hanover Inn**, the entertainment complex called **Hopkins Center**, and the **Hood Museum** (see below). The white information kiosk on the Green is staffed during summer months, starting point for historical and architectural tours Mondays and Thursdays at 2. Most visitors find their way into Baker Memorial Library to see the set of murals by famous Mexican painter José Orozco (which some alumni once demanded be removed or covered because of the artist's left-wing politics). When the kiosk is closed, guided tours are offered by the admission office in McNutt Hall by student members of Green Key.

Hood Museum of Art (603-646-2808), Dartmouth Green. An outstanding collection of art, ranging from Assyrian bas reliefs donated by missionary graduates in the 1850s, through works by Italian masters and American eighteenth- and nineteenth-century artists, to paintings by Rothko, Picasso, and Dartmouth graduate Frank Stella. There are frequently changing special exhibits. Open Tuesday–Sunday 11–5; Saturday until 8. Free.

Hopkins Center for the Arts (603-646-2422) has two theaters, a recital hall, art galleries for permanent and year-round programs of plays, concerts, film society showings. It serves as home base for the accomplished Dartmouth Symphony Orchestra.

Norwich   **Montshire Museum of Science** (649-2200), Norwich. Open Monday and Saturday 10–5; Sunday 1–5. Admission $4 per adult, $2 per child. Offshoot of a fusty old Dartmouth College museum that was filled with stuffed birds, this new facility (moved to larger quarters in late 1989) dramatizes both natural and theoretic sciences for all ages. Exhibits include more than 25,000 leaf-cutter ants and a Physics Playground. Many local field trips, special exhibits, and programs offered.

VILLAGES   **Norwich**, one of the prettiest towns in Vermont, was settled in 1761 by a group from Marshfield, Connecticut. It has always had close ties to Hanover (just across the bridge), with which it shares the

Larry Crowe

Hands-on science at Montshire Museum, Norwich

Dresden school district. Many Dartmouth faculty members live in Norwich, which once was the home for the American Literary, Scientific, and Military Academy founded in 1819 and named Norwich University in 1834; it moved to Northfield after the Civil War. The village is an architectural showcase for fine brick and frame Federal homes. Note the Seven Nations House across from the Norwich Inn, built as a commercial "tenement" in 1832.

Weathersfield Center. On a scenic, old, north-south road between Springfield and Route 131 stands this nearly secret gem of a hamlet with its brick 1821 Meeting House and Civil War memorial, a particularly sobering reminder of how many young Vermonters served and died (12 boys from this small village) in the war. The Weathersfield Historical Society, housed in the Reverend Dan Foster House, is nearby; open June–October, Wednesday–Sunday. It features a blacksmith shop.

Thetford has an unusual distinction in that the six different post offices established in the township are all functioning. Thetford Hill, site of Thetford Academy (and the Parish Players), is one of the most perfect hamlets left in the state.

Fairlee village is a plain cousin to its handsome twin—aristocratic **Orford**, New Hampshire (well known for its lineup of elegant Federal-era homes, some credited to Boston architect Charles Bulfinch), just across the river. But we like it better. Check out

Chapman's, a nineteenth-century pharmacy that has expanded in unusual directions under more than 40 years of Chapman ownership, and the Fairlee Diner, notably unchanged since the Roberts family assumed ownership in 1939. Summer camps and inns line nearby Lake Morey.

It's worth noting that Samuel Morey, a resident of Orford and a lumberman in Fairlee, was the inventor of the first steamboat: in 1793, 14 years before Fulton launched his *Clermont*, Morey was puffing up and down the river in a primitive craft barely big enough to hold him and his firewood. The remains of the little steamer are believed to lie at the bottom of Lake Morey, scuttled by its builder when the $100,000 in stock offered him by Robert Fulton turned out to be worthless. Morey also patented an internal combustion engine in 1825.

Bradford, where the Waits River flows into the Connecticut, is unique in Vermont because it is the only town to have been settled in the late 1760s without any deed, grant, or charter, thus setting an early example of the contrariness for which Vermont is famous. Bradford was home to James Wilson, an ingenious farmer who made America's first geographical globes in the early 1800s, and the birthplace of Captain Charles Cook, who commanded the battleship *Oregon* on its strategic 15,000-mile dash around Cape Horn from the Pacific to help defeat the Spanish at Santiago Bay in 1898. His exploit, on the heels of Commodore George Dewey's victory in Manila and Vermont Senator Redfield Proctor's jingoistic call for the liberation of Cuba, prompted the *Rutland Herald* to call this conflict "The Vermont-Spanish War." Today the town is chiefly known for its Annual Wild Game Supper (see *Special Events*).

Newbury and **Haverhill**. The northern reaches of the Upper Valley are defined by these two unusually handsome villages. Haverhill, New Hampshire, has a covered bridge (the oldest in New England) and double Commons, where all-day flea markets are held on the last Sunday of the month. Newbury, Vermont, also has a large, handsome Common, the scene of the late July Cracker Barrel Bazaar (see *Special Events*).

GREEN SPACE   **Wilgus State Park** (674-5422, 773-2657), 1½ miles south of Exit 8, I-91, off Route 5, Windsor. This small, quiet campground on the Connecticut River is ideal for canoeists since many lean-tos and tent sites are on the riverbank; car shuttle service available.

Springfield Nature Trail (where Weathersfield and Springfield meet). Fifty-five acres of fields and woods on the border of Springfield and Weathersfield have been developed by the Ascutney Mountain Audubon Society, an environmental group.

Ascutney State Park (674-2060), between Ascutney and Windsor on Route 5. Picnicking, trails, tent and trailer sites, lean-tos, paved road to summit. Granite was quarried here as early as 1808, and there was a popular summit house.

AIR RIDES AND BALLOONING   **Post Mills Airport** (333-9254), West Fairlee, is now owned by veteran balloonists Brian Boland and Ruth Ludwig, and they offer early morning and sunset rides year-round. On the summer evening we tried it, the balloon hovered above hidden pockets in the hills, and we saw a herd of what looked like brown-and-white goats that, on closer inspection, proved to be deer. After an hour or so, we settled down gently in an East Bradford farmyard. Champagne flights cost $150 per person year-round and are combined into reasonably priced weekend packages at Silver Maple Lodge. Airplane and glider rides also offered here and at **Kem Aviation** (886-8594) at Hartness State Airport in North Springfield.

BICYCLING   Ten-speed bicycles are available from **Silver Maple Lodge** (333-4326) in Fairlee. The river roads, especially Route 12A through Plainfield and Route 5 north from White River Junction all the way to Newbury, are favored by cyclists, usually flat and scenic. Eighteen-speed touring bikes are also available from **North Star Canoes**.

CANOEING   **North Star Canoes** (603-542-5802), Route 12A at Balloch's Crossing in Cornish, New Hampshire, just across the river from Windsor. John Hammond was shoeing a horse in front of his riverside barn the day we stopped by, and the canoes were there, too, ready for anyone to rent. John and Linda Hammond will shuttle you upstream for a half-day, all-day, or overnight (camping on an island) trip.

The **Ledyard Canoe Club** of Dartmouth College (603-646-2753) sponsors a variety of canoe and kayak events during the summer, including safaris to Maine and Connecticut, and kayak and windsurfer clinics. Membership open to the public.

This section of the Connecticut River is particularly seductive to paddlers, and three of our favorite inns—Haverill Inn, Stone House Inn, and Moose Mountain Lodge—collaborate to offer inn-to-inn canoe trips. For details, contact the Stone House Inn (see *Country Inns*).

Canoeing on the Connecticut River, a free, detailed guide focusing on this particular stretch of the river, is available from the Vermont Division of Recreation and Department of Water Resources Agency of Environmental Conservation, Montpelier 05602.

Connecticut River Watershed Council (603-448-2792), 312 1st NH Bank Building, Lebanon, New Hampshire 03766, offers guided, educational, day and overnight canoe trips along this stretch of the river, May–September.

Rental canoes are available from **Silver Maple Lodge** (333-4326), Fairlee. Also see **Inwood Manor** in the St. Johnsbury section of "The Northeast Kingdom."

GOLF   **Crown Point Country Club** (885-2703), Weathersfield Station Road; 18 holes, rolling terrain.

Windsor Country Club (674-6491), nine holes on Route 5, north of Windsor.

Hanover Country Club (603-646-2000), Rope Ferry Road, off Route 10, Hanover, New Hampshire. A classy, 18-hole course with pro shop and lounge, open May–October.

Lake Morey Inn Resort (333-4311 or 800-423-1211) features an 18-hole golf course on which the Vermont Open has been played for 35 years.

Bradford Country Club (222-5207); nine holes down by the river.

SWIMMING   **Union Village Dam Area**, west on Route 132 from Pompanoosuc, offers swimming, picnicking, and fishing.

Treasure Island (333-9625), Thetford, on Lake Fairlee, is a pleasant public beach with a tennis court; admission.

The beach at **Mill Pond in Windsor** is town-owned, open to the public for a fee.

Stoughton Pond between Downers and Amsden, south of Route 131 or north from Route 106, near Springfield Dam Lake. North Springfield Lake also offers picnicking and swimming.

FAMILY RESORTS   **Rutledge Inn & Cottages** (333-9722), Fairlee 05045, a Lake Morey family resort, with lots of activities. Nancy and Robert Stone have preserved the central lodge with its cheerful dining room, its lounge with bingo and cards, and its library. The rooms are in individual cottages by the lake, and there's an old-fashioned "casino" rec hall, a private beach, and an assortment of rowboats, canoes, and sailboats for use. Bountiful meals, served three times a day, are included in the per person rates: from $70 per day in the lodge to $95 in the best cottages, less for children; weekly rates; cheaper in May before the dining room opens.

Lake Morey Inn Resort (333-4311; 800-423-1211), Fairlee 05045. Perched on the shore of sparkling Lake Morey, this sprawling, year-round Avery family landmark has lots to offer: indoor and outdoor swimming pools, waterfront diversions, tennis courts, and cross-country ski and snowmobile trails in the winter, plus a good, player-friendly, recently-upgraded 18-hole golf course. The public rooms have an informal fifties atmosphere. One-night rates range from $83–$148 per person, MAP (including golf); two-night midweek senior, holiday, and seasonal specials from $74, plus group golf packages. Lakeside cottages available.

COUNTRY INNS   **The Inn at Weathersfield** (263-9217), Route 106 (near Perkinsville), Weathersfield 05151. If you're yearning for the New England edition of a cozy, English country inn or a French provincial *auberge,* here it is. This charming, porticoed eighteenth-century homestead and farm has been through several incarnations: as a stagecoach stop between Rutland and Nashua, New Hampshire; as a station on the Underground Railroad; and as an inn in 1961. There are

10 antique-furnished guest rooms and two two-room suites, all with private bath and several with working fireplaces. Five public rooms offer relaxation and browsing among the 4,000 books in the hosts' library. For working off the calories, an exercise room and sauna beckon; a pond and grass tennis court have been restored. For equestrians, the inn has box stalls and a paddock and can offer information about inn-to-inn carriage tours. Rates $175 per couple (suites $185–205), including breakfast, dinner, English tea, tax, and gratuity. To ensure tranquility, hosts Mary Louise and Ron Thorburn won't accept reservations for children under eight; older ones are welcome only if their behavior "will permit other guests to enjoy the quiet atmosphere of our dining and guest rooms" (see *Dining Out*).

Hartness House (885-2115), Orchard Street (off Route 143), Springfield 05156. Governor Hartness built the house in 1903 in the "Newport cottage" style on the bluff where the lathe-makers lived. He installed his own Turret Equatorial Telescope at the end of a 240-foot underground corridor connected to the mansion, which has served as the town's principal hostelry since 1954. It has spacious sitting and dining rooms and 45 guest rooms in the main house and attached wings, each with private bath, phone, color TV, $60–80 double. There's a heated swimming pool, lighted clay tennis court, 33 acres for cross-country skiing, and golf privileges.

Juniper Hill Inn (674-5273), RR 1, Box 79, Windsor 05069, off Route 5 on Juniper Hill Road. With a view of Mt. Ascutney and the Connecticut River Valley, this impressive 28-room mansion, built by Maxwell Evarts in 1901, combines Edwardian grandeur with the informal hospitality of its current proprietors, Jim and Krisha Pennino. Adult guests (and children over 12) can relax in the huge main hall, parlors, and cozy library. Nine rooms have fireplaces, and, of these, our favorite is number 7, done in white and blue. All are furnished in genuinely interesting antiques. Rates range from $80–115 per room, full breakfast included; MAP and five-day midweek plans available. Inn guests gather for meals around the immense table (original to the house) seating 20 (or they can choose to dine alone) in the pink dining room. The inn offers "Yankee Rambler" packages using rental canoes and 18-speed touring bicycles furnished by North Star Canoe Rentals (see *Canoeing*).

☞**The Stone House Inn** (333-9124), North Thetford 05054, is the old farmhouse centerpiece for canoeing inn to inn (see *Canoeing*), but it's a pleasant retreat year-round. Art and Diane Sharkey, both teachers, have been here since 1978, and the house, actually made from schist quarried across the river in Lyme and built in 1835, has an unusually comfortable, welcoming feel. There's a piano and fireplace in the living room and rockers on the wide, screened porch. The six guest rooms share baths; our favorite is in the back with

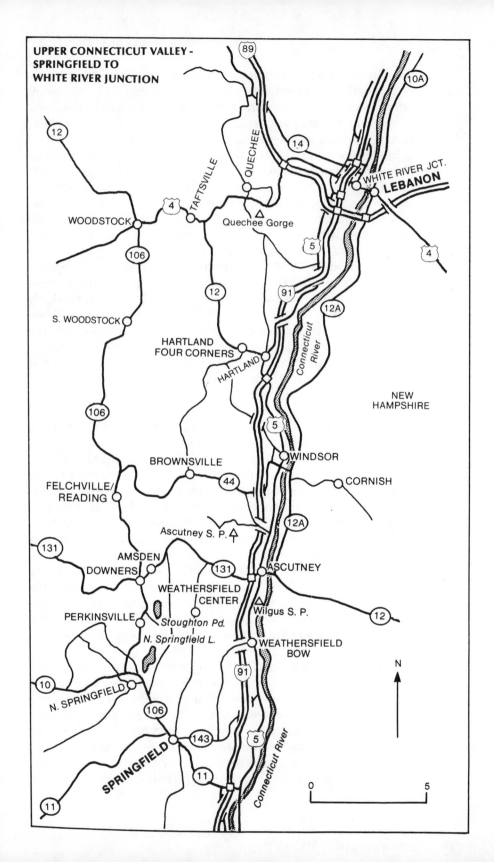

UPPER CONNECTICUT VALLEY -
SPRINGFIELD TO
WHITE RIVER JUNCTION

windows on the river. There are 12 acres in all, stretching flat and green to the river. $50 double, breakfast included.

Silver Maple Lodge & Cottages (333-4326; 800-666-1946), RR 1, Box 8, Fairlee 05045. Situated just south of the village on Route 5, Silver Maple was built as a farmhouse in 1855 and has been welcoming travelers for nearly 60 years. Now run by Scott and Sharon Wright, it has nine modestly priced, nicely appointed guest rooms in the lodge and five separate, pine-paneled, shaded hideaway cabins. The farmhouse has cheerful sitting rooms, screened porch, and a dining/ breakfast room where fresh breads appear with other continental breakfast goodies. Play horseshoes, croquet, badminton, or shuffleboard on the lawn, or rent a bike or canoe. Scott will also arrange a ride in a hot air balloon for you at neighboring Post Mills Airport. It's $450 per couple for two nights' lodging with breakfast and a champagne balloon ride. Scott grew up on a Tunbridge farm and takes pride in introducing visitors to Vermont. At $32–36 per couple with shared bath, $38–44 with private bath, and $42–48 with kitchenette, this is a great value. All prices include breakfast.

Lake House (333-4025), Route 244, Post Mills 05058. Built as an inn in 1870, this comfortable big house, a hundred yards from the shore of Lake Fairlee, has two rooms with private bath, ten shared. Rates for bed and full breakfast $75 per couple. Open all year.

TOWN INNS   Norwich Inn (649-1143), Box 908, 225 Main Street, Norwich 05055. Originally built as a stage stop by Jasper Murdock in 1797, this cheerful place now has 14 rooms in the main building plus a two-bedroom suite, and 7 rooms in a motel-like unit, all with private baths, telephones, and color cable TV. Sally Johnson, the new proprietor, has been redecorating the rooms, featuring stenciled walls and Williamsburg colors. Open for breakfast, lunch, and dinner, under a new chef. Rates range from $55–109 per room without meals, depending on the season; $59-81 per person, MAP.

The Hotel Coolidge (295-3118; 800-622-1124) deserves attention as one of the last of the old railroad hotels. Recently renovated, it has inexpensive accommodations and an above-average restaurant—in short, a "find" for the economy-minded traveler. $45–55 per room double. Be sure to look at the splendid Peter Michael Gish mural of Vermont history and life in the Vermont Room, painted in 1950 in exchange for room and board while the artist was studying with Paul Sample.

BED & BREAKFASTS   The Mill Brook (484-7283), Box 410, Route 44, Brownsville 05037. This 1890s farmhouse near Mt. Ascutney features antiques, art and crafts, and food. Three very casual sitting rooms and game area. Children and some pets welcome; limited smoking. Eight rooms, some with shared baths/showers. Kay Carriere is a food columnist, and breakfasts are special. From $30 single to $77 double with private bath in peak seasons.

The South View (484-7934), Roe Hill off Route 103 west and Ely Road, Brownsville. A secluded, contemporary, original Vermont Log Home, comfortably furnished by partners Denise Lanier and Susan Hines, provides five guest rooms; $35 per person including breakfast, afternoon and evening refreshments. Limited smoking; teens but not children or pets welcome.

House of Seven Gables (295-1200), 221 Main Street, Hartford 05001. A dramatic Victorian town house. $35–50 single, $55–70 double, with full breakfast.

Stonecrest Farm (295-2600), 119 Christian Street, Wilder 05088. Gail Sanderson's Greek Revival house has a long history of hospitality. Curved oak staircase, spacious beamed living room, five guest rooms, eclectically furnished with antiques. Rates from $90 including continental breakfast.

Long Meadow Inn (757-2538), Route 5, Wells River 05081, is a stately, red brick, porticoed Federal building that was once a stagecoach stop, now nicely restored by Roy and Ellen Canlon, with seven pretty guest rooms, three of which have fireplaces and private baths; rates $25–60 per room with full breakfast. Well-behaved children (but not pets) welcome; cash or checks, please.

Peach Brook Inn (866-3389), Doe Hill, off Route 5, South Newbury 05051. Ray and Joyce Emery have opened their spacious Colonial home with its splendid, panoramic view overlooking the Connecticut River. Four comfortable guest rooms: $40–50 with shared bath, $55–60 private, including full breakfast. No smoking.

FURNISHED HOMES   **Fahrenbrae Hilltop Retreat** (785-4304), Box 129, Thetford Hill 05074, has three attractive contemporary homes for rent, ideal for family vacations and reunions, completely furnished and equipped, with panoramic views. $80–125.

INNS WORTH CROSSING THE RIVER FOR   **Moose Mountain Lodge** (603-643-3529), Etna, New Hampshire 03750. Open June through October, December 26–mid-March. This is the most Alpine inn in all New England, perched high on a steep hill behind Hanover, just off the Appalachian Trail. Kay and Peter Shumway have been here since 1975 and obviously enjoy what they do, greeting guests like old friends and preparing memorable meals from only the freshest ingredients. Guest rooms are small but attractive with handmade spruce beds, shared baths. Inside and out, the lodge is pine, built from stones and logs cleared from this hill. The 300 acres include a deep pond just outside the door, ample woods, and meadows with long views. Summer diversions include canoeing (this is on the inn-to-inn tour), and in winter, there's cross-country skiing. The trick is getting up the hill (the hosts frequently assist guests). $75 per person MAP, $40 for children 12 and under.

Haverhill Inn (989-5961), Dartmouth College Highway (Route 10),

Haverhill, New Hampshire 03765. This is a classic, 1810 Federal-style house with canopied beds in its big, square rooms (private baths) with plenty to read about its surroundings, past and present. Grounds stretch invitingly out back, and the beautiful old village is just down the road. The river (this is part of the canoeing inn-to-inn tour) is just across the way. This is home for innkeeper Stephen Campbell, a computer systems manager at Dartmouth College. $65 double includes a full breakfast.

MOTELS   Since several kinds of transportation converge on White River Junction, it has a clutch of the major motor inns: **Holiday Inn** (295-3000); **Howard Johnson's Motor Lodge and Restaurant** (295-3015); the recently opened **Susse Chalet Inn** (295-3015, 800-628-7727), with 74 rooms and suites, heated pool, continental breakfast in the lobby, $59–65 double; and, across the river in Lebanon, New Hampshire, the **Sheraton North Country Inn** (603-298-5906).

DINING OUT   **The Inn at Weathersfield** (263-9217), Route 106 (near Perkinsville), Weathersfield. A five-course, prix fixe dinner ($25.95) is served every night except Wednesday, with reservations recommended. The menu changes daily, but one might choose the following: pumpkin apple soup, mushroom sautée in puff pastry, a marinated tomato and leek salad, sorbet, the inn's own pheasant with sauce chasseur ($2.50 extra), and dessert. A high English tea is open to the public as well as guests.

Ascutney 1799 House (674-6500), Routes 5 and 12, Ascutney, open year-round, Tuesday–Sunday, for lunch, dinner, and brunch. Traditional New England fare, featuring chowder and several versions of salmon, maple-glazed Cornish hen with cornbread-pecan stuffing, in the $12–15 range, plus a tavern menu.

Windsor Station Restaurant (674-2052), Depot Avenue, Windsor. This was the mainline station, now natural wood plus velvet and brass, serving reasonably priced lunch and dinner with entrées from chicken Kiev or Amandine and veal Madeira to the "Station Master" filet mignon topped with shrimp, asparagus, and Hollandaise sauce. A children's menu is available. $10.95–15.95.

☞**Skunk Hollow Tavern** (436-2139), Hartland Four Corners, off Route 12 north of I-91, Exit 9. People gather downstairs in the closest approximation of a true English pub in Vermont to play darts and backgammon and to munch on fish-and-chips, mussels, or pizza; generally excellent, more formal dining upstairs in the inn's original parlor. Open Wednesday–Sunday. Entrées $13–18.

La Poule à Dents at Carpenter Street (649-2922), in the historic 1820 House, Main Street, Norwich. Open for dinner Monday–Saturday and for lunch Monday–Friday, this attractive French restaurant, presided over by talented chef-owners Barry and Claire Snyder, offers a truly exceptional à la carte menu with dinner entrées from $16 and a prix fixe lunch for $10. There's also a bar menu, 5–midnight, and occasional special events such as a re-creation of "Babette's Feast" (at $100 per person).

Italian Gardens Restaurant (649-8824), Main Street, Norwich. The landmark Emerson House contains this "Italian restaurant with the French connection," serving lunch and dinner daily; closed Sunday. Antipasto could be followed by chicken tetrazzini with angel hair pasta, saltimbocca, or scampi. Entrées $9.50–$14.95.

Norwich Inn (649-1143), Main Street, Norwich, popular locally for lunch and dinner. Begin dinner with baked brie en croute or blackened carpaccio, followed by pork loin, poached salmon, or noisettes of lamb loin. Entrées $13.50–18.95.

D'Artagnan (603-795-2137) in the Ambrose Publick House, seven miles north of Hanover on Route 10, Lyme, New Hampshire, is probably the best (and most expensive) restaurant in this stretch of the Upper Valley. Decidedly French in atmosphere, it's open for dinner Wednesday–Sunday and for lunch on Sunday. A typical prix fixe dinner might include a light soup of oysters with curry or halibut quenelles to start, salmon with asparagus or duck breast, house salad, and dessert for $30. Reservations essential.

Also see the "Woodstock/Quechee Area" for Simon Pearce and the Quechee Inn, both in Quechee.

EATING OUT   Penelope's/McKinley's (885-9186), on the square, Springfield, is full of polished woods, stained glass, and greenery; homemade bread, soups, and desserts accompany beef, lamb, fish, and vegetarian dishes at very reasonable prices. Mexican food Wednesdays. Entertainment most weekends.

The Paddock (885-2720), Paddock Road, Springfield, 1/4 mile west of Route 5 and I-91. Continental and substantial American fare in a handsomely converted barn. Dinner 5–9, except Monday; Sunday noon–3, 5–8.

B.J. Bricker's (885-6050), River Street, Springfield, open daily for breakfast, lunch, and dinner. A 14 ounce T-bone or filet mignon goes for $9.95; children's menu; beer and wine.

Mr. G's (674-6902), Route 131, Ascutney, is open from 6 AM to 9; dinner specials from $5.95.

Cattleman's (674-2032), Route 5 south, Windsor, a roadside haven for steak, chicken, or fish, with a piano bar.

Than Wheeler's Coach's Corner (295-4847), Main Street, White River Junction. Offers good food at reasonable prices. Open from 11:30 AM until around midnight, closed Sunday. Weekend entertainment.

☞**Cashie's at the Hotel Coolidge** (295-3118), White River Junction. Lunch Monday–Friday, dinner Tuesday–Saturday. Several exceptionally well cooked selections, like "Gandy Dancer"—breast of chicken marinated in ground walnuts and served with an applejack cider sauce at $10.95.

The Third Rail (333-9797), Route 5, Fairlee. Open for lunch and dinner, except Mondays. A roadside (Route 5) house with a friendly pub (John Courage Ale on tap) and two dining rooms with booths and a large menu (burgers to steaks); also homemade pastas and some delectable surprises like bluefish papaillote and chicken Marsala.

Fairlee Diner (333-9798), Route 5, Fairlee. Open daily from 6 AM–9 PM, Sundays 8 AM–4 PM. There are still just six wooden booths and a dozen stools at a shiny formica counter, just the way they were in 1939 when the Roberts family acquired it. Soups and breads are made fresh every day, and the menu ranges from peanut butter and jelly sandwiches to chicken teriyaki. The family also operates Roberts' Country Kitchen, farther down Route 5 in East Thetford.

Colatina Exit (222-9008), Main Street, Bradford. Open daily from 5 PM. A real Vermont trattoria: candles in chianti bottles, Italian scenes on the walls, checked (green mind you) tablecloths, and a variety of pastas and pizzas, also entrées like blackened redfish with fettucini Alfredo.

Sala Thai in Windsor. A small, takeout Thai restaurant run by Michael and Anong Rive. Michael was serving with the Peace Corps in Thailand when he met Anong, who happened to be cooking at her mother's pushcart. Thai food features long-grain rice accompanied by either chicken, pork, or beef, plus vegetables. Beware of spicy entrées like Asian Fire Drill and Five Alarm Shrimp.

Happy Hours Restaurant (757-3466), Wells River. This solid, pine-paneled family restaurant in the middle of town is good for breakfast, lunch, and dinner at moderate prices. Fully licensed.

P&H Truck Stop (429-2144), Wells River. Just off I-91, a genuine truckers' haven, complete with showers and hearty grub. Popular with families as well.

Warners Gallery Restaurant (429-2120), Wells River. Lunch offers some surprises like vegetarian casserole, spinach lasagna, a mixed grill, and smothered chicken. Often crowded for dinner; reserve or be prepared to wait. A large salad bar and a good range of entrées.

ENTERTAINMENT   **Hopkins Center** (603-646-2422) stages year-round live performances, classic films, and concerts.

River City Arts (296-2505), headquartered in the landmark Briggs Opera House, White River Junction, stages professional and semi-professional theatrical productions year-round.

The Parish Players (785-4344), based in the Eclipse Grange Hall on Thetford Hill, is a vigorous young company with a growing reputation.

In the past few seasons, venues have burgeoned for folk, blues, and hard-to-label idiosyncratic performers. The **Lebanon Opera House** (603-448-2498) is one of the most active.

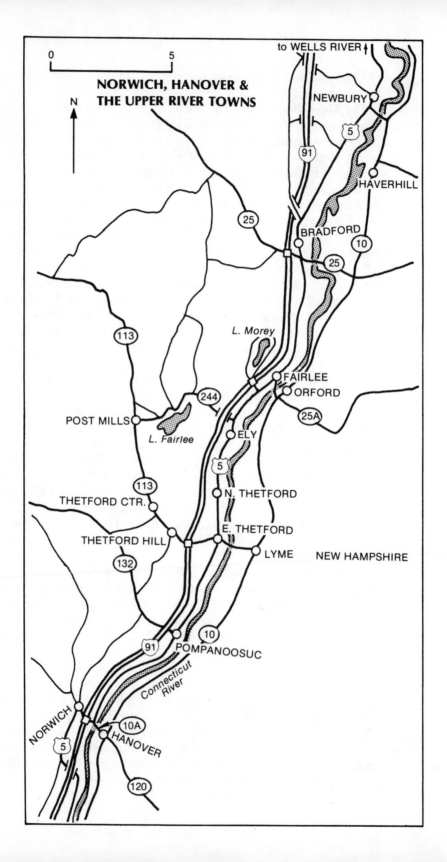

NORWICH, HANOVER &
THE UPPER RIVER TOWNS

0   5

N

to WELLS RIVER

NEWBURY

5

91

HAVERHILL

25

BRADFORD

25

10

L. Morey

113

FAIRLEE

244

ORFORD

POST MILLS

25A

L. Fairlee

ELY

5

113

N. THETFORD

THETFORD CTR.

E. THETFORD

THETFORD HILL

132

LYME

NEW HAMPSHIRE

10

91

POMPANOOSUC

Connecticut
River

NORWICH

10A

5

HANOVER

120

SELECTIVE SHOPPING   **Vermont Soapstone Company,** north of Perkinsville off Route 106 (look for sign). Soapstone griddles won't stick, and they retain heat amazingly. Soapstone is used for woodstoves and even kitchen sinks. Gift shop outlet open daily 9–5 except Sunday, May–December. Regular mill hours 9–4:30 weekdays, January–April.

Catamount Brewing Company (296-2248), 158 Main Street, White River Junction. Vermont's first brewery in 100 years produces quality ales. Open mid-June–mid-October; tours offered Tuesday, Thursday, and Saturday, and by appointment the rest of the year.

Vermont Salvage Exchange (295-7616), Railroad Row, White River Junction, for doors, chandeliers, moldings, mantels, old bricks, and other architectural relics.

Briggs Ltd. (295-7100), 12 North Main Street, White River Junction. Hunting supplies and Orvis tackle, as well as Woolrich and Pendleton clothing for men and women.

Pompanoosuc Mills (785-4851), Route 5, East Thetford 05043. Not too many years have passed since Dwight Sargeant began building furniture in his riverside house, a cottage industry that has evolved into a riverside factory employing 55, with showrooms throughout New England. Furniture is made to order, but there are seconds here. Open daily until 6, 12–5 Sundays.

R. Voake, Toymaker (785-2837), Route 133, Thetford Center, four miles from Exit 14, I-91. Hardwood toys in traditional and original designs made in the workshop where visitors can watch. Open 10–5 all year, but call ahead.

Lilac Hedge Bookshop (649-2921), Main Street, Norwich. Pleasant browsing for antiquarians, students, and "Dear Readers" of all kinds; large stock of not-so-new fiction, art, history, and regional titles, well arranged.

Stave Puzzles (649-1450), Main Street, Norwich. The handcrafted, wooden jigsaw puzzles made here are the Rolls-Royces of this pastime, some being cut and put together in multiple-choice fashion. Their prices are impressive, too: A 275-piece, 16-inch Snowflake costs $550. The 900-piece, 18-by-25-inch Bruegel wedding dance scene can be yours for $1,425. Stave also has some Petite Puzzles of famous paintings in the $140–215 class.

Chapman's Pharmacy (333-9709), Fairlee. Adele and Leland bought this old pharmacy and gradually expanded it. Lee was a renowned fisherman and fly-tier. The sports department, liberally garnished with stuffed trophies, still includes 10,000 hand-tied flies. The couple enjoyed wines, and there are now 500 labels. Adele (better known as Odie) collected antique linens and clothing, and there is now a wide selection, along with silver from Tasco, Mexico. There are also books: rows of old books, shelves of used paperbacks ($.35 with $.10 on returns), and books by area authors and illustrators. The store also stocks staples such as tubes of oil paint, night crawlers, and manila envelopes.

ANTIQUES   **The Windsor Antiques Market** (674-9336), 53 Main Street, Windsor. This Gothic Revival church houses 30 dealers in antiquities whose wares are particularly strong in period pieces (eighteenth and nineteenth centuries), American painting, folk art, and artifacts.

Exit 9 Antiques (574-9336), Route 5 north of Windsor. Seventeen dealers specializing in Victorian oak, also quilts and cut glass.

FARMS   **Cider Hill Farm** (674-5293), Hunt Road, 2½ miles west of State Street, Windsor. Growers of herbs and perennials, creators of herb wreaths, dry flower arrangements, herbal blends, and apple cider.

Cedar Circle Farm (785-4101), East Thetford. Famous for its four varieties of cantaloupes; also good for local peas and strawberries.

SPECIAL EVENTS   June–September: The ladies of Brownsville (West Windsor) have been serving up their famous baked bean and salad suppers since 1935, first for the benefit of the Methodist church, lately for the Grange and Historical Society. They start Saturdays in late June and run through the summer. People start lining up at 4 PM for the first seating at 5.

July: **Connecticut Valley Fair**, Bradford (third weekend). **Cracker Barrel Bazaar**, Newbury (last weekend), includes plenty of fiddling, church suppers, maybe a circus.   **Historic Windsor's Annual Antique Show** (usually held at Mt. Ascutney).

August: **Lyme Summer Revels**, Lyme, New Hampshire (early August); song and dance in a meadow.

October: The **Annual Vermont Apple Festival** (885-2779), Springfield, is held Columbus Day weekend and includes a craft show. **Festival Windsor** is an annual autumn celebration.

November: **Annual Wild Game Supper** in Bradford. The town nearly doubles its population of 1,700 on the Saturday before Thanksgiving, when hungry visitors pour into the Congregational church for this feast, now in its twenty-ninth year. Some 2,800 pounds of buffalo, venison, moose, pheasant, coon, rabbit, wild boar, and bear are cooked up by parishioners as roasts, steaks, hamburgers, stews, and sausage; devoured along with salad, vegetables, and gingerbread with whipped cream. Tickets ($15 adult, $7 for children) are limited to 1,000. Doors open at 3 PM. Reservations are accepted only on or after the "middle Monday of October," postmarked or in person. Write to: Game Supper Committee, Bradford 05033.

December: **Dickens of a Christmas** and **Christmas Revels** in Hanover.

MEDICAL EMERGENCY   Windsor (674-2112); Ascutney (542-2244); Norwich (643-3610); Hanover and White River Junction (911); Thetford/Fairlee/Bradford (353-4347).

Springfield Hospital (885-2151), 25 Ridgwood Road, Springfield. Mount Ascutney Hospital (674-6711), County Road, Windsor. The Dartmouth-Hitchcock Medical Center (603-650-5000) has moved from Hanover to One Medical Center Drive, off Route 120, between Hanover and Lebanon.

Woodstock/Quechee Area

WOODSTOCK

A moated village cradled in hills around the Ottauquechee River fourteen miles west of White River Junction on Route 4, Woodstock is one of the most cosmopolitan towns in the state and, justifiably, considered one of the half-dozen prettiest towns in America. It has been a popular year-round resort for a century: In the 1890s, summer folk settled into the old Woodstock Inn for the season or returned for lively winter sports parties; and in the mid-1930s, it was a mecca for eastern skiers because of its rope tow—the first in America (1934).

As the Shire Town of Windsor County since the 1790s, Woodstock attracted an influential and prosperous group of professionals who, with the local merchants and bankers, built the unusual concentration of distinguished Federal houses that surround the elliptical Green, forming a long-admired architectural showcase that has been meticulously preserved.

Woodstock produced more than its share of nineteenth-century celebrities, including Hiram Powers, the sculptor whose nude *Greek Slave* scandalized the nation in 1847, and Senator Jacob Collamer (1791–1865), President Lincoln's confidante who declared, "The good people of Woodstock have less incentive than others to yearn for heaven." George Perkins Marsh (1801–1882) helped found the Smithsonian when he was serving in Congress, was the U.S. minister to Turkey and Italy, and wrote the pioneering work on environmental conservation, *Man and Nature* (1864), which has long been regarded as the ecologists' Bible. John Cotton Dana was an eminent, early twentieth-century librarian and museum director, whose innovations made books and art more accessible to the public. The town still feels the influence of Frederick Billings (1823–1890), who became a famous San Francisco lawyer in the Gold Rush years and later was responsible for the completion of the Northern Pacific Railroad (Billings, Montana, was named for him in 1882). The Billings Mansion, a historic landmark and the boyhood home of George Perkins Marsh, and the prize Jersey dairy are now owned by Billings' granddaugh-

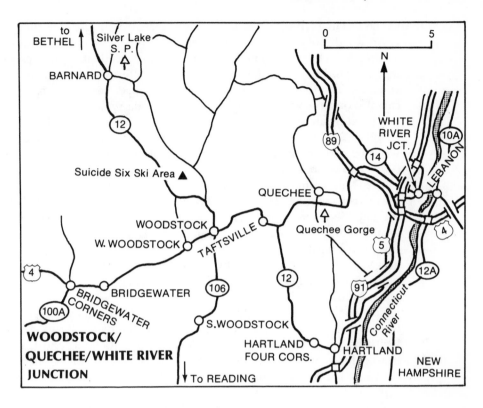

ter and her husband, Laurance S. Rockefeller. The Rockefellers are responsible for much of Woodstock's preservation, outlying green space, and recreational assets. Most of the village itself, and the hamlet of South Woodstock, are on the National Register of Historic Places, and plans are afoot to create a National Historic Park of the Billings Mansion and its surrounding forest.

GUIDANCE   The Woodstock Area Chamber of Commerce (457-3555), 4 Central Street, Woodstock 05901, keeps an information booth open on the Green from June through October (457-1042), which does its best to find beds in private homes for fall foliage leaf-peekers stranded without reservations (457-2389) and from which daily walking tours are conducted in season. The chamber annually publishes two useful free brochures, "Window on Woodstock" and "Where to Stay and Eat."

Woodstock Common magazine is published quarterly and is available locally without charge or from the Prosper Publishing Company, Box 206, Barnard 05031.

A detailed schedule of local events is posted daily on the blackboard at the corner of Elm and Central streets by the indefatigable "town crier," Frank Teagle.

TO SEE AND DO   The Billings Farm & Museum (457-2355), Route 12 north of River Road, holds a beautifully mounted series of exhibits demonstrating farm life in the 1890s: plowing, seeding, cultivating, harvesting, and storing crops; making cheese and butter; woodcutting and sugaring. The 1890 farm manager's house has been restored. Visitors can also observe what happens on a modern dairy farm. The tour is preceded by an imaginative audiovisual presentation. Open May 1–October 22 and for special events during the year, like Thanksgiving weekend and Christmas weekend celebrations, sleigh rally in mid-February, and periodic craft exhibits. Limited capacity; admission charge.

The Dana House (The Woodstock Historical Society, 457-1822) on Elm Street, completed in 1807 and occupied for the next 140 years by the notable Dana family, has an admirable collection of antiques, locally wrought coin silver, portraits, porcelains, fabrics, costumes, toys, and a barn full of early tools, stoves, skis, sleds, and a splendid go-to-meeting sleigh owned by the Billings family. Ask about the ghost. Museum shop. Open 10–5, May–October and winter weekends. Admission charge.

The Norman Williams Public Library (457-2295), on the Green, a Romanesque gem, donated and endowed in 1883 by Dr. Edward H. Williams, general manager of the Pennsylvania Railroad and later head of Baldwin Locomotives. It offers children's story hours, poetry readings, brown-bag summer concerts on the lawn. Open daily except Sundays and holidays.

The Green Mountain Perkins Academy and Institute (457-3974), Route 106 in South Woodstock, has exhibits related to its tenure as a famous school between 1848 and 1890. Open Saturdays 2–4:30 in July and August and by appointment.

The Vermont Institute of Natural Science (457-2779), 1.5 miles southeast of the village on Church Hill Road, has a rare herbarium collection, other exhibits of flora and fauna, the distinguished Pettingill Ornithological Library, nature trails, bird-banding station, a raptor center, and offers lectures and bird-fern-and-wildflower walks. Open year-round, Monday–Friday 9–4.

Pentangle Council on the Arts (457-3981) sponsors plays, films, concerts, ballet performances, and other touring shows at the restored Town Hall Theater.

COVERED BRIDGES   There are three in the town of Woodstock—the Lincoln Bridge (1865), Vermont's only Pratt-type truss, Route 4, West Woodstock; the Middle Bridge, in the center of the village, built in 1969 by Milton Graton, "last of the covered bridge builders," in the town lattice style (partially destroyed by vandalism and rebuilt); and the notable red Taftsville Bridge (1836), utilizing multiple king and queen posts and an unusual mongrel truss, Route 4 east. The Taftsville

Sheep shearing at the Billings Farm and Museum in Woodstock

John G. Fox

Bridge overlooks a hydro dam, still in use.

BICYCLING   **Bike Vermont** (457-3553), Box 207, Pleasant Street, Woodstock. Weekend and five-day midweek, inn-to-inn tours are arranged through central Vermont, including Grafton and Chester, Middletown Springs, Lake St. Catherine, Manchester, and the Connecticut River Valley. Twelve-speed Univegas are available for rent.

The Cyclery (457-3377), Route 4 in West Woodstock, has rentals; a marked bike path leads east from the village along River Road to Taftsville and its covered bridge.

GOLF AND TENNIS   The 18-hole **Woodstock Country Club** (457-2112) designed by Robert Trent Jones is part of the Woodstock Inn and Resort. Ten tennis and two paddle courts are available.

Vail Field. Two public tennis courts and children's playground.

HORSEBACK RIDING   Woodstock has been an equestrian center for generations, especially for the hardy Morgans, which are making a local comeback in South Woodstock.

The Green Mountain Horse Association (457-1509), Route 106, South Woodstock. Sponsor of the original 100-mile ride, an annual event around Labor Day that draws entrants from all over; shows, trials, and other popular events.

Kedron Valley Inn Stables (457-1480), Route 106, South Woodstock. Generally recognized as one of the best places to ride horseback—if you know how but don't happen to own a horse—in New England. Over the years, Paul and Barbara Kendall have pieced together a network of paths to link appealing inns. They lead riders over hiking and recreation trails, dirt roads, and meadows on one- to four-day tours that average 15 miles a day, six hours in the saddle. Prices, which include meals and lodging, range from $395 for a weekend to $1,225 for five nights, four days. Trail rides are also available by the hour ($20–25) and day ($120 includes lunch). Four-day, Woodstock-based clinics with a combination of lessons and riding are $750, including lodging.

SWIMMING   **Silver Lake State Park** (234-9451/773-2657), 10 miles north on Route 12 in Barnard, has a nice beach, and there's another smaller one right next to the general store.

The Woodstock Recreation Center has two public pools, mostly for youngsters.

WALKING AND HIKING   **Faulkner Park**, laid out by its donor, Mrs. Edward Faulkner, one of Woodstock's most thoughtful philanthropists, was modeled on Baden-Baden's "cardiac" walks; marked trails lead upward around Mt. Tom.

CROSS-COUNTRY SKIING   The **Ski Touring Center** (457-2114) at the **Woodstock Country Club,** Route 106 south of the village, part of the Rockresort properties, has mapped, marked, and groomed 47 miles of varied trails, from gentle terrain to forest and uplands, including

Mt. Tom and the Skyline Trail in Pomfret. Group and individual lessons; guided, four-hour picnic tours; rentals; sales room; lockers; bar restaurant (and dog-sled carts when the snow fails!).

Wilderness Trails (295-7620), Clubhouse Road at the Quechee Inn, has eight miles of track-set trails. Most of the trails are good for "entry-level" skiers and travel through the woods and meadows around Quechee Gorge, offering views of its waterfalls. Complete rentals, lessons available.

DOWNHILL SKIING   Suicide Six (457-1666), two miles north of the village on the Pomfret Road, now 50 years old, is the heir—on the other side of the slope—to the first ski tow in the United States, which was cranked up in 1934. The Face of Suicide Six, 655 feet vertical (operated for many years by Ski Hall of Famer, the late Bunny Bertram), is now part of the Woodstock Inn and Resort complex and has a roomy new base lodge finished with native woodwork. Its beginners' area has a complimentary J-bar; two double chair lifts reach 18 trails ranging from easy to "The Show Off" and "Pomfret Plunge." Lessons; rentals; restaurant.

ICE SKATING   Silver Lake, by the general store in Barnard.

Vail Field, Woodstock, maintained by local hockey and skating committee. Free, light for night skating. Woodstock Sports offers skate rentals (457-1568), 30 Central Street, Woodstock. $3 per day, $20 deposit. Sharpening ($1.50). Ski rentals also.

HEALTH SPA   The Sports Center (457-1160), part of the Woodstock Inn and Resort, Route 106, has indoor tennis and racquetball, lap pool, whirlpool, aerobic and state-of-the-art fitness equipment, plus restaurant and bar.

LODGING   The Woodstock Inn and Resort (457-1100; 800-223-7637), on the Green, is the lineal descendant of the eighteenth-century Eagle Tavern and of the famous "old" Woodstock Inn that flourished between 1893 and 1969 and put the town on the year-round resort map. Today's grand 143-room, air-conditioned, Colonial-style edition, owned by Laurance S. Rockefeller, reflects the owner's meticulous standards and was extensively remodeled in 1989–1991 with the addition of a townhouse wing, the luxurious Richardson Tavern, and expansion of the dining and meeting rooms. The comfortably furnished main lobby is dominated by a huge stone fireplace where five-foot birch logs blaze in the winter. There's a spiffy main dining room, plus coffee shop, library, gift shop, conference facilities, putting green, and swimming pool. Guests have access to the scenic 18-hole Woodstock Country Club for golf and tennis (it's a fine cross-country ski center in the winter) and to a splendid indoor Sports Center, plus downhill skiing at the historic Suicide Six area and wagon and sleigh rides. Current rates range from $125–245 double; up to $450 for spacious fireplace suites in the new Tavern Wing. Children under 14 free when staying in the same room with an adult; MAP available at $44 per person.

Check out their special packages: Serenity Season, Summer Sports, Wassail Weekend, and Ski Vermont Free, which includes lift tickets at Suicide Six, and others.

The Kedron Valley Inn (457-1473), Route 106, South Woodstock 05071. Max and Merrily Comins have gingered up the decor, appointments, and cuisine of this venerable mini-resort without depleting its nineteenth-century charm. The mellow brick main house and historic tavern, plus Vermont log motel unit, are supplemented by an acre-plus swimming pond with sandy beach and the adjacent Kedron Valley Stables—boarding, lessons, trail rides, indoor arena, surrey and sleigh rides in season. The freshly decorated 30 guest rooms, all with private bath, feature canopy and antique oak beds, some with fireplaces or Franklin stoves. There are so many examples of the Comins' collection of antique quilts on display that the dining room might have been named "The Quilted Pony," reflecting both the superior quality of the food (see *Dining Out*) and the inn's popularity with the horse people who are drawn to South Woodstock as an equestrian center. Room rates range from $73–101 per person double, MAP. Discounts available for midweek stays during nonholiday periods.

The Village Inn of Woodstock (457-1255), 41 Pleasant Street, is an informal, Victorian manse with fireplaces, oak wainscotting, pressed tin ceilings and all, plus bar and dining room. There are eight comfortable rooms, six with bath, $70–120 including continental breakfast. MAP available; midweek discounts.

The Lincoln Inn (457-3312), Route 4, West Woodstock. This 200-year-old, recently renovated farmhouse on the river, next to the covered bridge, has eight cheery guest rooms with baths, hand-hewn beams in the library, and a fine dining room. The gazebo is popular in summer, and sleigh rides, in winter. Rates: $160–200 double MAP, $99–140 B&B.

The Jackson House Inn (457-2065), Route 4, West Woodstock 05091. Hosts Jack Foster and Bruce McIllveen have further expanded this spacious 1890 farmhouse with the addition of a pond for swimming and trout fishing and a four-room housekeeping apartment due for completion in the summer of 1992. Filled with museum-quality antiques and objets d'art, this treasure house is more of an inn than a B&B, partly because of its pre-dinner wine, champagne, and hors d'oeuvre buffet, along with memorable breakfasts (poached eggs in puff pastry topped with chicken in a cream-sherry sauce, for example), both included in the fare. Each of the ten guest rooms is furnished in a different style and named accordingly, such as "Miss Gloria Swanson," in honor of the actress who hid out here in 1948 with her Rolls-Royce while her secretary stayed at the Woodstock Inn. The two mini-suites on the third floor ($160) are especially luxurious; the "Josephine Bonaparte" bedroom on the ground floor has a magnificent Empire mahogany and brass double bed. Rates: $120, $130, $160; $225 for the "Regency" apartment (with weekly or seasonal modifications). Smoke-free; two-day minimum on weekend and certain holidays; no pets or children under 14; cash or personal checks.

BED & BREAKFASTS   *In the Village*   ☞**Three Church Street** (457-1925). In one of the grander Federal houses near the Green, Eleanor Paine holds hospitable court, serving bountiful breakfasts (sometimes lunch in the summer and fall). There are spacious sitting rooms and 11 guest rooms, with private and shared baths ($68–95 B&B), plus swimming pool and tennis court. Pets welcome.

The Charleston House (457-3843), 21 Pleasant Street. Bill and Barbara Hough make this luxurious Federal brick town house appealing, with period furniture in seven bedrooms, all with private bath. $100-135, including full breakfast in the dining room or continental breakfast bedside.

Canterbury House (457-3077), 43 Pleasant Street. The Houghs also run this beautifully renovated, Victorian, antique-furnished house, seven rooms with baths and air-conditioning, $90–125 with full breakfast.

The 1860 Shire Town Inn (457-1830), 31 South Street, has three "old worldish" rooms with private baths, hearty country breakfast, $65–85.

Barr House (457-3334), 55 South Street. Kay Paul, the retired Woodstock Inn bartender, and Jim, the former fire chief, offer two charming rooms with shared bath in a trim saltbox. $40 single, $60 double including American breakfast and afternoon tea.

1826 House (457-1335), 57 River Street, two double rooms and one single, shared bath; German, French, and Russian spoken. $45–50.

The Woodstocker (457-3869), 61 River Street, has nine rooms with private baths, plus a whirlpool; two suites with living room, kitchen, and deck; $65–115 double with big buffet breakfast.

South of the Village   **Woodstock House** (457-1758), Route 106, three miles south of Woodstock. Three rooms with private bath, two shared; exposed beams, wide-board floors. Children welcome, but no pets or smoking. $50–70 with full breakfast.

Greystone Bed & Breakfast (484-7200), Box 85, Reading 05062, 11 miles south of Woodstock on Route 106. This restored 1830 stone Colonial has two elegant bedrooms, sharing a bath, and a full-floor suite with twin beds, sitting room with a queen sofa, and private bath: $85 for the bedrooms, $100 for two in the suite; lower midweek. Continental breakfast. Nonsmokers preferred. No pets.

The Peeping Cow (484-5036), Box 47, Reading 05062, 13 miles south of Woodstock on Route 106. This 1830 farmhouse is antique-furnished and is near a swimming hole. No TV, no pets, nonsmokers preferred. French and Spanish spoken. $60–75 double.

West Woodstock Area   Carriage House of Woodstock (457-4322), Route 4. Early American decor, seven rooms, six baths, $75 double. Children but not pets welcome.

Thomas Hill Farm (457-1067), Rose Hill, Greek Revival cape with three bedrooms, two with private baths, continental breakfast, $65–80. Children and pets not welcome.

Winslow House (457-1820), Route 4. Restored, antique-filled farmhouse, five rooms, four baths, $68–78, full breakfast; children and pets welcome.

Olsson's Guests (457-3087), Route 4. Two comfortable rooms in a family home; children welcome, no pets. $40 double.

Deer Brook Inn (672-3713), Route 4 west. Restored 1820 farmhouse with antique charm. Four spacious bedrooms with private baths; children but no pets. $65–85, full breakfast.

Troutbrook Acres (672-3716), Route 4, Bridgewater Corners. Attractive cabins, with continental breakfast in the farmhouse. Pets accepted. From $50 double.

East of the Village   ☞Applebutter Inn (457-4158), Taftsville. Authentically restored and attractively decorated Federal house with five downy bedrooms, two and one-half baths, living room with fireplace, $50–80 with natural-foods continental breakfast.

Beaver Pond Farm (436-2443), RR 1 Box 796, Woodstock. Up Hartland Hill Road 4.5 miles east of Woodstock, Beverly Garnett offers "lodging for horse and rider" in a Georgian Colonial on 122 acres, plus dressage ring and barn stalls; swimming, fishing, and canoeing in the six-acre pond; cross-country ski trails and riding trails linked to the Green Mountain Horse Association. No children under 10; three large rooms with fireplace and bath in each, $85–100 (depending on the season) with country continental breakfast.

FARM RETREAT   Six Willows Farm (436-2078), Box 88, Hartland Four Corners 05049, on Hartland Hill Road. Antique-furnished living room, 1–3 double bedrooms, kitchen (breakfast needs and staples supplied); tennis court, swimming pond, barn, and pastures. Horses, pets, children welcome. $85 for the first bedroom, $55 each additional; two-night minimum.

MOTELS   Braeside (457-1366), Route 4 east; 12 deluxe units, small heated pool. Shire Motel, 46 Pleasant Street, 18 units. Woodstock Motel (457-2500), Route 4 east, 15 units. Pond Ridge (457-1667), Route 4, West Woodstock, 12 units plus apartments. Ottauquechee Motel (672-3404), Route 4, West Woodstock, capacity 38.

DINING OUT   The Prince and the Pauper (457-1818), 24 Elm Street, Woodstock. Provides nouvelle and continental cuisine in a candlelit, elegantly rustic setting. Owner/chef Chris Balcer has, over the years, created and upheld consistently superior standards, now with daily menu changes. A recent sampling of the $28 prix fixe dinner included, for starters, smoked marlin, garnished with Raifort sauce and capers, fettucini Primavera, Escalope de Veau Forestiére (veal sautéed with oyster mushrooms, Madeira and crème fraîche), and Paillard of blackened tuna seared with Cajun spices. A boneless rack of lamb in puff pastry carried a supplement. Patrons tend to linger in the premium winebar, where one can also dine on the Bistro Menu (grilled entrecote with garlic herb butter, $12.95) or on exotic pizzas ($8.95). Open daily except for late fall and early spring vacations. One of the state's best; "worth every calorie and dollar," we said in the first edition of this book, and we have no reason to change our minds.

The Barnard Inn (234-9961), Barnard, 10 miles north of Woodstock on Route 12 in an impressive 1796 brick house, serves dinner in three beautifully appointed formal rooms. Owner/chef Sepp Schenker is renowned for his classic cuisine, stressing Swiss specialties and seasonal local produce (fiddleheads, morels, wild grapes, wild raspberries). Particularly recommended is the semi-boneless duckling, with various sauces, and veal scaloppine Parisienne, laced with a creamy sauce of mushrooms, white wine, and veal stock. Appetizers: $5.50–6.50; entrées $21.50–29.00 ($60 for Chateaubriand for two). Reservations essential. Closed Mondays, and it's wise to call ahead anyway to check whether it's open.

The Woodstock Inn and Resort (457-1100). The cheerfully contemporary main dining room, with its alcoves and semi-circular bay, is an especially attractive setting for the elaborate Sunday brunch buffet ($15.75) and ambitious, upper-bracket dinners. The latter might start with smoked pheasant and chestnut pâté or venison slivers with a salad of poached pears and hazelnuts, followed by baked apple smoked rack of lamb with tomato, mustard, and Zinfandel sauce ($20.50) or poached salmon and scampi ($19). Pastries and other desserts, subtle or lavish, are notable. Lighter fare is served at breakfast, lunch, and dinner in the Eagle Café.

The Kedron Valley Inn (457-1473), Route 106, five miles south of Woodstock, has won applause for its stylish "Nouvelle Vermont" cuisine. Appetizers include soups, pasta with basil pesto, oysters, escargots in puff pastry with fennel butter. Entrées range from chicken breast with honey, peaches, white wine, and scallions to the delectable house special, filet of Norwegian salmon stuffed with an herb seafood mousse, wrapped in puff pastry. Fresh vegetables are especially well prepared and subtly seasoned. Entrées in the $15–22 range.

The Lincoln Inn (457-3312), West Woodstock. Fireside Continental dining on such popular selections as broiled Norwegian salmon, lamb déjà vu (boneless loin with honey mustard), and roast duck with strawberry sauce. Open Tuesday–Sunday, plus Sunday brunch from 11. Entrées $12.95–18.95.

The Village Inn of Woodstock (457-1255), 41 Pleasant Street, Woodstock. This Victorian guest house serves dinner nightly, featuring roast Vermont turkey, roast duck, prime rib, or rack of lamb. Look for seasonal early-bird special and "Italian Nights." Entrées $12.95–20.75.

Bentley's Restaurant (457-3232), Elm Street, an oasis of Victoriana and plants, is open daily for lunch and dinner, featuring everything from brawny hamburgers and croissant sandwiches to veal Marsala and Jack Daniel's steak. Frequent live entertainment, disco dancing weekends. Entrées under $20.

EATING OUT   **Spooner's** (457-4022), Route 4 east (in the Sunset Farm Barn), is a natty, informal, relatively inexpensive restaurant specializing in beef, seafood, and a salad bar. Open daily for lunch and dinner.

Stone House Tavern (457-3609), Woodstock East (located in the basement of the 1834 Stone House), is a popular local hangout with a pleasant patio shaded with an awning in the summer. Soups, salads, burgers, steaks, veal, spareribs for lunch and dinner daily.

The Corners Inn (672-9968), Routes 4 and 100A, Bridgewater Corners. A casual place, featuring Italian dishes, open Wednesday–Sunday, which is all-you-can-eat "four pastas" night at $9.95.

Jade Garden (672-3133), Route 4 west. This exceptionally good Chinese restaurant featuring Mandarin and Szechuan dishes is the most recent addition to the gustatory scene. Shredded pork with Peking sauce and a house special pork, beef, chicken, and shrimp Subgum are outstanding. Open daily for lunch and dinner, plus takeouts.

Woodstock Country Club (457-2112). Light lunch.

Courtside (457-1160), in the Woodstock Inn and Resort Sports Center, Route 106 south, serves soups, salads, sandwiches, and luncheon specials in lofty surroundings or on the deck in summer,   11:30–3.

Mountain Creamery (457-1715), Central Street, serves breakfast daily 7–11:30, plus sandwiches and luncheon specials and homemade ice cream. Pies and cakes from their bakery are for sale.

Mia Cucina (457-4110), 47 Pleasant Street, is a unique source for exceptional Italian specialties, to savor on a small table inside or to order ahead for takeout; catering and special orders.

The Village Butcher (457-2756), 18 Elm Street, provides tasty deli specials to go, along with its top-flight meats, wines, and baked goods, plus homemade fudge.

The Wasp Diner, Pleasant Street, is unsigned, but if you can find it, join Woodstock's hard-working fraternity for breakfast or lunch at the counter.

Bentley's Florist Café (457-3400), 7 Elm Street, offers sandwiches, ice cream, cappuccino, and flowers.

The Dunham Hill Bakery, 61 Central Street, is a pleasant stop for pastries and coffee; breakfast and snacks daily.

SELECTIVE SHOPPING   Woodstock is full of antique and gift shops, boutiques, and specialty stores for toys, quilts, linen, sports and children's clothes, silver, leather, wool, and needlework. Among the established or unusual:

F. H. Gillingham & Sons (457-2100, 800-344-6668), Elm Street, owned and run by the same family since 1886, is something of an institution, retaining a lot of its old-fashioned general store flavor in which plain and fancy groceries, wine, housewares, and hardware for home, garden, and farm can be found. Mail-order catalog.

Gallery 2 (457-1171), in two locations (on Elm Street and around the corner on Central Street), has won special awards for its consistent promotion of the work of Vermont painters, sculptors, and glass blowers. Folk art and prints round out its distinctive examples of contemporary art.

The Looking Glass (457-1301), Central Street, stocks upscale children's clothing, featuring its locally made Elizabeth Anne collection.

Unicorn (457-2480), 15 Central Street, is a veritable treasure trove of unusual gifts, cards, games, toys, and unclassifiable finds.

Woodstock Potters (457-1298), Mechanic Street (off Central), is a studio workshop where Kathy Myers and Robin Scully make stoneware pottery and hand-painted porcelains.

The Yankee Bookshop (457-2411), Central Street, carries a large stock of hardbound and paperback books for adults and children, plus cards; features the work of local authors and publishers.

Who Is Sylvia? (457-1110), 26 Central Street, features vintage clothing and accessories.

Primrose Garden, 26 Central Street, vends dried and silk flowers, wreaths, and sweet-smelling things of all sorts.

The Vermont Workshop (457-1400), 73 Central Street, features a wide selection of gifts and crafts, furniture, rugs, and lamps.

Log Cabin Quilts (457-2725), 9 Central Street. Calicos, stencils, and supplies; imaginative works by Vermont artisans.

Gallery on the Green (457-4956), corner of Elm Street, features original art, limited edition prints, occasionally sculpture.

North Wind Artisans Gallery (457-4587), 81 Central Street, jewelry, glass, furniture, pottery, and weaving.

Minerva (457-1940), 61 Central Street, is a partnership of eight New England artisans who produce stoneware, porcelain, clothing, rugs, blankets, silver and gold jewelry.

Woodstock Gallery & Design Center (457-1900), Gallery Place, Route 4 east, shows and sells paintings, photographs, and prints; custom framing.

The Lamp Shop (457-2280), 47 Central Street, has a fine selection of antique lamp bases plus customized shades and some other antiques.

Motley's (457-5151), 67 Central Street, is an expensive "toy store for adults": bears, bears, and more bears, cornhusk dolls, stained glass, hand-painted furniture, prints.

HSI (457-3804), Routes 12 and 4, Taftsville. Factory outlet store for the designers and manufacturers of contemporary oak furniture.

Red Cupboard Gift Shop (457-3722), Route 4, West Woodstock, has a broad selection of Vermont-made gifts, jams, jellies, and maple products.

The Market Place at Bridgewater Mill (672-3332), Route 4, Bridgewater. When an 1825 woolen mill on the Ottauquechee finally gave up the ghost in the early 1970s, a local bootstrap effort was mounted to convert it to an indoor shopping center. **The Mountain Brewers** (672-5011) offer tasting tours daily, 10–6. **The Sun of the Heart Bookstore** (672-5151) is an especially appealing, bright shop with a well-selected stock of new books.

Taftsville Country Store (457-1135), Route 4 east. Recently refurbished and restocked, this local 1840 landmark carries carefully selected Vermont gifts as well as a good selection of cheese, maple products, jams, jellies, smoked ham and bacon, plus staples, Dunham Hill Bakery goodies, and a deli.

Sugarbush Farm (457-1757), Pomfret—Route 4 to Taftsville, cross covered bridge, go up the hill and turn left on Hillside Road, then follow signs. Sample seven Vermont cheeses, all packaged there. In season, one can watch maple sugaring.

ANTIQUES   Wigren & Barlow (457-2453), 29 Pleasant Street, is closed in the winter; **Church Street Antiques** (457-2628), west of the Green, is open daily; **Frasers'** (457-3437), Taftsville, for early Americana; **Pomfret Hollow Antiques** (457-1300), Cloudland Road, Pomfret, open Memorial Day through foliage by chance or appointment.

SPECIAL EVENTS   February (Washington's Birthday): A week of **Winter Carnival** events sponsored by the Woodstock Recreation Center (457-1502); concerts, Fisk Trophy Race, sleigh rides, square dance, Torchlight ski parade.

July the Fourth: **Crafts Fair,** music and fireworks display in the evening at the high school. **Woodstock Road Race,** 7.4 miles (457-1502).

Mid-August: Sidewalk sale.

Mid-October: **Apple & Crafts Fair.**

Early December: **Christmas Wassail Weekend,** which includes a grand parade of carriages.

MEDICAL EMERGENCY   Woodstock (911), Barnard (728-9600). **Ottauquechee Health Center** (457-3030), 32 Pleasant Street, Woodstock.

QUECHEE

Quechee, on Route 4, four miles east of Woodstock, once a thriving woolen mill town, has been almost completely swallowed in the past 20 years by the 6,000-acre Quechee Lakes Corporation, probably the largest second-home and condominium development in the state. As such enterprises go, this one has been well-planned, allowing for a maximum of green space, but hilltops crowned by town houses can't help but make rural preservationists wince. Still, it's an attractive colony of suburbanites. In the wake of this leviathan, village resources have been preserved and expanded, including a replicated covered bridge across the river near what was Downer's Mill.

GUIDANCE   The **Quechee Chamber of Commerce** (295-7900).

TO SEE AND DO   **Quechee Gorge**, Route 4, is one of Vermont's natural wonders, its 165-foot chasm bridged by a span that used to carry Woodstock Railroad trains. The nearby **Quechee Gorge Recreation Area** (295-2990/773-2657) has picnic grounds, tent and trailer sites, and trails leading down into the gorge, which should be approached carefully; at the north end of the gorge, under a spillway, is a fine, rockbound swimming hole, accessible by easy stages through the pine woods at the west end of the bridge.

Quechee Polo Club. Matches most Saturdays in July and August on the field near the center of the village.

Quechee Hot Air Balloon Festival (295-7900), late June. Ascensions, flights, races, craft show, entertainment.

Timber Village (295-1550), the biggest attraction at Quechee Gorge, Route 4, combines a country store, a 225-dealer antique mall, an arts and crafts center, Basket Mart, Christmas Loft, Sugar House and Cider Mill, an operating 1946 Worcester Diner, and a carousel and miniature train ride for kiddies. Miniature golf nearby.

Wilderness Trails (295-7620), Clubhouse Road at the Quechee Inn. Complete outdoor equipment rental for the whole family: daily bike trips, canoeing on the Connecticut River or Dewey's Mills Waterfowl Sanctuary, and fishing on Dewey's lake or with the Vermont Fly Fishing School.

LODGING   All places listed below are in Quechee (zip code 05059) unless otherwise noted.

Quechee Lakes Corp (rentals 295-1970), Box 277. House and rental condo properties include cable TV, fireplace or woodstove, fully

Quechee Gorge below former railroad bridge

equipped kitchens; some accommodations have Jacuzzi and sauna; rental fee includes linens, firewood, utilities. $315–700.

Carefree Quechee Vacations (295-9500, 800-537-3962), 50 Main Street, handles condo and townhouse rentals.

The Quechee Inn at Marshland Farm (295-3133, 800-235-3133), Clubhouse Road, is an extremely attractive, restored and enlarged eighteenth-century farmhouse, once the home of Vermont's first lieutenant governor. It's near the Ottauquechee River just above the dramatic gorge. The sitting and 24 guest rooms have a romantic aura, and the dining room is above average. Guests have access to the nearby Quechee Club for golf, downhill skiing, and swimming pool. The inn maintains its own 18 km of groomed cross-country ski trails (see also Wilderness Trails under *To See and Do*). Rates range from $148 double to $198 for the Lt. Governor's suite, peak season, MAP, lower midweek from November to May.

BED & BREAKFASTS   **Quechee Bed & Breakfast** (295-1776), Route 4. Eight comfortable guest rooms with private baths, $85–125 with full breakfast.

The Parker House (295-6077), Main Street, Quechee. This handsome Victorian mansion has four spacious guest rooms at $60–120 with continental breakfast, served in your room if you prefer. Formal dining, too (see *Dining Out*).

DINING OUT   **Quechee Inn at Marshland Farm** (295-3133), Clubhouse Road, Quechee. Open seven evenings a week, this romantically rustic dining room features, for example, smoked chicken turnovers, grilled eggplant tart, avocado with Boursin, or escargot as appetizers, and entrées that might include duckling with raspberry sauce, pork with peaches, venison loin with wild rice cakes, or New Zealand rack of lamb. Their French Silk Pie is not to be missed. Entrées $14–19.

Simon Pearce Restaurant (295-1470), The Mill, Quechee, is a cheerful, upbeat, contemporary place for consistently superior lunch and dinner, served with its own pottery and glass, overlooking the waterfall. The patio is open in the summer, and its Irish soda bread and Ballymaloe brown bread alone is worth a visit. Lunch entrées could be spinach and cheddar cheese in puff pastry or beef and Guiness stew; at dinner, duck with mango chutney sauce, veal with two-mustard sauce, or beef tenderloin pressed in cracked pepper and sautéed with brandy and mustard. Open daily. Dinner entrées $13.50-22.00.

Isabelle's at the Parker House (295-6077) serves a $24.95 prix fixe, three-course dinner—smoked salmon with crème fraîche and mustard, for example, followed by spinach, endive, and apple salad with a curry vinaigrette, and rack of lamb with a thyme and rosemary sauce. Bistro entrées from $5.95.

EATING OUT   **Rosalita's** (295-1600), Waterman Place, Route 4, is the area's

Tex-Mex hangout (with adobe walls and Mexican tiles) where you can quaff Dos Equis beer and cheese soup served in a deep-fried tortilla bowl, munch hamburgers or Nachos Fajita anytime, or add Louisiana blackened sole for a dinner entrée. Inexpensive (and should be).

Sevi's House of Seafood (295-9351), Route 4. In pleasant nautical surroundings, Mike and Sevi Guryel offer hearty, consistently well prepared dinners daily, featuring lobster, broiled scrod, baked stuffed shrimp, a broiled shore dinner, steak, or tender prime ribs, all accompanied by Greek salad. Their homemade New England clam chowder is rich, and daily specials are good values. From 4 to midnight, it's pizza time, in the lounge or takeout.

Wildflowers Restaurant (295-7051), Route 4, Quechee (near the gorge). An above-average road-food place, for breakfast, lunch, and dinner, often crowded with bus tours during the summer and early fall.

SELECTIVE SHOPPING   Simon Pearce Glass (295-2711), The Mill, Main Street, Quechee. Pearce, who operated his own glassworks in Ireland for a decade, moved here in 1981, acquired the venerable Downer's Mill, and is now harnessing the dam's hydro power for the glass furnace. Visitors can watch glass being blown and can shop for individual pieces from the retail shop, where seconds with imperceptible flaws are also stocked, along with handknit sweaters, quilts, and distinctive pottery. The shop is open from 10 to 5 daily; glass blowing can be viewed during those hours on weekdays and on summer weekends.

Antiques Collaborative (800-2-RARITY), Waterman Place, Route 4, three floors of some 90 dealers' selected stock displays.

The Fat Hat Factory (434-6646), Tucker Mountain Studios, Route 4 at Club House Road, has clothing and hats made in the old barn.

Laro's Farmstand, Route 4 between Taftsville and Quechee, open in summer and early fall, is a superior produce market that also sells well-selected wooden ware, woven placemats, syrup, honey, preserves, Ben and Jerry's ice cream, an unlimited variety of baskets, and a barn full of old things. Fresh corn on the cob roasted while you wait.

Scotland by the Yard (295-5351), Route 4, three miles east of Woodstock, imports tartans and tweeds, kilts, capes, coats, sweaters, skirts, canes, books, records, oatcakes, and shortbreads.

Talbot's Herb & Perennial Farm (436-2085), Hartland-Quechee Road, three miles south of the blinker off Route 4. Field-grown herbs, dried flowers and wreaths, greenhouse. Open daily 9–5, from early April through October.

Sugar Pine Farm (295-1266), Route 4, Quechee. Old and contemporary folk art and other gifts, in a 1740s replica house. Closed Wednesdays, usually open other days from 10:30.

III. Central Vermont

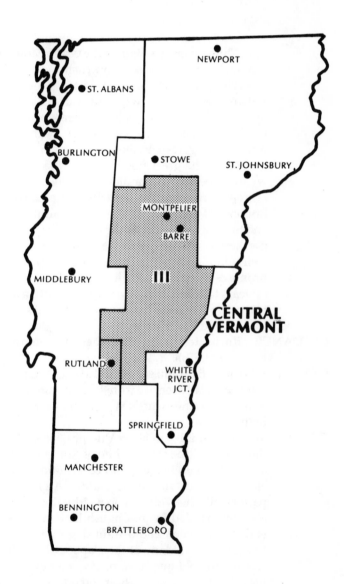

NEWPORT

ST. ALBANS

BURLINGTON

STOWE

ST. JOHNSBURY

MONTPELIER

BARRE

MIDDLEBURY

III

CENTRAL
VERMONT

RUTLAND

WHITE
RIVER
JCT.

SPRINGFIELD

MANCHESTER

BENNINGTON

BRATTLEBORO

The White River Valley

The White River rises high in the Green Mountains—near Bread Loaf Mountain, to be precise—and rushes down through the villages of Granville, Hancock, and Rochester, keeping company with Route 100 until Stockbridge, where its course dictates a dog leg in the highway. It then turns sharply northeast, carving a narrow valley for Route 107. This section is an especially challenging one for kayakers during spring freshets. Flowing through the village of Gaysville, devastated by the great flood of 1927, the White River reaches Bethel, where it begins to parallel Route 14 and I-89. Vestiges of an old railroad connecting Rochester to Bethel can occasionally be seen from Routes 100 and 107. As the river continues through the Royaltons and Sharon on its way to the Connecticut River, the input of its three northern branches swells its waters, making it particularly rich in swimming and fishing holes. A federal salmon hatchery in Bethel promises to make the White River even more attractive to fishermen in years to come. In the winter, the route from White River Junction to the upper reaches in Granville is heavily trafficked by skiers bound for the Mad River Valley.

GUIDANCE **Rochester Valley Chamber of Commerce** (434-3411), Box 143, Rochester 05767.

GETTING THERE By train: see *AMTRAK* in "What's Where."

By bus: Daily service from Boston, connecting in White River Junction with Connecticut, NYC service; stops in Sharon, South Royalton, Bethel.

TO SEE AND DO **South Royalton Village** 05068. Cupped between a bend in the river and the straight line of Route 14, this is a small but unusually attractive village gathered around an outsized Green with an elevated bandstand in the middle. A granite arch at one end of the park recalls the 1780 raid on nearby Royalton by more than 300 Indians commanded by an English lieutenant. A stagecoach inn at one end of the Green and a train depot on another recall later eras in village history. Many of the clapboard buildings within eyeshot, including the old inn, have received a new coat of paint and lease on life as part of Vermont's first and only law school, headquartered in a tower-topped old school building. Founded in 1972, accredited in

1975, Vermont Law School now has a full-time faculty of 27 and a student body of 465 men and women from around the country. Memorabilia from the town's colorful past can be seen in the Royalton Historical Society Museum (763-8830) in the 1840 Town House in Royalton, open by appointment.

Rochester, tucked into a narrow valley between the Green Mountains and the Braintree Range, is almost equidistant between—and just far enough from—Waitsfield to the north and Killington to the south, thereby escaping some of the ravages of resort development. It's still a quiet, unhurried sort of place, with a picturesque village Green and reclusive summer population. A drive through the Hollows, situated above the village on the flanks of the Braintree Range, provides superb views and a delightful alternation of field and forest. The largely uninhabited western portion of the town lies within the Green Mountain National Forest and is used by sportsmen, picnickers, and hikers. The Bingo area, in particular, offers swimming holes, abandoned town roads, cellar holes, and Civil War–era cemeteries to poke around in.

Joseph Smith Memorial and Birthplace, Sharon. One mile south of South Royalton, a marker on Route 14 points you up a steep two-mile hill to a complex maintained by the Mormon Church. Open year-round during daylight hours, this is a museum devoted to telling about the life of the founder of the Church of Jesus Christ of Latter Day Saints. A 38½-foot-high obelisk, cut from Barre granite in 1908, marks the site of the farm in which Joseph Smith was born in 1805 and lived until he was ten. Each foot on the shaft marks a year in the life of the prophet, who was murdered by a mob in Carthage, Illinois, in 1844. There are a total of 360 beautifully maintained acres here, including picnic tables and campsites.

Bethel National Fish Hatchery, Gaysville (Bethel). Established in 1977 to raise imprint salmon for the Connecticut River restoration program, the hatchery produces one million salmon smolts per year.

GREEN MOUNTAIN NATIONAL FOREST   Among the highlights in the Rochester district of the GMNF are the **Long Trail** and the **Texas Falls Recreation Area** (off Route 125), offering 17 picnic sites and an interesting series of cascades hollowed through bedrock. **Chittenden Brook** (off Route 73) is the developed campground near Rochester. A good short hike is from Brandon Gap north six-tenths of a mile to the cliffs of Mount Horrid, where there are views to the east. Because of the abundance of other things to do in this area, be sure to drop into the district ranger's office on Main Street in Rochester (767-4777, or RR 1, Box 108, 05767) and ask about their Recreation Opportunity Guides.

BOATING   While most of the White River is navigable in high water, the 20-mile stretch from Rochester to Bethel is especially popular with canoeists, tubers, and kayakers. A good place to put in is at the cement bridge just south of Rochester. Camping is available at Rud Memorial Park, seven miles from Bethel. The river has white water in spring and some steep grades.

GOLF   The White River Golf Club (767-GOLF/4653), RD 1, Box 137, Rochester 05767, Route 100, has been thoroughly upgraded within the past two years: nine holes, new clubhouse with a restaurant serving lunch (dinner by arrangement). Open May 1–October 31. Next to it is a golf driving range (767-3211).

FISHING   Trout abound at the junction of the Tweed and White rivers, downstream from Bethel, above Randolph and below Royalton. Fly-fishing enthusiasts find the Bethel area good for large rainbows and brown trout, while below Royalton there are bass, spring walleye, and trout. **Bud's Bait and Tackle Shop**, on Route 14 between Sharon and South Royalton, is a source of fishing tackle and supplies.

HIKING   There are two short nature trails near Granville Gulf. At Moss Glen Falls, the ½-mile loop on the west side of the road is more rugged than the 1-mile loop on the east side.

CROSS-COUNTRY SKIING   Trail Head Ski Touring Center (746-8038), Stockbridge. A total of 45 km of trails, 20 km set on flat, easy meadows and surrounding woodlands. Food, rentals, and instruction are available, along with guided tours, mountaineering, inn-to-inn tours.

   Nordic Adventures (767-3996), Box 155, Rochester 05767. Cross-country ski tours are tailored to your needs in the neighboring national forest and adjacent areas. Day-trips, inn-to-inn tours, instruction, and rentals.

LODGING   **Tupper Farm Lodge** (767-4243), RR 1, Box 149, Rochester 05767. An 1820s farmhouse on Route 100, known for its friendly atmosphere and good cooking. Roger and Anne Verme can accommodate 30 guests in 10 rooms with private baths. They cater to skiers and bicyclists with bountiful breakfasts and candlelit dinners. The swimming hole is across the road in the White River. $50 per person MAP, double occupancy.

   Harvey's Mountain View Inn (767-4273), Rochester 05767. Situated in the North Hollow area, this spot offers spectacular views of the Green Mountains and the Braintree Range. Don and Maggie Harvey have been specializing in farm-style family vacations for years and have developed a strong following, so book well in advance. Heated pool in summer. Open year-round. $35–55 per person MAP.

   Liberty Hill Farm (767-3926), Rochester 05767. This is a working, 100-head dairy farm set in a broad meadow off Route 100—a great place for families. Bob and Beth Kennett have two boys (aged 14 and 13 at this writing), and there are plenty of toys, three horses, some chicks, and kittens. There are seven guest rooms, four with shared baths; families can spread into two rooms sharing a sitting room and bath. Meals are served family-style, and Beth makes everything from

VTD

Tubers head for the White River, Rochester

scratch. In summer, you can hear the gurgle of the White River (good for trout fishing as well as its swimming hole) from the porch, and in winter you can ski off into the village across the meadows. $50 per adult, $25 per child under 12, MAP.

The Huntington House Inn (767-4868/3772), on the Green, Rochester 05767. A gracious 1806 village home has two, newly redecorated, two-room suites ($60) and a single ($50), all with private bath, breakfast included. The dining room is open to the public for dinner.

The Stockbridge Inn (746-8165), Box 45, Stockbridge 05772, Route 100. A handsome Victorian country home built by the grandson of Justin Morgan, the noted horse breeder; six comfortable guest rooms with private or shared baths, $40–90 per room depending on the season; full breakfast.

The Kincraft Inn (767-3734), PO Box 96, Hancock 05748. This is a handsome old home on Route 100 with six guest rooms, nothing fancy, but cozy spaces to spend the night. Downstairs there is a comfortable living room with an organ and a pleasant dining room; dinner is available by reservation, and breakfast is included in $22–30 per person B&B; family-style dinner by reservation for guests only. Innkeepers Ken and Irene Neitzel also have a showroom for Ken's handmade furniture.

Hawk North (746-8911, 800-832-8007), PO Box 529, Route 100, Pittsfield 05762. Hawk homes are nicely designed vacation homes, each hidden away in the woods on sites scattered between Hancock, Rochester, and Pittsfield. Rates vary wildly with the season. As of this writing, the winter rates are $215 (for a two-bedroom house) to $315 (for a four-bedroom house) per night. Inquire about special packages.

Fox Stand Inn (763-8437), Royalton 05063. An 1818 stage stop on Route 14, established as a restaurant, Jean and Gary Curley also offer five guest rooms (share two baths), $35–50 B&B.

Greenhurst Inn (234-9474), Bethel 05032. A Victorian mansion, it stands alone on the western fringe of Bethel, across Route 107 from the river. There are 13 guest rooms, seven with private baths; amenities include eight fireplaces and a library of 3,000 books; $50–95 double room with breakfast.

Poplar Manor (234-5426), Bethel 05032. Two miles west of Bethel on Route 107, this gracious, Federal-era home offers a family suite with two double beds, two rooms with twin beds, and one single; $26–38.

The New Homestead (767-4751), Rochester 05767. This handsome old house on the fringe of town has three rooms with private baths, two with shared. $40 double includes a sumptuous breakfast of home-grown ingredients.

Loalke Lodge (234-9205), Gaysville 05746. Olive Pratt serves family-style meals in her rustic log cabin that accommodates 20 (shared baths). $30 per person MAP, $20 EP.

The Columns Motor Lodge (763-7040), Sharon 05065. A small, neat motel attached to an old house. Located in Sharon Village, just off I-89; it has a nice gift shop and is across from both the general store and Brooksies Family Restaurant, a good way stop. $34–40 double.

Cobble House Inn (234-5458), off Route 107, Gaysville 05746. Set high on a hillside overlooking the White River, the capacious house built by Dr. Sparhawk in 1864 has been transformed into a distinctive, welcoming inn by the Bensons. There are two parlors, framed in natural woods, a dining room, and six period bedrooms with private baths, which go for $80–100, including full breakfast, tax, and gratuities. Dinner is served by reservation only, cooked by Beau Anne Benson, a graduate of the Academie de Cuisine of Bethesda, Maryland.

CONDOMINIUMS See "Killington/Pico Area" for **Hawk Mountain Condominiums** in Pittsfield, Stockbridge, and Rochester.

HOSTEL **Schoolhouse Youth Hostel** (767-9384), Main Street, Rochester 05767. This 150-year-old former church has long been a favorite of ski and bike groups, but drop-ins, including motorists, are also welcome. Open May 15–October 15; November 15–April 15.

DINING OUT **Annabelle's** (746-8552), Stockbridge. Located near the junction of Routes 100 and 107, this restaurant offers a memorable dining experience, in part because of its glass-walled light and plant-filled decor but primarily because the American–Continental entrées are imaginative and well prepared: $8.95–$15.00. Sunday brunch, family buffet, lunch, and tavern menu, too.

Cobble House Inn (234-5458), Gaysville. The top-drawer dinner menu changes weekly but includes hot rolls, salad, a pasta or pâté appetizer, and main entrée, which could be veal "Thief Style" (with sage, mushrooms, shallots, roasted pine nuts, and wine), chicken stuffed with brie, prosciutto ham with shallots and wine, or chicken Normandy, stuffed with apples, maple, spices, cream, and brandy. Open daily 6–9, in the summer; call ahead for reservations, especially in the winter. Main courses $18.25–25.00.

Huntington House Inn (767-4868), On the Park, Rochester. John Trautlein, co-owner with Mark Eichhorn, is the chef, and his training at La Verenne in Paris is evident in homemade pastas, seafood, local game, rack of Vermont lamb, and vegetarian specialties. Open Wednesday–Sunday 6–9; $14–18 for entrées. The inn and dining room are nonsmoking.

EATING OUT **Fox Stand** (763-8437), Route 14, Royalton. Homegrown beef and farm produce served in a landmark 1818 stagecoach inn. Lunch and dinner, Tuesday–Saturday; Sunday noon buffet.

Trail BBQ (763-2131), Route 14 north, South Royalton. Home-smoked ribs, chicken, beef, and hot dogs star in this takeout spot (picnic tables in the summer) run by Mark and Donna Green. Open 11:30–7:30 Tuesday–Sunday.

South Royalton House (763-8315), on the Green, South Royalton, serves tasty meat and vegetarian sandwiches, light meals, and dinner specials, indoors or out depending on the weather and time of year; check ahead to see when it's open.

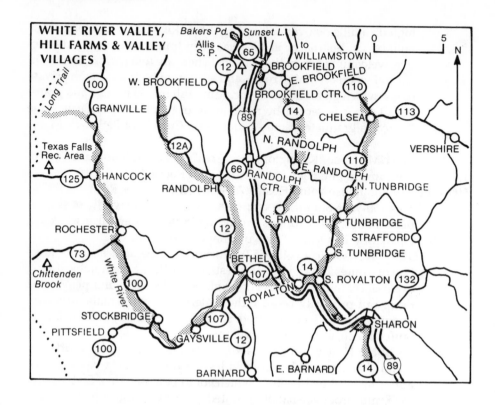

WHITE RIVER VALLEY, HILL FARMS & VALLEY VILLAGES

Brooksies Family Restaurant (763-8407), Sharon. A genuine family restaurant with counter service on one side and a slightly classier addition on the other. The diner opens early for breakfast and has a full lunch and dinner menu. Dinners on the restaurant side can begin with baked stuffed mushroom caps and include roast duckling flambé, filet mignon, or spaghetti with meatballs. Just off I-89, this is a traditional stop for many ski-bound families.

Vermont Sugar House, Inc. Located at the junction of Routes 14 and 107 in Royalton, a restaurant featuring pancakes and local syrup; Vermont cheese and other products are also sold.

Wilson's Creek House, junction of Routes 12 and 107; dependable for breakfast, lunch, supper; homemade bread.

SELECTIVE SHOPPING   **Tontine Press** (763-7092), RFD 2 (East Barnard), South Royalton 05068. Sabra Field's woodcuts of Vermont landscapes and people are among the most popular works of art presently produced in the state. The artist welcomes visitors (call before) in the studio attached to her home in the village of East Barnard—five miles up Broad Brook Road from the river road (cross the iron bridge at Tracy's Garage, on Route 14, just west of the general store in Sharon). The bright, distinctive prints are exhibited in the gallery at Tontine, where they are available as postcards or full-sized prints, either mounted or framed ($35–2,500).

Rathdowney (234-5157), Bethel, is the herb shop and garden where the firm's fragrant products are made. Books, gifts, and Vermont food products on sale, too. Open daily.

Camp Brook Corner Gallery (234-5030), RR 1, Box 615, Bethel, Route 12 north, features the paintings of Maryann Mayberry Davis; custom framing.

Frecks (765-8850), in South Royalton. Open weekdays 9–5, Saturdays 9–12, an old-fashioned family store selling clothes, stationery, toys, and an incredible variety of basics.

The Artists Guild (767-4610), Rochester Village, just across from the bank. A cooperative of primarily local artisans displaying a variety of crafts from jewelry to clothing. Open Thursday–Sunday.

Just Vermont Shop, junction of Routes 100 and 125, in the old Hancock Hotel building. Books, cards, preserves, T-shirts, Christmas decorations.

Je-Mel Wood Products (767-3266), on Route 100 in Granville, manufactures native wood products, and its retail store features its own finished and unfinished woodenware, including "seconds" and other gifts. Open daily year-round.

Vermont Only Village Store (767-4711), Route 100, Granville. Central Vermont's largest selection of Vermont-made products is housed in an old farmhouse; good for woodenware, toys, crafts, cards, books, clothing, baskets, smoked meats, cheeses, maple products, specialty foods, antiques.

Vermont Wood Specialties (767-4253), also on Route 100 in Granville, is the state's largest maker of wooden lazy susans, ice buckets, and other items, available at retail and wholesale, including "seconds." Shop open daily; factory on weekdays.

MEDICAL EMERGENCY   Bethel, Stockbridge (728-9600); Rochester (767-4211).

Hill Farms and Valley Villages

From Montpelier and Barre, four streams and parallel roads thread their way south through four valleys—separated by some of the most remote woodland and uncommercial farm country in all Vermont. Route 110 follows the First Branch of the White River through the classic farming towns of Chelsea and Tunbridge, flanked by high, open country and webbed with back roads where the sky seems very near. To the east, roads slope gently off this high plateau through the academic communities of Vershire and Strafford. To the west, Route 14 and Route 12 both traverse lonely valleys that steepen in spots into gulfs and are linked by a particularly rewarding road through the photogenic village of Brookfield. Further to the west, Route 12A follows the Third Branch of the White River along the base of the majestic Roxbury and Randolph ranges. Three streams and their three accompanying roads (Routes 12A, 12, and 14) meet like threads in a string purse in the town of Randolph—a combination of hill farms, a gracious old village in Randolph Center, and Randolph itself, the area's commercial center.

GUIDANCE **Randolph Chamber of Commerce** (728-9027), 66 Central Street, Box 9, Randolph 05060. Phone answered year-round, information center maintained at State Plaza, just off I-89 Exit 4 (next to the Mobil Station). Request a map brochure and business directory for the area. Good for information on the Randolph area. For leads on cottage rentals and details about special events in other communities, check with their respective **Town Clerks:** Brookfield (276-3352), Chelsea (685-4460), Tunbridge (889-5521), Strafford (765-4411). *The White River Valley Herald* (728-3232), Box 309, Randolph, carries local news and events for most of Orange County.

GETTING THERE Vermont Transit buses stop just off I-89 in Randolph; otherwise see "Barre/Montpelier Area."

VILLAGES **Randolph.** Randolph Center is clearly the oldest of the five Randolphs, a lineup of brick and clapboard Federal-era mansions along a main street that was cut unusually wide with the idea that this might be the state capital. Instead, it is now a soul-satisfying village in which life centers around Floyd's General Store and the nearby complex of Vermont Technical College, grown from the grammar school built here in 1806. A historical marker informs us that musician and schoolmaster Justin Morgan of Randolph Center brought a young stallion from Massachusetts to his home here in 1789 (Justin Morgan the man lies buried in the nearby cemetery; the grave of Justin Morgan the horse is marked by a simple stone off Route 110 in Chelsea). Randolph remains an unusually horsey community. But with the arrival of the railroad in the midnineteenth century, the population shifted from the Center to the valley three miles west, where a red brick Main Street now serves as a shopping, dining, and entertainment center for surrounding villages. Vermont Castings, housed in a nineteenth-century foundry hidden away down under the railroad bridge, claims to manufacture the world's best-selling cast iron woodstoves.

Brookfield. Easily one of the most picturesque four corners in all New England, this sleepy community belies its vivid past. Among its boasts are the state's oldest, continuously operating library (established 1791) and a house in which the Prince of Wales, father of Queen Victoria, not only slept but received a kick in the pants. Sunset Lake is traversed by a floating bridge, buoyed by 380 barrels (the lake is too deep to support a pillared span). During the summer, much of its traffic stops midway to fish, and on the last Saturday in January, it is a much-coveted viewing point for one of New England's last ice harvest festivals. A few of the village buildings now form Green Trails, an inn catering to bikers in summer, cross-country skiers in winter. Unfortunately, the sound of traffic on I-89 less than a mile from the village breaks the otherwise perfect sense of remoteness. Allis State Park a few miles west offers camping, picnicking, and a sweeping view.

Chelsea. Chelsea has been hailed as one of the few remaining bastions of "Vermont character." It is a town with an unusual survival rate of dairy farms and maple producers. It has a classic, steepled church and courthouse, a brick library and its own bank (since 1822), an abundance of Federal-era homes, and not one but two handsome Commons. An amazing number of services—post office, restaurant, barber, food stores, sewing shop, and fish and game office—are compressed into a small space. The commercial heart of town revolves around two twin 1818 brick buildings that house general stores.

Tunbridge. Some 20,000 people jam into this village of 400 souls for four days each September. They come for the World's Fair, said to originate in 1761 when the town received its charter from George III to hold two fairs each year. In fact, the fair dates back to 1867 when it was first sponsored by the Union Agricultural Society. Sited in a grassy, natural bowl by a bend in the river, the event still has everything an agricultural fair should have: a midway, livestock displays and contests, a Floral Hall, collection of old time relics, dancing, sulky racing, a fiddlers' contest, horse pulls, a grandstand, and more. Known as the "Drunkards Reunion" during a prolonged era when it was claimed that anyone found sober after 3 PM was expelled as a nuisance, it is now billed as a family event; drinking is confined to the parking lot and beer hall. The town also boasts five covered bridges, a fishing hole, and a photogenic brick Methodist Church (South Tunbridge).

Strafford. East from Tunbridge, the road climbs steeply through woods and fields, finally cresting and beginning its downhill run through a new kind of landscape: beautifully restored farms with ponds out back (pools would be too garish), stables, and other signs of wealth not evident back on the other side of the mountain. You are in Strafford, a physically beautiful community that has grown greatly in recent decades because it is within an easy commute of Dartmouth College and the Vermont Law School, also within the outstanding bi-state Dresden School District. Aristocratic homes—which include the Gothic Revival mansion built by US Senator Justin Morrill in 1848—are clustered along and below a sloping Common above which rises the exquisite white clapboard Town House, built in 1799. South Strafford is a crossroads community with an unusually pleasant general store at its center.

SIGHTS TO SEE   Justin Morrill Homestead (828-3226), Strafford. A striking, 17-room Gothic Revival mansion built by Justin Morrill, who served as a congressman and senator in Washington from 1855 until 1898 and is best remembered for the Land Grant Colleges Act. Morrill built this as his retirement home but never managed to spend much time here, because he kept getting reelected. It is a fascinating Victorian house, well maintained by the Vermont Division for Historic Preservation, free. Open mid-May–mid-October, Wednesday–Sunday 9:30–5:30.

Floating Bridge at Sunset Lake, Brookfield. First built in 1820 and replaced six times since, this is the only heavily used bridge of its kind in the country and very picturesque.

Marvin Newton House, Ridge Road, Brookfield Center. An eight-room house built in 1835, this displays historical exhibits for the area and serves as the site for weekly lecture programs in summer; open Sundays in July and August, 2–5.

Chandler Music Hall and Cultural Center (728-9878), Main Street, Randolph. A fine, acoustically outstanding music hall built in 1907, recently restored to mint condition, open year-round for musical and theatrical performances. The gallery here features changing exhibits of photography, art, and crafts. Saturday and Sunday 11–4.

Randolph Historical Society Museum (728-5398), Randolph. Located upstairs in the Police Station, this is a fine collection of local memorabilia, with emphasis on railroading; three rooms are furnished in circa

VTD

Ice harvesting at Brookfield's floating bridge

1900 style. Open June 4–October, Sunday 2–4, and by appointment.

Braintree Meeting House (728-9291), Braintree Hill Road. A great picnic spot with an early cemetery and views to the White Mountains. The building is open by appointment and on the first Sunday in August.

FARMS TO VISIT **Vermont Technical College** maintains a demonstration farm in Randolph Center (728-3395). Visitors can tour the sugarhouse, apple orchard, and dairy barn.

The Reynolds Farm (728-5297), East Randolph, the **Sprague Farm** (276-3453) and **Brookfield Farms** (276-3057), both in Brookfield, also the **Maple Ridge Sheep Farm** (728-3081) in Braintree, all welcome visitors.

COVERED BRIDGES There are five covered bridges in the town of Tunbridge: the Mill and Cilley bridges, both south of the junction of Route 110 with the Strafford Road, both built in 1883; the Howe Bridge (1879), east off Route 110 in South Tunbridge; and in North Tunbridge the 1845 Flint Bridge and 1902 Larkin Bridge, both east of Route 110.

In Randolph, two multiple Kingpost bridges, both built in 1904, are just off Route 14 between East Randolph and South Randolph.

In Chelsea, there is the Moxley or Guy Bridge, an 1886 Queenpost, east off Route 110.

SUGARHOUSES   These maple producers all sell syrup from their homes year-round and welcome visitors into their sugar shacks during March production periods.

Chelsea   **Nicholas Gilman** (685-2286), Route 110 north of the village, has a wood-fired evaporator, fed by buckets and pipeline.

Brookfield   **Robert Churchill** (276-3300), West Street, permits up to six at a time in his sugarhous

Randolph   **Silloway and Lambert Farms** (728-5253/4489), Boudro Road, Box 36, Randolph Center, welcomes up to 20 visitors at a time.

Vermont Technical College Farm (728-3395/3391), Route 66 east off I-89 invites visitors to tour sugaring operations.

Braintree   **Woodchuck Hollow Maples** (728-5770), Battles Road.

STATE PARK   **Allis State Park** (276-3175), Brookfield. Open May 30–September 15, a camping area with 22 sites, four with lean-tos, no hookups, each on a wooded loop road separate from the picnic area in which you can choose from tables on a windy hilltop or under a pavilion. A hiking trail (see *Hiking*) commands a fine view of the valley northward.

BICYCLING   This is some of the most rewarding biking country in Vermont. **The Brick Store** on the Common, Strafford (765-4441), offers repairs and touring advice but no rentals. Organized bicycle tours frequent The Three Stallion Inn in Randolph and Green Trails in Brookfield. Given the scenic north/south roads and choice of east/west links, also the abundance of back roads not shown on the state highway map, the potential for do-it-yourself tours is immense.

New England Bicycle Tours (728-3261, 800-233-2128), 41 South Main Street, Randolph, arranges inn-to-inn bike and canoe vacations in Vermont, New England, and Europe in partnership with the Swiss-based Baumeler Tours.

FISHING   **Baker's Pond** on Route 12 in Brookfield has a parking area and boat launch, good for trout fishing; there is a boat access on **Road Pond** in Williamstown and a canoe access on **Sunset Lake** in Brookfield, also stocked with trout; the floating bridge is a popular fishing spot.

GOLF   **Montague Course** (728-3806), nine holes, Randolph.

HIKING   In **Allis State Park,** Brookfield (off Route 12), a 2½-mile trail circles down through meadows, back up through woods. Access is from the fire tower beyond the picnic area; views are exceptional.

PICNICKING   See Allis State Park. Also Brookfield Gulf, Route 12 west of Brookfield: picnic facility, nature trail.

SWIMMING   Ask locally about various swimming holes in the first, second, and third branches of the White River. In Randolph Center, there is a man-made beach, bathhouse, and picnic area. At Lake Champagne, there is swimming at a private campground that charges admission. There is also a swimming pool at the recreational park in Randolph.

TENNIS   Green Mountain Tennis Center, Green Mountain Stock Farm (728-9122), Randolph.

CROSS-COUNTRY SKIING   Green Trails Ski Touring Center (276-3412), Brookfield. Forty km of trails meander around frozen ponds, through woods, and over meadows at elevations of 1,132–1,572 feet. A ski shop offering rentals and instruction is open weekends, holidays; inn-to-inn tours may also be arranged. Much, but far from all, of this trail system is within earshot of the highway.

Green Mountain Sports Center (728-9122), Randolph. More than 20 miles of groomed and tracked trails through woods and meadows; instruction and rentals available from the shop at Three Stallion Inn, marked from Route 66.

OTHER WINTER RECREATION   See *Northfield,* under "Barre/Montpelier Area" for downhill skiing.

Peak Pond Farm (728-5065), in Randolph Center, offers hay and sleigh rides.

LODGING   ☞Green Trails Inn (276-3412), Brookfield 05036. The unusual shape of this inn is explained by its history. It began as a scattering of rooms owned by friends and relatives of Jessie Fiske, a Brookfield native who became one of the first women professors at Rutgers University in New Jersey. The rooms were rented out to her students and associates who spent summers horseback riding and "botanizing" with Miss Fiske. The present inn consists of 15 rooms, some in a 1790s house called "The Lodge" (with one particularly appealing room that retains its early eighteenth-century stenciling), more in "The Inn," which offers a comfortable sitting room and dining room. Nine guest rooms have private baths, and there is an efficiency unit. While horseback riding is no longer offered, the trails are still good for walking almost all seasons that they aren't good for cross-country skiing (30 km are marked and groomed). The inn sits just across from the floating bridge on Sunset Pond (see Brookfield under *Villages*) and maintains its own small beach. Peter and Pat Simpson are your hosts, and rates in summer are $68 (shared bath) to $80 per couple with breakfast, plus 15 percent gratuity; MAP also available.

Three Stallion Inn (728-5575), off Route 66, Randolph 05060. Al and Betty Geibel host this attractive oasis for sports-minded people on 1,300 acres of rolling pasture and woodland, part of the Green Mountain Stock Farm. There's a spacious dining wing, and the sitting rooms in the old stone farmhouse can be adapted for conference use. In summer, this is a favorite for inn-to-inn bike tours, and in winter its Green Mountain Touring Center grooms 50 km of ski trails. There's an up-to-date fitness room, plus year-round Jacuzzi, two

tennis courts, and an outdoor lap pool. The adjoining nine-hole
Montague Golf Club is expanding to 18 holes; swimming and fishing
are possible on the Third Branch of the White River, which runs
through the property. The inn sponsors an annual mountain bike
race in mid-August. Rates from $50 (shared bath) to $75 double with
private bath, MAP and group packages available.

The Shire Inn (685-3031), Chelsea 05038. An exceptional, 1832
Federal-era brick mansion furnished with fine antiques, offering six
rooms, four with working fireplaces, all with private bath. $75–95
per couple B&B, $145–165 MAP. Dinner can be reserved a day in
advance. Innkeepers Jim and Marylee Papa have been here for eight
years and are delighted to direct guests wishing to explore the quiet
beauty of this region. The inn is right in the village of Chelsea (see
Villages), an easy stroll to both handsome Greens.

Watercourse Way (765-4314), Route 132, South Strafford 05070.
Lincoln and Anna Alden offer three rooms in this 1850 farmhouse
(wide pine floors, a flagstone fireplace). The property·backs on the
Ompomponoosuc River, and there is summer fishing, winter ski touring. $60 per couple, including a breakfast of fresh baked muffins and
fruit. A cut-your-own Christmas tree farm is an added attraction.

Birch Meadow Farm (276-3156), RD 1, Box 294A, Brookfield 05036,
East Street off Route 65 south, is Mary and Matt Commerford's
woodsy hideaway with three modern log cabins equipped for housekeeping, with TVs and woodstoves, plus a B&B suite in the main
house. $80 per couple, $15 each additional adult.

Rantree Farm Bed & Breakfast (728-5782), Braintree. A spacious
turn-of-the-century house set high on its own 150 (plus) acres with
expansive views. There are three guest rooms, one with private bath,
all nicely decorated. In summer, there's a swimming pond, in winter,
cross-country skiing. This is a small working farm with resident rab-
bits, chickens, sheep, and a horse. $60 per couple includes breakfast.

Placidia Farm Bed & Breakfast (728-9883), Braintree. This is an
apartment in a hand-hewn log home (deck, kitchen, bedroom, and
living room) on a large farm with its own pond; breakfast is served.
Rates on request.

DINING OUT   Shire Inn (685-3031), Chelsea, serves a superior five-course,
$32 prix-fixe dinner, by advance reservation and mostly family style,
at 7. Marylee Papa, the chef, features regional and other specialties
like Shire scallops with carroway, pumpkin soup, filet mignon with
cranberry brandy, baked pears, and even richer desserts.

Stone Soup Restaurant (765-4301), Strafford. Open Wednesday–
Sunday 6–11, dinner served until 9:15. Reservations strongly suggested. There is no sign for this elegantly rustic little restaurant that
has acquired a strong following over the past decade. There are daily
blackboard specials like maple country spare ribs and roasted Cor-

nish game hen. Main courses under $20. Personal checks, but no credit cards.

Three Stallion Inn (728-5575), off Route 66, Randolph. The attractive, expanded dining room here is open for lunch and dinner with a menu specializing in beef, veal, and seafood, such as a platter of shrimp, scallops, and crabcake, grilled swordfish, stir fries, chicken, and creative pastas; from $9.95 for chicken and scallop pesto Alfredo with fettucine to $13.50 for a 12-ounce rib eye with Jack Daniel's sauce. Open Tuesday–Saturday for lunch and dinner, also in summer for Sunday dinner, 4:30–9.

August Lion (728-5043), Randolph. Located on Main Street across from Chandler Music Hall in a nineteenth-century house with high tin ceilings, plants, and stained glass. At lunch the menu features soups, salads, and sandwiches; at dinner the specialty is Maine seafood, steak, pastas, and veal, accompanied by a bountiful salad bar with unshelled shrimp. Sunday brunch is especially popular. Closed Tuesdays. Main courses under $20.

EATING OUT **Chelsea Restaurant** (685-4838), open Monday–Saturday, 7 AM–8 PM, Sunday till noon. This cheery little place is fine for daily specials like beef and barley soup, plus a hot, tender pork sandwich for $3.75, sandwiches, and local gossip.

Lupine's (728-9397), Randolph. A family restaurant specializing in Italian specials, homemade fries, turkey and roast beef, desserts and muffins. Open for lunch except Sunday and Monday.

SELECTIVE SHOPPING **Vermont Castings** (728-3181, 800-22-STOVE), Prince Street, Randolph. Even if you are not interested in buying a wood- or coal-burning stove, the showrooms are worth a stop. Since its founding in the mid-1970s, the company has established a reputation for cast-iron stoves that keep a fire overnight, ornament the house, and do not take up much space. Their first model was the Defiant, followed by the smaller Vigilant and even smaller Resolute. Gas-fired stoves come from its European affiliate. Open weekdays 8–5.

Brookfield Gallery (276-3146), Box 450, Brookfield, near the Green Trails Inn. Connie Karal shows the work of 17 Vermont artists (including Helen Dillon) and crafters and has a distinctive selection of gifts. Open mid-May to Christmas.

SPECIAL EVENTS January (last Saturday): **Brookfield Ice Harvest Festival.** February: **Strafford Winter Carnival.**

March: Sugaring in an exceptional number of open sugarhouses.

May: **Chelsea Arts Day**—flea market covers both Greens; music, crafts.

July: July 4 parade in Strafford, a bigger one in Randolph. Chandler Players performance at Chandler Music Hall, Randolph.

July, August: Summer music school, workshops at the **Mountain School**, Vershire.

Early August: **Huntington Farm Show**, Strafford.

September: **World's Fair**, Tunbridge.

October (Columbus Day weekend): **Lord's Acre Supper**, sale and auction, Barrett Hall, Strafford.

November: **Annual Hunters' Supper**, Barrett Hall, Strafford.

MEDICAL EMERGENCY   Randolph (728-9600); Chelsea, Tunbridge (685-4545). **Chelsea Health Center** (685-4400), Chelsea. **Gifford Memorial Hospital** (728-4441), 44 South Main Street, Randolph.

Killington/Pico Area

Killington is the largest ski resort in the East. It boasts six mountains, the longest ski run and season in the Northeast, the longest gondola line in the country, and the most extensive snow-making in the world. Just down the road is Pico, "the friendly mountain": older, smaller, family-run and -geared. It's said that some 11,000 visitors can bed down within 20 miles of these two ski destinations.

The rugged lay of this land, however, precludes any chance of a traditional resort village. Killington is the second highest peak in the state: It is flanked by other mountains and faces another majestic range across Sherburne Pass. Although the road through this upland village has been heavily traveled since the settling of Rutland (11 miles to the west) and Woodstock (20 miles to the east), there was never much of anything here. In 1924, an elaborate, rustic-style inn was built at the junction of Route 4, the Appalachian Trail, and the newly established Long Trail. A winter annex across the road was added in 1938 when Pico installed one of the country's first T-bars. But the lumbering village of Sherburne Center was practically a ghost town in 1957 when Killington began.

Lodging is strung along the four-mile length of Killington's access road and on Route 4 as it slopes ever-downward through Mendon to Rutland. The hill village of Chittenden, sequestered six miles up a back road from Route 4, is blessed with a large reservoir and a few inns. Ski lodges are also salted along Route 100 north to the pleasant old town of Pittsfield. Killington's Northeast Passage chair lift from Route 100 also puts the inns of Plymouth within a few miles and those of both Woodstock and Ludlow within 14 miles.

In summer, this is exceptional hiking country. The view from the summit of Killington is also accessible via gondola and chair lift. Other things to do include visiting the restored village of Plymouth, birthplace of Calvin Coolidge, and the Alpine Slide at Pico. Killington offers its own tennis and golf packages, and a few inns have full resort facilities; a number have tennis courts and swimming pools. There is also summer theater and ballet, a series of musical, horsey, and other events, and—because this is still primarily a winter resort area—substantial savings on summer accommodations. See "Rutland and the Lower Champlain Valley" for more dining and lodging options.

GUIDANCE   See *Lodging* for the Killington (year-round) and Pico (ski season only) reservations services.

In summer: **Killington-Pico Area Association** (773-4181), Box 114, Killington 05751, maintains an information booth (775-7070) next to the Lothlorien in the small shopping complex, junction of Routes 100 north and 4, open June through foliage daily, 10–6.

GETTING THERE   By bus: Vermont Transit stops en route from Rutland to White River Junction at Killington Depot, Route 4 near the access road. Most inns will pick up guests.

By plane: The Lebanon, New Hampshire airport, served by Northwest and Delta airlines, is 39 miles to the east; also see Burlington, 85 miles to the northwest.

TO SEE AND DO   **Plymouth Notch Historic District** (672-3650), Route 100A, is dedicated to Calvin Coolidge. Open Memorial Day through late October, 9:30–5:00; admission charged. This tiny white clapboard hamlet is where the thirtieth president of the United States was born in 1872, worked on his father's farm, was awakened 52 years later at 2 AM one August morning to take the oath of office as successor to President Warren G. Harding, and was buried. A modest photo-history in the granite Visitors Center summarizes Coolidge's life. The old vehicles in the Wilder Barn, the plainly furnished homestead, the recreated general store that was run by the president's father are all tangible reminders of the simplicity and frugality of the Coolidge aura.

The Plymouth Cheese Company, founded by the elder Coolidge in 1890 and revived in 1960 by his grandson, John Coolidge (who summers in the village), welcomes visitors year-round (see *Selective Shopping*). Cheese is made weekdays and sold on the premises along with Common Crackers. The Wilder House, an old village home, serves soups and sandwiches in its pretty dining room and has counter service. Picnic tables available.

Pittsfield National Fish Hatchery (483-6618), Furnace Road. Open 8–4 daily. The Fish and Wildlife Service raises landlocked salmon and lake trout here.

PARKS AND FORESTS   **Calvin Coolidge State Forest** (672-3612), Plymouth 05056. A 16,165-acre preserve that offers 60 campsites including 35 lean-tos, a dump station, picnic area and shelter, hiking, and snowmobile trails. Killington Peak is actually within this area. Primitive camping is permitted in specified parts of the forest. Facilities are handy to the Calvin Coolidge Birthplace and to the Shrewsbury Peak Trail.

Gifford Woods State Park (775-5354), Sherburne 05751. One hundred fourteen acres located ½ mile north of Route 4 on Route 100: 47 campsites including 21 lean-tos, a dump station, picnic area, fishing access to Kent Pond, hiking on the Appalachian Trail (also near Deer Leap Trail); fees same as above.

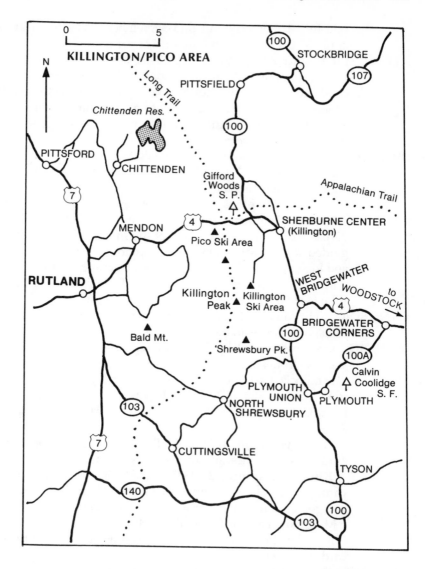

KILLINGTON/PICO AREA

0   5

N

Long Trail

STOCKBRIDGE

PITTSFIELD

Chittenden Res.

PITTSFORD

CHITTENDEN

Gifford Woods S. P.

Appalachian Trail

MENDON

SHERBURNE CENTER
(Killington)

Pico Ski Area

WEST BRIDGEWATER

WOODSTOCK

to

RUTLAND

Killington Peak

Killington Ski Area

BRIDGEWATER CORNERS

Bald Mt.

Shrewsbury Pk.

Calvin Coolidge S. F.

PLYMOUTH UNION

PLYMOUTH

NORTH SHREWSBURY

CUTTINGSVILLE

TYSON

Camp Plymouth State Park, off Route 100 at Tyson. Beach on Echo Lake picnic area, food concession.

AERIAL RIDE   Killington Peak. At 4,241 feet, this is the second highest mountain in the state, said to be the spot where a Reverend Samuel Peters in 1763 may have called the state "Verd monts." The summit restaurant serves also as terminal for the **Killington Gondola** (422-3333), which operates practically nonstop in the ski season, on weekends August–Labor Day and mid-September–Columbus Day (spectacular in foliage); $12 per adult, $8 per child 12 and under, $25 per family. The shorter ride to the summit on the **Killington Chairlift** runs daily, mid-July–Labor Day and mid-September–Columbus Day, $10 per adult, $6 per child 12 and under, $22 per family.

ALPINE SLIDE   Pico Alpine Slide (775-4346), Route 4, Sherburne. Memorial Day–Columbus Day, 10–5 in slower periods. $4 per adult, $3 per child age 6–12. Patrons ride a triple chair lift up and then slide down a total of 3,410 feet; the slide begins near the summit with a sweeping view of the valley to the west. Lunch and snacks are served in the base lodge at the bottom.

BICYCLING   Killington mountain bike rentals, tours (422-3333). The Killington Chairlift operates July 4–Labor Day and mid- through the end of September, hoisting bicyclists and their bikes to Killington Peak, accessing 25 miles of marked trails; rentals and guided tours available.

Vermont Mountain Bike Tours (746-8580), PO Box 685, Pittsfield 05762. Tom Yennerell was one of the first to offer guided and self-guided tours. Participants tour abandoned farm lanes, dirt roads, and logging trails. Packages include meals and lodging.

Mountain bike rentals are also available from **First Stop Ski & Bike** (422-9050), Route 4.

CANOEING   The Mustard Seed (483-6081), Dam Road, Chittenden, rents and transports canoes to the nearby reservoir.

FISHING   Licenses are available from the Sherburne Town Clerk, River Road, and also from sporting goods stores and state park rangers.

Landlocked salmon and trout can be had in Chittenden Reservoir; trout are the catch in Mendon Brook. There also is fishing in Kent Pond, Colton Pond, White River, Tweed River, and the Ottauquechee River.

The Tangled Line (773-0736), Route 4, is a source of fishing gear, guided fishing tours, and fly-fishing sessions.

GOLF   Killington Resort (422-3333 ext. 586), has its own 18-hole, 6,300-yard, par 72 course designed by Geoffry Cornish. Weekend clinics and golf packages. PGA professional instruction, rental clubs.

Mountain Top Golf School (800-445-2100), Mountain Top Resort, Chittenden. Pro Sam Snead offers sessions utilizing the resort's 300-yard practice range and putting green.

HIKING   Deer Leap Trail off Route 4 behind The Inn at Long Trail is the most popular short hike: a two-hour round-trip trek up a winding, steep path that yields a panoramic view from the top of a 2,490-foot cliff. See *Fifty Hikes in Vermont* (Backcountry Publications, Woodstock 05091).

For details about hiking the Appalachian/Long trails south from Sherburne Pass (Route 4) and the Long Trail north, consult *Guide Book to the Long Trail*, published by the Green Mountain Club.

Shrewsbury Peak. A rewarding, five-hour round-trip hike begins in the abandoned Northam Picnic Area on the steep, wooded North Shrewsbury Road off Route 100 south of West Bridgewater (see *Day Hiker's Guide to Vermont*).

Bald Mountain. This three-mile, three-hour round-trip hike is in Aiken State Forest, off Stratton Road from Route 4 in Mendon. The blue-blazed circle trail begins opposite the entrance to Tamarack Notch Camp.

Two local inns, **Mountain Meadows Lodge** and **Tulip Tree Inn**, cater to hikers on the "Hike . . . inn to inn" program; for details write: Churchill House Inn, RD 3, Brandon, Vermont 05733. **The Inn at Long Trail** also offers hikers a special rate (see *Country Inns*).

HORSEBACK RIDING **Mountain Top Stables** (483-2311), Chittenden; pony and trail rides, group and private instruction, sleigh rides.

Hawk Center (672-3811), at Salt Ash, Route 100, in Plymouth offers lessons, trail and hay rides.

SPA PROGRAM **New Life Fitness Vacations** (422-4302/800-228-4676), The Inn of the Six Mountains, PO Box 395, Killington 05751. Full weeks during the summer season, weekends in spring. Jimmy LeSage has been refining and fine-tuning his six-day fitness program since 1978. This was one of the first such programs in the country, and it's still one of the best we know of. It combines sensible eating and exercise that can be transposed to daily living. The daily regime begins with a pre-breakfast walk and includes low-impact aerobics, body conditioning, and yoga. In the afternoon, there's usually a hike. Meals are varied, and the emphasis is on high-fiber, low-fat foods. The stress is less on losing weight than on increasing energy and stamina. $895–1195 for six days double occupancy, $385–450 for a three-day weekend.

TENNIS **Killington School for Tennis** (800-343-0762), Killington. Weekend and five-day, midweek packages are available: Memorial Day to early September, using nine outdoor courts and the Village at Killington.

Cortina Inn (773-3331), Route 4, Killington. A resort with eight outdoor courts, also available to the public.

Summit Lodge (422-3535), Killington Road. Six outdoor courts available to guests, also to the public.

Public courts are also maintained by the towns of Chittenden and Sherburne.

CROSS-COUNTRY SKIING **Mountain Meadows Ski Touring Center** (775-7077), Killington. One of Vermont's oldest and most serious touring centers set high (1,500–1,800 feet) on the rolling acreage of the Mountain Meadows Lodge; 40 km total, 25 km set; instruction, rentals, also Telemark lessons and rentals. Tours of the backcountry available. $15 per day adult, $11 for children 10–15, children under 10 free, $5 for senior citizens.

Mountain Top Ski Touring Center (483-6089), Chittenden. A total of 110 km of trails (40 km set) begin at Mountain Top Inn, an ideal location at 1,495–2,165 feet with sweeping views of Chittenden Mountain and Reservoir; rentals and lessons, limited snow-making, and a log cabin warming hut in the woods at the intersection of trails; $12 for a full day.

Trail Head Ski Touring Center (see "The White River Valley").

Woodstock Ski Touring Center (see "The Woodstock Area").

Nordic Adventures (see "The White River Valley").

DOWNHILL SKIING   **Killington Ski Area** (422-3333, 773-1330), Killington. Among its boasts, Killington claims twice the uphill capacity of any other ski resort in the East. With six parking lots, six base lodges, six interconnected mountains, an entirely separate novice area, Killington is unquestionably big. Thanks to its three entry points and far-flung network of lifts and trails, the crowds are neatly dispersed throughout the area.

Lifts: six double chairs, four triple chairs, five quads (two are high-speed detachables), one 3½-mile gondola.

Trails and slopes: 107.

Vertical drop: 3,175 feet.

Snow-making: Services all 18 lifts from the six summits and connecting trails, meaning seven months of skiing.

Facilities: Six cafeterias, five ski rental shops, one mountaintop restaurant, four lounges.

Ski school: Accelerated Ski Method (a refined version of GLM that was developed here); one-day introduction to skiing program, two-

Killington/Bob Perry

Six mountains linked by 107 trails

and five-day programs available for all levels; novices have their own Snowshed Area; "terrain gardens" have been constructed as learning areas for various abilities.

For children: Children from six weeks are accepted in the nursery; the combination nursery and ski school program for ages 2–12 is available on a drop-in to seven-day basis; reservations required: 800-372-2007.

Special programs: a two-hour Meet the Mountain Tour, geared to varied ability levels, introduces patrons to the full extent of terrain within their ability levels. Offered 9:45 four days a week, December–mid-April, free with lift ticket.

Rates: Two-day adult $72, junior $36; five-day adult $160, junior $80; five-day lifts, lessons, and equipment, $313 adult, $157 junior.

Pico Ski Resort (775-4346 and 800-848-7325), Sherburne Pass, Rutland 05701. Dating back to 1937, this is a low-key, friendly, expanding area. It offers plenty of first-rate skiing on four mountains.

Lifts: two high speed detachable quads, two triple chairs, three double chairs, one T-bar, one Poma.

Trails: 40.

Vertical drop: 2,000 feet vertical, measured from base to 3,967-foot summit.

Snow-making: 82 percent of ski trails.

Facilities: Attractive base lodge, cafeteria, ski and rental shops, Last Run Lounge. Pico Resort Hotel, with shops, sports center, restaurant.

Ski school: ATM method, single lessons, two- to seven-day packages geared to all levels. Race camps.

For children: A nursery (from six months); ski school has its own cheerful building, adjacent to the base lodge, children aged three and up enroll in a full-day program that includes three ski lessons.

Special programs: Adult Racing Camp available on a five-day basis.

Rates: $37 per adult, $30 weekdays; $20 per junior (under 15), $18 weekdays; also half-day and multi-day rates.

ICE SKATING   See Cortina Inn and Summit Lodge under *Resort Inns*.

YEAR-ROUND   **Cortina Health Club** (773-3331), Cortina Inn, Route 4, Killington. Heated indoor pool, whirlpool, exercise room, saunas, massage, facials, exercise classes. Open daily 6 AM–10 PM. Special short-term memberships.

Summit Lodge Racquet Club (422-3535), Killington Road. Racquetball courts, instruction, racquet rental, volleyball, whirlpool, saunas, massage, ice skating, and skate rentals.

Mountain Green Health Club (422-3000), center of Killington Village. Located in the Mountain Green complex, a club with a 54-foot indoor lap pool, Jacuzzi, aerobics classes, steam rooms, sauna, massage. Open 10–10 daily.

The Woods Resort and Spa (422-3100, 800-633-0127), Killington

Road (near the bottom). Facilities include an unusually attractive lap pool with waterfall and Jacuzzi, an exercise room with Eagle equipment, and a full menu of spa treatments: massage, aqua-aerobics, herbal wrap, salt-glo loofah, Thalasso, and (our personal favorite) Parafango (mud treatment). Hours are 10–8 daily.

LODGING Killington Lodging Bureau (800-372-2007; 773-1330), 100 Killington Road, Killington 05751, open daily 8 AM–9 PM mid-November–May, in summer 8–5. The bureau keeps a tally of vacancies and makes reservations.

Pico Lodging Bureau (775-1927 and 800-225-PICO) offers a reservations service for more than 100 local lodging places during ski season.

RESORT INNS Cortina Inn (773-3331, 800-451-6108), Killington 05751. This modern luxury condominium hotel on Route 4 in Mendon is designed for the average American family willing to pamper themselves. Innkeepers Bob and Breda Harnish are enterprising hosts who offer a full summer program: tennis with pros using eight courts, a Fitness Center with whirlpools, saunas, exercise machines, and indoor pool, a game room, and special hiking, fishing, and picnicking expeditions. Year-round there is candlelight dining (open to the public) in the attractive, formal dining room and Theodore's Pub. The grounds include an extensive nature trail and a touring trail connecting with both the Mountain Meadows and Mountain Top trail networks in winter. Afternoon tea is served in the unusual two-story lobby that has a round hearth in the center and exhibit space for local sculpture and art in the gallery. There are 98 rooms, a variety of individually decorated spaces, some suites with fireplaces and whirlpool baths (#215 is immense), some with lofts, five wheelchair accessible. Rates: $84–114 per person MAP in winter, $84–129 per room (no meals) in summer.

Mountain Meadows Lodge (775-1010), Thundering Brook Road, Killington 05751. Open except early April–mid-June and mid-October–Thanksgiving. The main building is an 1856 barn, nicely converted to include an informal dining room, spacious living room, a BYOB bar, and game room. Run by the Scott family for 18 years and geared to families year-round, catering to hikers in warm weather months and cross-country skiers in winter, this is a hospitable, thoroughly relaxing kind of lodge. There are 18 guest rooms, all but three with private baths. In summer, there is a swimming pool and 100-acre Kent Lake that abuts the property, good for fishing and canoeing as well as swimming; the town tennis courts are just down the road. In winter, this is a major ski touring center (see *Cross-Country Skiing*). Winter rates are $53–63 per person MAP in a double room with bath; lower in summer, also family rates and for longer stays; there are a variety of packages winter and summer, including a rate for those hiking inn to inn.

Mountain Top Inn (483-2311, 800-445-2100), Chittenden 05737. Closed April–Memorial Day and weekends after Columbus Day until mid-December. Set on 500 rolling acres, overlooking Chittenden Reservoir and Mountain, this is one of Vermont's few truly self-contained resorts. Nicely rebuilt in 1977 when fire destroyed the old facility, it has been owned and managed by the Wolfe family for the past 50 years. There are 40 rooms, all with private bath, also a few chalets with maid service. Facilities include a heated pool, tennis, lawn games, sauna, canoeing, horseback riding, chip'n'putt golf, and, in winter, a major cross-country skiing center and trails with limited snow-making: $95–142 per person MAP, $65-115 per person B&B; packages and cheaper off season.

Summit Lodge (422-3535, 800-635-6343), Killington Road, Killington 05751. This is one of the zaniest inns in Vermont. An antique car festooned with a variety of other unexpected "objects" is parked in the lobby where one of the 45-room inn's two St. Bernard's is usually majestically ensconced. Facilities include whirlpools, saunas, tennis and racquetball courts, outdoor heated swimming pool (geared for winter use too), lawn games, and a courtesy bus to Killington lifts. There is also a year-round dining room and rathskeller, a library, gift shop, and a game room. From $75 per person MAP, many packages.

Grey Bonnet Inn (775-2537), Killington. Open except April 15–June 15 and October 15–Thanksgiving. A nicely designed modern lodge set off by itself on Route 100 north, just beyond the Route 4 junction. There are 42 standard rooms, each with two double beds and private bath, TV, phone, flowery curtains and spreads. Bill and Barbara Flohr have created plenty of relaxing space in two comfortable, spacious living rooms. Amenities include an indoor pool, sauna, exercise room, and cross-country trails that interconnect with Mountain Meadows. In summer, there is tennis, an outside pool, and walking trails. The dining room is large and inviting with a menu to match. $68 per person MAP midweek, $159 per person MAP on weekends in winter; less in summer. Add 15 percent gratuity.

Hawk Inn and Mountain Resort (672-3811 or 800-685-4295), Plymouth 05056. Over the past three decades, hundreds of Hawk homes and condominiums have been built on four different properties throughout Vermont. The largest of these is the Hawk Inn Mountain Resort complex, south of the Killington's Northeast Passage entrance on Route 100. Both the free-standing homes (salted away in the woods and on hillsides with splendid views), and the condo units are architecturally striking and luxuriously furnished and equipped. The 46-room, six-suite inn is a centerpiece. In summer, there is horseback riding, swimming and boating on Lake Amherst, and tennis. In winter, you can appreciate the indoor pool, ice skating, and sleigh rides. Hawk prices vary widely depending on the season and special packages. In winter, rates are $155–220 per couple in the inn, $330–520 in the town houses, $385–605 in the free-standing homes, less in summer, much less in off season. Rates include breakfast.

The Inn of the Six Mountains (422-4302, 800-228-4674), Killington Road 05751. An ambitious, 103-room, four-story Adirondack-style hotel with gabled ceilings, skylights and balconies, two-story lobby with a fieldstone fireplace. Common spaces include a second-floor sitting room and a third-floor library. There is also a spa with lap pool, Jacuzzis, sauna and exercise room, and a dining room. The only hitch here is the building's unfortunate location, right on the access road. And when we stayed here in August, bus groups predominated. $95–195 per night including breakfast.

COUNTRY INNS   **The Inn at Long Trail** (775-7181, 800-325-2540), Killington 05751. Closed May and June and November–Thanksgiving. This is the first building specifically built to serve as a ski lodge in New England. It began in 1938 as an annex to the splendid summer inn (see introduction to this section) that burned in 1968. Less elaborate than the original inn, its interior was also designed to resemble the inside of the forest as much as possible and so incorporates parts of trees and boulders. The 22-foot-long bar is made from a single log, and a protruding toe of the backyard cliff can be seen in both the pub and dining room. (The boulders seen from the dining room are said to be the oldest rocks in Vermont.) The 16 rooms are small but delightful, 14 with private baths, plus 6 two-room suites with their own fireplaces. Dinner is served nightly in the fall and winter, soup and salads during summer and fall from noon until 10 PM. There is Guiness on tap and Irish country and folk music on weekends in the pub, also a hot tub and ample space for relaxing near the hearth. Summer rates are $54–76 per couple B&B, in winter $294–374 per couple per weekend MAP, $325–406 per couple for a five-day ski week B&B. Gratuity is 15 percent MAP.

Tulip Tree Inn (483-6213), Chittenden 05737. This splendid home was built by inventor William Barstow, who retired here after selling his various holdings for $40 million right before the 1929 stock market crash. There is swimming, canoeing, and fishing in the Chittenden Reservoir just down the road, and in winter you can cross-country ski in town. Ed and Rosemary McDowell offer eight carefully furnished guest rooms, all with private bath, five with Jacuzzis. There is a big stone fireplace in the paneled den and a comfortable living room as well as a small tap room. Guests gather for drinks before a candlelight dinner that includes a soup, salad, sorbet, and then an entrée (pork medallions on our last visit) and dessert. Rosemary is the chef, and Ed serves. The couple then join guests for after-dinner conversation.   Rosemary is a superb cook. Rates are $60–105 per person, double occupancy, MAP. Add 15 percent gratuity.

Salt Ash Inn (672-3748), Plymouth 05056. This is one of the few surviving small, ski-oriented inns left. Built as an inn in the 1830s, it has 15 guest rooms, all with private baths and many with bunk space. There is a great little union pub in the former general store that retains the original grocery counter and wooden post office boxes (Calvin Coolidge picked up his mail); there are inviting places to sit around the circular hearth. The owners are Glen and Ann Stanford. Winter rates: weekends, $109–135 per couple MAP plus 15 percent gratuity; $68 per room midweek B&B.

The Vermont Inn (775-0708/800-541-7795), Killington 05751. Set high above Route 4 with a fine view of Killington and Pico mountains, this is a nineteenth-century farmhouse with a homey feel to its public rooms (there's a living room with woodstove, a great game room, and an upstairs reading room). In summer, there is a pool, tennis court, and lawn games. The sauna and hot tub are available year-round. Susan and Judd Levy are the friendly innkeepers. There are 16 guest rooms, 12 with private bath, one that's wheelchair accessible. $45–75 per person MAP in summer, $30–65 B&B; in winter $55–90 MAP, no B&B. Add 15 percent gratuity.

The Inn at Pittsfield (746-8943), Pittsfield 05762. Located in the center of the village on a handsome green, this double-porched old tavern is owned by Barbara Morris and Vicki Dubasi, enthusiastic innkeepers who offer seminars in interior floral arrangements. Each of the nine guest rooms (all private baths) has been individually decorated, and both breakfast and a multi-course dinner (with ambitious entrées like game hen topped with a tomato caper sauce) are served. The inn also serves as home base for Vermont Mountain Bike Tours (see *Bicycling*). $130 per couple MAP, plus 15 percent service; less midweek and for multi-day stays.

The October Country Inn (672-3412/800-648-8421), junction Routes 4 and 100A, Bridgewater Corners 05035. Handy to Killington (five miles from Northwest Passage lifts) and Woodstock (eight miles) as well as most of the things to do and see in this chapter, yet sequestered up a back road with hiking trails out back that lead to the top of a hill for a sweeping, peaceful view. Richard Sims and Patrick Runkel have opened up the farmhouse, created a large, comfortable living room with inviting places to sit around the hearth and around the big round table in the dining room, not to be confused with the other cheery dining room in which guests gather around long tables for memorable meals—which can be Greek, Hungarian, Chinese, Mexican, Italian, or occasionally, American; candlelit dinners include homemade bread, cakes, home-grown vegetables and herbs, and wine. Breakfasts are equally ambitious, geared to fuel bikers who frequent the inn in summer and skiers in winter. The 10 guest rooms vary in size, but all are carefully decorated and have private baths; $105–135 includes dinner and breakfast for two, $175–230 per couple per weekend. There are also single and children's rates.

LODGES   **The Cascades Lodge** (422-3731), Killington Road, Killington 05751.

Open year-round. A modern lodge just across the parking lots from the Killington lifts. The MacKenzie family has renovated and redecorated, creating an inviting living room adjoining the Wooden Nickel Lounge. This is an interesting space with a greenhouse, fern-filled corner, a grand piano, and a huge fieldstone fireplace. Rooms are standard with two double beds but mountain views. Facilities include an indoor pool, bar, whirlpool, exercise room, electronic games, and informal dining room serving breakfast and dinner, handy to the Killington lifts. In winter $42–74 per person per night, with breakfast; in summer $33–43 per person. Lunch and dinner also served in the Copper Penny restaurant.

Trailside Lodge (422-3532/800-447-2209), Coffee House Road, Killington 05751, off Route 100. This classic Vermont farmhouse, complete with crazy window, has grown a long way out back. A homey, old-fashioned, downhill ski-oriented place with a loyal following. Meals and the 28 rooms are family style with bunk beds (sleeping up to nine) or double, all with private bath. There's a hot tub and a big, comfortable living room. The place is geared to church and school groups, but families and individuals are welcome. It's a great place for a family reunion. (We suggest asking if and what groups are booked for the time you plan to be there.) $44–60 per person MAP in winter, $39 double (no meals) in spring and fall. Shuttle service is offered to the lifts.

Butternut on the Mountain (422-2000/800-524-7654), Box 306, Killington Road, Killington 05751. Open except May and June. A family-owned ski lodge with 18 large standard rooms with color TV and phone. Facilities include an indoor pool, whirlpool, fireside library and lounge, game room, laundry facilities, Mrs. Brady's Restaurant; $30 per person with continental breakfast, MAP and ski packages available.

CONDOMINIUMS   The Villages at Killington (422-3101 or 800-343-0762). There are a total of 500 condo units in a dozen different clusters, and the complex also includes the 96-room Villager Motor Inn and Sunrise Mountain Village, high on the mountain. In summer, with Snowshed Lodge offering dining and theater, this becomes a mini-resort in its own right, nicely landscaped and filled, primarily, with Florida retirees who have discovered the value of long-term rentals. In summer, golf packages are $69 per day, including greens fees and breakfast. Amenities include pools and whirlpools for each condo cluster. In winter, you can walk to the lifts, and while the village is not "slope-side" (it's a schlep or shuttle to the base lodge), you are right at the nerve center of Killington's vast lift and trail network. Winter rates, which include skiing, are $291–332 per couple in the Villager, $291–332 per night in the town houses, less for ski weeks and packages.

The Woods at Killington (422-3100, 800-633-0127), RR 1, Box 2210, Killington Road 05751. A complex of cluster and townhouse condominiums salted away in the woods on 100 acres around Terra Median, a combination check-in center, with an unusually attractive pool (with waterfall), steam room, and sauna. The units are the ultimate in condominium-style luxury: private saunas, two-person whirlpools, sound systems, washers and dryers, the works. Rates from $95 for a one-bedroom unit off season.

Hogge Penny Motor Inn (773-3200), PO Box 914, Rutland 05701. These well-constructed, attractive units can be rented as motel rooms or as part of a one- or two-bedroom condominium suite. The buildings command a spectacular view across the Otter Valley to the Taconics and are set well back from Route 4, surrounded by grounds that include tennis courts and pool. Each bedroom has a private bath, two double beds, and color TV, and each building includes a laundry room. There is a separate restaurant and tavern, also an office staffed round-the-clock. Winter rates are $57–96 per couple for a motel room, $89–139 for a one-bedroom suite; less in summer.

Pico Resort Hotel (775-1927 or 800-848-7325). In recent years, 152 slope-side units have mushroomed at the base of Pico, and they are well done: one-bedroom suites in the Village Square; two-, three-, and four-bedroom units in the Village with phones and marble-faced fireplaces. The sports center offers an indoor pool, Nautilus equipment, aerobics room, Jacuzzi, saunas, and lounge. Winter rates: a one-bedroom unit runs from $80 for a studio midweek to $360 for a three-bedroom loft unit on weekends.

MOTEL   **Farmbrook Motel** (672-3621), Route 100A, Plymouth 05056. An unusually attractive, 12-unit motel three miles from Coolidge's birthplace; the brook-side grounds have outdoor fireplaces, picnic tables. Rates: $44–52. Some rooms sleep five. Two kitchenettes.

DINING OUT   **Hemingway's** (422-3886), Killington. Between Linda's eye for detail in the decor and service and Ted's concern for freshness, preparation, and presentation of the food, the Fondulas have created one of the most elegant and rewarding dining experiences in Vermont. Chandeliers, fresh flowers, and floor-length table linens grace the high-ceilinged main room, while a less formal atmosphere prevails in the garden room and stone-walled wine cellar. Specializing in "regional, classic cuisine" with grilled pheasant with Beaujolais wine, and fillet of beef with morels. Closed Mondays and Tuesdays. Prix fixe $36.

Claude's (422-4030), Killington Road, is a frequent Taste of Vermont winner. Claude, the owner-chef, prepares appetizers such as escargots in garlic butter and smoked salmon ravioli, entrées of beef Wellington and rack of lamb perseille, and luscious Belgian chocolate mousse cake for dessert. Open Wednesday–Monday except off season when it's Thursday–Sunday.

The Countryman's Pleasure (773-7141), Mendon. Known for Austrian/German specialties: Veal Schnitzel Cordon Bleu, Sauerbraten, goulash, etc. The dining rooms occupy the first floor of a house, just off Route 4, opposite the Hogge Penny. Open 5:30–9 daily. The atmosphere is cozy, informal. Entrées $9.95–22.50.

Churchill's Restaurant (775-3219), Route 4, Mendon. Open for dinner only; closed Mondays. Vinnie Donnelly's is the one place "up on the mountain" that Rutland residents routinely drive to for their night out, and it's probably the area's all-round most popular restaurant with visitors too. Choose from book-lined alcoves in the main dining room, the cheerful pub, and a greenhouse-like area. The French onion soup au gratin is a favorite, along with the sole Rockefeller (fresh lemon sole wrapped around Maine crabmeat, spinach, onion, and garlic butter: $11.95), chicken Kiev, and New York sirloin steak. Leave room for chocolate mousse. A lighter pub menu is also available in the dining room.

The Vermont Inn (775-0708), Route 4, Killington. Open for dinner except Mondays. Chef Stephen Hatch has captured first place for the past two years in the Killington-Korbel Dine Around Award. It's a pleasant inn dining room with a fireplace and a varied menu that changes nightly. On an October Sunday, it included chicken Normandy (boneless breast of chicken sautéed with cider, applejack brandy, cream, and apples), cranberry glazed duckling, and fresh salmon poached and served with lobster veloute. Entrées $13.95–16.95.

Cortina Inn, Route 4, Killington. The large, attractive dining room is open to the public for dinner. The à la carte menu includes specialties like top sirloin with smoked bacon, shrimp scampi, grilled marinated lamb loin with port wine sauce, and salmon sautéed with rosemary garlic and tomato. Entrées include soup or salad and coffee, $13.50–20.00. (Watch for the New England Culinary Institute's arrival here.)

Inn at Long Trail (775-7181), Route 4, Killington. Open during ski and summer seasons. The dining room in this unusual inn (see *Country Inns*) looks out on the spotlit face of a steep cliff. A limited choice of entrées (examples: cornish game hen, prime rib, Guiness stew); all dinners include salad, bread, and vegetables; dinner served winter only, in summer, soups and salads all day from noon until 4 PM. Entrées $10.95–15.95.

Grist Mill (422-3970) at the Summit Lodge, Killington Road, Killington. Open for lunch and dinner. This is a new building, nicely designed to look like a grist mill that has always stood on Summit Pond (there's a 90-year-old water wheel). The space within is airy and pleasing, dominated by a huge stone hearth. The menu ranges from steaks and veal dishes through grilled swordfish to vegetable stir fry. Entrées $10.95–15.95.

EATING OUT   Casey's Caboose (422-3795), Killington Road. The building incorporates a circa 1900 snowplow car and a great caboose, housing the coveted tables in the place, but you really can't lose since the atmosphere throughout rates high on our short list of family dining spots; free buffalo wings in the bar 3–6, open daily from 3 PM, good for Italian and seafood dishes, as well as burgers, and the taco salad is a feast.

Powderhound's (422-4141), Killington Road. *The* best pizza on the mountain; take out to your condo or eat in the cheerful restaurant. Try the white pizza without tomato sauce or "Avalanche Pie" with ricotta, mozzarella, and fresh garlic; there are also burgers, salads, and Thai food.

Charity's 1887 Saloon Restaurant (422-3800), Killington Road. Open for lunch and dinner, for brunch (11:30–3) on Saturday and Sunday. Hanging plants, Tiffany shades, and plenty of gleaming copper and shiny wooden booths, this place is good for a Reuben or vegetarian casserole at lunch, for steak teriyaki, or for just onion soup gratinée for dinner; informal, satisfying.

Mother Shapiro's (422-9933), Killington Road. The most popular place on the mountain for breakfast (open at 7:30 AM), good for lunch and dinner too. A pubby, friendly place with big burgers and monster deli sandwiches, homemade soups, specials.

The Deli at Killington Corners (775-1599), Route 4, has the best, most generous daily specials and homemade soups to take out, such as roast pork with sauerkraut, lasagna. Open daily 6:30AM–9PM during ski season, 7–7 otherwise.

Back Behind Saloon (422-9907), junction of Routes 4 and 100 south. Open for dinner nightly and for lunch Friday, Saturday, and Sunday. A zaney atmosphere (look for the red caboose and antique Mobil gas pump), barnboard, stained glass, a big hearth. Specialties like venison Jack Daniels and Texas spareribs augment basic American fare: steaks and chicken, generous portions. Entrées on the high side ($10.95–18.50).

Sugar & Spice (773-7832), Route 4, Mendon. A rather unique pancake restaurant housed in a large replica of a classic sugarhouse and surrounded by a 50-acre sugarbush. Besides dining on a variety of pancake, egg, and omelet dishes, soups, and sandwiches, you can watch both maple candy and cheese being made several days a week. Open 7–2 daily, gift shop.

Blanche & Bill's Pancake House, Route 4, 1 mile east of junction with Route 100 south. "Serving breakfast anytime," 7 AM–2 PM, closed Monday and Tuesday. Blanche has been serving reasonably priced meals in the front rooms of her small house by the side of the road for over 10 years.

Marge & John's Country Breakfast, Route 4, Mendon. Closed Tuesday, otherwise open 7 AM–3 PM. Specializing in fresh sourdough bread French toast. Another roadside house with reasonable prices.

Mrs. Brady's (422-2020), Killington Road at Butternut Motor Inn. The atmosphere is casual and colorful, and the menu features a salad bar, steak, and seafood; includes a great American burger platter and gobbler (turkey on a grinder with stuffing and gravy), as well as baked stuffed lobster. There are also pasta, veal, and steak dishes, stir fries, plus pizza and a children's menu.

Donna's Country Kitchen (773-7974), Route 4, Mendon. Housed in their log home building, William and Dorothy Nicolai serve breakfast (available anytime), featuring all natural Belgian waffles with Vermont syrup and butter. There is also a standard burger and sandwich menu, take out or eat in. Open 7–3, with a snack bar 11–9.

The Corners Restaurant (672-9986), Bridgewater Corners. Favored by locals, a farmhouse specializing in Italian fare, a good bet any night; Sunday brunch also served. See the Woodstock area.

Penny Tavern (775-6620), a ways down Route 4 before the Rutland Mall (handy to the movies) in Mendon, attached to the Hogge Penny Motor Inn. Open for breakfast and dinner. A bright, eclectically decorated family restaurant, good for deli specials (even chopped chicken liver) for lunch, a full meal, or just soup and salad for dinner.

Also see "Rutland and the Lower Champlain Valley." Rutland is an exceptionally good "eating out" town.

APRÈS SKI   **The Wobbly Barn** (422-3392), Killington Road. A steakhouse (dinner: 5–11) with plenty of music, dancing, blues, rock'n'roll; ski season.

The Nightspot (422-9885), Killington Road. Dancing nightly to a DJ. Free ski tuning and happy hour hors d'oeuvres nightly.

McGrath's Irish Pub at the Inn at Long Trail (775-7181), Route 4. Live Irish music on weekends to go with the Guiness on tap and Gaelic atmosphere. It's a great pub with a 22-foot-long bar made from a single log and a boulder protruding from the back wall.

Pickle Barrel (422-3035), Killington Road. "Some of the finest rock'n'roll bands in the East."

SELECTIVE SHOPPING   Spread along Route 4 at the intersection of the Killington access road and Route 100 is a nice variety of shops all within walking distance of each other: **Bill's Country Store**, **Southworth's** (a wide selection of sports clothing and ski and tennis equipment), **Lothlorien** (Vermont products and crafts, fine gifts and souvenirs, selected wines and foods), and **Mountain Wine & Cheese Shop** (State Liquor Store). Across the road is the **Ski Shack**, a discount outlet for national brand sports wear. It's open year-round, seven days a week, 8–5:30.

Also see the Marketplace at Bridgewater Mill, in the Woodstock section, and the "Rutland and the Lower Champlain Valley" chapter.

Cheese: **The Plymouth Cheese Corp.** (672-3650), Box 1, Plymouth.

Open year-round but call ahead in winter. John Coolidge, son of Calvin, remains president of this business, which has been in the family since 1890. It's a true, old-fashioned Vermont granular curd cheese, carefully aged, available by mail order as well as by trip to the factory store.

Seward's Cheese. See "Rutland and the Lower Champlain Valley."

SPECIAL EVENTS   January–March: Frequent alpine ski races for all ages at Killington, Pico. **Fireworks** every Thursday.

May 1: **Annual May Day Fun Slalom**—limited to first 150 entrants.

Late May: **Annual Antiques Show**. A three-day event at Pico Base Lodge, Route 4.

June 1: **Annual June 1st Fun Slalom**—a three-day event at Pico.

July 4: Calvin Coolidge Birthday memorial, Plymouth.

July: **Killington Mountain Equestrian Festival**, two-week competition including North American Hunting and Jumping Championships.

July and August: **Killington Music Festival**, **Hartford Ballet**, and **Killington Playhouse**, which has performances five days a week at 8 PM, Saturday at 5, and children's performances.

July–mid-October: Aerial chair lift and gondola rides at Killington, Killington School for Tennis.

August: **Craft Show**, Killington.

Labor Day weekend: **Killington Stage Race**, cyclists compete for big stakes in the five-day event.

MEDICAL EMERGENCY (911) **Rutland Regional Medical Center** (775-7111), 160 Allen Street, Rutland. Also: 773-1700.

Sugarbush/Mad River Valley

There were farms and mills in this magnificent valley before Mad River Glen began attracting skiers in 1948, but the unique look and lifestyle of this community has evolved in the past 40 years, spawned by the three ski areas, just as truly as earlier villages took shape around their Greens. Early patrons at Mad River built themselves New England's first trailside homes, and in the early 1960s, Sugarbush built the region's first bottom-of-the-lift village. By the mid-1960s, new homes were being built each year—many in unconventional shapes by young architects eager to test new theories of solar heating and cluster housing. For their own enjoyment, the settlers—most of them sophisticated refugees from megalopolis—formed polo and fox hunt groups, built an arts center, an airport, and other amenities. For their livelihoods, they opened some delightful inns and two unusually tasteful shopping centers full of specialty shops. The shops plus a choice of restaurants are in the village of Waitsfield at the junction of roads to the three ski areas. In the village of Warren, five miles south, life revolves around a general store featuring French bread, fine wines, and deli salads.

The valley itself is a beauty: meadows stretching away from the banks of the river, rising to the Green Mountains on the west, the Roxbury Range on the east. In contrast to Stowe, the Valley never became a busy summer resort. Now, even though it can accommodate more than 6,000 tourists any night (substantially more than Stowe), you don't see them. Most are in condominiums ranged in tiers above Sugarbush Village or clustered away in the woods off the Sugarbush access road or off Route 100, the valley spine. Route 100 is so uncluttered that in summer tourists tend to drive right on through, seeing nothing more than the clump of specialty shops in Waitsfield.

As for skiing, the Valley rivals all comers. Between Sugarbush, Sugarbush North, and Mad River Glen, there are a total of 20 lifts servicing 99 trails. There are also five ski touring centers with a total of 260 km of cross-country trails. In summer and fall, there is hiking on the Long Trail as it traverses some of the highest peaks in the Green Mountains (Mount Abraham, Lincoln Peak, and Mount Ellen are all more than 4,000 feet high). There is soaring above the seven-mile wide valley and fishing and swimming in the Mad River itself.

GUIDANCE   **Sugarbush Chamber of Commerce** (800-82-VISIT or 496-3409), Box 173, Waitsfield 05673. A walk-in visitors center on Route 100 in Waitsfield, open year-round 9–5. After 5PM vacancies are posted in the rear, near the courtesy phone. Write for the free guides and lodging listings.

GETTING THERE   By bus: Waterbury is the nearest Vermont Transit stop.
By train: AMTRAK station in Waterbury.
By air: Burlington Airport is 45 miles; see "Burlington Region" for carriers.

GETTING AROUND   During ski season the Sugarbush Shuttle Bus offers a shuttle between lifts at Sugarbush South and Sugarbush North. Many inns have their own transport to the lifts. At night a "Fun Shuttle" runs between the resort and area restaurants.
Taxis: **Morf Transit**, 864-5588.

TO SEE AND DO   In winter, the Valley's magnets are its alpine and cross-country ski areas, but in summer there are no ski lifts running, no slides, no factory outlets, no focal point to converge on at all. Aside from two covered bridges, there are no attractions as such, just an unusual number of activities to pursue. Check the following list!

AERIAL LIFT   **Sugarbush Resort** (583-2381), Warren, operates its Green Mountain Express mid-June through September to the midmountain area of Sugarbush North. This is literally a leg up for hikers who want to sample the local ridgetop stretch of the Long Trail or for anyone who simply wants a view. The Glen House Lodge at the top of the lift offers a deck and refreshments. $8 adult, $5 children.

BICYCLING   Rentals of mountain bikes and guided tours from **Clearwater Sports** (496-2708), Route 100, Waitsfield; from **Mad River Bike** (496-9500). **The Mountain Bike Touring Center**, based at the Hyde Away Inn (800-777-HYDE and 496-2322), also offers guided tours. **Sugarbush Resort** (583-2381) offers mountain bike rentals for use on selected ski trails.

CANOEING   **Clearwater Sports** (496-2708). Barry Bender offers windsurfing rentals and lessons, learn-to-canoe and kayak programs, also a children's day program (age 9–13) and a five-day wilderness camp program for 9–13 year olds. Canoes and paddleboats are also on hand at Blueberry Lake.

FISHING   **Northland Trout Tours** (496-6572), RFD 1, Box 1649, North Fayston 05660, is a local guide service specializing in the Mad River, Dog River, the Winooski, and Lamoille. Half-day trips available; fly-fishing school, May–October. **Sugarbush Resort** also offers fly-fishing lessons and clinics.

GOLF   **Sugarbush Golf Course** (583-2722), Warren, at the Sugarbush Inn. An 18-hole, Robert Trent Jones course, PGA rate 42, par 72; $32, carts and lessons available.

MINI-GOLF   **Lots-O-Balls** (244-5874), Route 100, in Duxbury, between Waitsfield and Waterbury. Open in season from 11 AM, a great 19-

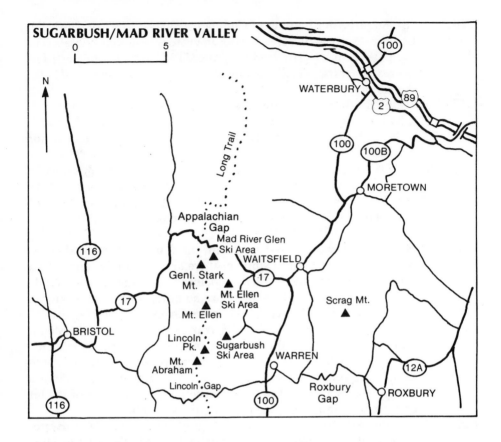

SUGARBUSH/MAD RIVER VALLEY

hole miniature golf course; $2 per adult, $1 per player aged five and under.

HIKING   **North Wind Inn-to-Inn Hiking Tours** (496-5771), PO Box 46, Waitsfield 05673. Clif and Dae Todd offer hiking tours throughout Vermont, a number in the valley itself; $275 for two days, $545 for four days includes lodging and meals. **Clearwater Sports** offers guided hikes, Wednesday–Saturday, 12–5, $15 per person.

   The Long Trail. For details—which you should have before attempting an actual hike—consult the *Long Trail Guide* or *Fifty Hikes in Vermont*. **Mount Abraham** can be reached from the Warren-Lincoln Highway 4.7 miles west of Route 100; since this is one of the most popular day hikes on the entire trail, be advised to come early (parking is limited). A five-mile, round-trip trail leads to the summit (4,052 feet) with views west across Lake Champlain to the Adirondacks, south as far as Killington Peak, north as far as Belvidere Mountain.

   Lincoln to Appalachian Gap. From Mount Abraham north to Lincoln Peak to Mount Ellen (4,135 feet); 11.1 miles, much of it above tree line; the Battell Shelter and Glen Ellen Lodge, maintained by the Green Mountain Club, offers bunkspace.

General Stark Mountain. A hike up to the 3,600-foot summit, 2.6 miles south of the Long Trail access at Route 17. In the 1940s when Mad River Glen opened, the road west from Waitsfield stopped here. There is an excellent view from Stark's Nest; the Theron Dean Shelter has bunks for four to six hikers, 1.4 miles west of Mad River Glen.

Scrag Mountain, Waitsfield (see *Day Hiker's Guide to Vermont*). From Waitsfield Village, take the East Warren Road through the covered bridge but bear left at the fork, turn right onto Cross Road and across the next intersection to the parking area. The three-hour, 4.2-mile round-trip hike is wooded, but the summit view of the Green Mountains across the valley is extraordinary.

HORSEBACK RIDING   Vermont Icelandic Horse Farm (496-7141), RR 376–1, Waitsfield 05673. Year-round. These strong, pony-sized mounts were brought to Iceland by the Vikings in 965 and to Vermont by Christina Calabrese, a young Swedish doctor who offers trail rides from Waitsfield Common up into high meadows and woods; half-day rides ($45 per person) frequently include a stop for a swim. The horses have an unusually smooth gait (their "tolt" is faster than a walk, gentler than a trot), ideal for the three-day treks that are also offered.

Summer Horsemanship School (496-6251), Dana Hill Road. May–October, certified instructor Meg Hilly-Anderson uses Centered Riding Techniques.

Sugarbush Resort (583-2381) also offers guided trail rides and pony rides on lower ski trails, July through foliage season.

POLO   Polo clinics are offered at **Holly Ward Barn** (496-3016), and there are polo matches twice a week during the summer, held either at **Schaffer Farm** on the East Warren Road, at the **Fly-in Field**, marked from Route 100 north of Waitsfield, or at the **Village Field** on Route 1001 in Waitsfield.

SOARING   Sugarbush-Warren Airport (496-2290), Warren. Respected as one of the East's prime spots for riding thermal and ridge waves; glider lessons, rides, food; open daily 9–5. The Sugarbush Soaring Association offers three-, five-, and ten-day "Soaring Camps" to anyone age 13 and up, but in limited numbers. Also 20- and 30-minute sailplane rides.

SUMMER DAY CAMP   Sugarbush Resort (583-2381), Warren. Sugarbear Day Care for children from six weeks to four years, and Camp Sugarbush for 5–10 year olds extends the kind of care available during the ski season to summer months. Activities include hiking, swimming, and trips to local attractions.

SWIMMING   Many condominiums and inns have their own pools. **The Sugarbush Sports Center** (see *Year-Round*) features a large, L-shaped outdoor pool with adjacent changing facilities, café, bar, and Jacuzzi. In the vicinity of Warren, the Mad River becomes a series of dramatic falls and whirlpools cascading through a gorge. The most secluded place is by the **Bobbin Mill** (the first right off Route 100 after the Lincoln Gap Road, heading south); park by the gravel pit and follow the path through the pines to a series of pools, all icy cold. Ask locally about the best spot for skinny dipping. The best area for kids is just south of Waitsfield off Route 100: There is a public parking area, small beach, a rock for jumping off, and muddy downstream clay for children to coat themselves with. Also, **Blueberry Lake** (496-6687) in Warren.

TENNIS   **Sugarbush Tennis School** (800-451-4213), using facilities at The Bridges (see *Resort*), the Sugarbush Sports Center (see *Year-Round*), and the Sugarbush Inn (see *Resort*), offers five-day clinics in conjunction with lodging; also a junior tennis camp in summer. Many local inns also have their own courts.

YEAR-ROUND   **Sugarbush Sports Center** (583-2391), Sugarbush Village, Warren. An outstanding complex consisting of indoor and outdoor pools, indoor and outdoor Jacuzzis, whirlpool, sauna, steamroom, exercise room, indoor squash, tennis, and racquetball courts, massage room, aerobics studio, 11-station Nautilus, and a full range of cardiovascular equipment. The nursery takes children six weeks and up. Open 6:30 AM–9:30 PM daily, weekly membership rates.

CROSS-COUNTRY SKIING   **North Wind Touring** (496-5771), PO Box 46, Waitsfield 05673. Clif and Dae Todd lead inn-to-inn ski and snowshoe tours around central and northern Vermont from January to early April. Tours range in duration from weekends to five days. Round-trip transportation from airport, bus, or train terminals is available, as are ski rentals.

    Tucker Hill Ski Touring Center (496-3202), Waitsfield 05673. A network of 40 km of trails, at elevations of 1,000–1,500 feet, radiate from the center located at the back of the Tucker Hill Lodge, open daily 8:30–5. Features young peoples' rental and retail equipment.

    Ole's Cross-Country Center (496-3430), Warren 05674. Sited at the airport on the East Warren plateau at altitudes of 1,200–2,450 feet: ten trails overlooking the valley, half wooded, half open, totaling 48 km, 32 km of them set. Change rooms and showers as well as food, sales, rentals, and instruction are available at the airport building; guided day tours and waxing clinics also offered.

    Sugarbush Inn Touring Center (582-2301), Sugarbush Access, Warren. Open, rolling terrain on a 10-km golf course trail is good for novices and ski racers. Some 25 more km of tracked trails wind through hardwoods and high meadows at elevations of 1,300–1,900 feet; instruction, change rooms, showers, Telemark instruction, and guided tours, all available along with equipment sales and rentals.

    Blueberry Lake Cross-Country Ski Center (496-6687), Plunkton Road, Warren. On the scenic, east side of the valley, a total of 23 km of tracked trails; instruction, rental, retail, repair, café, lodging, day

Ski slopes loom over Warren

care, change rooms, showers, guided tours, snow-making, lighted trail for night use.

Local trails: **Puddledock** in Granville Gulf State Reservation on Route 100, south of Warren: 3.5 miles of ungroomed trails marked with red, metal triangles; map available at the registration box. **The Long Trail**, 5.7 miles from the summit of Lincoln Peak to the top of Mad River Glen, should be attempted only by expert skiers using proper equipment, guided by instructors from a local touring center.

DOWNHILL SKIING   Sugarbush (information: 583-2381; ski report: 583-SNOW; lodging: 800-53-SUGAR). Two separate trail systems cascade down from two big-league peaks—3,975-foot Lincoln Peak at Sugarbush South and 4,135-foot Mount Ellen at Sugarbush North. The undeveloped swatch of mountain, the Slide Brook Area, separates these two areas. **Sugarbush** itself opened in 1958 as New England's first destination ski resort, complete with gondola, village shops, restaurants, and condominiums. It immediately acquired the following it wanted: wealthy "café society" New Yorkers, many of whom invested in trailside condos and still form a core clientele.

The second area, opened as Glen Ellen in 1963, is now **Sugarbush North**. Its Glen House Restaurant at 1,312 feet is a staging ground for a variety of trails off the top and is a favored spot for sunning. The two areas are not connected by any trail, but a shuttle bus provides frequent transfers. The area has changed hands several times in recent years but now seems to have the funding and necessary permitting. In 1990 three new quad chairs were added, along with many family-geared programs. Snow-making was also boosted on Sugarbush North, and all signs point to increased snow-making at Sugarbush South for the 1992–1993 season.

Lifts: 16 including three quads, three triple, and six double chair lifts.

Trails: 88.

Vertical drop: 2,600 feet.

Snow-making: 46 percent of trails.

Facilities: Cafeterias, lounges, ski shops, rentals, restaurants, sports center, condominiums.

Ski school: GLM, ATM, special teen program.

For children: nursery from infancy, special morning and afternoon programs.

Rates: $38 weekend, $35 midweek; junior $20.

Mad River Glen (496-3551), Waitsfield 05673. One of New England's oldest major ski areas, still retaining its enviable reputation as one of the most challenging yet friendliest places to ski. Its vertical drop puts it in the big league, yet the number of lifts and trails remain consciously limited; all trails funnel into the central base lodge area, the better for families—many of whom are now third-generation Mad River skiers—to meet. Many trails are off the ski map. A favored place for Telemarking.

Lifts: four chairs, including the country's only surviving single.

Trails and slopes: 30; expert, intermediate, novice.

Vertical drop: 2,000 feet.

Snow-making: 15 percent on novice slope and base areas.

Facilities: Base lodge cafeteria and pub, also the Birdcage, halfway up the mountain, serving sandwiches, drinks; ski shop, rentals.

Ski school: American Teaching Method (ATM).

For children: Cricket Club Nursery for three months–toddlers, SKIWEE (4–12) Junior Racing Program and Junior Mogul Program.

Rates: $26–30 per adult, $20 junior (14 and under), special half-day, multi-day, senior citizen, and student rates.

ICE SKATING   Sugarbush Inn offers skating on flooded tennis courts. Free day and night skating on the groomed hockey rink at **Tuckers Plants and Produce** on Route 100, also at **Brooks Recreation Field** off Brook Road in Warren.

SLEIGH RIDES   Lareau Farm Country Inn (496-4949), Route 100, Waitsfield. **Inn at the Round Barn Farm** (496-2276) also offers rides, as does **Whispering Winds Farm** (496-2819) on SouthHill Road in Moretown.

SUGARHOUSES   Palmer's Maple Syrup (496-3696), Waitsfield (East Warren Road, one mile from the covered bridge). Everett and Kathryn Palmer welcome visitors with homemade doughnuts during sugaring season; syrup available year-round.

Eastman and Darla Long (496-3448), Waitsfield (first left after Fayston Store on Route 17), set 10,000 taps, welcome visitors to their sugarhouse.

Paul and Marie Hartshorn (496-3471), Ox-Bow farm in Waitsfield (Route 100 sign), welcome visitors.

LODGING   **Sugarbush Reservations** (800-537-8427), Warren 05674, offers a year-round lodging service linked to 50 local inns and condos. Request its free "Directory pamphlet."

Mad River Glen (496-3551) also provides a winter lodging service and a directory. The **Sugarbush Chamber of Commerce** (see *Guidance*) also serves as a source of information about condo and second home rentals.

RESORT   **Sugarbush Resort** (800-451-4213), Warren 05674, now owns the **Sugarbush Inn & Country Townhomes**, itself a self-contained resort complex built around a semiformal inn with 46 inn rooms and 60 more condo units, plus a sports center with an indoor pool, Jacuzzi, tennis courts, and a conference center, as well as an 18-hole Robert Trent Jones golf course. The resort now also encompasses six more condo complexes including **The Bridges Resort and Racquet Club** (583-2922, 800-451-4213), yet another self-contained resort in its own right with indoor tennis, squash, an indoor pool, saunas, Jacuzzi and exercise room, and 100 condo-style units ranging from one to three bedrooms, each with fireplaces, sundecks, TV, phone, some with washers and dryers. Sugarbush Resort now also manages five more condominium complexes and a total of 36 tennis courts and 10 swimming pools. Special packages include golf, tennis, and ski weekends and five-day sojourns. Winter rates: $90–150 per person MAP. All rates are much less in summer when resort facilities include the Sugarbush Tennis School, trail and hay rides, and both the Sugarbush Day School (for ages 6 weeks to 10 years) and Camp Sugarbush for kids aged 5–10. A teen program is new in 1992.

COUNTRY INNS AND LODGES   ☞**Millbrook Inn** (496-2405), Route 17, Waitsfield 05673. Open except April, May, and early November. This nineteenth-century farmhouse is a gem. You enter through the warming room, actually warmed by a woodstove in winter. The living rooms invite you to sit down. The heart of the ground floor is, however, the dining room, well known locally as one of the best places to dine in the Valley. Each of the seven guest rooms is different enough to deserve its own name; all have stenciled walls, antique beds and bureaus. A ski lodge since 1948, Millbrook has become a true country inn under ownership by Joan and Thom Gorman who are constantly redecorating, fine-tuning. $46–70 per person, double occupancy MAP, $25–30 per person B&B in summer.

The Inn at Round Barn Farm (496-2276), East Warren Road, Waitsfield, is a landmark because of the remarkable round (12-sided) barn built in 1910, one of the few remaining. Jack and Doreen Simko have transformed the adjacent house into a very elegant bed and breakfast with just six guest rooms and built a lap pool in the bowels of the barn, which now serves as a conference and reception center. Guests have a wicker-filled solarium, stone terrace, and book-lined library. Rates range from $85 for the Jones Room, with a double spool bed and shower, to $125 for the Joslin Room with a canopied king and Jacuzzi. Prices include "gourmet breakfast, game room with TV and pool table, workout room, après ski edibles, Bach, Vivaldi, and goodnite [sic] chocolates." No smoking.

The **Sugartree Inn** (583-3211), Sugarbush Access Road, Warren 05674. This is an intimate, personal place with more than a touch of fantasy. It's a modern ski lodge, but Howard and Janice Chapman have done their utmost to create a country inn atmosphere. The Virginia-born couple were living in the Midwest when the Vermont bug bit them, and they have created the kind of New England atmosphere that the rest of the country expects to find. All 10 rooms have quilts that Janice has sewn, and many have canopy beds (all have private baths). The TV and fireplace are in the living room, and there are just four tables in the adjoining dining room; the idea is to bring guests together. At breakfast your waffles may be topped with fruit and whipped cream. $40–60 per person B&B plus 10 percent service.

The **Lareau Farm Country Inn** (496-4949), Route 100, Waitsfield 05673. A 150-year-old farmhouse set in a wide meadow by Route 100 and the Mad River offers 14 guest rooms, 10 with private baths, all nicely furnished with antique beds, quilts, and rockers. Dan and Susan Easley are warm hosts, and guests feel right at home, checking in via the kitchen and settling into the living room or onto the back porch, overlooking an expansive spread of lawn that stretches down to a great swimming hole, wide, deep, and clean. At this writing, the "Lareau Zoo" includes two horses (sleigh rides are offered in winter), three dogs, three cats, and a chicken. Guests are free to walk or ski the 67 acres, and Dan is happy to lead a tour for four or more guests. $40–50 per person includes a full breakfast; $30–40 in summer.

☞**Knoll Farm Country Inn** (496-3939), Bragg Hill Road, Waitsfield 05673. Closed in November and April. This genuine, working farm sits high above the valley but handy to everything, a half mile off Route 17 near its junction with Route 100. This is not the kind of place you simply stop at for a night's lodging. It's so beautiful—anytime of year—in the farm's high meadows that you won't want to leave. It's a good idea to reserve far in advance; Ann Day, a respected poet and photographer, has acquired a strong following since she began taking in skiers in 1957. Abundant meals are served family style, prepared from food raised on the 150-acre property. There is a classic old barn out back, and animals include Scotch Highland cattle and horses. The hosts are up early with barn chores, and guests are wel-

come to get in a ski tour, some snowshoeing, or hiking before breakfast. In warm weather, there is swimming in the 14-foot-deep pond.
Children over six are welcome. $50 per person MAP, double occu-
pancy.

☞**Mad River Barn** (496-3310), RR 1, Box 88, Waitsfield 05673. Phone
either Mad River Glen or Mad River Barn, and Betsy Pratt will probably answer. Betsy owns and manages both. The Barn is a classic
1940s ski lodge, complete with a massive stone fireplace and deep
leather chairs, a dining room filled with mismatched oak tables and
original 1930s art. The food (breakfast only in summer, dinner too in
winter) is fine, as are the pine-walled guest rooms, all with private
baths (those in the annex come with small kitchchenettes). In summer, the appeal of the place is enhanced by the pool, secluded in a
grove of birches, and the deck overlooking landscaped gardens, a
setting for weddings and receptions. In winter, a trail connects with
Mad River. In summer, rates with breakfast are $60 per couple and
children under 10 in the same room are free. In winter: $60–80 per
couple B&B, $130 MAP.

West Hill House (496-7162), RR 1, Box 292, Warren 05674. An
1860s farmhouse with a comfortable, ski lodge–style common room
and full breakfasts (great apple and cheese pancakes) served to guests
around the dining room table. Located away from the villages, up
above the golf course with plenty of walking and cross-country space
and long views; guest rooms with sumptuous baths, $65–85 double
in winter, $60–70 in summer and fall. Nina and Bob Heyd are helpful
hosts. No smoking.

Mountain View Inn (496-2426), Box 69, Waitsfield 05673. A typical
Vermont house by Route 17 that can accommodate 14 in nicely decorated rooms. Guests gather around the wood-burning stove in the
living room and around the long harvest table for dinner. Fred and
Suzy Spencer are genial hosts. Handy to Sugarbush North and Mad
River Glen, the inn's ski-touring trails tie into the extensive local
network. $50 B&B and $65 per person MAP in winter.

Waitsfield Inn (496-3979), Waitsfield Village 05673. This is a
Federal-era parsonage handy to village shopping. It offers 12 rooms
upstairs over the public dining room and the rambling posterior,
formerly an attached barn and woodshed, now an attractive area
with ample common space for guests. Managed by Dan Malloy, from
$50 per room B&B in summer, $70 in winter.

Pitcher Inn (496-3831), Warren Village 05674. Restaurant closes in
November and April. This is a find, and more than for breakfast (see
Eating Out). When this traditional-style guest house came up for sale
a few years ago, a group of local people chipped in to buy and to
create an authentically welcoming place. Jenny Duel is the friendly
innkeeper. There are 12 bright, comfortable rooms, sleeping a total of

20 people. Families are welcome. While breakfast is the big thing, lunch is also served seven days a week, dinners Thursdays through Sundays. The location is great, right in the middle of a traditional village, handy to cross-country ski trails and summer horseback riding and swimming. $25 single room, $50 double; $10 for third person in room; children under six free. Rates include a full breakfast.

Beaver Pond Farm Inn (583-2861), Warren 05674. This traditional Vermont farmhouse has a superb setting on a hillside overlooking a beaver pond and a rolling expanse of golf course. This was Bob and Betty Hansen's vacation home, and they have turned it into an elegant little inn with a formal dining room and attractive living room with a BYOB bar in one corner. In winter, they offer multi-course meals some nights, $17–20 prix fixe. In summer, there are tables on the large deck, and in winter you can ski right out the front door. Rates include a full breakfast. $40–45 per person per night on weekends (double occupancy); a minimum of two days is required in winter; midweek rates are 20 percent less. Downhill, cross-country, and golf packages are also available.

The Christmas Tree Inn (800-535-5622or 583-2211), Box 23, Sugarbush Access Road, Warren 05674. This is a modern ski lodge with a nice feel and reasonable prices. There are 12 inn rooms, from $50–75 per room in winter, $50 in summer, plus 24 new one-bedroom condominiums, each accommodating two to four people, from $100 per unit in summer, $100–130 in winter. This is a good spot for families, an informal sitting room with games and puzzles, in summer croquet, badminton, tennis, a small pool. Five-night ski weeks for $439.

The White Horse Inn (496-2476), Waitsfield 05673. One of the few lodging places located on German Flats Road connecting Sugarbush South and Sugarbush North , also handy to Mad River Glen. This is a modern ski lodge with 28 rooms, all with private bath. $30–45 per person B&B; group and MAP rates also available.

Valley Inn (800-638-8466 or 496-3450), Box 8, Route 100, Waitsfield 05673. This is the kind of friendly old ski lodge you *used* to find in Stowe: wooden walls, well-thumbed books, communal dining tables, comfortable furniture instead of antiques, but all private baths; $50–70 per person with two meals in winter, $35 B&B in summer (add 10 percent gratuity in summer, 15 percent in winter). The Stinsons have been the keepers of this inn for 20 years, creating a relaxed atmosphere that you feel the moment you walk into the huge living room; there is also a game room and bar with darts and a pool table.

Wilder Farm Inn (496-6541 or 800-344-9453), PO Box 397, Waitsfield 05673. This rambling farmhouse sits above Route 100 north of Waitsfield Village. It has nine rooms, seven with private bath. A library and large living room each have a fireplace and lots of cats to keep guests company. Hosts Chris and Mike Russo put out a varied and filling continental breakfast, included in $40–80 per room, varying seasonally.

Newtons' 1824 House Inn (496-7555), Box 159, Waitsfield 05673. North of the village on Route 100. Nicholas and Joyce Newton pride themselves on extravagant breakfasts (soufflés, fruit-filled crêpes). The 10-gabled house offers six bedrooms, all with private baths and some wonderful featherbeds (one king-sized), gracious drawing and dining rooms with fireplaces. The 52-acre property invites walking and cross-country skiing, and horses can be stabled in the barn. There's also an outstanding swimming hole just across the road. $37.50–52.50 per person includes breakfast and afternoon tea.

The Schultzes' Village Inn (496-2366), Moretown 05660. Located on Route 100, five miles north of Waitsfield, this is an exceptionally friendly, homey place with six guest rooms, including bunk rooms and doubles that can be mixed and matched as family suites. An exceptionally pleasant spa room with a whirlpool and sauna overlooking meadows. It is an ideal place for children since John and Annette Schultz have two of their own; available for groups of up to 20 who want to do their own cooking. Buffet dinner served (optional) Saturday night. $25 per person weekdays, $35 weekends and holidays, includes a full breakfast; children over five years pay their age.

Powderhound Lodge (800-548-4022 or 496-5100), Route 100, Warren 05674. The old roadside farmstead now serves as reception, living, and dining rooms—with a deservedly downstairs pub—for the 44 condo-style apartments clustered in back. Each of these consists of two rooms, one with two beds and another lounging/dining space with two more daybeds and a TV; token cooking facilities. There are also four motel units with phones, TV, and double beds. It's all nicely designed and maintained, a good deal for families and couples who like the privacy of their own space with an option to mix with fellow guests. Summer facilities include a swimming pool, clay tennis court, and lawn games, and there's a hot tub for year-round use, plus a winter shuttle to the mountain. $50–64 in summer, $110 weekends in winter with many two- and three-day (also midweek) packages.

Camel's Hump View Farm (496-3614), Box 720, Moretown 05660. Jerry and Wilma Maynard are native Vermonters who pride themselves on genuine hospitality. The snug old homestead has two living rooms with a double fieldstone fireplace. Guest quarters include one pleasant room with its own entrance and bath ($30 per person) and a bunk room ($25 per person); rates include a full breakfast; it's $10 extra for dinner.

Weathertop Lodge (496-4909), Route 17, Box 151, Waitsfield 05673. The atmosphere is that of a ski lodge rather than country inn, but it's appealing, especially to families, any time of year. The common room has a fieldstone fireplace, stereo, piano, cable TV, video games, and VCR. There's also a fitness center with its array of exercise machines and the hot tub and sauna. The nine rooms are standard—two double beds and a full bath—but Bill and Gail Mulconnery are methodically redecorating with warmer "country inn"-style fabrics and furnishings.

Wait Farm Motor Inn (496-2033), Waitsfield 05673. Eight motel units, four with kitchenettes, also two double rooms and one bunk room in the main house comprise this friendly family business; $25–35 per person.

Tucker Hill Lodge (496-3983), RFD 1, Box 147, Waitsfield 05673. A home built along traditional lines with a fieldstone hearth in the inviting living room and 21 nicely furnished guest rooms, 11 with private baths, and puffy quilts. There's also Eastman House, a restored three-bedroom, 1810 farmhouse with three fireplaces, geared to families and small groups. Handy to both Waitsfield Village and Sugarbush North, it has an away-from-it-all feeling enhanced by an extensive cross-country ski trail network up into the woods. $60–80 per perso, MAP. It is now owned by the Baron Group. $126–228 per night.

The Mad River Inn (496-7900), PO Box 75, off Route 100, Waitsfield 05673. A house with fine turn-of-the-century detailing, like fine woodwork and large picture windows with lace etchings in the living room. Furnished with an eye to fabrics, colors, and antiques; details like hand-stenciled hearts and a doll collection. $75 for the smallest room with shared bath midweek to $95 for the largest with private bath on a weekend, includes a "gourmet country breakfast" and afternoon tea. Children welcome. The house overlooks a meadow and the Mad River, and it's handy to a good swimming hole.

The Garrison (496-2352), Route 17, Waitsfield 05673. Motel rooms and condominium units with kitchens open onto an indoor swimming pool heated to 89 degrees year-round. There's an all-weather tennis court too; rates $19–40 per person depending on unit and season.

CONDOMINIUMS   The valley harbors more than 400 condominium units, many clustered around Sugarbush South, more scattered along the access road and some squirreled away in the woods. No one reservation service represents them all.

Sugarbush Resort (800-451-4213) manages seven complexes, all with access to the Sports Center. $109–420 for one- to three-bedroom units; many packages, cheaper in summer.

Sugarbush Village Condominiums (583-3000, 800-451-4326). This reservation service encompasses 13 condo complexes (including some of those managed by Sugarbush Resort), a total of 330 units. Units vary from studio units in the former Hotel Sugarbush and the adjacent, five-story Village Gate cluster to five-bedroom condominiums and town houses in Unihab. Rates are $105–230 per couple, less in summer. Note: These rates do not include access to the Sports Center.

The Battleground (496-2288 or 800-248-2101), Fayston (Waitsfield) 05673. An unusually attractive cluster of condominiums, each designed to face the brook or a piece of greenery, backing into each other and thus preserving most of the 60 acres for walking or ski touring (the area's 60-km network of trails is accessible); in summer there is a pool, tennis, paddle tennis, and a play area for children; Mad River Glen is just up Route 17; summer rates nightly (two-night minimum) for two-, three-, or four-bedroom units are $615–850 per week in summer, $1,035–1,430 per week in winter.

Ski Travel (800-451-4574), RR 1, Box 300B, Warren 05674. A reservation service representing most condominium clusters on the mountain, also local ski homes. Condos are priced from $100 for a one-bedroom in Middle Earth to $345 for a luxurious three-bedroom unit in South Village.

DINING OUT   Chez Henri (583-2600), Sugarbush Village. A genuine bistro. Twenty years ago, Henri Borel relinquished his position as food controller for Air France to open this snug, inviting café with a fireplace, a marble bar (imported from a Barre soda fountain), and terrace dining out front in summer. After dinner, the back room becomes a disco, open until 2 AM (nightly in winter, Friday–Sunday in summer). Year-round you can always find something light and delicious in the café from noon on: onion soup, Moules à la Provençale, or Coquilles Saint Jacques. Entrées in the more formal dining room include Les Supremes de Volaille (young chicken breast prepared differently every day); or rack of lamb broiled with thyme; specials change frequently so that long-time patrons can always find something new. Dinner entrées $12.50–18.00.

Millbrook Restaurant (496-2405), Route 17, Waitsfield. The attractive, unpretentious dining room in this roadside inn is the right setting for satisfying dining that ranges from garden lasagna to veal Roma (Vermont veal quickly sautéed with fresh sage, shallots, white wine, and mushrooms). There is always a choice of Indian entrées too, including locally raised lamb simmered in a rich curried sauce of cardamom, cumin, coriander, coconut, almonds, ginger, yogurt, and tomatoes. Entrées from $8.95 for cheese cannelloni to $16.95 for shrimp sautéed with garlic and butter or served in a spicy curry sauce.

Sam Rupert's Restaurant (583-2421), Sugarbush Access Road, Warren. Open for dinner only, year-round. The core of this building is a sugarhouse; it has gone through several changes but has evolved over the past decade under present ownership into a widely respected dining place in which a choice of seafood and vegetarian specialties, plus veal, duck, and lamb, is served amid greenery. A dinner here might begin with escargot en brioche with Spanish garlic herb sauce, followed by "farfalloni": strips of chicken breast and gulf shrimp sautéed with onions, roasted peppers, and tomatoes, finished with cilantro pesto and white wine, tossed with bow tie pastas and topped with Parmesan cheese. Entrées $9.95–18.50.

The Common Man (583-2800), German Flats Road, Warren. Dinner only, closed Mondays off season. This unusual, immensely popular landmark, destroyed by fire early in 1987, has been replaced by an equally elegant barn right down to the crystal chandeliers. You might begin with confit de canard, feast on bouillabaisse, hasenpheffer, or escalops of fresh Vermont raised veal, sautéed in Vermont butter and napped with a sauce of Vermont cream and wild local chanterelle mushrooms. Entrées $9.50–16.50

EATING OUT   **Jay's** (496-8282), Mad River Green Shopping Center, Route 100, Waitsfield. Open for breakfast, lunch, dinner, and Sunday brunch. When Jay Young sold the Sugarbush Inn to Sugarbush Resort, everyone assumed he would return to his native Bermuda. Not so. To their own surprise, the family discovered that they had been in "The Valley" so long that it was now home. So, in short order, Young's entrepreneurial savy had a new focus: a family restaurant with real flare. The space is bright and spacious, the chef is Walter Brink (formerly of the Sugarbush Inn), the menu is immense and reasonably priced. Dinner might be veal Piccata with lemon, capers, and white wine ($9.95), "Very British Fish and Chips" ($7.75), a boneless breast of chicken with artichokes, mushrooms, and white wine ($8.25), or "Jay's famous stuffed pizza for four" ($25). There's also a children's menu and a variety of specially blended coffees.

The Den (496-8880), just north of the junction of Routes 100 and 17 in Waitsfield. Open daily for lunch and dinner. The atmosphere is cheerful pubby: booths, stained glass. The menu is large, always includes a homemade soup and wide choice of burgers (all day) and a salad bar; at dinner there is also a choice of chicken and steak dishes with specials like poached salmon with smoked mussels in cream sauce. We recommend the Texas Three Alarm Chili.

Reveille at the Pitcher Inn (496-3831), Warren Village. Open weekdays 7–11, weekends 8–12. This pleasant village inn enjoys giving friends and neighbors an excuse to gather for breakfasts like Eggs Reveille (poached eggs with a slice of tomato and creamed spinach on an English muffin with hollandaise sauce), corned beef hash, French toast, pancakes, and waffles served with real Vermont maple syrup, or just about any kind of omelet you can think up. Lunch is also served daily and dinner Thursday through Sunday in season.

R.S.V.P. (496-7787), Bridge Street, Waitsfield Village, open daily from 11:30 AM for lunch and dinner. The decor is high 1950s, and the sandwiches—Vermont cob-smoked turkey in particular—are fine; plus, you can help yourself to salad by the pound. Try the pizza by the slice before you go for the whole pie.

Old Tymes Restaurant (496-3875), Route 11, Waitsfield. Originally Orr's Ark, one of the Valley's first inns, this farmhouse is an increasingly popular source of reasonably priced regional American cuisine. Completely destroyed by fire on July 4, 1991, the new building mimics its former design: three dinng rooms and a stone-fireplaced tavern. Summer lunches and dinners are also served on the deck. Try the Chesapeake crabcakes.

China Moon (583-MOON), Sugarbush Village. A first-rate Chinese restaurant with takeout and some unusual entrées like whole crispy fish Szechuan style ($10.95), and many-flavor chicken (poached, served with Szechuan peppercorn sauce, garlic, ginger, chili, and hot bean paste). Squid in chili oil and mock eel are also on the menu.

Flatbread Pizza Nights at Tucker Hill Lodge (496-3983), Route 17, Waitsfield. At this writing, the stone oven flatbread pizza is served Monday through Friday evenings (5:30–9:30) in the inn's bar/café. George Schenk built the stone ovens in which the pizzas are baked; he also personally smokes the meat and dries the tomatoes and herbs, and the dough is from organically grown wheat; pizza choices on a given night might include cheese (Vermont mozzarella) and herbs, Vermont pheasant and scallions, new world sausage, and sun-dried tomato and mushroom.

Miguel's Stowe Away (584-3858), Sugarbush Access Road, Warren. Serving meals 5:30–10. An offshoot of Stowe's successful Mexican Stowe Away. Pollo and pescado augment a choice of fajitas, chiles, enchiladas, and burritos, also good for sopas and ensaladas.

The Warren Store (496-3864), Warren Village. Open daily 8–7, Sundays until 6. Year-round the bakery produces French and health breads, plus croissants on Sunday, and the deli food is good for takeout salads and sandwiches, but in summer the appeal of this place as a place to eat out—on the deck out back, overlooking a waterfall—increases mightily.

Green Mountain Coffee Roasters. The café and expresso bar features croissants, pastries, and chocolate truffles to go with the coffee. See *Selective Shopping*.

APRÈS SKI   The Blue Tooth (583-2656), Sugarbush Access Road. A "mountain saloon" geared to ski season, closed in summer; après ski snacks and drinks, moderately priced dinners, live entertainment; a prime boy-meets-girl place.

Hyde Away, Route 17, Waitsfield. Open daily from 4 PM and for weekend breakfasts. A casual gathering place with reasonably priced entrées like lasagne verde and pepper steak, also nightly specials, a children's menu, and toy area.

ENTERTAINMENT   The Valley Players (496-3485), a local community theater company, produces three to four plays a year in their own theater just north of Waitsfield Village, Route 100.

Phantom Theater (496-5207), Box 341, Warren. Plays at the Odd

Fellows Hall, Monday theater workshops for adults in July and August (at the Warren Town Hall), and summer classes in theater skills for children (visitors welcome).

Edison's Studio (496-2336), Route 100 north, Waitsfield. First-run films shown, drinks and snacks served.

SELECTIVE SHOPPING   **Tulip Tree Crafts** (496-2259), Village Square, Waitsfield. Judy Dodds runs this exceptional store featuring folk art, pottery, antiques, cards, quilts. Judy herself is a fiber artist, specializing in quilted wall hangings. Her husband silk-screens T-shirts, and the shop offers an unusual variety.

The Troll Shop (496-2171), Route 100, Waitsfield. A long-time Valley source of ski and general sportswear.

Cabin Fever Quilts (496-2287), the Old Church, Waitsfield. Closed Tuesdays, otherwise open 10–5. Machine-sewn, hand-tied quilts come in a range of sizes and patterns, priced $175–400, also pillows, gifts, and quilt fabrics.

Kristal Gallery (496-6767), East Warren Road. Open year-round, daily 10:30–6. Hanni Saltzman mounts a genuinely interesting mix of oils and watercolors; in summer, there's also a sculpture garden.

Waitsfield Pottery (496-7155), Route 100 across from Bridge Street. Ulrike Tesmer makes functional, hand-thrown stoneware pieces, well worth a stop.

Luminosity Stained Glass Studio (496-2231), the Old Church, Route 100, Waitsfield. Since 1975, Barry Friedman has been fashioning Tiffany lampshades and a variety of designs in leaded and stained glass; the shop also carries some interesting jewelry.

Fosters (496-2549), Waitsfield, Bridge Street next to the covered bridge. Dress up in 1890s garb and pose for your picture. It's fun and something to keep.

Three Bags Full (496-4298), Route 100, Waitsfield. At the Black Sheep Farm, right on Route 100 south of the village, Bill and Ellen Austin sell pelts, yarns, fleeces, and retail lamb. There are also live lambs to see.

Rosie Borel's Lescalier (583-2666), Sugarbush Village. Literally a stairwell, crammed with French Provincial prints: cloth, clothes, purses, also exceptional pottery from the southern French town of Moustier.

All Things Bright and Beautiful (496-3397), Bridge Street. There are an incredible number of stuffed animals and unusual toys on two floors of this old village house.

Tempest Book Shop (496-2022), Village Square, Waitsfield. This family-run bookstore is a trove of titles in most categories, including children's books. We like their motto: "A house without books is like a room without windows" (H. Mann).

The Store (496-4465), Route 100, Waitsfield. Since its 1965 opening, this exceptional shop has grown tenfold, now filling two floors of an 1834 meetinghouse with superb early American, French, and English antiques, cookwear, tabletop gifts, collectibles, lifestyle books, Vermont gourmet products, and children's toys and books from around the world.

Mad River Canoe, Inc. (496-3127), Mad River Green, Route 100, Waitsfield. This is the home of the internationally known line of Mad River fiber glass, Kevlar, and Royalex canoes. The factory showroom is open Monday–Friday 9–5; factory seconds sold.

American Flatbread Factory (496-8856) at Lareau Farm Country Inn, Route 100, Waitsfield. A large stone-and-clay wood-fired oven produces flatbreads weekdays, 7:30-4. Visitors welcome for factory tours.

Warren Village Shops include the **Warren Store** (see *Eating Out*), known for its selection of wines, as well as food; a **More Store** upstairs sells assorted clothes, toys, and housewares. Next door, the **Parade Gallery** offers an affordable selection of prints and original art, and **Warren Village Pottery** (across from the covered bridge) displays hand-crafted stoneware pieces by Amalia Lang-Youngman. Nearby, **Warren Antiques** is open year-round with 4,000 square feet of furniture and toys.

Green Mountain Coffee Roasters, Mad River Green Shopping Center, Waitsfield. Open daily. Some 30 varieties of freshly roasted coffee; a pot of java (or whatever) is perpetually brewing. House specialties include La Minita Tarrazu from Costa Rica; a full line of coffeemakers are also sold. Café on premises.

SPECIAL EVENTS   Check with the chamber of commerce for weekly listings of special events.

Late February: **Sugarsap Run**—15-km cross-country race.

March: **March Madness**—special series of happenings to celebrate spring skiing. **Annual New England Telemark Festival.**

Late March: **Sugarbush Triathlon**—canoe, kayak, bicycle, cross-country ski race (more than 400 competitors).

July 4: Outstanding, long-standing parade and celebration, Warren Village.

July and August: Summer productions by the **Valley Players** and by **Phantom Theater** (see *Entertainment*).

Late July, early August: **Sugarbush Horse Show** and **Green Mountain Polo Tournament.**

Labor Day weekend: Celebration with crafts show.

Early October: **Fall Wave Soaring Encampment. Sugarbush Antique Car Show**.

December: Christmas celebration.

MEDICAL EMERGENCY   Ambulance (496-3600). **Mad River Valley Health Center** (496-3838).

Barre/Montpelier Area

Montpelier is the smallest and possibly the most livable of the nation's state capitals. It is a town of less than 9,000 people with band concerts on summer Wednesdays, high school playing fields just a few blocks from the capitol, and a bus depot so small that patrons frequently wait on the sidewalk. The gold dome of the statehouse itself is appropriately crowned by a green hill rising steeply behind it, and unless you follow the commercial strip along Route 302 to Barre, you are quickly out in the country—in the wooded Worcester Range to the north or the wilderness to the west; East Montpelier is a crossroads village.

Any attempt to understand the character of Vermont entails a visit to Montpelier: a stroll through the Vermont Museum (an extraordinary collection of things past, housed in a replica of a steamboat, Gothic-style hotel) and into the fine statehouse built of Vermont granite and marble. The surrounding nineteenth-century brick business and state office buildings harbor an increasing number of good restaurants and pleasant shops.

Why precisely this narrow floodplain of the Winooski was selected as Vermont's statehouse site in 1805 seems uncertain, as well as why it was named for a small city in the Languedoc region of France. The fact is, however, that Vermont's first legislators picked a town noted for its unusual number of whiskey distilleries and named it for a town best known for its wine and brandy. It's also true that Montpelier is unusually accessible, by roads both old and new, from every corner of central and northern Vermont.

A city of 9,824, surrounded by a town of 7,090, **Barre** (pronounced "berry") is larger than Montpelier, to which it is linked via the five-mile commercial strip of Route 302. Barre's Main Street is a perpetual bottleneck, and motorists caught in it may ponder the conspicuous absence of granite in the facades of the commercial buildings, most of which date from the 1880–1910 period when Barre became known far and wide for granite memorials. During that era, the community's population jumped tenfold, swollen by stonecutters and craftsmen from Scotland, Eastern Europe, Italy, and French Canada, not to mention England, Scandinavia, Spain, Germany, and the Middle East—a volatile mix of largely underpaid workers who elected a socialist mayor and were not afraid to strike for their rights or to shelter victims of strikes elsewhere. Around the time of World War I, the famous radical feminist, Emma Goldman, was arrested here. The quarries continue to employ some 2,000 people.

The granite quarries are southeast of town, primarily in Graniteville where Millstone Hill has been chipped and chiseled since 1812 when the bedrock was turned into millstones, doorstoops, and posts. In the 1830s, huge slabs were hauled by oxen to build the statehouse. It was only after the Civil War that the railway and a series of inventions enabled Barre to make its mark. The memorial stone business escalated after 1888 when the branch railroad finally linked the quarries to finishing sheds in the valley and to outlets beyond. Today, Barre continues to produce one-third of the country's memorial stones, for which its own Mt. Hope Cemetery serves as a museum. All but one of the major quarries are owned by Rock of Ages, a company that has long made its operations a showcase for visitors, who can view the unforgettable, surrealistic landscape of the quarries themselves, hear the roar of the drills, and watch ant-sized men chip away at the giant pits.

GUIDANCE   **Central Vermont Chamber of Commerce** (229-5711), Box 336, Barre 05641.

Vermont Chamber of Commerce (223-3443), Box 37, Montpelier 05601, is located off I-89, Exit 7 near its junction with Route 302 between Montpelier and Barre, 9–5 weekdays.

Vermont Travel Division (828-3236) has its main information center at 134 State Street, Montpelier.

GETTING THERE   By bus: Vermont Transit from Boston to Montreal, connecting with New York and Connecticut service.

By train: See *AMTRAK* in "What's Where."

By air: Eastern Express to Knapp Airport, flights from Boston.

Ground transfers: **Alpine Central Cab**, Barre; **Limousine by Jules** (476-8658, 476-6845).

TO SEE AND DO   **Vermont State House** (828-2228), State Street, Montpelier. Open Monday–Friday 8–4, closed holidays. July–October "Friends of the Vermont State House" offer tours Monday–Friday 10–3, otherwise by appointment. In 1805 when Montpelier was chosen as the "permanent seat of the legislature for holding all their sessions," it was on condition that the town give land for the capitol and get it built by 1808. The resulting building was nine-sided, three stories, with a cupola, warmed by a two-story stove. Legislators sat on plank seats at pine desks that were said to have been "whittled out of use" by the representatives' jackknives. The whole building had to be demolished in 1836 and was replaced by a granite Grecian temple designed by Federal-era architect Ammi Young. After it was virtually destroyed by fire, it was rebuilt along the same but larger lines, completed in 1857. Visitors are welcome to watch the legislature in action, January–mid-April. Note that the 150 state representatives and senators talk with their constituents while standing in the Hall of Flags or seated on the black walnut sofas (which cost $60 apiece in 1859) at either end. Larkin Mead's statue of Ethan Allen on the steps is Danby marble, and the handsome black-and-white floor of the lobby was quarried on Isle la Motte. The lobby is lined with portraits of Vermont-born heroes including Admiral George Dewey, Admiral Charles Clark (like Dewey, a hero of the Spanish-American War), and Calvin Coolidge, thirtieth president of the United States. The cannon on the front steps was captured from Hessians at the Battle of Bennington in 1777. The Roman lady atop the gold-leafed dome is, of course, Ceres, goddess of agriculture, also sculpted by Larkin Mead.

The Vermont Museum (828-2291), 109 State Street, Montpelier. Open weekdays, year-round 8–4:30; weekends also during July, August, and foliage season: 10–5. Donation. This outstanding state museum is maintained by the Vermont Historical Society, housed on the ground floor of the replica of the Pavilion Hotel, which occupied this site between 1870 and 1966. You climb the steps, cross the veranda as if you were a hotel guest, enter a Victorian lobby with horsehair and elaborately carved furnishings. Children and adults alike can enjoy the recently redesigned displays dramatizing Vermont history and the relics ranging from the state's first printing press to Ethan Allen's gun. There are also changing exhibits, a small gift store, and a large, excellent library of sourcebooks and genealogies.

T. W. Wood Art Gallery at the Vermont College Art Center (828-8743), in Montpelier, open Tuesday–Sunday, noon–4 PM. The gallery displays Civil War–era art by local artist Thomas Waterman Wood and has excellent shows of contemporary Vermont artists and craftspeople.

Mural of Vermont Life, National Life Insurance, Montpelier. This huge mural fills a wall of the lobby of the home office of National Life Insurance (founded by Admiral Dewey's father) on Memorial Drive, just off I-89, open weekdays 9–4:30. It is a monumental piece by Paul Sample, depicting the sweep of the state's present and past.

Barre Opera House (476-8188), corner of Prospect and Main streets. Built in 1899, after fire destroyed its predecessor, this elegant, acoustically outstanding, recently restored theater occupies the second and third floors of City Hall. Performances are scheduled mid-April through mid-October.

Rock of Ages Quarry and Craftsmen Center (476-3119), Graniteville. The Craftsmen Center, in which stone is polished and sculpted into memorials, is open year-round, Monday–Friday 8:30–3:30. The Visitors Reception Center a mile up the road, open May–October 8:30–5, has displays explaining the geology of granite; a path

Rock of Ages granite quarry is world's largest

leads you the short way out back to the state's oldest, 27-acre-wide quarry. From June–September, an open-car train departs every half hour, 9:30–3:30, for the working quarries farther up the hill.

Mt. Hope Cemetery, Route 14 just north of Barre. The memorials that stonecutters have sculpted for themselves and their families are among the most elaborate to be found anywhere in the world.

Barre Historical Society Museum (476-7550), Aldrich Library. An outstanding collection of nineteenth-century paintings, furnishings, and articles relating to Barre's stormy history are displayed upstairs in Barre's unusually fine library; by appointment.

Goddard College (454-8311), Plainfield. Founded in 1863, a progressive college with several buildings designed by students; frequent live entertainment, films, concerts.

NORTHFIELD   The town's midnineteenth-century commercial blocks suggest the prosperity that it enjoyed during the term its native son Charles Paine served as governor. Paine literally railroaded the Vermont Central Railroad through his hometown instead of the more logical Barre. The old depot, now a bank, stands at one end of the handsome Common. Today, the town's pride is Norwich University, a private, coed college of 1,000 cadets, which bills itself as "the oldest private military college in the U.S." In the Norwich University Museum in White Memorial Chapel, you learn that this institution sent more than 300 officers into the Civil War. It wasn't until 1867, however, that the college moved to Northfield from its original site in Norwich. More Northfield memorabilia as well as changing exhibits can be seen in the Northfield Historical Society museum housed in the Old Red Brick Schoolhouse, Stagecoach Road (open June–Labor Day, Sunday 2–5 PM).

East Roxbury Fish Hatchery, two miles south of Roxbury on Route 12A. This is a state hatchery in which salmon species are raised; children are allowed to feed the fish.

Drive from Roxbury to Warren. The road through Roxbury Gap, while not recommended in winter, is spectacular in summer and fall, commanding a breathtaking view of the Green Mountains from the crest of the Roxbury Range. Do not resist the urge to stop, get out, and enjoy this panorama. Ask locally about the hiking trail that follows the ridge line from the road's highest point.

COVERED BRIDGES   Off Route 12 to Northfield Falls stand three covered bridges: "The Station Bridge," spanning 100 feet, and "The Newell Bridge" are within sight of each other; further along Cox Brook Road is "The Upper Bridge" with a span of 42 feet.

GREEN SPACE   **Hubbard Park**. More than 110 acres in the upper reaches of Montpelier, primarily leafy, windy roads, good for biking, jogging.

BOATING AND FISHING   **Wrightsville Dam,** just north of Montpelier; **North Montpelier Pond,** with a fishing access off Route 14; **Curtis Pond** and **Mirror Lake** in Calais. **Nelson Pond** and **Sabin Pond** in Woodbury are both accessible from Route 14, as are **Valley Lake** and **Greenwood Lake** (good for bass and pike). **Stevens Branch** south of Barre offers brook trout. Also see nearby Marshfield and Groton for their facilities.

GOLF   **Montpelier Country Club** (223-2600), 9 holes.

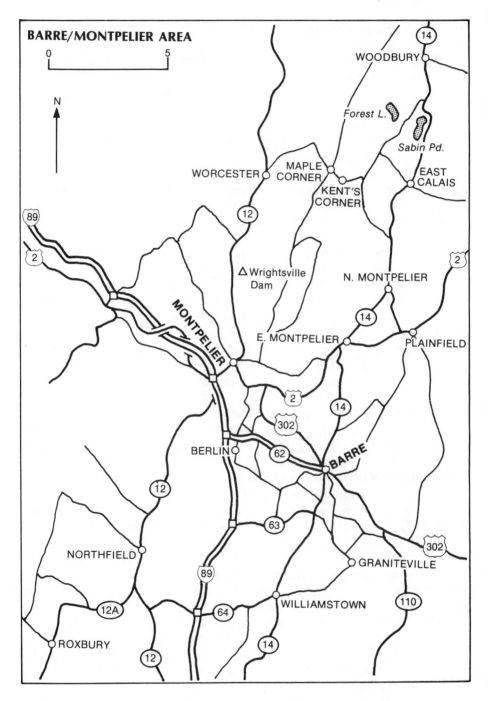

BARRE/MONTPELIER AREA

0   5

N

Barre Country Club (476-7658), 18 holes. Northfield Country Club, 9 holes.

HORSEBACK RIDING   Breckenridge Farm (476-8077), RR 1, Box 3490, Barre 05641. **East Hill Farm** (479-0858), Plainfield 05667, year-round lessons, no trail rides. **Whispering Winds Farm** (496-2819), South Hill, Moretown 05660.

HIKING   Guidance: The Green Mountain Club (223-3463), headquartered at 43 State Street, Montpelier, encourages general inquiries and trail description updates. See *Hiking* under "What's Where."

Spruce Mountain, Plainfield. An unusually undeveloped state holding of 500 acres, rich in bird life. The trail begins in Jones State Forest, 4.2 miles south of the village; the three-hour hike is described in *Fifty Hikes in Vermont* (Backcountry); also in *Day Hiker's Guide to Vermont* published by the Green Mountain Club.

Worcester Range north of Montpelier. There are several popular hikes described in the above books, notably Elmore Mountain in Elmore State Park (a three-mile trek yielding a panorama of lakes, farms, and rolling hills), Mount Worcester (approached from the village of Worcester), and Mount Hunger.

SWIMMING   Wrightsville Dam Recreation Area, Route 12 north; also numerous swimming holes in the Kents Corner area; also see Marshfield and Groton for their extensive facilities.

TENNIS   Wedgewood (223-6161), Granger Road, Berlin. Tennis, racquetball, swimming.

CROSS-COUNTRY SKIING   Montpelier Elks Ski Touring Center, contact Onion River Sports, Inc. (229-9409), 20 Langdon Street. This facility uses gently rolling golf course terrain, offers 10 km of set trails, instruction, rentals, food.

DOWNHILL SKIING   Lybrand Ski Area (485-5011), at Norwich University, Northfield. Open to the public; a reasonably priced area with rentals, instruction, two lifts.

LODGING   The Inn at Montpelier (223-2727), 147 Main Street, Montpelier. Vermont's capitol city now has an exceptional, truly capital place to stay. Two stately, adjacent Federal houses have been beautifully renovated and luxuriously furnished by Maureen and Bill Russell. Amenities include central air-conditioning, downstairs guest pantries for coffee and tea at any hour, in-room cable TV, bar service, small conference facilities. A marvelous Colonial revival veranda wraps around the brick Lamb-Langdon house for relaxing in clement weather. Of the 19 rooms, the deluxe chambers with fireplaces ($105–130) are just about the handsomest guest quarters in the state, as are the smaller king-, queen-, and twin-bedded rooms from $88, all with private baths and continental breakfast. About half the rooms are nonsmoking. Children over 10 welcome; no pets. (See also *Dining Out*.)

Days Inn (223-5252), 100 State Street, Montpelier, formerly the Landmark Tavern, has 103 newly renovated guest rooms and suites plus conference and banquet rooms, fitness facilities with an indoor pool, lounge, and dining room. Rates: $75–85 single, $85 double during the foliage season, $60–70 otherwise.

The Hollow Inn and Motel (479-9313), 278 South Main Street, Barre 05641. Peg and Bill Whitehouse add a personal touch to this combined inn and motel. From the south, use I-89 Exit 6 to Route 14, then one-half mile north; from Barre and the north, one mile south of the center of the city. The outdoor heated pool and Jacuzzi are surrounded by plantings, wood fences, and a natural stone wall, and boasts a summer kitchen and gas grill. The indoor Swallow Relaxation Center is equipped with whirlpool, sauna, and fitness equipment. Double room rates start at $65 ($95 for suites) depending on the season, including continental breakfast. All of the rooms have VCRs as well as TV, and videotapes can be rented. Fifteen new rooms with microwave and refrigerator. Discounts available for stays of more than three or seven consecutive nights. BYOB lounge.

The Autumn Crest Inn (433-6627), Box 1540, RFD 1, Williamstown 05679, Route 64 east from Exit 5 off I-89. Perched on a knoll, with a panoramic view across rolling pastures to distant ridges, Autumn Crest—a 46-acre horse farm—has been cheerily toned up by its new owners, Richard Casson and Kenneth Eden. The 18 guest rooms are comparatively plain (a refreshing change from so many other inn rooms that have been over-draped with "Laura Ashley"and other flowery fabrics) and have private baths and TVs. "Willow," on the ground floor, is equipped for the handicapped. One of the two semi-suites has a fireplace; "Pine" is the prettiest. There's a big fireplace in the spacious living room, and a fine dining room, open to the public. Guests enjoy the swimming pond, two night-lit tennis courts, and horseback riding in the summer; sleigh rides and 27 miles of cross-country ski trails in the winter. Rates: $68–88 double B&B, $98–118 MAP; holiday packages and midweek discounts in April. Children and pets welcome.

LaGue Inns (229-5766), RD 4, Box 1720, Montpelier 05602. Conveniently located on Exit 7 off I-89 near the Central Vermont Hospital and the Barre-Montpelier airport, this 80-unit motel has pleasant rooms, an outdoor pool, convention facilities for up to 300 persons, and Suzanna's Restaurant. $40–110.

Comfort Inn at Maplewood (229-2222), RR 4, Box 2110, Montpelier. A quarter of a mile off I-89 Exit 7, has 89 rooms, 18 two-room suites with kitchenette, and a VIP suite with whirlpool. Rates $59 single, $69 double, suites $89–200 on weekends, less midweek, with continental breakfast.

Vermont's third capitol, Montpelier

VTD

OTHER MOTELS **Brown Derby Motel & Restaurant** (223-5258), 101
Northfield Street, Montpelier; **Sir Anthony Motel & Round Table
Restaurant** (476-6678), 173 South Main Street, Barre; **The Heiress**
(479-3333), 573 North Main, Barre.

BED & BREAKFASTS **Montpelier Bed & Breakfast** (229-0878), 22 North
Street, Montpelier 05602. A ten-minute, half-mile walk from the capi-

tol, the Kitzmiller family offers six guest rooms and an efficiency suite decorated with antiques and quilts and silk-screen prints. Rates are from $25 single to $60 double, shared bath, with breakfast. Weekly rates available; no smoking, no pets.

The Schultzes' Village Inn (496-2366), Route 100B, Moretown, west of Montpelier. $25–35 per person; children are charged their age. Guests have use of a spa solarium and large kitchen. Full breakfast provided.

Betsy's Bed & Breakfast (229-0466), 74 East State Street, Montpelier, is an impressive, restored Queen Anne house in the town's Historic District. Spacious rooms with double beds, private baths, cable TV, and phones; generous breakfasts; $55 single, $60 double, with discounts for three nights or more. Children welcome, but no pets or smoking inside.

Northfield   **The Northfield Inn** (485-8558), 27 Highland Avenue. Aglaia and Alan Stalb have renovated a grand old 1902 hillside mansion, nicely landscaped with a gazebo overlooking the town and comfortable guest rooms that can be combined into family suites; antiques, brass or carved wood beds, European feather bedding; rates from $55 single to $85 double, $115 for a suite, including hearty country breakfast.

Long Way Inn (485-3559), RD 1, Box 1610, on Rabbit Hollow Road off Route 12A west of Northfield. Ginne and Allen Kelly welcome guests to this secluded, traditional/contemporary residence. Full breakfast, snacks; $50–75 per room.

Margaret Holland Inn (481-9867), near the Norwich campus; an old-fashioned guest house with four bedrooms at $25; no breakfast.

DINING OUT   **Tubbs Restaurant** (229-9202), 24 Elm Street, Jailhouse Common, Montpelier. This renovated jail is one of Vermont's outstanding places to eat. It is run by the New England Culinary Institute, whose student chefs produce delectable dishes for lunch and dinner. The menu, changing daily, might include duck consommé with fresh ginger, hot oysters with spinach and caviar, escalope of salmon with sorrel, veal steak with peppercorns and cognac. Dessert pastries and bread are baked by La Brioche, on the premises, which serves Monday–Friday 7:30–3:45, Saturday 7:30–1, indoors and on the patio. Tubbs itself is open for lunch Monday–Friday and for dinner Monday–Saturday. Closed for the institute's late November vacation. Dinner entrées under $20. Pub menu in its new Finch's Bar.

The Inn at Montpelier (223-2727), 147 Main Street. Inn guests and the public dine exceedingly well here. Start with Spinney Creek oysters, for example, or grilled chicken sausage with oriental peanut sauce, continue with Black Angus strip steak or rack of lamb roasted with a mustard-herb crust. Entrées $11.50–19, with daily specials from $9.50.

Philura's (479-0892), Barre-Montpelier Road, northeast side near Twin City Lanes, Berlin. This casual restaurant with antique signs and blackboard menu is a "find." Judy Jones presides over this oasis named for her husband's great-grandmother. Specialties include home-smoked trout Wilder and such hearty entrées as rack of lamb Emile with garlic and herb butter, pork Harold, tenderloins richly sauced with mushrooms, shallots, mustard, basil, white wine, and cream, or sea scallops baked with saffron, shallots, and brandy cream sauce. Sinful chocolate desserts or a frothy raspberry mousse. Dinners Tuesday–Saturday. Entrées $12.95–18.00.

The Autumn Crest Inn (433-6627), Route 64, Williamstown. The superb views from the wraparound dining room and porch are reportedly matched by the dinners prepared here nightly by chef Thomas Goullett, a graduate of the New England Culinary Institute. The menu changes almost daily but could include cream of broccoli soup with paprika and smoked Gouda cheese; smoked trout, salmon, and swordfish served with spinach tortellini in a pepper, caper, dill, tomato sauce; or Thai peanut curry roast loin of pork. For dessert, English Toffee cheesecake, or Maine raspberry chocolate cake. Main courses $12.50–17.00.

EATING OUT   **Elm Street Café** (223-3188), 38 Elm Street, Montpelier, around the corner from Tubbs, this more casual sibling is also operated by the Culinary Institute, serving breakfast, lunch, and dinner Monday–Saturday, at reasonable prices: baked Vermont cheddar in phyllo, Cajun barbecued shrimp, grilled pork tenderloin.

Horn of the Moon Café (223-2985), 8 Langdon Street, Montpelier. Open Monday 7–3; Tuesday through Saturday 7–9; Sunday 10–2. Smoking and sugar are out, innovative, vegetarian dishes definitely in: herb teas, local organic products, wheat bread, pancakes, tofu, soups, and salads predominate the inexpensive menu. Beer and wine served.

Chadwick's (223-2384), State Street, Montpelier. French classics alternate with California nouvelle in an agreeable setting. Sunday–Saturday 11:30–9.

About Thyme Café (223-0427), State Street, Montpelier. International flavors characterize the soups, salads, baked goods.

Country House Restaurant (476-4282), 276 North Main Street, Barre, serves modestly priced Italian specialties at lunch and dinner Monday–Saturday.

Jack's Backyard (479-9134), 9 Maple Avenue, Barre, "an adult watering & feeding place," serves a wide selection of inexpensive sandwiches, chili, crêpes, soups, quiche, salads for lunch, Monday–Saturday and Sunday brunch.

Julio's (229-9348), 44 Main Street, Montpelier. Good, reasonably priced Mexican food in a second-floor dining room, which used to be MJ's.

Vermont Dept. of Employment & Training Cafeteria (229-0311, ext. 146), open for lunch and dinner, serviced by students of the New England Culinary Institute, the best buy in town for breakfast and lunch.

Green Mountain Diner (476-6292), 240 North Main, Barre. Open 6 AM–9 PM, our choice of eating spots in town: friendly booths, a blackboard menu with specials like stew or Spanish pork chops; beer and wine served.

SELECTIVE SHOPPING   **The Artisans' Hand** (229-9492), 7 Langdon Street, Montpelier. Monday–Saturday 10–5. An exceptional variety of quality Vermont craftwork.

Bear Pond Books (229-0774), corner of Langdon and Main streets, Montpelier. One of the state's most inviting bookstores, heavy on literature, art, and children's books.

Capitol Stationers (223-2393), 29–31 Main Street, has a large stock of new books, with a strong Vermont and New England section.

Morse Farm (223-2740), County Road (the western extension of Main Street), Montpelier. Open daily, year-round except holidays. The farm itself has been in the same family for three generations. This is a place to come watch sugaring off in March; a large farmstand sells Vermont crafts and cheese as well as produce in summer, fall, and Christmas greens in December. Sugar on snow.

Bragg Farm (223-5757), Route 14, East Montpelier. Open daily, March 15–December 24 for maple products, Vermont crafts.

Knight's Spider Web Farm (433-5568), off Route 14 on Cliff Place, Williamstown Village. In season, visitors can see spider webs being collected and mounted; gifts and pine accessories. Open daily 9–6; January–March by appointment.

Danforth's Sugarhouse (229-9536), Route 2, East Montpelier. Maple products, including aromatic maple candles, miniature sugarhouses, wooden toys.

Great American Salvage Company (223-7711), 3 Main Street, Montpelier 05602. A treasure trove of antique architectural artifacts: doors, stained glass, columns, mantels, tubs—the motherlode for the company's Cooper Square branch in New York City.

SPECIAL EVENTS   Early June: **Vermont Dairy Celebration,** statehouse lawn.
June–August: **Montpelier City Band Concerts**, statehouse lawn.
July: **Midsummer Art and Music Festival**, Vermont College campus, sponsored by the Onion River Arts Council (229-9408).
Labor Day weekend: In Northfield: pageant, parade of floats, and Norwich cadets.
Late September: **Old Time Fiddlers Contest**, Barre Auditorium—

one of the oldest contests, attracting some of the East's best fiddlers.

Early October: **Vermont Apple Celebration**, statehouse lawn.

Late October: **Festival of Vermont Crafts**, Montpelier High School (Central Vermont Chamber of Commerce, 229-5711).

MEDICAL EMERGENCY　Barre (476-6675); Montpelier (911); Northfield (485-6666). **Central Vermont Medical Center** (229-9121), Berlin (off Route 302; Exit 7 off I-89).

IV. Lake Champlain Valley

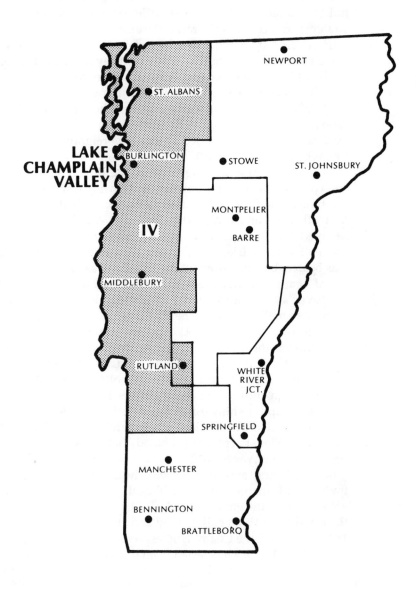

NEWPORT

ST. ALBANS

LAKE
CHAMPLAIN
VALLEY

BURLINGTON

STOWE

ST. JOHNSBURY

MONTPELIER

BARRE

IV

MIDDLEBURY

RUTLAND

WHITE
RIVER
JCT.

SPRINGFIELD

MANCHESTER

BENNINGTON

BRATTLEBORO

INTRODUCTION

Lake Champlain, one of the most beautiful inland waterways in America, flows—contrarily—north for 120 miles from Whitehall, New York, and drains into Quebec's Richelieu River. Covering 452 square miles, it is only 12 miles across at its widest point, but its historic, strategic, and commercial influence affects a broad area.

Discovered by Samuel de Champlain in 1609, the lake was controlled by the French until 1759 when Jeffrey Amherst, the legendary British officer, drove them out of Fort Carillon (renamed Ticonderoga) and Crown Point. Major Robert Rogers' Rangers were then trained at Crown Point for guerilla warfare against the French and Indian marauders, later dramatized in Kenneth Roberts' famous novel, *Northwest Passage*. Amherst ended French sovereignty in North America by capturing Montreal in 1760.

Early in the American Revolution, the British strategy to divide and conquer the northern colonies was thwarted when Ethan Allen's rambunctious Green Mountain Boys seized Fort Ticonderoga on May 10, 1775, and again when Benedict Arnold and a hastily assembled American flotilla engaged a heavier British squadron in the Battle of Valcour Island in October 1776. Arnold's outgunned navy was beaten, but this prong of the British invasion was blunted, frustrated again near Bennington, and finally brought to a halt when Burgoyne's army surrendered at Saratoga in October 1777. One of Arnold's small gunboats, the *Philadelphia*, sunk by the British off Valcour, was salvaged in 1935 and now reposes in the Smithsonian Institution as the oldest surviving American naval vessel.

In 1814, the British again tried to use Lake Champlain as an invasion route. The vigorous, 31-year-old Commodore Thomas Macdonough moved his headquarters from Burlington south to Vergennes and a shipyard at the mouth of Otter Creek where he quickly outfitted a small fleet, which barely managed to defeat British ships at Plattsburgh Bay—a bloody but decisive engagement that helped end the War of 1812.

Before, during, and after this war, the lake was the major artery for trade with Canada, much of it illegal, which in turn spawned the great nineteenth-century decades of Champlain steamboats. When the canal from Whitehall to Troy and the Hudson River opened in 1823, ports on Lake Champlain, especially Burlington, boomed. The age of the side-wheelers lasted from the launching of *The Vermont* in

1809 to the demise of *The Ticonderoga* (1906–1953); this stately, steel-hulled steamer has been preserved for posterity at the Shelburne Museum, after a remarkable two-mile, 65-day overland rail portage in the fall and winter of 1954–1955.

Ferries still ply the sparkling waters of the lake, providing spectacular panoramas of both the Adirondacks and the Green Mountains and magnificent sunsets. No longer a significant commercial waterway, Champlain offers exhilarating cruising and sailing opportunities. But recreational sailors beware: The lake's moods can change quickly from serenity to tempestuous squalls!

Bass, walleyes, yellow perch, northern pike, and other warm-water fishing has always been good; a recent restoration project improves the prospect for lake trout, steelhead rainbows, and landlocked salmon, north of the Sand Bar Bridge. Eel fishing has become a commercial venture, with most of the eel exported to Europe. Ice fishing is a winter passion for many.

Anglers may even spot "Champ," the elusive serpentine creature described by those who claim to have seen (and photographed) it as resembling its cousin, the "Loch Ness Monster."

Rutland and the Lower Champlain Valley

RUTLAND REGION

Rutland, Vermont's second largest city (18,435), is more than just a convenient commercial adjunct to the Killington-Pico ski resorts. Stolid, early Victorian mansions and streets criss-crossed with railroad tracks testify to nineteenth-century prosperity—when Rutland was known as "the marble city."

Today, city fathers are trying hard to reconstitute the downtown core, buoyed by the presence of General Electric and several other large employers. The daily *Rutland Herald,* oldest newspaper in the state, continues to win frequent journalism awards.

The long-established shops along Merchant Row and Center Street have held their own in recent years and number upwards of 100 within just a few square blocks; they include some genuinely interesting newcomers. This is, moreover, a good restaurant town.

Rutland is the business and shopping center for the Lower Champlain Valley, a broad, gently rolling corridor between New York state and the Green Mountains. In contrast to the rest of the state, this valley is actually broad enough to require two major north/ south routes. Route 7 is the busier highway. It hugs the Green Mountains and, with the exception of the heavily trafficked strip around Rutland, is a scenic ride. Route 30 on the west is a far quieter way through farm country and by two major lakes, Lake Bomoseen and Lake St. Catherine, both popular summer meccas.

Route 4 is the major east-west road, a four-lane highway from Fair Haven (see *Villages*), at the New York line, to Rutland, where it angles north through the middle of town before turning west again, heading uphill toward Killington. Route 140 from Wallingford to Poultney is the other old east-west road here, a quiet enough byway through Middletown Springs, where the old mineral springs form the core of a pleasant park.

GUIDANCE **The Rutland Region Chamber of Commerce** (773-2747), 7 Court Square, Box 67, Rutland 05701; visitors center open late May–mid-

October at the junction of Routes 7 and 4 (775-0831). The chamber supplies an illustrated "Vacation Guide."

The Vermont Office of Vacation Travel maintains a Welcome Center (open 8:30–5:30) on Route 4 near the New York line.

GETTING THERE   By car: Routes 7 and 4; 103 from Bellows Falls.

By bus: Vermont Transit, from Albany, Boston, and other points.

TO SEE AND DO   Also check the "Killington/Pico Area." **Chaffee Art Gallery** (775-0356), 16 South Main Street. Closed Tuesdays, otherwise open June–October 10–5 and November–May 11–4. One of the state's outstanding art galleries, representing 250 Vermont artists, a former private house listed on the National Register of Historic Places. It has permanent and periodic exhibits and a youth gallery for school displays. Traditional and contemporary paintings, sculpture, crafts, graphics, and photography are included.

Wilson Castle (773-3284), Route 3 from West Rutland toward Proctor. This 32-room, nineteenth-century stone "chateau" on a 115-acre estate is furnished with elaborate European and Oriental pieces, stained glass, and a variety of wood paneling. Guided tours given daily, mid-May–mid-October. Admission charge.

Vermont Marble Exhibit (459-3311 ext. 435), Route 3 from West Rutland, Proctor. Open daily 9–5:30, mid-May–mid-October. Admission charge. The first commercial marble deposit was discovered and quarried in Vermont in 1784. The Vermont Marble Company, formed

Downtown Rutland rooflines and nearby range

A.J. Marro

in 1870 when Redfield Proctor merged several quarries, has been one of the state's principal resources. Marble from Proctor and Danby was used for the US Supreme Court building, the Lincoln Memorial, and the Beinecke Library at Yale, among many other notable edifices. Proctor himself served as governor, United States senator, and secretary of war. Several other members of the Proctor family and chief executives of the company also filled the governor's chair, forming a political dynasty that lasted nearly a century. The company has been owned by the Swiss-based Pleuss-Staufer Industries since 1976. Nearly 100,000 people visit the marble exhibit every year, making it one of the biggest tourist attractions in New England. Featured are a special geological display, a gallery of bas-reliefs of American presidents, a movie, slide show, gift shop, replicas of the Pieta and The Last Supper, a sculptor-in-residence, and a factory viewing site to watch the various stages of transformation from rough-cut blocks to polished slabs.

The New England Maple Museum (483-9414), Route 7 north of Pittsford, has an attractive display of the history, production, and consumption of maple syrup, once called "sweet water," and its by-products. One can view the Danforth Collection of antique equipment, murals, and a 10-minute slide show, and there is a tasting area and gift shop. Mail-order service. Open daily 8:30–5:30, November, December, and March–May 10–4, closed January and February. $1.50 admission; group rates.

Norman Rockwell Museum (773-6095), Route 4 east, Rutland. Display of magazine covers, ads, and other published illustrations. Gift shop. Open daily 9–6. Admission charge.

Paul P. Harris Memorial, Route 7 south of Rutland, Wallingford. Paul Harris (1868–1947), founder of Rotary International while he was working in Chicago, was born in Wallingford and went to school in the small brick building on Main Street, where the local club meets Mondays at 6:30 PM.

Pittsford Fish Hatchery (483-2300), Furnace Brook Road, Pittsford, open 8–4 daily for viewing landlocked salmon.

VILLAGES   **Fair Haven**, located where Routes 4, 4A, and 22A intersect, is at the core of Vermont's slate industry. One of its earliest developers in the 1780s was the controversial Matthew Lyon, who started an iron works and published a newspaper called *The Scourge of Aristocracy*, in which he lambasted the Federalists. Elected to Congress in 1796, Lyon had scuffles on the floor of the House and criticized President Adams so violently that he was arrested and jailed under the Alien and Sedition Act. Lyon's case caused such a national uproar that this patently unconstitutional censorship law was soon rescinded; Lyon was reelected to Congress while still in jail and took his seat in time to cast the tie-breaking vote that made Thomas Jefferson president instead of Aaron Burr.

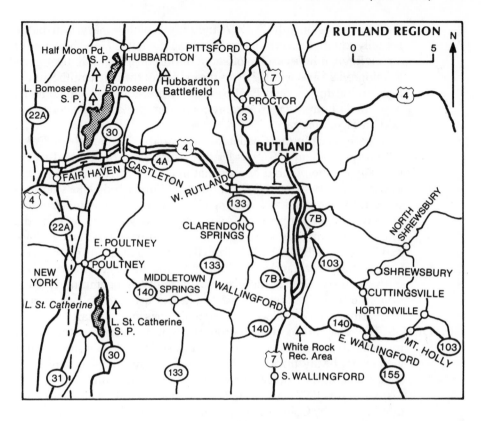

Around the spacious Green are three Victorian mansions (two faced with marble) built by descendants of Ira Allen.

Poultney, on Route 30, the home of Green Mountain College, also has significant journalistic associations: Horace Greeley, founder of the *New York Tribune*, lived at the venerable Eagle Tavern in East Poultney while he was learning the printing trade at the East Poultney *National Spectator* in the 1820s (and organizing a local temperance society). Working with him was George Jones, who helped to found the *New York Times* in 1851.

It's East Poultney that's the picturesque village worth detouring to see. The fine white **Baptist Church**, built in 1805, is the centerpiece, standing on a small Green surrounded by late eighteenth- and early nineteenth-century houses. The general store is also a classic and a source of good deli sandwiches. Its picnic benches are within earshot of the Poultney River, here a fast-flowing stream.

Castleton, at Routes 4A and 30, has triple historical significance: Ethan Allen and Seth Warner planned the capture of Ticonderoga here; on a nearby hill in Hubbardston, Colonel Warner's scrubby militiamen made a valiant rear-guard stand while halting the British invasion force on July 7, 1777, the only Revolutionary War battle actually fought on Vermont soil; and the town itself is a showcase of Greek Revival houses. One offshoot of the conspiratorial meeting in Remington's Tavern in 1775 was the exploit of the blacksmith Samuel Beach—Vermont's own Paul Revere—who reputedly ran some 60 miles in 24 hours to recruit more men from the countryside for the raid on Ticonderoga.

After the Revolution, Castleton grew rapidly. Thomas Royal Dake, who arrived about 1807, has left his hallmark of design and workmanship on the pillared houses that line Main Street, including the Ransom-Rehlen mansion with 17 Ionic columns and Dake's masterpiece, the Congregational Meeting House, now the Federated Church, with the lovely pulpit that Dake completed with his own funds. These heirloom houses are open for tours during Castleton's Colonial Days, usually held in late July. Between 1850 and 1870, the West Castleton Railroad and Slate Company was the largest marble plant in the country. During these years, a large Welsh community grew up in the area. The town is also the site of Castleton College, part of the Vermont State College system, which has an active arts center.

HISTORIC SITE   The **Hubbardton Battlefield** is in East Hubbardton, seven miles north of the posted Route 4 exit. A small, hilltop visitors center is open mid-May through mid-October, Wednesday–Sunday 9:30–5:30. Battle buffs won't want to miss the diorama and audiovisual display of this 1777 battle, detailing how a small force of Green Mountain Boys led by Colonel Seth Warner, together with a Massachusetts militia and a New Hampshire regiment, managed to defeat a far larger British contingent led by General Burgoyne.

LAKES   **Lake Bomoseen**, just north of Castleton, is a popular local summer colony. The lake gained notoriety in the 1930s because of Alexander Woollcott's summer retreat on Neshobe Island. The portly "Town Crier" entertained such cronies as Harpo Marx, who was known to repel curious interlopers by capering along the shore naked and painted blue.There are two state parks on its western shore.

Lake St. Catherine with lots of summer cottages.

STATE PARKS   **Bomoseen State Park** (265-4242/483-2314), Route 4 west of Rutland, Exit 3, five miles north on town road. Its 60 campsites and five lean-tos are set in a lovely wildlife refuge; beach, picnic area, nature program, and trails, boat ramp and rentals.

Half Moon Pond State Park (273-3848/483-2314), Fair Haven, off Route 4 west of Rutland, Exit 4, 7½ miles north on Route 30, 2 miles west on town road, 1½ miles south on town road. Wooded campsites around a secluded pond; rental canoes; hikes to High Pond, a remote body of water in the hills.

Lake St. Catherine State Park (287-9185/483-2314), 9½ miles south of Poultney on Route 30. Fifty-two campsites, sandy beaches, fishing, boat rentals, nature trails.

BOATING   Note boat rentals from the state parks on Lake Bomoseen and Lake St. Catherine (above).

GOLF   **The Rutland Country Club** (773-9153), a mile north of the business section on North Grove Street; 18-hole golf course on rolling terrain, restaurant.

Proctor Pittsford Country Club (483-9379), Corn Hill Road, Pittsford. 18 holes, lounge, and restaurant.

Lake St. Catherine Country Club (287-9341), Route 30, south of Poultney. Nine holes, lounge, and restaurant.

The Bomoseen Country Club (468-5581) in Castleton offers nine holes.

HIKING   **White Rocks Recreation Area**, Route 140 off Route 7 in Wallingford. Follow signs from the White Rocks Picnic Area. The big feature here is a 2,600-foot, conical white peak surrounded by quartzite boulders that retain ice and snow into the summer. We advise picking up a hiking guidebook (see *Hiking* in "What's Where") before starting out.

HORSEBACK RIDING   **Pond Hill Ranch** (468-2449), Pond Hill Road, Castleton, offers trail rides and hay rides.

HUNTING   **Tinmouth Hunting Preserve** (446-2337), Box 556, East Road, Wallingford, has 800 acres of varied cover where individual and group pheasant, partridge, and quail shoots can be arranged from September through March (except on Sunday). Five sporting clays shooting areas have been added.

SWIMMING   See **Lakes Bomoseen** and **St. Catherine**. There's also **Elfin Lake** beach, off Route 140 west, two miles southeast of Wallingford.

CROSS-COUNTRY AND DOWNHILL SKIING   See "Killington/Pico Area."

SLEIGH RIDES   **Pond Hill Ranch** (468-2449), Castleton. One- to three-hour rides.

SNOWMOBILE RENTALS   **Marina St. Catherine** (645-0410), Lake St. Catherine, Wells. Trails and fields.

LODGING   *In and Around Rutland*   **The Inn at Rutland** (773-0575), 70 North Main Street, Rutland. This is a large 1890s town house on Route 7 just north of the center of town. All 12 guest rooms have phones, private baths, and antiques. The differences are in size and position. We suggest a room in the back, away from Route 7. The woodwork in the dining room is exceptional, the living room is attractive, and the Quinns are eager to share their knowledge of where to dine and what to see in Vermont's funky, interesting second city. $65–95 single, $75–139 per couple, breakfast included.

The Silver Fox (438-5555), Route 133, West Rutland 05777. The nattily remodeled Elija Smith farmhouse is roughly 15 minutes southeast of Rutland, set in farm country. The formal canopy on an eighteenth-century farmhouse, the core of a dairy farm and still surrounded by fields, seems a shade bizarre. Inside the feel is elegant but not stiff enough to make hikers, bikers, and skiers feel uncomfortable. Pam and Gerry Blis have obviously enjoyed decorating each of the seven guest rooms, which include the ground floor Lilly Room and the hand-stenciled Sweetheart Room, with French doors dividing the bedroom with its four-poster from a sitting room complete with two Queen Ann stuffed chairs. All rooms have wide pine floors and private baths. Breakfast, served in a corner dining room with floor-to-ceiling windows, is included in the rates: $75–110. Add 15 percent gratuity. A multi-course dinner ($22–28, see *Dining Out*) is also available.

Fair Haven, Poultney, and the Lakes   **The Vermont Marble Inn** (265-8383), on the town Green, Fair Haven 05743. Swathed in tan marble and full of ornate marble fireplaces, and lavishly furnished in high Victorian style, Turkish carpets, crystal chandeliers, and bric-a-brac, this inn has attracted a lot of notice. Its 13 lofty bedrooms, with big four-poster or canopy beds, are named for authors: among them, Shakespeare, Elizabeth Barrett Browning, Oscar Wilde (twin beds), and George Bernard Shaw (in art deco style). Rates $145–175 per couple MAP (add 15 percent gratuity), B&B rates also available. The dining room has won a host of local admirers (see *Dining Out*).

Maplewood Inn (265-8039/800-253-7729), Route 22A south, Fair Haven 05743. A distinguished Greek Revival farmhouse, set in fields, decorated in period style, with common rooms that ramble on and on, from the cozy tavern (BYOB) and breakfast room to the parlor. The Blue Room, and the Oak and Hospitality "Pineapple" suites are especially attractive. The latter may be combined with the Rose Room at $155. Otherwise, rates are $65 (shared bath) to $95, including a full country breakfast. Innkeepers Cindy and Doug Baird brew their own beer and also sell home brew supplies.

The Stonebridge Inn (287-9849), 3 Beaman Street (Route 30), Poultney 05764, is a splendid, 1808 Greek Revival house. Renovated with a flair are five cheerful bedrooms (two with private bath, others share), two comfortable sitting rooms, and an attractive wainscotted dining room. Room rates are $64–84 double (private bath), including a three-course breakfast.

Tower Hall Bed and Breakfast (287-4004), Poultney 05764. Across from the Green Mountain College campus, this Queen Anne house with a turret, original woodwork, and stained glass has three bedrooms, one with private bath, adjacent to a sitting room with fireplace. $45–50 with continental breakfast.

Lake St. Catherine Inn (287-9347), Route 30 south, Poultney 05764. Here's a peaceful, cheerful, lakeside family retreat that might remind oldsters of happy days at a traditional summer camp. Set in a grove on the shore of this placid little spring-fed lake, and open May–October, this rustic 1920 inn offers a total of 35 rooms in the main lodge or in motel-like units. Guests can use paddleboats, Sunfish, and canoes without extra charge and relax on the sundeck or dock.

There's a big, comfortable living room/game room and an inviting lakeside deck. Patricia and Raymond Endlich are the friendly hosts. Rates $54–72 daily, per person, double occupancy, MAP (less between May 8 and June 18 and September 8–20); Early Bird, Mother's Day, Fisherman's, midweek, and other specials. Add 15 percent gratuity.

The Middletown Springs Inn (235-2198), Middletown Springs 05757, at the junction of Routes 140 and 133, 16 miles southwest of Rutland, is a most unusual, pure Victorian mansion on the Green of this quiet village. Eugene and Jayne Ashley are the new owners. A total of 10 rooms are divided between the main and carriage houses. $60–120 per couple includes full breakfast; add 15 percent gratuity. Dinner by arrangement.

South of Rutland   **White Rocks Inn** (446-2077), RR 1, Box 297, Route 7, Wallingford. This elegantly furnished farmhouse and its spectacular, landmark barn are on the National Register of Historic Places. The four guest rooms, each with private bath, have either king or double canopy beds, queen, or tiger maple twins and can be had for $65–85 double occupancy including full breakfast. The Milk House Cottage (with a whirlpool bath, living room, and full kitchen) is $125. Midweek and weekly rates are 10 percent less, slightly more in foliage and holiday seasons. Children over 10 and horses are welcome, but smokers are not.

The Green Mountain Tea Room (446-2611), RR 1, Box 400, Route 7, South Wallingford 05773. Built as a stagecoach stop in 1792, this plainly inviting hostelry on Otter Creek (also on Route 7), run by the Pino family, has five rooms and two baths at $55 double, including tea and breakfast. Children and dogs welcome.

Also see **Maple Crest Farm** and **Buckmaster B&B,** two outstanding bed & breakfasts secreted in the beautiful village of Shrewsbury Center just a dozen miles southeast of Rutland, described in "Okemo Mountain/Ludlow Area."

Other lodging includes the "old reliables": **Holiday Inn** (800-HOLI-DAY; 775-1911), Routes 7 and 4 south, includes Paynter's Restaurant, indoor pool, Centre Stage lounge; **Comfort Inn** at Trolley Square (775-2200), Route 7 south; **Howard Johnson's Motor Lodge** (775-4303), Route 7 south; **Day's Inn** (formerly Rutland Lodge: 773-3361). Also see "Killington/Pico Area."

DINING OUT   *Rutland*   Also see "Killington/Pico Area."

Casa Bianca (773-7401), 76 Grove Street. Open for dinner Tuesday–Saturday. Here's a friendly, homelike Italian restaurant with excellent food and a cozy atmosphere. Lee Ryan has been pleasing her faithful patrons for 25 years, cooking and chatting with the lucky patrons who find their way to her eight-table dining room (in summer, there are more tables on the porch). Entrées $10.95–26.95.

Grand Finale (775-1853), Route 4 east, Mendon. Easy to miss but very good. Yankee pot roast, veal Marsala, roast duck, thoughtfully prepared and served in suave, formal dining rooms, Monday–Saturday 5–9. Moderate.

The Silver Fox (438-5555), Route 133, West Rutland. This inn (see *Lodging*) offers "fine dining" by reservation (eight hours required). Dinner might begin with fettucini Alfredo or scallops over peaches, proceed with a caeser salad and an entrée of beef Wellington with béarnaise sauce or shrimp stuffed sole with lobster Newburg sauce. Hot fudge cream puffs or a choclate peanut butter torte are dessert specialties. Their prix fixe is $22–28.

Ernie's Grill at Royal's Hearthside (775-0856), 37 North Main Street (junction of Routes 4 and 7). Open 11–11. Ernie and Willa Royal have a reputation earned over the past decades. Actually, the couple retired briefly but came back to add a mesquite grill to augment their open-hearth specialties: prime ribs, chops, seafood, and lobsters. Entrées $12.95–23.95.

121 West (773-7148), 121 West Street. Open for lunch (except Sunday) and dinner. A large dining room geared to business lunches and Continental dining at dinner. Entrées usually include Weiner Schnitzel as well as roast Long Island duckling and roast prime rib. Entrées $9.95–16.95.

Fair Haven   **The Vermont Marble Inn** (265-8383), West Park Place. The stately dining room in this bastion of Victorian opulence holds only 10 tables, and the prices are quite reasonable considering the quality of the cooking. Chef Don Goodman changes the menu every two weeks or so, but starters could include chilled grilled duck sausage with curried apples and shallot-cherry confit. There are usually four entrée choices, which might include breast of chicken stuffed with wild rice and almonds in tarragon veloute sauce or sea scallops and Mahi-Mahi with julienne vegetables and basil sauce over saffron angel-hair pasta. Entrées $14.95–16.95, including salad, sorbet, and rolls.

Fair Haven Inn (265-4907), Marble and Adams streets. Open daily. An 1830s inn just off the Green houses this large, informal restaurant. Owner-chef John Lemnotis took this on as a retirement project but has now been here (occasionally providing Greek bouzouki music himself) for more than 20 years. Ask anyone about his Athenian cuisine: jumbo shrimp à la Greque, seafood Souvlakia, stuffed grape leaves, egg and lemon soup, baklava—the works. Entrées $10.95–16.95.

EATING OUT   *Rutland*   **Back Home Café** (775-2104), 21 Center Street. Upstairs café open for lunch and dinner; the downstairs Deli & Bakery also serves lunch. The café is funky and friendly with deep booths. The enormous lunch menu is big on burgers, omelets, and hot, open-faced sandwiches; luncheon specialties include sliced breast of turkey with asparagus and boursin cheese ($4.95) and a vegetarian casserole ($3.75). The dinner menu is also big on burgers but also includes sautéed scallops and fettucini, gourmet pizzas, and New York sirloin. The attached nightclub is the scene of live music and dancing on weekends.

Seasons Circle (773-3701), 24 Wales Street. Open except Sundays, Monday–Friday 7:30 AM–9 PM, Saturday 10–9. A small, attractive café with mauve walls and bentwood chairs specializing in crêpes (try the Italian Ricotta), soups, salads, and pastas, but there are also burgers and sandwiches.

MacLeods Compass Rose (773-5925), #2 Center Street Alley. Open for lunch and dinner except Sunday. A bistro atmosphere with a long bar (Long Trail beer on tap); small, pleasant dining spaces. Tacos and enchiladas at lunch, expanded versions for dinner along with entrées ranging from lasagna to baked sole.

The Seward Family Restaurant (773-2738), Route 7 north. Family run and geared, Seward's began as a dairy bar in 1946. Their own ice cream (34 flavors) are still the specialty of the house, along with Seward's cottage cheese, sour cream, and the cheddar cheese the family has been producing (see *Selective Shopping*) since the Civil War. The coffee shop has expanded into a full-scale restaurant, open for all three meals.

South Station (775-1736), at the Trolley Barn, 170 South Main, is open daily for lunch and dinner, specializing in prime ribs of beef and such munchies as fried potato skins, zucchini sticks, stuffed mushrooms, chicken wings, hearty soups, salads, burgers, and teriyaki beef or chicken, all at moderate prices.

Sawdi's Steak House (773-8124), Route 7 north. Open for dinner daily; a roadside landmark for more than 20 years specializing in char-broiled steaks, lamb, and seafood; an extensive children's menu.

The Sirloin Saloon (773-7900), Route 7. One in a Vermont mini-chain (there are three), this colorful restaurant (lots of glasswork, art, and gleaming brass) is a good bet for families. The menu runs from ground sirloin ($8.95) to prime rib ($16.50).

Panda Pavilion (775-6682/6794), at the entrance to the Rutland Mall, Route 4 east. Highly praised Szechuan–Hunan–Mandarin cuisine, like Double Happiness Chicken. Open 11:30–11 Monday–Saturday, 1–10 Sunday. Takeout service.

South of Rutland   **The Wallingford Block Family Restaurant** (446-2098), open except Mondays 11–9, housed in a great old Victorian building, corner of Routes 7 and 140. Pizza is the specialty, along with lasagna and garlic bread. Hefty grinders, sandwiches, big burgers, and other staples also available.

Lake Area   **Dockside** (273-3334), Route 30, two miles north of Route 4, Lake Bomoseen, is a popular, amiable fish and steakhouse right on the lake, serving lunch and dinner Tuesday–Saturday, and open Sundays 12–9.

Checkmate Restaurant (468-5841), Route 4A, Bomoseen. A family restaurant and dairy bar open daily for lunch and dinner, breakfast too on weekends. House specialties include crispy fried chicken and golden fried fish.

ENTERTAINMENT Year-round movies: **Rutland Area Cinemas** with two locations, "Westway 1-2-3-4" (438-2888), Route 4 in West Rutland, and "Studio 1&2" (775-1539) at the Rutland Mall on Route 4 east, both show first-run flicks.

SELECTIVE SHOPPING *Rutland* **The Opera House**, Merchants Row, downtown Rutland. Part of this old music hall has been converted into a sleek mini-mall of shops for gifts and clothes and housing, especially **The Book King**, a bright, well-stocked book shop.

Michaels Toys (773-1488), upstairs at 13 Center Street. Michael Divoll makes everything in the space, specializing in rocking horses in a variety of sizes. He also makes great wooden trucks, and, even if you don't want to buy one, this is a great place to visit, with a small art gallery on the side.

The Unnamed Bookstore and Antique Center, 110 West Street. Clint and Lucille Fiske, former owners of the Haunted Mansion Bookstore in Cuttingsville, have moved their stock of second-hand books, antique maps, and such to downtown Rutland.

Eastman's (773-8533), 68–70 Merchants Row. This is an unusually complete stationery and art supply store, also good for cards and calendars.

Tennybrook Square, 230 North Main Street, is a cluster of shops including a **Bass Shoe Outlet**, **Hathaway Shirt Outlet**, and **Country Quilt & Fabric**, which offers custom-made quilts and accessories, supplies and instruction books, and cotton calicos.

Charles E. Tuttle Company (773-8930), Main Street, facing the park, has one of the largest stocks of used and rare books in New England. Charles Tuttle began his publishing company in Tokyo right after World War II and has built it into a major supplier of beautifully produced books on Oriental art and other Asian subjects.

The Seward Vermont Dairy Deli Shop (773-2736), 224 North Main Street (Route 7). One corner of this vast restaurant (see *Eating Out*) showcases the cheddar cheese that has been produced by this family since the Civil War. The specialty is sharp cheddar, aged over nine months. Smoked cheddar and herbed cheddars are also available in wheels, blocks, and sticks and via mail order (call 259-2311 or write to Hill Country Food Products, PO Box 218, East Wallingford 05743). Maple syrup and creamed honey are also available. This is also the only source of old-fashioned cheese curd.

Boutique International, 85 North Main Street, has a large assortment of gifts from many countries.

Annie's Book Stop (775-6993), Trolley Square, 170 South Main Street. Before or after Ben & Jerry's browse here for new books and swap your paperbacks.

Along Route 4 East of Rutland   **Snowridge Outfitters** (775-6550), 155 Woodstock Avenue, Route 4 east, has two shops here: CB Sports clothes and an authorized Orvis retail store.

Truly Unique (773-7742), Route 4 east, has an uncommon collection of country antiques, Vermont products, and gifts.

Rocking Horse Country Store (773-7882), Route 4 east, combines Vermont food products (including its own homemade wine jelly), gifts, antiques, and collectibles.

North of Rutland   **Fred's Carpenter Shop**, Route 7 north, Pittsford 05763, is a center for dollhouses and miniature furnishings, accessories, scaled lumber, hardware, electrical systems, and wallpaper, plus dollhouse and furniture kits. Open Monday–Saturday 9:30–5, Sunday 11–5 or by appointment.

South of Rutland   **The Old Stone Shop**, Route 7, Wallingford. Open as a gift shop in the summer, this historic site was built in 1848 by the Batchellers, who had been making pitchforks and farm implements since 1808.

Vermont Industries maintains a genuine factory store offering real savings on its products. See "Okemo Mountain/Ludlow Area."

Fair Haven and Poultney   **Vermont Bean Seed** (265-4212), Fair Haven. This growing mail-order outfit has opened a retail store near its test garden. Call ahead for hours.

Heartstrings (287-9565), 27 College Street, Poultney, is a Victorian cottage country store with tinware, candles, potpourri, herbcrafts, teddy bears, etc.

SPECIAL EVENTS   Late February: **The Great Benson Fishing Derby**, sponsored by the Fair Haven Rotary Club: many prizes in several categories, including best ice shanty. Tickets for the Derby, PO Box 131, Bomoseen 05732.

Early August: **Art in the Park Summer Arts Festival,** sponsored by the Chaffee Arts Center (775-0356) in the Main Street Park, junction of Routes 7 and 4 east.

Labor Day weekend: **Killington Stage Race**, five events for bicycle racers.

Early September: **Vermont State Fair** (775-5200). Midway, exhibits, rodeo, races, demolition derby, and tractor pulls animate the old fairgrounds on Route 7 south of the city.

Mid-October: **Art in the Park Fall Foliage Festival,** sponsored by the Chaffee Arts Center (above).

MEDICAL EMERGENCY   Rutland Regional Ambulance Service (911); Rutland Fire Department Rescue Paramedics (911).

Rescue Squads: Fair Haven/Castleton (265-8800); Poultney (287-9510); Pittsford (773-1700); Wallingford (775-5555).

Addison County and Environs

Including Middlebury, Vergennes, Brandon, and Bristol

Addison County packs as much contrasting scenery within its borders as any county in the country.

It includes the high eastern wall of the Green Mountains, laced with hiking trails and pierced by four of the state's highest, most dramatic "gaps" (passes). The mountains drop abruptly through widely scattered hill towns—Lincoln, Ripton, and Goshen—into the only valley in Vermont that's so broad that you can't see one side from the other. And when you do, after traveling west through many miles of flat farmland and rolling orchard land, you can't believe what you see. Lake Champlain is far narrower here than up around Burlington, and the Adirondacks in New York seem higher and nearer, forming an improbable backdrop to cows, water, red barns, and apple trees.

Middlebury (population 8,000) is the county seat and hub of Addison County. It's also the home of prestigious Middlebury College, and one of Vermont's handsomest, liveliest, most welcoming communities. Inns and restaurants serve visitors as well as potential students and parents, and in recent years it has become a great place to shop.

Vergennes, midway between Middlebury and Burlington, is the smallest *city* (2,300 residents) in the United States. Although five miles inland, its history and present are linked closely to Lake Champlain. Otter Creek winds from the "city" to the lake, and the road leads to Basin Harbor, site of the area's premier resort and of the Lake Champlain Maritime Museum. We recommend the lake road south from Basin Harbor, by Button Bay State Park and the D.A.R. State Park to Chimney Point. The ruins of the eighteenth-century fort at Crown Point in New York are just across the Lake Champlain Bridge.

We prefer, however, to cross the lake at Larrabees Point. Route 74 winds down from Shoreham through orchards and ends at Teachout's, a general store built in 1836 from stones taken from Fort Ticonderoga. A small, car-carrying cable ferry makes the crossing to the fort itself in six minutes flat. Officially, the "Fort Ti Ferry" has held the franchise from the Vermont and New York legislatures since 1799, but records indicate the service was initiated by Lord Jeffrey Amherst in 1757 for use by his soldiers in the campaigns against the French. Its boast is "serving people and their vehicles since Mozart was three months old." The *M/V Carillon*, a sleek excursion boat, is based at the adjacent wharf. It traces the 1775 route used by Ethan Allen and his Green Mountain Boys to capture Fort Ticonderoga, cruising as far as Mount Independence in Orwell.

The Addison County Chamber of Commerce offers information about every corner of its domain, from Vergennes and Bristol on the north to Orwell on the south. The fine old town of Brandon, however, because the county line detours peevishly to avoid it, must tout its own horn (see *To See and Do*).

GUIDANCE   Addison County Chamber of Commerce (388-7951), 2 Court Street in the Painter House. Open Monday–Friday 9–5. This unusually large walk-in information center publishes a map/guide, stocks brochures, and refers visitors to a wide variety of lodgings, from inns and bed & breakfasts to seasonal cottages on Lake Dunmore. During foliage season, it is unusually resourceful in finding lodging for all comers.

The Brandon Area Chamber of Commerce (247-6401), Box 267, Brandon 05733, publishes a map/guide and maintains a seasonal information center near the Green.

The Bristol Area Chamber of Commerce, PO Box 291, Bristol 05443, publishes a pamphlet guide.

The Map & Guide for Middlebury and Addison County, published by Huntington Graphics ($2.50), is well worth buying for bicyclists, canoeists, fishermen, and other serious explorers.

GETTING THERE   By bus: Vermont Transit (864-6811/800-451-3292) stops in Brandon and Vergennes as well as Middlebury. This is the Burlington to Albany run, so New Yorkers and Bostonians must change in Rutland.

By car: The major north/south highway is 7, but we advise anyone from New York or Boston to approach through the Middlebury Gap (see details under *To See and Do*). From the west you can take the toll bridge at Chimney Point year-round or the seasonal ferries described below.

By ferry: Lake Champlain Ferry (864-9804) from Essex, New York, to Charlotte operates spring through fall, takes 20 minutes, and puts you just above Vergennes.

Fort Ticonderoga Ferry (897-7999), Larrabees Point to Fort Ticonderoga. Memorial Day weekend through June, 8–6 daily; July–Labor Day 8 AM–9 PM, then 8–6 through the last Sunday in October. Cars $5 one-way, $8 round-trip. See the introduction to this chapter.

TO SEE AND DO   *Middlebury*   Both the town (8,000) and Middlebury College (founded in 1800 and now one of the most sought-after private colleges) owe much to the energy and vision of Gamaliel Painter, a surveyor who settled here before the Revolution. Painter accompanied Ethan Allen on the Fort Ticonderoga raid and returned to Middlebury to become the town's principal landowner, sheriff, judge, and assemblyman. The fine mansion on Court Square belonged to Painter. Another benefactor was Joseph Battell, who owned thousands of acres of forest and mountain land that he left to the college and the state when he died in 1915. He was the proprietor of the famous old summit house, Bread Loaf Inn, now the nucleus for the summer Bread Loaf School writers' conference. Battell also owned a weekly newspaper in which he fulminated against the invasion of motor cars. Emma Hart Willard, who pioneered in the education of women, was another Middlebury luminary.

The town's proudest buildings—the courthouse, Middlebury Inn, and the fine Congregational church—are grouped, along with compact business blocks, around the Common. It's a short walk down Main Street to the churning Otter Creek falls, a centerpiece for dozens of shops that have proliferated in the old riverside mills and marble works on both banks of the river, connected by a footbridge. With the Vermont State Crafts Center as its anchor store, this is now one of Vermont's most interesting places to shop.

Middlebury College (388-3711) fills a 350-acre campus a short walk from downtown Middlebury. For visitors, its focal point is the new Center for the Arts, a facility similar to Dartmouth's Hopkins Center. It includes an art gallery exhibiting the college's distinguished, permanent collection of paintings and small sculptures by Hiram Powers, Francois Rude, Auguste Rodin, Medardo Rosso, and others, as well as notable landscapes and drawings, plus transient shows. It also houses a theater and concert hall.

The Sheldon Museum (388-2117), Park Street. Open Monday–Saturday 10–5, June–October 31; Wednesdays and Fridays 1–4 the rest of the year (the gift shop remains open weekdays 10–4). This 1829 marble merchant's house has no less than six black marble mantels and holds an intimate collection of furnishings, tools, household articles, clothes, books, games, and other artifacts portraying Vermont folkways, displayed in period rooms. A modern research ell has been added with a gallery for changing exhibits. There are also frequent special events. $2.50 per adult, $2 for seniors and students over 12.

The Vermont State Craft Center at Frog Hollow (388-3177). Open Monday–Saturday 9:30–5, Sunday afternoons, spring through fall. This nonprofit shop combines the natural beauty of Otter Creek falls, just outside its windows, with a dazzling array of the best art and crafts work in Vermont. More than 200 Vermont artisans are repre-

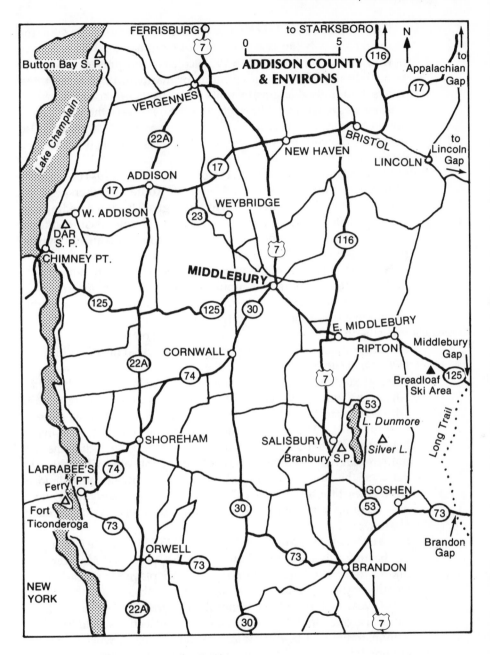

sented, and you can come away with anything from a 50-cent post-card to a $2,400 bed. A feast for the eyes, it's also a serious shopping source with an outstanding selection of pottery, woven clothing, hangings, jewelry, and woodwork, among other things.

The Vermont Folk Life Center (388-4964), 2 Court Square (in the Painter House, below the Chamber of Commerce). This relatively new organization (founded in 1984) collects and presents the traditional arts and folk ways of Vermont, primarily through taped interviews. It mounts changing exhibits and sells its publications.

The Congregational Church (1806–1809) is one of the state's most architecturally distinguished. Its architect, Lavius Fillmore, who also designed the church in Old Bennington, was obviously influenced by the work of Asher Benjamin.

Morgan Horse Farm (388-2011), open May–October, 9–4 daily. From Middlebury town square, head west on Route 125, then right on Route 23 (Weybridge Street) and follow signs. This is a breeding and training center operated by the University of Vermont. Guided tours of the stables and paddocks are available, along with an audiovisual presentation about the Morgan horse and farm. Admission.

The Battell House, on the park (now the community house), was built in 1816 for Horatio Seymour, senator from Vermont from 1821 to 1833. The end walls of this urbane mansion are capped by marble coping instead of the usual "carpenter's finish."

Vergennes Its site on an impressive falls and its handsome, early nineteenth-century commercial buildings suggest an unusual history. This is, in fact, one of the oldest, as well as the smallest, cities in the country. It was founded by Donald McIntosh in 1764 and later named by Ethan Allen for Count de Vergenne, the French minister of foreign affairs who was a strong supporter of the American Revolutionary cause.

In 1811–1812, Thomas McDonough used the Otter Creek basin just below the falls to build, in record time, three ships, including the 734-ton, 26-gun *Saratoga,* and equipped nine gunboats, with which he defeated the British fleet in Lake Champlain off Valcour Island in 1814. One of these gunboats, *The Philadelphia,* has been raised and is now residing in the Smithsonian Institution. A replica rides in Basin Harbor.

Lake Champlain Maritime Museum (475-2317), at the entrance to the Basin Harbor Club off Panton Road. Open mid-May through mid-October, Wednesday–Sunday 10–5. Displayed in an early nineteenth-century, one-room schoolhouse are objects that reflect the 10,000-year history of Lake Champlain, with emphasis on the latest nautical archaeological explorations. Evening lectures, field trips, and demonstrations of boat-building craftsmanship. A working replica of Benedict Arnold's 54-foot gunboat *Philadelphia,* built on the spot, was launched in 1991 and is on view.

Rokeby Museum (877-3406), three miles north of Vergennes on Route 7 in Ferrisburg. Open for guided tours at 11, 12:30, and 2, Thursday–Sunday, May–October, and by appointment for groups and researchers throughout the year. This is the home of Rowland E.

Robinson, the nineteenth-century author, illustrator, and naturalist. The eight rooms of exhibits in this Underground Railroad station for fugitive slaves contain furnishings and personal items from four generations of the Robinson family. Admission charge.

Brandon   A peaceful town of some 4,000 inhabitants and a heretofore underrated appeal, **Brandon** has an unusual array of eclectic nineteenth-century houses in an interesting mix of Federal and Victorian styles. Sited between Otter Creek and the Neshobe River, it was the home of Thomas Davenport, who invented and patented an electric motor in 1838, and the birthplace of Stephen A. Douglas (1813–1861), "the little giant" of the famous debates with Abraham Lincoln in 1858 when Douglas was senator from Illinois. Brandon's hospitality to travelers is growing with the addition of some interesting new places to stay.

Bristol   Billing itself as the "Gateway to the Green Mountains," Bristol is nestled at the foot of Lincoln Gap, at the junctions of north-south Route 116 (less heavily trafficked than Route 7) and east-west Route 17. Its broad Main Street is lined with a delightful mix of stores and restaurants, housed in a nineteenth-century building that leads to a square Green, complete with a fountain, park benches, and old cannon.

The local site to see is **The Lord's Prayer Rock** (on the south side of Route 17 entering Bristol from the east), a flat rock inscribed with the Lord's Prayer. A physician named Joseph C. Greene commissioned the inscription in 1891, presumably because he was still thankful for having reached that point safely when, as a youth, he was hauling logs over steep roads.

COVERED BRIDGES   **The Pulpmill Covered Bridge**, between Middlebury and Weybridge, near the Morgan Horse Farm, is the oldest in the state (1808–1820) and the last remaining two-lane span in use.

Halpin (1824). New Haven, two miles east off Route 7, highest bridge above the streambed.

Station Bridge, across Otter Creek in Cornwall (two miles east of Route 30 on Swamp Road), is a 136-foot towne lattice bridge built in 1836.

FORTS   **Mount Independence,** eight miles west of Orwell on the shore of Lake Champlain, Route 73 off 22A, facing Fort Ticonderoga, was a key fortification defending the colonies in 1776–1777, but unlike Ticonderoga the horseshoe battery was never reconstructed nor developed. This 400-acre woodlot remained neglected and almost inaccessible for 200 years until 1975, when it was opened to the public by the Vermont Division of Historic Preservation, which has been gradually restoring a sense of its importance.

Fort Ticonderoga (518-585-2821), Ticonderoga, New York. Open mid-May–mid-October daily. The eighteenth-century stone fort has been restored and includes a museum displaying weapons and uniforms. It was built by the French (named "Fort Carillon"), captured by English General Jeffrey Amherst, and held by the British until 1775, when Ethan Allen and his Green Mountain Boys took the fort by surprise, capturing the guns that eventually helped free Boston. The fort is easily accessible from Point Larrabee on the Vermont shore (see *Getting There* and *Boating*).

Crown Point State Historic Site (518-597-3666), Crown Point, New York. Open May–October, Wednesday–Saturday 10–5, Sunday 1–5. Free. Just across the Lake Champlain Bridge from Chimney Point, Vermont. Fifteen miles north of Fort Ticonderoga, Crown Point was once a far larger, more important fortification, and in 1775 it was the source of 29 pieces of canon captured by the Americans and hauled off to Boston. The complex includes eighteenth-century ruins and a visitors center.

On the Vermont shore, there are two related sites: **John Strong Mansion** (759-2309), West Addison, Route 17, west of 22A, open mid-May–mid-October, Friday–Monday 10–5. This is one of several substantial brick houses and buildings made of stone taken from the ruins of Fort Crown Point and skidded across Lake Champlain by oxen. General Strong, an early settler and Green Mountain Boy, built his (third) residence here in 1796, with brick from his own claypits on the "Salt Lick" where he first hunted deer. The house is now owned by the Daughters of the American Revolution and open to the public during the summer. Admission: $2 per adult, $1 seniors and students.

The Barnes Tavern, Route 125, Chimney Point, state-owned and full of historical interest, is open Wednesday–Sunday in the summer.

GAPS   **Middlebury Gap.** This is our favorite approach to Addison County from the southeast, and this stretch of Route 125 is more dramatic driving east to west. Begin in Hancock and stop at Texas Falls (see *Waterfalls*). The road quickly crests at its junction with the Long Trail, near the Middlebury Snow Bowl. Then it's all downhill through the woods until the huge, wooden Bread Loaf Inn (now part of Middlebury College) improbably appears. The Robert Frost Wayside Picnic Area and the Interpretive Trail are a short ways beyond. We also like to stop in the small, nineteenth-century cemetery a bit farther down, where a wind chime strikes softly in a row of maples. The picturesque hill town of Ripton is just below, and as the road continues to plunge into the valley, you briefly glimpse the Adirondacks in the distance.

Appalachian Gap, Route 17 east from Bristol, climbs steadily for four miles (past the Jerusalem General Store), eases off for a couple miles, and then zigzags steeply to crest at more than 3,000 feet yielding some spectacular views before dropping into the Mad River Valley.

Lincoln Gap. Follow Route 17/116 east from Bristol, but follow signs to Lincoln and on through Lincoln over the Gap Road, unpaved in sections. Again there are beautiful views, and you are quickly down in Warren (see "Sugarbush/Mad River Valley").

Brandon Gap. Route 73 is a high road over Goshen Mountain and through Brandon Gap. At the height of land, several wooded hiking trails are posted, and a rest area has been sited to catch the full majesty of Mount Horrid Great Cliff. The road then rushes downhill with Chittenden Brook, joining Route 100 and the White River below Rochester.

GREEN SPACE AND WATER   Lake Dunmore, in Salisbury between Brandon and Middlebury on Route 53 off Route 7, is a tranquil, 1,000-acre lake lined with simple summer cottages at the foot of Mt. Moosalamoo and its hiking trails. On the east shore road is **Branbury State Park** (247-5925), with a sandy beach, boating, snack bar, picnic grove, museum nature trail, and hiking to the Falls of Lana, Cascade and Silver lakes; likely to be crowded on weekends. Silver Lake is accessible only on foot.

Along Lake Champlain   **D.A.R. State Park** (759-2354/483-2314), eight miles west of Addison on Route 17, has a campground with 71 sites and a picnic area, with steps leading down to a smooth shale beach for swimming.

Button Bay State Park (475-2377/483-2314), on Panton Road just below Basin Harbor. Named for the unusual, buttonlike clay bank formations, with a splendid view across the lake to the Adirondacks; 72 campsites, picnic areas, swimming, fishing, nature museum, and trails.

Kingsland Bay State Park (877-3445), Ferrisburg. Marked from Route 7. Facilities include a picnic area on Lake Champlain, also a tennis court, hiking trails.

Dead Creek Wildlife Management Area (759-2397), 7 miles east of the D.A.R. State Park on Route 17, is a 2,800-acre semi-wilderness tract. Except for certain refuges, most of it is open to the public. The information booth is not always staffed, because the supervisor is generally in the field, but a self-guided tour folder is available.

In the Green Mountain National Forest   Robert Frost Country was a title officially bestowed on a wooded piece of the town of Ripton in 1983, because it was here, in a log cabin, that the poet summered for 39 years. This section of Route 125, between the old Bread Loaf Inn (part of the Middlebury College Campus) and the village, has been designated as the Robert Frost Memorial Highway, and there is also a Robert Frost Interpretive Trail and a Robert Frost Wayside picnic area near the road leading to the farm and cabin. The picnic area has grills and drinking water, and it's shaded by red pines that were pruned by Frost himself during summer visits. Just east of the wayside, a dirt road leads to the Homer Noble Farm. Park in the lot provided and walk past the farm to Frost's cabin (it's not open to the public). **The Robert Frost Interpretive Trail**, a bit west on the opposite side of Route 125, is an easy walk, just ³/₄ mile. It begins with a bridge across Beaver Pond (we actually saw a beaver here one time) and winds through   woods and meadow, by seven Frost poems mounted along the way. This trail is also popular with cross-country skiers and snowshoers and with July and August blueberry pickers.

WATERFALLS   **The Falls of Lana** near Lake Dunmore are particularly accessible and rewarding. The trail begins just south of the Branbury Park entrance, and it's just a half mile to the picnic area and falls.

Texas Falls, in Hancock, is easily accessible from the marked road, three miles east of the Middlebury Gap. It's a short drive to the parking area, and the series of falls are just across the road, visible from a series of paths and bridges. There's also a picnic area.

APPLE PICKING   September and October is Apple Time in Addison County, where visitors are welcome to pick their own (see *Apples* in "What's Where"). The orchards are particularly thick in and around Shoreham.

BICYCLE TOURING   **Vermont Bicycle Touring** (VBT) (453-4811), Box 711, Bristol 05443, is now the best-known and largest bike vacation organizer. The founder, John Freidin, originated the inn-to-inn concept in 1972 with a single weekend tour and wrote the perennially popular *25 Bicycle Tours in Vermont* (published by Backcountry Publications, Box 175, Woodstock 05091, $11.45 postpaid). Bill Perry, the owner and director, offers 55 different VBT tours, including 9 weekend trips, 11 inn-to-inn tours, and 9 special-interest and combination vacations. All of these are spelled out in the VBT brochure; they will also loan you a 17-minute videotape.

Bike & Ski Touring Center (388-6666), 74 Main Street, Middlebury, is a source for a variety of rental bikes. So is **Bicycle Holidays** (388-BIKE) in Middlebury.

Country Inns Along the Trail bike tours usually begin and end at Churchill House (see below), which has a limited number of 10- and 12-speeds for rent. Other inns are on the itinerary. Brochure from **Churchill House** (247-3300), RD 3, Brandon 05733.

BOATING   *Cruise*   The *M/V Carillon*, a 60-foot, 49-passenger replica of a 1920s Thousand Island luxury motor yacht, operates daily, May 10–October 20, from **Teachout's Lakehouse Store and Wharf** (897-5331) at Larrabee's Point. The 1¹/₂-hour cruise goes up to Hand's Cove, then across to Fort Ticonderoga (you can debark and catch a later boat), and on to Mount Independence and Mount Defiance, while the captain tells you what was happening along the route in the 1770s. $6.25 per adult, $4.25 per child, group rates.

MARINAS AND RENTALS   **Champlain Bridge Marina** (759-2049), West Addison, boat access, pump-out station for boats under 35 feet.

Chipman Point Marina & Campground (948-2288), Route 73A, has dockage for 60 boats, grocery store, pump-out station, game room, swimming, boat rentals.

Buoy 39 Marina (948-2411), Orwell.

Waterhomes (252-4422), West Shore Road, Lake Dunmore. Rents rowboats, canoes, motorboats, sailboats.

Lake Dunmore Kampersville (352-4501), in Salisbury, also rents rowboats, canoes, sailboats, and motor bugs.

FISHING   Otter Creek is a warm-water stream good for smallmouth bass and northern pike. The cooler Neshobe River, especially in Forest Dale, is better for trout, and rainbows can be found in the Middlebury River just below Ripton. The New Haven River below Bartlett's Falls is also good trout fishing.

GOLF   **Ralph Myhre Golf Course** (388-3771), just south of the Middlebury campus, is owned and operated by the college, 18 holes.

The Basin Harbor Club (475-2311), Vergennes, 18 holes.

Neshobe Golf Club (247-3611), Town Farm Road (just off Route 73). Open April–October, a full-service club, 18 holes.

HIKING   **The Green Mountain National Forest District Office** (388-4362), Route 7, Middlebury, offers pamphlet guide to 28 "Day Hikes" in the area.

Country Inns Along the Trail. Seven inns collaborate with Churchill House (247-3300) to provide lodging along an 80-mile stretch of the Long Trail.

SWIMMING   **Bartlett's Falls** in Lincoln, two miles east of Bristol on the road marked to Lincoln, just off the junction of Routes 116 and 17. This is a series of long, deep pools and a popular diving spot around the falls.

Middlebury Gorge, East Middlebury, off Route 125 just above the Waybury Inn, where the road suddenly steepens. A path leads in along the river.

Also see **Branbury**, **Button Bay**, **D.A.R.**, and **Kingsland Bay** state parks under *Green Space and Water*.

CROSS-COUNTRY SKIING   **Carroll and Jane Rikert Ski Touring Center** at the Bread Loaf Campus of Middlebury College (388-2759), Ripton, Route 125, 12 miles from the main campus, is owned and operated by Middlebury College. It has over 42 km of groomed trails in the area of the Robert Frost Farm and the college ski bowl. Elevations range from 975 to 1,500 feet. Rentals, accessories, repairs; $7 trail fee.

Blueberry Hill (247-6735), Goshen. Fifty km of tracked and groomed trails plus another 20 of outlying trails on elevations of 1,400–3,100 feet make this a fairly surefire cross-country mecca during even marginal seasons. $13 trail fee.

DOWNHILL SKIING   **Middlebury College Snow Bowl** (388-4356), 13 miles east of Middlebury on Route 125, at Bread Loaf, has three chair lifts, a total of 15 trails, 40 percent covered by snow-making. It also offers a ski school, rentals, restaurant. Closed December 25.

RESORT   **Basin Harbor Club** (475-2311), Box 7, Vergennes 05491, located on Lake Champlain five miles west of town, off Panton Road. Open mid-May – mid-October. This is Vermont's premier, family-run resort. The 700-acre retreat on Lake Champlain offers 121 rooms, most in cottages scattered along the shore. Since 1886, when they began taking in summer boarders, the Beach family has assiduously kept up with the times. Over the years, a large swimming pool, an 18-hole golf course, and even an airstrip have been added. Still, the handsome old farmhouse has been preserved. In summer, Dutchman's pipe climbs as it always has around the porch pillars, and three grand old maples shade the lawn, which slopes to the flower gardens and to the round harbor beyond. There are 18 rooms in the inn, 13 more in the attractive stone Harbor Homestead. The 77 cottages, geared to families (and well-behaved pets), vary in rate, depending on size and location. All have phones, and many have fireplaces, fridges, and wet bars. The lakeside units are worth the little extra, with views of the lake and Adirondacks that are so extraordinary it's difficult to tear yourself away from the window or deck, especially at sunset.

Basin Harbor manages to please both children and elderly couples. Youngsters can take advantage of the beach, elaborate playground, and lively, supervised (complimentary) children's program from 9 to 1, and younger children can also dine together and play until 9 PM. For those age 10 –15, there are golf and tennis clinics, movies, mixers, and video games in the Red Mill, the resort's informal restaurant off by the airstrip. Needless to say, those who like to dress for dinner have ample opportunity; men and boys over 12 must wear jackets and ties. The food is fine (see *Dining Out*). Rates, daily, per person with a full American Plan, are $95–150. Add 15 percent gratuity. Less for children. There are also Golf, Tennis, and Fall Foliage packages.

INNS   *In and Around Middlebury   05753*   **The Middlebury Inn** (388-4961, 800-842-4666), 14 Courthouse Square, has been the town's imposing chief hostelry since 1827. Innkeepers Frank and Jane Emanuel have now totally renovated the 74 guest accommodations and public rooms. Rooms in the main house are on two floors (there's a 1926 Otis elevator) and are furnished in reproduction antiques. They have private baths, cable color TV, air- conditioning, and direct-dial phones. There are also 20 motel units (15 are wheelchair accessible) with inn-style furnishings, and the adjacent Porter Mansion, full of handsome architectural details, has five Victorian rooms. The common rooms include a vast, comfortable lobby with a formal check-in desk and portraits of the Battell family and Robert Frost. Elegant afternoon tea and light dinners are available in the pubby Morgan Tavern, and all three meals are served in the pillared, wedgwood blue, formal din-

Basin Harbor, Vergennes, classic Lake Champlain resort

VTD

ing room. Thoughtful touches include readable books on shelves near guest rooms, umbrellas for guests' use next to the door, and complimentary muffins and juice in the lobby from 6:30 to 7:30 AM. Rates range from $80 to $142 double, including afternoon tea. Inquire about packages. Pets are welcome in the motel units at a small daily fee, and arrangements for babysitting can be made.

The Swift House Inn (388-9925), 25 Stewart Lane, was, until a few years ago, the family estate of the legendary philanthropist Jessica Stewart Swift, who lived to be over 100. Antiques, elaborately carved marble fireplaces, formal gardens, and other gracious amenities add to the charm of this 1814 mansion. Common space in the inn itself includes a lovely wicker-filled porch and cozy pub as well as an attractive living room. Dinner and breakfast are served in the cherry-paneled, main dining room or in the library. There are 10 guest rooms in the main house, five more in the annex, and another five in the renovated 1886 Carriage House. Rates per room range from $80 to $150 for suites with fireplaces, sitting area, whirlpool tub, and cable TV. Andy and John Nelson preside. Dinner is served Thursday–Monday year-round.

The Waybury Inn (388-4015), Route 125, East Middlebury 05740, is an inviting, historic, 14-room village inn, open all year. Bob Newhart never did sleep here, though guests sometimes ask for the "Loudons" because the exterior serves as the "Stratford Inn" on the veteran CBS series. There's no pool, but a swimmin' hole under the nearby bridge. The innkeepers are Marcia and Marty Schuppert, and the rates range from $80 to $115 double, including a full country breakfast. Two-night minimum stay on busy weekends and holidays. Luncheon is served on the enclosed porch July–October, dinner, in the dining room year-round.

The Chipman Inn (388-2390), Ripton 05766, Route 125 on the way to or from Bread Loaf and the Middlebury College Snow Bowl ski area, in the center of the tiny village of Ripton (population: 300), which consists of a schoolhouse, community meetinghouse and church, and a general store. This is an exceptionally attractive 1828 house with nine guest rooms of varying sizes (we suggest requesting one at the back of the house), all with private baths. Guests gather in the lounge/bar, around a very large old hearth, or settle into the sunny sitting room near the woodstove. The dining room is lit by candles and decorated with stenciled wallpaper. Innkeepers Joyce Henderson and Bill Pierce offer a five-course dinner on request (prix fixe $20), and both dinner and breakfast guests are encouraged to sit together at long tables. There is also a table for two. Rates are $93–108 per couple ($60 single) with breakfast. Closed in April and November.

In and Around Brandon   **The Brandon Inn** (247-5766), 20 Parker Street, Brandon 05733. Like the Middlebury Inn, this is a massive brick landmark overlooking its town Common. It dates from 1892, after fire destroyed its predecessor. Innkeepers Sarah and Louis Pattis have scaled down the number of guest rooms on the second and third floors from 46 to 28, refurbishing them nicely. Number 217, a two-room suite, is especially attractive, at $155 MAP. Other MAP rates: $65–75 per person double; September 18–October 18, $75–85 per person double, MAP, when a two-day minimum stay is required on weekends. The B&B rate is $45–70 per person. Children under 12 are free in their parents' room. There are sitting rooms upstairs as well as down, and some of the nineteenth-century furniture and a good deal of the atmosphere survive. The inn's five acres include a swimming pool and stretch of the Neshobe River, good for trout fishing. An 18-hole golf course is just up the way. Buses from New York, Boston, and Montreal still stop, as stages once did, at the front door.

The Churchill House Inn (247-3078), RD 3, Brandon 05733. Closed October–Christmas Day and mid-March–early May. Located west of the Brandon Gap on Route 73, and run by Roy and Lois Jackson, this old farmhouse has eight guest rooms furnished in nineteenth-century style, serves zesty dinners and breakfasts, and offers fly-fishing and canoeing, hiking, bicycling, and cross-country ski expeditions. Winter rates are $80 per person MAP; summer $75; fall $85 (add 15 percent gratuity). This is also the nerve center for the four-night inn-to-inn packages featuring either fly-fishing, hiking, or biking. Inquire too about special rates for weekend and midweek stays.

Blueberry Hill Inn (247-6735/6535 or 800-448-0707), Goshen 05733, on Forest Road 32 in Ripton. Over the past 20 years, Tony Clark has turned this blue 1820 farmhouse on a remote back road into one of New England's most famous country inns. The big lures are fine food and, in the winter, cross-country skiing. But there is more to it: a sure touch. The rooms—some with lofts, all with full baths—have their share of antiques but are not particularly large or luxurious. The common rooms are, however, sunny and inviting with geraniums blooming in the greenhouse off the kitchen and a stone fireplace in the dining room. Guests are encouraged to mingle, from morning coffee to evening hors d'oeuvres and dinner. This inn has long been known for its food, and current chefs more than deserve the reputation, producing elaborate, creative dinners featuring fresh, local ingredients. The cross-country ski center, with 70 km of groomed trails, tends to be snowy, thanks to its elevation, if there is any snow in Vermont. Rates are high: $105 per person MAP, double occupancy, plus 15 percent gratuity, half price for children 14 and under in same room. BYOB. No smoking. Closed November, April, and May.

MORE INNS ☞**The Shoreham Inn & Country Store** (897-5861; 800-255-5081), Route 74 west, on the Green, Shoreham 05770. This friendly, comfortable place is a great antidote if you've overdosed on Laura Ashley wallpaper and mints on the lacy coverlets of antique beds. Longtime innkeepers Cleo and Fred Alter offer, instead, comfortable, ungussied rooms, some with daybeds for families, and plenty of singles for the many bicyclists and hikers who frequent the inn. There are 11 guest rooms, or nine, plus a two-room suite, depending on how you look at it, with seven baths. The many-windowed inn, which dates from 1790, sits in the middle of a small village, surrounded by apple country and not far from Larabee Point. The living room and dining room are both filled with pictures, plants, and, frequently, the aroma of coffee, soup, or things cooking and baking in the kitchen. Guests gather around the long dining room table. Rates: $40 single with breakfast, $70 double. Closed November.

The Long Run Inn (453-3233), RD 1, Box 114, Bristol 05443. Only open May–October. This gabled village inn, located in Lincoln Center on the New Haven River, began life as a lumberjack's hotel soon after its construction in 1820 and offers access to hiking on Mount Abraham, to an "ol swimmin' hole," and to cross-country and bike trails. Now owned by Michael and Beverly Conway. Room rates: $50 per person double occupancy MAP. Children under 10 half price. Closed April and November.

BED & BREAKFASTS *In and Around Middlebury* ☞**Robert Frost Mountain Bed & Breakfast** (388-6042), East Middlebury 05740. Twenty years ago Arthur Lord built this house along traditional, late eighteenth-century lines, and he did it so well that you could fool any number of guests. Not far from either Middlebury or Ripton, it seems very far from everything, sequestered on 20 acres, on an unpaved road. Hosts Garcile and Arthur Lord can both trace their Vermont lineage way back, and they offer a taste of true Vermont hospitality. The two guest rooms are large and sunny, sharing an immaculate bath, and there's a large living room with fireplace and view of the garden, well stocked with books. $50 per couple includes a full breakfast, served in the open-beamed dining room in front of the hearth.

October Pumpkin (388-9525, 800-237-2007), Route 125, East Middlebury. You can't miss this pumpkin-colored, 1850s Greek Revival, and maybe you shouldn't. Eileen and Charles Roeder, longtime B&B hosts, decorated the rooms with early stencils, English and American antiques, whimsical wicker. Rates range from $50 (shared bath) to $75 for a room with a canopy bed and private bath. Either a continental or full breakfast is included, and polite pets are welcome.

Brookside Meadows (388-6429), RD 3, Box 2460, Middlebury, is a handsome and comfortable house set back from a quiet country road, just three miles from the center of town and Middlebury College. Linda and Roger Cole offer three bedrooms and a two-bedroom suite, all with private baths. The living room overlooks the garden and a roll of meadow. The rate, including tax and full breakfast, is $70.20 for a room, $129.60 for the suite occupied by four people.

Traditional bandstand on the green, Bristol

The Annex (388-3233), Route 125, East Middlebury. This tidy house across from the Waybury Inn offers six rooms, four with private bath. There's a small living room with TV and a dining room with one large table. Rooms are $50–60, $70 for the suite sleeping four, continental breakfast included. Smoke-free, no pets.

In Bristol 05443   **The Crystal Palace Bed & Breakfast** (453-4131), 48 North Street. Two blocks north of the Green, a Victorian-style house with six very clean guest rooms (three on the second and three on the third floor) sharing three baths. Retired IBM engineer Price and Christina Corney are your hosts; $60–65 per couple includes a full breakfast.

Also see **The Millhouse Bed & Breakfast** in Starksboro in the "Burlington Region."

In Vergennes 05491   **The Strong House Inn** (877-3337), Route 22A, Vergennes. This is a real beauty, built in the 1830s by Samuel Paddock Strong, a local worthy, in the graceful Federal style, with such fine workmanship as curly maple railings on the free-standing main staircase. Michelle and Ron Bring offer six bedrooms, all exceptional. The "Empire Room" has mahogany furnishings (queen-size bed), a working fireplace, and a private half bath ($80), but the sunny "English garden room" with its brass (shared bath) is also a find at $45. Samuel's suite with queen and double beds, a fireplace, meadow view, and sun room is $125 for four people. We also wouldn't mind settling for the English "Hunt" room with its sleigh bed or the Victorian room with its marble-top dresser, both $70 (private bath). Michelle and Ron Bring include a full breakfast in the rates. No smoking or pets indoors.

Emerson's Guest House (877-3293), 82 Main Street, Vergennes, is a spacious Victorian home with four large, airy bedrooms and gracious living areas, antiques, and extensive gardens. Rates are $35–65 per room, including a full breakfast. Pat and John Emerson have been welcoming guests since 1980.

Chimney Point House (759-2632), RD 3, Box 248, Vergennes. Located on the shore at the junction of Routes 125 and 17 near the bridge to Crown Point, New York, this Italianate house has wonderful woodwork and some original wall coverings. Three bedrooms with shared bath, formal Victorian parlor, $40–45, including continental breakfast.

In Brandon 05733   **The Old Mill Inn** (247-8002), Route 73, East Brandon 05733. This is an attractive farmhouse set above the Neshobe River, adjoining the Neshobe Golf Club (18 holes). Guests enter through a sunny breakfast room and find two large living rooms with wing chairs, a piano, a TV, and a pot belly stove. There's a sense of space here, both inside and out. The six rooms have private baths, stenciling, and rag rugs, iron bedsteads, and other carefully chosen antiques. Annemarie and Karl Schreiber include a full country breakfast for $65–95 per couple.

The Moffett House (247-3843), 69 Park Street. This is a spiffy, 1860s Victorian "painted lady," complete with tower and gables, long windows, inviting veranda, and superb detailing. The seven guest rooms vary widely, from smallish with shared bath to large with canopy bed and Jacuzzi tub; there's also a third-floor suite. The decor includes a number of stuffed teddy bears, and the rates, $65–85 per room, includes a full, multi-course breakfast.

Rosebelle's Victorian Inn (247-0098), 31 Franklin Street. A mansard-roofed house on a quiet side street. There's a small, high-ceilinged living room with a fireplace and TV and a large dining room, the setting for full breakfasts, featuring gourmet coffees and fresh, baked breads and muffins. All but one of the seven guest rooms share baths. Hostess Ginette Milot speaks French.

Brandon Ordinary (247-3969), 5 Pearl Street. David and Barbara Forrest's house is a Federal (1815) beauty with elegant twin parlors with fireplaces and porches. There are three guest rooms (one with private bath). Children and pets welcome, full breakfast included in $55 per room.

The Gazebo (247-3235), 25 Grove Street. This is another attractive in-town house, ca. 1865 classic, with a woodburning stove in the sitting room, comfortable rooms, private baths; hosts Joel and Janet Mondlak include a full breakfast at $55–75 per couple.

Blake House (247-3152), Route 73 east of town, a handsome 1825 stone house with two guest rooms. Frankly, no one was home when we stopped by, but it looked very attractive, and we like the brochure that states "children are always welcome." $60 per room includes continental breakfast.

MORE BED & BREAKFASTS   **Apple Valley** (897-7621), Smith Street, Shoreham 05770, is an 1820 house that includes the original eighteenth-century homestead. Layne and Bill Litleiholm offer a downstairs room with twin beds, private bath, and separate entrance for $55 ($35 single), also two upstairs rooms with double bed and semi-private bath for $45, including a complete breakfast. An additional single bed or crib is $15 extra.

Brookside Farms (948-2727), Route 22A, Orwell 05760. Guests breakfast in this columned Greek Revival mansion and are free to relax in the living room and browse in the 10,000-volume library. But only the suite (two bedrooms: $100 single, $150 per couple, $185 for three) is in the mansion itself. The remaining four rooms are in the vintage, 1810 "Guest House," approached through a garagelike antique shop. These seemed dark and unappealing for the price ($50 per person). Guests can observe the workings of the 300-acre dairy farm, which includes cross-country ski trails. Afternoon tea, lunch, and dinner by arrangement. Rates quoted include breakfast.

MOTELS   **The Adams Motel and Restaurant** (247-6644), Route 7, one mile south of Brandon, should really change its name, because it's not a motel but a shady campus of 20 cozy, one- or two-room cottages of the kind so familiar in pre-motel motoring days. Most of the cottages have fireplaces and TV, and there's a swimming pool plus miniature golf across the highway. Moderate. Open from late spring to November.

Brandon Motor Lodge (247-9594), Route 7, two miles south of Brandon, is nicely situated amid acres of front lawn, with a swimming pool and two tennis courts. This old reliable has been expanded. Room rates vary with the seasons, in the $40–55 range, depending on size and the day of the week. Holiday weekend rates may be higher and require a two-night minimum. Polite pets welcome. $38–55, more during holiday weeks.

Bristol Commons Inn (453-2326), junction of Routes 17 and 116, Bristol 05443. An attractive A-frame–style motel in a peaceful valley setting, one mile from the village of Bristol, with a restaurant, Rosemarie's, on premises. Room rates: $45–50 double occupancy; $58 for a room with a loft. Chip-putt green. Rosemarie's serves breakfast and northern Italian dinners. Open all year.

COTTAGES   *Lake Dunmore*   Some cottagers hope that the lake will remain off the beaten track; however, it's being "discovered," and here are some good bets:

Dunmore Acres (247-3126, 207-499-7491 off season), a former summer camp in a lovely setting, has nine two- and three-bedroom housekeeping cabins, a swimming pool, tennis court, rec hall, boat dock with canoe and rowboat. $55 per night for a two-bedroom cabin, $60 for a three-bedroom (two-night minimum), or $375 and $400 per week, respectively.

Lake Dunmore Lodge (352-4444), West Shore Road, Salisbury 05769, nicely situated on a point with 400 feet of shoreline, rents a substantial chalet with four bedrooms and two baths for $750 per week.

Sunset Lodge Cottage Colony (352-4290 April–November; 352-9054 November–April), West Shore Road, Salisbury 05769, has 22 simple cottages on the lake, five of which are available in the winter for ice fishermen. Lots of recreational equipment for children, with boats and bikes for rent. Call or write for reasonable rate schedule.

Note: The **Addison County Chamber of Commerce** (388-7951) has a list of rental cottages on both Lake Dunmore and Lake Champlain.

DINING OUT   *In Middlebury*   **Swift House** (388-2766). Dinner is served Thursday–Monday all year. Dine either in the paneled main dining room or in the more intimate library on elegant fare: perhaps hot wild mushroom salad to start ($4.75), then maybe rack of lamb with honey mustard glaze ($18.50), or roast pheasant with lemon, honey, and thyme ($17.50). Save room for chocolate mascarpone terrine with espresso cream ($4.25). Entrées begin at $14.50 for grilled loin of pork with bourbon peaches. Wine specials are available by the glass.

Woody's (388-4182), Five Bakery Lane, open daily 11:30–midnight. You have the sense of being wined and dined on a small, three-decker art deco ship beached on the bank of Otter Creek. Owner/chef Woody Danforth serves up salads and quiches midday, homemade breads and desserts, and lists among dinner entrées spicy Cajun or Bourbon shrimp. The menu changes nightly, and the wine list is extensive, as is the selection of imported and domestic beers. Dinner entrées from $9.

Mr. Up's (388-6724), on the Bakery Lane plaza, open daily, 11:30–midnight. Dine outside on the riverside deck or in the brick-walled, stained-glass, oak and greenery setting inside. The menu is equally colorful, ranging from chicken Piccata to Maryland crabcakes to Moroccan seafood stew. Dinner entrées range from $11.95 to $12.95. The menu also always includes "lighter fare" like calamari fra diavilo ($6.95) and overstuffed burritos ($6.50). There's a surprising wine choice.

The Waybury Inn (388-4015), East Middlebury, open for breakfast, lunch, and dinner. On any given night, half the patrons may be here because they've seen the facade on TV as the "Stratford Inn" in Bob Newhart's CBS series. The other half are here because they know this is one of the better places around Middlebury to eat. Entrées range from pasta primavera ($11.50) to grilled butterflied leg of lamb ($14.25). The dining room is attractive, and there's an inviting pub.

The Middlebury Inn (388-4961/4666) serves a big breakfast buffet, lunch in the Morgan Tavern or on the West Porch, and the wedgwood blue "Founders Room" dining room features candlelight dining. A popular appetizer here is fried Cabot cheese (deep-fried Vermont cheddar served with fresh marinara for dipping). The menu changes frequently but might include veal sautéed with shiitake mushrooms, sun-dried tomatoes and madiera wine, or "sole Paupiettes" (spinach, crabmeat, butter, and crumbs rolled in two fillets and baked with mornay sauce). Entrées, $8.95–17.50, include hot popovers and a trip to the salad bar.

Fire & Ice Restaurant (388-7166/800-367-7155), 26 Seymour Street. Open except Mondays 11:30 –9:30. "Good Food & Legal Vice," it says of itself; excellent lunch and dinner plus Sunday brunch in an informal stained-glass and mahogany setting. Closed Mondays. A local favorite since 1974 with a variety of special shrimp dishes as well as steaks. Entrées ($11.40–17.90) include the shrimp and seafood salad bar and breads.

The Dog Team Tavern (388-7651), a jog off Route 7, four miles north of Middlebury. Traditional New England fare (sticky buns, et al.) Open for dinner daily except Monday. Open for lunch late spring through foliage. Gift shop. Opened in the 1930s by Sir Wilfred Grenfell (1865–1940), the British medical missionary who established hospitals, orphanages, schools, and cooperative stores in Labrador and near the Arctic Circle. Entrées $8.50–14.95.

Café Chatillon (388-1040), ground floor of the Frog Hollow Mill, open for lunch, dinner, and light entrées. Filling the quarters and shoes of the old Otter Creek Café, with ever-changing menus featuring Vermont products, also fine wines and espresso. Dinner reservations appreciated.

Luigi's Little Naples (388-3385), 86 Main Street. Open for lunch and dinner, Tuesday–Saturday. An informal, storefront setting with a range of Italian dishes, from spaghetti and meatballs ($6.95) to ambitious lamb and veal dishes. Lunch from $4.95.

Emperor's Garden (388-3020), the Marble Works, Middlebury, open for lunch and dinner. An upscale oriental restaurant with lush greenery and fresh flowers, Szechuan, Hunan, and Cantonese cuisine. Inexpensive to moderate.

In Brandon   **The Brandon Inn** (247-5766). Open for dinner except Monday off season; lunch Tuesday–Saturday. Austrian-trained owner/chef Louis

Pattis makes dinner in his grand, old multi-pillared dining room; something of an event, with appetizers like chicken liver pâté with fresh fruit, entrées like stuffed quail with a brown sauce ($15.95) and rack of lamb with an herbal demiglaze ($19.95). Memorable desserts include a flourless chocolate cake with raspberry banana filling.

In Bristol   ☞ **Mary's** (453-2432), 11 Main Street. Open year-round except Mondays for lunch, dinner, and Sunday brunch (10:30–3). Highly and widely regarded as one of the most delectable restaurants in Vermont, this small storefront café is deftly decorated with mismatched tablecloths and original art. Among its unusual dinner offerings: pasta Alfredo with home-smoked salmon and local fiddleheads ($11 half, $14 full), lamb and eggplant curry ($13), and jumbo coconut shrimp with Key Lime sauce ($17). For lunch you might savor a pesto pizza to a Vermont Reuben (pastrami, sauerkraut, and Vermont cheddar with Russian dressing, broiled open faced). For brunch you can sample green eggs and ham (with spinach, ham, and spinach pesto, served with homefries and homemade toast).

In Vergennes   **Basin Harbor Club** (475-2311), Basin Harbor, off Panton Road, five miles west of Vergennes. If you don't stay at Basin Harbor, there's all the more reason to drive out for lunch or dinner to see the lakeside setting and savor the atmosphere. The food is fine too. The menu and dining room are both large. You might begin with smoked mussels with lemon dill sauce and dine on veal Marsala or lightly breaded bay scallops. The prix fixe menu also includes juice, salad, vegetables, fruit, cheese, and desserts ranging from jello to old-fashioned strawberry shortcake. The wine list is immense.

EATING OUT   *In Middlebury*   **Rosie's** (388-7052), one mile south of Middlebury on Route 7, is open daily (6 AM–9 PM in winter, until 10 May–November) and serves a lot of good, inexpensive food. This family mecca is said to expand every eight months or so to accommodate its fans. There's a friendly counter for those in a hurry or interested in the local gossip, and two large, cheerful dining rooms with stained-glass lights. We lunched on a superb beef and barley soup and a turkey salad on wheat. Dinner choices run from fish n' chips ($6.50) to Smitty's top sirloin ($10.50), and there are always stir fries.

Amigo's (388-3624), on the Green, serves Mexican specials from light snacks to full dinners, weekdays from 11:30, Sundays from 4.

Luigi's Deli Market (388-3385), 86 Main Street. Middlebury's Italian restaurant is also a source of takeout pasta, salads, and cheeses.

Calvi's, 42 Main Street. Open for breakfast, lunch, and dinner in summer, closes at 6 in winter. A classic, old-fashioned ice cream parlor and "news store" with a marble-topped counter and a scattering of tables; but the payoff comes in summer with the tables on the screened porch in back, overlooking Otter Creek. This is the perfect place for a banana split. Breakfasts run from oatmeal to omelets, and there are "dinner sandwiches," also pizza, homemade soup, and egg creams.

In Brandon   **Patricia's Restaurant** (247-3223), Center Street, open daily from 11 for lunch and dinner, 1–8 Sundays, when there's a senior citizen discount on complete dinners. Traditional fare like grilled pork chops ($9.50), fried haddock ($12.95), and Italian dishes ranging from cheese ravioli ($7.50) to spaghetti with hot sausage ($8.75).

In Bristol   **Rosemarie's** (453-2326), Routes 17 and 116, Bristol, is a superior, moderate Italian restaurant with specialties like fried calamari, escarole and bean soup, and conch.

Bristol Bakery & Café (453-3280), 16 Main Street. Open daily from 5 AM except Sunday when it's 6. An inviting storefront filled with the aroma of coffee and breads. Stop at least for a muffin and espresso and take home a loaf of sourdough bread; there are also blackboard luncheon specials.

Cubber's Restaurant (453-2400), 8 Main Street. Open daily. Decent pizza, also chili, soups, and salads; wine and beer served.

In Vergennes   **Vermont Pasta** (877-3413), 3 Green Street. Open for lunch, dinner, and Sunday brunch. A sibling of the Burlington restaurant with the same trendy atmosphere and winning menu. You can lunch on spinach mushroom lasagna and a variety of pastas, dine on Danish fettucini and shrimp ($9.95) or Vermont pasta primavera ($7.95).

SELECTIVE SHOPPING   *In Middlebury*   **The State Craft Center at Frog Hollow** (see the Middlebury section under To See and Do) has become the anchor store for an unusual mix of shops on both sides of the falls.

Sweet Cecily (388-3353), Frog Hollow Lane. Nancy Dunn, former Frog Hollow gallery director, has assembled her own selection of ceramics, folk art, hooked rugs, and other items from 100 craftspeople, including Mexican and Amish.

Frog Hollow Mill, a neighboring three-story stone mill houses two distinctive shops, **Middlebury Goodwares**, featuring kitchen and bath furnishings and gadgets, and **Black Hawk**, an upscale clothing store specializing in natural fiber sportswear for both men and women.

The vintage 1837 **Star Mill** also houses a variety of shops in which you can find anything from crystals to canoes. The shortcut from Frog Hollow up to Main Street is through the **Great Falls Collection** and **Mill Stream Toys**, two more eclectic and intriguing shops. Across the Marble Works Memorial (foot) Bridge, the 1890s stone buildings in which marble was once finished presently house a dozen shops, including **The Clock Shop** in which David Welch repairs and sells timepieces, specializing in antique pocket watches. There's also a **Vermont Only** outlet for Vermont products and souvenirs.

Woody Jackson's Holy Cow (388-6737) studio and workshop at 52 Seymour Street is a short walk beyond the Marble Works. Woody

Susan Leader Pottery, Vermont State Craft Center, Middlebury

himself, a Middlebury graduate whose Holstein products have become almost more of a symbol of Vermont than the state's seal, is usually on the premises. His black-and-white Holstein cows, immortalized on Ben & Jerry's ice cream cartons, decorate T-shirts, aprons, coffee mugs, boxer shorts, and more.

Danforth Pewterers (388-0098), also at 52 Seymour Street, are best known for their distinctive pewter buttons, found in stores throughout New England. Fred and Judi Danforth actually continue a family tradition begun by Revolutionary War hero Thomas Danforth II. They also make pewter jewelry, oil lamps, and tableware.

Back on Main Street don't miss **Lazarus Department Store** (388-2551), 22–26 Main Street (open Monday–Saturday 9–6), a wonderfully old-fashioned department store with a "sidewalk shop" discount corner on the second floor.

Vermont Bookshop (388-2061), 38 Main Street, was opened in 1947 by Robert Dike Blair, who is one of New England's best-known booksellers and the publisher of Vermont Books, an imprint for the poems of Walter Hard. Robert Frost was a frequent customer for more than two decades, and the store now specializes in autographed Frost poetry collections as well as current and out-of-print books about Vermont.

Otter Creek Old and Rare Books (388-3241), Main Street, is a book browser's delight: 40,000 very general titles.

Skihaus (388-6762), Battell Block, open daily, stocks sportswear of all kinds plus a ski shop for Nordic and Alpine gear.

Wood Ware (388-6297), Route 7 south of Middlebury, is the home of solid butternut door harps and dozens of other items. Open daily, May–October, or by appointment.

Harvest Hill (388-6412, 800-272-4212), Route 7 south. Vermont products.

Middlebury Antique Center (388-6229, in Vermont: 800-339-6229), Route 7 at the junction of Route 116 in East Middlebury. A fascinating variety of furniture and furnishings representing 50 different dealers.

In Brandon   **Brown's of Brandon** (247-3000), on the Green, has Vermont crafts, pottery, wall hangings, stenciled rugs, baskets, and books.

In Vergennes   **Kennedy Brothers Marketplace** (877-2975), just off Route 7, an attraction for many years for its factory outlet oak and pine woodenware, has expanded its quarters to include a Factory Marketplace with three floors of Vermont products, crafts, and antiques; plus a bakery, the **Owl's Basket Delicatessen** for eat-in or takeout soups, sandwiches, Ben & Jerry's ice cream. Discovery Craft Fair here in mid-October.

Collectors Emporium (877-3858), Route 7, New Haven, two miles south of Vergennes. A trove of collectibles: glass and china, furniture, miniatures, books.

In Bristol   **Deerleap Books** (453-4062), 5 Main Street. Daily except Mondays. A small, friendly, and carefully stocked bookstore that entices you to browse and to buy.

SPECIAL EVENTS   Early February: **The American Ski Marathon** a 25- or 50-km challenge that draws as many as 600 skiers.

Late February: **Middlebury College Winter Carnival** (388-3711). Ice show, concerts, snow sculpture.

Mid-March: The **Pig Race** winds up with a fine pork barbecue. Further information from Blueberry Hill.

July 4: Bristol hosts one of the most colorful Independence Day parades around.

Early July: A six-day **Festival on the Green,** featuring individual performers and groups such as the Bread & Puppet Theater.

Early August: **Addison County Field Days** (545-2488). Livestock and produce fair, horse show, lumberjacks, demolition derby, and other events.

MEDICAL EMERGENCY   Middlebury (388-3333); Shoreham (897-7777); Bristol (453-2401); Brandon (247-6828).

Burlington Region

Superbly sited overlooking Lake Champlain and the Adirondack Mountains, Burlington is Vermont's financial, communication, educational, and cultural center, a junior Boston with five colleges, an excellent medical center, electronic and engineering industries, and imaginative waterfront redevelopment. With an area population of over 100,000, Vermont's "Queen City" is the seat of Chittenden County, named for Thomas Chittenden, the one-eyed but foresighted first governor of the state (1777–1797).

Burlington was chartered in 1763, four years after the French were evicted from the Champlain Valley. Ethan Allen, his three brothers, and a cousin were awarded large grants of choice lots along the "Onion" (now Winooski) River. Ira Allen was responsible for securing in 1791 the legislative charter for the University of Vermont (UVM), from which the first class, of four, was graduated in 1804.

Ethan and Ira would have little trouble finding their way around the city today. Main streets run much as they did in the 1780s—from the waterfront uphill past shops to the school Ira founded (UVM now enrolls more than 10,000 students) and on to Winooski Falls, site of Ira's own grist- and sawmills.

Burlington's waterfront today resembles its early self more than it has for a century. Handsome, Federal-style commercial buildings now house shops and restaurants, and the Greek Revival mansion, designed by Ammi Young for the first president of the Rutland Railroad, now houses offices. The ferry terminal and neighboring Union Station are reminders of the city's late nineteenth-century boom period as a lumbering port, when the lakeside trains connected with myriad steamers and barges.

The neo-Victorian Burlington Boathouse is everyone's window on Lake Champlain, a place to rent a row- or sailboat, or simply to sit sipping a morning coffee or sunset aperatif, lunching or dining on the water. The adjacent Waterfront Park and promenade are linked by bike paths to a series of other lakeside parks (bike and roller blade rentals abound), which include swimmable beaches.

Halfway up the hill, the graceful Unitarian Church, designed in 1815 by Peter Banner (architect of Boston's famous Park Street

Church), still heads Church Street—now a bricked, traffic-free marketplace for four blocks. Benches and boulders (from different parts of the state), kiosks and street vendors pepper the promenade, and the buildings themselves—a mix of architectural styles—are filled with more than 100 shops and an unusual choice of restaurants.

Both Church Street and the waterfront now serve as settings for frequent, exuberant events. Music and theatricals in these venues augment performances at UVM's Royall Tyler Theater and at Main Street's Flynn Theater.

There's a lot of creative energy at work and play in Burlington these days, and the once rather stodgy city has such a yeasty atmosphere that a socialist mayor—the only one in the United States—was elected by ten votes in 1981 by what a *New Republic* writer recently called "the 'hipboisie,' the granola-chewing exemplars of backpack chic who have come here for the university and the mountains." Mayor Sanders was reelected in 1983, 1985, and 1987, however, by a substantial plurality of voters who crossed party lines. He is now serving Vermont in the United States House of Representatives.

A "Who's Who" of Burlington would include Ethan Allen Hitchcock, ambassador to Russia and secretary of the interior in the McKinley and Teddy Roosevelt administrations; John Godfrey Saxe, an enormously popular poet of the mid-1800s; Admiral Henry Mayo, commander of the Atlantic Fleet in World War I; James R. Angell, longtime president of Yale University; John Dewey, the educator whose philosophy revolutionized American teaching; A. Atwater Kent, pioneering radio manufacturer; U.S. Senator Warren R. Austin, the first American ambassador to the United Nations; Philip Hoff, the first Democratic governor of the state who served three terms after 1962; Patrick Leahy, Vermont's first Democratic senator, who was re-elected for a third term in 1986; and Madeleine Kunin, the Democratic governor from 1984 until 1990.

Our only complaint about Burlington is its amazing lack of downtown places to stay. Given both the waterfront's recent renewal and the abundance of handsome mansions arrayed in tiers along the city's upper slope, one would assume a choice of inns and bed & breakfasts would appear to meet the obvious demand. Not so. Fifteen years after its controversial debut, the seven-story Radisson remains the only in-town hotel. On a happier note, both business- and family-geared lodging, along with a variety of attractive bed & breakfasts, have proliferated in just the past few years, scattered through South Burlington, Williston, Winooski, Colchester, Essex Junction, and—moving just a bit farther out—Jericho, Bolton Valley, Richmond, Shelburne, Charlotte (pronounced sha-*lot*), Ferrisburg, and Starksboro—all areas described within this section.

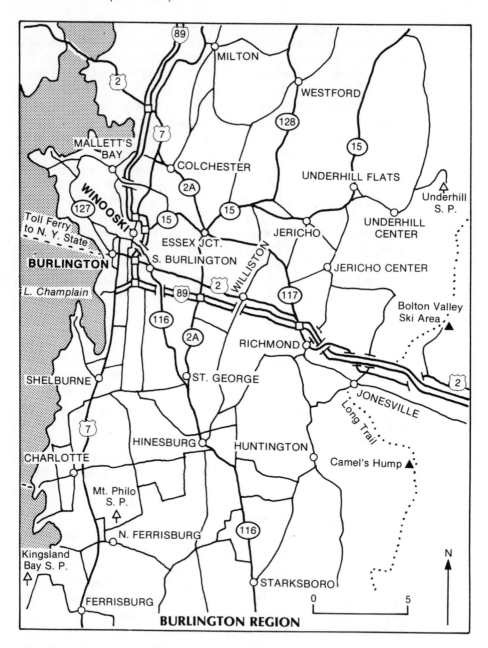

BURLINGTON REGION

GUIDANCE   The Lake Champlain Regional Chamber of Commerce (863-3489), 209 Battery Street (Box 453), Burlington 05402-0453. Write for brochure guides to lodging and dining. The waterfront office, open Monday–Friday 8:30–5 (also summer Saturdays dependent on volunteers), is a source of walk-in information.

The Information Gallery (658-6673) maintains a manned information kiosk downtown at the corner of Church and Bank streets, open 11–5, mid-May–mid-October. They supply a visitors' map and offer advice on dining, shopping, and lodging in Burlington and the upper Champlain Valley.

Newspapers: The daily *Burlington Free Press* and the weekly *Vermont Times*, the latter especially for reviews, political features, and entertainment notes.

GETTING THERE   By car: I-89, Routes 7 and 2.

By air: Burlington International Airport (863-2874) is just three miles from downtown, served by Continental Airlines, United Airlines,,, USAir, Northwest Airlines, and Delta Airlines.

By bus: Vermont Transit Lines (800-451-3292 in New York and New England), headquartered in Burlington, offers service to Albany, Boston, New York City, Montreal, Portland, and many points between.

By boat: **Lake Champlain Ferries** (864-9804). Between mid-May and mid-October, the LCTC car ferries make the one-hour crossing between Burlington and Port Kent, New York. They also ply between Charlotte, just south of Burlington, and Essex, New York; year-round service is offered between Grand Isle (see "The Northwest Corner") and Plattsburgh, New York.

By train: AMTRAK (800-USA-RAIL, or in Canada 800-4AM-TRAK). The Washington, D.C., to Montreal train stops at Essex Junction, five miles north of Burlington; the northbound train stops at 7:05 AM and southbound, it's 8:30 PM daily. The station is served by two cab companies and by Burlington CCTA buses.

PARKING   **Burlington Square Central Parking** (entrance from Cherry Street) is perhaps the easiest to find among a half-dozen downtown Burlington parking areas, all regulated by the city to charge $.25 per half hour, $4 maximum per day, no charge on Sundays. There are also ample meters within an easy walk of the waterfront and Church Street.

GETTING AROUND   **Chittenden County Transportation Authority** buses (864-0211). CCTA bus routes radiate from the corner of Cherry and Church streets (hub of the Church Street Marketplace), serving the Shelburne Museum, the airport, the ferry, and the Champlain Mill in Winooski as well as all the colleges and shopping areas. The fare is $.75, and transfers are free.

MUSEUMS   **The Shelburne Museum** (985-3344) is open daily 9–5 mid-May–late October, with daily 1 PM tours of selected buildings the rest of the year. This fascinating "collection of collections" portraying "the American spirit" was assembled discerningly after 1947 by the late Electra Havemeyer Webb and her husband J. Watson Webb. One can wander for a whole day or more through 35 buildings, most of them transplanted from other places in New England and Vermont. A separate guidebook is needed to describe all of these extraordinary collections of Americana, but here are a few highlights: a 1915 steam locomotive and private Palace Car presented to Governor E. C. Smith in 1890 by W. Seward Webb, then president of the Rutland Railroad; paintings of North American big game in the Beach Gallery; the sidewheeler Ticonderoga, in her basin near the Colchester Reef Light House; the Horseshoe Barn's marvelous carriages; the Castleton Slate Jail; Shaker Horsestand Shed; Dorset House and its decoys, Audubon game bird prints, and fowling pieces; General Store; Saw Mill; and the Webb Memorial Building, in which rooms from the Webb's New York apartment have been recreated, together with their distinguished art collection. There's a museum shop and cafeteria, electric trams for the footsore, and picnic areas. Something for everyone; lots of displays geared to children, such as a model circus parade. The visitors center is a rare round barn. $14 adult, $9 student, $6 child over 6; off season: $6 adult, $2.50 youth.

The Discovery Museum (878-8687), 51 Park Street, Essex Junction, is a special delight for children. Open daily, except Monday; call for hours. Nature, science, history, and art are conveyed in innovative, hands-on ways with the use of permanent and special exhibits, including computer terminals. Admission charge for adults.

At the University of Vermont   The Robert Hull Fleming Museum (656-0750), Colchester Avenue. Open 9–4 weekdays, except Monday, 1–5 Saturday and Sunday. Closed holidays. Dedicated in 1931 as a memorial to an alumnus of the university, this expanding gallery has varied collections of art, natural history, archaeology, and geology. Its holdings in ancient primitive art from several cultures and continents are especially notable. It has a well-selected retrospective collection of American portraits and landscapes, from the eighteenth century to contemporary works, and frequent special exhibits. The building was designed by the renowned firm of McKim, Mead, and White, who also designed UVM's Ira Allen Chapel (1927) and Burlington's City Hall.

Billings Library (1885), given to the university by Frederick Billings of Woodstock to house the extraordinary collection of books assembled by George Perkins Marsh (1801–1882), the Burlington lawyer who served as Congressman and diplomat and who wrote *Man and Nature* (1864), still regarded as the ecologist's bible. The Romanesque-style building is H. H. Richardson's last work.

Pringle Herbarium (656-3221). Open Monday–Friday 8:30–6. Dried plant specimens from around the world.

FARMS   Shelburne Farms (general information: 985-8686), off Route 7, Shelburne. Farm Store and Visitors Center (985-8442), open daily year-round, 9–5 (10–5 off season). The property is open for five 1½-

hour tours daily mid-May through mid-October, 10–5 ($5.50 per adult, $5 seniors, $2.50 per child aged 3–16). Most of the grand estate belonging to Dr. and Mrs. William Seward Webb (Lila Vanderbilt) in the 1880s and 1890s is now being used as an experimental farm and educational and cultural center, under the auspices of Shelburne Farms Resources, open to the public at specified times and for certain events. Comprising 3,800 acres at its zenith, this "duchy" was landscaped by the famous Frederick Law Olmsted (who also designed Central Park) and forested by Gifford Pinchot. The Webbs' 110-room summer "cottage" on a bluff overlooking Lake Champlain, the immense, five-story, 416-foot Farm Barn, and the Coach Barn, once occupied by prize Hackneys, are the nucleus of the present Webb family's nonprofit programs for continuing education in rural development, conservation, and the arts. The mansion itself has been restored as an inn and conference center (see *Inns*), and the farm's prize-winning cheddar cheese, made from its own herd of Brown Swiss cows, is sold, along with other Vermont products, in the Farm Store. A walking trail winds from the visitors center about one mile to the top of Lone Tree Hill for sweeping views of Lake Champlain and the Adirondacks.

Vermont Wildflower Farm (425-3500), Route 7 five miles south of the Shelburne Museum. Open April–October, 10–5:30 daily. A multimedia show June–October. Six acres of wildflowers in test fields and woodland settings; flowers and trees labeled along paths; a large gift shop and "the largest wildflower seed center in the East." Admission: $2 per adult, free 12 and under.

Taproot Morgan Horse Farm (482-2168), Falls Road, Hinesburg 05461. Charles and Charlotte Ross translated their passion for Morgans into a 200-acre stud farm for the famous breed where visitors (and potential buyers) are welcome.

HISTORIC SITES   The Ethan Allen Homestead (865-4556), off Route 127, in the Winooski Valley Park district just north of Burlington. Open for tours May to late October: in spring, Tuesday–Sunday 1–5; summer, Monday–Saturday 10–5, Sunday 1–5; fall, Tuesday–Sunday 1–5. Vermont's godfather has been memorialized here in the modest farmhouse where he lived out the last years of his turbulent life until his death in 1789. The restored homestead is surrounded by a working garden, and there's a fascinating multi-media show in the visitors center. $3.50 adults, $2.50 seniors, $2 ages 6–16.

Old Red Mill, off Route 117, Jericho Corners, a National Historic site, with a crafts shop. Open Monday–Saturday 10–5; Sunday 1–5, except January–March when it's only open Wednesday, Saturday, and Sunday. This tower-topped,1800s mill, set above a gorge, is one of the most photographed buildings in Vermont and appropriately houses prints and mementoes relating to one of the state's most famous photographers, Wilson A. "Snowflake" Bentley. A Jericho farmer who was the first person in the world to photograph individual snowflakes, Bentley collected more than 5,000 microphotos. The basement-level museum also tells the story of the many mills that once lined the Browns River's six sets of falls. Sales from the crafts store upstairs benefit preservation of the building, which is owned by the Jericho Historical Society. A 20-acre park behind the mill, along the river, offers picnic tables and hiking trails. Ask directions to Jericho Center, an unusually beautiful village Common with a general store and picnic tables.

Old Round Church, I-89 Exit 11, Richmond. This 16-sided building, one of the most unusual in the state, was constructed in 1812–1813 as a community meetinghouse. It's believed that 16 men each built one side, and the seventeenth man added the belfry.

Fort Ethan Allen, Colchester on Route 15. Constructed in 1893, it was used for a variety of military purposes until 1961. Although now owned by the University of Vermont and St. Michaels College, it still retains much of its historic character.

Williston Village Historic District on Route 2 includes a concentration of Greek Revival and Federal-style buildings built during the community's agricultural prosperity in the nineteenth century.

GREEN SPACE AND WATER   Winooski Valley Park District (863-5744). More than two dozen parks are included in this unusually wellrun park system, which includes three beaches (see *Swimming*), boat launches, tennis courts, and an extensive lakeside bike path; a good place for picnics and gazing at the two mountain ranges. Request a copy of the Burlington "Bike Paths & Parks" map.

The Green Mountain Audubon Nature Center (434-3068), Huntington. Trails wind through 230 acres of representative habitats (beaver ponds, orchards, and woodlands). Interpretive classes are given. Groups welcome to watch (and help) in its wood-fired sugaring. Open all year, but call ahead to confirm. Directions: turn right at Round Church in Richmond; go five miles south to Sherman Hollow Road.

Mt. Philo State Park (425-2390; 372-5060), Charlotte. A small mountaintop picnic and campground, with spectacular views of the valley, lake, and Adirondacks. A short but steep ascent off Route 7 (not recommended for trailers or large RVs); 15 campsites; $1 per adult admission.

Kingsland Bay State Park (877-3445), Ferrisburg 05456. West from Route 7 on Little Chicago Lane, about 1½ miles north onto Slang Road, 3 miles to Lake Champlain. Picnic areas, tennis courts on 130 acres.

BICYCLING   The Burlington Bike Path runs for 8.2 miles along the waterfront, from Oakledge Park on the south to the Flynn Estate at the mouth of the Winooski River. Bike and roller blade rentals are available from several sources along Main Street. This path is as well used for walking, running, and roller blading as well as biking.

BOAT CRUISES, CHARTERS   **"Spirit of Ethan Allen"** (862-9685), Perkins Pier, Burlington. Daily scenic, narrated, 1½-hour cruises, dinner and sunset cruises on Lake Champlain on this 149-passenger replica paddlewheeler. June–October 15.

McKibben Sailing Vacations (864-7733, 800-522-0028), 176 Battery Street, Burlington. Sail and powerboat charters, crewed or bare.

International Sailing School and Club (864-9065), 253 Lakeshore Drive, Colchester 05446, charges seasonal (May 2–October 31) membership fees, allowing unrestricted use of the club's sailboats, use of windsurfers, instructional workshop and clinics, sunset cruises, and club races. Weekend and six-day clinics available with lodging packages.

Burlington Community Boathouse (865-3377), foot of College Street, Burlington. Rowboats, Rhodes and Laser sailboat rentals, captained day sails, sailing lessons, fishing charters, June–October.

Red Finn Charters (862-7596), Box 31, Colchester 05446, offers a 24-foot Baha cruiser with electronics, tackle, and equipment.

Marble Island Resort (864-6800) offers hours, half- and full-day cruises aboard its motor yacht for up to six people.

DIVING   **Waterfront Diving** (865-2771), 214 Battery Street, Burlington, provides equipment rentals, instruction in snorkeling, underwater archaeology, and video, scuba, and charters to historic preserved shipwrecks.

HORSEBACK RIDING   **Elm Tree Stable** (878-0170), 162 Mill Pond Road, Colchester, offers hour-long trail rides ($10 per hour).

MARINAS   **Shelburne Shipyard** (985-3326), Harbor Road, Shelburne 05482. Complete repair facilities, some transient docking, winter storage, free pump-out, fuel, marine store, boat rentals and sales.

Malletts Bay Marina (862-4072), 228 Lakeshore Drive, Colchester 05446, full service, dockside and moorings, repairs.

Point Bay Marina (425-2431), Thompson's Point, Charlotte 05445. Complete repairs, dockage for 100, mooring for 75, marine store, fuel, free pump-out, rest rooms, showers.

See also: **Fischer's Landing** (425-2554), McNeil's Cove, Charlotte; **The Moorings** (862-8925), Lakeshore Drive, Colchester.

GOLF   **Burlington Country Club** (864-9532), South Prospect Street, 18 holes.

Marble Island Resort (864-6800), Marble Island Road, Malletts Bay, Colchester, 9 holes.

Rocky Ridge Golf Club (482-2191), St. George (five miles south on Route 2A from Exit 12 off I-89), 18 holes.

Kwiniaska (985-3672), Spear Street, Shelburne, 18 holes.

Williston Golf Course (878-3747), Williston, 18 holes.

SWIMMING   **North Beach Park** (864-0123), off North Avenue at Institute Road, Burlington (turn at the high school), provides tent and trailer sites plus swimming from a long, sandy beach, mid-May–October, vehicle charge. (Just before the park is the entrance to Rock Point, where the Episcopal Diocese of Vermont maintains Bishop Hopkins' Hall School, the Bishop's residence, a conference center, and an outdoor chapel.)

Other beaches: **Leddy Park**, also off North Avenue; **Oakledge Park**, off Route 7 south of the city, at the end of Flynn Avenue; **Red Rocks Park,** South Burlington's public beach on Queen City Park Road; **Bayside Beach** on Malletts Bay, Route 127 in Colchester. All have modest fees.

RACQUET SPORTS   **Olympiad Health, Racquetball and Aerobic Club** (863-4299), 70 Farrell Road, South Burlington. Also handball, squash, and outdoor pool available to nonmembers for daily fee.

Quarry Hill Tennis Club (862-5200), 360 Spear Street, South Burlington. Clubhouse, bar, seven outdoor courts, two pools, and Jacuzzi. Nonmembers daily fee.

Bolton Valley Resort, Bolton (434-2131).

CROSS-COUNTRY SKIING   **Bolton Valley** (434-2131). A 100-mile network of trails ranging in elevation from 1,600 to 3,200 feet. A total of 42 km are machine groomed, meaning tracked for the most part, rolled in others. There is a wide and gently sloping 3.6-mile "Broadway" and a few short trails for beginners, but most of the terrain is backwoods, much of it splendidly high, wilderness country. You can take an Alpine lift ($3) to the peak of Ricker Mountain and ski "Old Turnpike," then keep going on cross-country trails for a total of seven miles. There are rentals in Camp Bear Paw near Bolton Valley's condominiums, and experienced skiers are welcome to stay in the area's high huts by reservation. Telemarking is a specialty here, along with guided tours. $6 trail fee.

Bolton Valley to Trapp Family Lodge. This 12-mile ridge trail is one of the ultimate adventures available in New England ski touring. The trail was blazed in 1971 by Bolton Valley's Gardiner Lane and Johannes Von Trapp. It is used by a few groups every winter, recommended only for accomplished cross-country skiers. For details check either with Bolton Valley or Trapp Family Lodge (see "Stowe").

Camel's Hump Nordic Center (434-2704), 10 miles south of Exit 11 off I-89, Huntington. Located on the western flank of one of Vermont's most dramatic peaks, trails are challenging with some fine views: 50 km total, 30 km machine groomed. Elevations range from 1,100 to 2,300 feet; one 9-km trail drops 1,500 feet in its course. Rentals, child care, and lessons are offered.

Sherman Hollow (434-2057), Richmond. There are 40 km of one-way machine-tracked trails, 3.5 miles of them lit at night, elevation from 100 to 1,450 feet. This is the place for fitness buffs, complete with racing and training programs and an outdoor hot tub at the Main Lodge. There is also a lounge, change room and showers, rentals, instruction, and full-service dining. $8.

Catamount Family Center (879-6001), Williston. The 40 km of trails—30 of them machine tracked, 2 km lit—are on rolling terrain, geared to all abilities. Guided tours, rentals, instruction, warming hut. $12.

DOWNHILL SKIING   **Bolton Valley** (434-2131; lodging, 800-451-2131), Bolton 05477. This is a substantial ski mountain with the highest base elevation in the East and a nicely developed condominium complex with a sports center clustered around a hotel and base lodge. Geared to families with quality children's programs, it is actually owned by one enterprising local family who bought the whole 6,000-acre wooded preserve in 1964. The 44 ski trails here date back to the 1920s and are on 3,680-foot Bolton Mountain, which towers above its neighbors in a lonely stretch of country 20 miles east of Burlington, 20 miles west of Montpelier. Set atop a four-mile access road that is, in turn, a long way up Route 2 from anything else, it offers a genuinely self-contained resort atmosphere guaranteed to make you want to stay put for a week.

Also see **Smugglers' Notch** in "North of the Notch," the Stowe section, and "Sugarbush/Mad River Valley." A total of five major Alpine areas are within easy striking distance of Burlington.

SKATING   **Leddy Arena** (864-0123), Leddy Park, Burlington. Rentals.

SLEIGH RIDES   **Shelburne Farms** (985-8442) offers rides in 12–15-passenger sleighs. For a description of the setting, see *Farms*.

Whitcomb Farm Hayrides (879-6291), Essex Junction. Rides in a 15-passenger sleigh drawn by Belgian draft horses on a 600-acre dairy farm.

HOTELS   **The Radisson Hotel** (658-6500, 800-333-3333), 60 Battery Street, Burlington 05401. The view and location can't be beat. It's worth paying the extra $10 for a room overlooking the lake because few hotels anywhere offer a more dramatic panorama: Lake Champlain backed by the Adirondacks. Families may, however, prefer the cabana rooms in the back of the hotel on the plaza level, handy to the indoor swimming pool, outsized Jacuzzi, and fitness room. For guests on the top (seventh) floor, complimentary continental breakfasts and late afternoon, hot hors d'oeuvres are served with cocktails by a helpful concierge. Complimentary parking is offered in the adjacent garage, and the shops and restaurants of downtown Burlington are minutes away—on foot. In the hotel itself, the Village Green Café serves three daily, moderately priced meals, and Gérard's (see *Dining Out*) is one of the best-rated restaurants in the area but lacks the lake view available from Visions Lounge, featuring live evening comedy. Admittedly the seven-story, glass-faced building itself will never win an architectural award, but don't blame Radisson. Back in the early 1970s when this first high-rise hotel in Vermont was proposed, it caused such a local furor that the original, more ambitious design was replaced by something so generic it was difficult to object. Request a corner room, facing south as well as west. $95–135 double, but inquire about the $79 B&B rate and off season rates from $59. Complimentary shuttle service to the airport is offered.

The Sheraton-Burlington (862-6576, 800-343-6320), 870 Williston Road, Burlington 05401. With 310 rooms, this is now Vermont's largest hotel, and it has preempted the city's convention and trade show scene. It's set in campuslike grounds in South Burlington near the I-89 (Exit 14W), Route 2 interchange. Amenities include an indoor pool, Jacuzzis, a fitness center, an executive floor with complementary breakfast, evening hors d'oeuvres and concierge service. Facilities include Caroline's Restaurant, Baxter's Lounge nightclub, and a complimentary airport shuttle. Seasonal rates on request. $79–118 per room, more in high seasons.

The Inn at Essex (878-1100, 800-727-4295), 70 Essex Way (Route 15 east), Essex Junction 05452. Since the inn also serves as the second campus of the New England Culinary Institute of Montpelier, the food in the elegantly formal dining room, Butler's, and the sunny, casual Birch Tree Café is exceptional (see *Dining Out*). Each of the 97 rooms and suites has been individually decorated with country-chic wallpapers and fabrics. Thirty of them have working fireplaces; the Bridal Suite has a Jacuzzi as well. The large, wooden, neo-Colonial complex is sited in a commercial, suburban area handy to IBM but a good 20 minutes northeast of downtown Burlington. Facilities include a gracious conference center, linked to the hotel via an underground art gallery. Inquire about whether the indoor pool and fitness center and the tennis courts have been completed. In the interim, guests have access to a nearby fitness center. A free shuttle to the airport is also offered. $69–200 for rooms, $325–453 for suites. Inquire about special packages.

The Wilson Inn (800-521-2334, 879-1515), 10 Kellogg Road, Essex Junction 05452. This all-suite hotel has 32 units that combine bedroom, living room, and full kitchen (including microwave oven and automatic coffeemaker). Handy to IBM rather than Burlington (20 minutes away), it can work for families as well as business people. Amenities include a free breakfast buffet, a grocery shopping service, and access to the neighboring fitness center. Some handicapped units available: One-bedroom units are $81, and two-bedroom, $101; weekend specials, available most of the year, begin at $65.

Marriott Residence Inn (878-2001, 800-331-3131), Route 2A, Williston 05495. At Exit 12 off I-89, this glossy, all-suite motor hotel has an indoor pool, spa, and Sport Court; free breakfast buffet. The one-bedroom plus living room and kitchen suite is $117, and the duplex,two-bedroom penthouse suite, $142; but weekend rates ($79–99) are also available.

RESORTS   **Marble Island Resort and Conference Center** (864-6800), 150 Marble Island Road, Malletts Bay, Colchester 05446, is an attractive, 34-room resort on a peninsula. Notice the pink marble in the lobby, quarried on the spot. Guests have access to the nine-hole golf course, tennis courts, windsurfing, and lake cruises. Rooms are attractive, some with sleeping lofts, some lakeside. Amenities include a restaurant, fitness center, and two outdoor heated pools. On a reservation basis. Rates $95–140 per room with continental breakfast, tennis and greens fees; $80 off season.

Bolton Valley Resort (434-2131), Bolton Valley 05477. A mountaintop cluster of condominiums, a lodge, restaurants and shops, and a sports center set on 6,000 acres. In winter, this is a ski resort (see *Downhill Skiing* and *Cross-Country Skiing*), and in summer, the focus is on tennis, with formal programs for adults, a nursery for children aged three months to six years, and "Camp Bear Paw" for children 6–12. An outdoor pool, an extensive network of hiking trails, and a nearby 18-hole golf course are also part of the summer picture. Facilities include the 150-room slopeside hotel (some rooms have a fireplace and kitchenette) and 122 one- to four-bedroom condominium units. The sports center houses an exercise room, pool, tennis courts, and game room. Rates for double room in winter, $148–170 per person for two nights, includes all activities. Guests arriving by car from Burlington should take Exit 16 off I-89, follow Route 7 north for 1.9 miles, turn left on Blakely Road; continue for 3.7 miles and turn right on Marble Island Road; bear left at the fork and continue to the entrance sign.

INNS   **Shelburne House** (985-8498; 985-8686, mid-October–May), Shelburne 05482. Open mid-May–mid-October. For a peerless taste of restored Edwardian grandeur, being a summer guest in this stately home is not to be missed. The 60-room Queen Anne–style mansion was built by Seward and Lila Vanderbilt Webb on a bluff overlooking Lake Champlain. Completed in 1899, the house is the centerpiece of a 1,000-acre estate whose grounds were designed by Frederick Law Olmsted and forested by Gifford Pinchot. The property is being maintained by the present generation of Webbs as a working farm.

Guests have access to tennis, boating, a swimming beach, and walking trails. Turn-of-the-century furnishings predominate throughout the inn, where guests can browse in the library and dine well in the Marble Room with a spectacular view of the lake and Adirondacks. Rates for the 24 luxurious, individualized bedrooms (Louis XVI, Empire, Colonial, Dutch) are $150–225 single with private bath, $95–

130 single, shared bath; $155–230 double, private bath; $100–135 double, shared bath—all depending on size, location, and time of year. Modified American Plan is available at an additional $46 a day per person. Otherwise breakfast is $6–12, a box lunch $7.50, afternoon tea $3.50, and memorable dinners, $20 plus for entrées. All of this quickly adds up to one of the more expensive stays in the state, but it's a dreamy place and worth the trip back into tranquility. No smoking is allowed in the house except in the game room, complete with heavy, carved baroque furniture, pool table, and antlered trophies.

Black Bear Inn (434-2126), Bolton Valley 05477. The modern, ski lodge–style inn sits at 2,000 feet, adjacent to the Bolton Valley ski slopes. The 24 rooms are individually decorated, and amenities include a heated pool and access to Bolton Valley's Sports Club (indoor tennis, pool, etc.). $56–99 per couple without meals; breakfast and dinner served.

BED & BREAKFASTS   In the introduction to this chapter, we noted the recent rise of bed & breakfasts widely scattered around—rather than in—Burlington.

In Burlington   **Howden Cottage** (864-7198), 32 North Champlain Street, within walking distance of downtown shops, restaurants, and the waterfront. Two basic upstairs rooms share a downstairs bath and living room. $35 single, $45 double includes continental breakfast; no smoking.

Along Route 15 in Essex Junction, Jericho, and Underhill Village and Center

Country Comfort (878-2589), 36 Old Stage Road, Essex Junction. Located on a grassy plateau with distant mountain views and a great feeling of peace and space. This is a good-looking, well-kept home with a choice of private and shared bath, lots of walking space, sheep in the pasture. $55 with private bath, $50 for one of the two rooms that share a bath. Common space includes a living room with fireplace, and a full breakfast is included in the rates. Hosts Eva and Ed Blake will pick guests up at the nearyby AMTRAK station and take them to a local car rental office.

Homeplace (899-4694), RR 2, Box 367, Jericho 05465. The house is set in a hundred-acre wood. The guest area is separated from the family quarters. Four rooms share two baths (twin or double beds). Mariot and Hans (a UVM professor) Huessy are friendly, sophisticated hosts. From $40 single.

Eaton House (899-2354), Box 139, Brown's Trace, Jericho 05465, south of Jericho Center (ask directions from Route 15). Overlooking meadows, Sue Eaton's comfortable eighteenth-century house includes three guest rooms, ranging from a small double with oak furniture to a grand master bedroom with double beds, stenciling, and private bath. Rates are $50–70 double, breakfast included. Just a few miles north of I-89, this has a great away-from-it-all feel.

Henry M. Field House (899-3984), RR 2, Box 395, Jericho 05465. A high Victorian house, with a widow's walk, on Route 15 in the middle of Jericho Village. Hosts Mary Beth Perilli and Terrence Horan are teachers who take a lively interest in this interesting area. The house is set back from the road, and in warmer months, guests can relax on one of the three porches or stroll down to the Browns River through meadow and woods; $65 for a private and $55 for a shared bath includes continental breakfast and afternoon tea. No smoking.

Sinclair Towers Bed & Breakfast (899-2234), RD 2, Box 35, Underhill 05489. This is an elaborate, very Victorian "painted lady" with an in-town setting on Route 15. Furnishings are unusually lovely, suited to the house. All six rooms have private baths and air-conditioning. One is wheelchair accessible. $55–70 per couple includes a full breakfast and afternoon tea. Children over 12 welcome. No smoking.

Haus Kelley (899-3905), PO Box 49, Old West Bolton Road, Underhill Center 05490. A modern home but with a warm, country feel, a jolly hostess (Irene Kelley), handy to the great general store in Underhill Center and to some outstanding hiking in Underhill State Park. There's also a tennis court and a splendid view. $35 single, $45–55 double includes a full breakfast.

Fox Hill (899-4361), Underhill Center 05490. Marian and Bill Kuschel's contemporary house overlooks a pond in the foreground, and just about every room features large windows with views of Mount Mansfield in the distance. The two guest rooms share a sitting room and bath and can be rented either as a suite ($90) or separately (from $45), less by the week. Rates include a full breakfast, and the grounds have trails for walking and cross-country skiing.

In Richmond 05477   **The Richmond Victorian Inn** (434-4440), PO Box 652. On Route 2 in the village of Richmond, handy to both Bolton Valley and Burlington (one mile off I-89), this exceptionally clean and classy house has six guest rooms, three with shared and three with private baths, all individually decorated with brass beds and antiques and quilts; two connecting rooms with shared baths works for families; $50–85 double includes a full breakfast. Nonsmoking. Will pick up Appalachian Trail hikers.

In Charlotte 05445   **The Inn at Charlotte** (425-2934), 1188 State Road. A single-story house on Route 7, but the living area is at the back of the house, around the pool and tennis court and an attractive patio area. Letty Ellinger is a caterer and is happy to provide lunch and dinner on requests. She will also pack a picnic for guests to take on a hike in adjoining Mount Philo State Park (the views are of Camel's Hump and the Adirondacks). The decor is understated 1930s, elegant and soothing. $55–65 per couple with shared baths, $55–75 with private, full breakfast included. No smoking.

Green Meadows (425-3059), Mt. Philo Road. A restored Victorian house just east of Charlotte in a quiet valley. The decor is nutmeg-toned floors, small-print wallpaper, ruffled curtains, and many antiques. Louise Smith is a warm hostess, and you will also be greeted by a friendly Great Dane. No smoking. $75 per couple for the master bedroom with a Jacuzzi bath, $55 for any of the three other rooms, which share two baths. Rates include a breakfast of juice, fruit, pancakes, or homemade breads.

Horsford Gardens (425-2939), Route 7 (winter entrance from Greenbush Road). This is the bed & breakfast for botanists! And for someplace so handy to Burlington, it has an amazingly country feel. Founded in 1893 by Frederick H. Horsford, Horsford Gardens & Nursery is Vermont's oldest nursery. It continues as a source of perennials, grown in French-intensive–style growing beds. The nursery fields are full of lilacs and flowering crabapples, as well as hundreds of varieties of trees and shrubs. The 40-acre grounds include two ponds and several trails, creating a real country feel. Guest quarters are in a former (nicely renovated) barn and packing shed. There are just three rooms, one with private bath. Hosts are Paul and Erin Ostin. $58–78 per couple includes continental breakfast.

Charlotte's Webb (425-3341), RR 1, Box 1047, Greenbush Road. This is a splendidly converted, nineteenth-century barn with huge windows overlooking meadows and mountains. Gretchen and Stan Semuskie are your sophisticated hosts. $70 includes continental breakfast and state tax. There are two double and one single guest rooms sharing two baths.

In Starksboro 05487   **The Millhouse Bed & Breakfast** (453-2008), just off Route 116. While it's 25 miles from Burlington, this gem of a bed & breakfast isn't really in any other region (as defined by our chapters) either. The friends who tipped us off to it found it convenient enough to use while visiting their daughter at UVM. The house retains its graceful 1831 lines and sits just above a rushing brook, near enough so that the sound of the water is constant. The sleeping arrangements include the upstairs master bedroom (shared bath) and two suites, one with three bedrooms (a large twin bedroom and two small single rooms) and another composed of two double bedrooms. The house is tastefully, comfortably decorated with plenty of common space, including a great back porch. Rates include a breakfast buffet; $30–35 per person, a rate that's especially appealing to singles.

MOTELS   The several "strips" that radiate from Burlington—Shelburne Road (Route 7) to the south, Route 15 to the northeast, and Williston Road (Route 2) to the east— all have their share of motels. Among them: The rather unusual **Howard Johnson's Hotel** (865-2174),1720 Shelburne Road (Route 7), a five-story, 117-room hotel that's been an old reliable landmark; amenities include an indoor pool, sauna, whirlpool, exercise equipment, and restaurant.

The **Bel-Aire Motel** (863-3116), 111 Shelburne Road. Close to downtown, cozy, reasonably priced rooms, flower boxes and whitewashed exterior. **Susse Chalet** (879-8999/800-258-1980), Route 2A close to I-89, Exit 12 in Williston. Good value and location. **Yankee Doodle Motel** (985-8004) near Shelburne Museum; the **Anchorage Inn** (863-7000) with an indoor heated pool, Jacuzzi, and sauna in South Burlington; and the **Fairfield Marriott Inn** (228-2800) in Colchester, with an outdoor heated pool, are also good values.

DINING OUT   *Downtown*   Note: Burlington offers an unusually wide choice of restaurants that fall somewhere between our usual "Dining Out" and "Eating Out" categories. Many offer "dining out" atmosphere and food at (thanks to their largely student patronage) at "eating out" prices.

Déjà Vu Café (864-7917), 185 Pearl Street, is perhaps the city's best for classic and contemporary nouvelle cuisine in a dramatic setting. Polished wood and brass and ornate glass lamps create an ambience in which you can easily spend $100 on dinner for two. On the other hand, you can feast well off the bistro selections, and there are always moderately priced specials such as cassoulet Americaine, made with black beans and venison sausage. Open for lunch Monday–Saturday. Dinner nightly, Saturday and Sunday brunch. The desserts are exquisite. Entrées from $5.95 to $24.00.

Gérard's (864-5005), at the Radisson Hotel, has been transplanted from the shore of Mallett's Bay, along with its artfully presented, innovative cuisine that won the Taste of Vermont Grand Award. One might commence with escargots in puff pastry with fresh spinach and garlic sauce, or a warm duck salad, and continue with Norwegian salmon poached perfectly, wrapped in spinach, or roast duck with thinly sliced breast meat and a "confit" leg. Open for lunch, Monday–Friday, and for dinner nightly. Most dinner entrées are $16.

Sweetwater's (864-9800), corner of Church and College streets. Housed in a former and splendidly restored 1920s bank building, this is a deservedly popular spot, with continuous service weekdays from 11:30 to midnight, Sunday 10:30–10. Note the frescoe depicting a number of recognizable Burlingtonians cavorting down Church Street with Bacchus. You might lunch on a bison bacon burger or a salmon cake sandwich, dine on grilled duck steak ($14.95) or chicken Oscar (wood-grilled chicken, asparagus spears, and crabmeat, topped with a béarnaise sauce, $11.95). It's also possible to dine on Jamaican Jerk or Garlic Chicken for $7.95.

Sakura (863-1988), 2 Church Street, Vermont's first and only Japanese restaurant, opened in 1987, has drawn banzais of praise for its sashimi, sushi, tempuras, and entrées. Lunch Monday–Saturday, dinner daily. Reservations please. Entrées: $9.50–28.

☞**The Daily Planet** (862-9647), 15 Center Street. Open from 11:30

Lively Church Street Market Place scene, Burlington

Monday–Saturday, and from 4 on Sundays, until 2 AM most nights. The atmosphere is bright and casual with a solarium and airy dining room, both filled with small tables dressed in bright oil cloths at lunchtime, linen for dinner. Unusual soups of the day are a specialty, along with tapas, nachos, burritos, and entrées ranging from grilled lamb loin to Vietnamese seafood and a variety of pastas. Planet burgers and fajitas are also usually on the menu. Dinner entrées $8.95–13.95.

Bourbon Street Grill (865-2800), 213 College Street. Open for lunch and dinner daily. This trendy pink place (with plenty of artwork and greenery) is Burlington's Cajun corner. Appetizers include jambalaya ("a trial-size introduction into real Louisiana cooking") and beer-and-salsa-steamed mussels. Entrées like Cajun grilled chicken and cioppino (a San Francisco-style seafood stew) are priced from $11.25 to $14.95 and you can always nosh on Cajun popcorn shrimp and Cajun wings.

The Ice House (864-1800), 171 Battery Street. Open for lunch and dinner daily, Sunday brunch. Overlooking the Champlain ferry slip and marina, this was a pioneer in the city's upscale restaurant scene. It now gets mixed reviews, serves American regional dishes, including Vermont lamb and seafood, on two levels. Oyster bar. Reservations recommended. Entrées $13.50–19.50.

Whitecaps at the Boathouse (862-1240), Burlington Boathouse, Battery Park. Open year-round for lunch, but snack bar and deck closed September–May. Best known for Sunday brunch (11–2:30), this is also a great place for everyday feasting on the view of Lake Champlain and on dishes like roast turkey with all the fixings or a garlic ginger pork roast with green peanut sauce. Entrées run $11.25–12.50. Lighter fare also available.

Five Spice Café (864-4045), 175 Church Street. Open Monday–Saturday for lunch and dinner, Sunday 11–3 for Dim Sum brunch. The dishes are from a variety of Asian countries—Thailand, Vietnam, Indonesia, and India as well as China, and the spices are as hot as you care to take them. The atmosphere is appealing, and there's frequently live jazz.

Alfredo's Restaurant in the Alley (864-0854), off Church Street across from City Hall. Open for lunch weekdays, for dinner nightly from 5. A respectable trattoria featuring seafood as well as pasta. Specialties include seafood Cavelli (shrimps, scallops, and calamari sautéed in white wine with shallots and peppercorns) and a variety of lobster specials. Entrées $8.95–16.95.

In Colchester **Hearthside at the Marble Island Resort** (864-6800), 150 Marble Island Road, Malletts Bay. Open daily, but check ahead between mid-October and Easter. The resort's creamy, country-formal dining room is a glamorous setting for dinner, which might begin with smoked Idaho trout or clams Casino, followed by a caesar salad with fried oysters, a New England shellfish stew in a lobster and saffron sauce, sautéed veal rib eye with morels, cognac, and cream. At Sunday brunch, try a smoked fish platter, Finnan Haddie, or shrimp curry. Entrées range from $7.95–$15.95.

In Essex **Butler's** (878-1100), The Inn at Essex, Route 15, Essex Junction. Open for dinner nightly. In the deft hands of the New England Culinary Institute, the cuisine in this elegantly formal, green-walled room with high-backed, upholstered chairs is a visual as well as gustatory treat. Dinner might start with pheasant pie with field greens and proceed to pan-roasted partridge with couscous, currants, and wilted greens. Entrées $16.50–21.00.

In the adjacent Birch Tree Café, connected by the Chimney Point Lounge, lunch and dinner are served, including such specials as a sublime salmon en croute, carrot and egg linguine in horseradish sauce, or a grilled yellowfin tuna "burger" with pickled ginger. Entrées $8.95–11.50.

Shelburne Area **Shelburne House** (985-8498), Shelburne. Open for dinner by reservation from early June to mid-October, this turn-of-the-century manor (see *Inns*) offers imaginative cuisine in a magnificent setting—black-and-white marble floor, crimson flocked wallpaper, and a stunning sunset view of Lake Champlain and the Adirondacks. Canapés of Vermont smoked ham and Shelburne Farms cheddar are served with drinks. An unusual appetizer of fricassee of wild mushrooms could be followed by roast whole baby pheasant, sliced leg of veal with white wine and mushroom sauce, or chicken with spinach and pine kernel stuffing. Vegetables come from the farm's gardens, and one can't resist a peach almond pie with blueberry sauce. No smoking in the dining room, but smokers can have coffee served on the terrace or in the adjoining game room. Entrées from $20.

Pauline's Café & Restaurant (862-1081), 1834 Shelburne Road (Route 7 south), Shelburne. Open daily for lunch and dinner. Run by the talented Déjà Vu folks, it is well worth braving the strip development traffic for lunch or dinner daily. In the elegant simplicity of the downstairs café or the more formal upstairs dining rooms (one for smokers), subtle Continental and American cuisine is artfully presented in sensible portions. Entrées such as pork loin scaloppine with apricot, sherry, and herb sauce, loin of Vermont rabbit with artichoke hearts and mushrooms, or veal tenderloin with wild mushrooms. $13.95–21.95.

Café Shelburne (985-3939), Route 7, Shelburne. Open for dinner except Monday. Conveniently located across the road from the Shelburne Museum, this chef-owned and operated, authentically French bistro has been serving uncommonly good food since 1969. It's open for lunch and dinner Tuesday through Saturday. The chef was named Best National Seafood cook in 1988. This remains one of the better restaurants in the state. Entrées $15.00–18.50.

The 1810 Farmhouse Restaurant (877-2576/658-6622), Route 7, Ferrisburg, is a pleasant place for dinner in the summer, spring, and fall. Call ahead for information. Traditional New England fare at very moderate prices. Travelers can also browse around the 1824 covered bridge; the Little Red Cider Mill, in operation during apple season; the North Ferrisburg Railroad Depot; and the Old Covered Bridge Gift Shop. They also have a 213-acre Christmas tree farm.

Francesca's (985-3373), Route 7. Open daily for lunch, dinner, and Sunday brunch, this northern Italian restaurant in a trendy setting has a tempting selection of pastas, ravioli, veal, and shrimp. Entrées $8.00–17.50.

Perry's Fish House (862-1300), 1080 Shelburne Road, is a big, bustling, landlocked pier with an extensive menu of moderately priced seafood that attracts large numbers of Burlingtonians. Children's menu. Open daily 5–10, 4–10 Sunday. Entrées $7.95–16.25.

In Winooski **Waterworks** (655-2044), the Champlain Mill. Open for lunch and dinner. An attractive restaurant overlooking the dam spillway and rapids. You can dine outside, in a greenhouse area or surrounded by the ambiance of the old mill building. The large menu ranges from sandwiches to Weiner Schnitzel, steak, stir fries, and nightly specials. Entrées $8.95–14.95.

The Prime Factor (655-0300), the Champlain Mill. Open daily for lunch and dinner. A shade more formal than Waterworks, featuring, as might be expected, prime rib, also a 52-item soup and salad bar. Entrées $9.75–15.95.

At Bolton Valley   **Lindsay's** (434-2131), Bolton Valley, serves dinner daily except Monday, and features nouvelle American and Continental cuisine in a romantic, formal setting with a splendid view of sunsets. Appetizers might be crabmeat Alfredo or oysters Rockefeller. Entrées include veal Aramica, steak au poivre, tournedos with béarnaise. Entrées $10.95–18.95.

EATING OUT   *In Burlington*   **Leunig's Old World Café** (863-3759), Church and College streets. Open daily for breakfast, lunch, and dinner. A delightful European-style café with dark wood and gleaming coffee machines within, streetside tables without. Daily specials, great pastries.

The Rusty Scuffer (864-9451), 148 Church Street. Open nightly for dinner, except Sundays for lunch. A cheerful, pubby dining landmark, a favorite among locals, good for a lunchtime chili and cheese omelet or a crabbyburger or, for an evening, fried seafood platter or baked "stuft" chicken.

Shanty on the Shore (864-0238), 181 Battery Street. Open daily 11–11. Handy to the ferry with great inside and outside lake views; good for burgers and sandwiches as well as seafood platters, even escargot. A children's menu and choice of exotic drinks also offered.

India House (862-7800), 207 Colchester Avenue. Lunch and dinner Tuesday–Saturday, Sunday brunch. Traditional curries, chicken tandoori, and the like, plus puffy poori bread, all at moderate prices.

Vermont Pasta Restaurant (658-2575), 156 Church Street. Open daily for lunch and dinner and for Sunday brunch. An attractive storefront eatery featuring its homemade "pastabilities": fettucini (regular, spinach, fresh herb), linguini (regular, spinach, fresh herb, and tomato basil), angel hair (three varieties), orzo, tortellini, and ravioli. Dinner entrées include Vermont quail and potato gnocchi ($11.95) as well as spaghetti and meatballs, mushrooms, and jalapeños ($5.95).

Mirabelles (658-3074), 198 Main Street. A delightful bakery-eatery featuring tea, espresso, pastries, sandwiches, and light fare.

Henry's Diner (862-9010), 155 Bank Street, is a long-established, authentic diner around the corner from the Church Street Marketplace, where you can get the meat loaf and thick gravy you've been hankering for. Closed Monday.

Carbur's (862-4106), 115 St. Paul Street, has a 16-page menu, offering a hundred or so sandwich combos and many entrées. Lunch and dinner daily amid wood panels and stained-glass lamps. Inexpensive to moderate.

Bove's Café (864-6651), 68 Pearl Street. Open for dinner only on our last visit. An old standby for moderately priced Italian.

Burlington Bagel Bakery (658-0563), 139 St. Paul Street. Open daily for what you might expect: cream cheese, lox, hummus, kosher salamis, and more.

Brueggers Bagel Bakery (860-1995), 81 Church Street. Open daily. Three levels to eat and watch the passing scene, outside tables in the marketplace in summer.

The Vermont Pub and Brewery (865-0500), 144 College Street. Open daily 11:30 AM–12:30 PM. Housed in a modern building but with an old beer hall atmosphere (tile floor, huge bar, brass), specializing in ales and lagers brewed on the premises (brewery tours are offered Wednesdays at 8 PM and Saturdays at 4). The home brew is in small batches, available in draft; a variety of bottled beers and wines also available. The menu includes cornish pastie, mulligan stew, bratwurst, and fish and chips, also homemade soups and teriyaki chicken.

City Market Bakery Café "With a Vegetarian Accent" (658-5061), 211 College Street. Open for breakfast, lunch, and dinner daily, Sunday brunch 10–4. Another popular student congregating spot, also ideal for eating alone with a book or magazine. Each day features two unusual soups, also pizzas and calzones. The specials for each day of the week are printed up on Monday, for example, Wednesday: Hungarian potato cabbage soup and a choice of knishes, also Spanish chicken or linguini with tofu fall, for dinner, cashew stuffed chicken or tofu teriyaki.

In Winooski, Essex Junction, and Jericho   **Sneakers** (655-9081), 36 Main Street, Winooski, serves a great breakfast, Monday–Friday, lunch Monday–Friday, dinner Monday–Saturday, weekend brunch, plus jazz every Tuesday, bluegrass Wednesday. Breakfast options include eggs Benedict and freshly squeezed O.J., and the dinner special may be seafood or lamb.

Mary B's Tables (879-4627), 12 Railroad Avenue, Essex Junction. "Those in the know" relish the home cooking and bakery here at breakfast, lunch, and dinner weekdays.

Emma's (899-4828), Jericho East Complex, Route 15, Jericho. Open for lunch, brunch, and dinner, daily soup and quiche and hearty grilled Reubens, chocolate mousse cake.

Williston Road to Richmond   **Windjammer** (862-6585), 1076 Williston Road. A big, informal, relaxed, moderately priced steak and seafood house, with a glass-walled pavilion, mezzanine for drinks, boat-shaped salad bar; open for breakfast, lunch, and dinner weekdays, Sunday brunch and dinner. Children's menu.

The Checquers Country Restaurant (434-4203), junction of I-89, Routes 117 and 2, Richmond. This restored 1795 Georgian brick house was built by Governor Chittenden as a wedding present for his son;

note the unusual brick work, one of the only surviving examples in the state. Open daily for breakfast, lunch, and dinner. Chicken, seafood, steak in various combinations.

Daily Bread Bakery Café (434-3148), Richmond. People leave I-89 south just to drop by for breakfast, lunch, or Saturday and Sunday brunch, or even a slice or two of maple bread.

On Shelburne Road (Route 7 South) **Perry's Fish House** (862-1300), 1080 Shelburne Road. Open nightly for dinner. Another winner by the owners of the Sirloin Saloon chain and of Sweetwater's (see *Dining Out*). Locals swear by this place, featuring "fried favorites" and baked or broiled fish.

ENTERTAINMENT   **Vermont Mozart Festival Performances** (862-7352). Summer concerts in various settings—on ferries, at the Shelburne Museum and/or Shelburne Farms, at the Basin Harbor Club, in churches. Winter chamber series.

Flynn Theater for the Performing Arts (86-FLYNN), 153 Main Street, Burlington. This cultural showcase is a refurbished art deco movie house, now home to plays, musical comedies, jazz concerts, and lectures, many under the auspices of the George Bishop Lane Series.

St. Michael's Summer Playhouse (654-2507), St. Michael's College, Winooski. Vermont's only resident stock professional Equity theater; performances throughout the summer season.

The Vermont Symphony Orchestra (864-5741), 77 College Street, Burlington. One of the country's first statewide philharmonics presents a five-concert Chittenden County Series at the Flynn; outdoor summer pops at Shelburne Farms and elsewhere.

George Bishop Lane Series (656-3418) sponsors major musical and theatrical performances around town fall through spring.

Also see *Special Events* at the end of this chapter.

SELECTIVE SHOPPING   *In Downtown Burlington*   **The Church Street Marketplace.** Nearly a hundred stores, restaurants, and services line several blocks of Church Street, nicely paved, landscaped, closed to traffic, and enlivened by seasonal arts and crafts shows, weekend festivals, and street entertainers.

Burlington Square Mall. This vast indoor agora, mostly underground, has 80 stores stocking just about everything, linked to a parking garage and the Porteous Department Store. Several food stalls for grazers.

BOOKSHOPS   **Chassman & Bem** (800-NEWBOOK), 81 Church Street. Moved to larger, more central space at the heart of the Church Street Marketplace, this is a beautifully designed store, displaying 30,000 titles, also featuring recorded music, international magazines, stationery, and, in the back, a Viennese café. The shop's former quarters at the northern end of Church Street are now filled with Kids' Ink, a two-level store devoted entirely to children's books.

Other Church Street bookstores include **Little Professor** and the **Everyday Book Shop; Bygone Books**, 31 Main Street, is the place for old, out-of-print, and rare volumes. **What An Interesting Bookstore!** upstairs at 22 Church Street, offers Burlington's largest selection of New Age books.

CRAFTS   **Frog Hollow on the Marketplace**, Church Street, represents only a branch of the Vermont State Craft Center of Middlebury, a showcase for fine things crafted in the state, from furniture and art glass to hand-woven scarves.

Designers Circle (864-4238), Church Street, features beautifully crafted jewelry.

Bennington Potters North (863-2221), 127 College Street. Kitchenware, home furnishings, glass, woodenware, and "factory prices" on Bennington pottery.

CLOTHING   **Laura Ashley, Banana Republic, Michael Kehoe,Ltd.,** and **The Mayfair** are a few of the fine clothiers on and around Church Street.

OTHER SHOPPING   **Champlain Chocolate Company**, 431 Pine Street, the home of the American Truffle and other expensive candy, discounts some of its premium chocolates.

Cheese Outlet, 400 Pine Street. Sample their Vermont Velvet Cheesecake and Quiche Puff, made on the premises; factory store for Vermont and imported cheeses.

Webb & Parsons North (658-5123), 147 Main Street, is a gallery and museum shop for folk and "outsider" artists, plus hand-woven clothing, ceramics, glass, kinetic sculptures, all from Vermont artisans.

The Downhill Edge Store and Sailboarding School (862-2282), 65 Main Street, features high-performance sailboards, gives lessons, and offers rentals at Leddy Beach and the Marble Island resort.

Skirack (658-3313), 85 Main Street. A major source of cycling, running, roller blade, and cross-country ski gear and wear.

Sailworks (864-0111/372-6606), 176 Battery Street, has a retail store and gives private and group lessons at its Sand Bar Yacht Club, Sand Bar State Park, Route 2, where sailboards, sailboats, rowing shells, and canoes can be rented.

Peace on Earth Store, 21 Church Street, run by the city's active Peace and Justice Coalition, a source of alternative publications and third-world crafted items—jewlery, cards, clothing, etc.—all purchased from wholesalers committed to nonexploitation and social justice. The bulletin board is also worth checking.

Basketville, 152 Cherry Street. The third branch of this amazing Vermont-based chain, featuring every conceivable kind of basket and plenty of wicker.

In the Charlotte-Shelburne Area   **The Dakin Farm** (425-3971), Route 7, Ferrisburg (and the Champlain Mill, Winooski), is one of the principal purveyors of cob-smoked hams and bacon. This roadside store also stocks a variety of other Vermont food products and gifts.

African Imports (425-3137; 800-635-5009), Greenbush Road, Charlotte 05445. Lydia Clemmons specializes in authentic jewelry, soapstone carvings, batik, banana leaf prints, sisal mats and bags, masks, thorn carvings, and museum-quality items imported from Ghana, Kenya, Nigeria, Tanzania, and Zaire. Mail-order catalogue. Open Saturdays 9–5; daily in the summer.

The Vermont Wildflower Farm (425-3500), Route 7, Charlotte. This important source for wildflower seeds and planting advice is open daily, May–mid-October. There are self-guided pathways through acres of wildflowers (admission charge) and a gift shop.

Shelburne Farms Store and Visitors Center (985-8442) open daily year-round 9–5 (10–5 off season; see a full description of what this place is about under *To See*). The store features the prize-winning cheddar cheeses made from the milk of the estate's own Brown Swiss herd. A variety of Vermont products are also stocked.

Harrington's, Route 7, across from the Shelburne Museum, Charlotte, has been known for years by its delectable (and expensive) corncob-smoked hams, bacon, turkey, pork chops, and other goodies. The shop also displays an array of cheese, maple products, griddle cake mix, jams, fruit butters, relishes, baked goods, wine, and coffees.

The Shelburne Country Store, Route 7, encloses several gift galleries under the same roof—a sweet shop, foods, lampshades.

Vermont Teddy Bear Common, Route 7, Shelburne. The former Jelly Mill Common complex is now dominated by the factory and retail outlet for the Vermont Teddy Bear Company (800-829-BEAR), a Burlington-born firm that now produces 100,000 bears per year. These traditional teddies have moveable arms and legs, pull-proof eyes, and are 100 percent polyester (nonalergic) and washable. They come in three basic sizes, from 15 or 20 inches to 3 feet ($45–59); prices do not include clothing, tax, or shipping. The shop is open daily, and factory tours are offered.

Vermont's Own Products (985-2505), Tennybrook Square, Route 7, Shelburne, is a showcase for—you guessed it—all sorts of things made in Vermont: foods, pottery, jewelry, woolens, books, woodenware, quilts, crafts, toys, art.

Factory Outlet Center, Route 7, Shelburne Road. More than 20 stores.

Winooski   **The Champlain Mill** (655-9477), One Main Street, a creatively converted woolen mill, holds 30 smart shops, including the **Craft Center, Ltd.**, and the **Book Rack**, a well-stocked book shop, plus two good restaurants, bakery, and deli. **The Children's Pages** on the river level of the mill is a highly successful off-shoot of the Book Rack, exclusively devoted to children's titles.

Blackthorne Forge (655-7676), 94 West Canal Street. Assorted traditional fixtures, plus unusual sculptured clocks.

Also in Greater Burlington   **University Mall** (863-1066), Dorset and Williston streets (I-89, Exit 14E), South Burlington. Your basic shopping mall with 70 stores; Ames is the anchor.

Desso's General Store (899-3313), Brown's Trace Road, Jericho Center. A refreshing contrast to the commercial lineup along Shelburne Road, just minutes north of mega businesses in Essex Junction, Desso's stands on an oval, picture perfect Common, occupying a grey, wooden building that's architecturally difficult to describe. It's just a genuine, old-fashioned general store, open daily 5 AM–9 PM (9–8 on Sundays). Lil and Gerry Desso carry the usual fresh, frozen, and canned produce, plus socks, mittens, gloves, boots, etc. The syrup and beans (which, we can attest, bake up nicely) are local.

SPECIAL EVENTS   Memorial Day weekend: **Lake Champlain Balloon & Craft Festival**: 45 hot air balloons hover over the Champlain Valley Fairgrounds, dawn to dusk, many special events including skydivers, crafts fair, children's rides, fireworks.

Early June: **Arts Alive,** a showcase of Vermont artists.

Mid-June: **Discover Jazz Festival.** For four days, the entire city of Burlington becomes a stage for over 200 musicians.

Mid-June: **Lake Champlain International Fishing Derby.** For details about registration and prizes, check with the chamber of commerce.

Late June: **Green Mountain Chew Chew** at City Hall Park, a three-day food festival featuring over 50 area restaurants, continuous family entertainment.

Early July: Gala Independence Day celebrations on the Burlington waterfront; fireworks over the lake with live bands in Battery Park, children's entertainment, a parade of boats and blessing of the fleet.

Mid-July: **Vermont Reggae Festival,** free outdoor bands and ethnic foods, various locations around Burlington.

Mid-July–mid-August:**Vermont Mozart Festival** (see *Entertainment*).

Mid-August: **Shelburne Craft Fair**, Shelburne Farms.

Late August: **Champlain Valley Exposition**, Essex Junction Fairgrounds; a big, busy, traditional county fair with livestock and produce exhibits, trotting races, midway, rides, spun sugar candy—the works.

Mid-September: **Annual Harvest Festival**, Shelburne Farms. **Fools-A-Float**—a parade of land and sea craft, downtown Burlington.

Early October: **Marketfest:** a celebration of Burlington's cultural diversity.

Early December: **Christmas Weekend at the Shelburne Museum**—a nineteenth-century festival. Phone 985-3344 for specific dates and details.

December 31: **First Night** (863-6005). The end-of-the-year gala—parades, fireworks, music, mimes, and other performances that transform downtown Burlington into a happy "happening."

MEDICAL EMERGENCY   Burlington (911); Colchester (655-1412); Winooski/Williston (655-3212); Shelburne (911); South Burlington (656-4444); Charlotte (985-3233). **Medical Center Hospital of Vermont** (656-2345), Burlington. **Fanny Allen Hospital** (655-1234), 101 College Parkway, Winooski.

The Northwest Corner

Traveling between Burlington and the Canadian border, a motorist who wants more variety than I-89 has to offer can make another choice: to follow Route 7 to St. Albans and Swanton or to swing through the islands on Route 2, rejoining Route 7 just south of the border. With apologies to St. Albans, we can't help recommending that the wayfarer opt for the islands, Vermont's Cape Cod but as yet unspoiled.

THE ISLANDS

Once called the Isle of the Two Heroes, this sparsely settled land chain, composed of a peninsula (Alburg) and four islands (Isle la Motte, the two Heros, and Grand Isle), extends 30 miles south from the Canadian border into Lake Champlain. The views are spectacular: west to the Adirondacks in New York State and east to the Green Mountains, a dramatic wall seemingly rising just beyond the lake. This is Grand Isle County (Vermont's smallest, with a year-round population of 5,000), and it was homesteaded by Ebenezer Allen, Ethan's cousin, in 1783. Its farms and apple orchard—especially away from its high road (Route 2)—present a clearer picture of unspoiled Vermont than any other region except the Northeast Kingdom. Isle la Motte, known for its distinctive marble and stone houses, is particularly sleepy and well suited to exploring by bike.

GUIDANCE   The Lake Champlain Islands Chamber of Commerce (372-5683), South Hero 05486, publishes a list of accommodations, restaurants, marinas, campgrounds, and trailer parks.

GETTING THERE   From New York State on the north, Route 2 from Rouses Point, and from Vermont, Route 78 from Swanton (an exit on I-89). From Vermont on the south, I-89 Exit 17 to Route 2—which runs the length of the island.

Lake Champlain Ferries (864-9804) offer year-round, 12-minute crossings between Gordon's Landing in Grand Isle and Cumberland Head in New York State (crossing continuously 5 AM–1 AM).

TO SEE AND DO   St. Anne's Shrine (928-3362), Isle la Motte, Route 129. An open-sided chapel in a pine grove on the shore marks the site of Vermont's first French settlement in 1666. There are daily outdoor masses in the summer and Sunday services as long as weather permits. Near the public beach and picnic grounds is an impressive granite statue of Samuel de Champlain, commissioned for Vermont's Pavilion at Montreal's 1967 Expo. Facilities also include a cafeteria and a gift shop. The complex is maintained by the Edmundites, the order who runs St. Michael's College in Winooski.

Hyde Log Cabin, Route 2, Grand Isle. Built by Jedediah Hyde in 1783, the cabin was restored by the Vermont Board of Historic Sites in 1956 and leased to the Grand Isle Historical Society, which has furnished it with appealing, eighteenth-century artifacts-furniture, kitchenware, toys, tools, fabrics. Open July–Labor Day, 9:30–5:30 daily except Tuesday and Wednesday. Free admission; contributions welcome.

Isle La Motte Historical Society. Open July–August, 2–4 daily. This Old School Building and Blacksmith Shop has displays about the island's amazing past.

BICYCLING   With its flat roads (little trafficked once you are off Route 2) and splendid views, the islands are popular biking country. On the quiet west shore of Isle la Motte, **Champlain Islands Cycling** (928-3202), Old Quarry Road, rents bikes, from children's to 18-speed, mountain all-terrain cycles. They also have car racks and offer self-guided tours. **Island Cyclery** (372-3202) in South Hero also offers rentals and repairs.

BIRDING   Located on one of the major flyways for migrating birds, the islands are particularly rich in birdlife: herons, eagles, osprey, cormorants, among many. Prime birdwatching sites include the South Hero Swamp and Mud Creek in Alburg and the Sand Bar Wildlife Refuge across from Sand Bar State Park.

BOATING   Rental fishing boats are available in North Hero from **Anchor Island Marina** (372-5131/4763), **Charlie's Northland Lodge** (372-8822), which also rents canoes, and from **Tudhope Marine Company** (372-5545), which also offers ski and fishing rigs, party boats.

Tudhope Sailing Center and Marina (372-5320), at the bridge in Grand Isle, offers boat slips, sailing instruction, and charters.

Marina Internationale (372-5953), North Hero.

LAKE CRUISES   McBride Group Tours (372-4719, 862-6939), Box 92, North Hero 05486, offers Lake Champlain, Barge Canal, and Hudson River cruise package tours between New York City and Burlington aboard the motor cruiser *Dutch Apple* in July, August, and September for about $600 per person, double occupancy. The five-day, four-night trip includes charter coach return, hotel accommodations ashore, meals, an evening at the Saratoga races, and a visit to West Point, with narration by Captain Lynn Bottum.

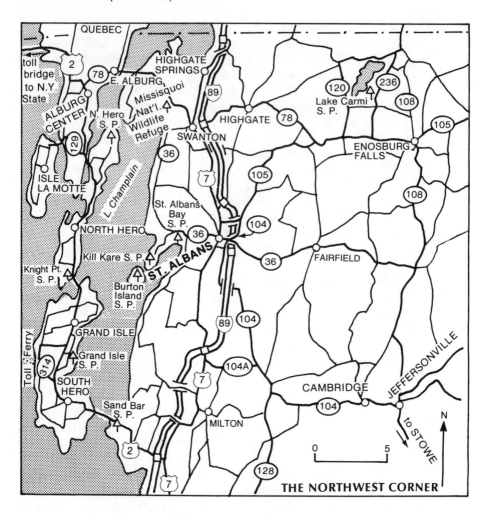

THE NORTHWEST CORNER

Captain Paul Boileau (372-4730, summer; 899-3104, winter), Box 97, Jericho Center 05465, takes up to six passengers on his 25-foot motorboat *Champ* on sunset cruises from the Sandbar Motel, South Hero, during July and August; $75 an hour for a minimum of two people, $25 each additional person.

FISHING   **Lake Champlain** is considered one of the finest freshwater fisheries in America. With the right bait and a little luck, you can catch trout, salmon, smelt, walleye, bass, pike, muskellunge, and perch. Don't expect the local fishermen to give away their favorite spots, but you can find hints, maps, and equipment at one of the many bait and tackle shops that dot the islands. Ask around if you would like to hire a guide. See *Boating* for rentals.

GOLF   **Alburg Country Club** (796-3586), Route 129, three miles west of South Alburg. Eighteen holes, gentle, shady terrain, snack bar.

Appletree Bay (372-5398), South Hero. Nine holes, rentals.

Wilcox Cove (372-8343), Route 2, Grand Isle. Nine holes, golf carts, pro shop, rentals.

PARKS AND FORESTS *Camping* **North Hero State Park** (372-8727), has 117 campsites on 399 acres, mostly in lowland forests with access to open fields, a beach, boat launch, and children's play area.

Grand Isle State Park (372-4300) has 155 campsites, including 33 lean-tos (no hookups) on 226 acres, with a beach, nature trail, and recreation building.

Day Use **Knight Point State Park** (372-8389) is located on the southern tip of North Hero, where many visitors have reported seeing Champ, the Lake Champlain monster. The park has a nature trail, a picnic shelter, and a sandy beach, from which you can watch sailboats and yachts pass through the drawbridge between the islands.

Sand Bar State Park (372-8240), fills to capacity on sunny weekends in the summer, but this arcadian oasis with its sandy beach and adjacent Waterfowl Area is a fine place to relax on weekdays.

LODGING   Here our usual lodging categories don't apply. What counts is location and ambience, and three places stand out on both counts:

☞**Shore Acres Inn and Restaurant** (372-8722 summer, 372-5853 winter), Route 2, North Hero 05474, has sweeping, peaceful, beautifully groomed grounds and 19 comfortable rooms facing the lake and the Green Mountains. There's a bar/lounge; breakfast and dinner served (see *Dining Out*). In winter there are four guest rooms in the annex, away from the lake. Susan and Mike Tranby worked hard to make this an exceptionally friendly as well as comfortable place to stay. Amenities include lawn chairs, a driving range, lawn games, and a half mile of private shore for swimming. Rooms in the motel, many of which have been recently upgraded (#18 has Sabra Field prints, a writing desk, fridge, and daybed), are available early May to late October, $66.50–95.00. In winter, it's $50 per couple B&B.

☞**Thomas Mott Homestead** (outside Vermont 800-348-0843, ext. 12, otherwise 796-3736), Route 78, Alburg. This white 1838 farmhouse with a splendid view of the Green Mountains is a real find. Hosts Pat and Dottie Schallert came from California to begin welcoming guests to Vermont's "West Coast" in 1988, and they still seem to take immense pride in the quality stay enjoyed by each visitor. Pat actually takes a photo of every guest to add to his album, and there's a large repeat clientele. Guests gather around an intriguing old Tailor's table for outstanding breakfasts, maybe an omelet or quiche with shrimp or French toast with fresh raspberries. You might want to linger in the common room with its hearth and games or on the porch (where dinner can be served by special arrangement) with its view. Quilts, old and new, brighten the house throughout. Choose from four guest rooms, each with private bath. The downstairs suite has lake views, a cathedral ceiling, and a twin daybed. Carrie's Room at the top of the stairs has a small sitting area and red-quilted twin beds. Laura's Room has two queen beds under the eaves, and Ransom's Rest (up to honeymoon standards) has its own fireplace and a balcony from which to enjoy the view. Amenities include complimentary Ben & Jerry's ice cream—10 flavors—always available in the kitchen fridge, with frosted glasses to go with them. A canoe and bicycles are also available to guests, and there are lawn games. At Christmas, Pat decorates the barn with white lights. Cross-country skiing on the frozen lake, he tells us, is a great antidote to winter cabin fever. $50–65 per couple B&B, $10 per extra person.

Ruthcliffe Lodge & Restaurant (928-3200), Isle la Motte 05463. Open Mother's Day to Columbus Day. Way out at the end of Old Quarry Road, this lakeside compound includes a small motel with seven units, each with two double beds and a view. The neighboring lodge has five small guest rooms opening onto the second-floor gallery above the (busy) dining room, each with a half bath but sharing one full bath. Mark and Kathy Infante are warm hosts, and the food is well known (see *Dining Out*); three meals a day are served. Swimming and fishing are out the front door; rental boats and bikes are available. $60 double, $360 weekly ($5 per extra person), $45 after Labor Day.

Others: **North Hero House** (372-8237, 201-439-3887, November 1–May 30), Route 2, North Hero 05474, has been deservedly popular for years. It is a venerable old inn at an old steamboat dock, offering rooms in the main house and three lakeside annexes, with a sturdy dock, sandy beach, tennis court, and sauna. Outboards, Sunfish, canoes, sailboards, and fishing tackle can be rented. There's a good restaurant and "Lobster on the Dock" Friday buffet. Rates range from $41–80 double in the main house; $80–97.60 in Cove House, Southwind, and Homestead right on the shore. Especially desirable is the Cobbler's Room ($97.60), which has a double and a twin bed, sitting room with fireplace, and a private screened porch. No credit cards.

Sandbar Motor Inn and Restaurant (372-6911), Route 2, South Hero 05486, has 40 pleasant units with kitchenettes and a larger cottage for six or more. The complex backs on water and also overlooks the lake across Route 2. Rates $45–85. Midweek discount for two or more days. Breakfast and dinner served. Open May through foliage.

The Terrys Lodge (928-3264), Isle la Motte 05463. A bit funky but a comfortable, friendly, family kind of place in a superb location: on a quiet road not far from St. Anne's Shrine, across a narrow road from the lake with a fine lakeside deck and swim raft. Most of the seven rooms in the lodge itself have lake views; we liked them all except #8. Breakfast and dinner (family-style) are served. There's also a four-unit motel, a housekeeping cottage, and housekeeping apartment

($350–400 per week) in the rear. Rental bikes and rowboats are available. From $58 (shared bath) to $60 (private bath) per couple with breakfast; motel units are $65 B&B, add $20 per couple for dinner.

Charlie's Northland Lodge (372-8822), Route 2, North Hero 05474, open all year, has three bedrooms with shared bath at $45–50 double. It's part of a nifty little complex that includes Northland Sporting and Gift Shop, tennis courts, boat and motor rentals, fishing licenses, bait and tackle. Housekeeping cottages available.

Wilcox Cove Cottages & Golf Course (372-8343 summer; 862-4913 winter), Route 314, mailing address: 3 Camp Court, Grand Isle 05458. This homey, lakeside cottage colony and nine-hole public golf course, less than a mile from the ferry, is a real find (adults preferred). Each of the 11 cottages has a living room, dining area, fully equipped kitchen, one bedroom with twin beds, bathroom with shower, and one or two screened porches. They are completely furnished except for sheets, pillowcases, bath and kitchen towels, and can be rented for about $330 a week including greens fees.

BED & BREAKFAST Ye Olde Graystone (796-3711), Route 2, Alburg, open except February. The renovated, stone 1827 home of Gordie and Kathy Jarvis, who run the adjacent lakeshore Goose Point Campground, has four comfortable rooms sharing two large baths, plus a spacious living room. Swimming pool, boat and canoe rentals. $55 per room with continental breakfast. Open winters by advance reservations. The house stands across Route 2 from the lake.

Paradise Bay Bed & Breakfast (372-5393), RR 1, Box 496-C, Kibbe Point Road, South Hero 05486. This is a very gracious new house with plenty of deck space overlooking the lake. The two guest rooms share a bath in a separate wing. $65 per couple includes a full breakfast. Guests have access to the swim dock, not bad just 25 minutes north of Burlington.

DINING OUT Shore Acres (372-8722), Route 2, North Hero. Reservations for dinner are a must much of the time. Also open for breakfast May through October and for lunch in July and August; dinner also served weekends until New Year's. The dining room's large windows command a sweeping view of the lake, with Mount Mansfield and its flanking peaks in the distance. It's a very attractive room with a large fieldstone hearth and areas for nonsmokers and (out near the bar) smokers. The nightly special might be Vermont lamb or fish baked in papillote. Fried scallops and shrimp, tenderloin steak, and charbroiled smoked pork chop with homemade applesauce are also on the menu. Entrées, which come with homebaked bread, a salad, and seasonal vegetables, are $8.95–16.95. The chocolate pie is famous.

Ruthcliffe Lodge (928-3200), Old Quarry Road, Isle la Motte. Open mid-May–mid-September. Be sure to reserve for dinner before you drive out to this rustic building, way off the main drag, overlooking the

VTD

Traditional maple sap gathering, Fairfield

lake. Dine in the pine-paneled dining room or outside on the deck. Owner/chef Mark Infante specializes in Italian dishes like veal Marsala ($16.95), but he's also known for barbequed ribs ($14.95) and marinated lamb kabobs ($15.95). Entrée prices include soup and dessert.

North Hero House (372-8237), Route 2, North Hero. Open mid-May through September. This historic old inn is known as a good bet for lunch as well as dinner (reserve). Although the dining room does not overlook the lake, it does feature a flower- and plant-filled greenhouse. The menu changes constantly, with entrées priced from $14 to $17. Friday night there's always a lobster feast down on the dock.

Sandbar Restaurant (372-6911), Route 2, South Hero. This is a large, attractive dining room with views up the lake. Steak is a specialty of the house—T-bone, top sirloin, and filet mignon all top the menu, chicken cordon bleu and scallops au vin are also on the menu. Entrées $11.25–15.00, including starch, vegetables, and salad.

EATING OUT   Cathy's Place, junction of Routes 2 and 129. Open for all three meals May through the Columbus Day weekend, weekends only in shoulder seasons. If I hadn't been starved I probably wouldn't have ventured into this white, shedlike place, but the number of local cars outside should have been a clue. It's great for homemade doughnuts, pie, specials like stuffed green pepper, plus all the basics.

Northern Café (796-3003), Route 2, Alburg. Open daily, 7 AM–9 PM. Nothing special from the road, but it can hit the spot when a grilled cheese or homemade soup is what you want. Dinner specials as well as predictable fare.

SELECTIVE SHOPPING   Apple Farm Market, South Hero. Open daily: apples, cider, pies, maple products, honey, preserves, cider doughnuts, eggs, cheese, and fruits in season. Their popular ice cream stand features a uniquely refreshing cider slush.

Hooting Owl Gift Shop, 33 West Shore Road, Grand Isle. A former hen house, now filled with Vermont-made gifts.

MEDICAL EMERGENCY   North and South Hero (372-4322). For Alburg (796-3409). Marine Emergencies (372-5590).

ST. ALBANS

Once an important railroad center and still the Franklin County seat, St. Albans (population 8,082), on Route 7, is showing signs of revitalization. Its firm place in the history books was assured on October 19, 1864, when 22 armed Confederate soldiers, who had infiltrated the town in mufti, held up the three banks, stole horses, and escaped back to Canada with $201,000, making this the northernmost engagement of the Civil War. One of the raiders was wounded and eventually died, as did Elinus J. Morrison, a visiting builder, who was shot by the bandits. The surviving Confederates were arrested in Montreal, tried, but never extradited; their leader, Lt. Bennett H. Young, rose to the rank of general. When he visited Montreal again in 1911, a group of St. Albans dignitaries paid him a courtesy call at the Ritz-Carlton!

GUIDANCE   The St. Albans Chamber of Commerce (524-2444), 132 North Main Street, St. Albans 05478.

TO SEE AND DO   The Franklin County Museum facing Taylor Park, open July and August, Tuesday–Saturday 2–5, was established by the St. Albans Historical Society in 1971 in a three-story brick schoolhouse erected in 1861. The Beaumont Room has been fitted up as a fascinating, old-time country doctor's office; one room has period costumes; and another houses Central Vermont Railroad memorabilia. Upstairs are farm tools, a maple sugaring exhibit, and other artifacts of the region. Admission is free; contributions appreciated.

Chester A. Arthur Birthplace, North Fairfield, a replica of the little house where the twenty-first (and usually underrated) president was born, can be found 10 miles east on Route 36 to Fairfield (open June–mid-October, Wednesday–Sunday and holidays, 9:30–5:30). In the visitors center, exhibits examine the controversy over the actual site of Arthur's birth, which impacted on the question of his eligibility to serve as president. Arthur's conduct as president in light of his reputation as a leading New York State political boss is also examined.

STATE PARKS   *Day Use*   **St. Albans Bay State Park**, four miles west on Route 36, is a good place for picnics, but the water is too shallow and weedy for decent swimming.

Kill Kare State Park (524-6021; 372-5060), once a fashionable summer hotel site and then, for years, a famous boys' summer camp. It can be crowded on weekends but blissfully quiet other days.

Camping   **Burton Island State Park** (524-6353), a lovely, 350-acre island reached from Kill Kare by park boat or by your own. Facilities include 42 campsites, including 22 lean-tos, 100 slip marina with electrical hook-ups and 20 moorings; campers' gear will be transported to the campsites by park vehicle. Fishing off this beautiful haven is usually excellent.

Lake Carmi State Park (933-8383/888-5733), Exit 19 off I-89, two miles on Route 104; 1.5 miles north on Route 105; three miles north of Route 108, in Enosburg Falls. Set in rolling farmlands, the 482-acre park has 178 wooded campsites, including 35 lean-tos and some on the beach of this sizable lake; nature trails; boat ramp and rentals.

Woods Island State Park (879-6565), two miles north of Burton Island. Primitive camping on an island of 125 acres. Five widely spaced campsites with no facilities, fires are not allowed. The island is unstaffed, although there are daily ranger patrols; reservations for campsites must be made through Burton Island State Park. There is no public transportation to the island; the best boat access is from Kill Kare.

GOLF   **Champlain Country Club** (524-9895), Route 7, three miles north of St. Albans. Nine holes, some terraced. Snack bar.

LODGING   **The Cadillac Motel** (524-2191), 213 South Main Street, St. Albans 05478, is a pleasant cluster of 41 units surrounding a swimming pool, with mini-golf, badminton, and a coffee shop in the summer. Rates $35–60.

The Champlain Inn and Motel (524-5956), 287 South Main Street, Route 7, St. Albans 05478 , has cable TV with free HBO, laundromat. $28–45 winter, $32–55 summer and foliage season.

RESTAURANTS   **The Blue Lion** (524-3060), 71 North Main Street. This venerable restaurant with its oak paneling and beams is approaching landmark status, for it hasn't changed in 60 years. Hearty American fare for lunch and dinner; inexpensive.

Jeff's Maine Seafood Market, at Main and Bank streets next to the Blue Lion, has a few tables and blackboard specials for lunch.

The Old Foundry Restaurant (524-9665), 3 Federal Street. Housed in one of the city's few 1840s buildings to have escaped the town's big 1895 fire, this is a great setting for traditional fare, like char-broiled rib steak or filet mignon (both $13.25), fried seafood, or char-broiled salmon steak ($12.95).

SPECIAL EVENTS   Early–Mid-April: **Maple Sugar Festival**—for three days, the town turns into a nearly nonstop "sugarin' off" party, courtesy of the local maple producers, augmented by arts and crafts and antique show and other events.

MEDICAL EMERGENCY   (911)

SWANTON

Settled by the French about 1700 and later named for a British captain in the French and Indian Wars, Swanton (population 4,622) is growing again after a long period of relative stagnation. During the First World War, the long abandoned Robin Hood-Remington Arms plant produced millions of rounds of ammunition for the Allied armies. At one end of the village Green dwell a pair of Royal swans. This park is the focus for the Swanton Summer Festival, the last week of July, with parades, band concerts, square dancing, arts and crafts shows. The tribal headquarters of the Abenaki are in the old railway depot.

GREEN SPACE AND WATER   **The Missisquoi National Wildlife Refuge** (868-4781), on the river's delta, lies two miles west of Swanton on Route 78 to East Alburg and the islands. Habitats are about equally divided between brushland, timberland, and marsh, through which wind Black Creek and Maquam Creek trails, adding up to about a mile and a half, or a two-hour ramble; both are appropriately marked for the flora or fauna represented. It's open most of the time, but call ahead to confirm.

RESORT   **The Tyler Place** (868-3301), Route 7, Highgate Springs 05460. Open May–late September. One of the country's oldest and most popular resorts continues to thrive on the 165-acre lakeshore spread for which an old spa hotel was once the centerpiece. At the height of the season, it is rather like a jolly, crowded cruise ship; its faithful partisans have been returning year after year for three generations of the Tyler family's management. They provide just about every conceivable form of recreation for adults and children from 2 to 17 years of age, with separate programs and dining for each group (special arrangements are made for infants). Accommodations vary, from cottages to the 1820 farmhouse, the 1890 Victorian guest house, and a modern inn. Each unit has two or more bedrooms, air-conditioning, and one or one-and-a-half baths. From late June to early September, package rates for adults range from $90 to $140 per person per day, and $51 to $61 for children, depending on age. During the spring, early summer, and fall, rates are 20–35 percent less.

LODGING   Royale Swans Country Inn & Motel (868-2010), Route 7 north, Swanton 05488. There are six rooms in a converted, 200-year-old farmhouse and 12 in the motel wing, all with private baths, connected to an indoor pool, spa, and sauna, at $40–55 per room. Summer, winter, weekend, midweek MAP packages. No smoking in the inn, dining room, or pool house.

RESTAURANTS   The Pines Restaurant (868-4819), Route 7, Highgate.

Almost Heaven (868-5009), Route 78. A tiny, upstairs eatery near the Common featuring homemade soups, chili, quiche, and dinner specials like marinated chicken breast ($9.95).

Swanton House of Pizza (868-3085), Merchants Row.

MEDICAL EMERGENCY   868-3320. **Northwestern Medical Center** (524-2161/5911), St. Albans.

V. Northern Vermont

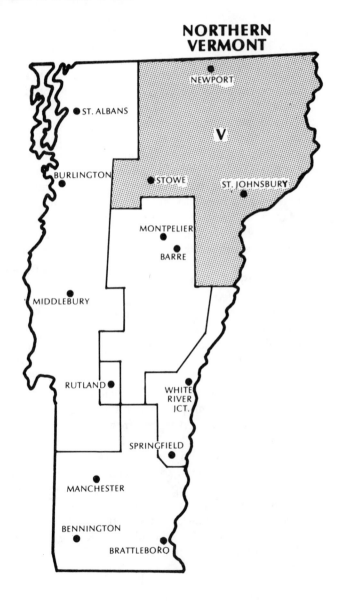

NORTHERN
VERMONT

NEWPORT

ST. ALBANS

V

BURLINGTON

STOWE

ST. JOHNSBURY

MONTPELIER

BARRE

MIDDLEBURY

RUTLAND

WHITE
RIVER
JCT.

SPRINGFIELD

MANCHESTER

BENNINGTON

BRATTLEBORO

Stowe and Waterbury

STOWE

Although it is no longer the state's biggest ski area, Stowe remains the "ski capital of the East" and Vermont's premier summer resort as well.

In its path up the spine of the state, Route 100 parallels many imposing peaks, but here, in the middle of this handsome village, it is joined by a road that angles off and climbs steeply right up over the shoulder of Vermont's highest mountain.

By the midnineteenth century, men were already taxing their imaginations and funds to entice visitors up onto the heights of Mount Mansfield, which bears an uncanny resemblance to the upturned profile of a rather jowly man. In 1858 an inn was built under the "Nose," a project that entailed constructing a 100-yard log trestle above a chasm and several miles of corduroy road made from hemlocks. In Stowe Village at this time, a hotel, the Mansfield House, accommodated 600 guests.

A number of Swedish families moved into Stowe in 1912 and began using their skis to get around. Then, in 1914, the Dartmouth College librarian skied down the Toll Road. Serious skiing, however, didn't begin until 1933 when the Civilian Conservation Corps cut a four-mile-plus trail just for that purpose, and the following year the town formed its own Mt. Mansfield Ski Club, setting up basic lodging near the bottom of the ski trail in a former logging camp. By 1937, a rope tow had been rigged from the camp to the top of the trail, powered by a Cadillac engine. It cost $.50 per day, $5 per season.

The Mt. Mansfield Company, formed in 1951 from the various small concerns that had evolved in the 1930s and 1940s to serve skiers, has come a long way but is still squarely rooted in its colorful beginnings. The company itself was for many years headed by Sepp Ruschp, the "crack skier" who left his native Austria—at the request of the Mt. Mansfield Ski Club—to become its ski instructor in 1936. And innkeepers still include the Von Trapp family, immortalized in the *Sound of Music*.

Although Stowe no longer boasts the greatest number of places to stay, it still represents the state's biggest concentration of inns; condominiums, while a growing phenomena, are scattered around the edges rather than setting the tone. The Stowe Area Association has been in business since 1936, matching visitors with lodgings they can afford and enjoy.

Stowe is a genuine, year-round resort, offering excellent skiing—both downhill and cross-country—in winter, and a superb golf course, tennis, theater, hiking, and fishing in summer, plus a wide variety of lodging, dining, and shopping. It is also an excellent pivot from which to explore northern Vermont: 30 miles from Burlington, just over the Notch from the little-touristed Lamoille Valley, and a short drive from both Montpelier/Barre on one hand and the Northeast Kingdom on the other.

GUIDANCE   The Stowe Area Association (253-7321, or toll-free reservations, 800-24-STOWE), Box 1230, Stowe 05672. Open daily Memorial Day–mid-October, 9–6, Thanksgiving–April, 8 AM–9 PM, and in the time between, 9–5. This service, housed in its own building in the middle

Stowe/Brownell

Stowe village and Mount Mansfield

of Stowe Village, keeps a tally of vacancies in more than 60 local lodging places and will make reservations; it also publishes seasonal guides listing most things in the area and is a walk-in source of advice about what's going on.

GETTING THERE   By bus: Vermont Transit/Greyhound stops in Waterbury with connections from Boston, New York, and points south.

By train: AMTRAK station in Waterbury.

By plane: The Stowe-Morrisville Airport, seven miles north, provides private plane services and charters. Burlington Airport, 34 miles away, is served by Continental from Newark, United Airlines from Chicago, USAIR from Pittsburgh, Syracuse, and Washington, D.C. The Montpelier-Barre Airport, 22 miles away, is served by Eastern Express from Boston.

Shuttle: Sullivan Transportation (253-9440, 800-548-7076), Box 544, Adams Mill Road, Moscow 05662, vans and limos make daily runs between Stowe and the Burlington Airport.

By car: From most points, I-89 Exit 10, and 15 minutes north on Route 100.

GETTING AROUND   During summer and winter months, trollies shuttle up and down the seven miles between the village and the mountain, 8–5:30. Special tours of the area are also offered.

TO SEE AND DO   Mount Mansfield. The highest point in Vermont, 4,393 feet high at the Chin, yields a truly spectacular view, accessible primarily in summer—unless you can clamber up to the summit from the Cliff House warming hut at the top of the gondola over ice and snow. In summer there are two easy ways up: the Toll Road and a four-passenger gondola.

The Toll Road (253-7311) begins 7seven miles up Route 108 from the village; look for the sign on the left just before the Inn at the Mountain. Open late May–mid-October, weather permitting, 9:30–5. $8 per car, $4 per repeat trip, and $5 per motorcycle; bikes and foot traffic free. First laid in the midnineteenth century, this steep, windy road leads to a hotel that served the public until 1957. (It was demolished in the mid-1960s.) This also served as a ski trail until the winter of 1981–1982, when the new novice area was created at Spruce Peak. The road terminates at the Mt. Mansfield Summit Station just below the Nose (4,062 feet), a small space serving cookies and cocoa and usually crowded with hikers. A half-mile Tundra Trail follows the Long Trail (red-and-white blazes on the rocks) north to Drift Rock (the trek should take 20 minutes); another mile along the trail brings you to the summit of Mount Mansfield (round-trip: two hours).

The Gondola (253-7311) operates mid-June–mid-October, weather permitting, 9–5; $8 per adult, $4 per child, round-trip; $4 per adult and senior citizen, $2 per child, one-way. The new eight-passenger gondola runs from the base lodge to the Cliff House, which serves light meals all day; a half-hour's trek brings you up to the Chin. However you get there, the view from the summit (the Chin) is spectacular on a clear day: To the west you see across 20 miles of farmland to Lake Champlain, east to the Worcester Range across the Stowe Valley, north to Jay Peak (35 miles distant) across the Lamoille Valley, and south, back along the Green Mountains to Camel's Hump. Mt. Washington is visible to the east, Whiteface to the west.

The Alpine Slide (253-7311), Spruce Peak Base Lodge, Mountain Road. Open late June to early September, 9:30–5, $5 per adult, $3.50 per child, $20 and $14 for five rides.

Bingham Falls, Mountain Road. On Route 108 (the Mountain Road), 1½ miles beyond the Toll Road turnoff, look for a widening in the shoulder and follow a well-beaten path to the right through the woods: water cascades through a flume and tumbles down through a series of chutes, falls, and pools.

Stowe Village. A classic, early nineteenth-century Vermont village with a spired, white meetinghouse at one end of Main Street and a brick stagecoach inn at the other, a satisfying variety of stores and restaurants all within an easy stroll. The former wooden high school (one block up School Street from Main), is now the **Helen Day Memorial Library and Art Center** (open Monday–Friday 2–5, also Wednesday 10–8, Saturday 10–12:30; closed Tuesday and Sunday; changing art exhibits). The Bloody Brook Schoolhouse next door is open July 4–Labor Day and during foliage season, also in early summer and in September, 1–3; small fee. A restored, one-room schoolhouse maintained by the Stowe Historical Society, which also has exhibits in the Memorial Building, Main Street. Open Monday–Friday 2–5.

COVERED BRIDGES   The Gold Brook Bridge in Stowe Hollow, also known as Emily's Bridge because Emily is said to have taken her life from it (different ways for different reasons in different stories) and reportedly returns to haunt it on dark occasions. There is another picturesque bridge across the Sterling Brook, off the Stagecoach Road, north of the village.

PARKS AND FORESTS   For fees and reservation rules, see *Campgrounds* in "What's Where."

Mt. Mansfield State Forest. The largest state forest—27,436 acres— much of which lies on the other (western) flank of the mountain.

Smugglers' Notch (253-4041), RFD, Stowe 05472. Ten miles up the Mountain Road (Route 108) from Stowe Village, open mid-May through mid-October: 38 campsites including 14 lean-tos. A few miles beyond the camping area, just beyond the highest point in this high, windy road—open only late May through November, weather permitting—is a turnoff with parking, toilet, and an information center; for details on the trails from this area, see *Hiking*;for background, see "North of the Notch."

Elmore State Park (888-2982), Lake Elmore 05657. Open mid-May–mid-October, 14 miles north of Stowe on Route 100, then east to Morrisville, south five miles on Route 12; 709 acres with a beach, bathhouse, rental boats, 64 sites for tents and trailers including five lean-tos, picknicking, hiking trail up Elmore Mountain.

SCENIC DRIVES   Not only is Stowe pleasantly sited for touring in all directions, it is also organized to offer visitors well-researched printed tours—11 trips ranging in length from 7.6 to 112 miles. Many of the roads are dirt byways that invite parking the car and strolling off through villages, across covered bridges, down to waterfalls, or whatever. Because most of the areas covered are included in other parts of the book, we omit details but strongly suggest you secure a copy of "Roads and Tours about Stowe" from the Stowe Area Association.

AIR RIDES   For hot air ballooning, inquire at Stoweflake Resort (253-7355). Soaring and airplane rides are available at the Stowe/Morrisville State Airport (888-7845).

BICYCLING   The equipage here is a mountain bike, and the rental sources are the **Mountain Bike** shop (253-7919), rear of the Depot Building, Main Street in the village; the bike shop at **Stowe Mountain Sports** (253-4896) in the Stowe Center Complex, Mountain Road; and **Stowe Action Outfitters** (253-7975), Mountain Road, which has canoe rentals also. Neophytes usually head for the **Stowe Recreation Path** (see *Walking*).

Umiak Outdoor Outfitters (253-2317, 800-479-3380), 1880 Mountain Road, Stowe, provides guided or personal mountain biking tours and rentals, plus canoe and kayak instruction and rentals, for the Winooksi and Lamoille rivers, from its retail center.

BOATING AND FISHING   Canoe rentals are available from **The Fly Rod Shop** (253-7346), two miles south of Stowe Village on Route 100, from **Stowe Action Outfitters** (see *Bicycling*), and also from **Buccaneer Country Lodge** (253-4772), 1390 Mountain Road. A printed guide to fishing, boating, and canoeing, provided by the Lamoille County Development Council (Box 577, Morrisville 05661) and available from shops. The Stowe Area Association describes canoeing and fishing on the Lamoille River, also in Lake Elmore, Lake Eden, Wolcott Pond, and Waterbury Reservoir, among others.

GOLF   **Stowe Country Club** (253-4269), an 18-hole course with a practice range, putting green, restaurant, bar, pro shop, lessons. There's a public golf course and driving range at the **Farm Resort** (888-3525), Route 100, six miles north of Stowe in Morrisville.

WALKING   **Stowe Recreation Path** is a new, 5.2-mile paved path that begins in Stowe Village behind the Community Church, winds up through corn fields, wildflowers, and raspberry patches, and parallels the Mountain Road but at a more forgiving pitch.

HIKING   Mount Mansfield. See the introduction to this section and *To See and Do* for a general description of Vermont's highest mountain. For walkers (as opposed to hikers), it's best to take the Toll Road or gondola up and follow the Tundra Trail described earlier. Serious hikers should at least purchase the weatherproof map of the Mount Mansfield region ($1.95) and can profit from the *Guide Book of the Long Trail* ($8.50), both published by the Green Mountain Club. A naturalist is on hand May–November along the heavily traveled, 2½-mile section of the Long Trail between the Forehead and the Chin; the Green Mountain Club maintains Butler Lodge, a half mile south of the Forehead, and Taft Lodge, below the Chin, as shelter for hikers.

Smugglers' Notch. The Long Trail North, clearly marked, is an easy, mile-plus hike to Sterling Pond, a beautiful spot at 3,000 feet, fish-stocked too. The Elephant's Head can be reached from the state picnic area on Route 108, a two-mile trail leads to this landmark—from which you can also continue on to Sterling Pond, and thence out to Route 108, but a couple miles above the picnic area. No one should drive through Smugglers' Notch without stopping at least to see the Smuggler's Cave and to clamber around on the rocks.

Other local hikes described in the pamphlet guide to "Hiking, Camping, Bicycling" provided by the Lamoille County Development Council (Box 577, Morrisville 05661) and available from the Stowe Area Association, also detailed in *Day Hiker's Guide to Vermont*, published by the Green Mountain Club: Belvidere Mountain in Eden, a 3½-hour trek yielding good views in all directions; Ritterbush Pond and Devil's Gulch, also in Eden, 2¾ hours round-trip; and Elmore Mountain in Elmore State Park, a 2- to 3-hour hike with spectacular views.

Camel's Hump, from Waterbury. This trail is detailed in *Fifty Hikes in Vermont* and takes you from Couching Lion Farm in Duxbury, a 6½-hour round-trip hike to the unspoiled summit of Vermont's third highest mountain.

Little River Trail System, Mount Mansfield State Forest, Waterbury. There are beautiful trails through the Ricker Basin and Cotton Brook area, once a settlement for 50 families who left behind cellar holes, stone fences, old cemeteries, lilacs, and apple trees.

Also see "Barre/Montpelier Area"for hiking in the Worcester Range.

HORSEBACK RIDING   Topnotch Stables (253-8585), Mountain Road. Trail rides, carriage lessons. **Edson Hill Manor** (253-8954), private lessons, trail rides.

POLO MATCHES June through September, Sunday afternoon polo matches begin either at 1 or 3 (check weekly calendar) at the Stowe Country Club Polo Field, off Mountain Road (turn just before Stoweflake Motel).

RAILROAD EXCURSION   **Lamoille Valley Railroad** (888-4255), Stafford Avenue, marked off Route 100 north of Morrisville Village (10 miles north of Stowe). This is a working railroad, hauling freight to and from points between Whitefield, New Hampshire, and Cambridge Junction, Vermont (93 miles). A portion of the rail route across the roof of Vermont was for many years served by the St.J&LC, known affectionately as the "Slow, Jerky & Long Coming." On selected days in summer (late June–Labor Day) and more frequently in fall (check current schedule) the line operates excursion trains. $15 adult, $5 children.

SWIMMING   Many lodging places have their own pools. The best swimming hole is **Forest Place** on the Notchbrook Road, marked on the Stowe map available from the Stowe Area Association. **Salzburg Inn** (253-8541) has an indoor pool and sauna available for a fee.

TENNIS   **The Racquet Club at Topnotch** (253-9308), four indoor, 11 outdoor courts, pro shop, instruction, videotape, 8 AM–11 PM.

   Mt. Mansfield Tennis Courts (253-7311), six well-maintained clay courts adjacent to the Inn at the Mountain, 8–6, available by the hour.

   Free public courts can be found at the town recreation area off School Street. A number of inns have courts available to the public; inquire at the Stowe Area Association (253-7321).

CROSS-COUNTRY SKIING   A 150-km network of trails adds up to some of the best ski touring in New England. Given the high elevation of much of this terrain, they tend to have snow when few areas do, and on windy, icy days, cross-country can be better in Stowe than downhill. All four touring centers honor the other's trail tickets (if you ski, not drive, from one to the next). In February of 1992, the interchangeable trail fee is $8.

   Mt. Mansfield Touring Center (253-7311), Mountain Road. Located near the Inn at the Mountain, this center offers 30 km of set trails, plus 25 km of backcountry trails, at elevations from 1,200 to 2,800 feet. It's possible to take the Toll House lift a ways up the Toll Road and ski down (a good place to practice Telemarking). You can also take the quad to a point near enough the summit to enable you to climb to the very top (via the Toll Road) for a spectacular view out across Lake Champlain; the descent via the Toll Road is relatively easy. Another beautiful trail circles Sterling Pond high in the Saddle between Spruce and Madonna mountains (accessible via chair lift). Connecting trails link this system with the Trapp Family Lodge and Top Notch trails.

   Trapp Family Lodge Cross-Country Ski Center (253-8511). Located on the Trapp Hill Road, off by itself in the upper reaches of the valley, this is one of the oldest and most beautiful commercial trail systems, 60 km of set trails at elevations of 1,100–3,000 feet. Lessons, equipment rental and sales, and outstanding pastries are all available, also guided tours.

Edson Hill Ski Touring Center (253-7371), Edson Hill Road. Relatively uncrowded, away on the uplands north of Mountain Road, offering 40 miles of set trails at elevations between 1,400 and 2,100 feet; instruction, rental, sales, full lunches, and guided tours available.

Topnotch Touring Center (253-8585), Mountain Road. Novice to expert trails, a total of 20 km; instruction, rental, café, and restaurant available, also change rooms.

Spruce Peak Alpine/Nordic Area (253-7311), Mountain Road. Cross-country is available on downhill trails with the purchase of a regular lift ticket.

Back-country Tours are offered by Umiak Outdoor Outfitters (253-2317), 1880 Mountain Road, as well as by the Mt. Mansfield Touring Center and Trapp Family Lodge.

DOWNHILL SKIING   **Stowe** (253-7311; snow report: 253-8521), Stowe 05672. See the introduction for the story of how the present Mt. Mansfield Company has evolved as a natural outgrowth of various enterprises serving skiers since the 1930s. In the winter of 1990–1991, the mountain company embarked on some long-overdue improvements, installing a fast new eight-passenger gondola, re-contouring trails, and improving snow-making. The old Mansfield base lodge still serves the largest network of trails, and the Spruce House, a short shuttle bus ride up Route 108, serves the novice area.

Lifts: New eight-passenger gondola, quad chair lift, triple chair lift, six double chair lifts, one surface.

Trails: 45 trails, also glade skiing; 23 percent expert, 58 percent intermediate, 19 percent novice.

Vertical drop: 2,350 feet on Mount Mansfield, 1,550 feet on Spruce Peak.

Snow-making: Covers 72 percent of the terrain trails served by nine of the 10 lifts.

Facilities: Three base lodges plus the Octagon and Cliff House at the top of the busiest lifts: cafeterias, rentals, ski shops, shuttle bus.

Ski school: 100 instructors; a lift especially designed for beginners at Spruce Peak where novices learn to make the transition from easy to intermediate trails.

For children: Day-care from two months. From three years up children can sign on for Winnie-the-Pooh day-care or a combo of care and lessons at Spruce Peak.

Rates: $39 per adult; $21 per child under 13; multiple-day discounts during nonholiday periods.

(Please note: For downhill skiing at **Smuggler's Notch**, see "North of the Notch": it is not accessible in winter from Stowe on Route 108.)

OTHER WINTER RECREATION   **Ice skating** is available at the Jackson Arena (253-6148) and on the pond at Commodores Inn (253-7131). Skates can be rented from Shaw's General Store (253-4040).

Sleigh rides are found at Stowehof, Edson Hill Manor, and The Trapp Family Lodge (see *Resort Inns*) and at Pristine Meadows (253-9877).

Snowmobiles can be rented at Nichol's (253-7239), also a source of information about local trails.

Snowshoe tours are offerd by Umiak (253-2317), Gale Farm Center, 1880 Mountain Road. Guided tours are also available from Bedside Tuners (253-7222)

East of Eden (635-2700), East Hill, Eden Mills, is a 150-acre "Winter Fun Park" one-half hour north of Stowe. It offers a 1,200-foot toboggan run, 10 kilometers of snowmobile trails (also rentals), floodlit ice skating, guided snowshoe tours, and a café.

Shaw's General Store is also a source of rental sleds.

HEALTH SPAS   **The Stowe Athletic Club** (253-2541), the Green Mountain Inn, PO Box 60, Stowe 05672. Facilities at the club, located in the rear of the Green Mountain Inn, include a whirlpool, sauna, outdoor pool, Nautilus system, massage, free weights, daily aerobics and stretch classes; stressing outdoor exercise (skiing, both downhill and cross-country, in winter, hiking and biking in summer).

The Spa at Topnotch (253-8585, eastern US 800-451-8686, Canada 800-228-8686), Box 1458, Mountain Road, opened in September 1989 under the direction of John and Ginny Lopis, former directors of the Arizona Canyon Ranch Spa. The 23,000-square-foot facility includes a new, 60-foot indoor pool, various exercise studios, personal service rooms for hydrotherapy, herbal and body wraps; a spa menu restaurant, art studio, and health and fitness library, plus the existing outdoor sports offered by the inn itself.

LODGING   Most accommodations are found either in Stowe Village or along—or just off—the 7¼-mile Mountain Road (Route 108) that connects it with the ski slopes. Winter rates are quoted, but they are 5–20 percent less by the five-day ski week, as much as half price in summer. The Stowe Area Association (see *Guidance*) publishes a booklet guide listing current rates and amenities offered by its member inns, lodges, motels, resorts, and condominium complexes. Unless otherwise noted, all places to stay are in Stowe 05672.

RESORT INNS   **Stowehof** (253-9722, 800-422-9722), two miles off Route 108. A fantasy world from the moment you step through its sod-roofed porte-cochere, supported by two maple trees. No two of the 47 guest rooms are alike (some suites, a few fireplace demi-suites with optional kitchenettes). The public rooms are filled with original details like the divining rod that located the water source for the building. Windows everywhere let in the magnificent view. Facilities include a Tap Room, a dining room known for nouvelle French dishes, tennis courts, a putting range, a delightful pool (with its own splendid view), sauna, and cross-country ski trails connecting with the larger network. An adjacent working farm has been added, where cattle can be seen and horses ridden. Rates are $80–110 per person MAP Friday and Saturday, but just $350 per person for a midweek, five-day ski package, four days of lifts included. In summer, a five-day midweek B&B package is $225 per person.

Topnotch at Stowe (253-8585; eastern US 800-451-8686; Canada 800-228-8686), PO Box 1260, Mountain Road, bills itself as "Vermont's world-class resort," and it's hard to quibble (though these days it would have to share the distinction with a few others). No matter: *Ski* magazine listed it as one of the world's "12 poshest ski hotels." Uncommonly comfortable rooms hold many amenities, including a runner's guide showing various routes, from an easy 1.7 miles to a challenging 5.8 miles. There are luxurious areas for lounging, the Bistro for lunch and light suppers, the convivial Buttertub Bar, and the stately, glass-sided, highly rated main dining room. A health and fitness spa has recently been added; contemporary sculpture surrounds the outdoor swimming pool. A major attraction for athletic guests is the big red farm barn across the road, which serves as a cross-country ski center in the winter (50 km groomed and connected with three other trails in Stowe), riding stable, indoor and outdoor tennis courts, and a handy skating rink.

Double room rates range from $90 per person off season MAP, $99–127 in summer; higher in winter. Several package plans are offered, including what may be the only "Tenniski" vacation. Suites, condos, and town houses available.

The Trapp Family Lodge (253-8511; 800-826-7000), off the Mountain Road, remains a fabled Austrian schloss with spectacular views, though somewhat more impersonal than it was before the original lodge burned and the Baroness Von Trapp died. The new 73-room lodge is Alpine-modern, with a charming greenhouse sitting room. On the slope below are tiers of condos and motel-type units. The inn's 1,700 acres constitute New England's most scenic cross-country ski terrain, with 60 miles of trails and splendid walks in the summer, plus tennis courts and a spring-fed pool. Summer rates range from $175–200 double, MAP, in the lower lodge; less in the spring; more in winter.

Edson Hill Manor (253-7371), off Mountain Road. Set in 300 cultivated acres on a high slope, this seductive place resembles the "English country" estate it once was. Many guests are drawn here because some of the amusing winter scenes of Alan Alda's *The Four Seasons* were filmed on its grounds. There are now 26 rooms, 11 in the stone manor and 15 close by, most with private baths and some with fireplaces, plus a cheery lounge and dining room. Other attractions are a stable, outdoor pool, stocked trout pond, and 40 km of cross-country trails. Not a good choice for groups. Summer rates range from $59–99 per room without meals; in winter, $70–90 per person MAP.

The Mount Mansfield Resort (800-253-4754; 253-7311), Mountain Road. The former Toll House Inn owned by the Mt. Mansfield Company and the closest lodging to the lifts: 34 rooms in the inn itself and 53 town houses, plus, 35 "lodges" (one-, two-, and three-bedroom, slopeside condominiums). Facilities include the Fireside Dining Room and Tavern, clay tennis courts, three swimming pools, the Mansfield Touring Center, and skiing on the Toll Road. $95 EP per person in a double room at the inn in summer; two- to four-day golf and five-day ski weeks available. Winter: $218 double to $385 for a 3-bedroom townhouse.

Green Mountain Inn (253-7301 and 800-445-6629), Main Street, Box 220. The brick and clapboard face of this landmark dates back to the 1830s, but it has been thoroughly and tastefully modernized. All 63 rooms, some in the inn and some in the motel annex out back, are nicely furnished in sturdy antique reproductions (including canopy beds) and Vermont watercolors. Two suites, one with whirlpool bath, can be converted into triples. The dining room is formal, and the Whip tap room is informal, overlooking the back garden and pool in summer, warmed by a hearth in winter. There are a number of inviting sitting rooms downstairs, and the spa (see *Health Spas*) offers full facilities and special weekend, five- and seven-day fitness plans. From $68 per person MAP and up, $35–90 per person EP.

Stoweflake Inn and Resort (253-7355; 800-253-2232), Mountain Road. The small ski lodge that the Baraw family opened some 28 years ago has mushroomed into a full-facility, 97-unit resort, including 24 townhouse units. There are bright, comfortable inn-style rooms in the original lodge and many nicely furnished motel rooms (besides its own motel wing, the resort includes the former Nordic Motor Inn). All rooms have cable TV, phones, and private bath, and common space includes a library and lobby with fireplaces and sitting area and a large living room with a sunken fireplace. Amenities include one outdoor pool, a sports center with indoor pool, a large meeting space, Jacuzzi, steam room, and two tennis courts, also badminton, volleyball, croquet, horseshoes, and a professional putting green and driving ranges. The links at the Stowe Country Club adjoin the property. Dining options include formal Winfields and the pubby Charlie B's. $68–118 per double room, $124–174 per couple MAP; town houses from $130 for a studio to $450 per day for a three-bedroom unit; five-day packages available both winter and summer.

Golden Eagle Resort Motor Inn (253-4811; 800-626-1010). The 12-unit motel that Herb and Ann Miller bought in 1963 has evolved through two generations into an amazing, 60-acre complex with 95 rooms, 15 apartments and chalets, some with fireplaces or Franklin stoves. Family-geared as well as owned, it offers a lot for children. In summer, there's a formal hiking and crafts program on selected days for 3–12 year olds, and on certain nights, year-round, there are evening movies with popcorn. Amenities include a state-of-the-art playground as well as an attractive health spa with indoor pool, large whirlpool, sauna, Universal exercise equipment, massage service, and exercise classes. There are also outdoor heated pools (swimming lessons are offered), a clay tennis court, fish-stocked ponds, shuffleboard, badminton, lawn games, and game rooms. Throughout, you have a sense of a well-run resort. A fifty-acre wildlife area with walking trails adjoins the area. $79–139 per room, $139–259 per night for suites, apartments, and chalets in winter; 10 percent less in summer, special packages year-round.

INNS AND LODGES   **Ten Acres Lodge** (253-7638, 800-327-7357, except in Vermont and Canada), Luce Hill Road, off the Mountain Road and near the entrance to the Von Trapp domain, this red clapboarded farmhouse radiates a luxurious, distinctive personality. It has 14 individually decorated guest rooms, 10 with baths, plus two guest cottages and two apartments, each with its own kitchen, fireplace, and private terrace from which to savor the marvelous view. There's also a pool, tennis court, and a dining room considered among the best in Stowe. Doubles range from $60–250 with breakfast, summer; $70–275, winter.

The Gables Inn (253-7730), Mountain Road. A sunny, welcoming inn with a total of 17 rooms, including 15 doubles, all with private bath, some in the motel. Sol and Lynn Baumrind have created a relaxing, informal atmosphere in the public rooms; after skiing, there is always a pot of soup in the ski room; dinner at 6:30 is candlelit. In summer, the sun porch is one of the most popular breakfast spots in town; there is also a pool and a hot tub. Winter rates are from $45 per person MAP; in summer, it's $55–78 per room EP.

Foxfire Inn (253-4887), Route 100 north of Stowe Village. This early nineteenth-century farmhouse is set on 70 wooded hillside acres. The five guest rooms have wide-board floors (several have exposed beams), furnished with antiques, each with private bath. A two- or three-bedroom cabin and a four-bedroom chalet, all efficiency units with fireplaces, are also available. Downstairs there is plenty of space for guests away from the large, public dining room, well respected for its Italian fare. $75 double per room includes a full breakfast.

The Yodler Motor Inn (253-4836), Box 10. Located at the corner of the Mountain Road and Route 100, the Yodler is a comfortable inn that has been in the same family for long enough to create an effortlessly friendly atmosphere. There are 53 rooms all told, some in the main house that dates from 1797, most in the motel annex in the back, which includes 3 efficiencies. There is a pleasant dining room, brightened with soft pinks and greens, specializing in buffets. There is also a lounge with fireplace, and summer amenities include a pool and tennis court. $36–110 per room, summer; $35–85 per person MAP in winter.

Scandinavia Inn and Chalets (253-8555), Mountain Road. Ed and Jan Griffiths have small children of their own and go out of their way to make other families feel welcome. Their gabled ski lodge has 18 motel-style rooms with bath and color TV; also two suites. In addition, there are three modern, A-frame–style chalets, each with a fireplace and three or more bedrooms, two or more baths. Guests enjoy use of the hot tub, sauna, game room, and outdoor pool. Swedish pancakes with lingonberries are the breakfast specialty. From $48 per room EP; special children's rates.

☞**Logwood Inn & Chalets** (253-7354, 800-426-6697), Edson Hill Road off Route 108. The first Stowe inn built specifically for skiers, this is a fieldstone and log lodge set back from the road amid birches and firs, its window boxes brimming with geraniums and petunias in summer. It's a real find for anyone who is looking for a traditional ski lodge atmosphere. Common rooms include a comfortable living room with a stone hearth, ski room, and game room with table tennis. There are 20 guest rooms, 13 with private bath, two family suites, two sharing a hall bath, two chalets (accommodating eight), and one apartment. The guest rooms have been brightened with country print curtains and quilts and—a plus even in Stowe in summer—have air-conditioning and back balconies and outside stairs down to the pool. In winter dinner is served, and guests gather beforehand for hors d'oeuvres served in front of the fire. In winter, $50–85 per person MAP, ski packages available; in summer, $55–65 per couple.

Timberholm Inn (253-7603), Cottage Club Road, Stowe (off Route 108). A delightful lodge off, but not far off, the beaten path, suited to couples who appreciate the beauty and peace of a gracious living room; there is a less formal game room and a total of ten rooms with private baths, also two-bedroom suites, complimentary soup and bread after skiing. BYOB; fall/winter rates including continental breakfast range from $60–90 per room.

Ski Inn (253-4050), Mountain Road, Stowe. Larry and Harriette Heyer has been welcoming guests in their gracious home—one of the handiest places to the lifts—since Pearl Harbor Day. The 10 guest rooms are bright, meticulously clean. There is a pine-paneled BYOB bar and attractive sitting and dining rooms. $40–50 per person MAP in winter; $35–50 per couple B&B in summer.

Fiddler's Green (253-8124), Mountain Road, Stowe. Less than a mile from the lifts, this pleasant, yellow, 1820s farmhouse has guest rooms tucked under the eaves; guests gather around the fieldstone hearth in the living room and the long table off the sunny kitchen. BYOB. In summer, B&B rates $30–56 per room; in winter, optional MAP is $30 (in a dorm) to $50 (with private bath) per person.

Bittersweet Inn (253-7787), Route 100 south, southern fringe of Stowe Village. This eighteenth-century brick farmhouse and converted carriage house is a find. Barbara and Paul Hansel offer seven rooms, including one suite, four with private bath. The house is right on Route 100, but there is a view and sense of space in the back. Space includes a comfortable living room, a game room with BYOB bar, a good-sized swimming pool, a large lawn, and a hot tub. Rates include a substantial continental breakfast with homemade pastries, and there is afternoon tea; hot après-ski soup in winter. $60–125 (for a two-bedroom suite sleeping four).

The Siebeness (800-426-9001 or 253-8942), 2681 Mountain Road. Sue and Nils Anderson are longtime Stowe innkeepers. Rooms are decorated in antiques, $60–90 breakfast included.

BED & BREAKFASTS   **The Inn at the Brass Lantern** (253-2229), Route 100 (where Charda's used to be), is a sparkling new guest house run by Mindy and Andy Aldrich, with nine (nonsmoking) rooms, comfortable sitting areas. $50–90 per room.

Some others: **Hadleigh House** (253-7703), three rooms, $55–65; **Raspberry Patch** (253-4145), four rooms, $55–60; **The 1860 House** (253-7351, 800-248-1860), five rooms (nonsmoking), pool, sauna, hot tub, $85–95. **Honeywood Country Lodge** (253-4124, 800-659-6289), twelve rooms and a two-room suite. $72–103 per couple.

MOTELS   **Commodores Inn** (253-7131, 800-44-STOWE), Route 100 south. This fairly recent addition to the hospitality scene is the work of longtime Stowe residents Bruce and Wendy Nourjian, both of whom are usually around to meet and greet guests. The 48 identical rooms are large (request one on the back, overlooking the lake), and there's a living room with fireplace, also two Jacuzzis and saunas and an outdoor pool.

The Stowe Yacht Club Steakhouse and Sport Lounge (a popular watering hole and spot for an evening burger) overlooks a three-acre lake on which model sailboat races are regularly held. Rates from $68 ($48 single) to $168 (double, MAP during Christmas week) include continental breakfast; special packages available.

Buccaneer (253-4772, 800-543-1293), Mountain Road. This is the former home of Olympian Billy Kidd. Twelve rooms, a condo, and a house all with TV, a small fridge, and coffee machine. Amenities include a hot tub, game room, a lounge with fireplace, ping-pong, and pool tables. $35–50 per person, including breakfast.

Die Alpenrose (253-7277, 800-962-7002), Mountain Road. A pleasant, small motel with just seven units, each with in-room coffee and fridge. $40–50 per room.

EFFICIENCY UNITS AND CONDOMINIUMS   More than two dozen Stowe properties include efficiency units. Here we list just a few outstanding options that are not attached to motels or inns.

And check these agencies: **All Seasons Rentals** (253-9872, 800-444-

7353), 35 condos, 40 houses; **Evans Realty** (253-8484), 50 condos, 60 houses; **Rentals at Stowe** (253-9786), 50 condos, 60 houses; **Sullivan Real Estate** (253-8132), 100 condos, 40 houses.

The Village Green at Stowe (253-9705; 800-451-3297). Seven nicely designed buildings set on 40 acres (surrounded by the Stowe Country Club links) contain 67 two- and three-bedroom town houses, all nicely, brightly furnished. A recreation building houses a heated indoor pool, Jacuzzi, sauna, game and changing room; there is also an outdoor pool and two tennis courts. Summer and fall rates begin at $140 per unit.

Stonybrook (253-9701), PO Box 311. Attractive condominium clusters are spread over 105 acres, with another 63 acres zoned forever as farmland. Units have two to four bedrooms; two bedrooms begin at $800 per week in summer, $1,200 per week in winter.

Kelly's Keep (253-9427), Mountain Road. Sequestered in the pines by Notch Brook, off the Mountain Road just a mile from the lifts, this is a unique complex splendidly built in the 1930s by a woman doctor; it contains five spacious apartments, each paneled, nicely decorated, equipped with hearths and sleeping from 4 to 14 people. Rates begin at $75.

Notch Brook (253-4882), off Route 108, RR 2, Box 1910, Stowe 05672. Sited in the shadow of Spruce Park with a spectacular view of Mansfield, an unusually well built (although why Vermont's premier architect, Robert Burley, designed them with flat roofs, no one seems to know) condominium complex of 50 units ranging from double rooms through three-bedroom town houses, most available by the day and week. Facilities include daily maid service, saunas, tennis, a pool, and winter shuttle service to the lifts; there is also a complimentary continental breakfast. Rates $60–260 for cabins built in 1836.

STATE SKI DORM AND HOSTEL   (253-4010) on the Mountain Road. Owned by the state's Department of Forests and Parks, this is the nearest lodging to the slopes, well built by the Civilian Conservation Corps in the 1930s. $24 MAP in winter, $6 per day in summer with AYH pass.

DINING OUT   **Edson Hill Manor** (253-7371), 1500 Edson Hill Road. Under new owners Eric and Jane Lande, the gracious (smoke-free) dining room at this low-key resort has quickly soared to the top of local restaurant ratings. The menu is traditional: grilled game hen or rack of lamb, pan-fried Vermont trout, sautéed salmon, and salmon sausage. You might want to start with oyster stew with spinach and sherry and finish with pumpkin cheesecake. Entrées run $16–21, appetizers, $4–8 and desserts $4–5. In winter dinner can be combined with a sleigh ride for two.

Isle de France (253-7751), Mountain Road. This is a classic French restaurant in the grand manner created by chef-owner Jean Lavina from New York's French Shack. Seated in a formal dining room worthy of a Ritz Hotel, one savors country pâté or escargots, smoked trout, followed by lobster Newburg, frogs legs, sweetbreads, Dover sole, or Chateaubriand for two. Entrées $14–45. There's also a tasty bar menu for much less. Closed Mondays.

Ten Acres Lodge (253-7638/9576), corner of Luce Hill and Barrows Road. The three small dining rooms in this attractive inn are extremely popular, deservedly so—some say the best in Stowe. The menu may include crabcakes with Dijon sauce or smoked salmon with buckwheat blinis, followed by bass baked in parchment, Texas antelope, or sautéed pheasant with gooseberries and Sauternes. The wine cellar is extensive. Reservations are a must. Smoke-free. Entrées $16–22.

Topnotch (253-8585), Mountain Road. Dinner in the lofty, glass-sided main room could begin with smoked salmon or trout with horseradish cream, or warmed breast of duck in five spices, and proceed to medallions of venison in a potato-peppercorn crust, fillet of beef with three peppercorn marinade, stuffed mushrooms and charon sauce, or grilled loin of lamb. Spa selections, too. Entrées $15.50–21.50.

Seasons at Stowehof Inn (253-9722). Contemporary American nouvelle cuisine in a dramatic, smoke-free setting, featuring Vermont quail, pheasant, lamb, veal, and an array of fine cheeses. Entrées $15–20.

The Yodler (253-4826), junction of Route 100 and the Mountain Road. The dining room is attractive, and if you like buffets, this one is a dandy: roast beef, baked beans, maple-cured ham, turkey with dressing, soup, seafood, beef Burgundy, salads, chicken, casseroles, etc., etc., etc., available every evening, 5:30–9 for $14.50.

Number One Main Street (253-7301), the Green Mountain Inn, open summers and winters and periodically other seasons, features a traditional roast turkey dinner plus seafood, prime rib, veal, chicken, and a Chef's Mixed Double of seafood sampler and a generous slice of roast beef. Entrées $10.95–17.50.

Villa Tragara (244-5288), six miles south of Stowe on Route 100. In this restored 1820 farmhouse, owner-chef Antonino Di Ruocco offers unusual pasta combinations, such as handmade ravioli filled with lobster in a sauce with bay scallops, scallions and saffron, and other specialties, like a filet mignon stuffed with mozzarella and prosciutto in a sauce with pancetta, chestnuts, and Madeira. Open Tuesday–Sunday. $35 five-course dinner by advance reservation, except Saturday; otherwise, under $15 for entrées.

EATING OUT **Restaurant Swisspot** (253-4622), Stowe Village. An old reliable, open from noon until 10 all year; soups, quiche, and fondue lovingly prepared. For lunch, there are tempting burgers with Swiss cheeses and a wide variety of sandwiches as well. Swiss cheese fondue and beef fondue Bourguignon for two are moderately priced; otherwise, inexpensive.

The Austrian Tea Room (253-8511) 10:30–5:30 daily is fully licensed, specializes in hot gluhwein and soups, sandwiches, and Bavarian desserts, served up by dirndl-clad frauleins. This attractive building is a part of the Trapp family complex. The view is spectacular, especially in summer from the terrace.

Stowe-Away Lodge and Restaurant (253-8972), Mountain Road. Imaginative Mexican dishes are the specialty in this snug old Vermont house, including crabmeat enchiladas, quesadillas, also tortillas stuffed with cheese, meat, and vegetables.

The Shed (253-4364), Mountain Road. Open daily for lunch and dinner, the most popular dining spot on the mountain, much expanded from its core eatery with its deep wooden booths, good for a beer or prime ribs. There's now a large, greenhouse-style dining room and an equally large menu that includes salads, tacos, baked onion soup, zucchini boats, barbecued ribs, and, of course, Shedburgers (now $4.40).

Whip Bar & Grill (253-7301), 11:30–9:30. Since recent remodeling, this space has lost a number of whips but nonetheless gained a good deal of charm. In summer, it is brightened by a view of lawns and the pool, and in winter there's a fire in the hearth. There is a blackboard menu, always a choice of grilled meats or fish, a raw bar, and specials ranging from pan-blackened fish to Montreal smoked meat with hot mustard. Dinner specials include marinated oriental black tip shark and fresh Vermont veal with fine herbs and cream. A low-calorie spa menu is available at all meals, and so are seductive desserts like Chocolate Sin.

McCarthy's Restaurant (253-8626), Mountain Road. This is where local people gather for breakfast and lunch; open 6–2 daily. There is a counter, a scattering of booths and tables, and a hefty deli section. The baking is fresh and breakfast is served all day; daily specials.

China Garden Restaurant (253-7756), Baggy Knees Shopping Center, Mountain Road. This Cantonese and Szechuan restaurant has a pleasant atmosphere and a large, reasonably priced menu that ranges from roast pork with bean sprouts to Peking duck. Specialties include hot and sour soup, pepper spareribs, chicken in garlic sauce, and squid with hot peppers.

Gracie's Restaurant (253-8741), Main Street, Stowe Village. A posh, pubby atmosphere in the middle of the village, open from 11:30 to "closing," specializing in seafood and spectacular desserts.

Stubb's Restaurant (253-7110), Route 108 at Edson Hill Road. Lamb, veal, beef, and fresh seafood abound. Dinner daily 6–10.

Whiskers (253-8996), Mountain Road. Steak, seafood, prime rib, and lobsters, served indoors or on an open deck, daily 5–10.

Trattoria La Festa (253-8480), Mountain Road. On the upper reaches of the Mountain Road with terrace dining in summer, a pleasant dining room, and a variety of pastas, chicken, veal, beef, and fish dishes in tomato and wine sauces.

Tanglewood's (244-7855), formerly Golden Horn East, marked from Route 100 north of Waterbury. American country cuisine, including clams casino with Vermont cheddar and bacon, smoked seafood bisque, mixed grill with house sausage. Lunch Tuesday–Saturday 11:30–2, Sunday 12–2; dinner Tuesday–Sunday.

APRÈS SKI   There are reputedly 60 bars in Stowe. For after-dinner dancing there is the **Rusty Nail** (hard rock), **B.K. Clark's** (a different group each week, frequently jazz and blues), and **Sister Kate's**, good for a variety of music and dancing. Look for après ski action at the **Matterhorn,** in the **Butter Tub** at Topnotch, at **Charlie B's**, and at **Mr. Pickwick's Pub**, source of one of Vermont's largest selections of beers (the better to wash down its beef steak and kidney pie).

ENTERTAINMENT   **Stowe Cinema & Projection Room Lounge** (253-4678), at the Stowe Center, Route 108. Standard seats and bar viewing area for first-run films.

Periodic productions by the **Lamoille County Players** at the Hyde Park Opera House.

Stowe Summer Stage (253-4325) at the Playhouse on the Mountain Road offers a series of summer musicals and Broadway favorites.

SELECTIVE SHOPPING   **Shaw's General Store** (253-4040), 207 Main Street. Established in 1895 and still a family business, a source of cheap socks as well as expensive ski togs and Vermont souvenirs.

Stowe Crafts Gallery, Mountain Road near the covered bridge. Outstanding crafts from throughout the country, winnowed from Jean Paul Patnode's many years of experience here. Jean Paul, who also operates the adjacent game shop, once explained to us how he happened to settle in Stowe: "I turned the corner at the light here one day in 1967 and felt like I was stepping into a tub of hot water. You know the nice comfortable feeling you get sometimes?"

Stowe Canoe and Snowshoe Co. (253-7398), River Road, marked from Route 100 in the Lower Village. A small shop showcases the work of this unusual company, producing quality mahogany ribbed canoes and the snowshoes and snowshoe furniture manufactured for many years under the Tubb name.

Exclusively Vermont (253-8776), Mountain Road near the covered footbridge; features wreaths, baskets, candles, soaps, lamps, rugs, patchwork, wooden toys, pottery, pewter, and selected specialty foods from artisans throughout Vermont.

Old Depot Shops, Main Street, Stowe Village, is a small indoor mall with some worthwhile corners, notably Pure Vermont Artistry, Bear Pond Book Shop, Purcell's Country Foods, and Stuffed in Stowe.

The Silver Den (253-8787), Main Street, Stowe. A small family business in a village house offers the largest selection of handcrafted jewelry in these parts.

Stowe Gems (in the village near the Helen Day Art Center). Barry Tricker polishes and sets exquisite stones, many from New England.

Lackey's Variety Store (253-7624), Main Street, Stowe Village, open 8:30–8:30 daily. This is "just a variety store," say its owners of more than 40 years. But it's the only one that's survived in this resort village, and it's an invaluable source of an incredible variety of essentials: nail clippers, india ink, shoe polish, scissors, not to mention patent medicine, artists supplies, and soda in bottles from an old-fashioned water-cooled cooler.

Moriarty's Hats & Sweaters (253-4052), Mountain Road. Many long years ago, Mrs. Moriarty began knitting caps for Stowe skiers, and her distinctive style caught on. It is now widely imitated, but the originals remain a Stowe tradition.

Samara (253-8318), West Branch Shops, Route 108. An exceptional selection of work by Vermont artisans; quilts, soft sculpture, jewelry, wooden toys, batik, stained glass, etc.

Wool and Feathers (near Helen Day), a source of beautifully woven clothing, also wool from local sheep. Other clothing too.

Misty Meadows Herb and Perennial Farm (253-8247), Stagecoach Road, offers potpourris, everlasting wreaths, seasonings and herbs, 9:30–5 daily.

Everything Cows and Country Candies (253-8779), Main Street, has homemade cream and butter fudge and "udder necessities" for cow lovers.

Pagan's House (253-2001), Main Street, features handknit woolens from Newfoundland and the Canadian Maritimes, plus Indian crafts and dolls.

The Fly Rod Shop (253-7346), Route 100, two miles south of Stowe, carries such name brands as Hardy, Marryat, and Cortland as well as its own Diamondback rods, which may be tried out at its casting pool. Rentals and fishing spot brochure.

The Spinning Wheel, Route 100 south. Chain saw artisans turn out an extraordinary array of wooden animals and humans: bears, a giant lobster, a charming piglet ($29). Other prices range from $75 to $750 for a larger-than-life wooden Indian, $4,000 for a moose.

The Notch Store, Route 108, at Smugglers Notch. Open in summer only, a co-op gallery specializing in painting, jewelry, hats, and sweaters.

Also see the **Johnson Woolen Mill** in "North of the Notch"; the short and scenic drive is certainly worth the effort.

Chainsaw art at the Spinning Wheel, Stowe

P. Jennison

ANTIQUES   A score of shops cluster around Stowe, including the **Stowe Antique Center** (253-9875), and, in Waterbury Center, **Sir Richard's Antiques** (244-8879), which has 14 dealers.

SPECIAL EVENTS   Mid-January: **Winter Carnival**—a week of one of the oldest and most gala village winter carnivals in the country: snow sculptures, sled dog races, ski races, public feeds.

Late February: **Stowe Derby**—a 10-mile race from the summit of Mount Mansfield to Stowe Village, usually about 300 entrants.

Easter Festivities: An Easter parade at Spruce Peak, Easter egg hunt.

May: Lamoille County Players present musicals at the Hyde Park Opera House.

July 4: **Stowe Marathon**. Separate festivities in the village of Moscow, too small for its own band, so they parade to the music of radios.

Mid-July: **Ben & Jerry's Hot-Air Balloon Festival**, Stowe Country Club.

Late July: **Stowe Performing Arts Summer Festival**—a week of concerts ranging from chamber to symphony, including bands and choral groups, presented in a number of places. **Lamoille County**

Field Days, a weekend agricultural fair in Morrisville—tractor pulling, crafts, children's rides. **Annual Stowe Craft Show**, three days.

Early August: **Annual antique and classic car rally**—three days.

Mid-August: **Grand Prix Horse Show.**

Late August: Lamoille County Players stage a musical in the Hyde Park Opera House.

September (last weekend): **Stowe Foliage Craft Fair**, Topnotch Field.

October (first weekend): **Stowe Foliage Antique Show and Fair.**

MEDICAL EMERGENCY   Stowe Rescue Squad, Police (911); Waterbury (244-5511); **Copley Hospital** (888-4231), Morrisville.

WATERBURY

"Ben and Jerry's Home Town," as this area is sometimes called, has achieved a friendly, untouristy distinction all its own, with several gastronomic attractions. It's near skiing in Stowe, of course, and in summer the Waterbury Reservoir is a great spot for swimming, boating, fishing, and camping. Once known only as the home of the state mental hospital, Waterbury has since become something of a state government satellite but retains its small town aura.

GUIDANCE   The **Waterbury Tourism Information and Reservation** (244-7466, 800-800-2224) has an information booth with a gazebo motif on Route 100 north, 200 feet from Exit 10 off I-89, at Billings Mobil station, attended during peak travel times.

TO SEE AND DO   **Ben & Jerry's Ice Cream Factory Tours** (244-5641), Route 100, Waterbury. No American ice cream has a story, let alone a taste, to match that totally Vermont-made sweet and creamy stuff concocted by high school buddies Ben Cohen and Jerry Greenfield. Over a decade ago, they began churning out Dastardly Mash and Heath Bar Crunch in a Burlington garage, and now they have outgrown this seemingly mammoth plant that threatens to outstrip the Shelburne Museum as Vermont's number one attraction. A half-hour tour of the plant is offered all year, Monday–Saturday 9–4. The big store, selling an amazing number of things relating to cows and Vermont, is open 9–5, and the Scoop Shop, 9–9 in summer, 9–5 in winter. The tour includes a multi-media show, a tour (from an observation platform) of the production room, and a free sample of one of the 34 "euphoric flavors." The grounds include picnic facilities and some sample black-and-white cows. $1 per head, children free.

Cold Hollow Cider Mill (244-8771, 800-3-APPLES), Route 100, Box 430, is one of New England's largest producers of fresh apple cider; visitors can watch it being pressed and sample the varieties. The retail stores in this big red barn complex stock every conceivable kind of apple jelly, butter, sauces, natural fruit preserves, honey, pancake mixes, pickles, and mustards, plus Vermont books and other gifts. Open daily 8–6, year-round.

Vermont Distillers (224-6255), junctions of Routes 2 and 100 in the Duxtown Industrial Park. This is the smallest distillery of spirits in the United States, producing Mad River Vodka, Mad River Light, Veranda Gin, Veranda Light, and Tamarack Liquer. Tours of the copper-pot still are available weekdays 10–2.

Little River Camping Areas (244-7103), RFD 1, Waterbury 05676. Six miles north of Waterbury on the Waterbury Reservoir: 64 campsites including six lean-tos, campers' swimming, hiking, rental boats, snowmobile trails.

HIKING & OTHER SUMMER SPORTS   There are marked trails up the nearby peaks of Pinnacle Ridge, Hunger Mountain, and Camel's Hump (part of the Long Trail); nine holes of golf at the Blush Hill Country Club, one of the more dramatic sites; swimming at the municipal pool and tennis on the town's four lighted courts.

LODGING   **Thatcher Brook Inn** (244-5911, 800-292-5911 in the US, 800-336-5911 in Canada), Route 100, RD 2, Box 62, Waterbury 05676. Although it sits right on Route 100, this big, handsome mansion manages to convey a real country inn atmosphere. There are 24 guest rooms, furnished comfortably and brightly, some with fireplaces, others with whirlpool baths. The dining room (see *Dining Out*) has established an enviable reputation; there is also Bailey's Fireside Tavern. No smoking allowed in guest rooms and no children under five years. $59–155 per double room B&B.

The Old Stagecoach Inn (244-5056), 18 North Main Street, Waterbury, a gracious 1826 village landmark with Victorian embellishments, has been restored and renovated, with a fireside dining room serving lunch and dinner and breakfast for guests. Room rates range from $35–95 per person B&B, depending on the season; less expensive dorm rooms available. No smoking, pets, or children under 10. Cash or checks preferred.

Holiday Inn (244-7822, 800-HOLIDAY), Exit 10 north, I-89. Outdoor pool, tennis court, sauna; 79 rooms, three suites. Squire's Restaurant, serving three meals. $60–130 per room including continental breakfast.

1836 Cabins (244-8533), Route 100 north, Waterbury Center 05677, are tucked into a pine forest whose logging roads become cross-country ski trails in winter. Completely furnished one- and two-bedroom units with kitchens, TV; telephones on request. Rates $69.50 for two, standard $89.50, deluxe; more over holidays, less off season.

BED & BREAKFASTS   **The Black Locust Inn** (244-7490, 800-366-5592), Route 100 north, an 1832 three-gabled home, renovated and air-conditioned by Anita and George Gajdos, has six rooms with private baths, polished wood floors, stained glass transoms. One twin-bedded room is

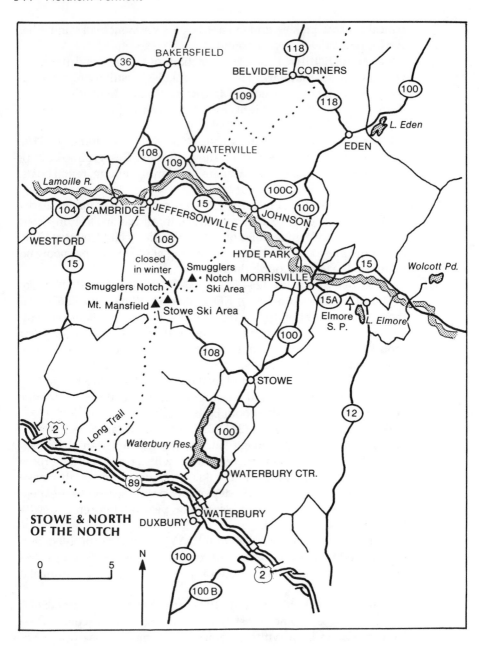

Map labels: BAKERSFIELD, 36, 118, BELVIDERE CORNERS, 109, 100, 118, L. Eden, WATERVILLE, 108, 109, EDEN, Lamoille R., 104, CAMBRIDGE, JEFFERSONVILLE, 15, 100C, 100, JOHNSON, WESTFORD, 15, 108, HYDE PARK, 15, Wolcott Pd., closed in winter, Smugglers Notch Ski Area, MORRISVILLE, Smugglers Notch, 15A, Mt. Mansfield, Stowe Ski Area, Elmore S. P., L. Elmore, 108, 100, Long Trail, STOWE, 2, 12, Waterbury Res., 100, 89, WATERBURY CTR., STOWE & NORTH OF THE NOTCH, DUXBURY, WATERBURY, 0 5, N, 100, 2, 100 B

handicap accessible. The large living rooms are decorated with oriental rugs, lace curtains; game area, books, music, and TV with videos. $59-95 with full breakfast and afternoon refreshments. Weekend and ski packages.

Grünberg Haus (244-7726; 800-800-7760), off Route 100 south, has

11 guest rooms in a secluded Tyrolean-style chalet; sauna, tennis court, and honor-system pub, plus library, greenhouse, warm-weather Jacuzzi. Formerly named the Schneider Haus, it's now run by Chris Sellers and Mark Frohman. Rates $50–80 B&B; "Adventure" packages—soaring, canoeing, skiing, golf, tubing, horseback riding, and bicycling available starting at $39 per person, double occupancy. No smoking, children under six.

The Inn at Blush Hill (244-7529, 800-736-7522), Blush Hill Road, off Route 100 (above the Holiday Inn), began life in 1790. Now operated by Pam and Gary Gosselin, it has six guest rooms and eclectically furnished common rooms, and the country breakfasts are served at an old farmhands' table in the kitchen. There's a spectacular view across the valley and reservoir (good for boating and swimming). Two rooms with private baths, one with fireplace: $55–100 with full breakfast and evening refreshments. Special rates available off season.

DINING OUT   The Inn at Thatcher Brook Falls (244-5911), Route 100, Waterbury. An extensive and ambitious menu includes barbecued Cornish game hen as an appetizer; tournedos with basil, tomato, and linguini, sautéed veal, roast duck with rosemary and thyme with blueberry and Grand Marnier sauce. Dinner nightly: $14.50–22.95.

Tanglewood's (244-7855), Guptil Road, marked from Route 100 north of Waterbury. American country cuisine, including clams casino with Vermont cheddar and bacon, smoked seafood bisque, mixed grill with house sausage, filet mignon with mushrooms and blue cheese butter, and other entrées (under $16). Lunch Tuesday–Saturday 11:30–2, Sunday brunch 11–2; dinner Tuesday–Sunday. Clambakes and other goodies to go; children's menus.

EATING OUT   Crust'n'Cauldron (244-5111), Park Row, Waterbury. Open 6–6 except Saturday when it's 6–2, closed Sunday. This brightly lit, unpretentious place has booths, formica-topped tables, and a counter. Blackboard specials include a variety of omelets, homemade soups, deli, and vegetarian dishes. The owner-chefs make all their own breads as well as pastries and soups, serve jug wine and herb teas.

Three South Cafe (244-8973), 3 South Street, Waterbury. Open weekdays 11:30–midnight; Saturday 5–9. A café atmosphere and nice choice of deli and hot sandwiches, soups, freshly brewed coffee, wine, and beer.

Arvad's Spirits and Light Fare, South Main Street, has ethnic dishes including Caribbean-style conch fritters.

SELECTIVE SHOPPING   Green Mountain Chocolate Company (244-8356), Route 100, north of Waterbury, is where former White House pastry chef Albert Kumin and his family create delectable truffles, fudge, cakes, and cookies. Closed Tuesdays.

Green Mountain Coffee Roasters (244-5621), 33 Coffee Lane.

Sample these now-famous blends at the factory outlet, 6:30–5 PM, Monday–Friday, 9–3 Saturday.

Shimmering Glass Studio (244-8134), Guptil Road off Route 100 north, open 10–6 except Tuesday. Custom-made stained-glass lampshades, fused glass boxes, vases, bowls, stained-glass panels by Susan Bayer-Fishman and other artists.

North of the Notch

Smugglers' Notch, the 2,162-foot-high pass traversed by Vermont's most dramatic road, is not in Stowe but rather in the little-appreciated town of Cambridge. Nestled at the northern foot of Madonna Mountain (a Siamese twin of Stowe's Spruce Peak) is the village of Jeffersonville, a gathering place for artists since the 1930s. Between the Notch and the village, motorists are startled by the unlikely vision of a condominium town rising out of nowhere. This is The Village at Smugglers' Notch, a self-contained resort accommodating some 1,800 people year-round, busiest in the winter when Morse Mountain, rising directly behind the complex, serves as a beginners' area for the three-mountain Smugglers' Notch Ski Area.

Although the highest reaches of Route 108 are closed (between Stowe and Smugglers' Notch Ski Area) from December to May, this area is actually less isolated than you might think, nearer to the Burlington airport than Stowe, also handy to AMTRAK at Essex Junction. Year-round, however, the feeling north of the Notch is totally different from the tourist-trod turf to the south. This is the Lamoille Valley, relatively open, gently rolling farm country beloved by fishermen, canoeists, and those who generally delight in the Vermont landscape, unembellished.

GUIDANCE **Smugglers' Notch Area Chamber of Commerce** (644-2239), Jeffersonville 05464, publishes an area directory and distributes information by mail and phone.

GETTING THERE By plane: See "Burlington Region." Given a 48-hour notice, The Village at Smugglers' Notch provides its own transfer for guests.

By train: AMTRAK stops at Essex Junction, 25 miles away, en route from Washington to Montreal.

GETTING AROUND A car is a must. When the Notch is closed in winter, the route to Stowe via Morrisville is 26 miles, but in summer via Route 108 it is 18 miles.

TO SEE AND DO **Smugglers' Notch.** During the War of 1812, Vermonters hid cattle and other supplies in the Notch prior to smuggling them into Canada to feed the British army—who were fighting the American army at the time. A path through the high pass has existed since

Indian days, but it wasn't until 1910 that the present road was built, which, with its 18 percent grade, is as steep as many ski trails, windier than most. Realizing that drivers are too engrossed with the challenge of the road to admire the wild and wonderful scenery, the state's Forest and Parks Department has thoughtfully provided a turnoff just beyond the height of land. An information booth here is staffed in warm-weather months; this is a restful spot by a mountain brook where you can picnic, even grill hot dogs. The Big Spring is here, and you can ask about hiking distances to the other local landmarks: the Elephant Head, King Rock, the Hunter and His Dog (an outstanding rock formation), Singing Bird, the Smuggler's Cave, Smuggler's Face, and natural reservoir. See *Hiking* in the Stowe section for details about the easy trail to Sterling Pond; also the trail to the Elephant Head.

Mount Mansfield (see the description under the Stowe section). The gondola, Alpine slide, and Toll Road are all within a dozen miles of Jeffersonville.

ART GALLERIES   Mary Bryan Memorial Art Gallery (644-5100), Main Street, Jefffersonville. Early June to late October, open daily 11–5. Built by Alden Bryan in memory of his wife and fellow artist Mary Bryan, this mini-museum has changing exhibits, featuring the works of artists who have worked in Jeffersonville.

Vermont Studio Center (635-2727), Johnson. Over the past eight years, this nonprofit center has absorbed 17 buildings in the village of Johnson. The lecture hall is a former meetinghouse, and the gallery, exhibiting the work of artists-in-residence, is in a former grain mill one street back from Main, down by the river. Some 50 professional artists from throughout the country are usually here at any given time. They come to take advantage of the studio space and the chance to learn from each other through lectures and critiques. Inquire about gallery openings and evening slide shows.

SCENIC DRIVES   Three loop routes are especially appealing from Jeffersonville:

(1) Route 108 through Smugglers' Notch to Stowe Village (18 miles), up the old Stage Coach Road to Hyde Park (be sure to see the old Opera House), and back through Johnson (see *Selective Shopping*).

(2) From Cambridge Junction (just north of Jeffersonville), Route 109 follows the Lamoille River north by a series of five covered bridges to Belvidere Corners; here take Route 118, which soon crosses the Long Trail (see *Hiking*) and continues to the village of Eden. Lake Eden, one mile north on Route 100, is good for swimming and boating; return on Routes 100, 100C, and 15 via Johnson.

(3) From Jeffersonville, drive west to the attractive village of Cambridge, south on Route 15 to Underhill Flats and Jericho—don't miss the photogenic Jericho gristmill, now the Old Red Mill gallery. Either

VTD

Maple Sugaring north of Smugglers Notch

continue through Essex Junction (note the Discovery Museum for children) to Burlington or simply return on Route 128 through Westford, where you can choose between the back road through the covered bridge or the paved highway via Route 104 back to Cambridge.

BICYCLING   Self-guided, inn-to-inn tours are offered by **Sterling Ridge Inn** (800-347-8266) in conjunction with inns in Montgomery and East Craftsbury. Shuttle service available.

CANOEING   The Lamoille River from Jeffersonville to Cambridge is considered good for novices in spring and early summer; two small sets of rapids. **Mannsview Inn** (800-937-MANN) rents canoes and offers shuttle service for groups up to 16. $40 per canoe; weekend packages available.

FISHING   See the Stowe section for description of Lamoille River fishing, boating guide. The stretch between Cambridge and Johnson is reputedly great fly- and spin-fishing for brown trout.

GOLF   **Wolf Run Country Club** (933-4007), Boston Post Road, Route 108, Bakersfield. Vermont's newest, and beautifully situated, course opened its nine holes in 1987.

Enosburg Falls Country Club (933-8951), Enosburg Falls, 9 holes.

HIKING   **Prospect Rock**, Johnson. An easy hike yielding an exceptional view of the Lamoille River Valley and the high mountains to the south. Look for a steel bridge to the Ithiel Falls Camp Meeting Ground. Hike north on the white-blazed Long Trail ¾ of a mile to the summit.

Belvidere Mountain, Ritterbush Pond, and Devil's Gulch. These are basically two stretches of the Long Trail; one heads north (3½-hours round-trip) to the summit of Belvidere Mountain, the other heads south (2¾-hours round-trip) to a rock-filled gulch filled with ferns. Both are described in the Green Mountain Club's *Guide Book to the Long Trail.*

HORSEBACK RIDING   **Cambridge Stables** (644-5568), Jesse Taylor, Box 61, Cambridge 05444. Overnight pack trips with horse, camping gear, and meals provided; also lunch and supper rides. Sleigh rides in winter.

Vermont Horse Park (644-5347/5444), center for the Smugglers' Notch Stables, offers guided trail rides, overnight tours, pony rides for kids, hay and sleigh rides.

LLAMA TREKS   **Northern Vermont Llama Treks** (644-2257), Waterville. Treks depart from the Village at Smugglers' Notch and head into the Mt. Mansfield State Forest. Half-day treks $25, full days $40 per person including a picnic lunch; family rates available.

PICNICKING   There are several outstanding roadside picnic areas:

(1) On Route 108, .2 mile north of the junction with Route 15 at Jeffersonville, there are picnic benches on the bank of the Lamoille.

(2) Route 108 south of Jeffersonville Village on the east side of the highway.

(3) On Route 108 in Smugglers' Notch itself; see Notch description.

(4) On Route 15, just 1.5 miles east of the Cambridge/Johnson line.

SWIMMING   **Brewster River Gorge**, accessible from Route 108 south of Jeffersonville (turn off at the covered bridge).

TENNIS   Courts at **Smugglers' Village**, and a summer program of clinics and daily instruction.

CROSS-COUNTRY SKIING   **Sugarhouse Nordic Center** (644-8851), Smugglers' Village. Narrow trails wind up and down through the trees, then climb meadows away from the resort complex, a total of 23 miles of set trails; rentals, repairs in the warming hut where there is cocoa on the woodstove; guided and night tours, lessons available.

Smugglers' Notch. The stretch of Route 108 that is closed to traffic for snow season is open to cross-country skiers. Guided tours are offered by the Sugarhouse Nordic Center.

DOWNHILL SKIING   **Smugglers' Notch** (644-8851), Jeffersonville. In 1956 a group of local residents organized "Smugglers' Notch Ski Ways" on

Sterling Mountain, a western shoulder of 3,640-foot-high Madonna.

In 1963 a high-powered group headed by IBM board chairman Tom Watson gained a controlling interest and began developing the area as Madonna Mountain, a self-contained, Aspen-style resort. Then, in 1973, it was acquired by Stanley Snider, the contractor whose company (Stanmar) had been building the modular condo units in the village. Today there are 305 units. It is also a major public ski resort, a natural snow bowl with a satisfying variety of terrain: beginners' trails on Morse Mountain (2,250 feet), some world-class trails and glade skiing on Madonna itself, along with intermediate runs that also predominate on Sterling Mountain.

The only way to the summit of Madonna, which commands one of the most spectacular views in New England—from Mount Washington to Mount Mansfield—is a 17-minute ride, the longest (coldest) chair lift in the East, and the way down can be via some of the region's steepest or longest runs. The ideal time to ski this mountain is early March, when it's relatively warm, and midweek, when it's empty. Obviously, this is a place you come, any time of ski season, for a five-day ski week—which automatically includes lessons for all members of the family.

Lifts: four double chair lifts, 2 surface

Trails: 56, including two 3½-mile trails; 41 percent expert, 43 percent intermediate, 16 percent beginner.

Vertical drop: 2,610 feet.

Snow-making: 100 percent on Morse and Sterling, 75 percent on Madonna.

Facilities: Mountain Lodge, base lodge with ski shop, rentals, cafeteria, pub. The reception center/ski shop at Morse Mountain has a Village Center, source of rentals and tickets; the complex also includes a ski shop and deli. Top of the Notch warming hut at the Sterling chair terminal.

Ski school: ATM method, group lessons at Morse and Madonna, beginners at Morse; Star Test to rate your own level of ability.

For children: Day-care for infants; Discovery Ski Camp for 3–6 year olds, all day with hot lunch, and two lessons with mountain games and races. Adventure Ski Camp for 7–12 year olds, all day with hot lunch and two lessons; games and races. Explorer Ski Program for 13–17 year olds, begins 1:15; lesson and evening activities.

Rates: $30 per day adults, $22 per junior (under 12). Kids six and under ski free.

ICE SKATING   **Smugglers' Village** rink (flooded tennis courts) is lighted at night.

RESORT   **Smugglers' Notch Village** (644-8851, US 800-451-8752, Canada 800-356-8679), Smugglers' Notch 05464. More than 300 condominium units in a variety of shapes ranging from town house to multi-story (ask about the newest, nicely designed units with Jacuzzis) can accommodate a total of 1,800 people. Geared to groups (facilities include a conference center) and to families, the resort offers a year-round combination of good things: skiing, swimming (the pool is protected by a heated bubble in winter), tennis, and a varied program of summer activities including a supervised children's activity schedule of fishing, horseback rides, movies, hikes, and games. Summer tennis and other packages are offered. The resort excels at catering to children, with a variety of very distinct facilities and programs geared to different ages. Alice's Wonderland, the nursery for newborns and tots, is particularly impressive, as is the program for teens. In winter, a Club Smugglers' five-day ski week includes lodging, skiing, lessons, use of tennis, pool, and sauna, a dinner out, and other extras from $365 per person, double occupancy; or from $1,095 for a family of four. In summer, a comparable program, including Discovery Camp Programs for youngsters, begins at $699 for a two-child family. Add 12 percent for combined state tax and service charge.

LODGES, INNS, AND BED & BREAKFASTS ☞**Smugglers' Notch Inn** (644-2412), PO Box 286, Jeffersonville 05464. Dating in part from the eighteenth century, a comfortable place that's been gentrified without losing its old-fashioned appeal. The living room retains its tin ceiling as well as its brick fireplace and remains a casual, inviting space with plenty of books and games. The 17 guest rooms all have private baths and country quilts. The low-ceilinged, columned dining room is known for Friday night smorgasboards but also serves breakfast daily and dinner every night but Monday. Virginia and Jeff Morgan are your hosts. $40 single, $55–85 double includes a full country breakfast.

   Sterling Ridge Inn (800-347-8266 or 644-8265), Junction Hill Road, Jeffersonville, two miles east off Route 108. Built in 1988 expressly as a small inn by Craig Kneeland, Sterling has four cheerful bedrooms with private baths and four that share two baths, making it ideal for families or weekend house parties. The lofty sitting/dining room has panoramic views of the mountains. The inn's 80 acres are webbed with 20 km of groomed, Nordic ski trails; mountain bikes and a canoe (with shuttle service) are also available. Full breakfast; lunch and dinner by arrangement. $25–35 per person, depending on the season; five-day ski package from $175 per person, double occupancy. No smoking.

   Mannsview Inn (800-937-MANN, 644-8321), Mountain Road, Jeffersonville 05464. The most popular spot in the house is the solarium, a greens-filled dining area off the open kitchen with a view of the mountains. Kelley and Bette Mann offer canoe trips on the Lamoille (see *Canoeing*). The six guest rooms share three baths. Children over 10 are welcome, and one room has an extra bunk. $50–70 per couple includes breakfast; $159 for two nights includes dinner as well. Ski, cross-country ski, and canoe packages also available.

Three Mountain Lodge (644-5736), Jeffersonville 05464. Built beautifully of cedar logs as a ski hostel for UVM students, this exceptional building is now primarily a restaurant but offers two family-geared rooms and one dorm-style room; shared baths. $45 per couple includes breakfast.

Jefferson House (644-2030), Main Street, Jeffersonville. Three bedrooms in a Victorian village house with original woodwork throughout the home, also a wraparound porch with swings and an upstairs deck. Hosts are Colette and Michael Jurnak. $40 double with complete breakfast.

Red Fox Alpine Lodge (644-8888), Junction Hill Road, off Route 108, Jeffersonville, is a delightfully informal place for families, foursomes, or groups of seniors, with indoor and outdoor recreation, including a swimming pool and hot tub, and a tavern with Franklin stove. There are three basic kinds of rooms, ranging from a standard double to dorm. Meals are usually served cafeteria style. Christopher and Anne-Edith Cameron are the helpful hosts. Flexible accommodations for up to 100 people; no private baths. September–November, $42 per room B&B; in winter, $89 weekend and $169 ski week. Children with parents pay $6, breakfast included. Add 2 percent service.

Windridge Inn (644-5556), Main Street, Jeffersonville. This is primarily a restaurant, but the four upstairs guest rooms are exceptionally nice. There is, however, no common space. $65–85 with full breakfast. Indoor/outdoor tennis available, plus the Cheval D'Or Restaurant (see *Dining Out*).

Kelldarra Bed & Breakfast (644-6575), Box 197, Jeffersonville 05464. A snug, brick 1826 house on the Waterville Road, six miles from Smugglers Notch. You enter through the large country kitchen and find a very attractive library and TV room. Of the four guest rooms, we prefer those upstairs under the eaves; one has a Jacuzzi. $50–70 with breakfast.

The Highlander Motel (644-2725), Route 108, Smugglers' Notch Road, Jeffersonville. There's an innlike atmosphere here, thanks to Tom and Kathy Kontos, who have 15 units, sauna, game room, café, cable TV, pool, and playground. Breakfast available, ski packages $50–64 per couple.

FAMILY FARM VACATION   Berkson Farms (933-2522), Enosburg Falls 05450. A mile north of the village on Route 108, this 600-acre dairy farm welcomes families year-round. The renovated, nicely maintained,130-year-old farmhouse, managed by Dick and Joanne Keesler, can accommodate 8–10 people in four crisp bedrooms, one of which has a private bath. There's a spacious living room and library as well as a comfy family and game room with TV and VCR. But the main attractions, especially for kids, are the cows, ducks, sheep, and goats, and sugaring in season. Cross-country skiing can be enjoyed, along with hay rides, local swimming holes, and golf at the nearby nine-hole Enosburg Falls Country Club. Rates are $45–55 B&B, weekly and children's rates also available.

DINING OUT   Le Cheval d'Or (644-5556), at the Windridge Inn, Jeffersonville. Master chef Ives Labbe has created a country French gourmet oasis here. He combines Vermont ham in a campagnarde terrine, for example, as an appetizer. Your entrée might be locally raised rabbit in a mustard sauce or two quails pan roasted and served with red cabbage braised with maple syrup. Prix fixe: $34 or à la carte with entrées from $19–26.

Smugglers' Notch Inn (644-2412), Jeffersonville. A large, old-fashioned, and appealing dining room, tin-roofed and decorated with paintings by patrons past; dinner nightly, locally esteemed for its Friday night buffet. An upscaled menu now includes escargots, veal Parmesan, Chef's Drunken Chicken (breast stuffed with Vermont cheddar and apples, baked with sherry), Steak au Poivre with cognac cream sauce. Entrées $10.95–16.95.

Three Mountain Inn (644-5736), Route 108, Jeffersonville. Open year-round, daily from 4 PM. The dining room of this log lodge is exceptionally attractive, with a large hearth and quilted tablecloths. Fish specials like grilled tuna with salad greens ($9.95), light fare, children's menu, music on weekends. Rack of lamb is $18.95, and veal Ste. Piere (with lobster meat in a tarragon cream sauce) is $17.95.

Stewart Hill (644-5525), Route 108 between the village and Smugglers'. Open for dinner only. The atmosphere is convivial and informal, and the specialties, Swiss. Also heart-healthy meals. Moderate.

Crown & Anchor (644-2900), Smugglers' Village. Housed in a New England–style house, one of the first structures built in the condo village, this is the most formal place to eat in town. The atmosphere is upscale English pub. Moderate.

The Somerset Inn (933-7771), Enosburg. A former flop house, newly revitalized as a restaurant serving lunch and dinner, so new it wasn't as yet open when we came through. We appreciate readers' reports.

EATING OUT   Windridge Bakery & Café (644-8207), Jeffersonville. A dry goods store until it became one of New England's outstanding bakeries and coffee shops; its baked goods were once distributed throughout the region but are now just available on a walk-in basis; open for breakfast at 8, serving until 4 PM. Ives and Carol Labbe of the Cheval D'Or now run it, and the menu is inspired: pasta salad, lamb stew, great chicken soup, daily specials.

☞**Persico's Plum & Main** (635-7596), Main Street, Johnson. Open 6 AM–8 PM weekdays, until 3 Saturday, 8–1 Sunday. Culinary Institute of America graduate Pat Persico could be writing his own ticket in Stowe, but this Johnson native would rather serve local folks along with the stray skier and leaf peeper. The breakfast specials might include apple cinnamon griddle cakes with home fries and syrup, and a bacon, cheddar, and onion omelet. The lunch menu covers the basics (a hot dog is $1.30 and a plain hamburger, $1.85) but the ingredients are fresh and the soup homemade. Dinner specials might include veal MacIntosh with apples, wine, and cream or broiled fresh lobster with steamed mussels ($12.95). Brunch specials might include fresh peach fritters with bacon and home fries or chicken puff pastry with a poached egg and fresh melon. The decor has changed little since the restaurant's previous life as the Johnson Diner. At this writing, a move downstreet is planned, perhaps because of the neighboring church, which precludes serving liquor.

Café Banditos (644-8884), Route 108, Jeffersonville, across from the Village at Smugglers' Notch. A spacious old house offers yet another family- and skier-geared dining option: "Ver-mex." Burgers, ribs, and homemade soups augment tacos, fajitas, and enchiladas. Children's menu.

Jana's Cupboard (644-5454), Jeffersonville. Open from 6 AM through dinner at the junction of Routes 15 and 109, a road stop with surprising quality homemade soups, salads, pies, country breakfasts with fresh rolls; takeout specials.

SELECTIVE SHOPPING   Johnson Woolen Mills (635-2271), Johnson 05656. Open year-round, except Sunday, 8–5; Saturday 9–4. Although wool is no longer manufactured in this picturesque mill, the fine line of clothing for which Johnson Woolen Mills has long been known is made on the premises. Dill Barrows, owner of the business that has been in his family since 1905, blames Vermont's strict environmental laws for the demise of his—and other—mills. This mill's label can still be found in sports shops throughout the country, and its famous, heavy green wool workpants, long a uniform of Vermont farmers, are especially popular in Alaska. Although there are few discounts at the factory store, the selection of wool jackets and pants—for men, women, and children—is exceptional. The mail-order catalog is filled with sweaters, wool ties, hunters jackets, blankets, and other staples available in the shop.

Vermont Rug Makers (635-2434), Route 100C, Johnson. Judy Paulette creates handwoven rugs in original designs and vibrant colors that have to be seen to be believed. The inventory in her small house (just beyond the Powerhouse Covered Bridge) is usually between 130 and 200 rugs, but many visitors leave having placed an order for custom-made combinations. No two rugs are alike, and while most seem more suitable as wall hangings than floor covers, all are machine washable, reportedly durable. They begin at $50.

Cambridge Herbary (644-2480), Box 84B, Jeffersonville 05464. Opens in May for the summer, 8:30–5, posted from Route 15 just east of Cambridge Village. Vermont native Sally Bevins minds her back road garden and shop, selling 88 different kinds of herbs in one shape or another, some woven into unusually beautiful dried wreaths or mashed into potpourri or perfumes; teas, vinegars, books on herbs, and herb gardening also sold.

Brewster River Mill (644-2987), Mill Street (Route 108), Jeffersonville. Open Memorial Day through fall foliage, daily. This distinctive, three-story plus cupola gristmill has been rebuilt by local welder David Albright. Using local lumber and an old barn from his father-in-law's farm, Albright and his family pegged the post-and-beam structure together, then installed a 1922 steam engine. The wares are stone-ground flour and meal, locally made syrup, honey and jams, and things locally crafted.

Smugglers' Creations Quilt Shop (644-5075), Route 108, Notch Road, Jeffersonville, has some 200 quilts on hand, created and sewn on the spot. The range of colors, designs, and prices is unbeatable. Catalog available on request.

Sculpture by David Stromeyer (933-2518), Enosburg Falls. Monumental, abstract, brightly painted steel pieces sited on the artist's 200-acre farm in the Cold Hollow Mountains. Visitors by appointment only.

Smugglers' Forge Craft Gallery (644-2054), Jeffersonville. Crafted items and antiques sold in a house on Route 108 between the village of Jeffersonville and the Notch.

Arthur's Department Store (888-3125), Morrisville. Arthur, Theresa, and their daughter Adrienne Breault do their buying in New York and Boston and have created an unexpectedly fine and friendly source of clothing and footware for men, women, juniors, and children. The Cellar Shop offers genuine bargains.

SPECIAL EVENTS **Lamoille County Players** (888-4507), call for summer schedule of productions.

Marchfest: Four weeks of special events in mid-March—Nordic, Alpine races, broomball tournaments, crafts shows, folk dances, snow sculpture, fireworks, ball—all at Smugglers' Village.

September: **Labor Day Festivities** in Cambridge—barbecue on the Green, flea market. Family road run (3.1 miles) from Jeffersonville to Cambridge along back roads.

MEDICAL EMERGENCY Jeffersonville, Johnson (635-7511); **Cambridge Regional Health Center** (644-5114); Cambridge Rescue (911).

The Northeast Kingdom

"You know, this is such beautiful country up here. It ought to be called the Northeast Kingdom of Vermont."

It was in 1949 that Senator George Aiken made this remark to a group in Lyndonville. Since then, word has slowly gotten around that that's what Vermont's three northeastern counties—Orleans, Caledonia, and Essex—should be calling themselves. This is, after all, a world unto itself, a last frontier: the state's most rural and lake-spotted corner, encompassing nearly 2,000 square miles. There are a few dramatic elevations such as Jay Peak on its northwestern fringe and Burke Mountain at its heart, but generally this is an open, glacially carved land of humped hills and rolling farmland, also some lonely lumbering country along the northern reaches of the Connecticut River. Neither of the ski areas draw patrons enough to change the look of the surrounding landscape. In the days of trains, there were many more summer hotels than there are now. Yet you can still stay in an unexpected range of places—from elegant country inns and full resorts through ski lodges, condominiums, and summer cottages to working farms. And all the amenities are here: golf, tennis, and horseback riding as well as hiking, fishing, canoeing, and, of course, skiing. But they may take some searching out, and in the process, you may stumble across some people and places of memorable beauty.

ST. JOHNSBURY AND BURKE MOUNTAIN AREA

St. Johnsbury is the largest community in the Northeast Kingdom. Thanks to the Fairbanks family, who began manufacturing their world-famous scale here in the 1830s, it is graced with an outstanding museum of natural and local history and a handsome Athenaeum. The general late nineteenth-century affluence that St. J (as it is affectionately known) enjoyed as an active rail junction and industrial center has been commemorated in ornate brick along Railroad Street and sloping Eastern Avenue, and in the fine mansions along Main

Street, set high above the commercial downtown. In the 1960s, when Fairbanks became a division of a conglomerate—which threatened to move the scaleworks south—townspeople themselves raised the money to subsidize a new plant. Which is all to say that this is a spirited town boasting the oldest town band in the country, a busy calendar of concerts, lectures, and plays, and all the shops and services needed by the inhabitants of the picturesque villages along the Connecticut River to the south, the rolling hills to the southwest, and the lonely woodlands to the east. Less than a dozen miles north, the wide, main street of Lyndonville is also lined with useful shops. Burke Mountain, a short way up Route 114, is accessible by car as well as by foot in summer and draws skiers from throughout the Northeast in winter.

GUIDANCE   Northeast Kingdom Chamber of Commerce (748-3678), 30 Western Avenue, St. Johnsbury 05819. A seasonal information booth is maintained at the corner of Main Street and Eastern Avenue, a source for lodging, dining, and general information for much of the Northeast Kingdom.

The Lyndon Area Chamber of Commerce (626-9696), PO Box 886, Lyndonville 05851, publishes a leaflet guide to its area and maintains a seasonal information booth on the Common.

GETTING THERE   By bus: Greyhound/Vermont Transit from Boston, New York, and Connecticut via White River Junction. Buses stop in Wells River, McIndoe Falls, Barnet, Lyndonville, and St. Johnsbury. There also are buses from Montpelier and St. Johnsbury to Danville, and from Montreal and Sherbrooke.

TO SEE AND DO   The Fairbanks Museum and Planetarium (748-2372), Main and Prospect streets, St. Johnsbury. Open daily, year-round, Monday–Saturday 10–4, Sundays 1–5; in July and August 10–6 on weekdays; admission: $2.50 per adult, $1.25 per child, $6 per family. Planetarium programs: weekends at 2:30 year-round (admission: $1), also in July and August, weekdays at 11 and 2:30.

This is still a wonderfully old-fashioned place. Its main hall, which is capped by a 30-foot-high, barrel-vaulted ceiling, is filled with some 3,000 stuffed animals in old-style glass cases. Ranged along the mezzanine above are treasures collected in the nineteenth century from throughout the world.

"I wish the museum to be the people's school . . . to teach the village the meaning of nature and religion," explained Franklin Fairbanks at the museum's 1890 dedication. There are exhibits from Africa, Oceania, and South America; small jewels like a letter dated "Vailima, June 19, 1891" from Robert Louis Stevenson to Annie Ide, deeding her his birthday because hers fell on Christmas. Stevenson had met the St. Johnsbury girl in Samoa, where her father was serving as US consul. There are also exhibits of local flora and fauna that change

VTD

Historic treasures at the Fairbanks Museum, St. Johnsbury

with the season, and exhibits on aspects of Vermont history. In the upstairs planetarium, which seats just 50 people, you learn about the night sky as it appears in the Northeast Kingdom. It should be noted, too, that the museum is a US weather observation station, and daily forecasts are a popular feature on Vermont Public Radio. There is also a fine little gift shop.

St. Johnsbury Athenaeum (748-8291), Main Street. Open Monday and Wednesday 9–8, closed Sunday, otherwise: 9:30–5. The big attraction is the art gallery in the rear of this fascinating public library. Said to be the oldest unaltered gallery in the country, it has a distinctly nineteenth-century feel. Smaller canvases and sculptures are grouped around the outsized painting, "Domes of Yosemite" by Albert Bierstadt. Natural light through an arched skylight enhances the effect of looking into the Yosemite Valley; this is the setting for chamber music concerts.

Shores Memorial Museum, Lyndon Center. Open Saturdays and Sundays in summer, 2–4. What you notice first is the portrait of Vanila Shores as a young woman. Both the girl's parents followed the poor scholar when she went to Bates College, again when she moved on to Smith College and then Johns Hopkins. Shores' house is now filled with Victorian—hair wreaths and horsehair couches, vintage clothing and old toys, notably tops once made in town and sold around the world.

Waterford Dam at Moore Reservoir. New England Power offers guided tours of the huge complex of turbines. There are also a boat launch and picnic sites here. The approach is from the New Hampshire side of the Connecticut River, just below Lower Waterford, Vermont, off Route 135.

VILLAGES   **Peacham**. High on a ridge overlooking the White Mountains, this is an old and proud village with a library at the four corners, a distinctive old academy building (the academy, alas, is defunct), and a fine historical collection housed in an early nineteenth-century house. Inquire at the town clerk's office about hours. It is a beautiful village, and there is fishing in its pond.

Barnet. An old Scots settlement, the village of Barnet itself is on a curve of the Connecticut River, almost lost today in a curious intertwining of I-91 and Route 5. **Pearson's General Store** marks the middle of town, and there is **Goodwillie House** (633-2542), built in 1790 by a Scottish pastor, later serving as a stop on the Underground Railroad, now housing the collections of the Barnet Historical Society. Drive east to Barnet Center to find Harvey's Lake (good for both fishing and swimming) and the **Karme-Choling Buddhist Meditation Center** (633-2384), a Tibetan Buddhist meditation center formerly known as the "Tail of the Tiger," one among a number of such houses established in the United States and Canada by Trungpa Rinpoche. From the road, this appears to be a traditional white farmhouse with red trim and a big barn but with a bright banner billowing in the wind. Inside, the house has been dramatically altered to let in the sun and a sense of the surroundings, to create a Tibetan-style temple and housing for guests who are welcome to stay overnight, for a "weekthun" or a "dathun" (month) of learning to meditate; solitary retreats can also be arranged, and drop-in visitors are welcome. Meditation aids are sold in the barn where meditation pillows are made.

Danville. Until 1855, Danville was the shire town of Caledonia County. It is an exceptionally beautiful town set high on a plateau around a large Green complete with bandstand, Civil War monument, and general store. The imposing town hall was built as the county courthouse, and the small, square Caledonia Bank is one of the safest strongholds around, thanks to devices installed when it was last held up in 1935. Danville is known primarily as headquarters for the American Society of Dowsers, who hold their annual convention here each September. In the red **Dowsers' Hall** (684-3417), open weekdays 9–4:30 (occasionally on weekends), you learn that dowsing is the knack for finding water through the use of a forked stick, a pair of angle rods, or a pendulum. Dowsing equipment and a wide selection of books are sold here. The American Society of Dowsers boasts 2,600 members in 27 countries. The owner of the **Danville Morgan Horse Farm** (684-2251) provides tours and enjoys talking about the breed. Call ahead.

West Danville is a crossroads (Routes 15 and 2) village. Hastings Store is a great, old-fashioned general store cum post office, and one of the world's smallest libraries sits across the road on Joe's Pond. There is a public beach with picnic and sanitary facilities here. The water from Joe's Pond (an old summer resort) is said to empty, eventually, into Long Island Sound, while that from Molly's Pond (a mile south, named for Joe's squaw) is said to wind up in the Gulf of St. Lawrence.

Cabot. Known during the War of 1812 for its distilleries (the whiskey was sold to the Canadians), this distinctly upcountry village is now famed for its cheese. **The Cabot Farmers Co-op Creamery** is Vermont's major producer, and its visitors center is a popular attraction (see *Selective Shopping*).

Lyndonville. A substantial old community that serves as a shopping center for smaller villages to the north. Since 1896, it's been the site of the Caledonia County Fair, and it's the home of Lyndon State College (1,000 students) and of Bag Balm (see *Selective Shopping*).

East Burke. A small village with a beautiful library and historical society building (The Old Museum, 626-9823, open June–October, Wednesday and Saturday afternoons, also by appointment), some attractive shops, and restaurants geared to skiers at Burke Mountain.

SUGARHOUSES   Rowell Sugarhouse (563-2756), Route 15, Walden. Visitors welcome year-round; maple cream and candy as well as sugar, also Vermont honey and sheepskins sold.

David and Myra Houston (223-7307), West Hill in Cabot; 250–500

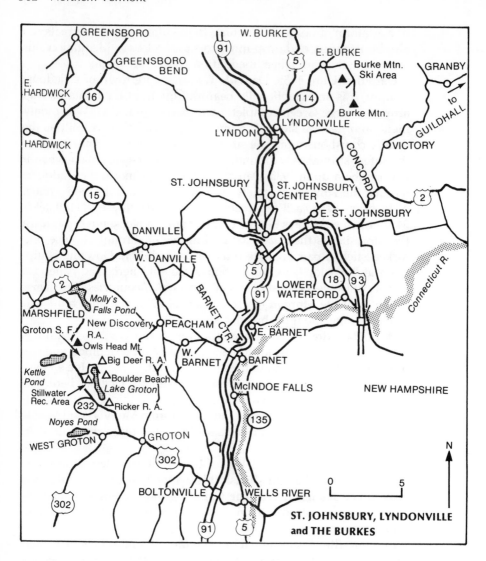

taps, buckets, gathered with oxen; up to 10 visitors at a time welcome during boiling off.

Tamarlane Farm (626-3265), Pudding Hill, Lyndonville. A family farm that prides itself on the quality of its syrup.

Maple Grove Maple Museum (748-5141), St. Johnsbury. May 30–late October; guided tours are offered daily 8–4:30 of "the world's largest maple candy factory." In business since 1904, this is an old-fashioned factory in which maple candy is made from molds. A film in the adjacent museum depicts maple production and displays tools of the trade.

       Goodrich's Sugarhouse (563-9917), just off Route 2 by Molly's Pond in East Cabot. A family tradition for seven generations, open to visitors March through December with a full line of award-winning maple products.

COVERED BRIDGES   All five within northern Caledonia County are in Lyndonville—one 120-foot, 1865 bridge across the Passumpsic, three miles north of town off Route 114, and one next to the Lynburke Motel, a genuine 1869 bridge moved from its original site; two others are in Lyndon Corner (one dating from 1879, the other from 1881, both west off Route 5), the fifth, in Lyndon Center on Route 122.

PARKS AND FORESTS   Groton State Forest, Marshfield 05658. A 25,623-acre preserve with four separate campgrounds, a beach area, yet another area for fly-fishing, and one for group camping. Access to all is from the "Marshfield-Groton Highway," Route 232.

       New Discovery Campground (584-3820). A total of 47 campsites, 14 of them lean-tos, beach privileges, hiking trails, primitive camping.

       Stillwater Campground (584-3822). On the west side of Lake Groton, a total of 63 tent sites, 16 lean-tos. Campers' beach and boat launch; rental boats, dump station.

       Ricker Pond Campground (584-3821). A total of 33 campsites, 22 lean-tos. On the south side of Ricker Pond; campers beach, rental boats, nature trail, dump station.

       Seyon Fly Fishing Area (584-3829). On Noyes Pond. Trout fishing with flies only from boats rented at the site.

       Kettle Pond (584-3820). On the south side of Kettle Pond; walk-in fishing, group camping, hiking, and snowmobiling.

       Boulder Beach Day Use Area (584-3820). A public beach, picnic area, snack bar, bathhouse.

       Victory Basin, alias Victory Bog. A 4,970-acre preserve administered by the Vermont Fish and Game Department, purchased in 1969 from the New England Power Company. It includes a 25-acre boreal bog with rare plant life, a total of 1,800 acres of wetlands, 1,084 acres of hardwoods, 71 acres of clearings and old fields. The dirt road access is via Victory; there are three parking areas: Mitchell's Landing, Lee Hill, and Damons Crossing.

SCENIC DRIVE   Burke Mountain. A 2½-mile auto road to the summit of Burke Mountain (3,267 feet) commands a sweeping view of the North Country; picnic areas are provided half-way and at the summit. Formerly the 10,000-acre Darling State Forest, donated to the state in 1933, the road was constructed by the Civilian Conservation Corps. The toll road ($2 per car, $1 per motorcycle) and campsites in the Sugar House Campground are open May 25–October 15.

       The Darling Hill Road from Route 114 in East Burke, five miles south to Route 114 in Lyndonville, follows a ridge past old homesteads, offers great views.

BIKE RENTALS　East Burke Sports (626-3215), behind Bailey's Store in East Burke Village, rents mountain bikes. So does **Richard Scheiber** (563-2252) on the South Walden Road in Cabot.

BOAT RENTALS　Injunjoe Motor Court (684-3430), West Danville; **Harvey's Lake Campground** (633-2213), West Barnet; **Village Sport Shop** (626-8448), Lyndonville.

**CANOEING　**This is canoeing country: down the Connecticut River itself and along the Moose River in Victory Basin. For rentals, check with the outlets listed under *Boat Rentals*.

　　　　Inwood Manor (633-4047), in East Barnet, not only rents canoes but offers shuttle service and inn-to-inn expeditions; meals, lodging, and shuttles included.

**FISHING　**See the pamphlet "Vermont Guide to Fishing" (available from the Vermont Fish and Game Department in Montpelier) for details about which fish are available where. Check the state highway map for local access points.

GOLF　St. Johnsbury Country Club (748-9894), open daily mid-May to October, nine holes.

HEALTH CLUB　St. Johnsbury Academy Field House (748-8683) has a pool, track, weight room with Nautilus and free weights, and three courts. These are open to the public at certain hours. Call ahead for times and rates.

LLAMA PACK TRIPS　Windy Hill Farm (584-3198), TR 37, Box 71 A, Groton 05046, sponsors llama expeditions—walking tours, day-trips, over-nights—from May 1 to October 31, through the Groton State Park and to other destinations. Rates: $45 per adult and children over 12 half-day, $70 full day; children under 12, free.

HORSEBACK RIDING　Sunny Brook Farm (467-3380), West Burke. Year-round instruction, summer horsemanship camp for girls.

　　　　Greenhope Farm (533-7772) in Walden also offers trail rides for experienced riders.

SWIMMING　Harvey's Lake in West Barnet; **Miles Pond** in Concord; public beaches in Groton State Forest; small beach at **Ticklenaked Pond** in Boltonville; **Joe's Pond** in West Danville; **Molly's Falls Pond** in Marshfield; public pools in St. Johnsbury and in **Powers Park** in Lyndonville.

CROSS-COUNTRY SKIING　Burke Mountain Ski Touring Center (626-8338), East Burke. Dashney Farm serves as a center with rentals, lessons, guided tours; 50 km of tracked trails at elevations between 1,100 and 2,200 feet.

　　　　Rabbit Hill Inn (748-5168), Lower Waterford. A total of 10 km of trails with views of the Connecticut River Valley; elevation between 900 and 1,900 feet. No rentals or instruction.

　　　　Groton State Forest. Snowed-over roads, good for 20 km of cross-country skiing.

DOWNHILL SKIING **Burke Mountain** (626-3305, reservations: 800-541-5480), East Burke 05832. The first ski trails on this majestic mountain were cut in the 1930s when it became a state park. In 1955, a Poma lift was installed to the summit, and a shelter and parking lot were opened. Long known as the "Vermonter's Mountain," it caters to local patrons, also to Canadians and Bostonians (Boston is less than four hours away via I-93). Bernd and Karin Schaefers, who took over the ski area in 1991, are making further improvements, with an eye toward giving it a flavor of their native Bavaria.

Lifts: one quad chair lift, one double chair lift, two Poma lifts, 1 J-bar.

Trails and slopes: 30 trails and three wide-open slopes, 20 percent novice, 20 percent advanced, the remainder intermediate.

Vertical drop: 2,000 feet.

Snow-making: 32 acres.

Facilities: Sherburne Base Lodge includes a glass-walled restaurant, as well as a cafeteria, both serving Bavarian specialties and beer. Another base lodge serves the upper portion of the mountain school, "Home of the carved turn," private and group lessons.

For children: a nursery for the four-month- to seven-year-old crowd; SKIwee, a supervised program for children aged 7–14. Burke Mountain Academy, a prep school for aspiring racers, claims to have developed more competitors for the U.S. Ski Team than any other American program.

Rates: $30 per adult, $20 per child 6–13; children 5 and under and seniors over 65, free; ski weeks and lesson packages.

LODGING **The Northeast Kingdom Chamber of Commerce** (748-3678) is a source of advice, and in foliage season, it does an outstanding job of finding beds, many of them in private homes, for stranded leaf peepers. Plan ahead for reservations.

INNS **The Old Cutter Inn** (626-5152), East Burke 05832. This is an 1845 farmhouse that has been an inn since 1969, with nine rooms, five with private bath, and a two-bedroom apartment next to the barn. A spotless, cozy inn with an excellent dining room, open to the public every night but Wednesday (when it still serves guests); fireside après ski in the cocktail lounge; heated swimming pool. Rates $48–60 double occupancy, $8 per extra person in room; $80–100 per person MAP for two days; multi-day packages; cheaper off season. Closed April and November. Pets are welcome with advance notice.

☞**The Wildflower Inn** (626-8310), Star Route, Lyndonville 05851. This is a fine old farmhouse set high on a ridge with a spectacular view, surrounded by its own 500 acres and famous for its sleigh rides. Four of the rooms are large, airy spaces upstairs in the house, sharing two baths. Eleven more have been fitted into the former carriage barn, and some of these have lofts with bunk beds (ideal for children). There are also a number of housekeeping "suites," plus the

School House—a honeymoon cottage—complete with whirlpool bath. Jim and Mary O'Reilly have five young children, and other children are particularly welcome here. There are plenty of animals—chickens, peacocks, a donkey, pony, kittens, and a dog. There is also a special children's corner, stocked with dress-up clothes and toys. The inn also offers some great adult spaces—an attractive parlor and library, stocked with games and the kind of books you really want to read. The landscaped pool commands a spectacular view of rolling hills. Dinner is a multi-course event (see *Dining Out*), but for families with children, there's the option of eating early with food on plates the moment they sit down. Breakfast is a three-course production, and tea is also served. $65–130 per couple, including breakfast and tea, more during foliage season; $5 for children 6–11; 10 percent service charge added.

Rabbit Hill Inn (748-5168; 800-76-BUNNY), Route 18, Lower Waterford 05848. John and Maureen Magee have injected new verve into this pillared landmark, an inn since 1834. All 20 rooms have their own private bath, all but two have views of the mountains, and five have working fireplaces. Each has been painstakingly furnished, complete with a "room diary." Summer swimming and fishing in a freshwater pond; winter cross-country skiing. $139–189 per couple, five-course, candlelit dinner included. Less off season.

Inwood Manor (633-4047), East Barnet 05821. This unusual looking inn once lodged workers of "the world's largest croquet factory." To find it, you turn east in East Barnet onto the Lower Waterford Road bridge, then north onto a plateau, from which the inn overlooks the Passumpsic. Peter Embarto is the friendly, longtime host. Dinner, served around a long, candlelit table, has the feel of a private party. Amenities include a large, swimmable trout pond. The inn sponsors canoeing excursions that can last for a day, a weekend, or five days. $45 single, $65 double includes breakfast. Dinner ($19.50) by reservation only.

OTHER LODGING   **Burke Green Guest House** (467-3472), East Burke 05832. An 1840 farmhouse with one twin-bedded and one double-bedded (an heirloom four-poster) room, and a room with four single beds. Guests have access to a family room with fireplace, also to a fridge and (summer) picnicking facilities. $42 double.

Mountain View Creamery (626-9924), Darling Hill Road, East Burke. Like the Wildflower Inn, this restored, landmark brick house on a 400-acre spread is part of the former 7,000-acre Darling estate, built as a working creamery with housing upstairs for the farm hands; seven tastefully decorated rooms with private baths. The quilts are made downstairs by Joan Fadden, who offers quilting courses. $90–120 per room, full country breakfast.

Creamery Inn Bed & Breakfast (563-2819), Cabot, is a Federal-style village home with three guest rooms, one with carefully restored original stenciling. $20–25 per person, including full breakfast and dinner by advance reservation.

Sherryland (684-3354), Danville 05828. A large, nineteenth-century farmhouse located on a pleasant country road about a mile south of the village Green. Five guest rooms are genuinely homelike. No meals; still only $25 double, $20 single, $5 per cot.

Raspberry Patch (684-3971), Peacham Road, Danville, is an 1806 farmhouse where Joan and Allen Vohden have two comfortable rooms for $45, including a "not just muffins" continental breakfast.

Injunjoe Court (864-3430), Route 2, West Danville. A venerable cottage colony overlooking Joe's Pond, open May 1–October 20. Moderately priced cabins with kitchenettes; swimming, boating, fishing.

The Village Inn of East Burke (626-3161), Box 186, East Burke 05832. A friendly bed & breakfast owned by Lorraine and George Willy. The three rooms are large enough to accommodate families, and all have private bath; common space includes a woodstove, books, and games. $38 single, $48.50 per couple includes a light breakfast served in your room.

The Looking Glass Inn (748-3052), RFD 3, Box 199, St. Johnsbury 05819. A brick, nineteenth-century bed & breakfast with antique double beds in all six guest rooms, on Route 18 toward Waterford. $55 per couple includes full breakfast.

Flower Cottage (748-8441), Lower Waterford 05848. Beryl and Eric Charlton never intended to open a bed & breakfast when they bought this rambling 1803 house in picturesque Lower Waterford Village. But then they never intended to sell the neighboring Rabbit Hill Inn either. It's just that someone offered them the right price for the inn and, after a few years, they began to miss hosting travelers. They offer two spacious guest rooms, each with private bath. $55 per couple includes a full breakfast.

Echo Ledge Farm Inn (748-4750), East St. Johnsbury. Fred and Dorothy Herman run this bed & breakfast on Route 2. Six rooms with private baths, on a farm established in 1793. Open year-round, $38–67 per room. Children over 10 welcome. Smoking discouraged.

Ha'Penny Gourmet (592-3310), Peacham (see also *Crafts*). Desi and Kati Kegl-Bognar, proprietors of the unusual Peacham Store, have three cozy bedrooms over it; $25–30 per person with breakfast; Hungarian specialties for dinner by reservation.

CONDOMINIUMS **Burke Mountain Condominiums** (626-3305, 800-541-5480), East Burke 05832. About 90 slopeside units in the rental pool are salted around the ski area's access roads. They range from studios to four-bedroom apartments accommodating 11 persons. All have woodstoves or fireplaces, TV, and trail access; $39 per person per night, two-night weekend ($41 holidays); $27 per person per night, five-night midweek stay.

MOTELS AND CABINS   **Fairbanks Motor Inn** (748-5666), 32 Western Avenue, St. Johnsbury 05819. A 45-suite facility with two double beds, larger and more tastefully furnished than most motels, with balconies overlooking a landscaped pool area. Amenities include room phones and cable TV; a continental breakfast is included in rate of $85 per room.

Mountain View Cabins (684-3814), Danville 05828. Five housekeeping cabins, one open year-round, comfortable and well kept, picnic facilities; $38 per couple.

Lynburke Motel (626-3346), Lyndonville 05851. A friendly motel with all the amenities: color TV, phones, a wax room, pool, restaurant, and lounge; six miles from Burke Mountain. $40 double.

Aime's Motel (748-3194), junction of Routes 2 and 18, East St. Johnsbury. Seventeen units, comfortable rooms with screen porches. Open May 15–October 20. Moderate.

DINING OUT   **The Wildflower Inn** (626-8310), between Lyndonville and East Burke on the Darling Hill Road. George Willy prepares the five-course dinners served in the inn's attractive dining room, one with a view off across rolling hills. Each night he features a particular wine, one that complements the choice of five entrées. Guests are invited to order and then stroll the lovely gardens, savoring the wine while waiting for the first course. On the day we stopped by, the night's menu included a choice of pan-seared ribeye steak, chicken Kiev, fresh broiled haddock. Entrées $10.95–20.00 range.

The Rabbit Hill Inn (748-5168), Route 18 in Lower Waterford. The elegant dining room holds just 11 tables. Both the food and atmosphere are carefully orchestrated here. There's candlelight and crystal, classical guitar and flute, and a choice of prix fixe dinners. On the night we stopped by, you could dine on steak Diane, chicken pesto, veal served with a lemon caper sauce, or swordfish with herb butter. A choice of appetizer or soup, bread, sorbet, salad, dessert, and beverage are included. $25 prix fixe.

Old Cutter Inn (625-5152), East Burke. Owner Fritz Walther prepares a few of his native specialties, like Rahmschnitzel (pork medallions, sautéed in butter with shallots, deglazed with white wine, and finished with fresh mushrooms in a light cream sauce). He is also known for his beef Wellington and veal dishes; there's a Sunday champagne brunch. Closed Wednesdays and in November and April. Entrées $15–20.

Creamery Restaurant (684-3616), Danville. Open Tuesday–Friday for lunch and dinner, and Saturday for dinner. A former creamery nicely converted into a gracious little restaurant that many feel is now the best in the St. J area; there is a blackboard menu featuring homemade soups and salads, pies, and a choice of meat and seafood dishes. Entrées in the $10–16 range.

Aime's (748-3194), junction of Routes 2 and 18, East St. Johnsbury. Open 7:30 AM–8:30 PM. Closed from Thanksgiving to April. A dependable, dining-out kind of place; specialties include pecan pie; children's menus. Aime's styles itself "the healthy food restaurant," prides itself on using fresh certified Angus beef, fresh seafood, sea salt, minimal sugar and salt, no MSG. Entrées under $18.

Tucci's Bistro (748-4778), 43 Eastern Avenue, St. Johnsbury. A photographer's studio in 1908, now a pleasant spot for lunch (Tuesday–Friday) or dinner (Tuesday–Sunday). Timpano is a house specialty, either as an appetizer or light meal. We won't begin to describe it. Try it for yourself. Entrées under $20.

EATING OUT **Rainbow Sweets Bakery and Café** (426-3531), Route 2, Marshfield. Generally open for breakfast and lunch, also for dinner Friday and Saturday. Closed Tuesday. This is a small but outstanding establishment with only five tables and a reputation that extends through much of central and northern Vermont, understandable when you sample the spanakopita, the broccoli quiche, gnocchi (potato pasta with homemade sauce), outstanding pizza, or sinful desserts concocted by William Tecosky, the baker-owner. Imported wines and beers available, along with espresso and herb teas.

The Pub Outback at Bailey's Store, East Burke Village, open daily 11–11. A trendy, appealing place with a variety of dining atmospheres, from the greenhouse to an upstairs gallery; sandwiches, salads, fresh popcorn, and a bar.

Dave's Not Your Average Diner (748-8888), Portland Street, St. Johnsbury. Dave bills this as a gourmet diner. Homemade soups, breads, herb teas, and specials. Open from 8–3.

Miss Lyndonville Diner (626-9890), Lyndonville. Open from 6 in the morning until supper, famed for its strawberry pancakes with whipped cream for breakfast, pie, homemade French toast, and jumbo eggs.

Miss Vermont Diner (748-9751), Memorial Drive, St. Johnsbury. Open from 6 AM through dinner weekdays, from 9 AM Saturday, 7–1 on Sunday. Under same ownership and very similar to the Miss Lyndonville, both are very popular; it's easier to get a seat in off-peak hours.

Danville Restaurant (684-3484), Danville Village. Housed in a village house, open 6 AM–9 PM, a family restaurant good for all three meals at reasonable prices in a friendly atmosphere; both counter and table service, from hamburgers to full course meals, daily specials.

St. Johnsbury Country Club (748-9894), Route 5, north of St. Johnsbury. The attractive clubhouse is open to the public for lunch; a good bet. Closed in winter.

Hilltopper Restaurant (748-7241), 43 Main Street, St. Johnsbury, open daily for breakfast through dinner, located conveniently down the street from the Fairbanks Museum and across the way from the Athenaeum, a good place to come with children.

The Wooden Horse (748-2540), 1 Caledonia Street, St. Johnsbury. Fine for oversized sandwiches and light suppers. Live music on Tuesday and Thursday.

Anthony's Restaurant (748-3613), 50 Railroad Street, St. Johnsbury. A cheerful, satisfying, family-style diner. Open 5:30 AM–9 PM weekdays, from 6 AM on Saturday, 7 AM–9 PM on Sunday. Try the "Woodsman," a memorable hamburger with Vermont cheddar, bacon, lettuce, tomato, and onions.

Eddie's Bakery & Luncheonette (748-3879), 159 Railroad Street, St. Johnsbury. Opens at 6 AM. One egg, any style, with homemade toast and coffee is $1.49. Good selection of homemade soups, sandwiches, and salads.

Lyndonville House of Pizza (626-8137), offers subs and pizzas. The nearby park makes a pleasant picnic spot.

F. Scott's (626-5557), 79 Broad Street, Lyndonville. Good selection of bar food in a nice atmosphere. The only singles scene in Lyndonville.

ENTERTAINMENT   Catamount Film and Arts Company (748-2600), 60 Eastern Avenue, PO Box 324, St. Johnsbury 05819. Established in 1975 as a nonprofit cultural organization serving northern Vermont and New Hampshire, Catamount stages a variety of "showcase events" at sites throughout the region, weekend film screenings at the Catamount Arts Center (the former St. Johnsbury post office), and changing shows in its gallery. Summer productions include performances of Circus Smirkus, participants in a summerlong circus workshop for area youths, aged 10–18.

St. Johnsbury Town Band concerts, weekly all summer at the bandstand in Town Hall Park. Monday 8 PM.

Lyndonville Town Band concerts, every Wednesday in the summer at 8 PM in the park.

Star Theater (748-4900/9511), 18 Eastern Avenue, St. Johnsbury. Cinemas 1-2-3; first-run movies.

Lyndon Corner Grange (748-8829) sponsors dances every Saturday night at the Grange Hall. A three-piece band plays for the over-50 crowd. BYOB, dancing begins at 9 PM. $3 admission, call for reservations.

Leonard's Auction Service (626-5883), Lyndonville. Auctions every Wednesday night, year-round, beginning at 6:30. Locals come by after dinner to read their newspapers and chat, all the while keeping a sharp eye on the block.

SELECTIVE SHOPPING: ANTIQUES   John M. Hale (748-2231), 13 Mill Street, St. Johnsbury, has a warehouse full of antique furniture, "as found" and restored.

BOOKS   **Green Mountain Books & Prints** (626-5051), 100 Broad Street, Lyndonville. A book lover's heaven: new and used books; many new, discounted titles, and a large stock of Vermont books; new and old prints; rare books. Open Monday–Thursday 10–4, Friday 10–6, Saturday 10–1.

Northern Lights Bookshop (748-4463), 79 Railroad Street, St. Johnsbury. A bright, lively bookstore with a creative flair for selecting stock.

CRAFTS   **Stephen Huneck Gallery** (748-5593), RFD 1, St. Johnsbury 05819. To find the home, workshop, and gallery of this increasingly famous folk artist, turn left at Spaulding District Road opposite the Fairbanks Scale factory on Route 2 east and drive a mile and a half; the old farmhouse and attached studios sit on a knoll on the right. Huneck's stylish, carved wooden animals and bold, fanciful furniture, panels, jewelry, and even Christmas tree ornaments are being widely exhibited and shown in the permanent collections of the Smithsonian and other museums.

Birdmen. Twin brothers Henry and Edmund Menard each maintain studios, one in Cabot (birthplace of both) on the back road from the village to Molly's Pond, the second farther down Route 2 in Marshfield. Henry (563-2501), and partner Mark Cote, specialize in exquisite, detailed bird carvings. He welcomes visitors in the house that he built, set in his commercial nursery that includes two acres of lilies (more than 100 varieties), at their best late June through August. Edmund (426-3310), who calls himself "Bird Man II," after the late Chester Nutting, the original Bird Man, produces small, impressively fantailed birds; he carves some 4,000 a year.

The Craft Shop at Molly's Pond, on Route 2, west of West Danville. Open May through December, closed Sundays; otherwise 10:30–5:30 (1–5:30 in winter). One of the state's outstanding little crafts shops, here for 26 years, specializing in original metal jewelry, fine pottery, weavings, blown glass, and prints—especially those by Mary Azarian who lives nearby. Shopkeeper Martha Price knows all the craftspeople personally.

Ha' Penny Gourmet, The Peacham Store (592-3310). Kati and Desi Bognar sell Vermont crafts, hand embroidery from Hungary, rugs from Afghanistan, wall hangings from Africa, locally made quilts, antiques and collectibles, and specialty foods. Gourmet food to take out. Their mail-order catalogue has many unusual items.

GENERAL STORES   **Danville General Store** (684-3691), on the Green, includes a collection of local crafts and foods, such as Clover Hill Farm fudge, Julie Kempton's children's clothes, Partridge Lane Woodworks, Marylyn Magnus' wool rugs. Mail-order catalogue.

Bailey's Country Store (626-3666), Route 114, East Burke. Open 6:30 AM–9 PM weekdays, 8–9 Sundays, closes at 8 in winter. This classic old general store has been nicely fancied up by longtime local residents Jeane and Jerry Bailey. There is now a cigar store Indian on the porch, and the second-floor gallery has been beautifully restored and displays work by local craftsmen. Downstairs are breads, pies, cookies, and coffee cakes baked daily right here, also a gourmet deli featuring cheeses and cold cuts, plus fresh fruits and vegetables and basic staples; a selection of wines, coffees, and teas and a back room full of wicker complete the scene.

GIFTS **Jacob's Ladder**, Route 302 in Boltonville near Wells River. A large, tourist-oriented shop full of New England crafts, baskets, penny candy, and general gift items.

OTHER SHOPPING **Cabot Farmers' Co-op Creamery** (563-2231), Cabot (see also Cabot under *Villages*). In addition to the tour of the plant, there's a great outlet store, featuring every conceivable variety of cheese products in several forms, plus spreads and yogurt, as well as other Vermont products.

Bag Balm, Route 5, Lyndonville. Developed in 1899 as an antiseptic ointment for cattle, Bag Balm proved particularly effective for chapped udders and is still used by Vermont farmers and their wives. In recent years, its campy, old-fashioned green tins began to appear in Madison Avenue pharmacies and ski resort boutiques, at three or four times the price they fetch locally. The factory is an old, red, double-porched building at the southern end of town, and the only sign on it reads "Visitor Information Ahead." Factory tours and sales are discouraged because the company, which turns out some 6,000 tins a day, has only four employees, so visit the Lyndonville Pharmacy, which stocks Bag Balm at realistic prices.

The Dairy Association Co., which also produces a hoof-softener and leather-care product, is owned by John Morris, who inherited the business from his father in 1933.

Maple Grove Maple Museum & Factory (748-5141), Route 2 east of St. Johnsbury (see *Sugarhouses*) is a source of a variety of gourmet maple-related products as well as syrup.

SPECIAL EVENTS February: **Snowflake Festival Winter Carnival**, Lyndonville-Burke. Events include a craft show, snow sculpture, ski races for all ages and abilities, sleigh rides, music, and art.

May: **East Burke: Annual White-Water Canoe Race** on the Passumpsic River, May 1.

June: **Lumberman's Day** at Burke Mountain.

July–October: **Farmers' Market**, Saturdays and Wednesdays 9–noon at the Middle School on Western Avenue.

July: **Strawberry Festival Dinner**, second Thursday at North Congregational Church; **St. J. Burklyn Summer Festival of Vermont Arts and Crafts**, Bandstand Park, Lyndonville. **Stars and Stripes Pageant**, Lyndonville, last weekend, big auction, parade featuring Bread & Puppet Uncle Sam, barbecue. **Hardwick Annual Fiddler's Contest**, also the last weekend.

VTD

Ready for showing, Caledonia County Fair, Lyndonville

August: **Caledonia County Fair,** Lyndonville; fourth weekend, Thursday–Sunday.

September: **Dowsers National Convention** (684-3410), Danville, second week, Tuesday–Sunday.

September–October: **Northeast Kingdom Fall Foliage Festival,** the last week in September or first in October. Six towns take turns hosting visitors; feeding them breakfast, lunch, and dinner; and guiding them to beauty spots and points of interest within their borders. In Walden, the specialty is Christmas wreath making; in Cabot, there is a tour of the cheese factory; in Plainfield, farm tours; in Peacham, sugar-on-snow parties in the hillside sugarhouse; in Barnet, there is usually a ham dinner at the Barnet Center Church, and in Groton, the wind-up **Lumberjack's Ball.** For details, contact the St. J. Chamber of Commerce.

December: **Burklyn Christmas Crafts Fair,** the first weekend. A major gathering of North Country craftspeople and artists in St. J.

MEDICAL EMERGENCY   748-3111. **Northeastern Vermont Regional Hospital** (748-8141), St. Johnsbury. **Lyndon State College Rescue Squad** (626-5053), Lyndonville.

LAKE COUNTRY

The Northeast Kingdom is blessed with some of the most beautiful lakes in Vermont. The largest of these is Memphremagog, stretching more than 30 miles from Newport, Vermont, to Magog, Quebec.

In the heyday of railroad passenger service, large wooden hotels sprang up near the shores of these lakes. In Newport, the 400-room Memphremagog House stood next to the railroad station (a site now filled by the Mobil gas station), Newport House was across the street where the Chittenden Bank now stands, and the New City Hotel stood where the Mini-Mart is now. Guests came by train from Boston and Philadelphia. Lindbergh came with his "Spirit of Saint Louis," and there was a race track and a paddle wheeler.

Newport is, admittedly, a shadow of its Victorian-era photos. The brick library, courthouse, and state building remain, but surviving stores have lost their mansards and towers. The bandstand, hotels, and station are gone, and there is no place to stay on the lake.

Memphremagog (with the stress on the last syllable) has a split personality. The two-thirds of the lake north of the Canadian border is not only French-speaking (although there are English pockets like Georgeville) but more of a resort area. Montreal is just an hour's drive from the French-speaking resort town of Magog, and Sherbrooke, a Canadian metropolis of 100,000, is much nearer—in stark contrast to the American end of the lake, which is literally the end of the road (I-91) from New York and Boston. It remains a delightful refuge for frugal flatlanders, especially for those who like to fish, hike, ride horseback, or generally steep themselves in the beauty of this high, rolling—still pastoral—countryside.

There are a number of smaller but beautiful lakes, notably Lake Willoughby, a long narrow sheet of shimmering water between the rock walls of Mount Pisgah and Mount Hor. It is generally considered the heart of the Northeast Kingdom.

GUIDANCE See *Lakes* for Barton Chamber of Commerce and Lake Willoughby Chamber of Commerce. Also, Nancy Kent runs a reservation service for lakeside cottages (525-6939, 800-NEK-AREA).

Greater Newport Chamber of Commerce (334-7782, FAX 334-8014), the Causeway, Newport 05855, serves much of this area, but a few of the towns and lakes have their own information sources or efficient town clerks, listed with their respective lakes. The Newport office is a friendly walk-in source of information, open daily year-round, shorter hours in winter.

Magog Bureau du Tourisme (819-843-2744), 1032 Principale Ouest,

Magog, Quebec J1X 2B6, Canada, serves the French-speaking shore-line. It's a good source of advice on area restaurants.

GETTING THERE   By bus: Vermont Transit from Canada and most US points; bus stops in Lyndonville, West Burke, Barton, Orleans, and Newport (but call for the latest schedules). Vermont Transit Bus Depot (334-2132), Jimmy Kwik Food Store, Coventry.

By car: Really the only way to get around. Note the link in I-93 that hooks up Lyndon Center, Barton, Orleans, Newport, and Derby Line directly with Boston: four hours to Derby Line.

GETTING AROUND   **Northeast Kingdom Tours** (334-TOUR), 3 Clough Street, Newport 05855, offers personalized bus tours of the region, by reservation, Monday–Wednesday in the summer, daily during foliage season.

TO SEE AND DO   **Bread and Puppet Theater Museum** (525-3031), Glover. Open March–November on Route 122 off Route 16. The internationally known Bread and Puppet Theater troupe lives together in a farmhouse on this back road, displaying the haunting puppet dwarfs, giants, devils, and other fantastic figures of good and evil. The puppets are the artistic expressions of Polish-born Peter Schumann, who lives with his wife Elka in a separate wooden house they built themselves. The vast meadow across the road is the scene of the annual Domestic Resurrection Circus (see *Special Events*), a free extravaganza in which the audience (of thousands) all receive free homemade bread and gibe at the expensive tickets and junk foods that accompany most current entertainment.

The Old Stone House Museum (754-2022), Brownington. Open daily May 15–October 15, 11–5, closed Wednesdays and Thursdays in May, June, September, October. $3.00 adults, $1.00 children. This is the Orleans County Historical Society Museum, housed in a four-story granite building dating back to 1836, built as a dormitory for a rural academy. It resembles the earliest dorms at Middlebury College from which Alexander Twilight, the school's principal and building's architect, graduated in 1823. Although he was dark-skinned, there is some question about whether Twilight was—as Middlebury College claims—the first Black graduate of an American college. There is no question about the beauty of the building and of the historical collections: rooms represent 10 of the 18 towns in Orleans County and also hold eighteenth- and nineteenth-century weapons, tools, paintings, furniture, and decorative arts. Brownington Village itself is a crossroads full of outstanding, early nineteenth-century buildings, the core of a once-proud hill town long since eclipsed by such valley centers as Barton, Orleans, and Newport. There are nineteenth-century gardens behind the Eaton House and a spectacular panorama from the wooden observatory set up in a meadow behind the church. A descriptive walking tour booklet is available.

St. Benoit du Lac (819-564-0027), Austin, Quebec. Open Monday–Saturday 9–11 and 1:15–4. This non-cloistered French Benedictine monastery, founded in 1911, is sited on the west shore of Lake Memphremagog at a fjordlike section. It's a handsome building, and the 60 resident monks welcome visitors for daily mass at 11 AM and vespers at 4:30 PM, at which Gregorian chants are sung. The monastery shop sells Gregorian music records, also apple cider wine, cheese, vestments, and religious articles made by the monks. The easiest route from Newport is via the North Troy border crossing; then through Mansonville, South Bolton, and Austin.

Jay Peak Tramway, for a spectacular overview of this region. See "Jay Peak Area."

LAKES   **Crystal Lake**. Guidance: **Barton Chamber of Commerce** (525-3701), Box 280, Barton 05822. Barton was once a railroad town with six passenger trains a day stopping in summer and depositing guests to fill big hotels in town or to be transported by boat livery to their gingerbread "camps" on Crystal Lake. The hotels are now gone, and the road to many of the cottages along the far shore is so rutted that outboards remain the best way to reach them. This is a beautiful little lake with a clifflike promontory on one side and public beaches at its northern rim. There is golf in nearby Orleans, and the interstate, Route 16, and Route 5 all cross here—making it an excellent pivot from which to explore the entire Northeast Kingdom and an attractive summer spot in which to locate for a week or more. The town of Barton itself packs an astounding number of services into its small downtown (see *Selective Shopping*). The Crystal Lake Falls Historical Association maintains the Pierce House Museum (525-6251) on Water Street, next to the old-fashioned office of the *Barton Chronicle*, an excellent little weekly covering much of Orleans and Essex counties.

Lake Willoughby. Guidance: **Lake Willoughby Chamber of Commerce,** PO Box 416, Barton 05822, publishes a brochure describing lodging options. Five-mile-long Willoughby is one of Vermont's most hauntingly beautiful lakes. Mounts Hor and Pisgah, which rise abruptly from opposite shores, create a fjord-like effect when viewed from the public beach in Westmore at the northern end, or from the southern tip. Mostly undeveloped, Willoughby is surrounded for much of its length by state forest. The view from Willoughby Cliffs is spectacular (see *Hiking*), the water is stocked with salmon and rainbow trout, and there is public boat access. It was a well-known resort area in the days of grand hotels and steamboats. Now it has a limited, loyal following of sailors and windsurfers (there is always a breeze here) and year-round fishermen. Lodging is limited but ranges from campgrounds to a posh new inn, with a choice of cottages in between.

Seymour Lake. This is a fair-sized, pleasant lake with cottages tucked away discreetly in the woods along its shore. There is a public

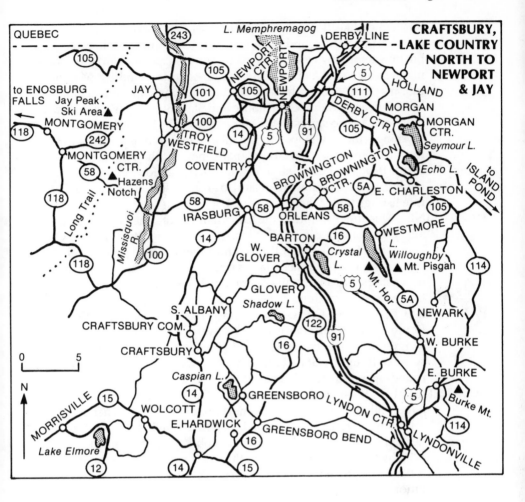

beach in the tiny village of Morgan Center, also the spot to rent boats for fishing for landlocked salmon. In winter, this lake is peppered with fishing shanties, and there is an untracked system of local cross-country trails.

Echo Lake. Much smaller than Seymour Lake and adjoining it on the south, this lake is circled by a dirt road and by gently rolling hills. White Birch Lodge is a small cottage colony with a private beach and boat rentals; guests will be met at the bus or plane in Newport (see *Lakeside Cottages*). There is also public boat access good for trout and landlocked salmon.

Lake Memphremagog. A 32-mile-long stringbean of a lake with only five miles within the United States. Memphremagog stretches north from Newport, a city of 5,500 people, a former logging and rail center that is enjoying a renaissance thanks to enterprising small businesses like Bogner of America, Sel-Bar Weaving (placemats), Newport Furniture, and American Maple Products. Main Street is a bustling shopping center, graced by some substantial gift and clothing stores as well as by its nineteenth-century Goodrich Memorial Library (334-8902), with its historical collections, and a matching red brick Orleans County Courthouse and State Building. From Prospect Hill—where the spires of St. Mary, Star of the Sea, tower above everything—the city slopes to the lake, which actually seems to surround it since the downtown area separates the lake proper from South Bay. The shoreline offers access points for sailing, canoeing, fishing, and swimming; there is also an 18-hole golf course. See separate listings under these categories.

DERBY LINE   This town straddles the Canadian border, the larger part actually possessing a different character and name (Rock Island, Quebec). The **Haskell Free Library and Opera House** on Caswell Avenue, a yellow brick, neo-classic structure with a handsome library downstairs, has an upstairs opera house in which audiences sit in the United States watching a stage in Canada.

PARKS AND FORESTS   **Crystal Lake State Park** (525-6205), Barton. Off Route 16 at the northern rim of Crystal Lake; facilities include a swimming beach, bathhouse, and picnic areas; children's swim lessons. **Willoughby State Forest**, Route 5A. A 7,000-acre preserve surrounding a dramatically beautiful lake (see *Hiking* and *Fishing*).

SCENIC DRIVES   **West Burke to Westmore**. The stretch of Route 5A along Lake Willoughby is one of the most breathtaking anywhere.

Bayley-Hazen Military Road. Begun at Wells River on the Connecticut River in 1776 by General Jacob Bayley, continued in 1778–1779 by General Moses Hazen, this road was a flop as the invasion route it was intended to be, but it served settlers well after the Revolution when it came time to establish towns in this area. Map still available from the Northeastern Vermont Development Association (748-5181), 44 Main Street, St. Johnsbury. The beautiful dirt stretch from Hazen's Notch to Lowell is noted in the "Jay Peak Area;" the next stretch to Albany is now a walking/riding trail. It continues unmarked through Craftsbury and is marked on its way through Greensboro, where a monument commemorates its story, reappearing in the St. Johnsbury area.

Route 105 west of Newport, as far as Richford , a sub-customs port and once an entry for Chinese railroad labor crews. You can return via Routes 118 and 58, but the Hazen Notch section is closed in the winter.

Hinman Settler Road from Derby Center to Brownington (mostly unpaved but good gravel). It's better to start from Derby as there are confusing forks from the other direction. The route terminates in Brownington Village historic district, from which a paved road leads to Orleans and I-91. To find this route, head south on Main Street,

Derby Center (Route 105). Where 105 curves sharply to the east at the lower end of the village, go straight to Brownington. You are rewarded by rolling hills and fields, sweeping vistas.

Holland-Morgan Loop. Take the paved road east from I-91, Derby Line exit. After several miles, the road makes an S-curve through tiny Holland Village and continues to Seymour Lake in Morgan. Here, take Route 111 to Derby Center.

SUGARHOUSES   **American Maple Products** (334-6516), Bluff Road, Newport. Tours offered Monday–Friday 8–11:30, 12:30–4, closed holidays. See a movie about maple production, sample and purchase the products that are distributed through most of the country under the Old Colony, Mrs. Appleyard, and Vermont Tea and Maple brands. A separate building to house historic maple exhibits is being planned.

Spates Maple Orchard (895-4012), Derby Line. Grant and Jeanne have 3,500 taps, use old and new methods.

Couture's Sugarhouse (744-2733), Route 100, Westfield. A modern sugarhouse with a wood-fired evaporator, open to the public whenever boiling. The maple shop at the farmhouse is open year-round.

The Sugarmill Farm (525-3701), Route 16 south of Barton Village. The Auger family have turned their former dairy farm into a combination maple museum, a working maple operation, a dairy parlor, and a gift shop selling local syrup and crafted items. Attractions include a horse-drawn wagon, a covered bridge, a film on sugaring, vintage farm and sugaring tools, and picnic tables. Sugar-on-snow is served in season.

BIKE RENTALS   **Lake Willoughby Bike Rental and Guided Tours** (525-6974), behind the Millbrook Store in Westmore, rents mountain bikes; guides lead visitors over the high, gravel roads around the lake. Mountain bikes can also be rented at the **Snowlines Lodge** (988-2822), Jay Peak.

BOATING   **Cruise Magog** (819-843-8068), Magog, offers summer round-trip lake cruises from the Canadian end to Newport in two, 50-foot steel or aluminum motor cruisers. Aluminum boats (14 feet) with 7½-hp motors, also pontoon and sailboats, may be rented at **Newport Marina** (334-5911), Farrants Point on Lake Memphremagog in Newport. Rental boats are also available from **Bill & Billie's Lodge** (525-6660) on Lake Willoughby, from **Lakeview Cabins** (525-4463) on Crystal Lake, and from **Trade Winds Country Store** (895-2975) on Lake Seymour.

FISHING   This is fine fishing country. The catch is landlocked salmon and brown, brook, lake, and rainbow trout, and you find them in dozens of ponds with boat access as well as in the lakes we describe here. The pamphlet "Vermont Guide to Fishing," prepared by the Vermont Fish and Game Department, available locally and by writing to the Vermont Travel Division in Montpelier, tells it all. For other guides consult *Fishing* under "What's Where." There is a state fish hatchery in Newark; Newark Pond has an access and is good for yellow perch

VTD

The pause that refreshes at Lake Willoughby

as well as trout. Rental boats, bait, and tackle are available at the sites listed under *Boating*. Lake Memphremagog is good for smelts, small-mouth bass, and walleyed pike as well as salmon and trout. Ice fishing is particularly popular on Memphremagog, Willoughby, and Seymour lakes and many of the rivers—notably the Passumpsic, Black, and Clyde rivers—are stocked with trout.

GOLF   **Newport Country Club** (334-7751), off Mt. Vernon Street, overlooking the lake. Eighteen holes, rentals, instruction, restaurant, April–November

   Dufferin Heights Golf Club (819-876-5528), Stanstead, Quebec. Nine holes, cart rentals, restaurant, May–November.

   Orleans Country Club (754-9392), Route 58, near Lake Willoughby, 18 holes, rentals, instruction, restaurant, April through November.

   Barton Golf Course (no phone), Telfer Hill, nine holes, cart rentals, low fees, April–September.

HIKING   **Mount Pisgah and Mount Hor**, Lake Willoughby. Named respectively for the place where the Lord sent Moses to view the Promised Land and for the place Moses's brother Aaron died after the Lord commanded him to go there, these twin mountains, separated by a narrow stretch of lake, form Willoughby Gap. Both are within the

7,000-acre Willoughby State Forest and offer well-maintained hiking trails. Mount Pisgah (2,751 feet) on the east side of the lake (access marked from Route 5A) has fairly short climbs yielding spectacular views of the White Mountains; trails up Mount Hor (2,648 feet) begin on the Civilian Conservation Corps road, 1.8 miles west of its junction with Route 5A, and also offer panoramic views of the Green Mountains to the west. For details, consult *Day Hiker's Guide to Vermont* and *Fifty Hikes in Vermont*.

Wheeler Mountain. The trail begins on the Wheeler Mountain Road, which leaves the north side of Route 5, 8.3 miles north of West Burke and 5 miles south of Barton Village. From the highway, the unpaved road climbs to the trailhead, 1.9 miles.

Bald Mountain. There are excellent views from the abandoned fire tower at the summit of this, the tallest, peak in the Willoughby Lake area. Trails ascend to the summit from both the north (Lookout's Trail, 2.8 miles) and from the south (Long Pond Trail, 2.1 miles). From the north side of Bald Mountain, you can hike on trails and wilderness roads all the way to the summit of Mount Hor, and Haystack Mountain (a side trip) has excellent views and two trails. Details can be found in *Day Hiker's Guide to Vermont* (see *Hiking* in "What's Where").

Hurricane Brook Wildlife Management Area, off Route 114, south of Norton Pond: 9,500 forested acres, also accessible via a gravel road past Holland Pond from Holland Village. A detailed map is available from the Fish and Game Department in Montpelier.

HAY RIDES AND SLEIGH RIDES   **Letourneau's Sugarhouse** (766-2646), Holland (northeast of Derby Line).

HORSEBACK RIDING   **Seldom Rest Riding Camp** (895-2868), Morgan Center. Open late June–Labor Day. Scenic trail rides, English and Western lessons, day camp, and live-in programs.

SAILBOARDING   Rentals and lessons are available from **Great Outdoors Trading Company** (334-2831), 73 Main Street, Newport.

SWIMMING   In Newport, at **Prouty Beach,** a public facility east of the city that also has tennis courts, picnic facilities, and campsites.

In Barton, at **Crystal Lake State Beach** just east of the village on Route 15, open daily in season 10–8; lifeguard, bathhouse, picnic facilities; and at **Pageant Park** a mile farther east on Route 16, a town-owned park open daily until 10 PM, also with a bathhouse and camping (primarily tenting).

Lake Willoughby has small public beaches at its northern and southern tips.

On Lake Seymour there is a public beach in Morgan Center, and on Caspian Lake there is a small beach in Greensboro.

Needless to say, there is also swimming at every pond and lake that offers fishing access.

CROSS-COUNTRY SKIING   Heermansmith Farm (754-8866), Coventry Village. A total 15 km of tracked trails, also rentals. The picturesque farm is also well known for its food (see *Dining Out*) and serves light lunches during ski season; there is also lodging. $3 trail fee.

DOWNHILL SKIING   See "Jay Peak Area" and "St. Johnsbury and Burke Mountain Area." On Lake Memphremagog, there is also Owl's Head (514-292-5592), Masonville, Quebec. There are 25 trails, including a steep expert run down the face of the mountain; snow-making covers 80 percent of the terrain, and there are six double chair lifts, one quad. Facilities include condominiums and a new apartment hotel, moderately priced.

LODGING   Top of the Hills Motel and Country Inn (800-258-6748), Route 105, Derby Road, Newport 05855. Comfortable Victorian farmhouse plus motel units; color cable TV, room phones; $55 per couple, subject to ARP/other discounts, including continental breakfast; discounted meals at Long Branch Restaurant next door.

   The Border Motel (766-2213, 800-255-1559), North Main Street, Derby 05829. A conveniently sited, pleasant motel ($49 double) with the Passport Pub and Border Dining Room, open daily.

   Derby Village Inn (873-3604), 46 Main Street, Derby Line. Tom and Phyllis Moreau have opened their handsome village home, with five double bedrooms upstairs, each with private bath and furnished with iron bedsteads and hooked rugs. Families are welcome, and dinner is served by reservation. From $40 for a former maid's room to $60 for the master bedroom, breakfast included. No smoking.

   ☞**Heermansmith Farm Inn** (754-8866), Coventry Village. This farm has been in the same family since 1807. Jack and Louise Smith offer three rooms upstairs in the snug, 1860s farmhouse that has become well known over the past few years as one of the region's leading restaurants. Since only dinner is served to the public, guests can enjoy the lounge by day. Light lunches are also served guests during winter; the inn's ski-touring network is open to the public. Summer: $40–50 per room, $10 more in ski season, including full breakfast.

   ☞**Fox Hall** (525-6930), RFD 1, Barton 05822. Ken and Sherry Pyden have transformed the main house at a former girl's camp into an upscale bed and breakfast. There are nine guest rooms, some round, some with fireplaces, all with antiques and views of Lake Willoughby. There are 76 acres, including lake frontage and a dock. Guests have access to canoes, paddleboats, and windsurfers, but they may never want to leave the wide, old, comfortable porch, which commands one of the most dramatic views in Vermont, right down Willoughby Gap. $70–$90 in peak season, less mid-October through June, full breakfast included.

   Willoughvale Inn (525-4123, 800-541-0588), Westmore (the address is RFD 2, Orleans 05860). There are eight upstairs rooms, one handicapped-accessible room downstairs, and four two-bedroom housekeeping cottages across the road on the lake. The large dining room is open to the public for dinner; breakfast is also available for guests. The original farmhouse here dates back to the mid-1800s, and by the early 1900s, it was a restaurant, its status until a few years ago when it was sold and sat vacant. Its current owners, Frank and Joan Symcak, have replaced the old building with a glossy new replica. $45–80 for a standard room, $95 for a deluxe room with lake view and a whirlpool built for two; $100–125 per night, $500–550 per week for the cottages, cheaper in winter. Golf packages offered.

Amberwood (525-3618), Route 5, Barton. This big yellow Victorian house on the hill across from the post office has three homey rooms and offers "Polish hospitality." $25 per person, including full breakfast; no smoking, children under 12, or pets.

Pauper's Manse (525-3222), RR 1, Box 96A, Barton 05822. Bill and Pat Britton offer four rooms (shared baths) in their fine old farmhouse set above meadows on the road from Willoughby Lake to Barton. $35–40 per night double includes breakfast.

Hunt's Hideaway (895-8322), Morgan 05853. Pat Hunt welcomes guests to her modern, split-level home; facilities include lawn games, a pool, playroom, and use of washing machine. The 100 acres are handy to Seymour Lake. There are two double rooms; $30 double includes breakfast.

Brick House (754-2108), PO Box 33, Route 14, Irasburg 05845. Madeleine Masseau and Rita Paquette welcome you to their Victorian brick house. The atmosphere is homey, the four guest rooms sharing two baths. $40–45 double, breakfast included, $5 extra for a one-night stay on Friday or Saturday.

Tester's Star Farm Bed & Breakfast (525-3814), Barton 05822. This snug old cape offers rooms at $40 double, $30 single, breakfast included; canoe available at hourly rates. Off Route 16, south of Barton Village.

Valley House Inn (754-6665), 4 Memorial Square, Orleans 05860. A 112-year-old, middle-of-town, wooden hotel, the likes of which you don't find any more. It's clean but not "restored." The walls are largely pressed tin, and the upstairs halls are wide and airy. The lobby still has its roll-top desk, safe, and stag heads. There are 30 rooms: from $35–60 double. (Higher rate means private bath.) Small dining room.

LAKESIDE COTTAGES   *On Lake Willoughby*   Millers Millbrook (525-6939, 800-NEK-AREA), Westmore (write RD 2, Orleans 05860). A cluster of housekeeping cottages on Lake Willoughby, available by the week in summer ($400–450); also available on a limited basis off season. Lakeside cottages have fireplaces and screened–in porches. Note the toll-free reservations number, which also serves other cottages and private houses around Lake Willoughby.

Mountain Lake Cottages and Resort (525-3072), Westmore (write

RFD 2, Orleans 05860). Ten log housekeeping cabins, built in two tiers along a steep slope (no beach) on the east side of Lake Willoughby, have fireplaces and two bedrooms. Tennis, lawn games, row boats. $500 in summer, $350 in spring and fall.

Perkins Hilltop Cottages (525-6988), Westmore (write RFD 2, Orleans 05860). Earle and Jeanne Perkins keep these eight heated cottages nicely landscaped. They are on the east side of Lake Willoughby, near but not on the lake, with access to an adjacent boat dock and private beach. No pets. Available May–October.

On Crystal Lake **Lakeview Cabins** (525-4463), Barton 05822. Eight housekeeping cottages accommodating one to five people, one or two bedrooms, also rooms in the house (from $25 per day); $42 per day for the cabins, $275 per week.

On Echo Lake **White Birch Lodge** (723-6271), RR 1, Box 28A, West Charleston 05872. The term "lodge" is misleading, because the central old building that once served meals is closed: This is a cluster of four, one- and two-bedroom cottages on Echo Lake. Facilities include a beach and boats (the catch is trout and salmon). $150–350 per week.

On Lake Memphremagog **Cottages at Strawberry Acres** (334-8635), PO Box 536, Newport 05455. Five well-spaced cottages on a quiet bluff overlooking Lake Memphremagog, with 650 feet of frontage including beach, are available from mid-April–mid-November from Rosemary Lalime. $300–350 per week for the two-bedroom to $400 for the three-bedroom.

INNS BEYOND THE BORDER **Cedar Gables** (819-842-4120), 4080 Magog Road (Route 108 at Cedar Lane), Box 355, North Hatley, Quebec, Canada, J0B 2C0. Sited on Lake Massawippi (just east of Memphremagog), 20 miles north of the border off Quebec Autoroute 55, this large, turn-of-the-century house offers a suite (a room with king-sized bed, a sitting room with woodstove, TV, and a private bath); a canopy double bedroom with window seat sharing a bath with a corner, lake-facing, king-sized bedroom; a very large, lake-facing, king-sized bedroom with a private bath including a bidet; and a first-floor bedroom with semi-private bath. There is a secluded sundeck on the lake, good for swimming, along with docks, swimming float, and canoes. Additional watercraft available at the nearby marina. North Hatley is an English-speaking resort village with a summer theater (see Piggery Theater under *Entertainment*). In winter, there are nearby cross-country trails and Alpine trails. Breakfast is included in the rate: $71–106 B&B (note: this is in Canadian currency and includes a 7 percent goods and services tax refundable to non-Canadians).

Auberge Ripplecove Inn (819-838-4296), PO Box 246, Ayer's Cliff, Quebec J0B 1C0. A small resort on Lake Massawippi offers a variety of accommodations, from antiques-furnished rooms in the inn to lakeside cottages. Facilities include tennis courts, an outdoor pool, paddleboats, and canoes; lake swimming and, in winter, sleigh rides and a choice of Alpine and cross-country skiing. Food is important here, and rates are $89–135 per person MAP per day, $345–562 per five-day week, Canadian currency.

DINING OUT · **Heermansmith Farm Inn** (754-8866), Coventry Village. Closed Tuesdays, otherwise open for dinner year-round. The farm itself is locally known for the quality of its produce, especially strawberries. The restaurant is the candlelit interior of the old farmhouse; a limited but quality menu specializing in fresh, poached salmon, roast duck with strawberry sauce, shrimp Dijonaise, and chicken saltimbocca. Entrées $10–16.

☞**Willoughvale Inn and Restaurant** (525-4123), Route 5A, Westmore. The dining room is spacious with large windows to maximize the view of Willoughby Gap. The chef is Michael LaCriux, formerly of Michael's in Derby Line, then the Landing in Newport, a magician in the kitchen. Start with Cockenoe Island oysters or smoked salmon, continue with braised shoulder of Vermont veal that melts in your mouth; entrée choices range from prime rib au jus and poached salmon through roast duckling to fresh Vermont-made tortellini. Farm-raised venison in season. Entrées in the $14.50–21.00 range, plus lower-priced Tap Room selections.

Forsthaus (334-7294), junction of Routes 105 and 14 in Newport Center, open for dinner only. A small German restaurant run by Gunter and Leoni Hartmann, which has already established an excellent reputation. $10–15.

Il Piano Scorza (334-1000), East Main Street (above the Village Bake Shoppe), Newport. Locally applauded, Italian "upper crust" specialties ($10–15) at dinner daily, lunch in the spring and summer, in imaginatively decorated quarters. The chef, Sam Sanzone, studied at the Culinary Arts Institute and the Cordon Bleu.

Long Branch Restaurant and Lounge (334-6430), Route 5, Derby Road, Newport. This locally popular roadhouse offers such entrées as sautéed chicken Dijon for $10.25 and cherry-orange curried pork at $10.95, plus Thursday and Friday luncheon specials. Open Sunday–Thursday 11–9; Friday and Saturday 11–10.

EATING OUT   **Candlepin** (525-6513). A classic roadside restaurant, a half mile north of Barton Village on Route 5. It's locally popular and good for three squares. The menu is huge, and there's a salad bar; also a small, quiet bar in the rear. The bowling lanes are in a converted barn out back.

5–16 Pizza (525-4066), Barton Village, open daily 11:30–9:30, from 12 on Sunday. This is a first-rate pizza place with some of the atmosphere left over from its previous life as a real Italian restaurant. There are the customary and "not so customary" pizzas, like Mexican and crab. You can also have spinach ricotta pie, calzones, grinders, and antipasto.

Country Comfort Restaurant (525-3758), Route 5A just northeast of the northern tip of Lake Willoughby. Open 7 AM–9 PM daily, 8–9 Sundays, year-round. A clean, pleasant spot specializing in home cooking, fresh seafood, basics like BBQ beef in a bulky roll and a Cancun combo: turkey, bologna, ham, bacon, cheese, lettuce, and tomato. Try the homemade pies. Beer and wine served.

Dot's Restaurant, Coventry (754-6668), Irasburg. Located on US Route 5, one mile south of Coventry Village. Dot Maxfield runs an inviting place with a varied menu. In summer, you can eat on the rear deck, overlooking rolling meadows.

Miss Newport Diner (334-7742), East Main Street. Open 5 AM–11 PM daily, except Saturday when it closes at 10:30 PM. Blueberry pancakes and fresh muffins are the specialty, along with homemade soup and friendly natives; choice of stools and booths.

The Border Motel Dining Room and Lounge (766-2213, 800-255-1559), Routes 5 and 105 in Derby. Seafood specials Friday night, veal, and chicken dishes, liquor license; reservations a good idea on Friday and Saturday nights.

Valley's Steak House (766-2100), junction of Routes 5 and 105, Derby. Home-cooked specials at lunch and dinner daily, plus a Sunday brunch buffet at $8.95.

Newport has more than its share of inexpensive, reliable places to eat. Besides those already described there are:

Nichelodean Café (334-8055), Newport. Oak, brass, arty prints, and a generally upscale pub atmosphere make this reasonably priced spot a find.

Rose's Deli & Café (334-5370), 742 East Main Street, Newport. A down-to-earth place for lunch and snacks in a converted automobile showroom, 6:30 AM–8 or 9 PM daily. Roselyn Houghten is the chef-owner, and specialties are basics like spaghetti and liver and onions with bacon. There are also grinders, soups, and sandwiches to go.

East Side Restaurant (334-2340), East Main Street, Newport, closed Mondays. A comfortable, conventional, locally popular place, open 7 AM–9 PM. The menu includes seafood, pork, poultry, beef, and homemade soups and pies; good for sandwiches (try a Mysterious Memphre). It is reportedly merging with the Landing, the only restaurant right on the lake.

The Brown Cow (334-7887), 900 East Main Street, open 6 AM–7 PM, except Sunday when it's 7–1. This is a nice spot to linger over breakfast (served all day); sandwich and salad lunches, reasonably priced dinners. Homemade ice cream on homemade pie.

Chez Marie (334-9908), 63 Main Street, open daily 5:30 AM–9 PM for steak, fried clams, prime rib, baked ham. Handicapped accessible.

ENTERTAINMENT   North Country Concert Association (723-6027), Box 601 in Newport, sponsors a dance, theater, and concert series in various locations throughout the area.

Piggery Theater (842-2191), North Hatley, Quebec. June–August, summer theater.

Northsong Chorus (895-2747), gives concerts at various times and places throughout the year.

The Westmore Association (525-3688) stages an entertainment series at the Community House in Westmore in July and August.

Merrill's Cinema I, II, and III (334-6830), Newport, is the local movie theater.

SELECTIVE SHOPPING   Barton Village. An exceptional shopping center with one of the Kingdom's few supermarkets, a serious garage, a laundromat with rocking chair, barber, the Franklin Store, and neighboring Pierce Pharmacy complete with soda fountain, which doubles as the state liquor store.

General Store of Barton (525-3735), open daily 8–8, for sports equipment and clothes, Vermont books, gifts, groceries, beer and wine, deli, hunting and fishing licenses.

Sugarmill Farm (525-3701), Route 16 south of Barton. This former dairy farm is now a combination maple museum and shop selling a variety of locally crafted items, as well as syrup.

Ethan Allen Furniture (985-8028), Orleans. This is a huge factory that offers tours to small groups (not recommended for children) and has a showroom.

Millbrook Store (525-4400), Westmore. Home of Willy, the Willoughby Lake Monster, available on a variety of T-shirts. Ed Ramsdell and Judy Miner also sell a wide selection of Christmas fantasy items, locally made gifts, and antiques.

Steffis Studio (754-6012), Irasburg Green. Steffi Huess crafts gold and silver jewelry, sells it along with other local arts and crafts right from the front room in her home.

American Maple Products (334-6516), Bluff Road, Newport. The outlet store discounts their Old Colony Brand syrup and maple sugar at an average of 10 percent below retail.

Ammex Tax-Free Shop (873-3323), Derby. At Exit 29 off I-91, this is a genuine, tax-free outlet for liquor, cigarettes, cigars, tobacco, perfumes, and gifts at 20–50 percent below retail.

Northwoods Outerware (334-1031), Newport. Located in the lakeside shopping center on the causeway, across from the info center. This is a genuine outlet specializing in Pedigree Skiwear (made in St. Albans) and nifty, Canadian-designed clothing for women and children.

Sel-Bar Weaving (334-6565) in the old South School, Glen Road, Newport, is a small factory store at the factory in which these distinctive cotton placemats are woven. They come in a great variety of colors.

Woodknot Books, 68 Main Street, Newport, offers a good selection of books, magazines, and VCR tapes.

Country Thyme Vermont (800-639-1370), Derby Road, specializes in handcrafted gifts and fine food gift baskets.

Great Outdoors Trading Company, Main Street, Newport. In summer, the store features an extensive array of fishing gear and sells fishing licenses; also offers guide service on the lake with an electronically equipped fishing boat. Its basement is a year-round outlet for Bogner and Slalom ski wear, both made in town. (Slalom is descended from a local 1891 overalls manufacturer and has been making ski wear since the 1920s.)

SPECIAL EVENTS   March: Sugaring throughout the region.

July: **Memphremagog International Aquafest**—a swim race from Newport to Magog in Canada (32 miles), also a water-ski tournament, parade, public suppers, and more. **Irasburg Church Fair on Irasburg Green.**

August: **Barton Fair**—old-fashioned event at the extensive fairground. **Domestic Resurrection Circus**—thousands of people converge on the meadows that form a natural amphitheater on the Bread and Puppet Theater's farm in Glover (525-3031). The weekend-long happening includes a variety of events, climaxed by the pageant of giant puppets parading on stilts. The theme is always the struggle between good and evil, justice and injustice. Free, black Polish bread is offered. Activities begin at 1 and go on until after dark; circus at 4 and parade at 7:45. **Old Stone House Day**—open house, picnic lunch, crafts demonstrations at the museum in Brownington Village.

September: **Banjo Contest**, last Saturday, in Craftsbury Common. **Fall Foliage Festival** on Lake Willoughby—triathlon, crafts show, fishing derby, and more.

MEDICAL EMERGENCY   Barton (525-3505); Derby, Derby Line, Morgan (766-2211); Orleans (754-6366); Newport (766-2211); **North Country Hospital & Health Center** (334-7331), Newport.

CRAFTSBURY COUNTRY

Of all the high, rolling country in the Northeast Kingdom, the open farmland around Craftsbury gives you the best sense of being on top of the world. The roads follow along ridges, and the fields roll away like waves to the mountains in the distance. This area, framed by Routes 14 on the west and 16 on the east, is webbed with gravel roads, spotted with small lakes and large ponds.

The resort village here is actually Greensboro, a turn-of-the-century summer compound on Caspian Lake. Craftsbury itself is a composite of scattered villages, most of which you drive through in a trice. It's Craftsbury Common that compels you to stop. So vast is the Common itself that it dwarfs the surrounding white homes, academy, and church. It's so high that the countryside drops away on all sides. A number of lodging places, ranging from farms and a sports center to the Kingdom's poshest inns, are found right around here.

Hardwick is the trading center for this area. Its Victorian Main Street is the sole reminder of the town's heyday as one of the world's largest granite processing places. The granite was actually in Woodbury, five miles south, from whence it arrived by rail. Thousands of skilled European craftsmen moved to town beginning in the 1870s and continuing into the 1920s; a number of French Canadians remain.

GUIDANCE   This area falls between the realms of the Kingdom's full-scale chambers of commerce. Most Craftsbury and Greensboro businesses belong to the **Hardwick Area Chamber of Commerce** (472-5906), an all-volunteer operation that maintains an information booth on Route 15 west of town in July and August. The phone number is that of the Hardwick News Center, a newsstand owned by Velda Laird. For cottage listings on Lake Parker in Glover, you can check with the **Barton Chamber of Commerce** (525-3701), Box 280, Barton 05822. If you are checking up on a particular event, you can try the **Craftsbury Town Clerk** (586-2823).

GETTING THERE   From the southeast (I-93 or I-91), take I-91 Exit 21 to Route 2 west and Route 15 to Hardwick, or take I-91 all the way to Barton (Exit 25), then south on Route 16. Be sure to ask your lodging place which way works better, because it can easily save a half hour.

TO SEE AND DO   **Bread and Puppet Theater Museum** (525-3031), Glover. Open March–November on Route 122 off Route 16. See "Lake Country."

Caspian Lake. Shaped like an hourglass, this is one Northeast Kingdom lake that has retained a following, summer in and summer out, for more than a century. The unusual purity of its water is checked three times weekly in season by its association of cottage owners— who include noted authors, educators, and socialites—all of whom mingle in Willey's Store, center of Greensboro. There is a public beach, also a combination beach, boathouse, and resort facility maintained by Highland Lodge, the only inn on the lake, now open year-round for cross-country skiers who can take advantage of its well-groomed and extensive trails. Greensboro also claims Vermont's oldest (nine-hole) golf course.

Craftsbury Common. Few places convey such a sense of tranquility and order. In summer, petunias bloom in the post office window boxes, and the green of the grass contrasts crisply with the white fence. In winter, the general whitewash of this scene contrasts with the blue of the sky. Throughout the year there are nearby places to stay and books to check out at the desk beneath the imposing portraits of Ebenezer and Samuel Crafts in the village library.

Unlike most North Country pioneers, Ebenezer was university educated (Yale, class of 1740). Forced to sell his tavern in Sturbridge, Massachusetts (the still-popular Public House), due to war debts, he made his way here over the Bayley-Hazen military road, eventually bringing his family and 150 of his Sturbridge neighbors this way on sleds. Ebenezer saw to it that a church and school were established soon after the saw and gristmills. His son Samuel, a Harvard graduate who served two terms as Vermont's governor, founded the Academy, which still serves as the public high school for the town. The Sterling College campus adds to the variety.

Visitors can meet Craftsbury residents in a number of ways. Many farms welcome paying guests or those who enjoy watching them "sugar"; some of the state's best maple sugar is sold at some of its lowest prices here, year-round. Two inns offer year-round lodging, and **Craftsbury Center**, a former prep school campus, offers basic accommodations, an extensive cross-country ski network in winter, and a varied year-round program of workshops for all ages in everything from wild mushroom identification and tapestry weaving to sculling and rock-climbing. The extensive web of well-surfaced dirt roads meandering in all directions is also beloved by bicyclists and horse riders.

Sights to see include the **John Woodruff Memorial Library** (586-9692) in East Craftsbury, a general store built in the 1840s by the grandfather of Miss Jean Simpson (recently deceased). She converted it into one of New England's most pleasant libraries; general titles are in the room once used for bolts of cloth and general groceries (old shelves and counters remain), and there is a special back room for youngsters, with a ping-pong table amid the books. Open Wednesday and Saturday 9–12, 2–5, and 7–9:30, and Sunday 12–1:30.

RAIL EXCURSIONS   In foliage season, one rail line originates in St. Johnsbury to the southeast, and the other begins in Morrisville to the west; both turn around in Greensboro Bend. For details on both, see "St. Johnsbury and Burke Mountain Area."

SCENIC DRIVES   This is one of the best areas in Vermont for "back-roading." For example, Greensboro Bend to Lyndon: An old ridge road with splendid views, the 17-mile Stannard Road is unpaved but usually well gravelled most of the way. Check locally, though, because there are occasional washouts.

Greensboro Village to East Hardwick: The road passes through Hardwick Street (that's the name of the hamlet), a fine collection of

Federal and Greek Revival houses; from Greensboro Village to Hardwick it makes a beeline through high and open farm country; and from Craftsbury Common north to Route 14 through Albany and Irasburg, it follows the rich farmland of the Black River Valley.

SUGARHOUSES   In Craftsbury: **Martin Calderwood** (586-2297), South Albany Road; 1,900 taps, gathered with a tractor and sled; arranges sugar parties on request. **Harry F. Sweat** (586-2838), 3,000 taps; arranges sugar parties, on the road from the Common to Craftsbury Center. **Bruce & Elizabeth Urie** (755-6713), South Albany Road; the sugar shack is right on this picturesque back road, across from the old red dairy barn; Stillmeadow Farm has been in the Urie family since the 1920s, and the syrup is outstanding and reasonably priced. **James and Annette Jones** (586-2292), one mile off Route 14, boil from 2,000 taps.

In Greensboro: **Peter and Sandra Gebbie** at Maplehurst Farm (533-2984) put out 7,000 taps and will arrange sugaring parties; syrup sold year-round in their friendly kitchen. **Beverly and George Young** (533-2964), Greensboro Bend, put out 1,100 taps and will arrange sugar parties.

BICYCLING   Craftsbury Sports Center (586-7767), Craftsbury Common, rents mountain bikes and offers bike tours of local roads and woods trails that are used as cross-country trails in winter. **Richard Scheiber** (563-2252), South Walden Road in Cabot, also rents bikes.

CANOEING   Craftsbury Sports Center (see above) rents canoes for use on Great and Little Hosmer ponds and on the Black River. Canoes are also made in the village by Horace Strong.

FISHING   Caspian and other lakes in this area are good for salmon, lake and rainbow trout, and perch. There are trout in the streams, too.

GOLF   Mountain View Country Club (533-9294), Greensboro, nine holes.

HORSEBACK RIDING   Greenhope Farm (533-7772) in Walden offers trail rides for experienced riders.

OTHER RECREATION   The Craftsbury Center also has stables and offers one-hour to weekend horseback safaris; plus programs in sculling, running, walking, Elderhostel, and Weight Loss Discovery sessions in the spring and fall.

SWIMMING   In Glover, **Shadow Lake Beach**, marked from Route 16, is a delightful spot. There is also a public beach on **Caspian Lake**, near Greensboro Village.

CROSS-COUNTRY SKIING   Craftsbury Sports Center (see above) grooms 53 km of its 100-km, marked and maintained trail system; offers rentals, instruction, lodging packages, and tours in conjunction with the Inn on the Common (see *Lodging*). **Highland Lodge** (533-2647), Greensboro. A total of 40 km of trails, 30 of them well groomed, traverse rolling fields and woods past farms and homes, through maple groves and evergreens. Instruction, rental, retail, and repair

John Brodhead

Cross-country skiers at Craftsbury Center

offered at the center adjacent to one of the Kingdom's best inns; ski weeks, guided tours offered. **Hilltop Cross-Country Center** (888-3710) in Wolcott offers a total of 25 km of set trails through gently rolling hills, woods, and open fields.

LODGING   The Inn on the Common (586-9619, 800-521-2233), Craftsbury Common 05827. The most regal lodging in the Kingdom is offered by Michael and Penny Schmitt. They have 18 exquisitely decorated guest rooms, some with fireplaces, some with canopy beds, in three Federal-style buildings close to the Common. Guests congregate in the library for cocktails at 7 and dine formally at long candlelit tables. Dinner might commence with a choice of pheasant soup or endive with veal pâté, and the entrées might include venison and a brace of quail; a choice of fine wines is available. In summer, you can take advantage of the solar-heated pool, the perennial gardens, lawn croquet, and tennis court, also of mountain bikes and canoes at the Craftsbury Sports Center, a nearby facility that teams up with the inn to offer cross-country ski tours in winter. $95–125 per person double occupancy, MAP, plus 15 percent service.

☞**Highland Lodge** (533-2647), Greensboro 05841. A fine, Victorian-era summer hotel that manages to be both airy in warm weather and cozy in winter, now managed by the second generation of Smiths (David, Wilhelmina, and Alex). A total of 60 guests can be accommodated between the lodge and ten cottages (three remaining open in winter). In summer, facilities include tennis and a pleasant beach with bathhouse and boats; in winter the draw is cross-country skiing on the extensive network radiating from the inn's touring center. Inside, there is plenty of space to read and get away from other guests, also nice corners in which to socialize; plenty of books, a grand piano, and a game room for children for whom there is an organized program (ages 4–9). In the lodge, $135–165 per couple, $35–45 per child depending on age, MAP; $165–190 per couple, $20–45 per child, in a cottage; rates include 15 percent gratuity. Open May 30–October 16; December 20–March 15.

Craftsbury Inn (586-2848), Craftsbury 05826, a village with a delightful general store, just downhill from Craftsbury Common. The handsome 1850 Greek Revival–style inn has a dignified, second-story, wraparound porch and unusually attractive public rooms, dressed with interesting artwork. There are ten guest rooms, also nicely decorated with heirloom and custom quilts and local art. Dinner is taken seriously. Rates $110–150 per couple, MAP. Midweek packages.

Craftsbury Bed & Breakfast (586-2206), Craftsbury Common 05827. Margaret Ramsdell welcomes guests to her farmhouse on Wylie Hill, one with views that (even by local standards) are hard to beat. Rooms are in the rear wing, sharing their own private gathering space, but guests are also drawn into the big kitchen with its glowing soapstone woodstove, backed by gleaming copper. Rates include a full farm breakfast (cinnamon-apple pancakes, eggs with cheddar cheese), $55–65 per couple ($35 single). The Catamount Ski Trail runs through the property.

Brassknocker Inn (586-2814), East Craftsbury 05826. Formerly the home of Craftsbury's leading family, now of the Richards family, the inn offers large, antique-furnished rooms, shared baths, a comfortable sitting room, and a large country kitchen; $50–75 double includes continental breakfast.

Finching Field Farm (586-1763), East Craftsbury 05826. Jeanette and Bob Mayer were B&B hosts in England, then in the Sugarbush area. Here they have four guest rooms (two with private baths). The common rooms are elegant, and there are seven acres, some exceptional plantings, and cross-country ski trails to Craftsbury Nordic Center and Highland Lodge. $60–75 per couple with shared bath, $50 single with shared bath, $20 for additional person in the room, a full breakfast and afternoon tea included.

Rowan Tree Keep (586-2513), Box 35, Craftsbury. Three romantic, antique-filled rooms share two baths; private dining, $40–55 per person.

The Brick House (472-5512/5104), Box 128, East Hardwick 05836. Judith Kane presides over this early nineteenth-century, two-story brick house on the edge of East Hardwick Village. There are three comfortably furnished bedrooms with shared bath (the beds have feather mattresses, feather pillows, and handmade quilts). The price includes a full breakfast served in a charming dining room and an English-style, wake-up tea tray, if desired. There are books, a fireplace, and dartboard in the sitting room, and amenities include woodland walks, trout fishing on the property, and a croquet court. Innkeeper Kane is British herself and serves English Cream Teas in the flower garden or gazebo Wednesday–Sunday afternoons (2:30–5), weather permitting. $50 per couple, $30 single, $10 for children under 12; "well-behaved pets" welcome.

Carolyn's Bed & Breakfast (472-6338), 15 Church Street, Hardwick 05843. An attractive Victorian village house with four large guest rooms sharing one-and-a-half baths. Tea and homemade English tarts served on arrival and to the public. A hearty breakfast included in $33–40 per person.

FARMS   ☞**Rodgers Dairy Farm** (525-6677), Glover 05839. Jim and Nancy Rodgers take in no more than 10 guests at a time, accommodating them in five guest rooms in their 1840 farmhouse. The night we stopped by, guests had congregated on the porch while they waited for a generous meal that was just about to be served in the spacious kitchen-dining area. The working dairy farm encompasses 350 acres not far from Shadow Lake. $40 per adult, $25 per child includes three meals; weekly rates are $200 per adult, $125 per child.

SPORTS CENTER   **Craftsbury Sports Center** (586-7767), Box 32, Craftsbury 05827. Accommodations are not the reason you come here. Lodging is in two large, dormlike buildings, each with nine large doubles and 31 smaller rooms sharing lavatory-style hall bathrooms. There are also two efficiency apartments and two larger rooms with private bath; two housekeeping cottages each sleep four. Three meals are served, buffet-style, in the dining hall. Guests come for the programs offered: running, sculling, walking, mountain biking, and cross-country skiing. Facilities include swimming at Lake Hosmer, exercise rooms, sauna, tennis courts, and 170 acres. Rates begin at $44–76 per person; weekend or six-night packages are available.

DINING OUT   **Elliot's Restaurant** (472-5470), Main Street, Hardwick. Dinner, Tuesday–Saturday. The dining room has a tin ceiling and stained-glass lighting fixtures, and there is a small, quiet bar area. Entrées $10–15.

Craftsbury Inn (586-2484), Craftsbury. Dinner is open to the public by reservation June–August. A small dining room with just eight tables and a choice of four entrées. Specialties include local lamb, pheasant and quail, fresh fish; home-baked French baguettes and unusual soups; grapefruit sorbet before the entrée; desserts. $10–20 for entrées.

Highland Lodge (533-2647), Greensboro. Open for breakfast, lunch, and dinner, served in the inn's attractive dining room. Dinner entrées ($10–20) might include roast sirloin Dijon, ocean catfish with tomato and wine, and chicken with peanut sauce. The meal might begin with wild mushroom and apple torte and end with chocolate cheesecake or Ishkabibble (brownie and ice cream with homemade hot fudge). Breakfast includes homemade granola, and lunch features interesting croissants, salads, and soups as well as the usual sandwiches. The inn's location and grounds make it a popular lunch destination.

EATING OUT   **In a Pig's Eye Café & Deli** (472-6297), Hardwick, is a small, surprisingly cosmopolitan place located in one corner of the old hotel building on Main Street. The menu is varied, including soups, salads, and sandwiches.

Village Restaurant (472-5701), junction of Routes 14 and 15, Hardwick, offers three squares in a basic, clean, comfortable, no-frills place in the center of town.

TEA   **The Brick House** (472-5512/5104), East Hardwick, serves other delicacies. A wide variety of teas are offered and served, of course, in a pot. The setting is the flower garden or gazebo, weather permitting, Wednesday–Sunday 2:30–5. Reservations appreciated.

ENTERTAINMENT   **Summer Music from Greensboro**, based at the Congregational Church, Greensboro, is a series of chamber and choral music concerts in July and August.

Craftsbury Chamber Players have brought chamber music to northern Vermont for 25 years. The six-week summer series runs mid-July–August, Thursday evenings, at the Hardwick Town House. There are also shorter, Thursday afternoon free concerts at the Town House. Most performers are faculty members at the Julliard School of Music in New York City.

SELECTIVE SHOPPING   **The Galaxy Bookshop** (472-5533), Hardwick. A full-service bookstore specializing in Vermont writers and unusual titles; an inviting place to linger that has recently doubled its space. (It's an outlet for Harry Besett's decorative ,"new age" hand-blown glass; the artist may be opening a retail studio of his own in Hardwick and can be reached at 472-5733.)

Stone's Throw Gardens (586-2805), Craftsbury, features displays of perennials and roses around a restored 1795 farmhouse; nursery open May 1–late August, Wednesday–Sunday.

Granite Hills Gallery, Hardwick Town House, Hardwick, an affiliate of the Craftsbury Chamber Players, features changing exhibitions.

The Old Firehouse (472-6166), downtown Hardwick, a mini-mall for antiques, yarn, crafts, and such, located in a nicely restored 1885 building, built as a church and later used as a firehouse.

Perennial Pleasures Nursery (472-5512), East Hardwick. Sited at

The Brick House and run by Rachel Kane, this unusual nursery specializes in authentic seventeenth-, eighteenth-, and nineteenth-century restoration gardens. There are two acres of flowering perennial and herb gardens, grassy walks and arbors; more than 375 varieties of plants are available.

The Old Forge (586-2826), East Craftsbury. Open daily, year-round, 10–5, 1–5 on Sunday; Scottish designer sweaters and other woolens.

Willey's Store, Greensboro Village. One of the biggest and best general stores in the state; an extensive grocery, produce and meat section, hardware, toys, and just about everything else you should have brought for a vacation but forgot.

The Miller's Thumb (533-2960), Greensboro Village. A former gristmill with a view of the stream below through a window in the floor, open June–mid-September, a gallery with crafts. Look for the branch store on Main Street, Hardwick (open year-round). Both stores are a trove of art, crafts, and gift items, many made locally.

Craftsbury General Store, Craftsbury Village. A genuine, old-style village store, under the same ownership for many years; a source of information about the area and a full stock of everything.

SPECIAL EVENTS   March: Open sugarhouses.

July: **Antiques and Uniques Fair** at Craftsbury Common.

July and August: **Circus Smirkus** (533-7443), Greensboro. A children's circus camp that stages frequent performances.

August: **Old Home Day**, Craftsbury Common. Second weekend: **Domestic Resurrection Circus**, Glover.

MEDICAL EMERGENCY   Craftsbury (472-6666), Glover (525-3505), see also Newport and St. Johnsbury sections.

JAY PEAK AREA

Jay Peak towers like a sentinel above a wide valley in which the state of Vermont and the province of Quebec meet at three border crossings and mingle not only in the waters of Lake Memphremagog but in general ambience. The sentinel itself has fallen to the French. The face of Vermont's northernmost peak is owned by Mont Saint-Saveur International, and more than half of the patrons at Jay Peak ski area hail from across the border. Montreal is, after all, less than two hours away.

From Jay's base lodge, a 60-passenger aerial tram runs summer as well as winter to the 3,861-foot summit—which yields one of the most spectacular views in the state: from Lake Champlain on the west, off across Lake Memphremagog to the north, across the Northeast Kingdom to the east, and back down the Green Mountains as far as Camel's Hump to the south.

In winter, storms sweep down from Canada or roll in from Lake Champlain, showering the clutch of mountains around Jay with truly dependable quantities of snow—a fact more pertinent to cross-country than downhill skiers in these days of snow-making. A total 100 km of trails link the five touring centers in the area. Aside from accommodations at Jay Peak itself, lodging is scattered along Route 242, which climbs steadily nine miles from Montgomery Center to the ski area, then dips as steeply the four miles down to Jay Village (named for John Jay who never saw it), which is just a crossroads inn, gas station, and general store. This land remains primarily farming and logging country with a special, haunting quality conveyed in water colors by Rudi Mattesich, also famed as the "father of American ski touring," who lives in nearby Troy.

In contrast to most ski resort areas, this one does not attract transients. Its innkeepers, restaurateurs, and shopkeepers are a mix of self-sufficient natives and the interesting kind of people who tend to gather in the world's beautiful back-and-behind places.

GUIDANCE   **Jay Peak Lodging Association** (326-4088, 800-882-7460), or the **Jay Peak Travel Service** (988-2611 or, outside Vermont, 800-451-4449), Jay 05859; sources of lodging information for the entire area. Open daily, 9–5 weekdays, until 7 on winter Saturdays, until 4 Sundays. **Montgomery Business Association** (326-4310), Box 18, Montgomery Center 05471. Much of this area is also covered by the **Newport Area Chamber of Commerce** (334-7782).

GETTING THERE   By plane: Burlington International Airport, one-and-one-half-hour drive.

By train: AMTRAK service to Burlington.

By bus: Greyhound and Vermont Transit service to Newport; host lodges generally pick up. From Montreal, the Jay Express makes daily runs.

TO SEE AND DO   **Jay Peak Tram**. The 60-passenger tram operates daily during ski season and late June–Labor Day, again in foliage season, 10–5.

Hazen's Notch. From Montgomery Center, an unpromising narrow road, Route 58, climbs steeply west, quickly changing to dirt. In winter, it is open only the first four miles and is a popular ski-touring spot (see *Cross-Country Skiing*). In summer, it is a beautiful road, dappled with sunlight through the thick foliage. A fine picnic spot has been provided near the height of land, close to a clear roadside spring. A historic site plaque says the road through the high pass was built by General Moses Hazen in 1778–1779, commissioned by George Washington himself. The road began in 1776, 60 miles to the southeast at Wells River on the Connecticut River, and was intended to reach St. John, Quebec. It was abandoned on this spot in April 1779, when the news that British patrols might use it as an invasion route (it was meant to work the other way) reached the camp at Hazen's Notch.

Montgomery Village. The most picturesque village in this area, Montgomery is nestled among the hills that rise abruptly on all sides. It began as a lumbering center and was for a long time one of the world's major producers of timothy grass seed culture. Today it is best known for the quality wooden toys made in Montgomery Schoolhouse, a green box of a building that stands on the triangular Green. The schoolhouse is open to the public; toys can be found in the ground floor shop (8 AM–4:30 PM, Monday–Friday). The town's historical collection is housed in an 1835 wooden church, open June–September at stated hours.

COVERED BRIDGES The town of Montgomery boasts a grand total of six town lattice covered bridges: one right in Montgomery Village over Black Falls Creek, one south on Route 118, another nearby but three miles off Route 118 on West Hill on an abandoned side road over a waterfall, another northwest on Route 118 over the Trout River, and two in Montgomery Center, both a mile west of Route 118 over the Trout River.

CANOEING The 86-mile-long Missisquoi River makes a complete loop around Jay, passes briefly through Quebec, and continues across Vermont to empty into Lake Champlain. The upper half of the river near Jay offers spring fastwater, and the lower reaches are gentle and broad, good spring and summer ground for beginners and for those who enjoy traversing outstanding rural landscape. Guided canoe trips are available from **Vermont Voyageur Expeditions** (326-4789), Montgomery Center 95471; specializes in family expeditions, combining canoeing with hiking and camping.

GOLF The **Enosburg Country Club** (933-8951) in Enosburg Falls maintains a nine-hole golf course on the north edge of the village.

FISHING The Trout River deserves its name; brook trout can also be found in the Missisquoi.

Jay Peak (800-451-4449 or 988-4363). The ski area has stocked its sizable snow-making pond with trout.

Also see "Lake Country."

MOUNTAIN BIKING The **Jay Peak Ski and Summer Resort** has opened a network of trails to experienced mountain bikers via its Aerial Tramway, which will transport them and their bikes to the 4,000-foot summit, from which several routes descend.

HIKING The Long Trail terminates its 262-mile route at the Canadian border, 10 miles north of Jay Peak, but the hike up Jay itself is what most hikers want. The most popular ascent is from Route 242, 1.2 miles east of the entrance to the ski area; the round-trip hike takes three hours. For details to this and to the section of the trail between Hazen's Notch and Route 242, also for the final, fairly flat leg to the border, see the *Guide Book of the Long Trail*, published by the Green Mountain Club, which maintains the trail and four shelters in this area. Hiking weekends, designed for people who have little hiking experience, are offered by **Vermont Voyageur Expeditions** (see *Canoeing*); they include guided treks along the Long Trail with dinner and lodging provided at local inns; also "walking weekends" and hiking combined with photography workshops.

SWIMMING   A number of local inns have their own pools. The most popular local swimming hole is at Jay Four Corners, downstream from the Route 101 bridge.

Jay Swim and Racquetball Club (988-2880). Day membership is available to the pool and courts.

CROSS-COUNTRY SKIING   **Hazen's Notch Ski Touring Center** (326-4708), Montgomery Center. Val Schadinger operates an outstanding touring center that offers meticulously tracked trails, some with fine views; also rentals, instruction, sports shop, Telemark slopes, café, changing rooms, lodging, guided tours. Trails are enjoyable well into March (elevation: 1,000–1,670 feet). $5 one day, $8.50 for two.

Vermont Voyageur Expeditions (326-4789), Montgomery Center. Sharon and Rolf Anderson offer weekend and three-day midweek guided tours, including inn-to-inn lodging and shuttle. The outfit also maintains a shop on Route 242 that serves as an informal touring center for the network of trails across the road in Alpine Haven. Rentals and instruction are available, along with the line of shell clothing that they produce. VVE also offers guided tours in the White Mountains and the Adirondacks.

The Snow Job (988-4464), Jay Village. Located next to the Jay Country Store, Mike Murphy rents as well as sells cross-country equipment and offers information about local touring trails.

Jay Peak Ski Touring Center (988-2611), Jay Peak. Some 25 km of trail are maintained at 1,800–2,915 feet, free use of the T-bar for Telemark practice; rentals and instruction available.

The Catamount Trail traverses the high terrain just south of Jay Peak; inquire at Hazen's Notch Ski Touring Center.

DOWNHILL SKIING   **Jay Peak** (988-2611 or 800-451-4449 including Canada). The original trails are stateside, on a shoulder of Jay Peak. Still considered some of the toughest runs in Vermont, they were carved 30 years ago by local residents. An enterprising Kiwanis group (it included the parish priest) convinced the Vermont legislature to reroute existing roads up over the high ridge from which Jay's access road arises, thus linking it to northwestern Vermont as well as to the Northeast Kingdom. They also imported an Austrian skimeister to create a true trail system and a ski school. Some 30,000 acres on and around Jay Peak were owned by Weyerhaeuser Corporation, and in the early sixties, the mammoth lumber company—based in Tacoma, Washington—acquired the ski area. It installed a Swiss-built tramway to Jay's peak, which it topped with a Sky Haus tram station, a building that emphasizes the crest of the summit and gives it a distinctly Matterhorn-like cap. Weyerhauser also built a large, sturdy, Tyrolean-style base complex, which includes a 48-room hotel, and it laid out a winding access road to be lined with chalets.

And there it sat. A major mountain offering outstanding lifts, trails, and one of New England's largest vertical drops (2,153 feet). In 1978 it was acquired by the Montreal-based owners of St. Sauveur, a lucrative Laurentian ski area. The rebirth of Jay as a destination rather than as a Montreal day-tripping place, is relatively recent. But under a dynamic new operations manager, lifts have been improved and condominiums have been proliferating. This is a great place for spring skiing, but beware of weekends when it's mobbed by Montrealers.

Lifts: 60-passenger tram; one quad chair, one triple, one double, two T-bars.

Trails and slopes: 39 trails, totaling more than 50 miles of skiing, spread over two peaks, connected by a ridge line.

Vertical drop: 2,100 feet.

Snow-making: 80 percent.

Facilities: Austria Haus and Tram Haus base lodges with cafeteria, pub, ski and rental shop. Sky Haus cafeteria at summit, nursery and day-care facilities; no charge for child care 9–9 for skiers staying at the mountain.

Ski school: US and Canadian certified instructors, adult and junior racing clinics.

For children: SKIwee program for 5- to 12-year-old group, kinderschool for age 2–5.

Rates: $31 per adult, $22 junior, $22 Vermonter. Two-day passes: $60 per adult, $44 junior; five-day passes: $130 per adult, $95 junior.

Snowboarding: Permanent half-pipe course; Jay is now Burton Board demo center; rentals, instruction for beginners for $29.

INNS AND LODGES   In summer, check with the **Greater Newport Chamber of Commerce** (334-7782), Box 632, Newport 05855. Note that Jay Peak itself divides this area into two distinct regions: the Jay Village side, oriented to Canada and Newport, and the Montgomery Center side.

Inglenook Lodge (988-2880), Jay 05859. Located one mile from the lifts, this is a modern ski lodge with a sunken living room, circular fireplace, and cathedral ceiling. There are 15 rooms with private baths, two bunkrooms. Facilities include an indoor pool, racquet courts, game room, and public dining room and pub. $52 per person MAP.

☞**Eagle Lodge** (326-4518), Montgomery Center 05471. One of the few Vermont inns run by Vermonters—three generations of the Scott family—this 1800 farmhouse offers 16 rooms and pleasant reading and game-playing corners near woodstoves. Meals are served buffet-style in the sun-filled dining room that overlooks a backyard trout pond, good for ice-skating in winter. Dinner is extra in summer, open to everyone by reservation; babysitting available on request, children are welcome. Rates: $45–55 per person MAP in winter (Jay Peak is just down the road); $25 per person B&B in summer.

Black Lantern Inn (326-4507, 800-255-8661), Montgomery 05470. A white-pillared, brick inn built in 1803 as the Montgomery Village stage stop. The bedrooms are small but nicely furnished, with private baths. Downstairs there is a small reading-talking area warmed by a handsome soapstone stove, a cozy taproom, and charming, seven-table dining room. Six suites with fireplaces and whirlpool baths have been added in the adjacent Burdett House. Innkeepers Rita and Allan Kalsmith set an elegant table. This is not a place for children. Beyond the porch is the lovely village to explore, and from the back, there is a view of Hazen's Notch. Rates $60–80 per person MAP.

Jay Village Inn (988-2634, 800-227-7452), Jay Village 05859. Bob and Jay Angliss have imbued this old lodge with real warmth. The public rooms include a lounge, with fireplace and a player piano, and a basement game room with ping-pong and pool tables, a dart board, and video games. The dining room is attractive and has a good local reputation. The 16 rooms upstairs are plain but comfortable, and there's an outdoor pool. $60–80 per room B&B. MAP available in ski season.

The Inn on Trout River (326-4391, 800–338–7049), Montgomery Center 05471. Built grandly by a lumber baron, this attractive village house offers 10 guest rooms with private baths, one suite with a brass bed and fireplace. There are also hearths in the dining room, library, and foyer. The dining room is formal (see *Dining Out*). Innkeepers Terry and Ray Wheeler have added touches like warm bath towels and robes for every guest. $66–95 per person MAP, $60 per room in summer.

Snowline Lodge (988-2822), Jay 05859. At the base of the Jay Peak access road, these 10 motel-style rooms are a good value, especially given their quality and the fireside pub and restaurant (specializing in steaks and burgers). $60–75 per double room B&B.

The Schneehutte Inne (988-4020, 800-445-0671), Route 242, Jay. One mile from the ski area, this place features lounge, game rooms; $35–43 per person MAP. Special rates for groups.

BED & BREAKFASTS   Woodshed Lodge (988-4444), Jay 05859. Located on Route 242, three miles from Jay Peak, a warm ski-lodge atmosphere with seven bedrooms, good for both couples and families. $32 per person B&B, with shared bath; $36 with private bath. (Dinner available by arrangement.)

North Troy Inn (988-2527), 15 Railroad Street, North Troy 05859. This handsome old home has cherry-paneled public rooms and nicely furnished guest rooms. Owners Russ and Julie Plourde are retirees from Westport, Massachusetts, where Russ's business was fixing cantankerous home machines like lawn mowers for grumpy owners. He finds it far more pleasant dealing with people who come to him for pleasure. $25 per person includes breakfast.

Rose Apple Acres Farm (988-4300), East Hill Road, North Troy 05859. There are four guest rooms in this comfortable house with its own 52 acres, good for cross-country skiing. Located 10 miles from Jay Peak, near a covered bridge on the Missisquoi River, good for fishing. $42–52 per room.

Friedlich Haus (744-6113, 800-992-0096), Pleasant Street, Troy. An 1870s house that Mitchell and Salona Privy now maintain as a bed & breakfast, offering three bedrooms with a shared bath, a large country kitchen, and living room.

Phineas Swann B&B (326-4306), Main Street, Montgomery Center. Cozy, bright Victorian with front parlor, TV, VCR. $60–70 per room.

HOUSEKEEPING UNITS   **La Maison Des Masters** (603-742-9428, 800-227-5974), Mountain Road, Jay. Two comfortably furnished, three-bedroom vacation units four miles from the ski area, fully equipped, with woodstoves, TV, VCRs. $150–185 per night.

Trilium Woods at Jay (988-4020, 800-445-0671), Route 242, Jay. Vacation town houses holding eight. Rates on request.

Alpine Haven (326-4567), Montgomery Center 05471. Eighty-two chalets, two to six bedrooms, fireplaces. Heated pool, tennis in summer, cross-country skiing on property in winter. From $125 per day.

Hazen's Notch Ski Touring Center Guest House (326-4708), Montgomery Center 05471. An old farmhouse offers a living room with woodburning stove, pleasant guest rooms, and a family-style kitchen. Cross-country trails radiate from the doorstep; under the same ownership as the adjacent touring center. $132–150 per night for nine people, less by the week.

DINING OUT   **Zack's on the Rocks** (326-4500), Montgomery Center. There is more than a touch of fantasy to this place. Zack (he was born "Zachadnykjon" in Blackstone, Massachusetts) frequently greets guests in purple garb. "I'm a frustrated actor," says Zack, who built this eyrie 29 years ago, using "all the things I like—marble, rocks. . . ." The predominant color is purple in many shades, and it extends to the soapstone stove. Zack dislikes the word "gourmet," but the fact is that patrons come back often because the food is superb. Entrées might include chicken banana or roast duckling with fruit sauce. There's no set menu. Dinner is by reservation only, 6–9, and there is music in Gussie's "After the Rocks" with Tom at the keys Friday and Saturday. Closed Mondays. The adjacent fantasy cottage for two with a fireplace in the bedroom and living room is usually reserved on weekends a season in advance. About $30 per person for dinner.

The Inn on Trout River (326-4391), Main Street, Montgomery Center. The dining room in this handsome old house is fairly formal, and the menu includes dishes like veal Malagasy with green peppercorns and baked rainbow trout. There is a glowing hearth and candlelight; a decent choice of wines. Dinner entrées $12.95–17.95; $7–12 in the Pub.

Hotel Jay (988-2611) at Jay Peak. Dinner is served 6–9, and reservations are a must in winter. The room itself is cheery, and the menu features dishes like veal Gruyere and filet of salmon Florentine; entrées include escargots Dijonaise and coquilles Saint-Jacques. Sunday brunch (fall and summer only) is big here. In summer, dinner is served only Friday–Sunday. Entrées under $20.

Black Lantern Inn (326-4507), Montgomery Village. "Continental cuisine" is nicely served by candlelight in the low-beamed dining room of this old inn. A strong local reputation. The menu might include stuffed shrimp, filet mignon with mushrooms and onions, and walnut-crusted sole. Entrées under $20.

Jay Village Inn and Restaurant (988-2643), Jay Village. A large, friendly dining room specializing in steak au poivre. Entrées $12.95–17.95.

EATING OUT   ☞The Belfry (326-4400), Route 242, Montgomery Center. Open 4 PM until late, nightly. An informal pub housed in an old schoolhouse with friendly wooden booths that patrons usually settle into for an hour or two. The soup is homemade, and there is a blackboard menu with daily specials like pan-blackened fish and grilled lamb chops, in addition to sliced London broil and BBQ chicken, salads, burgers, and fried mushrooms. Italian dishes Wednesdays.

J. R.'s Café (326-4682), Main Street, Montgomery Center. Open 6:30 AM–11 PM, later on weekends. Breakfast options include bagels and smoked salmon, eggs any style. Soups are a luncheon specialty, and at dinner, veal, pasta, and fresh fish are featured (there's a choice of liquor). Cheery, cozy, but frequently too crowded to get in.

Kilgore's General Store, Montgomery Center, across the way from J. R.'s. The soda fountain offers freshly baked bread for sandwiches, natural mayonnaise, and locàl greens, also egg creams.

ENTERTAINMENT   **Covered Bridges Theatre Company** (CBT), (326-4121), Route 118 on the western edge of Montgomery. A summer resident company performs a range of productions, from irreverent Shakespeare to comedy. The theater is an old barn.

Concerts on the Common, presented by the Montgomery Historical Society on Saturday evenings in July, August, and September in the Montgomery Village church.

APRÈS SKI   **Golden Eagle Lounge** at the base lodge of the mountain, the **Red Chair Pub** in Jay, the **Belfry** and **J.R.'s** in Montgomery.

SELECTIVE SHOPPING   **Kilgore's General Store** (326-4681), Main Street, Montgomery Center. A fine old store with an interior balcony, nicely restored with a classic soda fountain and cases stocked with healthy munchies (ideal for local hikers and bikers), a variety of organic foods, wines, and natural fiber clothing. Proprietor Morgan Davidson obviously has a sense of quality and a flare for display.

Vermont Voyageur Equipment (326-4789), Montgomery Center, Route 242. A quality line of shell parkas, pants, over-mitts, and overboots is made in the VVE shop, sold primarily by commission and mail order but also available on the spot. This cross-country skier wouldn't be without the mitts and boots, which are waterproof and effective. A mosquito-proof, light net jacket is popular with summer hikers and bikers. VVE also makes flags.

Self-Portrait Life Masks (326-4356), created for you individually by Maggie Sherman of Montgomery.

Jay Country Store (988-4040), Jay Village. Open daily with food and wine basics, also a deli, ice cream, and a coffee shop, plus a number of gift items and a whole room—The Christmas Loft—filled year-round with Christmas trimmings, cards, and presents.

The Snow Job (988-4464), Jay Village. Adjacent to the Country Store, a year-round sports shop: clothing, sports equipment, also ski rentals.

Kominsky's Bloomers (326-4505), Main Street, Montgomery Center, is filled with country afghans, fine linens, quilted wallhangings and calicos by Leslie Kominsky, and whimsical pottery.

Terry's Fine Woolens and Antiques (326-4118), Route 118, Montgomery Center, features Icelandic products.

SPECIAL EVENTS   January, last Sunday: **Hazen's Notch Ski Race.**

Mid-February: **Winter Festival**—varied events including a race from the summit of Jay Peak to Jay Village.

Mid-August: **Jay Day.**

October: **Octoberfest**: Art show, special events.

MEDICAL EMERGENCY   Montgomery (933-4000); **North Country Hospital & Medical Center** (334-7331), Prouty Drive, Newport.

ISLAND POND AND BEYOND

A sign in front of the city-sized Island Pond depot reads, "Pioneer railroad planner John A. Poor's dream of an international railroad connecting Montreal, Canada, with the ice-free harbor of Portland, Maine, became a reality on July 18, 1854, when the first through trains met at this great halfway point on the Grand Trunk Railway."

During the late nineteenth century and on into the early twentieth, Island Pond hummed with the business of servicing frequent passenger and freight trains transporting logs and wood pulp. It was

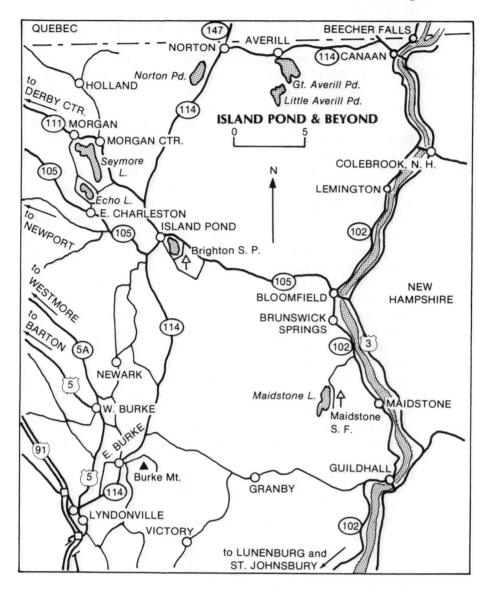

also a booming manufacturing center. No longer. Today it is a sleepy village on a two-mile-by-one-mile-long pond with a 20-acre island in its center.

For the traveler, Island Pond still looms large on the map, because you must pass through it to get to most places in Essex County. It also probably has more restaurants than the rest of the county put together, way stops before reaching the empty, lake-pocked land to the northeast (there's good fishing around Averill) and the hauntingly lonely stretch of the Connecticut between Guildhall and Canaan. Because this area is so sparsely populated, we have sketched our impressions of what lies along the obvious routes under *To See and Do*.

GUIDANCE   **Island Pond Chamber of Commerce** (723-4318), Box 255, Island Pond 05846, maintains a seasonal information center near the depot, also a year-round information service.

North Country Chamber of Commerce (603-237-8939), Colebrook, New Hampshire 03476, also serves this upper reach of the Upper Valley, including the Canaan, Vermont, area.

TO SEE AND DO   **Scenic Drive** From Island Pond, head north on Route 114. The Canadian National Railway's "Grand Trunk" line from Montreal to Portland, Maine, hugs the highway all the way to Norton. This railway was once Montreal's winter lifeline to Europe, since goods could not be shipped in or out of the frozen port of Montreal during the coldest months. The 16 miles between Island Pond and the border town of Norton is a lonely wilderness, much of the land owned by lumber and paper companies. About halfway to Norton, near the south end of long and slender Norton Pond, a gravel road to the left leads into the Bill Sladyk Wildlife Management Area, a vast, undeveloped wilderness frequented by hunters, fishermen, and loggers. Just before reaching the tiny village of Norton (opposite slightly larger Stanhope, Quebec), the forest thins out, and farmland reappears. Norton is the site of the notorious "Earth People's Park," a 1960s-style, loosely governed hippie commune that has survived but has dwindled from hundreds to perhaps two dozen residents. The road passes several farms, a school, and two stores, then swings abruptly eastward to avoid the imposing Canadian port-of-entry. Perhaps the most French Canadian town in Vermont, Norton is for practical purposes a satellite of nearby Coaticook, Quebec. Continuing eastward along the border, Route 114 re-enters the forest, passing a series of lakes, most of which are dotted with hunting and fishing camps. The largest of the lakes is Big Averill, which you can see by pulling off the road at Averill Village.

Shortly after passing Big Averill, you leave the St. Lawrence watershed and begin a rapid descent into the Connecticut River Valley. Halfway from Averill to Canaan, the road skirts the south shore of sizable Wallace Pond, almost entirely within the Province of Quebec.

Canaan, 14 miles east of Norton, is a pleasant pocket of civilization along the upper reaches of the Connecticut River. There are two villages. The first is Canaan itself, a village with a tiny Green and a lovely little Greek Revival building that houses the Alice M. Ward Memorial Library. A left at the junction of Routes 114 and 102 will take you a couple of miles north to Beecher Falls, another port-of-entry and a factory village, dominated by a huge Ethan Allen Furniture Plant, the company's original factory site (to arrange a tour, phone 266-3355). Occasionally in winter, you will hear Canaan mentioned on your weather report as the coldest spot in the United States for the day. (There is an official US weather observation station here.) Both villages hug the nascent Connecticut River, which originates in the Connecticut Lakes a few miles to the northeast in extreme northern New Hampshire.

From Canaan, you can choose driving southward on the more scenic Vermont side or via the faster New Hampshire side of the river. On the Vermont side (Route 102), you travel through river bottom farmland, reaching the bridge to Colebrook, New Hampshire, in just under 10 miles.

Colebrook is the only big town on this northernmost end of the river. It is the terminus of Concord Trailways from Boston, and it has a golf course, a Catholic shrine, and several blocks of shops and stores, amenities that are not to be found on the Vermont side of the river.

On the Vermont side, Route 102 continues south through Lemington, past the impressively long Columbia covered bridge, to the tiny village of Bloomfield. Along the way, the river valley alternately narrows and widens, and the road tunnels through forest, broken occasionally by farms, fields, and glimpses of impressive mountains. You pass the small town halls of Lemington, Brunswick, and Maidstone, but several of the townships, "gores," and "grants" are unorganized and have to be governed from Montpelier. At Bloomfield (consisting of one store, with adjoining snack bar), the "Grand Trunk" to Portland crosses the road, bound for North Stratford, New Hampshire, on the other side of the river. Here in January 1933, the lowest Vermont temperature ever (–50°F) was recorded.

Continuing south another 16 miles to Guildhall, Route 102 winds among the bluffs and oxbows of the ever-widening river. Glimpses of the White Mountains become more frequent. The town of Brunswick was once the site of a thriving mineral spring resort. The buildings are all gone, but the springs still run pure. Nearly halfway to Guildhall, a gravel road to the right leads to beautiful and isolated Maidstone State Park.

Entering Guildhall, we are informed by a billboard-sized sign that the town was "discovered" in 1754, chartered in 1761, and settled in 1764, making it the oldest town in northeastern Vermont (by contrast, Norton was not settled until 1860). We are further informed that the town has been the seat of Essex County since 1809. An attractive, square Green is flanked by a host of historically interesting buildings: a tiny courthouse, church, town hall ("the Guild Hall," 1798), and an ornate 1909 Classical Revival library with stained-glass windows. An unassuming white clapboard house serves as a county lock-up. There is also an attractive inn (see *Lodging*).

Two miles downriver from Guildhall, a town road marked "Granby" runs west off Route 102, beginning as a paved road but becoming gravel well before reaching the tiny hamlets of Granby and Gallup Mills, about eight miles from 102. This is wild, wooded, and boggy country, good for spotting moose and bear. Lumber camps and sawmills once peppered this area, and there was even a steam railway.

The road finally descends about eight miles west of Granby to reach Route 114, joining it a couple miles north of East Burke (see "St. Johnsbury and Burke Mountain Area"). Take Route 114 12 miles north through rolling, mixed farm and forest land to its junction with Route 105, two miles west of Island Pond.

STATE PARKS AND FORESTS   Brighton State Park (723-4360), Island Pond 05846. Located southeast of the village of Island Pond on the south shore of Island Pond and the west shore of Spectacle Pond. Facilities include 84 campsites, of which 21 have lean-tos; also a swimming beach, dump station, snack bar, picnic area, bathhouse, rental boats, nature trail, and naturalist in residence.

Maidstone State Forest (676-3930), near Bloomfield. Five miles south of Bloomfield on Route 102, then five miles on dirt road, this is a forest of maple, beech, and hemlock around a large lake, with a beach, picnic area, rental boats, picnic shelter, hiking trails, and 83 campsites, including 37 lean-tos.

Victory Basin. See "St. Johnsbury and Burke Mountain Area" *Parks and Forests.*

BOAT EXCURSION   Lady of the Lake (723-6649), offers a narrated tour of Island Pond. Check with Barnes Recreation.

CANOEING   The various lakes in northern Essex County offer a variety of wilderness canoeing experiences. The Upper Connecticut River offers conditions ranging from white water to smooth-as-glass. Ask the Island Pond and Colebrook chambers of commerce about conditions and rental possibilities.

FISHING   Quimby Country (see *Lodging*) is a self-contained resort that includes 70-acre Forest Lake and is a quarter mile from 1,200-acre Big Averill, both lonely and remote but good for trout and salmon; rowboats can also be rented here by the day. Boats are also available at both Brighton and Maidstone state parks. Check the pamphlet "Vermont Guide to Fishing" for details about which fish are available where. Check the state highway map for local access points. The Connecticut Lakes in adjacent extreme northern New Hampshire offer world-class trout fishing. Rental boats are available in Island Pond; check with the Lakefront Motel.

GOLF   There are no golf courses in Essex County. Closest in New Hampshire are the **Colebrook Country Club** (nine holes), **The Balsams** in Dixville Notch (18 holes, magnificent site), and the **Waumbec Country Club** in Jefferson (18 holes).

HIKING   **Bluff Mountain** (elevation 2,380 feet) looms over Island Pond to the north. It is a popular climb, with spectacular views. The trail starts from Route 114, north of the village. Inquire locally for directions.

Monadnock Mountain (elevation 3,140 feet) in Lemington, towers over the Connecticut River and Colebrook on the opposite shore. A trail runs west, beginning as a driveway off Route 102 near the bridge to Colebrook. An abandoned fire tower crowns the summit. Inquire at one of the houses near the trailhead about the exact location of the trail.

Bill Sladyk Wildlife Management Area, off Route 114, south of Norton Pond: 9,500 forested acres, also accessible via a gravel road past Holland Pond from Holland Village. A detailed map is available from the Fish and Game Department in Montpelier.

HORSEBACK RIDING   **Mountain Ridge Ranch** (723-6153/6578), south of Island Pond on Route 114, offers trail rides ($15 for 1½ hours), also pony rides for children.

SWIMMING   There are state facilities at Island Pond, a large beach that is sandy and shallow for quite a ways out, great for children, and at Maidstone Lake (small beach); nominal entrance fee charged.

SKIING   There are apparently no developed cross-country centers in northern Essex County. With all the wild, open land, one might find having to pay to ski somewhat appalling. There is a vast network of wilderness snowmobile trails that are marked by snowmobile clubs and open to skiers.

LODGING   **Quimby Country** (822-5533; off season: 717-733-2234), Averill 05901. About as north (less than three miles from Canada) and as east (10 miles from New Hampshire) as you can get in the Kingdom. This unique resort is a nineteenth-century lodge and grouping of 20 cabins overlooking 70-acre Forest Lake. It is also a quarter mile from 1,200-acre Big Averill, four miles from 400-acre Little Averill, and surrounded by its own woodland, in turn surrounded by forest owned by paper companies. Begun as a fishing lodge, Quimby Country evolved into a family-oriented resort under the proprietorship of Hortense Quimby, evoking a large following in the process. Fearful that the place might change when it came up for sale upon Miss Quimby's death, a number of regular guests formed a corporation and bought it. When the place is in full operation, mid-July–late August, the rates are $65–95 per adult, $40–50 per child depending on age, with all three meals; less in early July and in September. There is a full, organized program for children.

Guildhall Inn (676-3720), Box 129, Guildhall 05905. Built in the early 1800s and recently restored, this is a large, elegant old farmhouse with three rooms upstairs (shared bath), furnished with an assortment of country antiques. The site is on Route 102, just south of the Guildhall town Green. $30 single, $40 double, with breakfast.

Monadnock Bed & Breakfast (603-237-8216), One Monadnock

Street, Colebrook, New Hampshire 03576. Barbara and Wendell Woodard welcome you to their large, bungalow-style house just across the bridge from Lemington. Built around the turn of the century by a local lumber baron, the house contains some magnificent woodwork. The upstairs is reserved for guests and contains four bedrooms, a shared bath, and kitchenette (for early risers). Rates are $25, $35 double.

Lakefront Motel (723-6507), Cross Street, Island Pond 05846. A tidy, upscale, two-story motel right in the center of the village with sweeping views of Island Pond, which laps the edge of the property. There is no restaurant (there are enough within walking distance). The former bar-lounge with a fireplace has been converted into two two-bedroom apartments. Four of the 20 units have built-in kitchenettes. A small dock is reserved for motel guests, and just across a vacant lot is an extensive public recreation complex, including tennis courts, beach, picnic area, boat launch, lighted ice hockey rink, and children's playground. Marcel and Anita Gervais charge $55–70 for two people, depending on the season, $10 per extra person.

DINING OUT   ☞**Buck and Doe** (723-4712), Island Pond. Open for lunch and dinner, seven days a week. This very popular restaurant across from the old depot has a huge menu, and so are the portions. Specialties include a choice of fresh, broiled fish with lemon butter, including Gaspe salmon, breaded veal cutlet, and roast Long Island duckling. The dessert menu includes hot apple goody with ice cream. Ronnie, the late chef-owner, has been succeeded by his protégé, Dustin. Reservations suggested. Entrées $7.25–24.95 for a 24-ounce boned sirloin.

Quimby Country (822-5533), Averill (see *Lodging*). Open to the public for dinner by reservation only, offering a rotating menu of two entrées, plus a children's entrée; Sunday night buffet.

Sutton Place Restaurant (603-237-8842), 152 Main Street, Colebrook, New Hampshire. Open for lunch Tuesday–Saturday and dinner every night. Don and Carmela Kelsea have created an intimate dining place in the front parlors of a Queen Anne–style house in the center of town. Dinner entrées include steak, chicken, and seafood. Entrées under $20.

Candlelight Restaurant (266-8119), Beecher Falls. A full-service restaurant in newly rebuilt, overdecorated but comfortable quarters on the edge of the Connecticut River. Entrées under $20.

EATING OUT   **Jennifers** (723-6135), Island Pond, is a cheery little spot for hearty breakfasts, lunch, and dinner: roast turkey, $7.95; surf and turf, $10.95.

Northland Restaurant and Lounge (266-9947), Canaan. A large, clean, comfortable place offering three squares. The spacious, adjoining bar-lounge-dance floor hosts rock and country rock bands each Saturday evening.

MEDICAL EMERGENCY   Island Pond: 723-6262.

General Index

Lodging Index